A History of
TOKYO
1867—1989

EDWARD SEIDENSTICKER

A HISTORY OF
TOKYO
1867–1989

From EDO to SHOWA:
The Emergence of the World's Greatest City

Preface by **DONALD RICHIE**
Introduction by **PAUL WALEY**

TUTTLE Publishing

Tokyo │ Rutland, Vermont │ Singapore

Published by Tuttle Publishing, an imprint of Periplus Editions (HK) Ltd.

www.tuttlepublishing.com

Copyright © 2019 The Estate of Edward G. Seidensticker

Grateful acknowledgment is made to the following institutions for permission to publish illustrations supplied by them appearing on the following pages: Tokyo Prefectural Archives: pp. 296, 299, 307, 310, 313, 331, 335, 337, 338, 339, 350, 361, 370, 372, 380, 383, 391, 396, 406, 491, 534, and 552; Asahi Shimbum: pp. 318, 346, 355, 388, 402, 416, 431, 455, 467, 471, 474, 481, 505, 516, 548, 549, and 586; Asahi Hyakka Nihon no Rekishi: pp. 425, 428, 446, and 477; Asahi Graph: p. 432; Tokyo Prefectural Government: p. 605.

English translation by Edward Seidensticker of excerpts from Collected Works of Nagai Kafū. Originally published by Iwanami Shoten, Tokyo, Japan. English translation by Edward Seidensticker of excerpts from Collected Works of Takeda Rintarō, and excerpts from Collected Works of Kawabata Yasunari. Originally published by Shinchosha, Tokyo, Japan.

Grateful acknowledgment is made to the following for permission to reprint previously published material: Chuokoron-Sha, Inc.: English translation by Edward Seidensticker of excerpts from Collected Works of Tanizaki Junichirō. Copyright 1934 by Tanizaki Junichirō. Reprinted by permission of Chuokoron-Sha, Inc., 2-8-7, Kyobashi Chuo-ku, Tokyo 104, Japan. Keiso Shobo, Ltd.: English translation by Edward Seidensticker of excerpts from Collected Works of Takami Jun, Vol. XIX, 1974. Reprinted by permission of Keiso Shobo, Ltd., Tokyo, Japan.

Library of Congress Cataloging-in-Publication Data

Seidensticker, Edward, 1921-2007.
   Tokyo from Edo to Showa, 1867-1989 : the emergence of the world's greatest city : two volumes in one, Low City, High City and Tokyo rising / Edward Seidensticker ; introduction by Paul Waley ; preface by Donald Richie.
      636 p., [16] p. of plates : ill. (some col.), maps ; 21 cm.
   Includes bibliographical references and index.
   ISBN 978-4-8053-1024-3 (pbk.)
   1. Tokyo (Japan)--History--1868-1912. 2. Tokyo (Japan)--History--20th century. 3. Tokyo (Japan)--Social life and customs. 4. Tokyo (Japan)--Social conditions. 5. City and town life--Japan--Tokyo--History. 6. Social change--Japan--Tokyo--History. 7. Japan--History--Meiji period, 1868-1912. 8. Japan--History--Taisho period, 1912-1926. 9. Japan--History--Showa period, 1926-1989. 10. Capitals (Cities)--Case studies. I. Title.
   DS896.64.S425 2010
   952'.13503--dc22

                                 2010011099

ISBN 978-4-8053-1511-8

Distributed by

North America, Latin America & Europe
Tuttle Publishing
364 Innovation Drive
North Clarendon, VT 05759-9436 U.S.A.
Tel: 1 (802) 773-8930; Fax: 1 (802) 773-6993
info@tuttlepublishing.com
www.tuttlepublishing.com

Asia Pacific
Berkeley Books Pte. Ltd.
3 Kallang Sector #04-01/02
Singapore 349278
Tel: (65) 6280-1330; Fax: (65) 6280-6290
inquiries@periplus.com.sg
www.periplus.com

Japan
Tuttle Publishing
Yaekari Building 3rd Floor
5-4-12 Osaki Shinagawa-ku
Tokyo 141 0032
Tel: (81) 3 5437-0171; Fax: (81) 3 5437-0755
sales@tuttle.co.jp; www.tuttle.co.jp

22 21 20 19   5 4 3 2 1   1811CM

Printed in China

CONTENTS

Introduction   6

Preface   9

BOOK ONE
LOW CITY, HIGH CITY

Author's Preface   15

1. The End and the Beginning   23

2. Civilization and Enlightenment   43

3. The Double Life   101

4. The Decay of the Decadent   150

5. Low City, High City   186

6. The Taisho Look   247

BOOK TWO
TOKYO RISING

Author's Preface   281

7. The Days After   291

8. Happy Reconstruction Days   307

9. Darker Days   368

10. The Day of the Cod and the Sweet Potato   422

11. Olympian Days   495

12. Balmy Days of Late Shōwa   546

Notes   607

Index   615

INTRODUCTION

There can be few cities in the world that live, pulsate, and breathe through their geography as Tokyo does, few cities with a history that shifts through the creases of space as does that of Tokyo. This is particularly ironic in a city whose neighborhoods today hold few distinctive features and whose gentle topography has been all but obscured by batteries of buildings. But it was not always so, and what better way is there of writing Tokyo's history than by reflecting this shifting geography as neighborhoods prospered and declined while others, more aspirational, climbed up the socio-spatial ladder? This is precisely what Edward Seidensticker does in the pages of these two books, brought here together for the first time under one cover thanks to the efforts of a number of people, including Donald Richie, and the publisher.

Few books in whatever language are so suffused with the spirit of a city as Seidensticker's classic accounts, suffused with the spirit of the city, but also imbued with the wit of their author. These are not conventional histories. While they are written with a strong sense of history's ebb and flow, they are held together by their representation of the decline and marginalization of a way of life that was at the same time a part of town. Throughout these books, there is a sense of foreboding and of a fatal destiny being played out. But at the same time, there is a lightness of touch and an appropriateness of the chosen detail that provokes a smile, a chuckle, and a raised eyebrow on each reading.

This is definitely not anyone's Tokyo. It is Seidensticker's Tokyo. And Seidensticker's Tokyo starts in the Low City and moves out with it to embrace Asakusa. Much of these two volumes is dominated by the demise of the Low City and all that it stood for, until, that is, more recent years, when the deed is all but done and Asakusa consigned to the role of outpost for tourists. Many of Tokyo's districts have a part to play in these pages, indeed they are the principal characters, invested with a personality that can change with time but that is rooted in a sense of the almost atavistic attraction of the Low City and the parvenu presumption exhibited by the districts of the High City. So it is that we see the emergence of Ginza from obscurity in the shogun's city of Edo to shop window for all that was stylish and new. Nihonbashi, the old center of the merchants' city, was much more sedate, losing out slowly to the nearby district of Marunouchi. Roppongi gets short shrift as an upstart pleasure district that grew up as a result of US military facilities in the post-war period. Shinjuku and Shibuya are the back of beyond, to put it politely.

Alongside the districts, there are a number of buildings whose presence animates these books: the Twelve-Storys tower in Asakusa, destroyed in the great earthquake of 1923; Tokyo Central Station, inconveniently located in the center of the city; Frank Lloyd Wright's Imperial Hotel, which famously withstood the tremors; the city's main theatres, prominent among them the Kabukiza and the Shibuya Embujō. And people, too, whose lives have helped to shape the city and define its culture—people like Hattori Kintarō, the founder of Seikō, the watch-making company; or Josiah Conder, the British architect whose influence was seminal in the teaching of architecture in Japan; or Enoken, the most famous and best-loved of Asakusa's comedians; or the man called Suzuki who built a block in Shinjuku which he optimistically called Kabukichō. But the individuals whose presence most influences the tenor of these books are the many writers who have built at least part of their opus on Tokyo's ground, not only the likes of Tanizaki Jun'ichirō and Kawabata Yasunari, with whom many of us will already be familiar, but lesser-known authors such as Osanai Kaoru and Takami Jun.

This is a cultural and social history which for all its quirkiness is peppered with enlightening vignettes that create a wider context for Tokyo's history. It is built around a number of *leitmotifs*: corruption in high places; new cultures and technologies such as the department store; festivals, performances, theater; the geisha and the licensed quarters. But these two books are far from being orthodox history. They really belong to a genre of their own. It is hard not to reflect on the freedom Seidensticker must have felt writing about Tokyo. On the one hand, he was not translating, with its bondage to the original text. On the other, he was not writing as a historian, and so had no need to adopt the tools of the historian's trade. Nevertheless, he managed to capture in uncanny ways the telling details of historical change—the transition from feet to wheels in

Meiji Tokyo or the change in eating habits after the great earthquake when women started eating out in numbers. This is very much history as it was lived at the time, which is a history reflected in newspaper articles, on stage, in cafés. It is in fact an approach that has more in common with certain traditions of Japanese representations of places and of the past, a cross between topographical writing and satirical social and cultural history. But above all in reading these pages one feels subliminally the presence of Nagai Kafū, the writer whose wistful stories were translated by Seidensticker and whose cultural prejudices are, one senses, shared.

Paul Waley

PREFACE

Now that my friend of some fifty years is no more, I often think of him as I walk along the shores of the Shinobazu no Ike, near where we both lived, he up the hill in Yushima, me in Ueno by the pond. Shinobazu made a good meeting place because it was familiar to both of us and because the whole area had associations we liked.

These associations were mostly literary. Natsume Soseki had lived in the neighborhood when he wrote *I Am a Cat*, and Mori Ogai's house was still there (though now turned into a hotel) while Ed himself lived at the top of the steep street which Otama in Ogai's *Wild Geese* daily climbed.

Ed found the neighborhood still somehow literary and thought of himself as one of the last local bunjin. Not only did he concern himself with past literature, as in his translation of the *Genji Monogatari*, but also he loved the past for its own sake, as he demonstrated in his splendid, two-volume history of Tokyo. Yet he entertained a certain ambivalence toward the past, one he shared with us in the finest of all of his works, *Kafū the Scribbler*.

Just as Kafū disliked Meiji Japan until Taisho Japan turned out even worse, giving him then something to like about vanished Meiji, so Seidensticker disliked much of modern Japan until newer manifestations indicated something worse was on its way, at which point he would become nostalgic about what he had formerly disliked.

He collected these opinions in his feisty columns for the Yomiuri Shimbun, published in English as *This Country, Japan*, a title with a double meaning. It could be read simply as "this country" (*kono kuni*), or as "this country!" indicating an extreme degree of exasperation with Japan. His opinions and his way of arriving at them were so close to those of Kafū that is not surprising that Kafū the Scribbler is both an extraordinarily perceptive literary history and also a completely personal identification.

As I walk along the shores of Shinobazu no Ike I now think of the many times I met Seidensticker there, as he slowly wandered about, looking (though fatter) much like a latter-day Kafū himself. And when we talked about literature we always talked about Kafū. One of his regrets, he said, was that he had never met the great author. He knew Kawabata and Tanizaki, Mishima and others, but he had never met Kafū, the author he most admired.

Since Kafū was also my own favorite Japanese author, he became one of the things that Ed and I had in common. We also both favored a certain kind of English author who, like Kafū, had an immaculate style and an anomalous taste for the past: authors such as Thomas Love Peacock, Edward Lear, Lewis Carroll, Ronald Firbank.

And Jane Austen. We were both besotted with her six novels, read them all the time, even formed an unauthorized Jane Austen Society of Japan (along with Shulamith Rubinfein and Sheelagh Cluny), just for ourselves. Such tastes might be thought narrow but they had admirable results. Whenever I reread Seidensticker's *Genji*, I see that the tone, the mood, the feeling of this translation—its lightness, its rightness—owe much to his admiration for Jane Austen. She is standing there, just behind Murasaki Shikibu.

Sometimes in my evening walks around Shinobazu I would discover Ed on one of the benches, sitting there, regarding the pond. Sometimes he had been drinking (he liked *shochu*), sometimes not. Whichever, we always talked about the same things. I remember one such conversation. "I am delighted to see you," he said. "For I have something to tell you. My afternoon was spent with Abe Kobo and we spoke of his style, and he said that critics always said that the influence was Franz Kafka, but they were absolutely wrong. The real influence was *Alice in Wonderland*. Isn't that nice? Lewis Carroll!"

But then Seidensticker's physical problems began. He conquered his liking for *shochu*, but he had two hip replacements and could never properly walk after that. I would sometimes see him hobbling about Shinobazu of an evening, but gradually he stopped coming—he fell down too often. Instead we would meet, once a week or so, at an Ueno Indian restaurant we both liked and which he could reach by taxi.

Having much criticized Showa Japan while we were still in it, he was now praising the immediate postwar years because he found so much wrong with Heisei Japan. During our later meetings it was the contemporary young that irritated him the most with their laziness, their rudeness, their narcissistic ways. He remembered how much nicer the young people of Showa Japan had seemed, those he had formerly criticized just as bitterly. And we often (like Kafu, like all old people) remembered a kind of beauty which, whether or not it had actually existed, lived on in us.

Seidensticker was not only a bunjin and a splendid translator, he was also a man who (like Kafū) had the highest standards and was honest enough to criticize what he loved. He cared deeply for Japan, more so than many another foreigner, more so than many Japanese. Perhaps that was why he was on the shores of Shinobazu Pond on the day of the accident, April 26, 2007. It had been an unusually warm spring day with sun and the promise of summer. Now, as evening approached and the long shadows spread across the waters, it was perhaps because of a wish to enjoy this that he left the taxi and walked as best he could through the park on his way to the Indian restaurant and dinner with me and our friend Patrick Lovell.

Now when I take my stroll around the pond I always pass the small staircase down which he fell that day and fractured his skull. It is very short, just five steps, but falling from the top one was enough to put him into the coma that lasted four months to the day, ending with his death on August 26.

And then as I continue around the pond I see in the distance that someone is sitting on the bench where we used to sit. It has grown dark now—it is twilight, a star or two has appeared. I walk nearer to the seated person. I know that it is not my friend, Edward Seidensticker, but I wish it were.

Donald Richie

Used with permission of International House of Japan. This material originally appeared in the IHJ Bulletin and is an expanded version of an obituary which appeared in Japanese in the magazine Ueno, a publication for which Seidensticker regularly wrote.

BOOK ONE

LOW CITY, HIGH CITY

Tokyo from Edo to the Earthquake:
How the Shogun's Ancient Capital
Became a Great Modern City,
1867–1923

AUTHOR'S PREFACE

When young, I did not dedicate books. Dedications seemed overblown and showy. It is too late to begin; but if this book carried a dedication, it would be to the memory of Nagai Kafū. Though he was not such a good novelist, he has come to seem better and better at what he was good at. He was his best in brief lyrical passages and not in sustained narrative and dramatic ones. He is the novelist whose views of the world's most consistently interesting city accord most closely with my own. He has been my guide and companion as I have explored and dreamed and meditated upon the city.

I do not share his yearning for Edo, the city when it was still the seat of the Tokugawa shoguns and before it became the Eastern Capital. The Tokugawa Period is somehow dark and menacing. Too many gifted people were squelched, and, whether gifted or not, I always have the feeling about Edo that, had I been there, I would have been among the squelched ones.

I share Kafū's affection for the part of the city which had its best day then. The twilight of that day lasted through the succeeding Meiji reign and down to the great earthquake. It is the Shitamachi, the plebeian flatlands, which I here call the Low City. Meiji was when the changes that made Japan modern and economically miraculous were beginning. Yet the Low City had not lost its claim to the cultural hegemony which it had clearly possessed under the Tokugawa.

Many exciting things have occurred in the six decades since the earthquake, which is slightly farther from the present than from the beginning of Meiji. Another book asks to be written, about those decades and especially the ones since the surrender. Perhaps it will be written, but it would have to be mostly about the other half (these days considerably more than half), the hilly High City, the Yamanote. That is where the artist and the intellectual, and to an increasing extent the manager and the magnate, have been. If there is less in this book about the High City than the Low City, it is because one is not drawn equally to everything in a huge and complex city, and a book whose beginnings lie in personal experience does have a way of turning to what interests and pleases.

Kafū was an elegist, mourning the death of Edo and lamenting the emergence of modern Tokyo. With such a guide and companion, an elegiac tone is bound to emerge from time to time. The departure of the old and the emergence of the new are inextricably entwined, of course. Yet, because the story of what happened to Edo is so much the story of the Low City, matters in which it was not interested do not figure much. It was not an intellectual sort of place, nor was it strongly political. Another consideration has urged the elimination of political and intellectual matters: the fact that Tokyo became the capital of Japan in 1868. A distinction may be made between what occurred in the city because it was the capital, and what occurred because it was a city.

So this book contains little political and intellectual history, and not much more literary and economic history. The major exception in literary matters is the drama, the great love of the Edo townsman. The story of what happened to Kabuki is central to the story of the city, and not that of the capital. The endeavor to describe a changing city as if it were an organism is perhaps not realistic, since cities change in all ways and directions, as organisms and specific institutions do not. The subject here is the changing city all the same, the legacy of Edo and what happened to it. To a much smaller degree is it the story of currents that have flowed in upon the city because it was the capital.

Japanese practice has been followed in the rendition of personal names. The family name comes before the given name. When a single element is used, it is the family name if there is no elegant pen-name (distinguished in principle from a prosy one like Mishima Yukio), and the pen-name when there is one. Hence Kafū and Shigure, both of them pen-names; but Tanizaki, Kubota, and Shibusawa, all of them family names.

The staff of the Tokyo Metropolitan Archives was very kind in helping assemble illustrations. The prints, woodcut and lithograph, are from Professor Donald Keene's collection and my own, except as noted in the captions. I am also in debt to the Tokyo Central Library and the Toyo Keizai Shimpō. Mr. Fukuda Hiroshi was very helpful in photographing photographs that could not be taken across the Pacific for reproduction.

The notes are minimal, limited for the most part to the sources of direct quotations. A very important source, acknowledged only once in the notes, is the huge work called A *History of the Tokyo Century* (although it begins with the beginnings of Edo), published by the municipal government in the early 1970s, with a supplemental chronology published in 1980. Huge it certainly is, six volumes (without the chronology), each of them some fifteen hundred pages long. Uneven it is as well, and indispensable.

Guidebooks, four of them acknowledged in the notes, were very useful, the two-volume guide published by the city in 1907 especially so. Then there were ward histories, none of them acknowledged, because I have made no direct quotation from them. The Japanese are energetic and accomplished local historians, as much so as the British. Their volumes pour forth in bewildering numbers, those Japanese equivalents of the "admirable history of southeast Berks" one is always seeing reviewed in the *Times Literary Supplement.* Every ward has at least one history. Some are better than others, not because some are especially unreliable, but because some are better organized and less given to axegrinding.

I do not pretend to have been through them all, but none that I have looked at has been valueless.

The most important source is Nagai Kafū. To him belongs the final acknowledgment, as would belong the dedication if there were one.

E.S.
April, 1982

Tokyo in 1892

Tokyo in 1914

Chapter 1

THE END
AND THE BEGINNING

There was foreboding in Japan on September 1, 1923. September 2 would be the Two-Hundred-Tenth Day, counting from the day in early February when spring is held to begin. Awaited each year with apprehension, it comes during the typhoon season and the harvest. The conjunction of the two, harvest and typhoon, can mean disaster. The disaster of that year came instead on September 1.

The morning was warm, heavy, as most days of late summer are, with the shrilling of locusts. The mugginess was somewhat relieved by brisk winds, which shifted from east to south at about nine. A low-pressure zone covered the southern part of the Kantō Plain, on the fringes of which the city lies. The winds became stronger as the morning drew on. Rain fell, stopping at eleven. The skies cleared.

The city was awaiting the *don,* the "bang" of the cannon which since 1871 had been fired at noon every day in the palace plaza.

At one minute and fifteen and four-tenths seconds before noon, the great earthquake struck. The initial shocks were so violent that the seismographs at the Central Weather Bureau went out of commission. The surviving seismograph at Tokyo Imperial University made the only detailed record of the long series of quakes, more than seventeen hundred over the next three days. The epicenter was in Sagami Bay, southeast of the city. There was sinkage along a deep trough and a rising along the sides. The eastern limits of the modern city follow one earthquake zone, which runs along the Edo River and out into Tokyo Bay, and lie very near another, which crosses the wide mouth of Sagami Bay from the tip of the Chiba Peninsula to the tip of the Izu Peninsula. There had been a disastrous quake in 1855, centered on the Edo River zone, and a major though less disastrous one in the summer of 1894, also centered on the nearer of the two zones. It was assumed at that time that there would presently be another, and it is so assumed today, in 1982. Talk in 1923 of moving the capital to safer regions had been quieted by a proclamation from the emperor himself.

Between noon of September 1 and the evening of September 2, most of the Tokyo flatlands—the eastern sections of the city, the Shitamachi or "Low City"—went up in flames. The Low City produced most of what was original in the culture of Edo (as Tokyo had been known until the Meiji emperor moved there from Kyoto in 1867). Much of the Low City survived on the morning of September 1, and then, in forty hours or so, most of it disappeared.

Though we do not know how many died in the earthquake and the fires that followed, initial reports in the Western press almost certainly exaggerated. The *Los Angeles Times* informed a large and alarmed Japanese readership that half a million had died. The highest estimates today put the figure for Tokyo at something over a hundred thousand. Far more were killed in the fires than in the earthquake itself, and there seem to have been more deaths from drowning than from collapsed buildings.

Almost half the deaths, or perhaps more than half, if lower estimates are accepted for the total, occurred in an instant at a single place in the Low City, a park, formerly an army clothing depot, near the east or left bank of the Sumida River. Fires had started in several parts of the city soon after the initial shocks. There were whirlwinds of fire up and down the Sumida from midafternoon; the largest of them, according to witnesses, covered about the area of the Sumō wrestling gymnasium, the largest building east of the river, and was several hundred feet high. A flaming whirlwind came down upon the park at about four in the afternoon, and incinerated upwards of thirty thousand people who had fled there from the fires sweeping the Low City.

Akutagawa Ryūnosuke, the great writer of short stories and a man of strong suicidal impulses, liked to tell people that had he then been in his native Honjo, east of the river, he would probably have taken refuge where everyone else did, and been spared the trouble of suicide.

"In a family of nine, relatives of my wife, only a son, about twenty, survived. He was standing with a shutter over his head to ward off sparks when he was picked up by a whirlwind and deposited in the Yasuda garden. There he regained consciousness."

The traditional wooden house has great powers of resistance to wind, flood, and earthquake. It resisted well this time too, and then came the fires, leaving only scattered pockets of buildings across the Low City. The damage would have been heavy if the quakes alone had caused it, but most of the old city would have survived. Even then, seventy years after the arrival of Commodore Perry and fifty-five years after the resignation of the last Edo shogun, it was built mostly of wood. Buildings of more substantial materials came through the quakes well, though many were gutted by the fires. There has been much praise for the aplomb with which Frank Lloyd Wright's Imperial Hotel came through, built as it was of volcanic stone on an "earthquake-proof" foundation. It did survive, and deserves the praise; yet so did a great many other modern buildings (though not all). The Mitsukoshi Department Store suffered only broken windows from the quake, but burned as brightly as the sun, people who saw it said, when the fires took over. That the Imperial Hotel did not burn brightly was due entirely to chance.

It is difficult to judge earthquake damage when fires sweep a city shortly afterwards. Memories shaken and distorted by the horror of it all must be counted on to establish what was there in the brief interval between quake and fire. The best information suggests that after it was over almost three-quarters of the buildings in the city had been destroyed or seriously damaged, and almost two-thirds of them were destroyed or gutted by fire. The earthquake itself can be held clearly responsible only for the difference between the two figures.

Fifteen wards made up the city; a single one remained untouched by fire. It lay in the High City, the hilly regions to the west. In five wards the loss was above 90 percent and in a sixth only slightly less. The five all lay in the Low City, along the Sumida and the bay. The sixth lay mostly in the Low City, but extended also into the hills. In Shitaya Ward, half Low City and half High City, the flat portions were almost completely destroyed, with the line of the fires stopping cleanly at the hills. Had Ueno Park in Shitaya been hit as the erstwhile clothing depot was, the casualty lists might well have doubled.

Determining the number and cause of the fires has been as difficult as distinguishing between earthquake damage and fire damage. The best estimate puts the total number at upwards of a hundred-thirty, of which well over half could not be controlled. Most of the damage occurred during the first afternoon and night. It was early on the morning of September 2 that the Mitsukoshi was seen burning so brightly. Nineteen fires, the largest number for any of the fifteen wards, began in Asakusa, east of Shitaya. By the morning of September 3 the last of them had burned themselves out or been extinguished.

Ruins in Asakusa, including the Twelve Storys, after the earthquake.

It is commonly said that the chief reason for the inferno was the hour at which the first shocks came. Lunch was being prepared all over the city, upon gas burners and charcoal braziers. From these open flames and embers, common wisdom has it, the fires began.

But in fact many fires seem to have had other origins. Chemicals have been identified as the largest single cause, followed by electric wires and burners. This suggests that the same disaster might very well have occurred at any hour of the day. The earthquake of 1855 occurred in the middle of the night. Much of the Low City was destroyed then too. Most of the damage was caused by fire—yet in the mid-nineteenth century there were no electric lines and probably few chemicals to help the fire on. Fires will start, it seems, whenever buildings collapse in large numbers. No fire department can cope with them when they start simultaneously at many points on a windy day. Tokyo is now a sea of chemicals and a tangle of utility wires. It is not as emphatically wooden as it once was, to be sure, but the Low City, much of it a jumble of small buildings on filled land, will doubtless be the worst hit when the next great earthquake comes.

Among the rumors that went flying about the city was the imaginative one that an unnamed country of the West had developed an earthquake machine and was experimenting upon Japan. There were, nevertheless, no outbreaks of violence against "foreigners," which in Japan usually means Westerners. Instead, the xenophobia of the island nation turned on Koreans.

The government urged restraint, not to make things easier for Koreans, but because the Western world might disapprove: it would not do for such things to be reported in the Western press. Rumors spread that Koreans were poisoning wells. The police were later accused of encouraging hostility by urging particular attention to wells, but probably not much encouragement was needed. A willingness, and indeed a wish, to believe the worst about Koreans has been a consistent theme in modern Japanese culture. The slaughter was considerable, in any event. Reluctant official announcements put casualties in the relatively low three figures. The researches of the liberal scholar Yoshino Sakuzō were later to multiply them by ten, bringing the total to upwards of two thousand.

Not all the things of Edo were destroyed. The most popular temple in the city, the great Asakusa Kannon, survived. An explanation for its close escape was that a statue of the Meiji Kabuki actor Danjūrō, costumed as the hero of *Shibaraku* (meaning "One Moment, Please"), held back flames advancing from the north. But fire did destroy the Yoshiwara, most venerable of the licensed quarters that had been centers of Edo culture.

Several fine symbols of Meiji Tokyo were also destroyed. The old Shimbashi Station, northern terminus of the earliest railroad in the land, was among the modern buildings that did not survive. The Ryōunkaku (literally "Cloud Scraper"), a twelve-story brick tower in Asakusa, had survived the earthquake of 1894, when many a brick chimney collapsed and brick architecture in general was brought into disrepute. It had been thought earthquake-proof, but in 1923 it broke off at the eighth story. The top storys fell into a lake nearby, and the rest were destroyed the following year by army engineers.

The great loss was the Low City, home of the merchant and the artisan, heart of Edo culture. From the beginnings of its existence as the shogun's capital, Edo was divided into two broad regions, the hilly Yamanote or High City, describing a semicircle generally to the west of the shogun's castle, now the emperor's palace, and the flat Low City, the Shitamachi, completing the circle on the east. Plebeian enclaves could be found in the High City, but mostly it was a place of temples and shrines and aristocratic dwellings. The Low City had its aristocratic dwellings, and there were a great many temples, but it was very much the plebeian half of the city. And though the aristocracy was very cultivated indeed, its tastes—or the tastes thought proper to the establishment—were antiquarian and academic. The vigor of Edo was in its Low City.

The Low City has always been a vaguely defined region, its precise boundaries difficult to draw. It sometimes seems as much an idea as a geographic entity. When in the seventeenth century the Tokugawa regime set about building a seat for itself, it granted most of the solid hilly regions to the military aristocracy, and filled in the marshy mouths of the Sumida and Tone rivers, to the east of the castle. The flatlands that resulted became the abode of the merchants and craftsmen who purveyed to the voracious aristocracy and provided its labor.

These lands, between the castle on the west and the Sumida and the bay on the east, were the original Low City. Of the fifteen Meiji wards, it covered only Nihombashi and Kyōbashi and the flatlands of Kanda and Shiba. Asakusa, most boisterous of the Meiji pleasure centers, was scarcely a part of the old city at all. It lay beyond one of the points guarding approaches to the city proper, and was built initially to serve pilgrims to its own great Kannon temple. Later it was linked to the theater district, and was a part of the complex that catered to the Yoshiwara licensed quarter, yet farther to the north.

Today everything east of the Sumida is regarded as part of the Low City, but until Meiji only a thin strip along the east bank of the Sumida was so considered, and not even that by everyone.

The heart of the Low City was Nihombashi, broadest of the lands first reclaimed by the shogunate. Nihombashi set the tone and made the definitions. Nihombashi proper, the "Japan Bridge" from which the district took its name, was the spot where all roads began. Distances from the city were measured from Nihombashi. A proper resident of Nihombashi did not have to go far east, perhaps only as far as the Sumida, perhaps a few paces beyond, to feel that he had entered the land of the bumpkin. The Low City was small, tight, and cozy.

It changed a great deal between the resignation of the last shogun and the earthquake. As time runs on, new dates for the demise of Edo are always being assigned by connoisseurs of the subject. In 1895, we are told, or in 1912, Edo finally departed, and only Tokyo remained. Yet even today the Low City is different from the High City, and so it may be said that even today something of Edo survives. The earthquake was all the same a disaster from which the heart of the Low City did not recover. Already before 1923 the wealthy were moving away from Nihombashi, and vitality was departing as well. The earthquake accelerated the movement to the south and west, first apparent in the rise of Ginza. Today the most prosperous centers for drinking and shopping lie beyond the western limits of the Meiji city.

Tokiwa Bridge, Nihombashi, in early Meiji. Later site of the Bank of Japan

Nihombashi and the Low City in general were conservative. There was, of course, resentment at the rigid Tokugawa class structure, which put the merchant below everyone else. By way of fighting back, a satirical vein in the literature and drama of the Low City poked fun at the High City aristocrat, but never strongly enough to make the urban masses a threat to the old order. The Edokko, the "child of Edo," as the native of the Low City called himself, was pleased to be there "at the knee" of Lord Tokugawa, and the shogunate was wise enough to take condescending notice of the populace on certain festival days. When the threat to the regime eventually came, it was from the far provinces, and the Edokko was more resentful of the provincial soldiers who became the new establishment than he had ever been of the old.

He may be taxed with complacency. The professional child of Edo has descendants today, and they are proud of themselves to the point of incivility. They tend to divide the world between the Low City and other places, to the great disadvantage of the latter. The novelist Tanizaki Junichirō, a genuine Edokko, born in 1886 of a Nihombashi merchant family, did not like his fellow Edokko, whom he described as weak, complaining, and generally ineffectual. Yet the Low City of Edo had high standards and highly refined tastes, and if exclusiveness was necessary to maintain them, as the years since have suggested, that seems a small price to pay.

Kyōbashi, to the south of Nihombashi, included Ginza, which came aggressively forward to greet the new day. An artisan quarter under the old regime, Ginza stood at the terminus of the new railway and eagerly brought new things in from Yokohama and beyond. Tanizaki and others have described the diaspora of the Edokko, with Nihombashi its chief victim, as the new people came in. It can be exaggerated, and one suspects that Tanizaki exaggerated for literary effect. He made much also of the helplessness of the Edokko before the entrepreneur from the West Country. Yet many an Edo family did very well. Among those who did best were the Mitsui, established in Nihombashi since the seventeenth century. Not many children of Edo had been there longer. The demographic and cultural movement to the south and west was inexorable all the same, and more rapid after the earthquake.

The High City was much less severely damaged than the Low City. The growing suburbs, many of them later incorporated within the city limits, were hurt even less. Through the years before and after the earthquake, industrial production remained fairly steady for Tokyo Prefecture, which included large suburbs as well as the city proper. Within the fifteen wards of the city, it fell sharply in the same period. The suburban share was growing.

With the Low City pleasure quarters lost in the fires, those of the High City throve. They did not have the same sort of tradition, and the change meant the end of something important in the life of the city. The novelist Nagai Kafū—not, like Tanizaki, a real son of Edo, both because he was not from the merchant class and because his family had not been in the city the three generations held necessary to produce one—was even so an earnest student of Edo and Tokyo. All through his career (he was born in 1879 and died in 1959) he went on lamenting the fact that the latter had killed the former; and all through his career, with lovable inconsistency, he went on remembering how Edo yet survived at this and that date later than ones already assigned to the slaying. Though he is commonly considered an amorous and erotic novelist, his writings are essentially nostalgic and elegiac. The pleasure quarters were central to Edo culture, and it was in those conservative regions if anywhere that something of Edo survived. So it was natural that they should be his favorite subject. He had many harsh things to say about the emergent pleasure centers of the High City, and their failure to keep sex in its place—pleasurable, no doubt, but not the only thing at which the great ladies of the older quarters thought it necessary to excel. The old quarters were genuine centers of the higher arts.

The seventy-seventh of the Chinese sexagenary cycles came to a close in 1923. When Cycle Seventy-seven began, in 1864, the Tokugawa shogunate was in its final convulsions. The short administration of the last shogun was soon over, and the "Restoration," as it is called in English, occurred. Edo became Tokyo, with the Meiji emperor in residence. "Restoration" is actually a bad translation of the Japanese *ishin*, which means something more like "renovation" or "revitalization."

Edo could not have known, at the beginning of the Cycle Seventy-seven, that Lord Tokugawa would so soon be in exile. Yet there were ample causes for apprehension, not the least of which was the presence of the foreigner. He obviously did not mean to go away. At first, upon the opening of the ports, foreigners seem to have been greeted with friendliness and eager curiosity. Presently this changed. A Dutch observer dated the change as 1862, subsequent to which there were many instances of violence, including the stoning of an American consul. The Dutchman put the blame upon the foreigners themselves, an unruly lot whom the port cities attracted. The Edo townsman seems to have had little to do with the violence; his feelings were not that strong. Yet he seems to have agreed with the rustic soldiers responsible for most of the violence that the barbarian should be put back in his place, on the other side of the water.

Early in 1863, the new British legation was destroyed by arsonists of the military class—among them Itō Hirobumi, later to become the most prominent of Meiji statesmen. The legation had been built in the part of the city closest to the relative security of Yokohama. It was not yet occupied, and nothing came of plans for other legations on the same site. The Edo townsman seems to have received news of the fire with satisfaction.

Edo was not, like the great capitals of Europe, a commercial center in its own right, with interests independent of and sometimes in conflict with those of the sovereign. More like Washington than London or Paris, it was an early instance, earlier than Washington, of a fabricated capital. Technically it was not the capital at all, since the emperor remained in Kyoto through the Tokugawa centuries. It was, however, the seat of power. The first shogun established himself there for military reasons, and the commercial and artisan classes gathered, as in Washington, to be of service to the bureaucracy. It was an enormous bureaucracy, because the Tokugawa system required that provincial potentates maintain establishments in the city. The Edo townsman was happy, on the whole, to serve and to make money. He saw enough of the bureaucracy to know that its lesser members, at least, looked upon his own life with some envy.

Land-use maps, though they disagree in matters of detail, are consistent in showing a very large part of the city given over to the aristocracy and to temples and shrines, and a very small part to the plebeian classes, mercantile and artisan. If the expression "aristocracy" is defined broadly to include everyone attached in some fashion to the central bureaucracy and the establishments of the provincial lords, then the Edo townsman occupied perhaps as little as a fifth of the city. Not even the flatlands commonly held to be his abode belonged entirely to him. The banks of the Sumida were largely aristocratic all the way to Asakusa. The aristocracy possessed most of the land east of the river, and very large expanses as well in eastern Nihombashi and to the east of Ginza. There were extensive temple lands along the northern and southern fringes of the flatlands. A half million townsmen were crowded into what was indeed a small part of the city, scarcely enough to make up two of the present inner wards, or four of the smaller Meiji wards.

In the late eighteenth and early nineteenth centuries, Edo was probably the largest city in the world. The population was well over a million, perhaps at times as much as a million and two or three hundred thousand, in a day when the largest European city, London, had not yet reached a million. The merchant and artisan population was stable at a half million. The huge military aristocracy and bureaucracy made up most of the rest. There were also large numbers of priests, Buddhist and Shinto, numbering, with their families, as many as a hundred thousand persons; and there were pariahs, beneath even the merchants, the lowest of the four classes established by Tokugawa orthodoxy. There were indigents and transients. And finally there were entertainers, accommodated more and more uncomfortably by the Tokugawa regime as it moved into its last years.

Pictures of Edo—woodcuts and screens—make it seem the loveliest of places to live. Elegant little shops are elegantly disposed among temples and shrines, each of which offers a range of amusing sights and performers, jugglers and acrobats and musicians and swordsmen, and perhaps a tiger or an elephant brought from abroad in response to the exotic yearnings of a sequestered populace.

Prominent in such representations are the main streets of Nihombashi. They suggest a pleasant buzz of life, which indeed there must have been, but they do not reveal the equally probable crowding of the back streets. The main or "front" streets were for the better shops and the wealthier merchants. Lesser people occupied the alleys behind, living in rows of shingled huts along open gutters, using common wells and latrines.

The old city did not fill the fifteen wards of the Meiji city, much less the twenty-three wards of the present city. "It is Edo as far as the Kaneyasu," said the Edo maxim, with reference to a famous shop in the Hongō district, not far from the present Hongō campus of Tokyo University. There the provinces were said to begin, even though the jurisdiction of the city magistrates extended somewhat farther; and today the Kaneyasu is practically downtown. The city extended no more than a mile or two in most directions from the castle, and a considerably shorter distance before it reached the bay on the east. In a fifth or so of this limited area lived the steady and permanent populace of a half million townsmen, a twentieth, roughly, of the present population, on much less than a twentieth of the present land. In the back alleys the standard dwelling for the artisan or the poorer tradesman was the "nine-by-twelve," two rooms, one of them earth-floored, with nine feet of frontage on the alley and extending twelve feet back from it. The wealthier merchants lived, some of them, as expansively and extravagantly as the aristocrats of the High City, but lesser inhabitants of the Low City lived with mud, dust, darkness, foul odors, insects, and epidemics. Most of the huts in the back alleys had roofs of the flimsiest and most combustible sort. They burned merrily when there was a fire. The city was proud of its fires, which were called *Edo no harm*, "the flowers of Edo," and occurred so frequently and burned so freely that no house in the Low City could expect to last more than two decades. Some did, of course, and some have survived even into our day, but actuarial figures announced doom at intervals of no more than a quarter of a century.

It is easy to become sentimental about Edo and the beautiful way of life depicted on the screens. Nostalgia is the chief ware offered by the professional Edokko. But Meiji was an exuberant period, and even for the most conservative inhabitant there must have been a sense of release at its advent.

Tanizaki had a famous vision after the earthquake of what the rebuilt city would be like. He was in the Hakone mountains, some forty miles southwest of Tokyo, when the earthquake struck. He rejoiced in the destruction of the old city, and looked forward to something less constricting. Since he doubtless had the Nihombashi of his boyhood in mind, and the mood of Edo was still strong in that place and in those days, we may feel in his musings something of what the son of Edo must have felt upon leaving Edo and the repressive old regime behind.

Lafcadio Hearn once said that a person never forgets the things seen and heard in the depths of sorrow; but it seems to me that, whatever the time of sorrow, a person also thinks of the happy, the bright, the comical, things quite the opposite of sorrowful. When the earthquake struck I knew that I had survived, and I feared for my wife and daughter, left behind in Yokohama. Almost simultaneously I felt a surge of happiness which I could not keep down. "Tokyo will be better for this!" I said to myself....

I have heard that it did not take ten years for San Francisco to be a finer city than before the earthquake. Tokyo too would be rebuilt in ten years, into a solid expanse of splendid buildings like the Marunouchi Building and the Marine Insurance Building. I imagined the grandeur of the new metropolis, and all the changes that would come in customs and manners as well. An orderly pattern of streets, their bright new pavements gleaming. A flood of automobiles. The geometric beauty of block towering upon block, and elevated lines and subways and trolleys weaving among them, and the stir of a nightless city, and pleasure facilities to rival those of Paris and New York.... Fragments of the new Tokyo passed before my eyes, numberless, like flashes in a movie. Soirees, evening dresses and swallowtails and dinner jackets moving in and out, and champagne glasses floating up like the moon upon the ocean. The confusion of late night outside a theater, headlights crossing one another on darkly shining streets. The flood of gauze and satin and legs and illumination that is vaudeville. The seductive laughter of streetwalkers beneath the lights of Ginza and Asakusa and Marunouchi and Hibiya Park. The secret pleasures of Turkish baths, massage parlors, beauty parlors. Weird crimes. I have long had a way of giving myself up to daydreams in which I imagine all manner of curious things, but it was very strange indeed that these phantasms should be so stubbornly entwined among sad visions of my wife and daughter.

In the years after the Second World War, one was frequently surprised to hear from the presumably fortunate resident of an unbombed pocket that he would have been happier if it too had been bombed. A lighter and airier dwelling, more consonant with modern conveniences, might then have taken its place. The Edo townsman must have shared this view when the gates to the back alleys were dismantled and, after disappearing in fires, the alleys themselves were replaced by something more in keeping with Civilization and Enlightenment, as the rallying call of the new day had it.

Meiji brought industrial soot and other forms of advanced ugliness, and Nagai Kafū's laments for a lost harmony were not misplaced. But it also brought liberation from old fears and afflictions. In the spring of

Kotsukappara execution grounds

1888 services were held on the site of the old Kotsukappara execution grounds, in the northern suburbs, for the repose of the souls of those who had been beheaded or otherwise put to death there. The number was then estimated at a hundred thousand. The temple that now stands on the site claims to comfort and solace two hundred thousand departed spirits. If the latter figure is accepted, then about two persons a day lost their lives at Kotsukappara through the three hundred years of its use—and Kotsukappara was not the only execution grounds at the disposal of the Edo magistracy. The Meiji townsman need fear no such judicial harshness, and he was gradually rescued from epidemics and fires as well.

There was also spiritual liberation. The playwright Hasegawa Shigure, a native of Nihombashi, thus described the feelings of her father upon the promulgation, on February 11, 1889, of the Meiji constitution: "His joy and that of his fellows had to do with the end of the old humiliation, the expunging of the stigma they had carried for so many years as Edo townsmen."

One should guard against sentimentality, then; but there is the other extreme to be guarded against as well. The newly enlightened elite of Meiji was strongly disposed to dismiss Edo culture as vulgar and decadent, and the latter adjective is one commonly applied even now to the arts and literature of the early nineteenth century.

Perhaps it was "decadent," in a certain narrow sense, that so much of Edo culture should have centered upon the pleasure quarters, and it is certainly true that not much late-Edo literature seems truly superior. The rigid conservatism of the shogunate, and the fact that the pleasure quarters were the only places where a small degree of democracy prevailed (class did not matter, only money and taste), may be held responsible for the decadence, if decadence there was. As for the inadequacy of late-Edo literature, good taste itself may have been more important than the products of good taste.

Because of its exquisite products we think of the Heian Period, when the Shining Genji of the tale that bears his name did everything so beautifully, as a time when everyone had good taste. But it is by its nature something that not everyone possesses. Courtly Heian and mercantile Edo must have been rather similar in that good taste was held to be important and the devices for cultivating it were abundant.

Edo culture was better than anything it left to posterity. Its genius was theatrical. The *chanoyu*, the tea ceremony, that most excellent product of an earlier age, was also essentially theatrical. In the hands of the affluent and cultivated, it brought together the best in handicrafts, in painting, and in architecture, and the "ceremony" itself was a sort of dance punctuated by ritualized conversation. The objects that surrounded it and became a part of it survived, of course, but, whatever may have been the effect on the minds and spirits of the participants, the occasion itself was an amalgam of beautiful elements put together for a few moments, and dispersed.

So it was too with the highest accomplishments of Edo—and the likening of an evening at the Yoshiwara to an afternoon of tea is not to be taken as jest. In both cases, the performance was the important thing. The notion of leaving something behind for all generations was not relevant. Much that is good in the Occidental theater is also satisfying as literature, but writings for the Tokugawa theater, whether of Edo or of Osaka, tend not to be.

The best of Edo was in the Kabuki theater and in the pleasure quarters, whose elegant evenings also wore a theatrical aspect. It was a very good best, a complex of elements combining, as with *chanoyu*, into a moment of something like perfection. The theater reached in many directions, to dominate, for instance, the high demimonde. The theaters and the pleasure quarters were in a symbiotic relationship. The main business of the Yoshiwara and the other quarters was, of course, prostitution, but the preliminaries were theatrical. Great refinement in song and dance was as important to the Yoshiwara as to the theater. There were many grades of courtesan, the lowest of them an unadorned prostitute with her crib and her brisk way of doing business, but letters and paintings by the great Yoshiwara ladies turn up from time to time in exhibitions and sales, to show how accomplished they were.

The pleasure quarters were culture centers, among the few places where the townsman of affluence could feel that he had things his way, without censorious magistrates telling him to stay down there at the bottom of an unchanging social order. The Yoshiwara was central to the culture of Edo from its emergence in the seventeenth century as something more than a provincial outpost.

The elegance of the Yoshiwara was beyond the means of the poorer shopkeeper or artisan, but he shared the Edo passion for things theatrical. The city was dotted with Yose, variety or vaudeville halls, where he could go and watch and pass the time of day for a very small admission fee. There he found serious and comic monologues, imitations of great actors, juggling and balancing acts, and mere oddities. At no expense whatever there were shows on festival days in the precincts of shrines and temples. A horror play on a summer night was held to have a pleasantly chilling effect; and indeed summer, most oppressive season for the salaried middle class of the new day, was for the Edo townsman the best of seasons. He could wander around half naked of a warm evening, taking in the sights.

He did it mostly on foot. A scarcity of wheels characterized Edo, and the shift from feet to wheels was among the major revolutions of Meiji. The affluent of Edo had boats and palanquins, but almost no one but draymen used wheels. More than one modern Japanese city has been described as "the Venice of Japan," and the appellation might have been used for Edo—it was not as maritime in its habits as Venice, and the proportion of waterways to streets was certainly lower, but there was a resemblance all the same. Edo had a network of waterways, natural and artificial, and the pleasantest way to go to the Yoshiwara was by boat. Left

Pleasure boats moored in the northern suburbs in winter, early Meiji

behind by movements and concentrations of modern power, Venice remained Venice. Not Edo. No Japanese city escaped the flood of wheeled vehicles, and there really is no Venice of modern Japan. *Something* more of the Edo canal and river system might have survived, however, if the city had not become the political center of the modern country, leading the way into Civilization and Enlightenment.

In late Edo the resident of Nihombashi had to go what was for him a long distance if he wished a day at the theater or a night in the Yoshiwara. The theaters and the Yoshiwara were there side by side, leagued geographically as well as aesthetically in the northern suburbs. The Yoshiwara had been there through most of the Tokugawa Period. It was popularly known as "the paddies." The Kabuki theaters were moved north only in very late Edo, when the shogunate had a last seizure of puritanical zeal, and sought to ease its economic difficulties by making the townsman live frugally.

Asakusa was already a thriving center because of its Kannon temple, and it had long been the final station for wayfarers to the Yoshiwara. Now it had the Kabuki theaters to perform a similar service for. In the last decades of Edo, the theaters and the greatest of the pleasure quarters both lay just beyond the northeastern fringe of the city, and Asakusa was that fringe. The efforts of the shogunate to discourage indulgence and prodigality among the lower classes thus had the effect of making Asakusa, despite its unfortunate situation in watery suburban lands, the great entertainment district of the city. This it was to become most decisively in Meiji.

The Kannon drew bigger crowds of pilgrims, many of them more intent upon pleasure than upon devotion, than any other temple in the city, and a big crowd was among the things the city loved best. Crowds were their own justification, and the prospect of a big crowd was usually enough to make it even bigger. When the Yoshiwara was first moved north in the seventeenth century, the Kannon sat among tidal marshes, a considerable distance north of Nihombashi, and beyond one of the points guarding access to the city proper. That is why the Yoshiwara was moved there. The shogunate did not go to the extreme of outlawing pleasure, but pleasure was asked, like funerals and cemeteries, to keep its distance.

The same happened, much later, to the theaters. The Tempo sumptuary edicts, issued between 1841 and 1843, were complex and meticulous, regulating small details of the townsman's life. The number of variety halls in the city was reduced from upwards of five hundred to fifteen, and the fifteen were required to be serious and edifying.

Ladies in several trades—musicians, hairdressers, and the proprietresses of archery stalls in such places as the Asakusa Kannon—were held to be a wanton influence, and forbidden to practice.

In 1842 the Kabuki theater was picked up and moved to the northern limits of the city, a five-minute walk nearer Asakusa than the Yoshiwara. Kabuki was enormously popular in the early decades of the nineteenth century. The more successful actors were cultural heroes and leaders of fashion and taste, not unlike television personalities today. When two major theaters burned down, permission to rebuild was denied, and the possibility was considered of outlawing Kabuki completely. There was disagreement among the city magistrates, and a compromise was reached, permitting them to rebuild, but far from their old grounds. The suburban villa of a daimyo was taken over for the purpose. There the theaters remained even after the reforming zeal had passed, and there they were when Edo became Tokyo, and the Meiji Period began.

So Asakusa was well placed to provide the city of the new era with its pleasures. It has declined sadly in recent decades, and its preeminence in late Edo and early Meiji may have been partly responsible. People had traveled there on foot and by boat. Now they were to travel on wheels. The future belonged to rapid transit and to places where commuters boarded suburban trains. Overly confident, Asakusa chose not to become one of these.

It is of course a story of gradual change. The city has always been prone to sudden change as well, uniformly disastrous. It cannot be said, perhaps, that disasters increased in frequency as the end of Edo approached. Yet they were numerous after the visit of Commodore Perry in 1853, an event which many would doubtless have listed first among them. A foreboding hung over the government and the city.

The traditional system of chronology proceeds not by a single sequence, as with B.C. and A.D., but by a series of era names, which can be changed at the will of the authorities. In premodern Japan, they were often changed in hopes of better fortune; when one name did not seem to be working well, another was tried. The era name was changed a year after the Perry visit, and four times in less than a decade before the Meiji Restoration finally brought an end to the agonies of the Tokugawa.

Half the Low City was destroyed in the earthquake of 1855. There were two great fires in 1858 and numbers of lesser but still major fires through the remaining Tokugawa years, one of which destroyed the Yoshiwara. The main redoubt of the castle was twice destroyed by fire during the 1860s. Rebuilding was beyond the resources of the shogunate.

A lesser redoubt, hastily and roughly rebuilt after yet another fire, became the Meiji palace, and served in that capacity until it was destroyed again, early in the new era. A fire which destroyed yet another of the lesser redoubts was blamed on arson. The Meiji emperor spent most of his first Tokyo decades in a Tokugawa mansion to the southwest of the main palace compound. It later became the Akasaka Detached Palace and the residence of the crown prince, and is now the site of the guest house where visiting monarchs and prelates are put up.

There were, as there had always been, epidemics. It was possible to see ominous portents in them too. A nationwide cholera epidemic in 1858 was laid to the presence of an American warship in Nagasaki.

The opening of the ports meant the arrival of the foreign merchant and missionary, and the undisguised adventurer. The Tokugawa regime never got around to lifting the anti-Christian edicts of the seventeenth century, but Christianity was tolerated so long as the congregations were foreign. Inflation followed the opening of the ports. The merchant was blamed. On a single night in 1864, ten Japanese merchants were killed or injured, in attacks that must have been concerted.

"Rice riots" occurred in the autumn of 1866 while the funeral of the fourteenth shogun was in progress. The coincidence was ominous. In-

Doughnut cloud forms above the Central Weather Bureau in Kōjimachi as fires sweep the Low City after the earthquake

deed, everything about the death of the shogun was ominous, as if the gods had withdrawn their mandate. He had been a very young man, barely past adolescence, and his election had quieted factional disputes which now broke out afresh. He died of beriberi in Osaka, the first in the Tokugawa line to die away from Edo.

The riots began in Fukagawa, east of the Sumida River, as peaceful assemblies of poor people troubled by the high cost of food. In a few days, crowds were gathering in the flatlands west of the river, so large and dense as to block streets. There were lesser gatherings in the hilly districts as well, and four days before the climax of the funeral ceremonies violence broke out. Godowns (as warehouses were called in the East) filled with rice were looted, as were the shops of *karamonoya*, "dealers in Chinese wares," by which was meant foreign wares in general and specifically the products beginning to enter the country through Yokohama. It was in the course of the disturbances that the American consul was stoned, at Ueno, where he was observing the excitement.

What had begun as protests over economic grievances were colored by fright and anger at the changes that had come and were coming. The regime was not seriously endangered by the disturbances, which were disorganized and without revolutionary goals, but the anti-foreign strain is significant. Though the past may have been dark and dirty, the city did not, on the whole, want to give it up.

Yet the Tokugawa regime had brought trouble upon itself, and upon the city. The population had begun to shrink even before the Restoration. In 1862 relaxation was permitted of an institution central to the Tokugawa system, the requirement that provincial lords keep their families and spend part of their own time in Edo. Families were permitted to go to their provincial homes. There was a happy egress. The Mori of Nagato, most aggressive of the anti-Tokugawa clans, actually dismantled their main Edo mansion and took it home with them. It had stood just south of the castle, where a vacant expanse now seemed to mark the end of an era.

Widespread unemployment ensued among the lower ranks of the military, and a great loss of economic vitality throughout the city. An attempt in 1864 to revive the old system, under which the families of the daimyo were in effect held hostage in Edo, was unsuccessful. It may be that these changes did not significantly hasten the Tokugawa collapse, but they affected the city immediately and harshly. They plainly announced, as did the presence of foreigners, that things would not be the same again.

In 1863 the fourteenth shogun, Iemochi, he whose funeral coincided with the rice riots, felt constrained to go to Kyoto, the emperor's capital, to discuss the foreign threat. The dissident factions were clamoring for immediate and final expulsion. Iemochi was the first shogun to visit Kyoto since the early seventeenth century. Though he returned to Edo for a time, the last years of his tenure were spent largely in and near Kyoto. His successor Keiki (Yoshinobu), the fifteenth and last shogun, did not live in Edo at all during his brief tenure.

The Tokugawa system of city magistrates continued to the end, but the shogun's seat was for the most part without a shogun after 1863. The city could not know what sort of end it would be. The shogun was gone, and his prestige and the city's had been virtually identical. Would someone of similar qualities take his place, or would Edo become merely another provincial city—a remote outpost, even, as it had been before 1600? The half-million townsmen who remained after the shogun and his retainers had departed could but wait and see.

Chapter 2

CIVILIZATION AND ENLIGHTENMENT

The fifteenth and last shogun, no longer shogun, returned to Edo early in 1868.

Efforts to "punish" the rebellious southwestern clans had ended most ingloriously. The Tokugawa regime did not have the resources for further punitive expeditions. The southwestern clans already had the beginnings of a modern conscript army, while the Tokugawa forces were badly supplied and perhaps not very militant, having had too much peace and fun in Edo over the centuries. Seeing the hopelessness of his cause, the shogun resigned early in 1868 (by the solar calendar; it was late 1867 by the old lunar calendar). He himself remained high in the esteem of the city. Late in Meiji, when his long exile in Shizuoka was at an end, he would be invited to write "Nihombashi" for that most symbolic of bridges. Subsequently carved in stone, the inscription survived both earthquake and war. The widow of his predecessor was to become the object of a romantic cult. A royal princess married for political reasons, she refused to leave Edo during the final upheaval.

Politically inspired violence persuaded retainers of the shogunate to flee Edo. The provincial aristocracy had already fled. Its mansions were burned, dismantled, and left to decay. Common criminals took advantage of the political violence to commit violence of their own. The city locked itself in after dark, and large sections of the High City and the regions near the castle were unsafe even in the daytime.

The lower classes stayed on, having nowhere to go, and—as their economy had been based on serving the now-dispersed bureaucracy—little to do either. The population fell to perhaps half a million immediately after the Restoration. The townsmen could scarcely know the attitude of the new authorities toward the foreign barbarians and intercourse with barbarian lands. Yokohama was the most convenient port for trading with America, the country that had started it all, but if the new regime did not propose to be cosmopolitan, then placing the capital in some place remote from Yokohama would be an act of symbolic importance. Some did indeed advocate making Osaka the capital, or having Osaka and Edo as joint capitals.

Even when, in 1868, Edo became Tokyo, "the Eastern Capital," the issue was not finally resolved. By a manipulation of words for which a large Chinese vocabulary makes the modern Japanese language well suited, a capital was "established" in Edo, or Tokyo. The capital was not, however, "moved" from Kyoto. So Kyoto, which means "capital," could go on performing a role it was long accustomed to, that of vestigial or ceremonial capital. The Meiji emperor seems to have gone on thinking of Kyoto as his city; his grave lies within the Kyoto city limits.

Some scholars have argued that the name of the city was not changed to Tokyo at all. The argument seems extreme, but the complexities of the language make it possible. The crucial rescript, issued in 1868, says, insofar as precise translation is possible: "Edo is the great bastion of the east country. Upon it converge the crowds, and from it one can personally oversee affairs of state. Accordingly the place known as Edo will henceforth be Tokyo."

This could mean that Edo is still Edo, but that it is now also "the eastern capital," or, perhaps, "the eastern metropolitan center." Another linguistic curiosity made it possible to pronounce the new designation, whether precisely the same thing as a new name or not, in two ways: "Tokei" or "Tokyo." Both pronunciations were current in early Meiji. W. S. Griffis's guide to the city, published in 1874, informs us that only foreigners still called the city Edo.

The townsmen who stayed on could not know that the emperor would come to live among them in Tokyo, or Tokei. The economic life of the city was at a standstill, and its pleasures virtually so. The theaters closed early in 1868. Few came asking for the services of the Yoshiwara. Forces of the Restoration were advancing upon the city. Restoration was in fact revolution, and it remained to be seen what revolution would do to the seat of the old regime. The city had helped very little in making this new world, and the advancing imperial forces knew that the city had no high opinion of their tastes and manners. Gloom and apprehension prevailed.

The city waited, and the Meiji armies approached from the west. One of the songs to which they advanced would be made by Gilbert and Sullivan into the song of the Mikado's troops. It was written during the march on Edo, the melody by Omura Masujirō, organizer of the Meiji armies. The march was halted short of the Hakone mountains for conferences in Shizuoka and in Edo. It was agreed that the castle would not be defended. The last shogun left the city late in the spring of 1868, and the transfer of city and castle was accomplished, bloodlessly, in the next few days. Advance parties of the revolutionary forces were already at Shinagawa and Itabashi, the first stages from Nihombashi on the coastal and inland roads to Kyoto.

Resistance continued in the city and in the northern provinces. Though most of the Tokugawa forces scattered through the city surrendered, one band took up positions at Ueno, whence it sent forth patrols as if it were still in charge of the city. The heights above Shitaya, now Ueno Park, were occupied by the great Kan-eiji, one of the Tokugawa mortuary temples, behind which lay the tombs of six shoguns. The holdouts controlled the person of the Kan-eiji abbot, a royal prince, and it may have been for this reason that the victors hesitated to attack.

In mid-May by the lunar calendar, on the Fourth of July by the solar, they finally did attack. From early morning, artillery fire fell upon Ueno from the Hongō rise, across a valley to the west. It was only late in the afternoon that the south defenses were breached, at the "Black Gate," near the main entrance to the modern Ueno Park, after a fierce battle. Perhaps three hundred people had been killed, twice as many among the defenders as among the attackers. Much of the shelling seems to have fallen short, setting fires. Most of the Kan-eiji was destroyed, and upwards of a thousand houses burned in the regions between Ueno and the artillery emplacements. The abbot fled in disguise, and presently left the city by boat.

* * *

If we may leave aside linguistic niceties and say that Edo was now Tokyo and the capital of Japan, it was different from the earlier capitals, Nara and Kyoto. It was already a large city with a proud history. Edo as the shogun's seat may have been an early instance of a fabricated capital or seat of power, but it had both Chinese and Japanese forebears. Nara and Kyoto had been built upon rural land to become capitals; there had been no urban class on hand to wish that the government had not come. So it had been with Edo when it first became the shogun's seat, but when it became the emperor's capital there were the centuries of Edo to look back upon. The proper son of Edo had acquired status by virtue of his nearness to Lord Tokugawa, and when he had the resources with which to pursue good taste, he could congratulate himself that he did it impeccably. Now came these swarms of bumpkins, not at all delicate in their understanding of Edo manners.

> Destroyed, my city, by the rustic warrior.
> No shadow left of Edo as it was.

This is Tanizaki Junichirō, speaking, much later, for the son of Edo. It is an exaggeration, of course, but many an Edo townsman would have echoed him.

The emperor departed Kyoto in the autumn of 1868. He reached the Shinagawa post station, just south of the city, after a journey of some three weeks, and entered the castle on the morning of November 26. Townsmen turned out in huge numbers, but the reception was reverent rather than boisterous; utter silence prevailed. By way of precaution against the city's most familiar disaster, businesses requiring fires were ordered to take a holiday. Then the city started coming back to life. Despite its affection for Lord Tokugawa, it was happy to drink a royal cup. Holidays were decreed in December (the merchant class of Edo had allowed itself scarcely any holidays); two thousand five hundred sixty-three casks of royal sake were distributed through the city, and emptied.

The emperor returned to Kyoto early in 1869, after the pacification of the northern provinces. He was back in Tokyo in the spring, at which time his permanent residence may be said to have begun. He did not announce that he was leaving Kyoto permanently, and the old capital went on expecting him back. It was not until 1871 that the last court offices were removed from Kyoto, and most of the court aristocracy settled in Tokyo. Edo castle became what it is today, the royal palace, and Tokyo the political center of the country. Until 1923 there was scarcely a suggestion that matters should be otherwise.

The outer gates to the palace were dismantled by 1872, it having early been decided that the castle ramparts were exaggerated, and that the emperor did not need such ostentatious defenses. Several inner gates, though not the innermost, were released from palace jurisdiction, but not immediately dismantled. The stones from two of the castle guard points were used to build bridges, which the new regime favored, as the old had not.

Initial policy towards the city was cautious, not to say confused. In effect the Edo government was perpetuated, with a different terminology.

The north and south magistrates, both with offices in the flatlands east of the castle, were renamed "courts," and, as under the Tokugawa, charged with governing the city in alternation.

A "red line" drawn in 1869 defined the city proper. It followed generally the line that had marked the jurisdiction of the Tokugawa magistrates. A few months later the area within the red line was divided into six wards. The expression "Tokyo Prefecture," meaning the city and larger surrounding jurisdiction, had first been used in 1868. In 1871 the prefecture was divided into eleven wards, the six wards of the inner city remaining as before. In 1878 the six were divided into fifteen, covering an area somewhat smaller than the six inner wards of the city today and the two wards immediately east of the Sumida. There were minor revisions of the city limits from time to time, and in 1920 there was a fairly major one, when a part of the Shinjuku district on the west (not including the station or the most prosperous part of Shinjuku today) was brought into Yotsuya Ward. The fifteen wards remained unchanged, except in these matters of detail, until after the Second World War, and it was only in 1932 that the city limits were expanded to include thirty-five wards, covering generally the eleven wards, or the Tokyo Prefecture, of 1872. The red line of early Meiji takes some curious turns, jogging northwards above Asakusa, for instance, to include the Yoshiwara, and showing in graphic fashion how near the Yoshiwara was, and Asakusa as well, to open paddy land. The Tokyo Prefecture of early Meiji was not as large as the prefecture of today, and the prefecture has never been as large as the old Musashi Province in which Edo was situated. The Tama district, generally the upper valley of the Tama River, which in its lower reaches was and is the boundary between Tokyo and Kanagawa prefectures, was transferred to Kanagawa Prefecture in 1871. Because it was the chief source of the Tokyo water supply and an important source of *building materials as well,* there was earnest campaigning by successive governors to have it back. In 1893 it was returned, and so the area of the prefecture was tripled. The Izu Islands had been transferred from Shizuoka Prefecture in 1878 and the Ogasawara or Bonin Islands from the Ministry of the Interior in 1880. The Iwo Islands were added to the Ogasawaras in 1891, and so, with the return of the Tama district two years later, the boundaries of the prefecture were set as they remain today. Remote though they are, the Bonin and Iwo Islands, except when under American jurisdiction, have continued to be a part of Tokyo. It is therefore not completely accurate to say that Okinawa was the only prefecture invaded during the Second World War.

A still remoter region, the Nemuro district of Hokkaido, was for a time in early Meiji a part of Tokyo Prefecture. The economy of the city was still in a precarious state, because it had not yet been favored with the equivalent of the huge Tokugawa bureaucracy, and the hope was that these jurisdictional arrangements would help in relocating the poor.

Tokyo Prefecture was one of three *fu*, which might be rendered "metropolitan prefecture." The other two were Osaka and Kyoto. Local autonomy was more closely circumscribed in the three than in other prefectures. They had their first mayors in 1898, almost a decade later than other cities. Osaka and Kyoto have continued to be *fu*, and to have mayors as well as governors. Tokyo became a *to*, or "capital district," during the Second World War, the only one in the land. Today it is the only city, town, or village in the land that does not have a mayor.

On September 30, 1898, the law giving special treatment to the three large cities was repealed, and so October 1 is observed in Tokyo as Citizens' Day, the anniversary of the day on which it too was permitted a mayor. He was chosen through a city council voted into office by a very small electorate. The council named three candidates, of whom one was appointed mayor by imperial rescript, upon the recommendation of the Ministry of the Interior. It became accepted practice for the candidate with the largest support in the council to be named mayor. The first mayor was a councilman from Kanda Ward, in the Low City. Tokyo has had at least two very famous mayors, Ozaki Yukio, who lived almost a century and was a stalwart defender of parliamentary democracy in difficult times, and Gotō Shimpei, known as "the mayor with the big kerchief," an expression suggesting grand and all-encompassing plans. Though it cannot be said that Gotō's big kerchief came to much of anything, he is credited by students of the subject with having done more than any other mayor to give the city a sense of its right to autonomy. He resigned a few weeks before the great earthquake to take charge of difficult negotiations with revolutionary Russia, but his effectiveness had already been reduced considerably by the assassination in 1921 of Hara Takeshi, the prime minister, to whom he was close. Before he became mayor he had already achieved eminence in the administration of Taiwan (then a Japanese possession) and in the national government.

The first city council was elected in 1889, the year other cities were permitted to elect mayors. There were three classes of electors, divided according to income, each of which elected its own councilmen.

Some very eminent men were returned to the council in that first election, and indeed lists of councilmen through successive elections are worthy of a body with more considerable functions. The Ministry of the Interior had a veto power over acts of the city government and from time to time exercised the power, which had an inhibiting effect on the mayor and the council. Fukuzawa Yukichi, perhaps the most successful popularizer of Civilization and Enlightenment, the rallying call of the new day, was among those elected to the first council. Yasuda Zenjirō, founder of the Yasuda (now the Fuji) financial empire, was returned by the poorest class of electors.

The high standards of the council did not pervade all levels of government. There were scandals. The most sensational was the one known as the gravel scandal. On the day in 1920 that the Meiji Shrine was dedicated (to the memory of the Meiji emperor), part of a bridge just below the shrine collapsed. Investigation revealed that crumbly cement had been used, and this in turn led to revelations of corruption in the city government. The gravel scandal coincided with a utilities scandal, and the mayor, among the most popular the city has had, resigned, to be succeeded by the famous Gotō Shimpei. Tokyo deserves the name it has made for itself as a well-run city, but City Hall does have its venalities from time to time.

The Meiji system, local and national, could hardly be called democratic, but it was more democratic than the Tokugawa system had been. It admitted the possibility of radical departures. Rather large numbers of people, without reference to pedigree, had something to say about how they would be governed. Meiji was a vital period, and gestures toward recognizing plebeian talents and energies may help to account for the vitality. The city suffered from "happy insomnia," said Hasegawa Shigure, on the night the Meiji constitution went into effect.

Her father made a speech. The audience was befuddled, shouting, "No, no!" when prearranged signals called for "Hear, hear!" and vice versa; but it was happy, so much so that one man literally drank himself to death. It is an aspect of Meiji overlooked by those who view it as a time of dark repression containing the seeds of 1945.

The population of the city increased from about the fifth year of Meiji. It did not reach the highest Edo levels until the mid-1880s. The sparsely populated High City was growing at a greater rate than the Low City, though in absolute terms the accretion was larger in the Low City. The new population came overwhelmingly from the poor rural areas of northeastern Japan. Despite its more stable population, the Low City had a higher divorce rate than the High City, and a higher rate than the average for the nation. But then the Low City had always been somewhat casual

The Meiji emperor, photographed in 1872

toward sex and domesticity. It had a preponderantly male population, and
Tokyo continues to be one of the few places in the land where men outnumber women. The High City changed more than the Low City in the
years between the Restoration and the earthquake, but when sons of Edo
lament the death of their city, they refer to the dispersal of the townsman
and his culture, the culture of the Low City. The rich moved away and so
their patronage of the arts was withdrawn, and certain parts of the Low
City, notably those immediately east of the palace, changed radically.

Change, as it always is, was uneven. Having heard the laments of the
sons of Edo and turned to scrutinize the evidence, one may be more surprised at the continuity. The street pattern, for instance, changed little

between Restoration and earthquake. In his 1874 guide to the city, W. E. Griffis remarked upon "the vast extent of open space as well as the lowness and perishable material of which the houses are built." Pictures taken from the roof of the City Hall in the last years of Meiji still show astonishing expanses of open land, where once the mansions of the military aristocracy had stood. Photographs from the Nikolai Cathedral in Kanda, taken upwards of a decade earlier, show almost unbroken expanses of low wooden buildings all the way to the horizon, dissolving into what were more probably photographic imperfections than industrial mists.

One would have had to scan the expanses carefully to find precise and explicit survivals among the back alleys of Edo. Fires were too frequent, and the wish to escape the confines of an alley and live on a street, however narrow, was too strong. Yet one looks at those pictures taken from heights and wonders what all those hundreds of thousands of people were doing and thinking, and the very want of striking objects seems to offer an answer. The hundreds of thousands must have been far closer to their forebears of a hundred years before than to the leaders, foreign and domestic, of Civilization and Enlightenment.

Even today the Low City is different from the High City—tighter, more conservative, less given to voguish things. The difference is something that has survived, not something that has been wrought by the modern century.

It was considered very original of Charles Beard, not long before the earthquake, to characterize Tokyo as a collection of villages, but the concept was already familiar enough. John Russell Young, in attendance upon General and Mrs. Grant when they came visiting in 1879, thus described a passage up the river to dine at an aristocratic mansion:

> The Prince had intended to entertain us in his principal town-house, the one nearest the Enriokwan, but the cholera broke out in the vicinity, and the Prince invited us to another of his houses in the suburbs of Tokio. We turned into the river, passing the commodious grounds of the American Legation, its flag weather-worn and shorn; passing the European settlement, which looked a little like a well-to-do Connecticut town, noting the little missionary churches surmounted by the cross; and on for an hour or so past tea houses and ships and under bridges, and watching the shadows descend over the city. It is hard to realize that Tokio is a city—one of the greatest cities of the world. It looks like a series of villages, with bits of green and open spaces and inclosed grounds breaking up the continuity of the town. There is no special character to Tokio, no one trait to seize upon and remember,

except that the aspect is that of repose. The banks of the river are low
and sedgy, at some points a marsh. When we came to the house of
the Prince we found that he had built a causeway of bamboo through
the marsh out into the river.

The city grew almost without interruption from early Meiji to the
earthquake. There was a very slight population drop just before the First
World War, to be accounted for by economic disquiet, but by the end of
Meiji there were not far from two million people. Early figures, based on
family registers, proved to be considerably exaggerated when, in 1908,
the national government made a careful survey. It showed a population
of about a million and two-thirds. This had risen to over two million by
1920, when the first national census was taken. The 1920 census showed
that almost half the residents of the city had been born elsewhere, the
largest number in Chiba Prefecture, just across the bay; and so it may be
that the complaints of the children of Edo about the new men from the
southwest were exaggerated. In the decade preceding the census (the figures are based upon family registers) the three central wards seem to have
gained population at a much lower rate than the city as a whole. The most
rapid rate of increase was in Yotsuya Ward, to the west of the palace. The
High City was becoming more clearly the abode of the elite, now identified more in terms of money than of family or military prowess. Wealthy
merchants no longer had to live in the crowded lowlands, and by the end
of Meiji most of them had chosen to leave. Asakusa Ward stood first both
in population and in population density.

Tokyo had been somewhat tentatively renamed and reorganized, but
it passed through the worst of the Restoration uncertainty by the fourth
or fifth year of Meiji, and was ready for Civilization and Enlightenment:
Bummei Kaika. The four Chinese characters, two words, very old, provided the magical formula for the new day. *Bummei* is generally rendered
as "civilization," though it is closely related to *bunka,* usually rendered
as "culture." *Kaika* means something like "opening" or "liberalization,"
though "enlightenment" is perhaps the commonest rendering. Both words
are ancient borrowings from Chinese. As early as 1867 they were put together and offered as an alternative to the dark shadows of the past.

"Examining history, we see that life has been dark and closed, and that
it advances in the direction of civilization and enlightenment." Already
in 1867 we have the expression from the brush of Fukuzawa Yukichi,
who was to coin many another new word and expression for the new
day. Though in 1867 Fukuzawa was still a young man, not far into his

thirties, the forerunner of what was to become his very own Keiō University had been in session for almost a decade. No other university seems so much the creation of a single man. His was a powerful and on the whole benign personality. In education and journalism and all manner of other endeavors he was the most energetic and successful of propagandizers for the liberal and utilitarian principles that, in his view, were to beat the West at its own game.

For the Meiji regime, *Bummei Kaika* meant Western modes and methods. Though not always of such liberal inclinations as Fukuzawa, the regime agreed that the new formula would be useful in combatting Western encroachment. Tokyo and Osaka, the great cities of the old day, led the advance, together with the port cities of the new.

The encroachment was already apparent, and it was to be more so with the arrival of large-nosed, pinkish foreigners in considerable numbers. The formal opening of Edo was scheduled to occur in 1862. Unsettled conditions brought a five-year delay. The shogunate continued building a foreign settlement all the same. Tsukiji, on the bay east of the castle and the Ginza district, was selected for reasons having to do with protecting both foreigner from native and native from foreigner. Isolated from the rest of the city by canals and gates and a considerable amount of open space known as Navy Meadow, the settlement was ready for occupation in 1867. The foreign legations, of which there were then eleven, received word some weeks after the Restoration that the opening of the city must wait until more equable conditions prevailed. The government finally announced it towards the end of the year. Several legations, the American legation among them, moved to Tsukiji.

The gates to the settlement were early abandoned, and access became free. Foreigners employed by the government received residences elsewhere in the city, in such places as "the Kaga estate" *(Kaga yashiki),* the present Hongo campus of Tokyo University. Others had to live in the Tsukiji quarter if they were to live in Tokyo at all. Not many of them did. Tsukiji was never popular with Europeans and Americans, except the missionaries among them. The foreign population wavered around a hundred, and increasingly it was Chinese. Though small, it must have been interesting. A list of foreign residents for 1872 includes a Frenchman described as an "equestrian acrobat." Among them were, of course, bad ones, opium dealers and the like, and the gentle treatment accorded them by the consulates aroused great resentment, which had the contradictory effect of increasing enthusiasm for Civilization and

Enlightenment—faithful application of the formula, it was felt, might persuade foreign powers to do without extraterritoriality.

The two chief wonders of Tsukiji did not lie within the foreign settlement. The Tsukiji Hoterukan was across a canal to the south. The New Shimabara licensed quarter, established to satisfy the presumed needs of foreign gentlemen, was to the north and west, towards Kyōbashi.

The Hoterukan could only be early Meiji. Both the name and the building tell of the first meetings between Meiji Japan and the West. *Hoteru* is "hotel," and *kan* is a Sino-Japanese term of roughly the same meaning. The building was the delight of early photographers and late print-makers. One must lament its short history, for it was an original, a Western building unlike any building in the West. The structure, like its name, had a mongrel air, foreign details applied to a traditional base or frame. The builder was Shimizu Kisuke, founder of the Shimizu-gumi, one of the largest modern construction companies. Shimizu was a master carpenter, or perhaps a sort of building contractor, who came from a province on the Japan Sea to study foreign architecture in Yokohama.

Although the Hoterukan was completed in early Meiji, it had been planned from the last days of Tokugawa as an adjunct to the foreign settlement. It took the shape of an elongated U. Records of its dimensions are inconsistent, but it was perhaps two hundred feet long, with more than two hundred rooms on three floors, and a staff numbering more than a hundred. Tokugawa instincts required that it face away from the sea and towards the nondescript Ginza and Navy Meadow; the original design, taking advantage of the grandest prospect, was reversed by xenophobic bureaucrats, who wished the place to look more like a point of egress than a point of ingress. There was a pretty Japanese garden on the bay side, with a tea cottage and a pergola, but the most striking features of the exterior were the tower, reminiscent of a sixteenth-century Japanese castle, and walls of the traditional sort called *namako*, or "trepang," dark tiles laid diagonally with white interstices.

From the outside, little about it except the height and the window sashes seems foreign at all, though perhaps an Anglo-Indian influence is apparent in the wide verandas. Wind bells hung along chains from a weathervane to the corners of the tower. The interior was plastered and painted in the foreign manner.

Through the brief span of its existence, the Hoterukan was among the wonders of the city. Like the quarter itself, however, it does not seem to have been the sort of place people wished to live in. It was sold in 1870 to a consortium of Yokohama businessmen, and in 1872 it disappeared in the great Ginza fire. (It may be of interest to note that this calamity, like the military rising of 1936, was a Two-Two-Six Incident, an event of the twenty-sixth day of the Second Month. Of course the later event was dated by the solar calendar and the earlier one by the old lunar calendar; yet the Two-Two-Six is obviously one of those days of which to be apprehensive.) The 1872 fire began at three in the afternoon, in a government building within the old castle compound.

Fanned by strong winds, it burned eastward through more than two hundred acres before reaching the bay. Government buildings, temples, and mansions of the old and new aristocracy were taken, and fifty thousand people of the lesser classes were left homeless. It was not the largest fire of the Meiji Period, but it was perhaps the most significant. From it emerged the new Ginza, a commercial center for Civilization and Enlightenment and a symbol of the era.

Then there was that other marvel, the New Shimabara. For the accommodation of the foreigner a pleasure quarter was decreed. It was finished in 1869, among the first accomplishments of the new government. The name was borrowed from the famous Shimabara quarter of Kyoto. Ladies arrived from all over the Kantō district, but most of them came from the Yoshiwara. In 1870, at the height of its short career, it had a very large component indeed, considering the small size of the foreign settlement and its domination by missionaries. It followed the elaborate Yoshiwara system, with teahouses serving as appointment stations for admission to the grander brothels. Upwards of seventeen hundred courtesans and some two hundred geisha, twenty-one of them male, served in more than two hundred establishments, a hundred thirty brothels and eighty-four teahouses.

The New Shimabara did not prosper. Its career, indeed, was even shorter than that of the Hoterukan, for it closed even before the great fire. A report informed the city government that foreigners came in considerable numbers to look, but few lingered to play. The old military class also stayed away. Other pleasure quarters had depended in large measure upon a clientele from the military class, but the New Shimabara got only townsmen. In 1870 fire destroyed a pleasure quarter in Fukagawa, across the river (where, it was said, the last of the real Edo geisha held out). The reassigning of space that followed led to the closing of the New Shimabara. Its ladies were moved to Asakusa. There were no further experiments in publicly sponsored (as opposed to merely licensed) prostitution.

The most interesting thing about the quarter is what it tells us of changing official standards. In very early Meiji it was assumed that the foreigner, not so very different from the Japanese, would of course desire bawdy houses. Prudishness quickly set in, or what might perhaps better be described as deference to foreign standards. When the railway was put through to Yokohama, a land trade resulted in a pleasure quarter right beside the tracks and not far from the Yokohama terminus. Before long, the authorities had it moved away. Foreign visitors would think it out of keeping with Civilization and Enlightenment.

The foreign settlement seems to have been chiefly a place of bright missionary and educational undertakings. Such eminent institutions as Rikkyō University, whose English name is St. Paul's, had their beginnings there, and St. Luke's Hospital still occupies its original Tsukiji site.

The reaction of the impressionable townsman to the quarter is as interesting as the quarter itself. The word "Christian" had taken on sinister connotations during the centuries of isolation. In appearance so very Christian, the settlement was assumed to contain more than met the eye.

At about the turn of the century Tanizaki Junichirō was sent there for English lessons. Late in his life he described the experience:

> There was in those days an English school run by ladies of the purest English stock, or so it was said—not a Japanese among them… Exotic Western houses stood in unbroken rows, and among them an English family named Summer had opened a school. At the gate with its painted louver boards was a wooden plaque bearing, in Chinese, the legend "Bullseye School of European Letters." No one called it by the correct name. It was known rather as "The Summer." I have spoken of "an English family," but we cannot be sure that they were really English. They may have been a collection of miscellaneous persons from Hong Kong and Shanghai and the like. They were, in any event, an assembly of "she foreigners," most alluring, from eighteen or nineteen to perhaps thirty. The outward appearance was as of sisters, and there was an old woman described as their mother; and there was not a man in the house. I remember that the youngest called herself Alice and said she was nineteen. Then there were Lily, Agnes, and Susa [sic]… If indeed they were sisters, it was curious that they resembled each other so little…
>
> Even for us who came in groups, the monthly tuition was a yen, and it must have been considerably more for those who had private lessons. A yen was no small sum of money in those days. The English lived far better, of course, than we who were among the unenlightened. They were civilized. So we could not complain about the tuition…

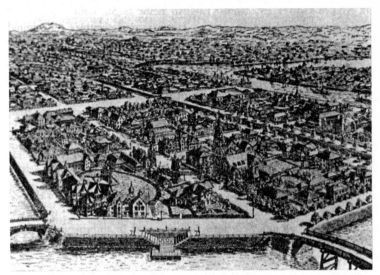

Bird's-eye view of Tsukiji foreign settlement

Wakita spoke in a whisper when he told me—he had apparently heard it from his older brother—that the she foreigners secretly received gentlemen of the Japanese upper classes, and that they were for sale also to certain Kabuki actors (or perhaps in this instance they were the buyers). The Baikō preceding the present holder of that name, he said, was among them. He also said that the matter of private lessons was a strange one, for they took place upstairs during the evening hours. Evidence that Wakita's statement was not a fabrication is at hand, in the "Conference Room" column of the *Tokyo Shimbun* for January 27, 1954. The article, by the recently deceased actor Kawarazaki Gonjūrō, is headed: "On the Pathological Psychology of the Sixth Kikugorō." I will quote the relevant passage:

"There was in those days an English school in Tsukiji called the Summer. I was sent to it. The old Uzaemon and Baikō, and Fukusuke, who later became Utaemon, had all been there before me, and it would seem that their object had to do less with the English language than with the Sanctuary of the Instincts. Among the Summer girls was a very pretty one named Susa. She was the lure that drew us."

Later Sasanuma, to keep me company, also enrolled in the Summer. The two of us thought one day to see what the upstairs might be like. We were apprehended along the way, but we succeeded in catching a glimpse of florid decorations.

Here is a description of Tsukiji from another lover of the exotic, the poet Kitahara Hakushu, writing after the settlement had disappeared in the earthquake, not to return:

> A ferry—off to Boshū, off to Izu?
> A whistle sounds, a whistle.
> Beyond the river the fishermen's isle,
> And on the near shore the lights of the Metropole.

This little ditty written in his youth by my friend Kinoshita Mokutarō, and Eau-de-vie de Dantzick, and the print in three colors of a Japanese maiden playing a samisen in an iris garden in the foreign settlement, and the stained glass and the ivy of the church, and the veranda fragrant with lavender paulownia blossoms, and a Chinese amah pushing a baby carriage, and the evening stir, "It's silver it's green it's red," from across the river, and, yes, the late cherries of St. Luke's and its bells, and the weird secret rooms of the Metropole, and opium, and the king of trumps, and all the exotic things of the proscribed creed— they are the faint glow left behind from an interrupted dream.

The foreign settlement was rebuilt after the Ginza fire, but not the Hoterukan. As the reminiscences of Hakushū tell us, there were other hotels. The Metropole was built in 1890 on the site of the American legation when the latter moved to the present site of the embassy. The Seiyōken is recommended in Griffis's guide of 1874. It was already in Tsujiki before the first railway was put through, and food fit for foreigners was brought from Yokohama by runner. The Seiyōken enterprise survives as a huge and famous restaurant in Ueno.

The Tsukiji foreign settlement lost its special significance when, at the end of the nineteenth century, revision of "the unequal treaties" brought an end to extraterritoriality. By way of bringing Japan into conformity with international practice in other respects as well, foreigners were allowed to live where they chose. The quarter vanished in the earthquake and fire of 1923, leaving behind only such mementoes as St. Luke's.

Very soon after the Restoration the city set about changing from water and pedestrian transport to wheels. A significant fact about the first stage in the process is that it did not imitate the West. It was innovative. The rickshaw or jinrickshaw is conventionally reviled as a symbol of human degradation. Certainly there is that aspect. It might be praised for the ingenuity of the concept and the design, however, and if the city and the nation were determined to spin about on wheels, it was a cheap, simple, and clean way of getting started. Though the origins of the rickshaw are not entirely clear, they seem to be Japanese, and of Tokyo specifically. The most widely accepted theory offers the names of three inventors, and gives 1869 as the date of the invention. The very first rickshaw is thought to have operated in Nihombashi. Within the next few years there were as many as fifty thousand in the city. The iron wheels made a fine clatter on rough streets and bridges, and the runners had their distinctive cries among all the other street cries. The populace does not seem to have paid as close attention as it might have. Edward S. Morse, an American professor of zoology who arrived in the tenth year of Meiji to teach at the university, remarked upon the absentminded way in which pedestrians received the warning cries. They held their ground, as if the threat would go away.

Some of the rickshaws were artistically decorated, and some, it would seem, salaciously, with paintings on their rear elevations. In 1872 the more exuberant styles of decoration were banned. Tokyo (though not yet the provinces) was discovering decorum. Runners were required to wear more than the conventional loincloth. Morse describes how a runner stopped at the city limits to cover himself properly.

For a time in early Meiji four-wheeled rickshaws carrying several passengers and pushed and pulled by at least two men operated between Tokyo and Yokohama. There are records of runners who took loaded rickshaws from Tokyo to Kyoto in a week, and of women runners.

From late Meiji the number of rickshaws declined radically, and runners were in great economic distress. On the eve of the earthquake there were fewer than twenty thousand in the city proper. The rickshaw was being forced out to the suburbs, where more advanced means of transportation were slower in coming.

It was an excellent mode of transport, particularly suited to a crowded city of narrow streets. It was dusty and noisy, to be sure, but no dustier and in other respects cleaner than the horse that was its first genuine competitor. An honest and good-natured runner, not difficult to find, was far less dangerous than a horse. Most people seem to have liked the noise—leastways Meiji reminiscences are full of it. Rubber tires arrived, and the clatter went away, though the shouting lingered on. The best thing about the rickshaw, perhaps, was the sense it gave of being part of the city.

Even this first and simplest vehicle changed the city. The canals and rivers became less important, and places dependent on them, such as old and famous restaurants near the Yoshiwara, went out of business. Swifter means of transportation come, and people take to them. Yet it seems a pity that the old ones disappeared so completely. The rickshaw is gone today, save for a few score that move geisha from engagement to engagement.

In its time the rickshaw itself was the occasion for the demise of another traditional way of getting about. The palanquin, which had been the chief mode of transport for those who did not walk, almost disappeared with the sudden popularity of the rickshaw. It is said that after 1876, with the departure for Kagoshima of the rigidly conservative Shimazu Saburō of the Satsuma clan, palanquins were to be seen only at funerals and an occasional wedding. The bride who could not afford a carriage and thought a rickshaw beneath her used a palanquin. With the advent of motor hearses and cheap taxis the palanquin was deprived of even these specialized functions.

The emperor had his first carriage ride in 1871, on a visit to the Hama Detached Palace, where General and Mrs. Grant were to stay some years later. Horse-drawn public transportation followed very quickly after the first appearance of the rickshaw. There were omnibuses in Yokohama by 1869, and not many years later—the exact date is in doubt—they were to be seen in Ginza. A brief span in the 1870s saw two-level omnibuses, the drivers grand in velvet livery and cocked hats. The first regular route led through Ginza from Shimbashi on the south and on past Nihombashi to Asakusa. Service also ran to Yokohama, and westwards from Shinagawa, at the southern edge of the city. The horse-drawn bus was popularly known as the Entarō, from the name of a vaudeville story-teller who imitated the bugle call of the conductor, to great acclaim. Taxis, when their day came, were long known as *entaku,* an acronym from Entarō and "taxi," with the first syllable signifying also "one yen."

The horse trolley arrived in 1883. The first route followed the old omnibus route north from Shimbashi to Nihombashi, and eventually to Asakusa. In the relentless advance of new devices, horse-drawn transportation had a far shorter time of prosperity than in Europe and America. There was already experimentation with the electric trolley before the horse trolley had been in use for a decade. An industrial exposition featured an electric car in 1890. In 1903 a private company laid the first tracks for general use, from Shinagawa to Shimbashi, and later to Ueno and Asakusa. The electric system was very soon able to carry almost a hundred thousand passengers a day, for lower fares than those asked by rickshaw runners, and so the rickshaw withdrew to the suburbs. Initially in private hands, the trolley system was no strong argument for private enterprise. There were three companies, and the confusion was great. In 1911, the last full year of Meiji, the city bought the system.

Horse-drawn buses in Ginza Bricktown, from a print by Hiroshige III
(Courtesy Tokyo Central Library)

The confusion is the subject of, or the occasion for, one of Nagai Kafū's most beautiful prose lyrics, "A Song in Fukagawa" (Fukagawa no Uta), written in 1908. The narrator boards a trolley at Yotsuya and sets forth eastwards across the city. As it passes Tsukiji, an unplanned but not unusual event occurs, which sends him farther than he has thought to go.

The car crossed Sakura Bridge. The canal was wider. The lighters moving up and down gave an impression of great activity, but the New Year decorations before the narrow little shops and houses seemed punier, somehow, than in Tsukiji. The crowds on the sidewalks seemed less neat and orderly. We came to Sakamoto Park, and waited and waited for a sign that we would be proceeding onwards. None came. Cars were stopped in front of us and behind us. The conductor and motorman disappeared.

"Again, damn it. The damned powers gone off again." A merchant in Japanese dress, leather-soled pattens and a cloak of rough, thick weave, turned to his companion, a redfaced old man in a fur muffler.

A boy jumped up, a delivery boy, probably. He had a bundle on his back, tied around his neck with a green kerchief.

"A solid line of them, so far up ahead you can't see the end of it."

The conductor came running back, change bag under his arm, cap far back on his head. He mopped at his brow.

"It might be a good idea to take transfers if you can use them."

Most of us got up, and not all of us were good-humored about it.

"Can't you tell us what's wrong? How long will it be?"

"Sorry. You see how it is. They're stopped all the way to Kaya-bachō…"

Caught in the general rush for the doors, I got up without thinking. I had not asked for one, but the conductor gave me a transfer to Fukagawa.

So Kafū finds himself east of the river, and meditates upon the contrast between that backward part of the city and the advanced part from which he has come. He yearns for the former, and must go back and live in the latter; and we are to suppose that he would not have had his twilight reverie if the trolley system had functioned better.

The rickshaw changed patterns of commerce by speeding people past boat landings. The trolley had a more pronounced effect, the Daimaru dry-goods store being a case in point. It was one of several such establishments that were to develop into department stores. Established in Nihombashi in the eighteenth century, it was in mid-Meiji the most popular of them all, even more so than Mitsukoshi, foundation of the Mitsui fortunes. "The Daimaru," said Hasegawa Shigure, "was the center of Nihombashi culture and prosperity, as the Mitsukoshi is today." In her girlhood it was a place of wonder and excitement. It had barred windows, less to keep burglars out than to keep shop boys (there were no shop girls in those days) in. Sometimes a foreign lady with foxlike visage would come in to shop, and the idle of Nihombashi would gather to stare. But the Daimaru did not lie, as its rivals did, on a main north-south trolley line. By the end of the Meiji it had closed its Tokyo business and withdrawn to the Kansai, whence only in recent years it has returned to Tokyo, this time not letting the transportation system pass it by. It commands an entrance to Tokyo Central Station.

For some, Nagai Kafū among them, the trolley was a symbol of disorder and ugliness. For others it was the introduction to a new world, at once intimidating and inviting. The novelist Natsume Sōseki's Sanshirō, a university student from the country, took the advice of a friend and dashed madly and randomly about, seeking the rhythms of this new world.

Construction of a railway, financed in London, began in 1870. The chief engineer was English, and a hundred foreign technicians and workers were engaged to run it. Not until 1879 were trains entrusted to Japanese crews, and then only for daylight runs. The first line was from Shimbashi, south of Ginza, to Sakuragichō in Yokohama, a stop that still

Daimaru Department Store, Nihombashi. Woodcut by Kiyochika

serves enormous numbers of passengers, though it is no longer the main Yokohama station. The Tokyo terminus was moved some four decades later to the present Tokyo Central Station, and the old Shimbashi Station became a freight office, disappearing in 1923.

The very earliest service, in the summer of 1872, was from Shinagawa, just beyond the southern limits of the city, to Yokohama. The Tokyo terminus was opened in the autumn, amid jubilation. The emperor himself took the first train He wore foreign dress, but most of the high courtiers were in traditional court dress; Western dress was still expensive and very difficult to come by. Among the notables present was the king of Okinawa.

The fare was higher than for a boat or horse-drawn bus. Everyone wanted a ride, but only the affluent could afford a ride daily. Eighty percent of the passengers are said to have been merchants and speculators with business in Yokohama. The first tickets carried English, German, and French translations. From 1876 on, there was only English.

It was in 1877 that an early passenger, E. S. Morse, made his famous discovery of the shell middens of Omori, usually considered the birthplace of Japanese archeology. The train took almost an hour to traverse its twenty-five kilometers, and Omori was then a country village offering no obstructions, and so, without leaving his car, Morse was able to contemplate the mounds at some leisure and recognize them for what they were.

The Tokyo-Yokohama line was the first segment of the Tokaidō line, put through from Tokyo to Kobe in 1889. Unlike the Tokaidō, the main line to the north was built privately, from Ueno. It was completed to Aomori, at the northern tip of the main island, in 1891. By the turn of the century private endeavor had made a beginning at the network of suburban lines that was to work such enormous changes on the city; in 1903 Shibuya Station, outside the city limits to the southwest, served an average of fifteen thousand passengers a day. When it had been first opened, less than two decades before, it served only fifteen.

Shimbashi Station possessed curious ties with the Edo tradition. The Edo mansion of the lords of Tatsuno had stood on the site. Tatsuno was a fief neighboring that of the Forty-seven Loyal Retainers of the most famous Edo vendetta. The Forty-seven are said to have refreshed themselves there as they made their way across the city, their vendetta accomplished, to commit suicide.

If the railroad caused jubilation, it also brought opposition. The opposition seems to have been strongest in the bureaucracy. Carrying Yokohama and its foreigners closer to the royal seat was not thought a good idea. If a railroad must be built, might it not better run to the north, where it could be used against the most immediately apparent threat, the Russians? Along a part of its course, just south of the city, it was in the event required to run inland, because for strategic reasons the army opposed the more convenient coastal route.

Among the populace the railway does not seem to have aroused as much opposition as the telegraph, about which the wildest rumors spread, associating it with the black magic of the Christians and human sacrifice. People seem to have been rather friendly towards the locomotive. Thinking that it must be hot, poor thing, they would douse it with water from embankments.

By the eve of the earthquake there were ten thousand automobiles in the city, but they did not displace the railroad as railroad and trolley had displaced the rickshaw. In one important respect they were no competition at all. When the railroad came, the Ukiyo-e print of Edo was still alive. The art, or business, had considerable vigor, though many would say that it was decadent. Enormous numbers of prints were made, millions of them annually in Tokyo alone, almost exclusively in the Low City. Few sold for as much as a penny. They were throwaways, little valued either as art or as investment. Nor were technical standards high.

Artists did not mind and did not expect their customers to mind that the parts of a triptych failed to join precisely. Bold chemical pigments were used with great abandon. Yet Meiji prints often have a contagious exuberance. They may not be reliable in all their details, but they provide excellent documents, better than photographs, of the Meiji spirit. Losses over the years have been enormous. Today such of them as survive are much in vogue, bringing dollar prices that sometimes run into four figures, or yen prices in six figures.

The printmakers of early Meiji loved trains and railroads. Many of the prints are highly fanciful, like representations of elephants and giraffes by people who have never seen one. A train may seem to have no axles, and to roll on its wheels as a house might roll on logs. Windows are frivolously draped, and two trains will be depicted running on the same track in collision course, as if that should be no problem for something so wondrous. The more fanciful images can seem prophetic, showing urban problems to come, smog, traffic jams, a bureaucracy indifferent to approaching disaster.

Sometimes the treatment was realistic. The manner of Kobayashi Kiyochika, generally recognized as the great master of the Meiji print is

Train on Takenawa embankment. Woodcut by Kiyochika

both realistic and effective, as beautiful a treatment of such unlikely subjects as railroads, surely, as is to be found anywhere.

Kiyochika was born in Honjo, east of the Sumida, in 1847, near the present Kyōgoku Station and not far from the birthplace of the great Hokusai. The shogunate had lumber and bamboo yards in the district. His father was a labor foreman in government employ. Though the youngest of many sons, Kiyochika was named the family heir, and followed the last shogun to Shizuoka. The shogun in exile was himself far from impoverished, but many of his retainers were. Kiyochika put together a precarious living at odd jobs, one of them on the vaudeville stage. Deciding finally to return to Tokyo, he stopped on the way, or so it is said—the details of his life are not well established—to study art under Charles Wirgman, the British naval officer who became Yokohama correspondent for the *Illustrated London News*. Missing nothing, Kiyochika is said also to have studied photography under Shimooka Renjō, the most famous of Meiji photographers, and painting in the Japanese style as well.

His main career as a printmaker lasted a scant five years, from 1876 to 1881, although he did make an occasional print in later life. In that brief period he produced more than a hundred prints of Tokyo. The last from the prolific early period are of the great Kanda fire of 1881, in which his own house was destroyed. (That fire was, incidentally, the largest in Meiji Tokyo.)

All the printmakers of early Meiji used Western subjects and materials, but Kiyochika and his pupils (who seem to have been two in number) achieved a Western look in style as well. It may be that, given his Westernized treatment of light and perspective, he does not belong in the Ukiyo-e tradition at all.

The usual Meiji railway print is bright to the point of gaudiness, and could be set at any hour of the day. The weather is usually sunny, and the cherries are usually in bloom. Kiyochika is best in his nocturnes. He is precise with hour and season, avoiding the perpetual springtide of his elders. His train moves south along the Takanawa hill and there are still traces of color upon the evening landscape; so one knows that the moon behind the clouds must be near full.

The prints of Kiyochika's late years, when he worked mostly as an illustrator, are wanting in the eagerness and the melancholy of prints from the rich early period. The mixture of the two, eagerness and melancholy, seems almost prophetic—or perhaps we think it so because we know what was to happen to his great subject, the Low City. His preference for nocturnes was deeply appropriate, for there must have been in the life of

Shrine near the Yoshiwara. Woodcut by Inoue Yasuji, after Kiyochika

the Low City this same delight in the evening, and with it a certain apprehension of the dawn.

The lights flooding through the windows of Kiyochika's Rokumeikan, where the elite of Meiji gathered for Westernized banquets and balls, seem about to go out. Lights are also ablaze in the great and venerable restaurant outside the Yoshiwara, but they seem subdued and dejected, for the rickshaws on their way to the quarter do not stop as the boats once did. In twilight fields outside the Yoshiwara stands a little shrine, much favored by the courtesans. Soon (we know, and Kiyochika seems to know too) the city will be flooding in all around it. Other little shrines and temples found protectors and a place in the new world, but this one did not. No trace of it remains.

Kiyochika had a knack one misses in so many travel writers of the time for catching moods and tones that would soon disappear. Other woodcut artists of the day, putting everything in the sunlight of high spring, missed the better half of the picture. Kiyochika was a gifted artist, and that period when Edo was giving way to Tokyo provided fit subjects for the light of evening and night. He outlived the Meiji emperor by three years.

The importance of the waterways declined as the city acquired wheels and streets were improved. The system of rivers, canals, and moats had been extensive, drawing from the mountains to the west of the city and the Tone River to the north. Under the shogunate most of the produce brought into the city had come by water. At the end of Taishō, or three years after the earthquake, most of it came by land. This apparent shift is something of a distortion, since it ignores Yokohama, the international port for Tokyo. The decline of water transport is striking all the same. There was persistent dredging at the mouth of the Sumida, but Tokyo had no deep harbor. It could accommodate ships of not more than five hundred tons. All through the Meiji Period the debate continued as to whether or not the city should seek to become an international port. Among the arguments against the proposal was the old xenophobic one: a harbor would bring in all manner of foreign rogues and diseases. What is remarkable is that such an argument could still be offered seriously a half-century after the question of whether or not to have commerce with foreign rogues had presumably been settled.

The outer moats of the palace were filled in through the Meiji Period, and the Tameike reservoir, to the southwest of the palace, which had been among the recommended places in guides to the pleasures of Edo for gathering new herbs in the spring and, in high summer, viewing lotus blossoms and hearing them pop softly open, was allowed to gather sediment. Its military importance having passed, it became a swamp in late Meiji, and in Taishō quite disappeared.

The system of canals was still intact at the end of Meiji, and there were swarms of boats upon them and fish within them. Life on the canals and rivers seems to have been conservative even for the conservative Low City. An interesting convention in the woodcuts of Meiji is doubtless based upon fact. When bridges are shown, as they frequently are, the roadway above is generally an exuberant mixture of the new and the traditional, the imported and the domestic; on the waters below there is seldom a trace of the new and imported.

Pleasure-boating of the old sort almost disappeared. Advanced young people went rowing on the Sumida, and the university boathouse was one of the sights on the left bank. A 1920 guide to Japan, however, lists but a single *funayado* in the city. The *funayado,* literally "boat lodge" or "boating inn," provided elegant boating for entertainment on the waters or for an excursion to the Yoshiwara. The boats were of the roofed, high-prowed sort, often with lanterns strung out along the eaves, that so often figure in Edo and Meiji woodcuts. Since the customer expected to be entertained as well as rowed, the *funayado* provided witty and accomplished entertainers, and so performed services similar to those of the Yoshiwara teahouses. As the network of canals disappeared, some of them made the transition into the new day and became the sort of restaurant to which geisha are summoned, but a great many merely went out of business. Ginza and Kyōbashi were the southern terminus for passage to the Yoshiwara. The *funayado* of that region were therefore among the ingredients from which the Shimbashi geisha district, still one of the finest in the city, was made.

Connoisseurs like Nagai Kafū said that Edo died of flood and fire, but it may be that the loss of boats and waterways had an even more destructive effect on the moods of Edo. Kafū himself implies as much when, in an elegiac evocation of late Edo, he has a famous writer set forth from a *funayado* and take stock of events. He is a victim of the puritanical edicts of the 1840s, and a quiet time on the Sumida is best for surveying the past and the future. The wheels of Meiji disrupted old patterns and rhythms. There was no longer the time or the inclination to put together a perfect outing, and so the arts of plebeian Edo were not in demand as they once had been.

This is not to say that the moods of the Sumida, so important to Edo, were quite swept away. They were still there, if somewhat polluted and coarsened. A "penny steamer" continued to make its way up and down the river, and on to points along the bay, even though it had by the time of the earthquake come to cost more than a penny. Ferries across the river were not completely replaced by bridges until after the Second World War. The most conservative of the geisha quarters, Yanagibashi, stood beside the river, and mendicant musicians still had themselves paddled up and down before it. One could still go boating of a summer night with geisha and music and drink. The great celebration called the "river opening" was the climactic event of the Low City summer.

In 1911 and 1912 the playwright Osanai Kaoru published an autobiographical novel called *Okawabata (The Bank of the Big River,* with reference to the Sumida). Osanai was a pioneer in the Westernized theater. Some years after the earthquake he was to found the Little Theater of Tsukiji, most famous establishment in an energetic and venturesome experimental-theater movement. Like Nagai Kafū, whose junior he was by two years, he was a sort of Edokko manqué. His forebears were bureaucratic and not mercantile, and he had the added disability that he spent his early childhood in Hiroshima. Such people often outdid genuine Edokko, among whom Tanizaki Junichirō could number himself, in

The Yaomatsu restaurant on the Sumida, looking towards Asakusa

affection for the city and especially vestiges of Edo, abstract and concrete. *The Bank of the Big River* has the usual defects of Japanese autobiographical fiction—weak characterization, a rambling plot, a tendency towards self-gratification; but it is beautiful in its evocation of the moods of the Sumida. The time is 1905 or so, with the Russo-Japanese War at or near a conclusion. The setting is Nakasu, an artificial island in the Sumida, off Nihombashi.

> Sometimes a lighter would go up or down between Ohashi Bridge and Nakasu, an awning spread against the sun, banners aloft, a sad chant sounding over the water to the accompaniment of bell and mallet, for the repose of the souls of those who had died by drowning.
>
> Almost every summer evening a boat would come to the stone embankment and give us a shadow play. Not properly roofed, it had a makeshift awning of some nondescript cloth, beneath which were paper doors, to suggest a roofed boat of the old sort. Always against the paper doors, yellowish in the light from inside, there would be two shadows... When it came up the river to the sound of drum and gong and samisen, Masao would look happily at Kimitarō, and from the boat there would be voices imitating Kabuki actors...
>
> Every day at exactly the same time a candy boat would pass, to the beating of a drum. Candy man and candy would be like distant figures in a picture, but the drum would sound out over the river

in simple rhythm, so near that he might almost, he thought, have reached out to touch it. At the sound he would feel a nameless stirring and think of home, forgotten so much of the time, far away in the High City. The thought was only a thought. He felt no urge to leave Kimitarō.

The moon would come up, a great, round, red moon, between the godowns that lined the far bank. The black lacquer of the river would become gold, and then, as the moon was smaller and whiter, the river would become silver. Beneath the dark form of Ohashi Bridge, across which no trolleys passed, it would shimmer like a school of whitefish.

The old wooden bridges, so pretty as they arched their way over river and canal, were not suited to heavy vehicular traffic. Wood was the chief material for wider and flatter bridges, but steel and stone were used for an increasing number of important new ones. Of 481 bridges in the city at the end of the Russo-Japanese War, 26 were steel and 166 were stone. The rest were wood. A new stone Nihombashi was dedicated in 1911. It is the Nihombashi that yet stands, and the one for which the last shogun wrote the inscription. He led the ceremonial parade, and with him was a lady born in Nihombashi a hundred years before, when there were yet four shoguns to go. The famous Azuma Bridge at Asakusa, often called "the

Azumabashi, Asakusa. From a lithograph dated 1891

big bridge," was swept away by a flood in 1885. A steel Azuma Bridge with a decorative superstructure was finished in 1882, occasioning a great celebration at the dedication, geisha and lanterns and politicians and all. It quickly became one of the sights of the city. The floor was still wooden at the time of the earthquake. It caught fire, as did all the other bridges across the river; hence, in part, the large number of deaths by drowning.

Nagai Kafū accused the Sumida, which he loved, of flooding twice annually. "Just as when summer gives way to autumn, so it is when spring gives way to summer: there are likely to be heavy rains. No one was surprised, for it happened every year, that the district from Senzoku toward the Yoshiwara should be under water."

So begins the last chapter of his novella *The River Sumida*. It is an exaggeration, and in other respects not entirely accurate. Late summer and autumn was the season for floods. The rains of June are more easily contained than the violent ones of the typhoon season. The passage of the seasons so important to Kafū's story required a flood in early summer. Records through the more than three centuries of Edo and Meiji suggest that the Sumida flooded on an average of once every three years. It may be that, for obscure reasons, floods were becoming more frequent. In the last half of Meiji the rate was only a little less than one every two years, and of eight floods described as "major, two were in late Meiji, in 1907 and 1910.

The flood of 1910, commonly called the Great Meiji Flood, submerged the whole northern part of the Low City, eastwards from the valleys of Koishikawa. Rising waters breached the levees of the Sumida and certain lesser streams. Asakusa, including the Yoshiwara and the setting of the Kafū story, suffered the worst damage, but only one of the fifteen wards was untouched, and the flood was a huge disaster. The damage has been calculated at between 4 and 5 percent of the national product for that year. Kafū liked to say that Edo disappeared in the Great Flood and the Yoshiwara fire of the following year. The flood was the occasion for the Arakawa Drainage Channel, to put an end to Sumida floods forever (see page 257).

Of all Meiji fires, the Ginza fire of 1872 had the most lasting effect upon the city. From it emerged the new Ginza.

Ginza had not been one of the busier and more prosperous sections of mercantile Edo. Compared to Nihombashi, farther north, it was cramped and narrow, caught between the outer moats of the great Tokugawa citadel and a bay shore occupied in large measure by the aristocracy. The great merchant houses were in more northerly regions. Ginza was a place of artisans and small shops.

W. E. Griffis gave a good account of what he saw there in 1870, before the fire. It contained no specific reference to Ginza, but a long walk, on his first visit to the city, took him from Tsukiji and the New Shimabara (which he wrongly calls the Yoshiwara) to Kanda. It must have been the Ginza district through which he first strolled.

> I pass through one street devoted to bureaus and cabinets, through another full of folding screens, through another of dyers' shops, with their odors and vats. In one small but neat shop sits an old man, with horn-rimmed spectacles, with the mordant liquid beside him, preparing a roll of material for its next bath. In another street there is nothing on sale but bamboo poles, but enough of these to make a forest. A man is sawing one, and I notice he pulls the saw with his two hands toward him. Its teeth are set contrary to ours. Another man is planing. He pulls the plane toward him. I notice a blacksmith at work: he pulls the bellows with his foot, while he is holding and hammering with both hands. He has several irons in the fire, and keeps his dinner boiling with the waste flame... The cooper holds his tub with his toes. All of them sit while they work. How strange! Perhaps that is an important difference between a European and an Asian. One sits down to his work, and the other stands up to it...
>
> I emerge from the bamboo street to the Tori, the main street, the Broadway of the Japanese capital. I recognize it. The shops are gayer and richer; the street is wider; it is crowded with people.
>
> Turning up Suruga Chō, with Fuji's glorious form before me, I pass the great silk shop and fire-proof warehouses of Mitsui the millionaire.

Ginza had once been something of a theater center, until the Tempō edicts of the 1840s removed the Kabuki theaters to the northern suburbs. Theater quickly returned to the Ginza region when it was allowed to, after the Restoration, but the beginning of Ginza as a thriving center of commerce and pleasure came after the fire.

The governor decided that the city must be made fireproof, and the newly charred Ginza offered a place to begin. An English architect, Thomas Waters, was retained to build an entire district of red brick. The government subsidized a special company "for building and for the management of rentals." The rebuilding took three years, when it could have been accomplished in the old way almost overnight. Rather proud of its fires, the old city had also been proud of the speed with which it recovered.

There seem to have been at least two brick buildings in the Ginza district even before the great fire, one of them a warehouse, the other a shop, "a poorer thing than the public latrines of later years," says an eminent authority on the subject. When the rebuilding was finished there were almost a thousand brick buildings in Kyōbashi Ward, which included Ginza, and fewer than twenty in the rest of the city. An 1879 list shows a scattering of Western or Westernized buildings through most of the other wards, and one ward, Yotsuya in the High City, with none at all.

The hope was that the city would make itself over on the Ginza model, and become fireproof. Practice tended in the other direction. Only along the main street was a solid face of red brick presented to the world. Very soon there was cheating, in the form of reversion to something more traditional. Pictures from late Meiji inform us that Bricktown, as it was called, lasted longest in what is now the northern part of Ginza. Nothing at all survives of it today.

The new Ginza was not on the whole in good repute among foreigners. Already in the 1870s there were complaints about the Americanization of the city. Isabella Bird came visiting in 1878 and in 1880 described Tokyo as less like an Oriental city than like the outskirts of Chicago or Melbourne. She did not say what part of the city she had reference to, but almost certainly it was Ginza. Pierre Loti thought that Bricktown had about it *une laideur americaine*. Philip Terry, the English writer of

Ginza Bricktown, with trees

tour guides, likened it, as Griffis had likened Nihombashi, to Broadway, though not with Griffis's intent to praise. "Size without majesty, individuality divorced from all dignity and simplicity, and convenience rather than fitness or sobriety are the salient characteristics of this structural hodge-podge." Not much of Bricktown survived when Terry wrote, in 1920. What did survive was the impression of a baneful American influence; and the original architect was English.

The city was of two minds about its new Ginza. Everyone wanted to look at it, but not many wanted to live in it. In a short story from early in this century, Nagai Kafū described it as a chilling symbol of the life to come.

The initial plans were for shops on the ground floors and residential quarters above, after the pattern of merchant Edo. The new buildings were slow to fill. They were found to be damp, stuffy, vulnerable to mildew, and otherwise ill adapted to the Japanese climate, and the solid walls ran wholly against the Japanese notion of a place to live in. Choice sites along the main street presently found tenants, but the back streets languished, or provided temporary space for sideshows, "bear wrestling and dog dances" and the like. Among the landowners, who had not been made to relinquish their rights, few were willing or able to meet the conditions for repaying government subsidies. These were presently relaxed, but as many as a third of the buildings on the back streets remained empty even so. Vacant buildings were in the end let go for token payments, and cheating on the original plans continued apace. Most Edo townsmen could not afford even the traditional sort of fireproof godown, and the least ostentatious of the new brick buildings were, foot for foot, some ten times as expensive. Such fireproofing measures as the city took through the rest of Meiji went no farther than widening streets and requisitioning land for firebreaks when a district had been burned over.

Despite the views of Miss Bird and Loti, the new Ginza must have been rather handsome. It was a huge success as an instance of Civilization and Enlightenment, whatever its failures as a model in fireproofing. Everyone went to look at it, and so was born the custom of Gimbura, "killing time in Ginza," an activity which had its great day between the two world wars.

The new Ginza was also a great success with the printmakers. As usual they show it in brilliant sunlight with the cherries in bloom; and indeed there were cherries, at least in the beginning, along what had become the widest street in the city, and almost the only street wide enough for trolleys. There were maples, pines, and evergreen oaks as well, the pines at intersections, the others between.

It is not known exactly when and why these first trees disappeared, leaving the willow to become the great symbol of Ginza. The middle years of Meiji seem to have been the time. Perhaps the original trees were victims of urbanization, and perhaps, sprawling and brittle and hospitable to bugs, they were not practical. Willows, in any event, took over. Hardy and compact, riffled by cooling breezes in the summer, they were what a busy street and showplace seemed to need. Long a symbol of Edo and its rivers and canals, the willow became a symbol of the newest in Tokyo as well. Eventually the willow too went away. One may go out into the suburbs, near the Tama River, and view aged specimens taken there when, just before the earthquake, the last Ginza willows were removed.

With the new railway station just across a canal to the south, the southern end of what is now Ginza—it was technically not then a part of Ginza—prospered first. From middle into late Meiji it must have been rather like a shopping center, or mall, of a later day. There were two bazaars by the Shimbashi Bridge, each containing numbers of small shops. The youth of Ginza, we have been told by a famous artist who was a native of the district, loved to go strolling there, because from the back windows the Shimbashi geisha district could be seen preparing itself for a night's business. One of the bazaars kept a python in a window. The python seems to have perished in the earthquake. From the late Meiji Period into Taishō, Tokyo Central Station was built to replace Shimbashi as the terminus for trains from the south. It stood at the northern boundary of Kyōbashi Ward, and so Ginza moved back north again to center upon what is now the main Ginza crossing.

At least one building from the period of the new Ginza survives, Elocution Hall (Enzetsukan) on the Mita campus of Keiō University. Fukuzawa Yukichi invented the word *enzetsu,* here rendered as "elocution," because he regarded the art as one that must be cultivated by the Japanese in their efforts to catch up with the world. Elocution Hall, put up in 1875 and now under the protection of the government as a "cultural property" of great merit, was to be the forum for aspiring young elocutionists. It was moved from the original site, near the main entrance to the Keiō campus, after the earthquake. It is a modest building, not such as to attract the attention of printmakers, and a pleasing one. The doors and windows are Western, as is the interior, but the exterior, with its "trepang walls" and tiled roof, is strongly traditional. In its far more monumental way, the Hoterukan must have looked rather thus.

The great Ginza fire of 1872 is rivaled as the most famous of Meiji fires by the Yoshiwara fire of 1911, but neither was the most destructive. The Ginza fire burned over great but not consistently crowded spaces. The Kanda fire of 1881, the one that brought an end to Kiyochika's flourishing years as a printmaker, destroyed more buildings than any other Meiji fire. And not even that rivaled the great fires of Edo, or the Kyoto fire of 1778. Arson was suspected in the 1881 fire, as it was suspected, and sometimes proved, in numbers of other fires. It was a remarkable fire. Not even water stopped it, as water had stopped the Ginza fire. Beginning in Kanda and fanned by winter winds, it burned a swath through Kanda and Nihombashi, jumped the river at Ryogoku Bridge, and burned an even wider swath through the eastern wards, subsiding only when it came to open country.

In a space of fifteen years, from early into middle Meiji, certain parts of Nihombashi were three times destroyed by fire. Great fires were commonest in the early months of the year, the driest months, when strong winds often came down from the north and west. (The incendiary raids of 1945 took advantage of these facts.) Much of what remained of the Tokugawa castle burned in 1873, and so the emperor spent more than a third of his reign in the Tokugawa mansion where the Akasaka Palace now stands. He did not move back into the palace until 1889. There were Yoshiwara fires in 1871, 1873, 1891, and 1911, and of course in 1923.

The great Yoshiwara fire of 1911

But Kanda has in modern times been the best place for fires. Of five great Meiji fires after a central fire department was organized in 1880, four began in Kanda, two of them within a few weeks of each other in 1881. The great Yoshiwara fire was the fifth. Only one Taishō fire, that of 1923 excepted, was of a magnitude to compete with the great Meiji fires. It too began in Kanda. No other Taishō fire, save again that of 1923, was remotely as large. The flowers of Edo were finally withering.

It was not until early Taishō that the fire department was sufficiently well manned to fight fires without amateur help. The disbanding of the old volunteer brigades did not come until after the earthquake. A ceremonial trace of them yet survives in the *dezomeshiki,* the display of the old panoply and tricks that is a part of the Tokyo New Year. Half the trucks owned by the department were lost in the earthquake, the first of them having been acquired five or six years before.

The Low City lived with the threat of fire. Only the wealthy had fireproof godowns. The lower classes kept emergency baskets ready in conspicuous places, and dug pits under their floors with ingenious arrangements that caused flooding when heated, and so, it was hoped, preserved such valuables as had been put away in time.

The young Tanizaki and his friends found an interesting use for the baskets.

> They were oblong and woven of bamboo, about the size of a small trunk, and they were kept where everyone could see them, awaiting an emergency. In the Kairakuen they were kept in a storeroom that had been the Chinese room. For us, as we played at our games, they became the cribs of the courtesans. Three and four of us would take turns in a basket as ladies and their companions. Gen-chan and I were lady and companion any number of times. I do not remember that we did much of anything but lie face to face for a few minutes. Then it would be the turn of another lady and companion to produce staring and snickering.
>
> I think that the origin of the game was probably in reports that Gen-chan had from the cooks about the Susaki quarter. The game delighted us, in any event. Day after day we would play it, the fire-basket game, as we called it.
>
> "Let s have another go at the fire baskets," someone would say.

E. S. Morse, the American zoologist who taught at the imperial university in early Meiji, was a great connoisseur of fires and firefighting methods.

Nearly every house has a staging on the ridge-pole with a few steps leading to it. Here one may go the better to observe the progress of a conflagration... When endangered by the approach of a conflagration the heavy window shutters and the doors of the fireproof building are closed and clay is then plastered over the cracks and chinks. Before closing it up, a number of candles are placed in a safe spot on the floor within and are lighted, thus gradually consuming all the oxygen and rendering ignition less likely.

Morse was initially contemptuous of Tokyo firefighting methods, but moved towards admiration as he became more knowledgeable. Of the first good fire to which he was witness, he said, among other things:

The stream thrown was about the size of a lead pencil and consisted of a series of independent squirts, as there was no air chamber as with our hand engines. The pumps were square instead of cylindrical and everything so dry, having hung in the sun for weeks, that more water spurted up in the air from the cracks than was discharged through the pipe... The fire companies are private and each company has a standard-bearer... These standard-bearers take a position as near the fire as possible, on the roof even of a burning building, and the companies whose standard-bearers are in evidence get a certain amount of money from the owners of the buildings saved.

In a note added for publication, he provided more sophisticated information, to the effect that the chief work of the firemen was not to put fires out but to prevent their spreading, and that the purpose of the little streams of water was not to extinguish the fire but to preserve the firemen.

By 1879, when he ran two miles at five o'clock one April morning to observe a fire, admiration was predominant.

The extent of the conflagration showed how rapidly it had spread, and the wooden buildings partly burned indicated that the work of firemen was not so trivial as foreigners supposed it to be; at least to check the fire in a high gale must have required great effort and skill. The fact is that their houses are so frail that as soon as a fire starts it spreads with the greatest rapidity, and the main work of the firemen, aided by citizens, is in denuding a house of everything that can be stripped from it... It seems ridiculous to see them shoveling off the thick roofing files, the only fireproof covering the house has; but this is to enable them to tear off the roofing boards, and one observes that the fire then does not spring from rafter to rafter. The more one studies the subject the more one realizes that the first impressions of the fireman's work are wrong, and a respect for his skill rapidly increases.

Given the fact that the fire brigades were largely manned by carpenters, a certain conflict of interest might be suspected; but they seem to have done their work bravely and, within the limits of the materials they had to work with, well.

Fire losses declined as Meiji gave way to Taishō. An accompaniment, or so the children of Edo often saw it, was a loss of harmony in traditional architecture. Kafū lamented it, and so did the novelist, playwright, and haiku master Kubota Mantarō, who may be numbered among Kafū's disciples. Kubota was a true son of Edo, born in 1889 in Asakusa (Tanizaki was born in Nihombashi three years earlier) to a family of craftsmen and shopkeepers. He stayed in Asakusa until the fires of 1923 drove him away, and, though he never moved back, spent most of the four decades that remained to him in various parts of the Low City. Sadness for the Low City and what the modern world did to it dominated his writing in all the several forms of which he was master. He had the right pedigree and unswerving devotion to the cause; and so he may be called the most eloquent spokesman for that loquacious band, the sons of Edo. Tanizaki was a better novelist, but he spoke on the whole grouchily of his native Low City. Writing in 1927, Kubota lamented the disappearance of the *hinomi*, the "firewatcher" or staging noted by Morse on the ridges of Tokyo houses.

> Among the things that have disappeared from all the blocks of Tokyo is the *hinomi*. I do not mean the fire ladder or the firewatch tower. I mean the *hinomi* itself. I do not know about the High City, but in the Low City, and especially on the roofs of merchant houses in busy and prosperous sections, there was always a *hinomi*. It was not only a memento of Edo, so ready with its fires. In the days when the godown style was the ideal in Japanese architecture, the *hinomi* was, along with the board fence, the spikes to turn back robbers, and the eaves drains, an indispensable element giving form to a Japanese house. And such fond dreams as the thought of it does bring, of Tokyo under willows in full leaf.

It may seem silly to mourn for appurtenances that proclaim a building, and indeed a whole city, to be a firetrap. Yet Kubota's remarks, and similar remarks by other mourners for Edo such as Nagai Kafū, have substance. Despite the failure of the city to take advantage of the Ginza model, it gradually made itself more resistant to fire, and the result was a great increase in ugliness. "Fair to look at is the capital of the Tycoon," said Sir Rutherford Alcock, who was in Edo during the last years of the Tycoon, or shogun. No one could call the Tokyo of our day a fair city, though it contains beautiful things. Coming upon a surviving pocket of Edo or Meiji, one sees in the somber harmonies of tile and old wood what has been lost.

The domestic and commercial architecture of Tokugawa Japan varied with the region. Except for warehouses, it was almost always of wooden frame construction, one or two storys high. The Kansai region favored paints and stains much more than did the Kantō and its greatest city, Edo. In Edo there were several kinds of roofing. The more affluent merchant houses were heavily roofed with dark tiles, while humbler dwellings had thatched or shingled roofs, the best kind of fuel for the fires that were always getting started. The wooden fronts of the unpainted houses and shops of Edo, often with delicate lattices over the windows, turned to rich shades of brown as they aged, and the roofs were of neutral tones to begin with.

Only an eye accustomed to austere subtleties could detect the reposeful variations upon brown and gray which a Low City street must have presented. That is probably why one looks in vain through writings by early foreign visitors for descriptions of what the Low City looked like (as distinguished from its effect upon the other senses). Even E. S. Morse, the most discerning and sympathetic of them, is far better at street cries and the buzz of life and quaint curiosities than he is at the expanses of wood and tile that he must have passed every day. Isabella Bird went through the wards east of the river in her quest for unbeaten tracks. She tells us nothing about them, though they must have been among the urban places of early Meiji where the old harmonies were least disturbed. Perhaps if she had known that they all were to go (and to do so more rapidly than unbeaten tracks), she might have tried a little to describe them.

The very first Western buildings, such as the British legation and the Hoterukan, were not fireproof. They were built by Japanese, accommodating old Japanese techniques to what were presumed to be Western needs and sensibilities. The first period of pure Western building may be held to begin with the new Ginza. It is often called the English period. Thomas Waters gave advice for Ginza, and Josiah Conder, the most famous of foreign architects active in Meiji Japan, put up buildings all over the city. The work of Japanese architects, inconspicuous during the English period, began to appear again in mid-Meiji. The most eminent were

Conder's pupils. A Japanese architect designed the first Imperial Hotel, which opened on a part of the present site in 1890. The grandest buildings of late Meiji and early Taishō—the Bank of Japan, the Akasaka Palace, the Imperial Theater, Tokyo Central Station—were by Japanese.

Conder, born in 1852, came to Japan early in 1877, retained by the Ministry of Technology. He taught architecture at the College of Technology and later at the university. A student of Japanese painting, he was especially good at fish.

He was a very important man. No other foreign architect who worked in Japan, not even Frank Lloyd Wright, was as influential as Conder, and probably none will be. He was a highly eclectic and not particularly original architect, but he was enormously successful as a teacher. The grand style in public building derives from him. His most famous work was an early one, the Rokumeikan, which gave its name to a span of years in mid-Meiji. Begun in 1881 and finished in 1883, the Rokumeikan was a state-owned lodging and gathering place for the cosmopolitan set. It was also, in those days when the "unequal treaties" were the great sore to be healed, a means of demonstrating to the world that the Japanese were as civilized and enlightened as anyone else, and so need not put up with such indignities as extraterritoriality.

The name means "House of the Cry of the Stag." It is a literary allusion, to a poem in the oldest of Chinese anthologies, the *Shih Ching*, and

The Rokumeikan

it signifies a hospitable summons to illustrious guests, and the convivial gathering that ensues. The Hama Palace, which had a semi-Western guest house even before the rebuilding of the Ginza, had earlier provided lodging for such guests, among them General Grant; it was in a bad state of repair, however, and otherwise considered unsuited to the needs of foreigners. So the Rokumeikan was put up, on the site of a Satsuma estate in Hibiya, by then government property, across from what was to become Hibiya Park.

It was a two-story structure of brick, in an Italianate style, most splendid for the time, with about fifteen thousand square feet of floor space. It had a ballroom, a music room, a billiard room, a reading room, suites for illustrious guests, and a bathtub such as had never before been seen in the land: alabaster, six feet long and three feet wide. Water thundered most marvelously, we are told, from the faucets.

Pierre Loti, who attended a Rokumeikan ball on the emperor's birthday in 1885, thought that, all flat, staring white, it resembled a casino at a French spa. He may have been dazed. He was taken by rickshaw, he says, from Shimbashi Station through dark, solitary streets, and arrived at the Rokumeikan about an hour later. One can easily walk the distance in ten minutes.

The great day of the Rokumeikan must be discussed later. It became the Peers Club once its vogue had passed (though the unequal treaties had not yet disappeared), and then the offices of an insurance company. After further changes it was torn down, on the eve of Pearl Harbor, to make way for a cluster of temporary government buildings. A far more delicate structure than the Imperial Hotel (the second one, designed by Frank Lloyd Wright) on the same Satsuma lands, it too survived the earthquake.

Perhaps the best notion of what it was like is to be had from a still-surviving Conder building, the Mitsui Club in Mita near Keiō University. Finished in 1915, the Mitsui Club is larger, but it is similarly provided with wide verandas and colonnades. Pictures suggest that the Rokumeikan, at least its front elevation, was more ornate—busier—than the Mitsui Club. Verandas do not run the whole length of the Mitsui Club as they apparently did that of the Rokumeikan, columns are fewer and farther apart, and the eaves and the roof do not, as with the Rokumeikan, call attention to themselves. Yet the Mitsui Club is probably of all buildings in the city the one most like the lost treasure. The first Imperial also echoed the Rokumeikan. A part of the same panorama, it must have seemed very much what it was, the work of the faithful and reverent disciple.

Conder put up many buildings, only a few of which remain. He supervised the building of the Nikolai Cathedral in Kanda, which was finished in 1891, after the design of a Russian professor. Seriously damaged in the earthquake, the Nikolai is now squatter and solider than it was before the disaster.

The Imperial and the Ryōunkaku, the "cloud scraper" of Asakusa, opened for business within a week of each other. Popularly called the Asakusa Twelve Storys, the Ryōunkaku was the building that lost its top storys in the earthquake and was then demolished by army engineers.

If the Rokumeikan was the great symbol of the Meiji elite and its cosmopolitanism, the Twelve Storys was in late Meiji the great symbol of the masses and their pleasures. Asakusa was by that time the busiest center of popular entertainment. The Twelve Storys symbolized Asakusa. Kubota Mantarō wrote:

> In days of old, a queer object known as the Twelve Storys reared itself over Asakusa.
>
> From wherever you looked, there it was, that huge, clumsy pile of red bricks. From the roof of every house, from the laundry platform, from the narrowest second floor window, there it was, waiting for you. From anywhere in the vastness of Tokyo—the embankment across the river at Mukōjima, the observation rise at Ueno, the long flight of stone steps up Atago Hill, there it was, waiting for you, whenever you wanted it.
>
> "Look—the Twelve Storys."
>
> So we would say, at Mukōjima or Ueno, or on Atago Hill. There was quiet pleasure in the words, the pleasure of finding Asakusa. That was what the Twelve Storys meant to Asakusa, a new pleasure each time, the pleasure of knowing Asakusa and its temple.
>
> And yet how clumsy, in illustrated guides, in prints of the Eastern Capital … how clumsy, above cherries fairly dripping with blossoms.
>
> Those cheap prints bring nostalgia for Asakusa as it was, the Asakusa of memory. In memories from my childhood it is always even thus, in the bosom of spring. The rich sunlight, the gentle winds, the green willow shoots, they speak always and only of spring; and as my eyes mount in pursuit of a wavering dragonfly or a stray balloon, there it is, the Twelve Storys, dim in mists.

The Twelve Storys was built by Japanese with the advice of an Englishman named William Barton. Some sources say that it was 320 feet high, some 220. The latter figure seems the more likely. It was in any event the highest building in the city, almost twice as high (even if the

The Asakusa Twelve Storys

lower figure is accepted) as the Nikolai Cathedral. It contained many interesting and amusing things, and, along with a tower on Atago Hill, was the place to go for a view of the city.

Octagonal, of red brick, the Twelve Storys had the first elevator in the land, imported from the United States; it took passengers, twenty of them at a time, to the eighth floor. The elevator was thought dangerous, and shut down after two months. On the second to eighth floors, wares from the world over were for sale. There was a Chinese shop with goods from the China of the Empress Dowager and sales girls in Chinese dress. The ninth floor contained diversions of a refined sort, such as art exhibitions. The tenth floor served as an observation lounge, with chairs scattered

Panoramic photograph by Ogawa Isshin,

about. All of the floors were well lighted—the building was described as a tower of light—but the eleventh floor especially so. It had rows of arc lights inside and out. The top floor, also for observation, was provided with telescopes. For all these delights the entrance fee was a few pennies.

The Twelve Storys may have boasted the first elevator, but the first one to continue operating seems to have been in Nihombashi, some sources say in the Bank of Japan, some in the Mitsui Bank. Nihombashi was itself both progressive and conservative, enlightened and benighted. It divided cleanly in two at the main north-south street, the one that crossed the Nihombashi Bridge. In early Meiji the place for Civilization and Enlightenment would of course have been the Ginza Bricktown. At the end of Meiji it might well have been the western portions of Nihombashi. The Bank of Japan, under construction there for eight years and finished in 1896, was the grandest of piles. To the east was the Mitsui Bank, south of which lay the Mitsukoshi department store, stone-built and several floors tall by the end of Meiji.

The main Nihombashi street passed to the east of them, and across it and a few paces towards the bridge lay the fish market. The conjunction was remarkable; nowhere else in the city was the sudden leap back into

taken from atop the City Hall: northeast quadrant

the past, or, if one preferred, the leap in the other direction, into the new world, more apparent than here. (For the problem of the fish market, see below, pages 94-95.) The view eastwards from the Mitsukoshi was over an almost unbroken expanse of low wooden buildings and the dark back streets of Tanizaki's boyhood. Change had come to them, in the form, for instance, of rickshaws, but not much else; if one did not like brick, stone, and bright lights, one could turn eastwards up one of the narrow streets and walk to the river and beyond, and be scarcely troubled at all by modern contrivances.

To the west, the new Bank of Japan looked grandly towards the palace ramparts over the almost empty spaces of "Mitsubishi Meadow." The original bank building survived the earthquake and survives today, the southwest portion of a much larger complex. A domed central hall runs east and west and two colonnaded wings extend to the south. It was to have been entirely of stone, but the Nagoya earthquake of 1891 persuaded the architect that brick would be safer. Two other buildings by the same architect survived the earthquake and down to our day—Tokyo Central Station and the Daiei Building, originally Imperial Hemp, a thin triangle somewhat reminiscent of the Flatiron Building in New York.

Southeast quadrant of panorama from City Hall

The Bank of Japan complex is held to mark the beginning of a new phase in Meiji architecture—the design and construction of buildings by Japanese architects, quite without foreign assistance, in the courtly and classical styles of Europe. This is probably true enough in a general way, though not absolutely so. There is a tiny building in front of the National Diet, put up in 1891, and thought to be the earliest stone structure designed by a Japanese. Though scarcely monumental, it is certainly classical. It is no more than four yards square, and looks like a tomb that is trying to look like a Roman temple. It houses the prime bench mark for measuring elevation, a bench mark that was two hundred eighty-six millimeters lower after the 1923 earthquake than before.

Great changes were coming, meanwhile, to the Mitsubishi Meadow, also known as Gambler's Meadow. The meadow (the Japanese term might also be rendered "wasteland") lay within the old outer moat of the castle, or palace. Such of its buildings as survived the Restoration disturbances served as the bureaucratic center of early Meiji. The offices gradually moved out, and in 1890 the meadow was sold as a whole to the Mitsubishi enterprises. The army, which then owned the land, needed money for installations on the outskirts of the city, and first proposed selling the tract to the royal household. This body, however, was in straitened circumstances, and unable to pay what the army asked. So the land went

to Mitsubishi. It is the present Marunouchi district, where the biggest companies strive to have their head offices. When such early visitors as Griffis remarked upon the great expanses of empty lands in the city, Marunouchi (which means something like *intramuros,* "within the walls") must have been among the places they had in mind. The Mitsubishi purchase was considered a folly. If the government did not want the place, who would? In very late Meiji it was rejected as a possible site for a new Sumō wrestling stadium. The children of Edo who provided Sumō with its spectators could not be expected to go to so desolate and forbidding a place. It was a day, wrote the poet Takahama Kyoshi,

> when people spoke of the row-houses, four in number, on the Mitsubishi Meadow, otherwise the abode of foxes and badgers. Here and there were weed grown hillocks from aristocratic gardens. The murder ot O-tsuya was much talked about in those days…
>
> Marunouchi was a place of darkness and silence, of loneliness and danger. If one had to pass the Meiji Life Insurance building, a black wilderness lay beyond, with only the stars to light it. Darkness lay over the land on which Tokyo Central Station now stands, and on towards Kyōbashi, where a few lights were to be discerned.

The murder of O-tsuya dates the description. It occurred in 1910, and was indeed talked about, one of the most famous of Meiji crimes. The corpse of a young lady, identified as Kinoshita O-tsuya, had been found one November morning near the prefectural offices. Her murderer was apprehended, quite by accident, ten years later.

Late in Meiji, Ogawa Isshin, one of the more famous of Meiji photographers, took panoramic photographs from the City Hall, on the site of the present prefectural offices in Marunouchi. On most sides of the City Hall appear empty expanses, very unlovely, as if scraped over by some landmover ahead of its time. In a southwesterly direction, scarcely anything lies between the City Hall and the Hibiya crossing, at the southeast corner of the palace plaza. The aspect to the north is even more desolate. There are a few barracks-like buildings, but for the most part the City Hall and the Bank of Japan, off on the western edge of Nihombashi, face each other across an expanse of nothing at all. To the northwest are the first of the new Mitsubishi buildings. Yet at the end of Meiji, Marunouchi still looked very hospitable, on the whole, to foxes, badgers, and gamblers. Only the view to the east towards the Ginza district, beyond the arches for the new elevated railroad, is occupied, most of it in what seems to be a rather traditional way. The remains of Ginza Bricktown do not show.

Mitsubishi was even then filling in the emptiness. In 1894, Conder finished the first of the brick buildings for what came to be known as the Mitsubishi Londontown. More than one architect worked on the district, and suggestions of more than one style were to be detected while Londontown yet survived. The first buildings lay along the street that runs past the prefectural offices from the palace moat. When this thoroughfare had been imposingly lined with brick, there were extensions to the south and then the north, where at the end of Meiji the new Tokyo Central Station was going up. Marunouchi took a quarter of a century being filled, and the newest buildings of Londontown did not last much longer than a quarter-century more. No trace survives today of the original rows of brick. Mitsubishi tore them all down in the years after the Second World War, perhaps a little too hastily. A surviving Conder building would be splendid public relations.

The preeminence of Marunouchi as a business district was assured by the opening of the new station in 1914, at which point it replaced Ginza as "the doorway to Tokyo." Goto Shimpei, director of the National Railways, he who was to become the mayor with the big kerchief, told the architect to produce something that would startle the world. The brick building, three towers and joining galleries said to be in a French style, is not very startling today. It was once more ornate, however, and grander in relation to its surroundings. The central tower, now topped by a poly-hedron, was originally domed; the dome was badly damaged in 1945. In 1914 the station looked off towards the palace over what had been finished of Londontown. Perhaps the most startling thing about it was that it did front in that direction, rather than towards the old Low City, which, thus eloquently told that it might be damned, was separated by tracks and a moat from the station.

This curious orientation has been explained as a show of respect for the palace and His Majesty. Certainly Mitsubishi and its meadow ben-efited enormously from the arrangement. There was nothing explicitly corrupt about it, but the smell of collusion is strong. So it is that eco-nomic miracles are arranged. To many it seemed that the naming of the station was itself an act of arrogance, implying that the other stations of the city, including Shimbashi, were somehow provincial. Kyōbashi and Nihombashi, east of the station, felt left out of things, and continued to board their trains at Shimbashi. It was friendlier and almost as con-venient. In 1920 a decision was finally reached to give Tokyo Central a back or easterly entrance, but at this point the Low City proved unco-operative. Quarreling between Kyōbashi and Nihombashi about the lo-cation of the necessary bridge was not settled until after the earthquake, which destroyed most of both wards.

Only after the earthquake were tracks laid from Tokyo Central to Ueno, whence trains depart for the north. By then Tokyo Central was un-shakably established as the place where all trains from the south stopped and discharged their crowds. Even today, one cannot take a long-distance express from the north through Tokyo and on to the south and west with-out changing trains. It is rather as Chicago was back in the days when Americans still traveled by rail. The traveler from San Francisco had to change in Chicago if he wished to go on to New York. The traveler south-wards gets off at Ueno and boards again at Tokyo Central. Economic rea-sons can be offered to explain the tardiness with which Tokyo and Ueno were joined. The right-of-way passes through densely populated regions laid waste by the earthquake and fire, far more heavily used in Meiji than those between Shimbashi and Tokyo Central or north of Ueno; but the effect was to assure that Mitsubishi Meadow would become worth ap-proximately its weight in gold. The governor of Tokyo has recently an-nounced his opposition to a new express line from the north extending

Tokyo Station from Nihombashi, about 1915

all the way to Tokyo Central. Thus a curious gap yet remains in one of the best railway systems in the world.

Another Meiji revolution was that which dispelled the shadows of Edo. It has happened everywhere, of course—dark medieval corners have become rarer the world over—but it happened more rapidly in the Japanese cities than in Europe and America. There are those, Tanizaki among them, who have argued that dark places were central to Japanese aesthetics, and that doing away with them destroyed something of very great importance. In his famous discourse on shadows, a subject dear to him, Tanizaki speculated on the course modern inventions might have taken had the Japanese done the inventing. Shadows would not have been done away with so brusquely.

Edo already had the kerosene lamp. Tokyo acquired gaslights sixty years later than London, and so the gaslit period was that much shorter. A leading Meiji entrepreneur named Shibusawa Eiichi proposed that the first gaslights be in the Yoshiwara. His reasons seem to have been aesthetic and not moral, and certainly it would have been appropriate for that center of the old, shadowy culture to lead the way into the new. But before this could happen the great Ginza fire intervened, and the rebuilt Ginza became the obvious place for the new brightness. In 1874 eighty-five gaslights flared, and became the marvel of the city, from Shiba along the main Ginza street as far north as Kyōbashi. By 1876 there was a line of gaslights all the way from Ginza to Asakusa, and westwards from Ginza towards the palace as well.

The first experiments with electric lighting were not entirely successful. The main attraction at the opening of the Central Telegraph Office in 1878 was an electric bulb, which burned out in fifteen minutes, leaving the assembly in darkness. In 1882 an arc light was successfully installed before the Ginza offices of the Okura enterprises. The crowds seen gazing at it in Meiji prints give not the smallest sign that they share Tanizaki's grief at the extinction of shadows. (It was, to be sure, only much later that he wrote his essay; in his youth he too loved lights.)

The effect upon the arts was profound, and probably most profound upon the theater. By at least 1877 Kabuki was gaslit, and a decade later had its first electric lights. Today it is dazzlingly bright, and to imagine what it was like in the old shadowy days is almost impossible.

Having left shadows behind, Tokyo seemed intent upon becoming the brightest city in the world, and it may well have succeeded. A series of industrial expositions became the ground for testing the limits.

"Sift civilization to the bottom of your bag of thrills," wrote the novelist Natsume Sōseki in 1907, "and you have an exposition. Filter your exposition through the dull sands of night and you have blinding illumination. If you possess life in some small measure, then for evidences of it you go to illumination, and you must cry out in astonishment at what you see. The civilized who are drugged with civilization are first aware that they live when they cry out in astonishment." It is the late-Meiji view of someone who was himself becoming weary of Civilization and Enlightenment; but it is not wrong in identifying "illumination" (the English word is used) with the soul of Meiji. Turning up the lights, much more rapidly than they had been turned up in the West, was indeed akin to a quest for evidence of life. Freed from the black Edo night, people gathered where the lights were brightest, and so at nightfall the crowds commenced heading south to Ginza from a still dark Nihombashi.

Tanizaki did not become a devotee of shadows until his middle years. In his boyhood Nihombashi was more amply provided with them than he wished. "Even in the Low City there were few street lights. The darkness was rather intimidating. I would return after dark from my uncle's house a few blocks away, scampering past certain ominous places. They were lonely places of darkness, where young men in student dress would be lurking in wait for pretty boys." Tanizaki himself was abducted by an army officer who had the "Satsuma preference," as it was called, and taken to the Mitsubishi Meadow, where he made a perilous escape.

Like the trolley system, the electric power system advertized the confusion of a city growing and changing too rapidly, and the inadequacies of private enterprise. In late Meiji the city had three power companies, in sometimes violent competition. Charges were not for power consumed but for the number of bulbs, which system of course provided encouragement for keeping all bulbs burning at all times. The same house might have a power supply from more than one company, and there were fistfights among linemen when a house changed from one company to another. Two mayors, one of them the famous parliamentarian Ozaki Yukio, were forced to resign because of their inability to impose order in this situation. Proposals for public ownership came to nothing. Finally, in 1917, an accord was reached dividing the city and the prefecture among the three companies. The city did presently buy a part of the system, and was providing power to extensive regions in the High City at the time of the earthquake.

Enlightenment was not immediately successful in dispelling shadows, and smells proved even more obstinate. In 1923 the central fish market stood where it had for almost three hundred years, right beside the Nihombashi Bridge, almost across the street from the Mitsukoshi Department Store and only a few steps from the Mitsui Bank and the Bank of Japan.

As early as the opening of Shimbashi Station, there were earnest endeavors to beautify the main street leading north through Nihombashi. The market was forbidden to use the street, and every effort was made to keep dealers out of sight. Yet the establishment sent its odors through much of Nihombashi and Kyōbashi. There were only two latrines, at the eastern and western ends of the market, remote from the convenience of busy fish dealers. Fish guts were left for the crowds to trample. Each time there was a cholera epidemic the market was blamed, and a clamor arose to move it where it might have the space (should it choose to use it) to be more sanitary and less smelly. Cholera germs were in fact traced to the market in 1922, and authorities closed it for several days.

It had been proposed in 1889 that the market move eastwards to the river, the move to be accomplished by the end of the century. There was strong opposition. A complex system of traditional rights stood in the way of expeditious removal. Nothing happened. In 1923 almost four hundred persons are thought to have died there in the post-earthquake fires that finally decided the matter. The market reopened, first in quarters by the bay and a few months later on the site it now occupies in Tsukiji, a short distance south of where the foreign settlement would be had it survived the earthquake. Most of the fish sold in the last years of the Nihombashi market were brought there by land. What came by water had to be reloaded for transport up the canal. The new site, by the harbor and only a short distance from the freightyards where the old Shimbashi terminus had been, was far more convenient. It was just across a canal from the Hama Palace, but the day was long past when eminent foreigners stayed there. The present emperor, an uncomplaining man, was then regent.

Sewers scarcely existed at the end of Meiji. Kanda had a tile-lined ditch for the disposal of kitchen wastes, but body wastes were left to the *owaiya* with his dippers and buckets and carts and his call of *owai owai* as he made his way through the streets. It was still a seller's market at the end of Meiji; the *owaiya* paid for his commodity. The price was falling rapidly, however, because the growth of the city and the retreat of farmlands to greater distances made it more and more difficult for the farmer to reach the inner wards. The problem grew to crisis proportions in the Taishō Period, as the seller's market changed to a buyer's and in some parts of the city it was not possible to get rid of the stuff. Shinjuku, on the western edge of the city, was known as the anus of Tokyo. Every evening there would be a rush hour when great lines of sewage carts formed a traffic jam.

The water supply was more sophisticated. It long had been. The Tokugawa magistracy had done virtually nothing about sewers, and the Meiji governors and mayors did little more, but there was a venerable system of reservoirs and aqueducts. The Low City was still heavily dependent on wells at the end of Meiji, however, making the problem of sewage disposal not merely noisome but dangerous as well. Water from wells was murky and unpalatable, and so water vendors made the rounds of the Low City, buckets hanging from poles on their shoulders, a wooden Boat in each bucket serving as a simple and ingenious device to keep the water from spilling.

It has been customary, this century and more, for the person who sees the city after an absence to remark upon the dizzying changes. W. E. Griffis, back in Tokyo a few weeks before the Ginza fire and after about a year in the provinces, found the city "so modernized that I scarcely recognize it... Old Yedo has passed away forever." Edo has gone on passing away ever since.

Certainly a comparison of the central Ginza district at the beginning and end of Meiji, of the Mitsubishi Meadow east of the palace, or the western part of Nihombashi, tells of devastating (if one wishes to call it that) change. Scarcely anything present at the beginning of the period, apart from streets, canals, and rivers (or some of them), is present at the end. Not only the visitor, but the native or old resident could remark upon the devastation.

"Bridges were rebuilt, there were evictions after fires, narrow streets were widened," said the novelist Tayama Katai in 1917. "Day by day Edo was destroyed."

Some streets were indeed widened, especially towards the end of Meiji, to make way for the trolley and to provide firebreaks. Others disappeared. The back alleys, the *uradana* of Edo, had been altogether too crowded and dark, and when it became possible to spread out even a little the townsmen quickly did so. Photographs and other graphic materials inform us that the extreme closeness of Edo was early, and happily, dispensed with. The most straitened classes, when they could put together the means, would rather be on a street, however narrow, that led somewhere than on a closed alley.

Yet even today, after numerous minor disasters and two huge ones, the Tokyo street pattern is remarkably like that of Edo. On the eve of the earthquake the traveler could still complain that the city was alternately a sea of mud and a cloud of dust. The surfaced street was still a novelty. In certain heavily commercial parts of the Low City the proportion of streets to total area actually declined in the last two decades of Meiji. Such widening as occurred was not enough to compensate for the loss of back alleys.

In 1915 the mayor found a curious excuse for inaction in the matter of parks, an excuse that tells much of life along the narrow streets. More than nine-tenths of the city was still wooden, he said, and most of the wooden houses were but one story high, each with its own little park. So public parks were not needed as in the cities of the West. It is good bureaucratic evasion, of course, but there must have been truth in it. Most of the streets had to be only wide enough for rickshaws to pass, and an occasional quarrel between runners when they could not was rather fun. The Edo townsman had long been accustomed to thinking of only the central portion of the street as public in any event. The rest could be devoted to greenery, especially to such plants as the morning glory, which gave a delicious sense of the season and did not require much room. The back streets may indeed have been like little parks, or fairs. Edo had always been the greenest of the large cities, and the morning glory might have been as good a symbol as the abacus of the Low City and its concerns.

Improved transportation had by the end of Meiji brought the Low City and the High City closer together. The aristocratic wife of Edo scarcely ever went into the plebeian city, though instances are recorded of well born ladies who attained notoriety by becoming addicted to the theater and actors. Now they commonly went shopping in Ginza or Nihombashi. Kabuki became an object of wealthy High City attention. Its base was more general. It was no longer the particular pride and treasure of the Low City.

In another sense, the division between high and low was accentuated. Class distinctions, measured in money and not pedigree, became clearer. The wealthy moved away from the Low City. Still in Tanizaki's childhood, the mansion of the entrepreneur Shibusawa Eiichi was an object of wonderment, looking somewhat Moorish on a Nihombashi canal. The great flood of 1910 destroyed many of the riverside villas of the wealthy—which were not rebuilt—but the last such place did not disappear until after the Second World War. The process was one of gradual evacuation, leaving the Low City with vestiges of a professional middle class, but no one from the old military and mercantile elite or the new industrial elite. Wealth went away and the self-contained culture of the Low City went too.

This is not to say that the Low City and the High City became alike. The *Shitamachi jōchō,* the "mood of the Low City," still existed, in the

The Shibusawa mansion, Nihombashi

row upon row of wooden buildings and in the sense of neighborhood as
community. But the creative energies had waned. The arts of Edo became respectable, and the lesser plebeian ranks, stranded in the Low City
when the wealthy moved away, were not up to creating anything of a dis-
reputability delicate and intricate enough to match the tradition. It was
as in the old castle towns that had been cultural centers of some note: the
new and original things were being done elsewhere.

In early Meiji, as industrialization got underway, factories were scattered
over the city. By the end of Meiji a pattern had emerged: three-quarters
of the factories were in the bay-shore wards, Kyōbashi and Shiba, and the
two wards east of the river. Tokyo lacked the prominence in manufacturing that it had, by the end of Meiji, in finance, management, and (vague
word) culture. Yet Meiji may be seen as a period of concentration, and the
time when this one city emerged as a place of towering importance. Edo
was important, having in its last century pulled ahead of its Kansai rivals,
culturally at least. Tokyo by the end of Meiji was far more important.

On the eve of the earthquake the city had about a sixteenth of the
population of the country and about two-fifths of the economic capital.
Osaka had almost as many corporations as Tokyo, but less than half as
much capital. A quarter of the total bank deposits were in Tokyo. Within
the city, the wealth was concentrated in three wards: Kojimachi, which
contained the palace and the Mitsubishi Meadow, and Kyōbashi and Nihombashi to the east. Four-fifths of all Japanese companies with capitalization of five million yen and more had their headquarters in one or
another of three wards.

In one curious cultural respect Tokyo lagged behind the nation. There
was far greater reliance upon private education at the primary level than
in the nation at large. In 1879 Tokyo contained more than half the private elementary schools in the country. Despite its large population, it
had fewer public schools than any other prefecture except Okinawa. The
"temple schools" of Edo had the chief responsibility for primary education in early and middle Meiji. It was only towards the turn of the century that the number of pupils in public schools overtook the number in
private schools. The reason would seem to be that the Meiji government
could not do everything at once, and the system of private elementary
education was so well developed in Edo that it could be made to do for a
time. Ahead at the end of Edo, Tokyo was consequently neglected. The
public schools had the greater prestige. Higuchi Ichiyō's novella *Growing
Up,* about a group of children on the edge of the Yoshiwara, informs us

of the inferiority and resentment which the ordinary child felt towards the privileged ones in the public schools.

In higher education, Tokyo prevailed. The western part of Kanda was by the end of Meiji all students and universities, and so was a large part of Hongō. In more general cultural matters, the century since the Meiji Restoration may be seen as one of progressive impoverishment of the provinces, until eventually they were left with little but television, most of it emanating from Tokyo. This process was far advanced by 1923; Tokyo was big-time as Edo had not been. While the cities of the Kansai might preserve their own popular arts and polite accomplishments (and for reasons which no one understands have produced most of the Japanese Nobel laureates), it was in Tokyo that opinions and tastes were formed. It was because Tokyo was so much the center of things that Tanizaki's decision to stay in the Kansai after the earthquake was so startling. All other important literary refugees quickly returned to Tokyo, and even Tanizaki in his last years was edging in that direction.

When, in 1878, the fifteen wards were established, they more than contained the city. They incorporated farmland as well. At the turn of the century two-thirds of the city's paddy lands were in Asakusa Ward and the two wards east of the Sumida. Half the dry farmlands were in Shiba and Koishikawa, the southern and northern fringes of the High City. Farmland had virtually disappeared by the end of Meiji. Attrition was especially rapid late in the period. In 1912, the last year of Meiji, there was only one measure of paddy land within the fifteen wards for every two hundred fifty that had been present but a decade before, and one measure of dry farmland for every three hundred.

The situation was similar with fishing and marine produce. The last authentic "Asakusa laver" (an edible seaweed) had been produced early in the Tokugawa Period. In early Meiji most of the nation's laver still came from outlying parts of Tokyo Prefecture. By the end of the period the prefecture produced none at all, save for the Izu Islands and beyond. The largest fishing community was at Haneda, beyond the southern limits of the city. *Sushi* is still described in restaurants as being *Edo-mae*, "from in front of Edo"—that is, from Tokyo Bay—but very little of it in fact was by the end of Meiji. None at all is today.

So a great deal changed in Meiji, and a good deal remained at the end of Meiji for the earthquake to destroy. In 1910, or whatever the chosen year, one could have joined all the sons of Edo in lamenting the demise of their city, and one could as well have rejoiced at all the little warrens of unenlightenment still scattered over the Low City. It is not possible to weigh change and tradition and decide which is the heavier.

To rejoice in what remained might, in the end, have been the less discommoding course. Recovering from his shock on perhaps the seventh or eighth of September, 1923, many a son of Edo must have lamented that he had not paid better attention to what had until so recently been all around him.

Chapter 3

THE DOUBLE LIFE

Civilization and Enlightenment could be puzzling, and they could be startling too.

In Japan one always hears about "the double life," not as suggestive a subject as it may at first seem to be, and indeed one that can become somewhat tiresome. It refers to the Japanese way of being both foreign and domestic, of wearing shoes and sleeping on floors. The double life is at best an expense and an inconvenience, we are told, and at worst a torment, leading to crises of identity and such things.

Looking about one and seeing the calm, matter-of-fact way in which the Japanese live the double life, one can dismiss the issue as intellectual sound and fury. The world has been racked by changes, such as the change from the rural eighteenth century to the urban twentieth, and, compared to them, the double life does not seem so very much to be tormented by. Yet there can be no doubt that it lies beyond the experience of the West. The West went its own way, whether wisely or not, one step following another. Such places as Tokyo had to—or felt that they had to—go someone else's way.

The playwright Hasegawa Shigure came home one day and found that she had a new mother. Had her old mother been evicted and a new one brought in to replace her, the change might have been less startling. What Shigure found was the old mother redone. "She performed the usual maternal functions without the smallest change, but she had a different face. Her eyebrows had always been shaved, so that only a faint blue-black sheen was where they might have been. Her teeth had been cleanly black. The mother I now saw before me had the stubbly beginnings of eyebrows, and her teeth were a startling, gleaming white. It was the more disturbing because something else was new. The new face was all smiles, as the old one had not been."

The women of Edo shaved their eyebrows and blackened their teeth. Tanizaki, when in his late years he became an advocate of darkness, developed theories about the effect of the shadows of Edo upon the spectral feminine visages created by these practices. Whatever may be the aesthetic merits of tooth-blackening, it was what people were used to. Then came a persuasive sign from on high that it was out of keeping with the new day. The empress ceased blackening her teeth in 1873. The ladies of the court quickly followed her lead, and the new way spread downwards, taking the better part of a century to reach the last peasant women in the remotest corners of the land. If the Queen and the Princess of Wales were suddenly to blacken their teeth, the public shock might be similar.

E. S. Morse did not record that his rickshaw runner was other than good-natured at having to stop at the city limits and cover his nakedness. The relationship between tradition and change in Japan has always been complicated by the fact that change itself is a tradition. Even in the years of the deepest Tokugawa isolation there had been foreign fads, such as one for calicos, originally brought in as sugar sacks, and later much in vogue as kimono fabrics. There had always been great respect for foreign things, which needed no justification. The runner probably felt no more imposed upon by this new vestmental requirement than by the requirement that he be cheerful and reasonably honest. There was, moreover, a certain sense of proportion. Hasegawa Shigure's mother was shamed by the neighbors into thinking that she may have gone too far. She did not return to tooth-blackening, but she did return to a traditional coiffure. The pompadour that had been a part of her new image was a subject of hostile criticism. The neighborhood was not yet ready for it.

If they sought to do what was expected of them, however, the lower orders must have occasionally wondered just what the right thing was. So many acts that had seemed most natural were suddenly uncivilized. A tabulation survives of misdemeanors committed in the city during 1876. "Urinating in a place other than a latrine" accounts for almost half of them. Quarreling and nudity take care of most of the remaining five or six thousand. Not many people were inconvenienced by other proscriptions, but they suggest all the same that one had to tread carefully. Cutting the hair without permission seems to have been an exclusively feminine offense. There is a single instance of "performing mixed Sumō, snake shows, etc." The same pair of miscreants was presumably guilty of both, etc. There are eight instances of transvestism, a curious offense, since it had long been a part of Kabuki, and does not seem to have troubled people greatly in more private quarters. Hasegawa Shigure tells in her reminiscences of a strange lady who turned up for music lessons in Nihombashi and proved to be a man. The police were not summoned, apparently, nor was the person required to discontinue his lessons.

Mixed bathing was banned by the prefecture in 1869. Indifference to the order may be inferred, for it was banned again in 1870 and 1872. Bathhouses were required to have curtains at their doors, blocking the view from the street. Despite these encumbrances, the houses were very successful at keeping up with the times. Few plebeian dwellings in the Low City had their own baths. Almost everyone went to a public bath, which was a place not only for cleansing but for companionship. The second floors of many bathhouses offered, at a small fee, places for games and for sipping tea poured by pretty girls. These facilities were very popular with students. From mid-Meiji, the nature of bathhouses seems to have become increasingly complex and dubious. The bathing function lost importance as private domestic baths grew more common, while second floors were sometimes converted to "archery ranges" (the pretty girls being available for special services) and drinking places. The bathhouse had earlier been a sort of community center for plebeian Edo, a relief from crowding and noise, or, perhaps, a place that provided those elements in a form somewhat more appealing than the clamor of home and family. Now it was a new and rather less innocent variety of pleasure center.

In the fiction of late Edo the barbershop, like the bathhouse, had been a place for watching the world go by. The new world spelled change here too. Western dress was initially expensive, but the Western haircut was not. The male masses took to it immediately; the other masses, as the example of Hasegawa Shigure's mother tells us, more slowly. The Meiji word for the most advanced way of cutting the hair was *zangiri* or *jangiri*, meaning something like "random cropping." The old styles, for aristocrat and commoner alike, had required shaving a part of the head and letting the remainder grow long, so that it might be pulled into a topknot. Already in 1873, the sixth year of Meiji, a newspaper was reporting that about a third of the men in the city had cropped heads.

"If you thump a *jangiri* head," went a popular ditty of the day, "it sounds back 'Civilization and Enlightenment.'" The more traditional heads echoed in a more conservative way, and some even carried overtones suggesting a revocation of the Restoration and a return to the old order.

The first new-style barbershop opened in 1869. It was in Ginza, which had new things even before the fire. The barber had learned his trade in

Up-to-date geisha, by Ogawa Isshin, 1902

Yokohama, and his first customer is said to have been the chief of a fire brigade. This seems appropriate. Firemen were among the more traditional of people, noted for verve and gallantry, and figuring prominently in the fiction and drama of Edo. So it often seems in Meiji: tradition and change were not at odds; the one demanded the other.

By 1880, two-thirds of the men in the city had randomly cropped heads. The figure had reached 90 percent a scant six years later, and by 1888 or 1889 only the rare eccentric still wore his hair in the old fashion.

The inroads of the Western barber were far more rapid than those of the Western tailor. It was not until the day of the flapper that women really began to cut their hair and let it down. Liberated Meiji women went in for a pompadour known as "eaves," from its way of projecting outwards in a sheltering sweep. A few geisha and courtesans adopted Western dress from mid-Meiji, and several wore what was known as the "shampoo coiffure," from its resemblance to hair let down for washing and not put back up again. The first beauty school was opened early in the Taishō Period, by a French lady named Marie-Louise. Others quickly followed.

The English expression "high-collar" came into vogue from about the turn of the century. At first it was derisive, signifying the extremely and affectedly foreign. A lady's coiffure was high-collar if it was thought to he too sweeping and eaveslike. A suggestion of dandyism still clings to the expression.

Some rather surprising things were high-collar, in the broad sense of innovative. Items and institutions which one might think to be very old and very Japanese have their origins in Meiji, under the influence of Civilization and Enlightenment. The word *banzai* is an old one, but the shouting of it on felicitous occasions seems to have occurred first with the promulgation of the Meiji constitution, in 1889. The popularity of Shinto weddings also dates from Meiji. The first marriage broker set up business in Asakusa in 1877. It may be that the police box, so much a part of Japan since Meiji, has its origins in certain Edo practices, but just as probably it began with the guards at the gates of the legations and the foreign settlements. The first private detective agency is believed to have been founded in 1891. Private detectives now seem to be everywhere, and they are so sophisticated that their relatively recent origins are cause for wonderment.

Traffic on the left side of the street also appears to have been a Meiji innovation. There had not been much vehicular traffic in Edo, but bridge signs give evidence that such as there was had been expected to pass on the right. In early Meiji, police orders—probably under the influence of the British, at the forefront of Civilization and Enlightenment in so many ways—required carriages to pass on the left.

Reading a line of horizontal print from left to right was a Meiji innovation. Not imposed by authority, the practice gradually and uncertainly came to prevail. Two adjoining Nihombashi financial establishments might have signs reading in contradictory fashion, one in the old direction, right to left, the other in the new. On the same train the description of the route would read right to left and the no-smoking sign left to right.

Beer, which has now replaced sake as the national drink, even as baseball has replaced Sumō as the national sport, made its appearance early in Meiji. The first brewery was in Tokyo, just south of the Hibiya parade grounds, not far from where the Rokumeikan and the Imperial Hotel later arose. The first beer hall opened in Kyōbashi on the Fourth of July in 1899, celebrating the end of the "unequal treaties."

Until very recently, the system of house numbers was so chaotic that ancient uncodified custom seemed the most likely explanation. In fact, however, there were no house numbers at all until Meiji. The sense of place centered upon the *machi* or *chō*, which might be rendered "neighborhood." A few streets had popular names and today a few have official names, but the neighborhood continues to be the central element in an address. Before Meiji there was nothing else. If more detailed information was required as to the site of a dwelling, only description could be offered—"two houses from the retired sealmaker in the second back alley," and the like. House numbers were observed by early travelers to the West, and thought desirable, and assigned helter-skelter as new houses went up and old houses wished numbers too.

The want of system has been remedied somewhat in recent years, so that Number 2 in a certain neighborhood will usually be found between Number 1 and Number 3; yet the consciousness of place continues to be by tract or expanse and not by line. Though it provides its pleasures, and sometimes one has a delicious sense of adventure in looking for an address, a system of numbers along a line is without question more efficient than one of numbers scattered over an area. The chaos of the Meiji method was a product of Civilization and Enlightenment, however, and not of benighted tradition, which eschewed house numbers.

What is now the most ubiquitous of Japanese accessories, the calling card, is a Western importation. The first ones are believed to have been brought from Europe in 1862 by a Tokugawa diplomatic mission. In the 1903 edition of their guide to Japan, Basil Hall Chamberlain and W. B. Mason describe Tokyo as having "a tranquil and semi-rural aspect owing to the abundance of trees and foliage." Compared to most Japanese cities, and especially Osaka, Tokyo is indeed a city of greenery. Yet the planting of trees along streets is a modern innovation. In the premodern city there had been some public trees (as they might be called) along waterways. The Yanagiwara, the "Willowfield" along the Kanda River, even predated the Tokugawa hegemony. Virtually all the trees and grasses of the old city were in pots or behind walls, however, and the pines, cherries, maples, and oaks of Ginza were the first genuine street trees.

Western things tended to make their first appearance in the treaty ports. Yet many an innovation was first seen in Tokyo. Yokohama may have had the first lemonade and ice cream, but Tokyo had the first butter and the first Western soup.

The first artificial limb in the land was bestowed in Yokohama upon a Tokyo Kabuki actor, the third Sawamura Tanosuke. Dr. J. C. Hepburn, a pioneer medical missionary and the deviser of the Hepburn system of romanization (still in use despite modifications in detail), amputated a gangrenous leg and then sent to America for a wooden one, which arrived and was fitted in the last full year before Meiji. Tanosuke lost his other leg and a hand before he finally died, in 1878. He went on acting to the end.

Men were in most respects quicker to go high-collar than women. It was so in the cutting of the topknot, and it was so as well in the discarding of traditional dress. The phenomenon is to be observed elsewhere in Asia. It has to do, probably, with the decorative functions assigned to women, and also with somewhat magical aspects assigned to Western panoply and appurtenances. Whether or not the business suit is more businesslike than the kimono, people are bound to think it is, because the wearer has been better at business.

There may have been a few geisha with bustles and flounces and the shampoo coiffure, and these were the proper accouterments for a well-placed lady of the upper classes on her way to the Rokumeikan. Yet even for upper-class ladies the emphasis in the late years of the century shifted from Western dress to "improvement" of the Japanese kimono. Though hot-weather dress became Westernized more quickly than dress for the cooler seasons, most lady strollers in Ginza still wore Japanese dress on the eve of the earthquake. Some two-thirds of the men were in foreign dress, which was very expensive in the early years, and attainable only by the wealthy and the bureaucracy (for which it was mandatory). The military and the police were the first to go Western. The change had begun before the end of the shogunate. By 1881, there were two hundred tailoring and dressmaking establishments in the city, more than half of them in Nihombashi.

The emperor's buttons and the empress's bracelets and bodkins arrived from France in 1872. Traditional court dress was abolished by the Council of State that same year, though most court officials were still in traditional dress at the opening of the Yokohama railroad. Willingness to wear Western dress was more prevalent among men than among women, and among the upper classes than the lower.

Even at the height of the Rokumeikan era (for a description of that building see pages 82–83), when the world was being shown that the Japanese could do the Western thing as well as anyone else, there seems to have been more determination than ardor. Newspaper accounts inform us that the dance floor at some of the more celebrated events was dominated by foreigners, and Pierre Loti informs us that Japanese ladies, when coaxed out upon the floor, were correct but wooden.

Rokumeikan parties did not have much to do with the life of the city. They belonged in the realm of politics and the highest society, and if the sort of person who took his pleasures at Asakusa ever set foot in the place, it was doubtless as a servant or a delivery boy. Such affairs do not belong to the story of what happened to Edo and all its townsmen. Yet the Rokumeikan era was such an extraordinary episode, or series of episodes, that to dismiss it as political and really too high-class would be to risk letting the Meiji spirit, at its most ardent there in Tokyo whether of the city or not, disappear in an excessively rigid schema.

The building itself is gone, and historical treatment of the era runs towards dryness. The life of the place is best sensed in the works of woodcut artists who, not themselves of high society, can have attended few if any Rokumeikan soirees. They make the best years of the Rokumeikan, and especially the ladies in their bright, bright dresses, seem utterly charming. Had one lived through those years, however, and been among the lucky few on the invitation lists, one might well have found the Rokumeikan hard work, no more charming than the doings of the Ladies' Benevolent Society today. The flounces and bustles might not be so much fun had they been photographed rather than made into prints. They came when the art of the Ukiyo-e was having its last show of vigor, and lent themselves well to the bold pigments favored by Meiji artists.

The Rokumeikan seems to have been the idea of Inoue Kaoru. When Inoue became foreign minister in 1879, treaty reform was among the great issues. He was of the Nagato clan, which with the Satsuma clan had been the principal maker of the Restoration. In 1881 his good friend and fellow Nagato clansman, Itō Hirobumi, emerged as the most influential figure on the Council of State. Both were young men as politicians go, Itō in his late thirties, Inoue in his early forties. They had gone together some years before the Restoration to study in England. When, in 1885, Itō became the first prime minister with the title that office still bears, Inoue was his foreign minister. They saw Europeanization as the best way to get rid of the unequal treaties, and most particularly of extraterritoriality. Among the details of the movement was the Rokumeikan.

Whatever other ideas he may have had, Inoue is best remembered for conceiving of the Rokumeikan. The charm of the place, in addition to the bustles and flounces, lies largely in an element of fantasy. What politician, one asks, could possibly have thought that such a hardheaded person as the British minister would be so moved by a few Westernized balls at the Rokumeikan that he would recommend treaty revision to the home office? Yet that is what the Rokumeikan was about. In the episode is all the eagerness and wishfulness of young Meiji.

Records are not consistent as to the number of guests invited by Inoue for his opening night. There may have been upwards of a thousand, with several hundred foreigners among them. The facade was a great expanse of branches and flowers, dotted with flags and the royal crest. The garden glittered rather than blazed, with myriads of little lights, each shining chiefly upon a miniature stag. In the hallway were two stags formed from leafy branches. The great staircase was solidly embanked with chrysanthemums. Wishing to seem European in every respect possible, Inoue had the orchestra play to what would have been a fashionable hour in a European capital, but well beyond the hour when the son of Edo would have headed for home or settled in for the night. Accordingly, there was a special train to accommodate guests from Yokohama.

Almost everything for which the Rokumeikan provided the setting was new. Invitations addressed jointly to husbands and wives were an astonishing innovation—the son of Edo would not have known what to say. The Rokumeikan saw garden parties and evening receptions, and in 1884 there was a big charity bazaar. This too was very new. The old order had managed charities differently; it might have been thought proper to give largesse of some sort to a deserving individual who was personally known to the donor, but the trouble of a bazaar to benefit faceless strangers would have seemed purposeless. The 1884 bazaar lasted three days, and ten thousand tickets were sold. At the end of it all, the head of the Mitsubishi enterprises bought the unsold wares. The chief organizer was a princess (by marriage) belonging to a cadet branch of the royal family, and many another great lady of the land was on the committee.

Whether done easily or not, dancing was the main thing to do at the Rokumeikan. Ladies and gentlemen were expected to appear in foreign dress, so much less constricting than Japanese dress, and so flattering to the foreigner. Beginning late in 1884, ladies and gentlemen gathered for regular and studiously organized practice in the waltz, the quadrille, and the like. Two noble Japanese ladies were the organizers, and the teachers were of foreign extraction.

The grand climax of the Rokumeikan era did not occur at the Rokumeikan itself, but serves well by way of summing up. In 1885 Itō Hirobumi, still prime minister, gave a huge masked ball at his Western mansion. Again, reports on the number of guests vary widely, ranging from four hundred to over a thousand. Foreign dress was not required, and numbers of eminent Japanese guests took advantage of this fact. Itō himself was a Venetian nobleman, but Inoue was a Japanese buffoon, and the Home Minister a Japanese horseman. The president of the university came as the poet Saigyō, who had lived some seven centuries earlier.

Itō was involved shortly afterwards in an amorous scandal, an affair with a noble lady who was another man's wife. The Itō cabinet became known—and the appellation is no more flattering in Japanese than in

English—as "the dancing cabinet." Itō held on as prime minister until 1888, but the fresh bloom of the Rokumeikan was passing. The antiquarian example of the university president seems to suggest that not everyone who went there was enthusiastic.

Strongly elitist from the outset, the Rokumeikan became the target of growing criticism, some of it spiteful and emotional, some of it soundly realistic. There were incidents, the Normanton incident of 1886 most prominent among them. The Normanton was a British freighter that sank off the Japanese coast. All the survivors were British, and all twenty-three Japanese passengers drowned. The captain was tried by consular court in Kobe and acquitted. He was later sentenced to a short prison term by the Yokohama consulate, but the sentence did not still public outrage. Extraterritoriality was becoming intolerable. The Rokumeikan and all its assemblies were accomplishing nothing towards the necessary goal.

The end of the decade approached, and it came to seem that the Rokumeikan had no friends anywhere. Itō's political career did not end with the scandal and his resignation, but Inoue never really came into his own. Demagogues of the radical right and leaders of the "people's rights" movement on the left were at one in thinking that the Rokumeikan must go. In 1889 it was sold to the Peers Club, and so began the way into obscurity and extinction that has been described. The name will not be forgotten. During its brief period of prominence the Rokumeikan was among the genuinely interesting curiosities the city contained. It has fascinated such disparate writers as Akutagawa Ryunosuke and Mishima Yukio.

Though the enthusiasm with which the grand men of the land went out courting Europe and America had passed, the vogue for big parties did not pass. Three thousand five hundred guests were present at a party given by a shipowner in 1908, at what had been the Korakuen estate of the Mito Tokugawa family. Another shipowner gave a remarkable party in 1917, by which time the art of party-giving had advanced beyond mere imitation of the West. He had been tigerhunting in Korea, and his two hundred guests, assembled at the Imperial Hotel, were invited to sample tiger meat.

Government offices were first provided with chairs in 1871. Later that year it became unnecessary to remove the shoes before gaining admission. Shoes were quickly popular with both sexes. Schoolgirls in full Japanese dress except for what appear to be buttoned shoes are common in Meiji prints. Clara Whitney, an American girl who lived in Tokyo from 1875, was distressed to see, at the funeral in 1877 of the widow of the fourteenth shogun, a band of professional mourners in traditional dress and foreign shoes. In early Meiji there was a vogue for squeaky shoes. To produce a happy effect, strips of "singing leather" could be purchased and inserted into the shoes.

Student uniforms of the Western style were adopted for men in mid-Meiji, and so came the choke collars and the blackness relieved only by brass buttons that prevailed through the Second World War. At the outset, school uniforms were not compulsory. Rowdiness was given as the reason for the change. Curiously, there had been a period earlier in Meiji when students were *forbidden* to wear foreign dress. Rowdyism seems to have been the reason then too, and the fact that foreigners were distressed to see students wandering about in foreign underwear.

It was not until the Taishō Period that the masses of students, young and older, changed to Western dress. A graduation picture for a well-known private elementary school shows all pupils in Japanese dress at the end of Meiji. A picture for the same school at the beginning of Shōwa (the present reign) shows most of the boys and about half the girls in Western dress. The middy blouse that continues to be a standard for girl students on the lower levels did not come into vogue until after the earthquake.

At the end of Meiji, the old way of dress yet prevailed among students, though the enlightened view held that it was constricting and inconsistent with modern individualism. When male students chose Western costume, they often wore it with a difference. A flamboyant messiness became the mark of the elite, and a word was coined for it, a hybrid. The first syllable of *bankara* is taken from a Chinese word connoting barbarity, and the remainder from "high-collar," signifying the up-to-date and cosmopolitan. The expression, still used though uniforms have virtually disappeared from higher education, means something like sloppily modern.

High-collar aspects of food had been present since early Meiji, especially the eating of meat, a practice frowned upon by Buddhist orthodoxy. It is recorded that Sumō wrestlers of the Tokugawa Period ate all manner of strange things, such as monkeys, but the populace at large observed Buddhist taboos. The beef-pot was among the radical Meiji departures, and among its symbols as well. Pigs, horses, and dairy products, almost unknown before Meiji, now entered the Japanese diet. So too did bread, which was not thought of as a staple until about the time of the earthquake. In Meiji it was a confection. A Japanized version, a bun filled with bean jam, was inexpensive and very popular among students.

The city had a slaughterhouse from late Tokugawa, first in the hills of Shiba, then, because of local opposition, on the more secluded Omori coast, beyond the "red line" that defined the jurisdiction of the city magistrates. The students at Fukuzawa's Keiō University seem to have been inveterate eaters of beef, as was most appropriate to that Westernizing place. Yet they had their inhibitions. Reluctant to be seen in butcher shops, customers would receive their orders through inconspicuous windows. When a butcher entered the Keiō gates to make deliveries, he would be greeted with the clicking of flints that was an ancient cleansing and propitiatory ritual.

Chinese cuisine was also new to the city, though it had long been present in Nagasaki. It is so ubiquitous today, and in many ways so Japanized, that one might think it most venerable. The first Chinese restaurant in Tokyo opened for business only in 1883. It was the Kairakuen in Nihombashi, where Tanizaki and his friends played at whores and cribs. Where the beef-pot seems to have caught on without special sponsorship, the Kairakuen, like the Rokumeikan, had wealthy and powerful promoters, who thought Chinese cooking a necessity in any city worthy of the name.

There were pig fanciers. Pigs commanded high prices. The tiny creatures known as Nanking mice also enjoyed a vogue. But the rabbit vogue was more durable and more intense, a rage of a vogue indeed. Though it spread all over the country, its beginnings were in Tokyo, with two foreigners, an Englishman and an American, who, situated in the Tsukiji foreign settlement, offered rabbits for sale. They also offered to make plain to the ignorant exactly what a rabbit connoisseur looked for in a particularly desirable beast. The rabbits were to be patted and admired, as dogs and cats are, and not eaten. A society of rabbit fanciers was formed. Rabbits with the right points brought huge prices, far greater, by weight, than those for pigs. Large floppy ears were much esteemed, as was the *sarasa*, or calico coat. A person in Shitaya was fined and jailed for staining a white rabbit with persimmon juice.

Imports from distant lands increased the rabbit count, and encouraged speculation and profiteering. In 1873, a year in which the population of domestic rabbits in the central wards reached almost a hundred thousand, authorities banned a meeting of the society of rabbit fanciers. Later that year they banned the breeding of the rabbits themselves, and imposed a tax to discourage possession. The vogue thereupon died down, though foreigners were observed thereafter selling French rabbits in Asakusa. Newspapers regarded the consular courts as too lenient, and so the rankling issue of extraterritoriality came into the matter. So did one of the great social problems of early Meiji, because the lower ranks of the military aristocracy—who had great difficulty adjusting to the new day—were the chief losers from the profiteering.

The enthusiasm for foreign things waned somewhat in mid-Meiji. In the realm of personal grooming there was a certain vogue for "improving" Japanese things rather than discarding them for the Western. This nationalist reaction was by implication anti-Western, of course, but it was not accompanied by the sort of antiforeign violence that had been common in late Tokugawa. There were such incidents in early Meiji, but usually under special circumstances. When, in 1870, two Englishmen who taught at the university were wounded by swordsmen, W. E. Griffis was on hand to help treat them. Initially he shared the anger and fear of the foreign community, but eventually he learned of details that shocked his missionary sensibilities and caused him to put the blame rather on the Englishmen. They had been out womanizing. What happened to them need no more concern the God-fearing citizen of Tokyo than a similar incident at the contemporary Five Points slum need concern a proper citizen of New York. Two men from southwestern clans were executed for the assaults, some have thought on insufficient evidence. Sir Harry Parkes, the formidable British minister, was about to depart for home, and it was thought necessary (or so it has been averred) that something memorable be done for the occasion. One of the two condemned men retracted his confession, which did not in any event agree with the evidence presented by the wounds.

Out of fashion for some decades after Prince Itō's masked ball, dancing became wild and uncontrolled, by police standards, in the years after the First World War. Another new institution of the Rokumeikan period, the coffee house, also left its early primness behind. A Chinese opened the first one near Ueno Park in 1888. Descriptions of it suggest that it may have been a sort of gymnasium or health club, with coffee offered as an invigorating potion. The transcription of "coffee" had a sort of devil-may-care quality about it. Today the word is generally written with two characters that have only phonetic value, but the founder of the Coffee House chose a pair signifying "pros and cons," or perhaps "for better or for worse." The English word has continued to designate the beverage, while the French came to signify a place where stylish and affluent gentlemen (without their wives) went to be entertained by pretty and accommodating young ladies. It was among the symbols of the Taishō high life.

Though sea bathing was not completely unknown in Meiji, ladies' bathing garments became good business only in Taishō. Immersion in natural bodies of cold water has long been a religious observance, but it was not until recent times that the Japanese came to think it pleasurable. When Nagai Kafū describes a summer beach of late Meiji it is notable for its loneliness, even a beach which now would be an impenetrable mass of bodies on a hot Sunday afternoon. In his memoirs Tanizaki describes an excursion to the Shiba coast, to a beach situated almost exactly where the expressway now passes the Shiba Detached Palace. The purpose of the outing seems to have been more for clamdigging than for bathing. In late Meiji there was an advertising campaign to promote the district and induce people to come bathing in its waters (then still clean enough for bathing, even though the south shore of the bay was becoming a district of factories and docks). Among the points made in favor of sea bathing was that it was held in high esteem by foreigners.

Eminent foreigners began coming to Tokyo at an early date. They were on the whole treated hospitably. An exception was the czarevitch of Russia, who was wounded by a sword-swinging policeman, though not in Tokyo, when he paid a visit to Japan in 1891. The very earliest was the Duke of Edinburgh, who came in 1869. Others included German and Italian princes, Archduke Franz Ferdinand, and a head of state, the King of Hawaii. William H. Seward called in 1870. The Meiji government felt more immediately threatened by Russia than by any other nation. Seward suggested an Alaskan solution to the Russian problem: buy them out. Pierre Loti was probably the most distinguished literary visitor of Meiji, but such attention as he received—his invitation to the Rokumei-kan, for instance—had less to do with his writing than with his diplomatic status as a naval attaché.

The eminent foreigners most lionized were without question General and Mrs. Ulysses S. Grant. On a round-the-world journey, they reached Nagasaki by cruiser in June, 1879, and were in Tokyo for two months, from early July to early September. They were to have visited Kyoto and Osaka, but this part of their schedule was canceled because of a cholera epidemic. The guard along the way from Yokohama was commanded by Nogi Maresuke, who became, in the Russo-Japanese War, the leading military immortal of modern times, and demonstrated the extent of his loyalty to the throne by committing suicide on the day of the Meiji emperor's funeral. For the Grants there was a reception at Shimbashi Station, before which a display of hydrangeas formed the initials "U.S.G."

A parade during General Grant's visit in 1879. Woodcut by Kunichika
(The Metropolitan Museum of Art: gift of Lincoln Kirstein, 1962)

Japanese and American flags decorated every door along the way to the Hama Palace, where the party stayed, and where the governor honored them with yet another reception. Receptions were held during the following weeks at the College of Technology and Ueno. The former is said to have been the first soiree essayed by the Japanese, whose ways of entertaining had been of a different sort. There were parades and visits to schools and factories, the sort of thing one gets on a visit to the New China today. The general planted a cypress tree in Ueno. It came through the holocausts of 1923 and 1945, and yet survives, providing the background for an equestrian statue of the founder of the Japanese Red Cross. Mrs. Grant planted a magnolia, which survives as well. There was classical theater, both Kabuki and Nō, and there was the most festive of summer observances, the "opening of the Sumida" in July. The general viewed it in comfort from an aristocratic villa, it being a day when there were still such villas on the river. The crowds were twice as large as for any earlier year in Meiji, despite the fact that the weather was bad. Fireworks and crowds got rained upon. All manner of pyrotechnical glories were arranged in red, white, and blue. The general indicated great admiration.

The general and the emperor saw a good deal of each other. The general paid a courtesy call on the Fourth of July, the day after his arrival.

They had breakfast together after a troop review on July 7, and met again at the great Ueno reception in August. Also in August, they had a long and relatively informal meeting in the Hama Palace. The general argued the virtues of democracy, though with a caution against too hasty adoption of this best of systems. He expressed the hope that the Japanese would be tactful and considerate of Chinese sensibilities as they took over the Ryūkyū Islands, claimed by both countries. A few days before his departure, he took his leave of the emperor.

Though overall the visit was a huge success, there were a few unpleasant incidents. Clara Whitney overheard a catty Japanese lady remark "that General Grant is treated so much like a god here that a temple should be erected immediately." Towards the end of his stay there were rumors of an assassination plot, but they proved to be the inventions of a jealous Englishman. The 1879 cholera epidemic, by no means the only such epidemic in Meiji, had led to the building of the first isolation hospitals in the city. Rumors spread similar to earlier ones about telegraph poles (see p. 65): the hospitals were for purposes of snatching livers, General Grant being ready to pay a handsome price for a liver.

These were minor details, however. On the whole, the city seems to have loved the general and the general the city.

The high point of the visit, for the historian of the event if not for the general himself, was his evening at the Kabuki. He went to the Shintomiza near Ginza, the most advanced theater in the city. Carpets and lacquered chairs had been carried in from the Hama Palace. Three royal princes were in attendance, as was the prime minister. The play was called *The Latter Three Years' War in the North*. Minamoto Yoshiie, the victorious general in that war (a historical event), resembled the visiting general in a most complimentary manner: he behaved with great courtliness and magnanimity towards his defeated adversary.

The theater manager, accompanied by Danjūrō, the most famous actor of the day, stepped forth in frock coat during an entr'acte to thank the general for a curtain he had donated. The climax was a dance performed against a backdrop of flags and lanterns. Some of the musicians wore red and white stripes, others stars on a blue ground. Then appeared a row of Yanagibashi geisha, each in a kimono of red and white stripes drawn down over one shoulder to reveal a star-spangled singlet. Japanese and American flags decorated their fans.

"Ah, the old flag, the glorious Stars and Stripes!..." Clara Whitney wrote in her diary. "It made the prettiest costume imaginable... We looked with strong emotion upon this graceful tribute to our country's flag and felt grateful to our Japanese friends for their kindness displayed not only to General Grant but to our honored country."

*   *   *

Next to General and Mrs. Grant, the foreigner who got the most attention from the newspapers and the printmakers was probably an Englishman named Spencer, who came in 1890, bringing balloons with which he performed stunts, once in Yokohama and twice in Tokyo. The emperor was present at the first Tokyo performance. Parachuting from his balloon, Spencer almost hit the royal tent, and injured himself slightly in his efforts to avoid it. He drew huge crowds at Ueno a few days later, and this time landed in a paddy field. An American named Baldwin tried to outdo him the following month, with aerial acrobatics and a threatening smoky balloon. Spencer is the one who is remembered, to the extent that he was given credit by the printmakers for stunts that apparently were Baldwin's. The following year the great actor Kikugorō appeared on the Kabuki stage as Spencer, in a play by Mokuami. Coached by a nephew of Fukuzawa Yukichi, he even essayed a speech in English. There was a vogue for balloon candies, balloon bodkins, and, of course, balloon prints. Since the Japanese had been launching military balloons for more than a decade, it must have been the parachuting and stunting that so interested people— or perhaps they enjoyed seeing a foreigner in a dangerous predicament.

W. E. Griffis, who felt that those two grievously wounded Englishmen (see page 113) deserved what they got, said that the same judgment applied to all attacks upon foreigners of which he was aware. It may be true. The attack on the czarevitch may not seem to fit the generalization as well as it might, but the assailant could have argued that Russia itself was behaving provocatively. Violence was also directed at Salvation Army workers, and much the same justification might have been offered—the army itself was provocative.

An American colonel of the Salvation Army arrived and set up an office in the summer of 1900. Very soon afterwards he published a tract called *Triumphant Voice (Toki no Koe)*, addressed to the ladies of the Yoshiwara. It exhorted them to flee their bondage, and offered help to those who responded positively. The brothel keepers attempted to buy up all copies. A Japanese worker for the Salvation Army was pummeled by a Yoshiwara bully boy as he hawked *Triumphant Voice*. Two men tried to rescue a lady from the Susaki quarter, and they too were attacked. This charitable endeavor attracted the attention and support of the newspapers. A reporter succeeded in rescuing a Yoshiwara lady, whereupon fleeing the quarters became something of a fad. The Salvation Army announced that during the last months of 1900 there were more than a thousand refugees in Tokyo alone. The figure is not easy to substantiate, but publicity was enormous. The vogue presently passed, and the Salvation Army was not afterwards able to match this initial success.

The "double life," that mixture of the imported and the domestic, was certainly present from early Meiji and indeed from late Tokugawa, for people to enjoy and to be tormented by. Eminent foreigners came, objects of admiration and emulation, and once Civilization and Enlightenment had been accepted as worthy, it must have been difficult to see pinching shoes and injunctions to urinate indoors as other than important. Through most of Meiji, however, the cosmopolitan part of the double life was the part added, the frills attached somewhat selfconsciously and discarded when a person wanted to be comfortable. The big change, the domestication of the foreign, began in late Meiji, at about the time of the Russo-Japanese War, and the advertising man and the retail merchant may have been responsible for it. Perhaps it would have occurred without their aggressive urgings. Yet the old drygoods store became the modern department store in late Meiji, and in the change we may see how the double life itself was changing. Civilization and Enlightenment were no longer much talked of in late Meiji, but it was hard for anyone, in the dingiest alley east of the river, not to know what the Mitsukoshi and the Shirokiya were offering this season.

Advertising is a modern institution. The canny merchant of Edo had been aware of its merits, and there are well-known stories of Kabuki actors who promoted lines of dress. Edo was a closed world, however, in which vogues, led by the theater and the pleasure quarters, spread like contagions. People knew their stores, and stores knew their people. Even the largest and richest were highly specialized. Faster transportation led to the development of a wide clientele, gradually becoming something like national. At the same time came the idea of offering everything to everyone.

Through most of Meiji, the old way prevailed. The big shops specialized in dry goods. The customer removed his footwear before stepping up to the matted floor of the main sales room. There was no window shopping. If the customer did not know precisely what he wanted, the clerk had to guess, and bring likely items from a godown. Aristocratic ladies from the High City did not go shopping in the Low City. Clerks came to them from the big "silk stores," or from smaller establishments that would today call themselves boutiques.

The Mitsui dry goods store, presently to become Mitsukoshi, had a fixed schedule of prices from early in its history. Haggling seems to have been common in early Meiji all the same, and a mark of cultural differences. The clans of the far southwest had made the Meiji revolution, and were the new establishment. Their ways were frequently not the ways of Edo and Tokyo. Their men took haggling as a matter of course, and the shopkeepers of Edo resisted it or acceded to it as their business instincts advised them. At least one old and well-established dry goods store bankrupted itself by the practice. Mitsui held to its fixed schedule, and survived.

The last decades of Meiji saw the advent of the department store. In many of its details it represented the emergence of a Western institution and the retreat of the traditional to the lesser realm of the specialty store. Certainly there was imitation. The big Mitsukoshi store of the Taishō era, the one that burned so brightly after the earthquake, was an imitation of Wanamaker's. If the department store symbolized the new city, however, it remained a Japanese sort of symbol. Department stores sold their wares by drawing crowds with culture and entertainment as well as merchandise. They were heirs to the shrine and temple markets, shopping centers ahead of their time.

Mitsukoshi's famous glass display cases

Mitsukoshi and Shirokiya, at opposite approaches to the Nihombashi bridge, led the way into the great mercantile transformation. Edo methods predominated until about the turn of the century. They did not disappear even then, but the big dealers quickly moved on to mass sales of myriad commodities.

Mitsui, or Mitsukoshi, had entered Edo from the provinces in the seventeenth century. Shirokiya had opened for business in Nihombashi a few years earlier. Mitsukoshi has fared better than Shirokiya in the present century, but it would be facile to see in this the commonly averred victory of the provincial trader over the son of Edo. Both enterprises had been a part of Edo from its earliest years. Mitsukoshi was better at advertising and "image-making" than Shirokiya. Though purveying almost everything to almost everyone, it has preserved a certain air of doing so with elegance. In late Meiji, standing face to face across the bridge to which all roads led, the two sought to outdo each other with bold new innovations. Shortly after the Russo-Japanese War of 1904-1905 Mitsui added a second floor, with showcases. These were innovations so startling that they were for a time resisted. Edo had done its shopping on platforms perhaps two or three feet from the ground, with no wares on display.

Although Mitsukoshi was ahead in the matter of showcases and elevated shopping, Shirokiya was ahead in other respects. In 1886 it became the first of the old silk stores to sell Western clothes. It had one of the first telephones in the city, which, however, was kept out of sight, in a stairwell, lest it disturb people. It provided the country with its first shop girls. All the clerks in the old dry goods stores had been men. From about the time it became Mitsukoshi, which was registered as the legal name in 1904, Mitsui began selling hats, leather goods, and sundries. Then, having withdrawn to a back street because the main north-south street through Nihombashi was being widened, Mitsukoshi reopened on the old site in 1908, with the makings of a department store. Shirokiya replied with a new building, four storys and a tower, in 1911. It had game rooms and the first of the exhibition halls that give the modern Japanese department store certain aspects of a museum and amusement park. In 1914 Mitsukoshi completed a grand expansion, into the building that burned after the earthquake. The new Mitsukoshi was a five-story Renaissance building, not the highest in the city, but the largest, it was said, east of Suez, and very modern, with elevators, central heating, a roof garden, and even an escalator.

The Mitsukoshi of 1914 was not a very interesting building, at least from the outside, but the Shirokiya must have been a delight, built as

Shirokiya Department Store, Nihombashi, after 1911

it was in an eclectic style that looked ahead to the more fanciful effusions of Taishō. The building of late Meiji does not survive, but in photographs it seems the more advanced and certainly the more interesting of the two. Yet Shirokiya was less successful than its rival in keeping up with the times.

Mainly, Mitsukoshi was the better at the big sell. Already at the turn of the century, a life-size picture of a pretty girl stood in Shimbashi Station inviting everyone to Mitsukoshi. Early in Taishō the store joined the Imperial Theater in a famous advertising campaign. The slogan was the only one still remembered from the early years of Japanese advertising. "Today the Imperial, tomorrow Mitsukoshi." Inviting the public to spend alternate days at the two establishments, it was very successful. In the Taishō period Mitsukoshi had a boys' band known to everyone. It is said to have been the first nonofficial band in the nation. The boys wore red and green kilts.

Despite all this innovation, the department stores were far from as big at the end of Meiji as they have become since. The old market was still healthy. Neighborhood stores offered most commodities and had most of the plebeian trade, the big Nihombashi stores still being a little too high-collar. Yet the department stores worked the beginnings of a huge

Matsuzakaya Department Store in Ueno

cultural shift, so that the city of late Meiji seems far more familiar than the city of late Tokugawa. They were not the only enterprises of their kind in the city. Kanda and Ueno each had one, both of them to advance upon Ginza after the earthquake.

The problem of what to do with footwear was not solved until after the earthquake, and the delay was in some measure responsible for the slowness of the big stores to attract a mass clientele. Footwear was checked at the door in traditional fashion, sometimes tens of thousands of items per day, and replaced by specially furnished slippers. On the day of the dedication of the new Nihombashi bridge, still in use, Mitsukoshi misplaced five hundred pairs of footwear. For this reason among others the department store was a little like the Ginza bricktown: everyone wanted a look at it, but it would not do for everyday. It was on the standard tour for *onobori*, country people in for a look at the capital. The presence of Mitsukoshi, indeed, along with certain patriotic sites now out of fashion, is what chiefly distinguishes the Meiji Tokyo tour from that of today.

There was another kind of shopping center, also new in Meiji, and the vexing problem of footwear has been offered to explain its very great popularity from late Meiji into Taishō. The word *hankōba* is a Meiji neologism that seems on the surface to mean, with exhortatory intent, "place for the encouragement of industry." It actually signifies something like "bazaar" or "emporium." Numbers of small shops would gather under a roof or an arcade and call themselves a *hankōba*. In the years when the old dry goods stores were making themselves over into department stores, the bazaars were much more popular, possibly because the customer did not have to remove his shoes or clogs. The great day of the bazaar was late Meiji. When the department stores finally emerged as a playground for the whole family, on whatever level of society, bazaars went into a decline.

The first bazaar was publicly owned. It opened in 1878, selling products left over from the First Industrial Exposition, held at Ueno the preceding year. Its location was for the day a remote one, at the northern end of what would become the Mitsubishi Meadow, just east of the palace. Two bazaars dominated the busy south end of Ginza, near which the main railway station stood until early Taishō. The building of the present Tokyo Central Station displaced the crowds and sent the bazaars into a decline. In the fourth decade of Meiji, however, there were three bazaars in Kanda and seven in Ginza. By 1902 there were twenty-seven scattered over the city. Nine years later there were only eleven, and in 1913, the first full year of Taishō, only six.

No establishment has called itself a *kankōba* since the 1950s, but the *kankōba* must have been not unlike the shopping centers that are a threat to the Nihombashi stores today. For all the newness of the word, the kankōba also had much in common with the neighborhood shopping district of Edo. There is continuity in these things, and what seems newest may in fact be tradition reemerging.

* * *

The department stores and the bazaars were in it to make money, but they also provided pleasure and entertainment. So it was too with the expositions. People were supposed to be inspired and work more energetically for the nation and Civilization and Enlightenment, but expositions could also be fun.

The Japanese learned early about them. The shogunate and the Satsuma clan sent exhibits to the Paris fair of 1867, and the Meiji government to Vienna in 1873 and the Centennial Exposition in Philadelphia.

The Japanese experimented with domestic fairs early in Meiji, one of them in the Yoshiwara. The grand exhibition that called itself the First National Industrial Exposition occurred at Ueno in 1877, from late summer to early winter. The chief minister was chairman of the planning committee. He was a man of Satsuma, and the Satsuma Rebellion was just then in progress; and so the import of the exposition was highly political, to demonstrate that the new day had arrived and meant to stay, in spite of dissension. The emperor and empress came on opening day and again in October, a month before the closing. The buildings were temporary ones in a flamboyantly Western style, with an art gallery at the center and flanking structures dedicated to farming and machinery and to natural products. Some of the items on display seemed scarcely what the Japanese most needed—a windmill, for instance, thirty feet high, straight from the drylands of America. Almost a hundred thousand items were exhibited by upwards of sixteen thousand exhibitors. The total number of visitors was not much less than the population of the city.

Other national exhibitions were scattered across Meiji. As a result of the second, in 1881, Tokyo acquired its first permanent museum, a brick structure designed by Josiah Conder, begun in 1878 and not quite finished in time for the exposition. The fourth and fifth expositions, just before and after the turn of the century, were held in Kyoto and Osaka. The sixth, in 1907, at Ueno once more, remains the grandest of the Tokyo series. Coming just after the Russo-Japanese War, it had patriotic significance, and therapeutic and economic value as well. Economic depression followed the war, and a need was felt to increase consumption. The main buildings, Gothic, in the park proper, were built around a huge fountain, on six levels, surmounted by Bacchus and bathed in lights of red, blue, and purple. Although the architecture was for the most part exotic, the prestige of Japanese painting had so recovered that the ceiling of the art pavilion was decorated with a dragon at the hands of the painter Hashimoto Gahō, who was associated with such fundamentalist evangelizers for the traditional arts as Ernest Fenollosa and Okakura Tenshin.

A water chute led down to the lower level, on the shores of Shinobazu Pond, where special exhibitions told of foreign lands and a growing empire. There was a Taiwan pavilion and a Ryūkyū pavilion, the latter controversial, because ladies from the pleasure quarters were present to receive visitors and make them feel at home. They were considered an affront to the dignity of the Ryūkyūs, whose newspapers protested.

It was the Sixth Exposition that inspired Natsume Sōseki's famous remarks about illumination (see page 93). Indeed, all the expositions were makers of taste. The more fanciful architectural styles of Taishō derive quite clearly from two expositions, held at Ueno early and midway through the reign.

Ueno, the place for expositions, is one of five public parks, the first in the city, established in 1873. The public park is another Meiji novelty introduced under the influence of the West. The old city had not been wanting in places for people to go and be with other people, but the idea of a tract maintained by the city solely for recreation was a new one. We have seen that at least one mayor thought such places unnecessary. He had a good case. The city already possessed myriads of gardens, large and small, and temples, shrines, cemeteries, and other places for viewing the flowers and grasses of the seasons.

The fact that one such place, in the far south of the city, was chosen by the shogunate as the site for the British legation was among the reasons for public satisfaction at the destruction of the unfinished building. A succession of temples occupied most of the land from what is now Ueno Park to the Sumida.

There were fewer such public spaces as time went by; and so the principle that the city had a responsibility in the matter was an important departure. The grandest of Edo temples are far less grand today. Had public parks not come into being, the loss of open space as religious establishments dwindled might have been almost complete.

A foreigner is given credit for saving Ueno. Almost anything might have happened to the tract left empty by the "Ueno War," the subjugation in 1868 of holdouts from the old regime. Before that incident it had been occupied by the more northerly of the two Tokugawa funeral temples, the Kan-eiji. With branch temples, the Kan-eiji (named for the era in early Edo when it was founded) extended over the whole of "the mountain"—the heights to the north and east of Shinobazu Pond—and low-lying regions to the east as well, where Ueno Station now stands. Six of the fifteen shoguns are buried on the Kan-eiji grounds. The grave of Keiki, the last, is nearby in the Yanaka cemetery.

The attacking forces destroyed virtually the whole of the great complex. What is the main hall of the Kan-eiji today was moved in 1879 from the provinces to the site of a lesser temple. A gate is the only relic of the central complex, although a few seventeenth-century buildings, among the oldest in the city, still survive in the park. The public had been admitted to the Kan-eiji during the daytime hours. The precincts were, then as now, famous for their cherry blossoms.

After the fighting of 1868, Ueno was a desolate but promising expanse, more grandly wooded than it is today. The Ministry of Education wanted it for a medical school. The army, the most successful appropriator of land in early Meiji, thought that it would be a good location for a military hospital. It was at this point that the foreign person offered an opinion.

Dr. E. A. F. Bauduin, a Dutchman, had come to Japan in 1862. He was a medical doctor, and during his career in Japan served as a consultant on medical education in Nagasaki and Edo, and at the university in Tokyo. The Ministry of Education summoned him from Nagasaki for consultations in the matter of making the Ueno site a medical school. Quite contrary to expectations, he argued instead that Ueno would make a splendid park, and that the medical school could just as well go in some other place, such as the Maeda estate in Hongō, now the main campus of Tokyo University.

This view prevailed. In 1873, Ueno became one of the first five Tokyo parks. The others were the grounds of the Asakusa Kannon, the Tokugawa cemetery at Shiba, some shrine grounds east of the river, and a hill in the northern suburbs long famous for cherry blossoms. Of the four parks in the city proper it was the only one that was not otherwise occupied, so to speak, and it has had a different career than the others. It was transferred to the royal household in 1890, and returned to the city in 1924, to honor the marriage of the present emperor. Today it is officially called Ueno Royal Park. Shinobazu Pond to the west, a remnant of marshlands that had once spread over most of the Low City, was annexed to the park in 1885.

Ueno has not entirely escaped the incursions of commerce. Though the scores of little stalls that had established themselves in the old temple precincts were closed or moved elsewhere, the huge Seiyōken restaurant is the chief eyesore on an otherwise pleasing skyline. (An 1881 poster informs us that the restaurant is in Ueno Parque.) The original park now includes the campus of an art and music college. The Tokugawa tombs were detached from the park in 1885.

Yet Ueno has remained very much a park, less greedily gnawed at than Asakusa and Shiba have been. For a decade in mid-Meiji, until 1894, there was a horseracing track around Shinobazu Pond, a genteel one, with a royal stand. The emperor was present at the opening. The purpose, most Meiji-like, was not pleasure or gambling but the promotion of horsemanship in the interests of national defense. Woodcuts, not always reliable in such matters, seem to inform us that the horses ran clockwise.

Ueno Park had the first art museum in the land, the first zoo, the first electric trolley, a feature of one of the industrial expositions, and, in 1920, the first May Day observances. (There have been 53 as of 1982; a decade's worth were lost to "Fascism.") In a city that contains few old buildings, Ueno has the largest concentration of moderately old ones. It was saved by royal patronage, and, ironically, by the fact that its holocaust came early. The arrangements of early Meiji prevailed through the holocausts of 1923 and 1945.

Besides Edo survivals, the park, broadly defined to include the campus of the art college, contains the oldest brick building in the city. It has just passed its centennial. The oldest concert hall, of wood, is chronically threatened with dismemberment. The oldest building in the National Museum complex, in a domed Renaissance style, was a gift of the Tokyo citizenry, put up to honor the wedding of the crown prince. The present emperor was already a lad of seven when it was finished. The planning, collecting of funds, and building took time. What has become the great symbol of the park, recognized all over the land, is also a relic of Meiji. The bronze statue of Saigō Takamori, on the heights above the railway station, was unveiled in 1898. The original plans had called for putting it in the palace plaza, but it was presently decided that Saigō, leader of the Satsuma Rebellion, at the end of which, in 1877, he killed himself, had not yet been adequately rehabilitated. His widow did not like the statue. Never, she said, had she seen him so poorly dressed.

Huge numbers of people went to Ueno for the industrial expositions, and soon after it became a park it was again what it had been in Edo, a famous place for viewing cherry blossoms. Under the old regime the blossoms had been somewhat overwhelmed by Tokugawa mortuary grandeur, however, and singing and dancing, without which a proper blossom-viewing is scarcely imaginable, had been frowned upon. A certain solemnity seems to have hung over the new royal park as well. Blossom-viewing places on the Sumida and on the heights to the north of Ueno were noisier and less inhibited. Indeed, whether or not because of the royal association, Ueno seems early to have become a place of edification rather than fun.

Asakusa was very different. The novelist Saitō Ryokuu made an interesting and poetic comparison of the two, Asakusa and Ueno. Ryokuu's case was similar to Nagai Kafū's: born in the provinces in 1867 or 1868 and brought to Tokyo as a boy of perhaps nine (the facts of his early life are unclear), and so not a son of Edo, he outdid the latter in his fondness for the Edo tradition. His way of showing it was different from Kafū's. He preferred satire to lyricism, and falls in the proper if not entirely likeable tradition of Edo satirists whose favorite subject is rustic ineptitude in the great pleasure palaces of the metropolis. He is not much read today. His language is difficult and his manner is out of vogue, and it may be that he was the wrong sex. Women writers in a similarly antique mode still have their devoted followings.

Some of his pronouncements deserve to be remembered. Of Ueno and Asakusa he said: "Ueno is for the eyes, a park with a view. Asakusa is for the mouth, a park for eating and drinking. Ueno puts a stop to things. From Asakusa you go on to other things. In Ueno even a Kagura dance is dour and gloomy, in Asakusa a prayer is cheerful. The vespers at Ueno urge you to go home, the matins at Asakusa urge you to come on over. When you go to Ueno you feel that the day's work is not yet finished. When you go to Asakusa you feel that you have shaken off tomorrow's work. Ueno is silent, mute. Asakusa chatters on and on."

Ueno was the largest of the five original parks. Of the other four, only Asukayama, the cherry-viewing place in the northern suburbs, has managed to do as well over the years as Ueno in looking like a park. The notion of what a park should be was a confused one. The Edo equivalent had been the grounds of temple and shrine. The park system of 1873 tended to perpetuate this concept, merely furnishing certain tracts a new and enlightened name. Ueno was almost empty at the outset and presently became royal, and ended up rather similar to the city parks of the West.

Asakusa, on the other hand, resembles nothing in the West at all. It was the third largest of the original five, more than half as large as Shiba and Ueno, and several times as large as the two smaller ones. What remains of the Edo temple gardens is now closed to the public, and of what is open there is very little that resembles public park or garden. The old park has in legal fact ceased to be a park. A decree under the Occupation, which liked to encourage religious institutions provided they were not contaminated by patriotism, returned the park lands to the temple. Yet the technicalities by which it ceased to be a park had as little effect on its career as those by which it had become a park in the first place.

The original Asakusa Park was expanded in 1876 to include the gardens and firebreak to the west. There was further expansion in 1882, and the following year "the paddies," as the firebreak was called, were excavated to make two ornamental lakes. The reclaimed wetlands were designated the sixth of the seven districts into which the park was divided. In the Meiji and Taishō periods, and indeed down to Pearl Harbor, "Sixth District" meant the music halls and the movie palaces and the other things that drew mass audiences. The Sixth District had its first theater in 1886, and, in 1903, Electricity Hall, the first permanent movie theater in the land. Among the other things were a miniature Mount Fuji, sixty-eight feet high, for the ascent of which a small fee was charged, and a rope bridge across the lakes, to give a sense of deep mountains. The

Fuji was damaged in a typhoon and torn down the year the Twelve Storys, much higher, was completed, on land just north of the park limits. Among those who crossed the bridge was Sir Edwin Arnold, the British journalist best remembered as the author of *The Light of Asia*. Several urchins tried to shake him and a lady companion into one of the lakes. The workmanship of the bridge reminded him of the Incas.

By the turn of the century, the Sixth District was a jumble of show houses and archery stalls—the great pleasure warren of a pleasure-loving city. It may be that the change was not fundamental, for the "back mountain" of the Asakusa Kannon had already been something of the sort. The Sixth District was noisier, brighter, and gaudier, however, and its influence extended all through the park. Remnants of the old Asakusa, shrinking back into it all, spoke wistfully to the few who took notice.

Kubota Mantarō, poet, novelist, playwright, and native of Asakusa, wrote of the change wrought by the cinema:

> Suddenly, it was everywhere. It swept away all else, and took control of the park. The life of the place, the color, quite changed. The "new tide" was violent and relentless. In the districts along the western ditch, by the Kōryūji Temple, somnolence had reigned. It quite departed. The old shops, dealers in tools and scrap and rags, the hair dresser's and the bodkin and bangle places—they all went away, as did the water in the ditch. New shops put up their brazen signs: Western restaurants, beef and horse places, short-order places, milk parlors. Yet even in those days, there were still houses with latticed fronts, little shops of uniform design, nurseries with bamboo fences, workmen from the fire brigades. They were still to be observed, holding their own, in a few corners, in the quiet, reposed, somehow sad alleys of the back districts, in the deep shade of the blackberry brambles behind the grand hall.

Asakusa had its gay and busy time, which passed. The lakes grew dank and gaseous in the years after the surrender, and were filled in. The crowds ceased to come, probably more because of changes in the entertainment business and new transportation patterns than because of what had happened to the park. It might be argued that Asakusa would have fared better if it had not become an entertainment center. If the old park had gone on looking like a park, then Asakusa, like Ueno, might still have its lures. As to that, no one can say—and it may be that if we could say, we would not wish the story of Asakusa to be different. It was perhaps the place where the Low City had its last good time. Nowhere today is there quite the same good-natured abandon to be found, and if people who remember it from thirty years ago may properly lament the change, the laments of those who remember it from twice that long ago are, quite as properly, several times as intense.

It is another story. Asakusa is an instance of what can happen to a public park when no one is looking, though the more relevant point may be that it never really was a park. As an episode in intellectual history, it illustrates the ease with which words can be imported, and the slowness with which substance comes straggling along afterwards. In 1873 Tokyo could face the other capitals of the world and announce that it too had public parks; but it was not until two decades later, when the city acquired land suitable for a central park (if that was what was wished) that the possibility of actually planning and building a park seemed real. The double life, in other words, was gradually reaching down to fundamentals. What had happened at Ueno had happened more by accident than forethought, and not much at all had happened at Asakusa—except that the purveyors of pleasure had had their cheerful and energetic way.

Since the rise of Marunouchi, Hibiya Park, along with the public portion of the palace grounds abutting it on the north, has been the central park of the city—perhaps more important, because of easy access to Ginza, than Ueno. In early Meiji it was not a place where a townsman would have chosen to go for a pleasant walk, and it did not become a public park until thirty years after the original five. Lying within the outer ramparts of the castle, it was at the end of the Tokugawa regime occupied by mansions of the military aristocracy. While the castle grounds nearby were being put to somewhat helter-skelter use by the new government and ultimately, after their time of providing homes for foxes and badgers, were left as public gardens or turned over to the commercial developers, Hibiya was a parade ground. It was cleared for the purpose in 1871, and there, a year later, the emperor first reviewed troops. It seems to have been fearfully dusty even after the Rokumeikan and the Imperial Hotel were built to the east, for a scorched-earth policy was deemed in accord with modern military methods. In 1893 the army, which had acquired more suitable spots on the western fringes of the city, announced its intention of turning Hibiya over to the city by stages. Hibiya Park was opened in 1903.

Initially it was thought that the present Hibiya park lands would become the bureaucratic center. Planning to that effect began after the burning of the palace in 1872. There was no hesitation about rebuilding the palace on the site of the old castle, and in 1886 a government planning office proposed a concentration of government buildings on the parade grounds. The advice of the Germans was invited. Two eminent architects arrived and drew up plans for a complex of highly ornate buildings. A big hole was dug, at great expense, before it was concluded that the soil would not really bear the weight of all that echt Western brick and stone, and that lands farther to the west might be more suitable. Though German prestige slid, we may be grateful for the results. Without the excavation Tokyo might lack a central park (as Osaka does). The German plans, modified in the direction of simplicity, found use in the government complex that did presently come to be. The original plans have been described as seven parts Nikkō (with reference to the most florid of the Tokugawa tombs) and three parts Western.

Some liked the new park, some did not. Nagai Kafū, on his return from France in 1908, found it repellently formal. It became so favored a trysting place, however, that the Kōjimachi police station felt compelled to take action. On the summer night in 1908 when a dozen or so policemen were first sent into the park, they apprehended about the same number of miscreant couples, who were fined. Hibiya is usually referred to as the first genuinely Western park in the city and in Japan. That is what Kafū so disliked about it—he did not think that Westernization worked in any thing or person Japanese but himself.

In fact a good deal of the park is fairly Japanese, and it contains relics of all the eras—trees said to be as old as the city, a fragment of the castle escarpment and moat, a bandstand that was in the original park, a bronze fountain only slightly later. The bandstand has lost its original cupola and the park has changed in matters of detail; yet of all the major parks it is the one that has changed least. Perhaps the fact that it was Western in concept as well as in name may be given credit for this stability.

*   *   *

The area officially devoted to parks grew slightly through Meiji and Taishō, but remained low compared to the cities of the West with which comparison is always being made. (It is high compared to Osaka.) In the last years of Taishō, the total of open spaces, including temples, shrines, and cemeteries, offered each resident of the city only one four-hundredth as much as was available to the resident of Washington. Even New York, whose residents were straitened in comparison with those of London and Paris, boasted forty times the per-capita park area that Tokyo did.

Yet there is truth in the excuse given by that Taishō mayor for the shortage of tracts officially designated as parks. While public parks were not pointless, they may have seemed much less of a necessity than they did in Western cities. Besides the tiny plots of greenery before rows of Low City houses, there continued to be a remarkable amount of unused space, especially in the High City, but in the Low City as well.

Kafū could be lyrical on the subject of vacant lots.

I love weeds. I have the same fondness for them as for the violets and dandelions of spring, the bell flowers and maiden flowers of autumn. I love the weeds that flourish in vacant lots, the weeds that grow on roofs, the weeds beside the road and beside the ditch. A vacant lot is a garden of weeds. The plumes of the mosquito-net grass, as delicate as glossed silk; the plumes of foxtail, soft as fur; the warm rose-pink of knotgrass blossoms; the fresh blue-white of the plantain; chickweed in flower, finer and whiter than sand: having come upon them does one not linger over them and find them difficult to give up? They are not sung of in courtly poetry, one does not find them in the paintings of Sōtatsu and Kōrin. They are first mentioned in the haiku and in the comic verse of plebeian Edo. I will never cease to love Utamaro's "Selection of Insects." An ukiyo-e artist sketched lowly grasses and insects quite ignored by Sinified painters and the schools of Kyoto. The example informs us how great was the achievement of haiku and comic verse and the ukiyo-e. They found a subject dismissed by aristocratic art and they made it art in its own right.

Far more than the plantings in all the new parks around the outer moat and behind the Nikolai Cathedral, I am drawn to the weeds one comes upon in vacant lots.

An important addition was made in Meiji to the lists of shrines, some of them not so very different from parks. Kudan Hill, to the west of the Kanda flats and northwest of castle and palace, was once higher than it is now. It once looked down over the swampy lands which the shogunate early filled in to accommodate merchants and artisans. The top half or so was cut off to reclaim the swamps. Barracks occupied the flattened top in the last Tokugawa years. In 1869 it became the site of a *shōkonsha*, a nationally administered "shrine to which the spirits of the dead are invited," or, in a venerable tradition, a place where the dead, and the living as well, are feasted and entertained. The specific purpose of several such shrines scattered over the country was to honor those who had died in line of duty "since the Kaei Period." This is a little misleading. Commodore Perry came in the Kaei Period, and there may seem to be an implication that he was resisted with loss of life, which he was not. The real intent was to honor those who died in the Restoration disturbances. As other conflicts and other casualties occurred, the rosters expanded. They include three Englishmen who died in the battle of Tsushima, at the climax of the Russo-Japanese War, as well as other surprises. Not many now remember that Japanese lives were lost in the Boxer Rebellion. It is of interest that Tokyo names on the growing rosters ran consistently below the national average.

The son of Edo was not as eager as others to die for his country. In 1879 the Kudan *shōkonsha* became the Yasukuni Jinja, "Shrine for the Repose of the Nation." It was in the Edo tradition, combining reverence and pleasure. There was horseracing on the grounds before the Shinobazu track was built. In 1896, the grandest equestrian year, 268 horses participated in the autumn festival. The last meet took place in 1898, and the track was obliterated in 1901. The shrine continued to be used for a great variety of shows, artistic and amusing, such as Sumō tournaments and Nō performances. A Nō stage built in 1902 survives on the shrine grounds, and a lighthouse from early Meiji. The latter served to guide fishing boats—for there were in those days fishing boats within sight of the hill.

A military exhibition hall was put up in 1882, a grim, Gothic place. It contained a machine gun made by Pratt and Whitney and presented to the emperor by General Grant. The Yasukuni had ten million visitors annually during and just after the Russo-Japanese War. Though the figure fell off thereafter, it continued to be in the millions. The shrine was more of a park, as that term is known in the West, than Asakusa. To those Japanese of a traditional religious bent it may have seemed strange that expanses of protective greenery extended to the southeast, southwest, and northwest of the palace—Hibiya Park, the Sanno Shrine (a very old one), and the Yasukuni Shrine—while the businessmen of the Mitsubishi Meadow were custodians of the most crucial direction, the northeast, "the devil's gate."

Tokyo grew the most rapidly of the large Japanese cities. At the close of Meiji, there can have been few foxes and badgers left in the Mitsubishi Meadow, lined all up and down with brick, and not many weeds can have survived either. Yet the fact remains that Tokyo was, by comparison with the other large cities of Japan, even Kyoto, the emperor's ancient capital, a place of greenery. Tanizaki's wife, a native of Osaka, asked what most struck her on her first visit to Tokyo, replied without hesitation that it was the abundance of trees. The paddies had by the end of Meiji withdrawn from the gate of the Yoshiwara, and they have been pushed farther and farther in the years since; but it was still a city of low buildings, less dense in its denser regions than late Edo had been. So it has continued to be. Perhaps, indeed, it contains the most valuable unused land in the world—the most luxurious space a weed, and even an occasional fox or badger, could possibly have.

There is another sense in which the city was still, at the end of Meiji, near nature, and still is today. The rhythm of the fields and of the seasons continued to be felt all through it. Everywhere in Japan Shinto observances follow the seasons. (It may be that in the United States only the harvest festival, Thanksgiving, is similarly bound to nature.) In deciding which among the great Japanese cities is, in this sense, most "natural," subjective impression must prevail, for there are no measuring devices. When Tanizaki's Makioka sisters, from an old Osaka family, wish to go on a cherry-blossom excursion, they go to Kyoto. They might have found blossoms scattered over Osaka, of course, but Osaka, more than Tokyo, is a place of buildings and sterile surfaces. From one of the high buildings, it is an ashen city. Having arrived in Kyoto, the sisters seem to have only one favored blossom-viewing spot near the center of the city, the grounds of a modern shrine. All the others are on the outskirts, not in the old city at all.

One is left with a strong impression that Tokyo has remained nearer its natural origins, and nearer agrarian rhythms, than the great cities of the Kansai. This fastest-growing city did remarkably well at preserving a sense of the fields and the moods of the seasons. At the end of Meiji the Tokyo resident who wished to revel under the blossoms of April might have gone to Asukayama, that one among the five original parks that lay beyond the city limits, but he could have found blossoms enough for himself and several hundred thousand other people as well at Ueno or along the banks of the Sumida. Nothing comparable was to be had so near at hand in Osaka or Kyoto.

Places famous in early Meiji for this and that flower or grass of the seasons did less well at the end of Meiji. Industrial fumes ate at the cherries along the Sumida, and clams, the digging of which was a part of the homage paid to summer, were disappearing from the shores of Shiba and Fukagawa. (The laver seaweed of Asakusa, famed in Edo and before, had long since disappeared.) Even as the city grew bigger and dirtier, however, new places for enjoying the grasses and flowers came to be.

Every guide to the city contains lists of places to be visited for seasonal things. Going slightly against the natural pattern, these things begin with snow, not a flower or a grass, and not commonly available in quantity until later in the spring. The ornamental plants of midwinter are the camellia and a bright-leafed variety of cabbage, but neither seems to have been thought worth going distances to view. The Sumida embankment was the traditional place for snow viewing. There were other spots, and in the course of Meiji a new one, the Yasukuni Shrine, joined the list. Probably snow has been deemed a thing worth viewing because, like the cherry blossom, it so quickly goes away—on the Tokyo side of Honshu, at any rate.

At the beginning of Meiji, the grasses and flowers of the seasons were probably to be found in the greatest variety east of the Sumida. One did not have to go far east to leave the old city behind, and, having entered a pastoral (more properly, agrarian) village, one looked back towards the river and the hills of the High City, with Fuji rising grandly beyond them. These pleasures diminished towards the end of Meiji, as the regions east of the river fell victim to economic progress. Kafū seems prescient when, in a story from very late Meiji, he takes a gentleman and a geisha to view some famous peonies in Honjo, east of the river. They are disappointed, and the disappointment seems to tell us what the future holds for the peonies and indeed all these regions east of the river. Yet as the peony lost ground in Honjo it gained elsewhere: famous peony places have been established nearer the center of the city.

Another generous disposition of blossom-viewing and grass-viewing places lay along the ridge that divided the Low City from the High City. From here one looked eastwards towards the river and the fields. At the southern end of the ridge was the site of the British legation that never came to be. Ueno and Asukayama, famous spots for cherry blossoms, both stood on the ridge.

The viewing places along the ridge fared better in Meiji than did those east of the river. Ueno gradually ceased to intimidate, as it had under the shoguns, and so moved ahead of Asukayama and the Sumida embankment as the favored place for the noisiest rites of spring. The part of the ridge that lay between Ueno and Asukayama, inside and outside the city limits, was the great Edo center for nurseries, for potted chrysanthemums and morning glories and the like. The pattern has prevailed through the present century. These establishments have been pushed farther and farther out, so that not many survive today in Tokyo Prefecture, but the northern suburbs are still the place for them.

Early in the spring came the plum blossom. To admire it in early Meiji one went to Asakusa and Kameido, a slight distance beyond Honjo, east of the Sumida. Kameido is also recommended for wisteria in May. The Kameido wisteria have survived, but there are plums no longer, either in Kameido or in Asakusa. The plum is the personal blossom, so to speak, of Sugawara Michizane, a tragic and quickly deified statesman of the tenth century, who is the tutelary god of the Kameido Shrine. If his flower has gone from Kameido, a plum orchard has since been planted at another of his holy places, the Yushima Shrine in Hongō. So it is that the flowers and grasses cling to existence, losing here and gaining there. Towards the end of *The River Sumida* Kafū has his sad hero go walking with an uncle to Kameido, and the poignancy of the scene comes in large measure from an awareness already present, then in late Meiji, of what progress is doing to the district. It lies in the path of economic miracles.

In April came the cherry, which might be called the city's very own blossom. It has long been made much of, for the swiftness of its blooming and of its falling appeals to the highly cultivated national sense of evanescence. In the years of the Tokugawa hegemony the cherry became the occasion for that noisiest of springtime rites. Goten Hill, overlooking the bay at the southern edge of the Meiji city, is no longer found on early Meiji lists of blossom-viewing places. That was where the British legation had been put up and so promptly burned down. The most popular Meiji sites for the cherry blossom were Asukayama, remotest of the original five parks; Ueno; and the Sumida embankment. Two of the three have declined as the city and progress have engulfed them, while Ueno, nearest of the three to the center, thrives. It still draws the biggest crowds in the city and doubtless in all of Japan.

The peach and the pear come at about the same time, slightly later in the spring. They are dutifully included in Meiji lists of things to see, but the Japanese have not made as much of them as the Chinese, whose proverb has the world beating a path to a door with a blooming peach or pear. It would be easy to say that they are too showy for Japanese taste, but the chrysanthemum and the peony, both of them showy flowers, are much admired. Perhaps observance of the passing seasons was becoming less detailed, and the peach and the pear are among the lost details. There were no famous places within the city limits for viewing either of the two. In the case of the pear, one was asked to go to a place near Yokohama (the place where, in 1862, Satsuma soldiers killed an Englishman, prompting the British to shell Kagoshima). There were other flowers of spring and early summer—wisteria, azaleas, peonies, and *yamabuki*, a yellow-flowering shrub related to the rose.

Certain pleasures of the seasons were not centered upon flowers and grasses, or upon a specific flower or grass. For plucking the new shoots and herbs of spring, the regions east of the river and the western suburbs were especially recommended. For the new greenery of spring there were Ueno and the western suburbs. For the clams of summer there were the shores of the bay, at Susaki and Shibaura, where Tanizaki and his family went digging. Insects were admired, and birds. Fireflies, now quite gone from the city save for the caged ones released at garden parties, were to be found along the Kanda River, just below Kafū's birthplace. They were also present in the paddy lands around the Yoshiwara, to the north of Ueno, and along the banks of the Sumida, where no wild fireflies have been observed for a very long time. Birds were enjoyed less by the eye than by the ear. Two places in the city are called Uguisudani, Warbler Valley, one in Shitaya and the other in Koishikawa. *Horeites diphone*, the warbler in question, may still be heard in both places. For the cuckoo there was a listening point in Kanda, near the heart of the old Low City, and another near the Maeda estate in Hongō, to which the university presently moved. For the voice of the wild goose one went beyond the Sumida, and also to the Yoshiwara paddies and to Susaki, beside the bay in Fukagawa. For singing autumn insects, the western suburbs were recommended.

In high summer came morning glories, lotuses, and irises. The Meiji emperor's own favorite iris garden, on the grounds of what is now the Meiji Shrine, was opened to the public a few years after his death. The morning glory has long had a most particular place in the life of the Low City. It was the omnipresent sign of summer, in all the tiny garden plots and along the plebeian lanes, a favorite subject, as principal and as background, in the popular art of Edo. The place to go for Meiji morning glories was Iriya, to the east of Ueno Park. It still is the place to go, but it has suffered vicissitudes in the century since its morning glories first came into prominence. In early Meiji, Iriya was still paddy land, and among the paddies were extensive nurseries. One looked across them to the Yoshiwara, the great houses of which kept villas in the district. The last of the nurseries left Iriya, no longer on the outskirts of the city, in 1912, and so too, of course, did excursions for viewing and purchasing morning glories. They have returned in the last quarter of a century. For the morning-glory fair in early July, however, the plants must be brought in from what are now the northern outskirts of the city.

A famous lotus-viewing spot was lost in the course of Meiji. Tameike Pond in Akasaka was allowed to become silted in, and presently built over. Shinobazu Pond, the other Meiji place for viewing and listening to

Shinobazu Pond, Ueno

lotuses (some say that the delicate pop with which a lotus opens is imagined, others say that they have heard it), survived Meiji, despite expositions and horse racing, and yet survives, despite the years of war and defeat, during which it was converted to barley fields. In Meiji and down to the recent past there were extensive commercial tracts of lotus east of the river, grown for the edible roots. They too were recommended in Meiji for lotus-viewing, and today they have almost disappeared.

The eastern suburbs were, again, the place to go for "the seven grasses of autumn," some of them actually shrubs and only one a grass as that term is commonly understood in the West. The chrysanthemum, not one of the autumn seven, was featured separately. Dangozaka, "Dumpling Slope," just north of the university in Hongō, was a famous chrysanthemum center that came and went in Meiji. Chrysanthemum dolls—chrysanthemums trained to human shape—were first displayed there in 1878. They figure in some famous Meiji novels, but by the end of Meiji were found elsewhere, first at the new Sumō stadium east of the river, and later in the southern and western suburbs. (Also, occasionally, in a department store.) The grounds of the Asakusa Kannon Temple were famous for chrysanthemums early in Meiji, but are no longer.

Asuka Hill, noted for its cherry blossoms, was the best place near the city for autumn colors. At the end of the year there were hibernal moors to be viewed, for the wasted moor ended the cycle, as snow had begun it. Had nature been followed literally, the sequence could as well have been the reverse; but an ancient tradition called for the wasted and sere at the end of the cycle of grasses and flowers. For the best among sere expanses, one went to Waseda, in the western suburbs.

It is not surprising, though it is sad, that so many famous places of early Meiji for the things of the seasons are missing from late-Meiji lists. Gone, for instance, are the night cherries of the Yoshiwara, popular in the dim light of early Meiji. It is more surprising that many places remain, in a larger, smokier city. A guide published by the city in 1907 gives a discouraging report on the Sumida cherries, even then being gnawed by industrial fumes and obscured by billboards. Yet it has a ten-page list of excursions to famous places in and near the city. Arranged by season, the list begins with felicitous New Year excursions, "all through the city," and ends with New Year markets, "Nihombashi, Ginza, etc." Snow-viewing tides the cycle over from one year to the next, and the Sumida embankment is still preeminent among places for indulging. Most if not quite all of the flowers and grasses are covered, from the plum (twenty-nine places recommended, all in the city and the suburbs, with a new place, the Yasukuni Shrine, at the head) to wasted moors (none left in the fifteen wards—only the western and northern suburbs). The twenty-three places for viewing cherry blossoms are headed, as they would have been at the end of Edo, by Ueno and the Sumida embankment. The sixty-page section on "pleasures" includes cemeteries and graves. They are chiefly for those of an antiquarian bent, of course, but a Japanese cemetery can also be pleasant for observing the passage of the seasons.

A person of leisure and some energy could have filled most of his days with the round of annual and monthly observances. The same guide contains a five-page list of monthly feast days at shrines and temples, and only on the thirty-first day of a month would there have been nowhere to go. In this too, tradition survives. No month in the lunar calendar had thirty-one days, and no thirty-first day in the solar calendar has been assigned a feast. Besides monthly feast days, most shrines had annual festivals, boisterous to the point of violence, centering upon the *mikoshi* "god-seats," portable shrines borne through the streets and alleys over which the honored god held sway. The god-seat sort of festival was among the great loves of the son of Edo, who, it was said, would happily pawn his wife to raise the necessary funds. Some of the god-seats were huge. Weaving down narrow streets on the shoulders of manic bearers who numbered as many as a hundred, they could go out of control and

crash into a shopfront. Sometimes this happened on purpose. In Asakusa, especially, such assaults were welcomed: it was thought that if a god
in his seat came crashing through the front of a shop, the devils must
depart through the rear.

Some shrines and temples had annual markets, perhaps the most remarkable of them being the Bird Fair, the Tori no Ichi, on the days in
November that fell on the zodiacal sign of the bird. It was held at several
"eagle shrines" throughout the city, the most famous and popular of them
just outside the Yoshiwara. Bird days occur either twice or three times
in a month, and when they occurred in November the throngs at the
Yoshiwara were enormous. They threatened the pillars of heaven and the
sinews of earth, said Higuchi Ichiyō in the best of her short stories. It was
believed that years in which November contained three bird days were
also years in which "the flowers of Edo," the conflagrations, flourished.

Though obviously the motives were mixed for crowds so great and
boisterous, it was essentially a shopkeepers' fair, and a part of the townsman's culture. The day of the bird was chosen from among the twelve
because the Japanese love a pun. *Tori*, "bird," also means "taking in"
or "reaping," and ornamental rakes were purchased at the market, as a
means of assuring a profitable year. The rake merchants added a pleasant twist: to insure the flow of profits, a larger rake must be purchased
every year. Bird fairs have declined in recent years, largely because the
traditional business of the Yoshiwara has been outlawed. They have not,
however, disappeared.

But many observances that must have been very amusing are gone. One
no longer hears, for example, of "the watch of the twenty-sixth night."
On that night in the Seventh Month under the lunar calendar (which
would generally be August under the solar), people would gather along
the coasts and in the high places of the city, waiting for the moon to rise.
If it emerged in a triple image, presently falling back into a single one, it
presaged uncommonly good luck. The watch lasted almost until dawn,
since the twenty-sixth is very near the end of the lunar cycle. Devices were
therefore at hand for enhancing the possibility of the triple image.

Annual observances were closely tied to the agrarian cycle even when
they did not have to do specifically with the flowers, the grasses, the
birds, and the insects. A sense of the fields has survived, despite the expansive ways of the city that had driven wasted moors from the fifteen
wards by the end of Meiji, and eaten up most of the paddy and barley
lands. Spring began in two ways, the lunar and the solar. The lunar way
is now hardly noticed, but the solar way survives, with spring beginning,

to the accompaniment of appropriate ritual, midway between the winter solstice and the vernal equinox. So it was that the city was awaiting the Two Hundred Tenth Day when the earthquake came.

Lists of "great festivals," the boisterous shrine affairs centering upon god-seats, always come in threes. The Kanda festival and the Sannō festival in Akasaka, to the southwest of the palace, are to be found on most Edo and Meiji lists of the big three.

The Sannō festival has fared badly in this century. Certainly it was among the great festivals of Edo, accorded condescending notice by Lord Tokugawa himself. The Sannō was the shrine to which baby Tokugawas were taken to be presented to the company of gods. It seemed to lose vigor as Tameike Pond, above which the shrine stood, silted in and was developed. Akasaka became a wealthy residential district and a place of chic entertainment, much patronized by the bureaucracy. The affluent bourgeoisie and the bureaucracy do not have much truck with shrine festivals, affairs of the Low City and the lower classes.

The Kanda festival had a troubled time in Meiji, for curious reasons, telling of conservatism and traditionalism. Two gods had in theory been worshipped at the Kanda Shrine. One of them was a proper mythological deity whose name scarcely anyone knew. The other was Taira Masakado, a tenth-century general who led a rebellion in the Kantō region. Unlike most Japanese rebels, he attempted to set himself up as emperor; the usual way has been to take the power but not the position. In 1874 the shrine priesthood, in somewhat sycophantic deference to the emperor cult of the new day, petitioned the governor to have Masakado removed, and another proper mythological entity brought from the Kashima Shrine in Ibaragi Prefecture. The festival languished. The demotion of Masakado, for whom a secondary shrine was presently built, is thought to have been responsible—this despite the fact that the arrival of the new deity, the other proper one, was boisterous. Resentment does seem to have been strong. Everyone had thought of the Kanda Shrine as belonging to Masakado, and he had a devoted following in his own East Country, whose inhabitants had for centuries been victims of Kyoto snobbishness. By 1884 old divisions and resentments were thought to have sufficiently healed that a good old-fashioned festival might be held. It was, and there was a typhoon on the second day, which the newspapers attributed to Masakado's anger. The press was frivolous, but one reads serious intent behind it. The Kanda festival never quite came into its own again.

If some observances disappeared in Meiji, others emerged into prominence, some quite new, some revivals, some revisions of the old. New Year celebrations culminated in a military parade, something new, and a review of the fire brigades, something old given a new turn. The latter had been banned for a time as dangerous. The danger was to the firemen who, dressed in traditional uniforms, did daring things high upon ladders. The old brigades were losing their practical significance, although it was not completely gone until after the earthquake. The New Year review was becoming show and no more, albeit exciting show, and aesthetically pleasing as well. It has survived, and seems in no danger now of disappearing.

Observances now so much a part of the landscape that they seem as venerable as the landscape itself frequently turn out to be no older than Meiji. The practice of taking small children to Shinto shrines in mid-November is an instance. Its origins are very old indeed, for it grew from the primitive custom of taking infants to a shrine at a certain age to confirm that a precarious bit of life had taken hold. It had been mainly an upper-class ritual in Edo, and did not begin to gain popularity in the Low City until mid-Meiji. The flying carp of Boys' Day must unfortunately be associated with militarism. They came into great vogue from about the time of the Sino-Japanese War. Boys' Day, May 5, is now Children's Day, and the first day of summer by the old reckoning. Girls' Day, March 3, is not a holiday.

Some of the god-seat festivals were very famous and drew great crowds, but they were essentially local affairs, gatherings of the clan (the word *ujiko*, "member of the congregation," has that literal significance) to honor its Shinto god. There were other Shinto festivals of a more generally animistic nature, affairs for the whole city. The two biggest occurred in the summer, in the Sixth Month under the old calendar, transferred to July under the new. Both honored and propitiated the gods of nature, Mount Fuji in the one case and the Sumida River in the other, upon the commencement of the busy summer season, when both would be popular and a great deal would be asked of them.

The Sumida and Fuji were not the only river and mountain that had their summer "openings," but they were the most famous and popular. Besides honoring animistic deities, the observances had practical significance. The opening of the Sumida meant the beginning of the hot weather, and of the pleasures associated with seeking coolness upon the waters. The opening of Fuji, or any other mountain, was the signal for the summer crowds, less of a religious and more of a hedonistic bent as time went on, to start climbing. It was not considered safe earlier in the season, because of slides and storms. Both openings are still observed, the Fuji one now at the end of June, the Sumida one at a shifting date in

July. Boating upon the Sumida is not the pleasure it once was, of course. The throngs upon Fuji are ever huger.

In the Edo and early Meiji periods there was a strongly religious element in an ascent of Fuji. The mountain cult was important from late Edo. The opening of the mountain was and is observed at several Fuji shrines through the city. Some may be recognized by artificial hillocks meant to be small likenesses of Fuji. Believers could with merit ascend one of them if an ascent of the real mountain was impractical.

The most popular of the Fuji shrines is just north of Asakusa, to the east of the Yoshiwara. Several days in early summer (a single day is not incentive enough for moving the giant trees and rocks that are offered for sale) there are garden fairs north of Asakusa, and great crowds.

The Sumida had always had a special significance for the city. All the wards of the Low City but one either bordered it or fell but a few paces short of it, and the elegant pleasures of Edo could scarcely have done without it. The summer opening, at Ryōgoku Bridge, was a time of boats and splendid crowds and fireworks. Purveyed by two venerable and famous makers, each of which had its claque, they were of two kinds, stationary displays near water level, and rockets. General Grant joined the crowds in 1879. E. S. Morse was there earlier, and described what he saw with delight:

> At the river the sight was entrancing, the wide river as far as the eye could reach being thickly covered with boats and pleasure barges of all descriptions. We had permission to pass through the grounds of a daimyo, and his servants brought chairs to the edge of the river for our accommodation. After sitting for a few minutes we concluded to see the sights nearer, and at that moment a boat came slowly along the bank, the man soliciting patronage. We got aboard and were sculled into the midst of the crowds. It would be difficult to imagine a stranger scene than the one presented to us; hundreds of boats of all sizes—great, square-bottomed boats; fine barges, many with awnings and canopies, all illuminated with bright-colored lanterns fringing the edge of the awnings... It was a startling sight when we got near the place to see that the fireworks were being discharged from a large boat by a dozen naked men, firing off Roman candles and set pieces of a complex nature. It was a sight never to be forgotten: the men's bodies glistening in the light with the showers of sparks dropping like rain upon them, and, looking back, the swarms of boats, undulating up and down, illuminated by the brilliancy of the display; the new moon gradually setting, the stars shining with unusual brightness, the river

dark, though reflecting the ten thousand lantern lights of all sizes and colors, and broken into rivulets by the oscillations of the boats.

Clara Whitney went too, and had mixed feelings:

> The Sumida stretched out before us, and for nearly a mile up and down it was covered by myriads of boats, from the clumsy canal boat to the gay little gondola dancing like a cockle shell on the tiny wavelets… Millions of lanterns covered the river as far as we could see until the sober Sumida looked like a sea of sparkling light… It was altogether a very pretty sight—the brilliantly lighted houses, the illuminated river, the gay fireworks, and crowds of lanterns held aloft to prevent their being extinguished… Like a stream of humanity they passed our perch and Mama and I spoke with sadness of their lost and hopeless condition spiritually.

There were, of course, changes in the festive pattern through Meiji and on into Taishō. New Year celebrations were less elaborate at the end of Meiji than at the beginning. Certain customs quite disappeared, such as the use of "treasure boats" to assure a good outcome for the "first dream of the year," which in turn was held to augur good or ill for the whole year. Treasure boats were paintings of sailing-boats manned by the Seven Gods of Good Luck or other bearers of good fortune. A treasure boat under a pillow, early in the New Year, assured the best sort of dreams. Conservative merchants paid particular heed to such matters, and so the simplification of the New Year may be taken as a sign of emergent modernism in commercial affairs. Meiji New Year celebrations lasted down to the "Bone New Year" on the twentieth of January, so designated because only bones remained from the feasts prepared late in the old year. They have gradually been shortened, so that little now happens after the fourth or fifth. In late Meiji there was still a three-day "Little New Year" centering on the fifteenth. The fifteenth is now Adults' Day, vaguely associated with the New Year in that it felicitates the coming of age. Under the old system New Year's Day was, so to speak, everyone's birthday. Reckoning of age was not by the "full count," from birthday to birthday, as it usually is today, but by the number of years in which one had lived. So everyone became a year older on New Year's Day.

Still, with all the changes, the flowers and grasses, the god-seats and the shrine fairs, survived. New Year celebrations became less prolonged and detailed. The advent of spring became less apparent in the eastern suburbs as industrial mists replaced natural ones. Nurseries were driven farther and farther north, and presently across the river into another prefecture. Yet the city remained close to nature as has no other great city in the world. In midsummer, for the festival of the dead, people returned in huge numbers to their villages, and those who could not go had village dances in the city. It was the double life at its best. Civilization and Enlightenment had to come, perhaps, but they did not require giving up the old sense of the earth. It is a part of Japanese modernization which other nations might wish to emulate, along with managerial methods and quality control and that sort of thing. No one can possibly have attended all the observances that survived from Edo through Meiji. It is a pity that no record-keeper seems to have established who attended the most.

The moods of a place will change, whatever its conscious or unconscious conservatism. The exotic and daring becomes commonplace, and other exotic and daring things await the transformation. Tolerance grows, the sense of novelty is dulled, and revolutions are accomplished without the aid of insistent revolutionaries. The old way did not go, but more and more it yielded to the new. The shift was increasingly pronounced in the last years of Meiji, after two ventures in foreign warfare.

If a native who departed Tokyo in 1870, at an age mature enough for clear observation and recollection, had returned for the first time forty years later, he would have found much to surprise him. He might also have been surprised at how little change there was in much of the city. The western part of Nihombashi and Kanda had their grand new banks, department stores, and universities, while fires played over the wooden clutter to the east. So too with trendier, more high-collar Kyōbashi: the new Ginza went as far as the Kyōbashi bridge, where the shadows of Edo took over.

He would have found ample changes, certainly: the new Ginza, the government complex to the south of the palace, the financial and managerial complex to the east. Scarcely a trace remained of the aristocratic dwellings that had stood between the outer and inner moats of the castle. He would have found department stores in place of the old "silk stores" (though he would still have found silk stores in large numbers as well), and an elevated railway pushing into the heart of the city, through what had been the abode of daimyo, badger, and fox.

He might have been more aware of a change in mood, and had more trouble defining it.

There was great insecurity in the early years of Meiji. Nagai Kafū describes it well in an autobiographical story titled "The Fox." The time is the aftermath of the Satsuma Rebellion. The place is Koishikawa, the northwest corner of the High City, above the Kōrakuen estate of the Mito Tokugawa family.

The talk was uniformly cruel and gory, of conspirators, of assassinations, of armed robbers. The air was saturated with doubt and suspicion. At a house the status of whose owner called for a moderately imposing gate, or a mercantile house with impressive godowns, a murderous blade could at any time come flashing through the floor mats, the culprit having stolen under the veranda and lain in wait for sounds of sleep. I do not remember that anyone, not my father or my mother, gave specific instructions, but roustabouts who frequented our house were set to keeping guard. As I lay in my nurse's arms through the cold winter night, the wooden clappers of the guards would echo across the silent grounds, sharp and cold.

Some of the disorder was mere brigandage, but most of it was obviously reactionary, directed at the merchant and politician of the new day, and reflecting a wish to return to the old seclusion. Of a piece with the reactionary radicalism of the 1930s, it suggests the gasps and convulsions of the dying. Already the Rokumeikan Period was approaching, and the high-water mark of Civilization and Enlightenment. The serving women in the Nagai house read illustrated romances of the old Edo variety, and we know that their children would not. At the beginning of the Rokumeikan Period the revolution known as the Restoration was not yet complete and thorough. The violence was nationalistic in a sense, stirred by a longing for the secluded island past, but it suggests an afterglow rather than a kindling.

The Meiji Period was sprinkled with violence. It was there in the agitation for "people's rights" and the jingoism that inevitably came with the first great international adventure, the Sino-Japanese War of 1894-1895. The *sōshi* bully-boys of the eighties and nineties were a strange though markedly Japanese combination of the expansive and the narrow. They favored "people's rights" and they were very self-righteous and exclusive. "The Dynamite Song," "The Chinks," and "Let's Get 'Em" were among their favorite militant songs. Not many voices were raised against the xenophobia, directed this time at fellow Orientals, save for those of a few faltering Christians. The disquiet of Kafū's boyhood was probably more serious, in that people lived in greater danger, but it was less baneful, something that looked to the past and was certain to die. The mood of the city at the end of the century was more modern.

Despite economic depression, it would seem to have been festive during the Sino-Japanese War. We hear for the first time of roistering at Roppongi, on the southern outskirts of the city, and so have the beginnings of what is now the most blatantly electronic of the city's pleasure centers. Roppongi prospered because of the army barracks it contained. What is now the noisiest playground of self-indulgent pacifism had its beginnings in militarism. The ukiyo-e print, also more than a little militarist and nationalist, had its last day of prosperity. Anything having to do with the war would sell. The great problem was the censors, who were slow to clear works for printing. Great crowds gathered before the print shops, and pickpockets thrived. The Kyōbashi police, with jurisdiction over the Ginza district, sent out special pickpocket patrols. No Japanese festive occasion is without its amusing curiosities. A Kyōbashi haberdashery had a big sale of codpieces, strongly recommended for soldiers about to be exposed to the rigors of the Chinese climate.

There was ugliness in the "Chink"-baiting and perhaps a touch of arrogance in the new confidence, and one may regret that Roppongi ever got started, to drain youth and money from less metallic pleasure centers. Yet, despite casualties and depression, the war must have been rather fun for the city.

The Russo-Japanese War of 1904-1905 was a more somber affair. The boisterous war songs of the Sino-Japanese War were missing. Nor were the makers of popular art as active. Pounds and tons of prints survive from the Sino-Japanese War; there is very little from the Russo-Japanese War. It may be said that the ukiyo-e died as a popular form in the interbellum decade. Dark spy rumors spread abroad. Archbishop Nikolai, from whom the Russian cathedral in Kanda derives its popular name, felt constrained to request police protection, for the first time in a career that went back to the last years of Edo.

The rioting that followed the Portsmouth Treaty in 1905 was a new thing. It was explicitly nationalist, and it seemed to demand something almost the opposite of what had been demanded by the violence of Kafū's boyhood. Japan had arrived, after having worked hard through the Meiji reign, and now must push its advantage. The politicians—the violence said—had too easily accepted the Portsmouth terms. The war itself had of course been the first serious engagement with a Western power. That it should have been followed by a burst of something like chauvinism is not surprising. Yet rioting could more understandably have been set off by the Triple Intervention that followed the Sino-Japanese War and took away some of the spoils. The early grievance was the greater one, and it produced no riots. The mood of the city in 1905 was even more modern.

On September 5, 1905, the day the Portsmouth Treaty was signed, a protest rally gathered in Hibiya Park. For the next two days rioting was widespread, and from the evening of the fifth to the evening of the sixth it seemed out of control. The rioters were free to do as they wished (or so it is said), and the police were powerless to stop them. Tokyo was, albeit briefly, a city without government. There were attacks on police boxes, on government offices, on the houses of notables, on a newspaper, and on the American legation. (Today the American embassy is an automatic target when anything happens anywhere, but what happened in 1905 was unprecedented, having to do with Theodore Roosevelt's offices as peacemaker.) Ten Christian churches were destroyed, all of them in the Low City. Casualties ran to upwards of a thousand, not quite half of them policemen and firemen. The largest number occurred in Kōjimachi Ward, where it all began, and where the largest concentration of government buildings was situated. Some distance behind, but with enough casualties that the three wards together accounted for about a third of the total, were two wards in the Low City, Asakusa and Honjo, opposite each other on the banks of the Sumida. It would be hard to say that everyone who participated did so for political reasons. Honjo might possibly be called a place of the new proletariat, now awakening to its political mission, but Asakusa is harder to explain. It was not rich, but it was dominated by conservative artisans and shopkeepers.

In some ways the violence was surprisingly polite. None was directed at the Rokumeikan or the Imperial Hotel, both of them symbols of Westernization and right across the street from Hibiya Park. Too much can be made of the attack on the American legation. It was unprecedented, but mild, no more than some shouting and heaving of stones. So it may be said that the violence, though widespread and energetic, was neither as political nor as threatening as it could have been. There was an element of the festive and the sporting in it all. There usually is when violence breaks out in this city.

Yet the Russo-Japanese War does seem to mark a turning point. Edo had not completely disappeared in the distance, but the pace of the departure began to increase. Our old child of Edo, back in 1910 after forty years, might well have been more surprised at the changes had he gone away then and come back a decade later. The end of a reign is conventionally taken as the end of a cultural phase, but the division between Meiji and Taisho would have been clearer if the Meiji emperor had died just after the Russo-Japanese War, in perhaps the fortieth year of his reign.

The Russo-Japanese War was followed by economic depression and, for the city, the only loss in population between the Restoration disturbances and the earthquake. Kōjimachi Ward, surrounding the palace, lost population in 1908, and the following year the regions to the north and east were seriously affected. When next a war came along, it brought no surge of patriotism; the main fighting was far away, and Japan had little to do with it. In an earlier day, however, there would have been huge pride in being among the victors. The city and the nation were getting more modern all the time.

Chapter 4

THE DECAY
OF THE DECADENT

People like to think themselves different from other people; generally they like to think themselves superior. In the centuries of the Tokugawa seclusion, the Japanese had little occasion to assert differences between themselves and the rest of the world, nor would they have had much to go on, were such assertion desired. So the emphasis was on asserting differences among various kinds of Japanese. The son of Edo insisted on what made him different from the Osakan. He did it more energetically than the Osakan did the converse, and in this fact we may possibly find evidence that he felt inferior. Osaka was at the knee of His Majesty, whereas Edo was merely at the knee of Lord Tokugawa. Today it is Osaka that is more concerned with differences.

Aphorisms were composed characterizing the great Tokugawa cities. Some are clever and contain a measure of truth. Perhaps the best holds that the son of Kyoto ruined himself over dress, the son of Osaka ruined himself over food, and the son of Edo ruined himself looking at things.

This may seem inconsistent with other descriptions we have heard of the son of Edo, such as the one holding that he would pawn his wife to raise funds for a festival. There is no real inconsistency, however. What is meant is that Edo delighted in performances, all kinds of performances, including festivals and fairs. Performances were central to Edo culture, and at the top of the hierarchy, the focus of Edo connoisseurship, was the Kabuki theater. On a level scarcely lower were the licensed pleasure quarters. So intimately were the two related that it is difficult to assign either to the higher or the lower status. The great Kabuki actors set tastes and were popular heroes, and the Kabuki was for anyone (except perhaps the self-consciously aristocratic) who had enough money. The pleasure quarters, at their most elaborate, were only for male persons of taste and affluence, but the best of what its devotees got was very similar to what was to be had at the Kabuki. The difference between the two might be likened to the difference between a performance of a symphony or opera on the one hand and a chamber concert on the other.

It has been common among cultural historians to describe the culture of late Tokugawa as decadent. It definitely seemed so to the bureaucratic elite of the shogunate, and to eager propagandists for Civilization and Enlightenment as well. That it was unapologetically sensual and wanting in ideas seemed to them deplorable. They may not have been prudes, exactly, but they did want things to be edifying, intellectual, and uplifting, and to serve an easily definable purpose, such as the strengthening of the state and the elevating of the commonweal. If certain parts of the Edo heritage could be put to these purposes, very well. Everything else might expect righteous disapproval.

There is a certain narrow sense in which anything so centered upon carnal pleasure ought indeed to be described as decadent. However refined may have been the trappings of the theater and of its twin the pleasure quarter, sex lay behind them, and, worse, the purveying of sex. Perhaps something of the sort may also be said about the romantic love of the West. The high culture of Edo, in any event, the best that the merchant made of and for his city, is not to be understood except in terms of the theater and the pleasure quarters. What happened in these decadent realms is therefore central to the story of what happened to the Meiji city.

We have seen that General and Mrs. Grant visited the Kabuki in the summer of 1879. Probably the general did not know that he was participating in the movement to improve the Kabuki. It had already been elevated a considerable distance. Had he come as a guest of the shogunate, no one would have dreamed of taking him off to the far reaches of the city, where the theaters then were, and having disreputable actors, however highly esteemed they might be by the townsmen of Edo, perform for him and his Julia. His aristocratic hosts would not have admitted to having seen a performance themselves, though some of them might on occasion have stolen off to the edge of the city to see what it was like. It belonged to the townsman's world, which was different from theirs. Making it a part of high culture, which is what "improvement" meant, had the effect of taking it from the townsman and his world.

The Shintomiza, which the Grants visited, was managed by Morita Kanya, the most innovative of early Meiji impresarios. The Kabuki had been removed from the center of the city to Asakusa in that last seizure of Tokugawa puritanism, a quarter of a century before the Restoration.

There, remote, the three major theaters still stood when the Restoration came. All three were soon to depart, and none survives. The Nakamuraza, which stayed closest to the old grounds, was the first to disappear. It was still in Asakusa Ward, near the Yanagibashi geisha quarter, when in 1893 it was destroyed by fire one last time. The Ichimuraza stayed longest on the Asakusa grounds, and survived until 1932, when one of repeated burnings proved to be its last.

The Moritaza left Asakusa most swiftly and with the most determination, and led the way into the new day. It took the new name Shintomiza from the section of Kyōbashi, just east of Ginza, to which Kanya moved it.

He had long harbored ambitions to return his theater to the center of the city. He thought to make the move in stealth, because he wanted none of his Asakusa colleagues to come tagging after him. He preferred to be as far as possible from the old crowd, and especially from such sponsors of the Kabuki as the fish wholesalers, who were likely to oppose his reforming zeal. The Shintomi district was his choice for a new site because it was near Ginza and because it was available, nothing of importance having come along to take the place of the defunct New Shimabara licensed quarter. There were bureaucratic difficulties. His petition would be approved, he was told, only if it was presented jointly by all three theaters. By guile and determination he was able to obtain the seals of the other two managers. He moved just after the great Ginza fire, the rebuilding from which put Ginza at the forefront of Civilization and Enlightenment.

The first Shintomiza looks traditional enough in photographs, but certain architectural details, such as a copper-roofed tower, were a wonder and a pleasure to the Kabuki devotee. In the pit (though they are not apparent in woodcuts) were several dozen chairs, for the comfort of those who chose to attend in Western dress. Kanya's first Shintomiza burned in 1876. The theater visited by General Grant was opened in 1878.

Kanya was an enthusiastic improver—in content, in techniques, and in managerial methods. He introduced bright new lights, and theater evenings. Kabuki had been staged only during daylight hours, on moral grounds, it seems, and also for the practical reason that the fire hazard increased as darkness came on. With the opening of his second Shintomiza he greatly reduced the number of theater teahouses, with a view to eliminating them altogether. The teahouse functioned as a caterer and ticket agency, monopolizing the better seats. Kanya's endeavor to get rid of the teahouses was in the end a complete success, although it took time.

The Shintomiza

Only complete control of the box office would permit a rationalization of managerial methods. With little exaggeration, it might be said that he looked ahead to the impersonal efficiency of the computer. Old customs can be slow to disappear, however, when people find them a little expensive and time-consuming, but not unpleasant. That they should die was probably more important to entrepreneurs like Kanya than to the Low City Kabuki devotee. (Traces of the old system survive, even today, in box-office arrangements for Sumō wrestling.) In his boyhood Tanizaki Junichirō was taken to a more modern and rationally organized theater, the Kabukiza, and it still had teahouses. Tanizaki was born in 1886, almost a decade after the opening of the second Shintomiza.

> I remember how my heart raced as we set out by rickshaw, my mother and I, southwards from Nihombashi towards Tsukiji. My mother still called the Shintomi district Shimabara, from the licensed quarter of early Meiji. We crossed Sakura Bridge, passed Shimabara, where the Shintomiza then stood, and turned from Tsukiji Bridge to follow the Tsukiji canal. From Kamei Bridge we could see the dome of the Kabukiza, which was finished in 1889. This would have been perhaps four or five years later. There were eleven theater teahouses attached to the Kabukiza. Always when a play was on they had awnings

draped from their roofs. We had our rickshaw pull up at the Kikuoka, where we would rest for a time. Urged on by a maid, we would slip into straw sandals and hurry over the boardwalks to the theater. I remember how strangely cold the smooth floor of the theater was as I slipped from the sandals. A cold blast of air always came through the wooden doors of a theater. It struck at the skirt and sleeves of a festive kimono, and was at one's throat and stomach like peppermint. There was a softness in it, as on a good day in the plum-blossom season. I would shiver, pleasantly.

Kanya spent a great deal of money on important officials and foreign visitors. On opening day of the second Shintomiza in 1878 all manner of notables, dressed in swallowtails, were set out upon the stage on chairs. The prime minister and the governor were among them, and so were most of the actors to whom the future belonged.

As an innovator, Kanya experimented boldly to bring modern elements into the Kabuki repertoire. The ninth Danjūrō became famous for his "living history," which sought to introduce literal reality into the properties and costumes of historical plays, while the fifth Kikugorō was renowned for his "cropped-head pieces"—plays with modern settings, distinguished by enlightened haircuts. Among Kikugorō's roles were the celebrated murderesses Takahashi O-den and Hanai O-ume, and Spencer the balloon man. Kanya even experimented with foreign performers and settings. Clara Whitney witnessed his most ambitious attempt at the cosmopolitan, A *Strange Tale of Castaways,* in 1879. A foreign lady from Yokohama trilled, "delightful on the high notes. But the best parts were spoiled because the Japanese, who thought it was something unusually funny, would laugh aloud…. I was quite out of patience." The experiment was a financial disaster, and Kanya's enthusiasm for Western things waned thereafter.

Kikugorō's balloon ascent did not join the Kabuki repertoire, but Kanya's experiments in stagecraft had a profound effect on the form. Near-darkness had prevailed in Edo, and he started it on its way to the almost blinding illumination of our time. The second Shintomiza had gaslights, but it may be that Kanya was not the very first to use them. E. S. Morse thus describes a visit to a theater, probably one of the two that still remained in Asakusa, in 1877:

Coming up the raised aisle from the entrance, several actors stride along in a regular stage strut and swagger, the grandest of all having his face illuminated by a candle on the end of a long-handled pole held by a boy who moved along too and kept the candle constantly before the actor's face no matter how he turned.... There were five footlights, simply gas tubes standing up like sticks, three feet high, and unprotected by shade or screen, a very recent innovation; for before they had these flaring gas jets it was customary for each actor to have a boy with a candle to illuminate his face.

Conservative actors still attempt to follow old forms as they are recorded in Edo prints and manuscripts; but bright lights have changed Kabuki utterly. Kanya also introduced evening performances, permitted because the bright new lights were regarded as less of a fire hazard than the dim old lights had been. From Edo into Meiji, theaters sometimes opened as early as seven in the morning, to pack in as much as possible before dusk. We can but imagine how heavily the shadows hung over the old Kabuki, natural light and candles doing little to dispel them. Perhaps Kabuki was improved by the efforts of people such as Kanya, perhaps it was not; but certainly it was changed.

Kanya was a zealous reformer in another sense. The "movement for the improvement of the theater" had two aims in his most active years: to abolish what was thought to be the coarseness and vulgarity of late Edo, and to make the Kabuki socially acceptable, a fit genre for upper-class viewing, let the lower classes follow along as they could and would.

As early as 1872, there were bureaucratic utterances informing the Kabuki that it must cease being frivolous and salacious and start being edifying. Danjūrō—to his great discredit, many will say—was a leading exponent of improvement. Wearing striped pants and morning coat at the opening of the second Shintomiza, he read a statement on behalf of his fellow actors: "The theater of recent years has drunk up filth and reeked of the coarse and the mean. It has discredited the beautiful principle of rewarding good and chastising evil, it has fallen into mannerisms and distortions, it has been going steadily downhill. Perhaps at no time has the tendency been more marked than now. I, Danjūrō, am deeply grieved by these facts, and, in consultation with my colleagues, I have resolved to clean away the decay."

Improvement became an organized movement during the Rokumeikan Period, shortly after *The Mikado* was first performed in London. There seems to have been a link between the two events. *The Mikado* was the talk of the Rokumeikan set, which thought it a national insult. Proper retaliation, it seems, was the creation of a dramatic form that foreigners *had* to admire, in spite of themselves. The Society for Improving the Theater had among its founders the foreign minister and the education minister. The wantonness of the old Kabuki must be eliminated. An edifying drama, fit for noble ladies, domestic and foreign, must take its place.

These purifying endeavors had little permanent effect on the Kabuki repertoire. Danjūrō presently moved away from "living history," which had never been popular. Many found it incomprehensible. The novelist Mori Ogai advised the spectator to stuff his ears with cotton upon entering the theater. Danjūrō was all right to look at, he said, but dreadful to listen to.

Yet for better or for worse, the endeavor to make Kabuki socially acceptable did succeed. The emperor's presence always conferred the badge of respectability; he dutifully viewed what he was told to, and one form of entertainment after another received the badge. He went to see Sumō wrestling in 1884 at the Hama Palace; the grand match was, most fittingly for all, a draw. He viewed certain offerings of the variety halls—and in 1887 he attended a presentation of Kabuki, at the foreign minister's residence. Kanya was in charge of the arrangements, and Danjūrō headed the cast. The first performance, at which the emperor was present, lasted through the afternoon. The emperor did not leave until almost midnight. Danjūrō grumbled to Kanya that no actor could be expected to perform well with a truncated *hanamichi* (the processional way by which actors approach the stage through the pit), but of course he could not, on such an occasion, decline to go on. (Actors grumbled similarly, but likewise went on, when Kabuki came to New York in 1960.) On the second day the empress had her viewing, and on two succeeding days other members of the royal family, including the empress dowager, had theirs. The emperor was taciturn in his reaction, declaring merely that he found Kabuki unusual, but the empress wept so profusely at a play about the murder of a child that Kanya, alarmed, urged the actors to try understatement.

In Edo and the Tokyo of Meiji, the most highly esteemed Kabuki actors had enormous popularity and influence. They set styles, such as that for a certain kind of umbrella, which quite swept the place. Huge crowds, of which Tanizaki himself was sometimes a part, turned out for the funerals of famous actors.

Still in late Meiji, after the turn of the century, the Kabuki was, along with the licensed quarters, the form on which the high world of the Low City centered. At the end of Meiji a lumber merchant from east of the river, as in Osanai s novel *The Bank of the Big River* (see pages 69-70), could still be a patron of the arts. One would not come upon his kind today. If modern actors have patrons, they are from the entrepreneurial aristocracy of the High City. In this fact is the measure of the success of the improvers in "improving" Kabuki and its actors, making them artists in an art acceptable to the elite. In the process, old ties were cut. The Kabuki and the demimonde are still close, but the demimonde too has cut its ties with the Low City. One would not be likely to find a person from east of the river among the big spenders.

Danjūrō is often reproved for obsequiousness and for indifference to the plebeian culture that produced Kabuki. Whether or not he is to be blamed for what happened, one may see the dispersal of the old mercantile culture in the changing sociology of the theater.

Morita Kanya's day of prosperity had already passed when Spencer came and Kikugorō took his balloon ride. It was at the Kabukiza that he took it. Opened in 1889, on the site east of Ginza where it still stands, the Kabukiza had a generally Western exterior, in a quiet Renaissance style. Some details suggest a wish to incorporate traditional elements as well. A fan-shaped composition on the central pediment looks in photographs like the ridge piece of a shrine or godown. Inside, the chief difference from the Shintomiza was in size: the Kabukiza was much larger. The great day of the former did not return and, immediately upon its opening, the Kabukiza became what it has been for almost a century, the chief seat of Tokyo Kabuki. Managerial methods were ever more modern, though the old teahouses were allowed in limited numbers, and yet

The Kabukiza, in a 1902 lithograph

humbler establishments as well, street stalls for which Ginza was still famous in the years after the surrender.

The improvers still were not satisfied. Even after the opening of the Kabukiza, they lacked a place where a gentleman might enjoy, in gentlemanly company, the traditional theater. So, in the last full year of Meiji, the Imperial Theater was opened beside the palace moat, on the western edge of Mitsubishi Meadow. Plans were begun in 1906. Shibusawa Eiichi, most energetic and versatile of Meiji entrepreneurs, was chairman. He was born in 1840, in what is now a part of metropolitan Tokyo. To the true son of Nihombashi he may have been a bumpkin, but his case further demonstrates that Osaka people were not the only successful ones in emergent Tokyo. He was everywhere, doing everything, among the organizers of the Bank of Japan, the First National Bank (the first incorporated bank in the land), the Oji Paper Company, Japan Mail Lines (N.Y.K.), and the private railway company that put through the first line to the far north. His was the somewhat Moorish house (see page 97) that seemed so strange to the young Tanizaki and other children of Nihombashi. Among the other organizers of the Imperial Theater were Prince Saionji and Prince Itō.

The first Imperial, which survived the disaster of 1945, was a highly Gallic structure of marble, hung with tapestries, and provided with seventeen hundred Western-style seats. Initially it had a resident Kabuki troupe, but it never really caught on as a place for Kabuki. The High City liked it better than did the Low City, which had a happy simile: seated in the Imperial, one felt like a cenotaph in a family shrine. The Imperial was the place for gala performances when, in the years before the earthquake, celebrities like Pavlova began appearing.

Theater was meanwhile becoming a big business, one which Osaka dominated. The theater and journalism, indeed, provide the best instances of the conquest of Tokyo by Osaka capital that is commonly averred and not easy to prove. It may be that Osaka money did best in fields of high risk and low capitalization. The Shōchiku company of Osaka bought the Shintomiza and another Tokyo theater in late Meiji, and in 1912 the Kabukiza. Shōchiku has dominated Kabuki ever since—but of course Kabuki has become a progressively smaller part of the city's entertainment business.

The large theaters were not the only theaters, nor was Asakusa bereft of Kabuki with the departure of the three major establishments. The name Miyatoza inspires great nostalgia, for that theater is held by many a connoisseur to have been the true heir to the Edo theater. It stood for forty years north of the Asakusa temple and park, very near the site of the big three. In 1896 a bankrupt theater was reopened under the name Miyatoza and new management, that of the enterprising Kanya. Miyato is an old name for the Sumida River. By the end of the century the important names in Meiji Kabuki were much too important to be associated with such a place, but many lesser and more traditional actors played there, as did most of the actors to be important in Taishō. The Miyatoza was destroyed in 1923, as the flames advanced upon the Asakusa Kannon but were held back by Danjūrō's statue (see page 27). It was rebuilt, and did not finally close until 1937. The lovelorn hero of Kafū's novella *The River Sumida* goes to the Miyatoza in search of forgetfulness. Asakusa has had nothing like it since. Nor, indeed, has Tokyo.

In 1873 the city issued regulations limiting the number of "proper theaters" to ten. These were theaters that had the appurtenances of grand Kabuki: *hanamichi* processional ways, revolving stages, drawn (as opposed to dropped) curtains, and teahouses. Smaller "Kabuki huts" were also permitted. By the end of Meiji the accumulated count of proper theaters, as one went and another came, was more than double the prescribed ten. The theater was a risky, unstable business, but some survived all the same. Except when rebuilding after fires, the Ichimuraza and the Moritaza stayed in business through the whole of Meiji. Two Kabuki theaters founded in Meiji yet survive, the Meijiza in Nihombashi and the Kabukiza. Neither is in its original building. The origins of the former lie in the years of the first Shintomiza, and so it has passed its centennial.

Kabuki was made proper and even elegant. In a sense, too, a kind of democratization was at work. The affluent bourgeoise from the High City does not at all mind being seen at a Kabuki opening with a Low City geisha a few seats away. The one is not demeaned and the other is perhaps somewhat elevated. Yet the form, as an institution, a play of social forces, has changed utterly; and because it was so crucial to the culture of the city, that has changed as well. The change was of course gradual. Yet something important happened when the Meiji emperor viewed Kabuki and so bestowed upon it the ultimate cachet. Something important happened again when the Imperial Theater was opened, and the gentry finally had a place where they could watch the old theater comfortably, among people who knew them and whom they knew. The Low City had lost an element of its culture that had but a few decades before been of supreme importance. Other people and places gained, but the loss of something that harms scarcely anyone, and has a refining and even ennobling effect upon many, is sad. In later days the son of Edo may have ruined himself watching baseball. That seems a comedown, somehow, from ruining himself watching Kabuki.

Kabuki was the liveliest of the arts cultivated by the Edo townsman. It was expensive, however, and did not attract people as did the Yose, or variety halls. The term Yose, which has been tendered above as "vaudeville," is in fact an abbreviation of a word signifying "a place that brings in the crowds." The heart of it was the monologue, sometimes serious and edifying, sometimes comic. It was the genuinely popular theater.

The average admission for Kabuki ran seven and eight times that for Yose, not including the levies of the teahouses. The cheapest possible day at the Kabuki was twice as expensive as the average for Yose. Attendance at Yose consistently ran four and five times as high as attendance at the Kabuki theaters; and yet total revenues were smaller. The less affluent son of Edo, when he wished to be away from the noise and clutter of home, went to either a bathhouse or a Yose theater.

"There were no electric trolleys and no busses and taxis," wrote the playwright Osanai Kaoru late in his life. "Only horse trolleys ran along the main streets of the Low City. It was a very rare occasion indeed when the Tokyo person set out for Ginza or Asakusa after dark. He would for the most part range no farther than the night stalls in the neighborhood or perhaps a temple or shrine fair. Yose was his one real diversion. It was a bore to stay at home every night, and he could hardly go on a constant round of calls. Even the stroll among the night stalls was denied him on a rainy evening. So what he had left was Yose."

The sedentary father of a geisha in Osani's *The Bank of the Big River* goes off every afternoon to the serious, edifying sort of Yose. The playwright Hasegawa Shigure, who grew up in Nihombashi, describes a person in her neighborhood who spent his mornings at the bathhouse and in the afternoon had a good rest in a Yose hall.

The number of such places fluctuated through Meiji, but it was never under a hundred in the fifteen wards, and sometimes it ran as high as two hundred. The greatest concentration was in the less affluent wards of the Low City. In Shiba there were seventeen houses in 1882, and sixteen are listed in a guide published by the city in 1907. In Kanda there were twenty-two and seventeen, respectively.

The best Yose monologues may claim to be literature. Sanyūtei Enchō, the most famous of Meiji performers, is held by the literary historians to have been a pioneer in the creation of a modern colloquial prose style. Born in 1839 in the Yushima section of Hongō, the son of that Entarō who gave his name to the horse-drawn trolley and part of it to the taxi, he was active to the end of the nineteenth century. Like the great Danjūrō of the Kabuki, Enchō has had his critics, and for a similar reason: he too harbored a penchant for "improving," for making his genre acceptable to high society. He did edifying historical pieces (one of them about Queen Elizabeth) and adaptations from Western literature, clearly in an attempt to raise it to the level of high culture, suitable for noble gentlemen and ladies, and for the international set as well—to achieve for Yose, in short, what such improvers as Danjūrō were achieving for Kabuki. Perhaps he was also like Danjūrō in that his popularity did not quite match his fame. He was very good at publicizing himself. Recent scholarship has cast doubt upon the theory that he too was summoned to perform in the royal presence. The chronology does not accord, it seems, with what is known of the emperor's round of engagements. Perhaps, late in his life, Enchō made the story up, and no one saw any reason to doubt him.

Yose did not become excessively proper despite Enchō's efforts. It was not, like Kabuki, taken over by the upper classes and made over into an assembly at which a person of the lesser classes, an artisan or a shopkeeper, was likely to feel uncomfortable. Today it is performed in the National Theater (at rather unfriendly hours), but it survives in the Low City as well. When the writer Nagai Kafū—in rebellion against the High City and intent upon losing himself in low, traditional places—sought to become a Yose performer, a spy tattled upon him, and he was dragged home and presently sent into exile beyond the ocean. It is true that the family's reactions to his plans for a career as a Kabuki playwright were no more positive, but it seems likely that, had he persisted and avoided exile, his chances would have been better in improved Kabuki than in still benighted Yose.

Enchō's achievements were considerable all the same. His was only the biggest name among the many that made for Yose its last golden age. It began to decline from about the turn of the century, although it may be said that the Meiji flowering was in any event not as fine as that of late Edo. The puritanical reformers of the mid-nineteenth century, identifying pleasure with decay, had allowed only one Yose house for every thirty that earlier dotted the city. The Meiji total never reached the highest Edo total, upwards of five hundred. Edo is said, with only slight exaggeration, to have had a Yose house for every block.

Though it has declined grievously since late Meiji, enough remains that we may imagine what Yose was like in the best years of Edo and Meiji. By any standard it was superior to the popular entertainment of our day. A good storyteller, whether of the edifying or the amusing sort, was a virtuoso mimic. The *katsuben* narrator for the silent movies, a remarkable and uniquely Japanese performer, may be seen as successor to the Yose man of the great days. He too took (and still does, vestigially, in the surviving Yose halls) all the parts, distinguishing among them with most remarkable skill. Mass entertainment has come to be dominated by the popular singer and the talk man, neither of whom tries to be other than himself, occasionally interesting and often not. It is perhaps inevitable that this should happen as the mass has grown and the tightness of the Low City been dissipated. The story of decline is a sad one all the same.

The few houses that survive today (there are no more than a half-dozen in the city) are large by Meiji standards, holding several hundred people. The typical Meiji house was cozier, more neighborly, perhaps occupying the space up some back alley that had once accommodated a private house or two, now lost to fire or wind or rot. The great masters of Meiji Yose are said to have striven for small, intimate audiences. A hundred was the ideal size. Fewer than a hundred led to an appearance of unpopularity, and more than a hundred to a loss of rapport. When a theater became too popular, the leading performers would turn their duties over to disciples and wait for more manageable circumstances.

*   *   *

The son of plebeian Edo and Tokyo had many things besides Kabuki and Yose to look at and go bankrupt over. The grounds of the larger shrines and temples were often pleasure centers. The Asakusa Kannon, busiest of them all, was one vast and miscellaneous emporium for the performing arts. As Basil Hall Chamberlain and W. B. Mason observed in the 1891 edition of their guide to Japan:

> On no account should a visit to this popular temple and the grounds *(Kōenchi)* surrounding it be omitted; for it is the great holiday resort of the middle and lower classes, and nothing is more striking than the juxtaposition of piety and pleasure, of gorgeous altars and grotesque ex-votos, of pretty costumes and dingy idols, the clatter of clogs, cocks and hens and pigeons strutting about among the worshippers, children playing, soldiers smoking, believers chaffering with dealers of charms, ancient art, modern advertisements—in fine, a spectacle than which surely nothing more motley was ever witnessed within a religious edifice.

And again:

> The grounds of Asakusa are the quaintest and liveliest place in Tokyo. Here are raree shows, penny gaffs, performing monkeys, cheap photographers, street artists, jugglers, wrestlers, life-sized figures in clay, venders of toys and lollipops of every sort, and, circulating amidst all these cheap attractions, a seething crowd of busy holiday-makers.

The skill of jugglers, acrobats, magicians, paper cutters and folders, and the like was so remarkable that Japanese performers had already traveled abroad, to acclaim, before the Restoration. There are records of fat women and peacocks, pleasing to the child of Edo, from the very earliest years of the city. In the last decades of the shogunate, Asakusa was the most thriving pleasure center, for it had the Yoshiwara and the theaters in addition to its great temple. There were other centers, near the two Tokugawa mortuary temples at Ueno and Shiba, for instance, and across the river in Honjo, where the Ekōin Temple, erected in memory of those lost in the great fire of 1657, had become a place for cheering departed spirits as well as for remembering them. Asakusa, Ueno, and Ryōgoku, where the Ekoin is situated, had the most thriving of the *hirokōji,* the "broad alleys," originally cleared as firebreaks and scattered through the city. The broad alleys of Ueno and Ryōgoku did not fare well in Meiji, as Asakusa prospered more and more. The stalls and shows were presently moved from the immediate environs of the temple to the western edge of what had become Asakusa Park.

Some of the shows seem to have been inelegant, even grotesque. At Ryōgoku there was a man greatly skilled at breaking wind. For some years a spider man turned up on all the big Asakusa feast days. He had the head of an aged adult, a body some two feet tall, and the arms and legs of an infant. He was very popular. Also at Asakusa was a woman who smoked with her navel. The painter Kishida Ryūsei, born in 1891, described a puppet show in the Ginza of his boyhood, in which a she-devil slashed open the stomach of a pregnant woman and ate the foetus—or rather, being a doll, not up to the ingestion, announced that she would take it home for dinner. (It was Ryusei who—see page 76—informed us of that particular Ginza pleasure, peeping in upon Shimbashi geisha as they made ready for a night.)

Many of the shows were free, some of them to aid in the hawking of medicines and the like, while some were willing to accept whatever pennies the viewer felt like tossing down. The larger shrines had stages for

Kagura, "god performances," which also were free, and sometimes, as Tanizaki's reminiscences inform us, not very godly.

> Kagura has all but disappeared from the shrines of Tokyo, festive performances are probably even rarer. The modern child would probably think it stupid beyond description, but I am filled with almost unbearable longing for the very feel of them, those naive dances to drum and flute, the dancers masked as fool and as clown, on a long spring day in Nihombashi... The troupes would also perform for this and that banquet, but the one I saw most frequently offered skits on the grounds of the Meitoku Inari Shrine, very near our house, on the eighth of every month, the feast day, in the evening. A genuine "god dance" would sometimes be offered to the presiding deity, but more commonly there were skits. The performers were amateurs with other occupations. One of them functioned as head of the company, and even had a stage name, Suzume. All the others referred to him as "the master."
>
> About then, which is to say the autumn of 1897, there occurred in Ochanomizu the murder of Kono, a very famous one that will doubtless be remembered by other old persons my age. A man from Fukushima named Matsudaira Noriyoshi, aged forty-one, who lived in Ushigome, murdered his common-law wife, Kono, who had been a serving woman in a geisha quarter and had accumulated a little money. He murdered her on the night of April 26, the Bishamon Fair, and mutilated her face to prevent identification. Wrapping the naked body in a straw mat and tying it with ropes, he set it rolling down the slope at Ochanomizu towards the Kanda River. It stopped some five feet short and was immediately found. There was an enormous stir. Noriyoshi was soon apprehended. The newspapers of course made a huge thing of the incident, and in this and that shop and in stalls on the day of the Suitengu fair I often saw card-sized pictures of Kono's mutilated face among the usual pictures of actors and geisha. Kono was forty, a year younger than Noriyoshi. The line where her eyebrows had been shaved was "iridescent," it was said, and she was "like a cherry still in fresh leaf." That the new avant-garde theater should take the incident up was inevitable. Already in June at the Ichimuraza the troupe headed by Ii Yōhō and Yamaguchi Sadao presented a "sensational" (or so it was proclaimed) version, along with A *Comical Tour of Hell*... It was perhaps a month later that I saw the Suzume troupe do the affair on the Kagura stage of the Meitoku Inari, in imitation of Yamaguchi and Kawai, who were the murderer and his victim at the Ichimuraza... Noriyoshi ... throttled her. Then, with the greatest

concentration, he carved several trenches on her face, and, lifting her head by the hair, showed it to all of us. It seems strange that such a play should have been done on the grand Kagura stage of a shrine, and it does not seem strange at all, for it was a day when Kono's face, on display in all the stalls, upset no one.

All the best-loved crimes of Meiji became material for the theater, and all of them, probably because the dramatic possibilities were heightened, involved women. A murdered woman, such as Kono, made good theater and good popular fiction, and a murderess was even better. There was, for example, Harada Kinu, known as "O-kinu of the storm in the night," a reference to her last haiku, composed as she set out for the Kotsukappara execution grounds:

> A storm in the night.
> Dawn comes, nothing remains.
> A flower's dream.

She was beheaded early in the spring of 1872. Heads of criminals were still put on display, in the old fashion. On his first trip from Yokohama to Tokyo, W. E. Griffis saw some, near the southern limits of the city. The newspapers reported that O-kinu's head possessed a weird, unearthly beauty. The concubine of a minor daimyo, she was left to fend for herself after the Restoration. She became the mistress of a pawnbroker and fell in love with a Kabuki actor, whom, in accepted style, she purchased. The affair proved to be more than a dalliance.

One winter morning in 1871 she fed the pawnbroker rat poison, that she might live with the actor. She did so until apprehended. One may pity O-kinu, for she belonged to the class that suffered most in the revolution called Restoration.

The most famous of Meiji murderesses, vastly popular on stage and in fiction, was Takahashi O-den, who was beheaded in the Ichigaya prison in 1879 by the executioner who dispatched O-kinu. She too came from the lower ranks of the military class. The story of her misdeeds has probably been exaggerated by writers of popular fiction. She is charged with more than one poisoning before she committed the crime that took her to Ichigaya. Evidence in support of the charges is slight, and she was convicted only of slitting the throat of a used-clothes merchant in an Asakusa inn. She did it for the sincerest of motives: after the Restoration she had made her way chiefly by prostitution, and she robbed the merchant to pay the debts of her chief patron. Hers was the last case assigned to the

The execution of Takahashi O-den. from an 1879 woodcut

famous executioner. He did it badly, wounding her before the final cut. There were horrible screams, according to newspaper accounts.

O-den, too, composed a final poem:

> I wish to be no longer in this hapless world.
> Make haste to take me over, O ford of the River of Death.

Her grave may be visited in the Yanaka Cemetery, where the poem is cut upon the stone. The little plot of earth is a sad one, beside a public lavatory, clinging precariously to the edge of the cemetery, given only cursory notice in guides that account for all the famous graves, such as that of Kafū's grandfather. The stone is not unimposing, however, and it is replete with bittersweet irony. It was erected in 1881 from contributions by most of the famous theatrical and journalistic persons of the day, and the man who collected the funds was Kanagaki Robun. Robun had rushed into woodcut print with a sensational story of her life a scant month after her execution. (He did a quickie on General Grant before the general had even departed the city.)

Among these dangerous women the most romantic was Hanai O-urae, the only one of the three who survived to enjoy her fame. It is generally agreed that she was less criminal than victim. She too came from the low ranks of the military class. After service as a geisha in Yanagibashi and Shimbashi, she opened a place of her own, near the river in

Nihombashi. She was tormented by a former employee, Minekichi by name (it is a name with a nice ring to it), who wanted to take over both her and her business. One night early in the summer of 1887, answering a summons to meet him on the bank of the canal that ran through her part of Nihombashi, she stabbed him thrice with his own butcher knife, beneath the willows, in a gentle rain. A troublesome and less than romantic detail is that she, and not he, may at the outset have been in possession of the knife. She was sentenced to life imprisonment and freed in 1903. In her last years she joined a troupe of traveling players; her most popular role was that of herself in her finest moment. She died in 1916, in a Yotsuya slum.

The performers who played murderer and victim in the drama described by Tanizaki were both men. So it will be seen that many conventions of Kabuki were retained by the "avant-garde" theater of the day, in spite of its aim to make the theater more Western and realistic. Men still played female roles.

In 1890 the chief of the Tokyo prefectural police let it be known that men and women might appear on the stage together. One of the two great Kabuki actors, improver Danjūrō, supported the policy, and the other, Kikugorō, opposed it. The Kabuki stage continued to be exclusively masculine. The new policy was revolutionary all the same, in a day when so many mixed things, such as bathing and wrestling, were held to accord ill with Enlightenment.

Women had never been absent from the performing arts. They had quite dominated the parlor varieties found at their best in the pleasure quarters. There were well-known actresses in late Meiji, and fullblown celebrities, symbols of their day, in Taishō. *Musumegidayū,* Osaka theater music *(gidayū)* performed by pretty girls *(musume)*, was enormously popular in Meiji, especially among students, who seem to have found it erotic. In 1900, when the vogue was at its peak, there were more than a thousand *musumegidayū* performers in Tokyo.

Music was less disposed than other arts to go Western. The *musumegidayū* vogue passed, not so much because it was overtaken by Western forms as because other traditional forms came into fashion. Yet already in Meiji are to be found the beginnings of modern popular music, which, with its volatile trendiness, may be distinguished from folk music and from the various forms of stage music, popular or otherwise, as well.

The street minstrel known as the *enkashi* had his beginnings in the Tokyo of mid-Meiji and was still to be seen for perhaps a half-dozen years after the earthquake. He was such a part of late Meiji and of Taishō that he can scarcely be omitted from graphic and dramatic attempts to convey the mood of the day. The word *enkashi* may be written in two ways, one of them conveying merely "singer," the other something like "singer of amorous songs." The *enkashi* was Western at top and at bottom—bowler hat and shoes—and always accompanied himself on a violin. The remainder of his dress was Japanese. He would stand on a street corner and sing topical songs in return for pennies. The repertoire was in part amorous, but it was also strongly political and satirical. There were war songs and there were songs of a righteous nature criticizing the customs and manners of the day. Perhaps the nearest thing to a hit was called "The Voice of the Pine." In a satirical vein, it criticized the decadent ways of girl students, and might have been called anti-amorous. Fujiwara Yoshie, later to become the most famous of Japanese opera singers, got his start as an *enkashi,* in attendance upon the man who did the voice of the pine.

Three things to ruin oneself in the viewing of—the theater, cherry blossoms, and Sumō wrestling—were held to be the great delights of Meiji Tokyo. Sumō is a very ancient sport, its origins traceable, according to the earliest chronicles, to prehistory. It is more complex and sophisticated than at first sight it seems to be. The rules are simple: when a wrestler touches the ground with any part of himself save the soles of his feet, or when he is forced from the ring, he loses. It may seem that size is the only important thing, for the wrestlers in recent centuries have been huge. The hugest on record, however, have not been the most successful. There are delicate skills having to do with balance and timing.

Early in Meiji, change touched Sumō. Like so many things of Edo, it was meant for masculine enjoyment. In the last years of Edo, women were admitted to the audience only on the final day of a tournament. There seem to have been religious reasons for this exclusion, having to do vaguely with ritual purity. From 1872 women were admitted on every day except the first, and from 1877 they were admitted every day. The Sumō ring continues, however, to be sexist. No woman may step inside. When, recently, a boxer with a lady manager fought in the Sumo stadium, the manager was required to manage from a distance.

Sumō, as we have seen, was made respectable by a royal viewing. This happened in 1884, at the Hama Palace. Sumo had seemed in early Meiji to be declining, but in late Meiji it enjoyed popularity as never before. This was probably due less to royal notice than to the emergence of two uncommonly skilled wrestlers, one of whom fought to the famous draw in the royal presence.

In 1909 Sumō acquired the biggest sports arena in the city and indeed in the whole Orient, a great improvement over the shelters in which tournaments had earlier been held, they were so flimsy that competition had to be called off in bad weather. The new arena was named Kokugi-kan, "Hall of the National Accomplishment," and Sumō has since been thought of as that, although baseball might in recent years have better claimed the sobriquet. Before construction was begun in 1907 there was a lengthy hunt for a site. Marunouchi, the Mitsubishi Meadow, was considered, but rejected as too remote from the traditional Sumō base in the Low City. The promoters finally decided on an old tournament site at the Ekōin, east of the river. The Meiji building was gutted by fire in 1917, badly damaged in the earthquake, and afterwards rebuilt on the same site.

Sumō was modernized in another way. The "human rights" of wrestlers became a burning issue. Some thought the old authoritarian methods of training and management inappropriate to the new enlightened age. The Tokyo band of professional wrestlers, based at the Ekōin, split over the issue in 1873. The rebellious faction, advocating human rights, withdrew to Nagoya. Back in Tokyo soon after, it held its tournaments at Akihabara, south of Ueno. In 1878 the police intervened, being of the view that two rival bands in the same city had disruptive possibilities. The factions were brought together under a system of government licensing, although a number of wrestlers of advanced views refused to participate.

The rebels became the establishment, and were themselves presently the victims of a strike. This occurred in 1895. The immediate occasion was a contested decision, but the authoritarian ways of the people in control were the real issue. The strike succeeded in that the head of the family, who had been among the rebels of the earlier day, was shorn of his powers. Sumō has continued to be very conservative all the same. Managerial methods, long similar to those of the theater, have remained close to their origins.

Early in Meiji (the precise date is a subject of scholarly dispute) there occurred an event of great moment. Few events have affected the lives of more Japanese. A stick and several hard balls arrived in Yokohama, bringing baseball to Japan. The first games were somewhat aristocratic. They were played on the grounds of a mansion on the southern outskirts of Tokyo belonging to the Tayasu, an important branch of the Tokugawa clan. The early years of Japanese baseball were dominated by the Shimbashi Club, named from the railway station and yards. It included numbers of Americans in the employ of the government. The work of the catcher seems to have been hazardous, for neither mitt nor protector had come with the stick and balls.

By mid-Meiji there were several clubs here and there around the city, and school teams as well. The last years of the century were dominated by the First Higher School, most elitist of institutions. Baseball was still somewhat elegant and high-collar, but it was on the way to becoming business as well. Waseda and Keiō universities, whose teams are today not quite amateur, had their first engagement in 1903. The mood in the stands grew so murderous towards the end of their 1906 series that they did not meet again until late in the following reign.

An international game, believed to have been the first, took place in 1896 between a team of Japanese schoolboys and an American team from Yokohama. The Japanese won. A Japanese university team went to the United States in 1905, and two years later the first foreign team, semi-professionals from Hawaii, came to Japan. On that occasion an admission fee was charged for the first time.

In 1890 there was an international incident, demonstrating even earlier than the Waseda-Keiō fanaticism how important baseball had become to the Japanese. During a game between Meiji Gakuin and the First Higher School an excited American dashed onto the field. He proved to be a missionary from the Meiji Gakuin faculty. After a pummeling by students from the First Higher School, he was arrested for disturbing the peace. A consular trial seemed in prospect, extraterritoriality yet prevailing. The view of the arbiter that both sides were at fault was accepted, however, and so the matter ended. It was long before the two schools were once again on friendly terms.

Baseball was something very new, a team sport. Traditional sporting encounters had been man-to-man. One can only speculate upon why baseball, among all the possible foreign importations, was chosen to become (as indeed it did) the national accomplishment. A prophet in early Meiji might have given cricket the better chance, for anglomania was strong. Today cricket is almost the only major foreign sport that does not interest Japanese at all.

Having had its beginnings in Tokyo, Japanese baseball is now everywhere. Like so many things, it continues to be dominated by Tokyo. The Tokyo Giants have a nationwide following that is rivaled by no Osaka team, and a Waseda-Keiō series still arouses passions such as are aroused by no other amateur (if somewhat professional) encounter.

Sumō became "the national accomplishment" in late Meiji, but its great popularity had to do less with nationalism than with the attributes and accomplishments of certain wrestlers. Judō, on the other hand, as distinguished from the earlier *jujitsu* (more properly *jujutsu)*, fell definitely into the category of martial arts, and had strongly nationalist connotations. Its origins lie in mid-Meiji, in a temple of the Low City. The two words, *judō* and *jujitsu,* are almost synonymous, *judō* being a development of *jujitsu* in the direction of "the way," the Chinese Tao, with emphasis upon spiritual training and upon utter concentration and dedication. Perhaps more remarkable than *judō* itself were the organizing skills of the founder, Kanō Jigorō. The huge following which *judō* came to have meant a return to tradition, which in Japan often means nationalism. Yet the growing popularity of baseball, also in the last decades of Meiji, informs us that the nationalism of those years was not the sort of revivalism that wished to return to the old isolation and reject importations.

With engaging openness and a regard for reality, the guide published by the city in 1907 includes the licensed quarters in its pleasure section, along with the theater and other places to see things, and with graves and cemeteries as well.

The licensed quarters had a rather bad time of it in Meiji. They had been important cultural centers, and, though prostitution continued to flourish, they declined badly as places of culture. Nowhere was the decay of the decadent more in evidence than here. The playwright Osanai Kaoru stated the matter well.

One has no trouble seeing why playwrights of Edo so often set their plays in the Yoshiwara. It was the fashion center and the musical center of Edo. In the dress of the courtesans and in the dress of their customers as well were the wanton colors and designs for all the latest rages. The brightness of the samisen when the ladies were on display, the quiet sadness of the old schools of music, Katō and Sonohachi: one no longer has them at the Yoshiwara. The courtesan has degenerated into a tasteless chalk drawing, the stylish clientele has given way to workmen's jackets and flat-top haircuts and rubber boots, and mendicant musicians *[enkashi]* who play "Katyusha's Song" on the violin. The Yoshiwara of old was the veritable center of Edo society. The daimyo with his millions, the braves of whom everyone was talking, robbers in the grand style who aimed at aristocratic houses, all of them gathered in the Yoshiwara. When an accidental meeting was required, therefore, the Yoshiwara was the obvious place to have it occur. No playwright would be silly enough to put the Yoshiwara of our day to such use. A chance encounter under the lights of the beer hall at the main gate would most likely involve a person with a north-country accent and a home-made cap, and his uncle, in the city with a petition to the Ministry of Commerce and Agriculture. The customer sweetening his coffee with sugar cubes in a Western-style salon, given a farewell pat on his new muslin undershirt, would most likely be a numbers man in a visor cap, or a wandering singer of Osaka balladry who does the outskirts of town. No one could think of the Yoshiwara as in the slightest degree a romantic setting.

This passage is quoted by Kubota Mantarō, who remarks that the decay was still more pronounced after the earthquake. "Katyusha's Song," commonly held to be among the earliest examples of popular music, had first been sung by Matsui Sumako, most celebrated of Taishō actresses (see below, page 267), in a stage version of Tolstoy's *Resurrection*. After the earthquake, says Kubota, it gave way to "Arabian Love Song."

The demimonde did not disappear or even decline, but it changed. The best of music and the dance, not inferior to that of the Kabuki, with which it shared a great deal, had indeed been found in the quarters, and especially the oldest and largest of them, the Yoshiwara. It was what the big spender wanted and got. There were both male and female geisha, but the performing arts of the quarters were largely the province of women, as those of the Kabuki were exclusively the province of men.

The elegant word for the bright centers of the demimonde has long been *karyūkai,* which an earlier edition of the principal Japanese-English dictionary defines as "a frivolous community," and the most recent edition, with less flourish, "the gay quarters." The expression means literally "streets of flower and willow." It comes from Li Po, the great Tang poet, who made the flower and willow similes for the ladies of the demimonde. For the purist there was a distinction between the two which has largely been forgotten, the flower being the courtesan and the willow the geisha.

The distinction was never widely respected, and even when it was accepted in theory it quickly ran into trouble in practice. *Geisha* is one of the most difficult words in the Japanese language to grasp and define. Literally it is "accomplished person." Nagai Kafū lamented the degeneration of the word and the concept, especially in the "geisha" quarters of the Meiji High City. Some geisha doubtless had a nunlike dedication to their artistic accomplishments, but many would have had trouble naming any that they possessed. They were for sale if the price and the asker were right. The grander of Edo courtesans, on the other hand, were sometimes very accomplished indeed, as little designs and billets-doux which survive from their hands demonstrate most clearly.

For all these imprecisions, the geisha and the courtesan had different places in the elaborate organization of the Edo Yoshiwara. To the former was entrusted the early part of a big evening, music and dance often of a very high quality, and to the other the more carnal business of the smaller hours.

As Meiji moved on towards Taishō, the geisha languished in the licensed quarters even as she thrived elsewhere. The licensed quarters became places of prostitution and little else, and for a more elegant sort of evening the affluent pleasure-seeker went rather to one of the geisha quarters. The change is seen most clearly in the fate of the *hikitejaya,* literally "teahouses that take one by the hand." Central to the organization of the old quarters, the "teahouses" were guides to and intermediaries for the bordellos proper. Houses of high grade did not receive customers directly, nor did the wealthy merchant, as he set forth upon an evening of pleasure, think of going immediately to a brothel. Preparations were made by a teahouse, to which the customer went first, there to be taken by the hand; and so ties between teahouse and geisha, male and female, were close. The teahouses were in large measure guardians of the old forms, and as they declined prostitution became almost the exclusive business of the quarters.

The number of licensed prostitutes declined through Meiji, unlicensed prostitution flourished, and, as Nagai Kafū did not tire of telling

A brothel in the Yoshiwara, as rebuilt after the Great Fire of 1911

us, certain geisha quarters, especially in the High Town, were little better than centers of prostitution. More to the point than this decline in
the rolls of the professionals is the sharp decline in the number of teahouses. A successor institution, the *machiai,* prospered as the teahouses
declined. Originally antechambers to tea cottages, *machiai* became places
of assignation and presently restaurants to which geisha were summoned.
"Streets of flower and willow" came presently to mean geisha quarters,
as the old teahouses, the *hikitejaya,* and also the boathouses that had
seen people so elegantly and comfortably to the Yoshiwara, merged with
or gave way to the new *machiai.* It is not to be thought that the geisha
quite disappeared from the Yoshiwara, where, indeed, some of the most
talented and accomplished geisha of the Taisho period plied their trade.
Geisha from all over town came to them for lessons.

The first thing that Civilization and Enlightenment did to the Yoshiwara and the other licensed quarters was to "liberate" their courtesans.
An order of liberation was handed down by the Council of State, the
high executive of the new government, late in 1872. It seems to have
been a direct result of the *Maria Luz* affair, which gave international
prominence to the licensed quarters. The captain of the *Maria Luz,* a
Peruvian ship, was in 1872 convicted by a Yokohama court of running
slaves, specifically Chinese coolies. In the course of the recriminations
the Japanese were accused by the Peruvians of being slave traffickers
themselves, their chief commodity being the ladies of the Yoshiwara and
the other licensed quarters.

So the ladies of the quarters were liberated legally whether or not they
wished to be, or had other means of subsistence. Stern measures were
taken for the repression of "private," which is to say unlicensed, prostitution. The aging aunt in Kafu's *The River Sumida* had gone to the uncle
for help when she was liberated, and was among the fortunate ones, for
he married her.

There were other marks of enlightenment in the quarters. An 1874
newspaper reported that the young men who traditionally patrolled the
night with wooden clappers, urging vigilance against fires, had taken to
using trumpets. Not well received, the practice was soon abandoned. A
fad for Western dress coincided with the Rokumeikan period. An enterprising bawdy house had Western beds in some of its rooms. The same
house had a somewhat cosmopolitan staff, which included the first Oki-
nawan courtesans active in Tokyo.

With liberation, the old brothels became *karizashiki,* literally "rooms
for rent," and the crisis passed. The old trade was permitted under a new

jargon, the ladies now in theory being free agents. They were permitted to do business in the rented rooms, so long as they were licensed. Six centers in and around the city had rooms for rent: the four "post-stations," Shinagawa, Shinjuku, Itabashi, and Senjū, which were the points of entry into the old city; and the Yoshiwara and Nezu (just north of Ueno). Prosperity returned as the new system proved as functional as the old. "A thousand houses, four thousand women, seven districts," went a saying of mid-Meiji, declaring the proportions of the trade. (Senjū had traditionally been counted as two post-stations, because roads from the north converged there as they entered the city; hence "seven districts.")

The Yoshiwara, the largest district, dwindled alarmingly in early Meiji, and after a decade or so began to revive. The number of houses on the eve of the Sino-Japanese War was still smaller than in the last years of Edo, though some of them were larger and more ornate houses by far than Edo had ever seen, grand edifices, indeed, of four and five storys, with chandeliers, stained glass, and the like.

The quality of the several districts may be gauged from the importance to each of its teahouses. It was considerably higher at the Yoshiwara than at Nezu, the next largest district. Of the old post-stations, Shinagawa maintained the highest ratio of teahouses to brothels, though it was lower than at the Yoshiwara and about the same as that at Nezu. Shinagawa had been the most particular of the Edo post-stations, because it commanded the most important point of access to the city, from the south and west, and the most demanding clientele, from the Kansai. What these facts tell us is that the old forms were more perdurable at the Yoshiwara than elsewhere. While there were teahouses there was at least a possibility that an evening at the Yoshiwara would not be given over entirely to fleshly things.

By the end of Meiji there were no teahouses at all in Itabashi, where the inland road from the Kansai entered the city. It was the smallest of the districts, notably unsuccessful at coming to terms with the new age. At Shinjuku, the most triumphantly successful of the old post-stations in this regard, there were only nine teahouses serving fifty-eight establishments with "rooms for rent." At the Yoshiwara the number was a dozen times as large. The Yoshiwara was, after all, in its fashion, a guardian of tradition.

It had its own cycle of festivals, closely tied to the seasons. Observances were less punctilious and elaborate in Meiji than during the last years of Edo, and less still so as Meiji progressed. In late Edo there had been grand processions of courtesans, so laden with robes and ornaments and elevated upon pattens to such heights that they had to be supported.

These processions honored the flowers of the seasons, and especially the cherry blossoms of the third day of the Third Month under the lunar calendar, the iris of the fifth day of the Fifth Month, and the chrysanthemums of the ninth day of the Ninth Month. A curious custom known as "heaped bedding," *tsumi yagu,* was still to be seen in Meiji, though less frequently and less elaborately than in Edo. The great courtesans demonstrated their popularity and the wealth of their patrons by public displays of bedding. It was a curious custom, and it must have been very erotic as well. The bedding, especially commissioned for display, was in gold and silver brocades and colored silks of extreme gaiety.

At least three Yoshiwara events still attracted whole families, men, women, and children. The main business of the quarter prospered, of course, but could hardly account for the throngs. More innocent amusements included the "night cherry blossoms," which the whole quarter turned out to view, and much of the city, and especially the Low City, as well. In late summer and early autumn the quarter set out lanterns in memory of an eighteenth-century courtesan of great popularity and sensitivity and high attainments, while dances known as Niwaka were performed on wheeled stages that moved up and down the main central street. They were sometimes humorous and sometimes solemnly dramatic, and the performers were the geisha, male and female, of the quarter. For obscure reasons, the observance declined sadly in late Meiji. Then on the two or three "bird days" of November came the Bird Fair, observed throughout the city but with an especial crowding at the Eagle Shrine just outside the quarter. On the days and nights of the fair the back gates of the quarter were opened to roisterers and the curious in general—on other days the main north gate was the only point of egress and ingress. The press and the stir were wondersome. Higuchi Ichiyō thus described them in her novella "Growing Up."

> Not given to letting such chances pass, young men poured into the quarter from the back gates. The main gate was quiet, and so it was as if the directions had suddenly reversed themselves. One trembled lest the pillars of heaven and the sinews of the earth give way in the roar. Gangs pushed arm in arm across the drawbridges and into the Five Streets, plowing the crowd like boats plowing their way up the river. Music and dancing, shrill cries from the little houses along the moat, and samisen in the more dignified heights, a delirious confusion of sounds that the crowds would not soon forget.

In the spring of 1881, when the cherry blossoms were in their greatest glory, a new main gate of wrought iron was dedicated. The inscription

The Yoshiwara Main Gate as it was in late Meiji and early Taishō

was a Chinese poem by Fukuchi Genichirō, president of the Tokyo prefectural council. He was paid the equivalent of fifty thousand dollars, thought by some excessive. No one in the quarter, male or female, failed to attend the dedication. The poem, two lines of eight Chinese characters each, may be rendered thus:

> The deepening of a springtide dream. A teeming street overcast by
> cherry blossoms.
> First tidings of autumn. Twin rows of lanterns down the street.

It refers, of course, to the first two of the three great annual Yoshiwara observances.

So the old pleasure quarter, greeting the visitor with Chinese poetry from an eminent hand, was still in mid-Meiji a place of some culture; but it was declining. The great fire of 1911, the last full year of Meiji, dealt a grievous blow. On April 9, just one day short of three decades after the dedication of the iron gate, the Yoshiwara was almost completely destroyed. Two hundred brothels and teahouses were lost, within a few score of the total number. The quarter was rebuilt, but in a manner that appeared to demonstrate what may be expected in such cases, or to illustrate the proposition that the worst thing the West did was to make things easy and inexpensive. Old methods were discarded. They were too dear and too troublesome. The results of the rebuilding had a certain charm when they were in the whimsically ornamental style of Taishō, but when simple and utilitarian, tended to be merely dull. With what remained of the old they formed a rather motley stylistic triad. The loss of the teahouses left a permanent scar. Very little of high culture remained. The Yoshiwara became what it was to be until the outlawing of prostitution on April Fool's Day, 1958, a place of just that and nothing more. Kafū exaggerated when he said that the Low City of Edo died in the flood of 1910 and the Yoshiwara fire of 1911, but the old Yoshiwara never really recovered its earlier, if decadent, glory.

None of the Five Mouths, as the post-stations fringing the city were called, lay within the fifteen wards of the Meiji city. A part of Shinjuku was incorporated into Yotsuya Ward just before the earthquake, and Shinagawa lay just beyond the southern tip of Shiba, the southernmost ward. The other two were more remote. (As has been noted, there were actually only four "mouths," Senju at the north being counted twice.) Though not central to the culture of Edo as the Yoshiwara was, they provided essentially the same pleasures and services. Each made its way through the Meiji era in a different fashion, and so they offer interesting variations upon the theme of change.

Shinagawa was the busiest of the four (or five), and second in size only to the Yoshiwara among the quarters of greater Edo. Very conservative, the Shinagawa station and quarter sought to remain apart from the new day. In this endeavor it was perhaps too successful. It was left alone, and dwindled to insignificance.

There was strong opposition in Shinagawa to the Shimbashi-Yokohama railroad. It ran along the coast, partly on fills, to the present Shinagawa Station, in Shiba Ward. Had it continued on the coast it would have passed very near the quarter. Instead it passed some distance inland. The quarter itself doubtless had less influence than the army on these arrangements, but a result was that the district around the new railway station prospered, and the old post-station, the "mouth," was isolated. It survived as a pleasure quarter, but a certain determination was required to get to it. This was true also of the Yoshiwara, and doubtless had something to do with the decline of that place as a cultural center. The rashness of choosing to stand apart from new traffic patterns was apparent earlier, however, in the case of Shinagawa. Where the Yoshiwara had always had its own very special attractions, Shinagawa had flourished only because it was beside the main Tōkaidō highway. The Shinagawa district lost population in late Meiji. It grew again in Taishō, but pleasure centers for the new city were by then emerging elsewhere. A private railway put through the district in the early years of this century was not enough to relieve the isolation, because there was no transfer to and from the main government line. This did not come until after the earthquake. The automobile age brought traffic back to Shinagawa, for the highway to Yokohama followed the old Tōkaidō, but by then it was too late. There were other places to go. In late Meiji and early Taishō the old Shinagawa station presented the curious picture of a bawdy district, with a few geisha to give it tone, cut off from the world by an encirclement of temples.

The case of Shinjuku was quite the opposite. It had been a relatively unimportant way station in the Tokugawa period, and even in mid-Meiji, when Shinagawa was being left behind, it was the smaller of the two quarters. It lay on the road to the province of Kai, the present Yamanashi Prefecture. The principal inland route to the Kansai now passes through Yamanashi, but did not then. The number of customers who might be expected to wander in from the highway or pass one last night on the road before venturing into the city was small. Shinjuku, meaning "New Station," was the parvenu among the Five Mouths, put together when the older Takaido station came to seem a bit too far out to serve as a first stop on the way to Kai.

Shinjuku was a lonely place under the Tokugawa. It did not immediately spring into prosperity with the beginning of the new day. Like Shinagawa, it was circumvented by the new transportation system. The railway that ran north and south along the western fringes of the city passed slightly to the west of it, even as the Tōkaidō line passed west of the Shinagawa quarter. There were two important differences, however: the old station, the "mouth," lay between the new station and the city, and within easy walking distance, and so the stroller need not have such a strong sense of purpose to get there as to reach Shinagawa; and the new station was to become an extremely important transfer point for commuters, the most important, indeed, in all the land. A private railway line, later bought by the government railways, was opened from Shinjuku westwards to Tachikawa in 1889.

The growth of Shinjuku as a residential district proceeded so briskly that it was the only significant annexation to the city through the Meiji and Taishō Periods. Its prosperity brought the decline of such geisha districts, nearer the city, as Yotsuya and Kagurazaka. The old pleasures of the way station also got lost in the prosperity. The bawdy houses, very conspicuous on the main highway westwards from the city, embarrassed the bright new Shinjuku. There were plans, very long in the formulation, to put them out of sight on back streets. With the assistance of fires, the plans were well on the way to fruition when the earthquake came, making relocation easier. The old quarter gradually dwindled, though it survived long enough to be outlawed on that memorable April Fool's Day of 1958.

Itabashi was the earliest of the Five Mouths to fall into a decline. By the middle years of Meiji it had fewer houses and ladies than Shinjuku, and no teahouses at all. The old highway on which it stood, the inland route to the Kansai, had been important; especially in the years after Perry, it accommodated grand processions fearful of the exposed seashore route, among them that of the royal princess who traveled east to become the wife of the fourteenth shogun. Itabashi fell in the revolution that put everyone on wheels. There are still traces of the old post-station, but one has to hunt for them. Most of the old quarter was destroyed by fire in 1884. Though it was partly rebuilt, the old business continued to decline. After the earthquake Itabashi began to attract commuters and developers, not customers for the old quarter. It does not, like Shinagawa, seem to have striven to be left behind by the new day, but somehow it was.

Senjū provided two of the Five Mouths. There were two clusters for pleasure and lodging, known as the Upper Station and the Lower, on either bank of the Arakawa River (as the upper reaches of the Sumida are called) and Senjū did more than double duty as a way station. Three important roads converged upon it: from Mito, seat of one of the "three Tokugawa houses"; from the far north; and from Nikkō, mortuary shrine of the first and third shoguns. Of all of them, it best gives a sense today of what an old way station was like. Senjū never languished like Itabashi nor throve like Shinjuku, and it did not, like Shinagawa, seek to reject the swift new wheels. In between, it has kept more of its past than any of the others.

The traveler from Edo usually proceeded northwards on foot, having arrived at Senjū on foot or by boat, as the great poet Bashō did in the seventeenth century. The modern road to the north does not follow the old road, which, therefore, escaped widening. There was another road, farther to the west, for grand official processions to Nikkō, and so Senjū did not get exceedingly important people, as Itabashi and Shinagawa did. Probably nothing made by man is old enough to have been seen by Bashō as he set out on his narrow road to the north, but there are yet patches of richly brown latticework and heavily tiled roofs, to suggest the sort of road it was. To reach Asakusa and Shitaya, the first considerable areas of dense population, the traveler still had to pass extensive farmlands. Senju was thus fairly safe from the fires that so frequently afflicted the city.

The last of the districts, Nezu, on the fringes of Hongō, was an inconvenience in early Meiji, for it lay just down the hill from the old estate of the Maeda, lords of Kanazawa, which became the campus of the Imperial University. The proximity was not thought appropriate, since the young men of the university were the future of the nation. They must be kept from temptation, at least within walking distance. The Nezu quarter could simply have been closed, but that posed another problem: Such facilities were necessary to a city absorbing great floods of unattached young men from the country. Edo always contained more men than women, and Tokyo continues the pattern. So in 1888 the Nezu quarter was moved bodily to Susaki, which means something like "sandbar," filled land in Fukagawa near the mouths of the Sumida. Great celebrations on the occasion of the removal let everyone know where the quarter had gone. Through the remainder of Meiji and indeed down to the outlawing of prostitution, the transplanted quarter was the chief rival of the Yoshiwara as a "nightless city." After the fires of early Meiji, it may have looked more like the Yoshiwara of Edo than did the Yoshiwara itself. Photographs and prints show low buildings in good traditional taste, comparing well with the Yoshiwara and its tendency towards the flamboyant. The old customs seem to have survived better at Susaki than at the post-stations.

As Meiji came to an end and Taishō began, the flower and willow of the old system were drifting apart. The flower was the more carnal of the two, the willow or geisha the more artistic and spiritual. The flower came to dominate the licensed quarters, while the willow was preeminent in the geisha quarters. *Machiaijaya,* literally "rendezvous teahouse," is what is usually referred to by the English term "geisha house." A Japanese word exists that may be literally rendered "geisha house," but it is not commonly used, and is more likely to be found in bilingual dictionaries than in the purely Japanese sort. The inference is strong that it is a translation from English for the convenience of foreign persons. The rendezvous teahouse, in any event, developed into an elegant restaurant to which geisha were summoned. Lest it seem that the music and dance of Edo declined absolutely as they declined in the six licensed quarters, the geisha districts ask to be looked at.

Edo had its "geisha of the town," distinguished from the geisha of the licensed quarters. Some of the "town" districts still present through Meiji were very old, going all the way back to the seventeenth century. Some of the most flourishing quarters, on the other hand, had their beginnings only in Meiji. A census of geisha, both those attached to the licensed quarters and those of the town variety, shows that they were concentrated, not surprisingly, in the Low City. Three-quarters were in four of the fifteen wards: Nihombashi, Kyōbashi, Shiba, and Asakusa. Geisha quarters were scattered over the flatlands, and in the hilly regions at least one, Kagurazaka, commenced operations at about the time Commodore Perry arrived. Other districts grew up in the High City of Meiji. They were neither as expensive nor as elegant, on the whole, as the best of the Low City districts.

The two great geisha districts of Meiji were Yanagibashi and Shimbashi. The Yanagibashi district, on the right bank of the Sumida south of Asakusa, was the Meiji quarter most esteemed by the connoisseur of old ways, and much reviled, as well, by those who thought that it was squandering its legacy. Narushima Ryūhoku's *New Chronicle of Yanagibashi* (*Ryūkyo Shinshi)* is a classic among satirical writings of the new age, as Ryūhoku himself was a classic son of Edo, one of the professionals. Ryūhoku, an "elegant sobriquet, suggests affinities with Yanagibashi. Literally, "North of the Willows," it derives from Yanagiwara or "Willowfield," the banks of the Kanda River near its confluence with the Sumida. Born in Asakusa in 1837, of a family of minor bureaucrats, Ryūhoku lived for some years to the north of Yanagiwara, and a slight distance to the west of Yanagibashi, "Willowbridge." Yanagibashi is thought, though without complete certainty, to have taken its name, as Ryūhoku took his sobriquet, from Yanagiwara.

He was in attendance upon two shoguns. Though he was for a time under house arrest because of critical remarks about persons in high places, he was given important assignments, such as seeking to keep the blue-eyed peril at bay. He served in a capacity roughly equivalent to that of Foreign Minister. With the collapse of the shogunate he was of course out of work and, like so many other men of the losing side, he went into journalism.

The first part of *New Chronicle of Yanagibashi* was written in 1859 and expanded in 1860. The Yanagibashi district had been in existence since the late eighteenth century, but its best age was in the last decades of Edo. The first section of the chronicle, starting with the premise (which must have had great immediacy in those years after the arrival of Perry) that we cannot be certain of the morrow, chronicles the standards and practices of the quarter in great detail. It is of a genre common and popular in late Edo, a display of connoisseurship that may have been helpful to the adolescent son of Edo embarking upon a career as a spendthrift, but may seem a touch self-satisfied and even pretentious to the outsider.

The work would probably be forgotten, save among specialists and bibliographers, had it not been for the advent of Meiji, a development not pleasing to experts on pleasure among the sons of Edo. Ryūhoku wrote a second installment in 1871. Both installments were published in 1874. A third installment, written in 1876, was banned, and Ryūhoku spent a time in jail because of it. The acerbity of the satire apparently passed limits. Only the introduction survives. Ryūhoku continued his journalistic career after his release, and died in 1884, securely established among the Edokko.

The chief interest of the *Chronicle* is in its account of what Meiji did to Yanagibashi. The first section tells us what it was like in the days of good taste and deportment. Then came the depredations of the new establishment. There are accounts of the violent and boorish ways of the new men, of parties at which people talk politics and ignore the geisha and her accomplishments, of speakers of English, of liberators and improvers. The geisha of the old school has no place in the new world, and the new variety is more interested in money than in art, and not easy to distinguish from the prostitute. She buys copies of the official gazette to determine how much her clients make, and has trouble identifying the father of her child. Thus has the corruption advanced, the decay of the decadent, even so early in Meiji. The son of Edo can only lament, and remember.

Ryūhoku's chronicle was extremely popular, although it is written in a highly sinified and ornate prose, remote from the tastes of our day. It is one of several works which were said to have forced up the price of paper. However valid his strictures may have been, Yanagibashi boasted famous and accomplished geisha through Meiji and beyond. Among the prosperous quarters of Meiji, it continued to be the one that had the closest ties with the old mercantile elite. Shimbashi and later Akasaka were the haunt of the new bureaucrat and businessman, while it was to Yanagibashi that the *danna* went, the Low City shopkeeper or wholesaler. (If he was really successful he probably no longer lived in the Low City, but that was another matter.) Yanagibashi was still the nearest of the quarters to Edo. It was favored by its situation, on the Sumida, just above Ryogoku Bridge, where that finest of summertime observances, the opening of the river, took place. Fukagawa, most storied of the quarters of late Edo, lay on the opposite bank. Only at Yanagibashi could a singer of amorous balladry be expected to come rowing his way up to a *machiai,* or a geisha and her customers to go boating among lanterns and samisen. The Sumida was in those days still fairly odorless.

Yanagibashi was the principal geisha quarter of very late Edo and early Meiji. With the rebuilding of Ginza, Shimbashi came to rival it. The new people, bureaucratic and entrepreneurial, formed the Shimbashi clientele.

A concentration of government buildings lay just to the west, and the big companies had their offices to the north. Shimbashi was among the places where the modern league of business and government, admired by some and reviled by others, took shape. It served the new establishment.

There had been "town geisha" in Shimbashi and Ginza from about the time of the Perry visit, and that watery region was a center for the *funaya-do* (see page 69). Shimbashi had its tradition then, but its great day began some twenty years after the Restoration. In late Meiji it was the quarter most favored by persons of money and power. The Shimbashi archetype was the country girl with energy and ambition, and a certain ruthlessness as well, in contrast to the Yanagibashi geisha, who inherited, or so it was said, the self-sacrificing pluck and verve of the Fukagawa geisha.

There were other geisha quarters, and they suffered vicissitudes. Old ones went, new ones came. The count of such quarters (as distinguished from the licensed quarters that deteriorated so grievously through Meiji) ran to almost thirty from Meiji into Taishō. Osanai Kaoru, in his novel about the banks of the big river, caught the last days of the big spenders from the Low City. There were still big spenders, but they were far less likely to be from regions near at hand. In what happened to the quarters, licensed and otherwise, is a measure of what was happening to the old mercantile culture in general. It was being scattered, dissipated.

The two disasters at the end of Meiji, the flood of 1910 and the fire of 1911, certainly worked great damage on the Low City. If one is intent upon finding a date for the death of Edo, one could do worse than follow Kafū and set it in the last years of Meiji.

It may be, however, that we are too easily disposed to see the death of a much-honored head of state as the end of an era. Events at the end of his reign or early in the next are taken as watersheds and given a prominence in cultural history that they might not otherwise have had. Kafū himself went on finding remnants of Edo to almost the end of his life, usually near the banks of the Sumida. His native High City interested him much less. There remained a difference between the two divisions of the city, for all the dilution and dispersal of Edo culture. He may have been wiser when he sought evidences of life than when he professed to know exactly the date of the demise of Edo.

The weakening of its old pleasures has been more pronounced in the last half of the Tokyo century than it was in the first. The son of Tokyo who had money to spend continued to do it as the son of Edo had, on the theater and closely allied pursuits. The Imperial Theater opened late in Meiji, of course, and then there were the movies, and Pavlova, but the pastimes that took his money continued to be largely traditional. If the Yoshiwara offered fewer of them on the eve of the fire than on the eve of the Restoration, and fewer after the fire than before, they were still to be had in places like Yanagibashi. Even today it is an insensitive person who, wandering the Low City of a long spring evening, does not come upon intimations of Edo.

It may be objected that the life of Edo and Meiji was not all pleasure. If a son of Edo spent himself into bankruptcy at the theater and in the pleasure quarters, his family did not really think that he had done the city and the family honor. The proper merchant had a severe code, and disinheritance was likely to come before bankruptcy. To insist upon pleasure as central to the culture of the city, and upon the decay of the way of pleasure as symptomatic of wider decay, may therefore be a distortion.

Yet a sense of evanescence hung over Edo in its finest day even as it hung over the Heian capital of a millennium before. The best things did not last. They were put together of an evening and vanished in the morning sunlight. The difference was that the Heian aristocrat had things his way. If he wished to fuss over perfumes and tints, there was no one to gainsay him. The merchant risked rebuke and even seizure, neither of them happy eventualities. His pleasures had to be more clandestine. He had his way only when he patronized actors and went to the pleasure quarters. This did not mean that he was a person whose taste was inferior to that of the Heian noble.

Meiji had its two sides. One cannot believe that Hasegawa Shigure dissembled when she described her father's exultation at the removal of the Edo stigma. Boundless new energies were liberated. To dwell upon inequity and repression is to miss this very important fact. Perhaps, facing braver and broader worlds, the son of Edo was ashamed that so much of his attention had gone into things so small. The big new things were often coarser things, however. The pleasure quarters presently lost their geisha, and the geisha presently lost their accomplishments.

The world of the geisha may have been a cruel one, as the world of the dedicated Kabuki actor was. No one should be sentenced to involuntary service in such a world. Yet it is a pity that people ceased submitting, and that no one was left to appreciate the sacrifice. The son of Edo knew a good geisha and an accomplished actor when he saw one. Less art and discrimination go into the making and appreciating of a Ginza bar girl and a first baseman.

Chapter 5

LOW CITY, HIGH CITY

The old Tōkaidō highway from Kyoto and Osaka ran through Ginza and crossed one last bridge, Kyōbashi, "Capital Bridge," before it came to its terminus at the Nihombashi bridge. The boundary between the two wards, Nihombashi and Kyōbashi, crossed the old highway at a point halfway between the two bridges. They have since been combined to make Chūō Ward, which means Central Ward, and indeed they were central to the Low City, the only two wards that lay completely in the Low City by any definition.

Seen together they have an agreeably solid and stable shape, from the Hama Palace at the southwest to Ryōgoku bridge at the northeast. When they are separated into the two Meiji wards, a difference becomes apparent. Because it keeps reaching out into lands reclaimed from the bay, the southern half, the Kyōbashi half (with Ginza inside it), has the more expansive look today. In early Meiji and in Edo it was the constricted half.

Both districts were largely cut off from the Sumida and the bay by bureaucratic and aristocratic establishments. Yet it would have been possible at the beginning of Meiji to walk the mile or so northeastwards across Nihombashi from the outer moat of the palace to the river and see no aristocratic walls. Only two or three hundred yards eastwards, across the Ginza district in southern Kyōbashi, one would have bumped into the first of them. Whether so planned or not, the Tokugawa prison in the center of Nihombashi was as far removed on all sides from the aristocracy as any point in the city. On land-use maps of late Edo, Nihombashi seems the only district where the townsman had room to breathe. By the end of Meiji the upper classes, whether of the new plutocracy or the old aristocracy, had almost completely departed the Low City, and so Nihombashi, solidly plebeian from the outer moat to the river, looks yet more expansive. So does Kyōbashi, filled out by reclamation and largely relieved of the aristocracy.

A new distinction took the place of the old. Nihombashi was rich and powerful (though the shogunate in theory granted no power to merchants), the heart of commercial Edo. There the rich merchant lived and there the big stores were, Mitsui and Daimaru and the like. Kyōbashi was poorer and more dependent on the patronage of the aristocracy, a place of lesser shopkeepers and of artisans.

This was the historical difference. In Meiji the difference was between the new and the old, the modern and the traditional. After the opening of the Tokyo-Yokohama railroad and its own rebuilding, Ginza, in southern Kyōbashi, emerged as the part of the city most sensitive and hospitable to foreign influences. Nihombashi remained the center of the mercantile city, though toward the end of Meiji Marunouchi had begun its rise.

It is a simplification. The northern part of Kyōbashi, beyond the Kyobashi Bridge, did not plunge into the new world as eagerly as Ginza to the south did, and Nihombashi was at once conservative and the site of the modern buildings most celebrated by ukiyo-e artists. The Hoteru-kan in Tsukiji, the southeastern part of Kyōbashi, was the earliest such building and certainly much celebrated, but it lasted a very short time. Blocks of brick, not individual buildings, were what the artists liked about Ginza. Nihombashi provided them with their best—and largest—instances of Civilization and Enlightenment.

The Mitsui Bank in Nihombashi

So it is a simplification. Yet if one had wished a century ago to wander about in search of what it was that Meiji was departing from, one would have been wise to choose Nihombashi. If the quest was for the city of the future, Kyōbashi would have been the better choice. At a somewhat later date one could have gone to the Rokumeikan, in Kōjimachi to the west, but that was an elite sort of place, not for everyone every day. One needed an invitation, and social ambitions would have helped too.

Much about the Meiji Ginza, and the Rokumeikan as well, is charming in retrospect. One would have loved being there, and one must lament that nothing at all survives, save those willow trees out by the Tama River. Much of the charm is in the fact that all is so utterly gone, and if to the person with antiquarian tendencies Ginza is today pleasanter than certain other centers of the advanced and the chic, that is because it is less advanced and chic than they. A century ago it would have been the most extremely chic of them all. Nihombashi on the contrary was the place with the coziest past, and, except for the parts nearest the palace and later the central railway station, the place most reluctant to part with that past. Today one must go farther to the north and east for suggestions of the old city that in Meiji were within a few minutes' walk of the foreign settlements.

At the proud forefront of Civilization and Enlightenment, the inner, affluent side of Nihombashi was later blessed with the new Bank of Japan, finished in 1896, and said to be the first genuinely foreign building of monumental proportions put up entirely by Japanese. Nihombashi was thus the financial center of the country, more modern, in a way, than Ginza even after Bricktown was built, because it was there and in government offices that the grand design for modernity was put together.

These modern structures, and the big department stores as well, were within a few paces of the Nihombashi bridge. Right there northeast of the bridge was also the fish market. It is striking in late Meiji how little of the modern and Western there is in a northeasterly direction from the bridge, off towards the Sumida. When, after the earthquake, Tanizaki rejected Tokyo and moved to the Kansai, he did it in a particularly pointed manner because he was rejecting his native Nihombashi, the very heart of the old city.

Nihombashi occupies the choice portion of the land earliest reclaimed from tidal marshes, the first Low City. It looks ample on Meiji maps, right there at the Otemon, the front gate of castle and palace. It is bounded on the north and east by water, and cut by the Nihombashi River,

The Nihombashi Fish Market, about 1918

The First National Bank in Nihombashi

the busiest canal in the city. All this water suggests commerce. It is less watery than the wards east of the river, but the latter look, on maps of the Meiji city, as if they were still in process of reclamation, while Nihombashi looks as if reclamation had been accomplished long ago, and the canals left from the marshes for good, productive reasons. Very little of Meiji remains in Nihombashi, and scarcely anything of Edo. Already in Meiji the wealthy, liberated from old class distinctions and what had in effect been a system of zoning, were moving to more elegant places. Already, too, Ginza and Marunouchi were rising to challenge its entrepreneurial supremacy. Yet there is something conservative about the air of the place. It has welcomed grand commercial and financial castles in the modern manner, but it has not welcomed glitter. It has never flashed as Ginza has, or been a playground like Asakusa.

In photographs looking eastwards from the Mitsukoshi Department Store, across the main north-south street, there is little on the eve of the earthquake that could not have survived (whether after all those fires it did or not) from Edo. There are modern buildings on the east side of the street, which was the great dividing line, and there is a financial cluster north of the Nihombashi River, where the Yasuda Bank, now the enormous Fuji, started growing; there too, at the juncture of the Nihombashi and the Sumida, the Bank of Japan had its first building, designed by Condor. For the most part, however, low roofs and wooden buildings in the grid pattern of the earliest years stretch on to the Sumida. It was among the parts of the Low City that had a smaller proportion of streets to buildings at the end of Meiji than at the beginning, and it looks that way. It is as if the snugness of Edo were still present, even though one knows that it could not have been. Vast numbers of country people had moved in and people like the Mitsuis had moved out, and the diaspora of the children of Edo (made so much of by people like Tanuaki) was well underway. Still the sense one has of conservatism is not mistaken.

The western part of Nihombashi did not begin going really modern until fairly late in Meiji. On the whole, Nihombashi was slower to change than Ginza or Marunouchi. The Nihombashi River was still at the end of Meiji lined by the godowns, some of them converted into dwellings, that had always been a symbol of the district and its mercantile prosperity. The Tanizaki family lived for a time in a godown. E. S. Morse wrote enthusiastically of converted godowns, which were doubtless ingenious, but other accounts inform us that they were as damp and badly aired as ever the Ginza bricktown was.

A row of merchant houses in Nihombashi, about 1919

The aristocracy did not occupy much of old Nihombashi, and neither did the religions. There were shrines, though what was to become the most famous and popular of them, the Suitengū, Shrine of the Water God, was moved from another part of the city only in early Meiji. There were a few Buddhist temples, most of them founded in Meiji, half of them on the site of the old Tokugawa prison, dismantled in 1875. Initially they had a propitiatory function.

Nihombashi was not without pleasures, but moderate about them, perhaps in this regard nearer the Tokugawa ideal than Asakusa or Ginza. Not since the removal of the Yoshiwara to the northern paddies after the great fire of 1657 (the occasion also for moving most Nihombashi temples to the paddies) had Nihombashi provided the more elaborate and expensive of pastimes. Nevertheless, it was in the Hamachō geisha quarter, near the river in Nihombashi, that O-ume romantically murdered Minekichi. Hamachō was a modest quarter compared to Yanagibashi in Asakusa Ward to the north and Shimbashi to the south. Of the major theaters in the city today, the Meijiza in Nihombashi has the longest history. Probably at no time, except perhaps briefly when rivals were rebuilding from fires, could it have been described as the premier theater of the city. Yet it has survived, eminent but not supreme. This seems appropriate to conservative, steady Nihombashi.

The Mitsui Bank in Nihombashi, by Kiyōchika

The Mitsui Bank and the First National Bank of early Meiji were both torn down at about the time the new Bank of Japan was going up. Printmakers contrived to show the two buildings in isolation, or perhaps to imagine what they would have been like had it been possible to view them in isolation. Photographers could not or did not achieve the same effect. There can have been nothing like them in Edo, except perhaps, in a very vague way, the castle keep. Yet they do not look out of place. They are as if imagined by someone who had never actually seen a Western building (in fact the builder of both had studied in Yokohama), and whose idea of the Western was the traditional made bigger and showier.

There is nothing Japanese about the Bank of Japan. It is a pleasing enough building, but it is obviously the creation of someone who had studied Western architecture well and did not presume to have ideas of his own. Very much the same can be said of the Mitsui buildings that went up on or near the site of the early Meiji bank. Only the Bank of Japan and some bridges—one of them the main Nihombashi Bridge itself and one of them, the Tokiwa, the oldest stone bridge in the city—survive from Meiji. The brick Mitsui buildings and the new stone building of the First National Bank have long since gone the way of their more fanciful predecessors.

The early buildings would obviously not have lent themselves to the purposes of increasingly monstrous economic miracles. Yet both institutions, the Mitsui Bank and the Daiichi Kangyō Bank, as it is now, are so hugely rich that they could have set aside their first sallies into Western design as museums, and so enabled us to see for ourselves something that cannot be quite the same in photographs and prints—something confused, perhaps, but also lovable, like a child trying to look regal in clothes brought down from the attic. Of course, since most of Nihombashi was lost in 1923, it is likely that the two buildings would have vanished then even if the mercies of the banks had been more tender.

So Nihombashi did not stand apart from all the Meiji changes. There were changes that were still invisible. Nihombashi may to this day perhaps be called the financial center of the city and the land, for it has the Bank of Japan and the stock exchange; but big management has for the most part moved elsewhere. Neither of the two banks that so delighted the printmakers has its main offices in Nihombashi. The beginnings of the shift may be traced to late Meiji. Rival centers were growing, to the south and west; the big movements in the modern city have consistently been to the south and west.

The novelist Tayama Katai came to Tokyo in 1881 as a boy of ten, and was apprenticed to a publishing house in Nihombashi. More than half a century later he mused upon the contrast between the old Nihombashi and Ginza, and between the parts of Nihombashi, bustling commerce on the one hand and stagnation on the other.

> There was not a day when I did not cross the Nihombashi and Kyōbashi bridges. A dank, gloomy Nihombashi main street, lined mostly with earthen walls, as against the bricks of Ginza, across Kyōbashi. Entaro horse-drawn omnibuses sped past, splashing mud and sending forth trumpet calls. On the right side a short distance north of the Nihombashi Bridge...two or three doors from each other, were two large bookstores, the Suwaraya and the Yamashiroya, their large, rectangular shop signs dignified and venerable, of a sort that one sees in Edo illustrations. Yet what gloomy, deserted stores they were! Two or three clerks in Japanese dress would always be sitting there, in abject boredom, and I did not once see a customer come in to buy a book. The contrast with the house on the corner, the Echigoya, forerunner of the Mitsukoshi, could not have been more complete. One can still find the latter, I believe, in old pictures, a one-story building with a long veranda, livening the district with an incessant shouting. It sounded rather like *"Owai, owai."* Customers were seated in rows, and the noise emerged from clerks ordering apprentices to get wares from the godown. Not only the Echigoya: on a corner towards the north and east was the yet larger Daimaru, and from it came that same *"Owai, owai"*...

Ginza was then in the new style, with what were called its streets
of brick, but from Kyōbashi to Nihombashi and on to Spectacle Bridge
there was scarcely a building in the Western style…

I was in Peking some years ago, and the crowding and confusion
outside the Cheng-yang Gate—a pack of little shops and stalls, by-
standers munching happily away at this and that—reminded me of
early Meiji. It was indeed no different from the stir and bustle, in
those days, at the approaches to the Nihombashi Bridge.

All up and down the main Nihombashi street there were shops
with displays of polychrome woodcuts…

Off towards Asakusa were shops with displays of something approaching erotica. I was somewhat surprised—no, I should say that
I would stand on and on, fascinated, as if, in that day when there
were no magazines worthy of the name, I were gazing at life itself,
and the secrets deep within it. But I doubt that the approaches to the
Nihombashi Bridge of Edo were in such disorder. In the confusion
something still remained of very early Meiji. I grow nostalgic for it,
that air of the degenerate.

Nihombashi was wealthy, and it was poor and crowded. It had its
gloomy back streets, lined by windowless godowns, and it had its entertainment quarter, off towards the river, on land once occupied by the aristocracy. Land in Nihombashi was, or so the popular image had it, worth
its volume in gold, but for a decent garden in any of the lands reclaimed
by the shogunate one had to import loam from the hills. Great care and
expense went into little gardens squeezed in among the godowns. Besides
gardeners, there were dealers in earth—not land but *earth*—brought in to
make mossy gardens. By late Meiji the very wealthy had left, but it was still
not uncommon for the middle ranks of the mercantile class to have houses
and gardens in Nihombashi even if they owned land in the High City.

Tanizaki wrote about the dark back streets of eastern Nihombashi,
only a short walk from the entertainment districts. If he remarked upon
the contrast with Ginza on the south, Hasegawa Shigure contrasted it
with Kanda, on the north. She had an aunt in Kanda, and it was there
that she had glimpses of the West not to be had in Nihombashi.

She took me to see the Nikolai Cathedral, then under construction.
It was when I stayed with her that I first heard the sound of violin
and piano and orchestra. In our part of the Low City such sounds and
such instruments were quite unknown. So it was that I first caught
the scent of the West. Kanda was where the students had their dens,
where the intelligentsia, as we would call it today, assembled.

Katai thought the confusion of Nihombashi unlike Edo. The reminiscences of Shigure, who was born in Nihombashi in 1879, make it sound very much like Edo as it has remained in art and fiction.

> On a late summer evening the breeze would come from the river as the tide rose. Hair washed and drying, bare feet, paper lanterns, platforms for taking the evening cool, salty cherry-blossom tea—all up and down the streets, under the stars, was the evening social, not to be savored by the rich ones and the aristocrats. It was easier and freer than the gathering in the bathhouse. The rows of houses were the background and the streets were the gathering place. If a policeman happened to be living in one of the row houses, he would become a human being once more, and join the assembly, hairy chest bare, kimono tucked up, a fan of tanned paper in his hand. He would not reprove the housewife if too much of her was exposed, and took it as a matter of course that the man next door should be out wearing nothing but a loincloth…
>
> Shinnai balladry would come, and *Gidayū*, and koto and samisen together. They were not badly done, for they had a knowledgeable audience. Strange, wonderful, distant strains would emerge from the gardens of the teahouses… The samisen and the koto duos were mostly played by old women, most of them from the old Tokugawa bureaucratic class.
>
> Just as in the lumberyards of Fukagawa no native was until the earthquake to be seen wearing a hat, so too it was in my part of Nihombashi. Down to the turn of the century a hat was a rare sight. The only hatted ones were men of affluence in party dress.

Photographs from late Meiji of eastern Nihombashi give an impression of changelessness, low-tiled roofs stretching on and on, but it is perhaps somewhat misleading. Edo must have been even thus, one thinks, and one forgets that the low roofs stretched over a wider expanse at the end of Meiji than at the end of Edo. The abodes of the less affluent stretched now all across Nihombashi to the river, as they had not in Edo. Such places of pleasure as Nihombashi did have—the quarter where Minekichi got stabbed, the shrine that had the liveliest feast days—stood mostly on land once occupied by the aristocracy. The departure of the aristocracy was not in any case the loss that the departure of the wealthy merchant class was. Though the pleasure quarters had been heavily dependent on the furtive patronage of the aristocracy, it had not provided open patronage, and it had remained aloof from the city around it. So perhaps an irony emerges: the changes that occurred in eastern

Nihombashi Bridge looking east, 1911

Nihombashi through Meiji may have been of a reactionary nature. The area may have been more like the Low City of Edo at the end of Meiji than at the beginning.

Nihombashi was proud of itself, in a quiet, dignified sort of way. The young Tanizaki was infatuated with the West and insisted upon rejection of the Japanese tradition, but he never let us forget that he was from Nihombashi. Perhaps more in Meiji than in Tokugawa it was the place to which all roads led—for a powerless court in Kyoto still then had powerful symbolic import.

Pride in self commonly brings (or perhaps it arises from) conservatism. In certain respects Nihombashi, especially its western reaches, was every bit as high-collar, as dedicated to Civilization and Enlightenment, as Ginza. Yet it was far from as ready to throw away everything in pursuit of the new and imported. If Nihombashi and Ginza represent the two sides of Meiji, conservative and madly innovative, Nihombashi by itself can be seen as representative of contradictions that were not after all contradictions. Now as in the seventh and eighth centuries, when China came flooding in, innovation is tradition.

It has continued to be thus, even down to our day. The last Meiji building in Ginza has just been demolished. The Bank of Japan yet stands. Nihombashi itself—which is to say, the corps of its residents—has probably had less to do with the preservation of the latter than the Ginza spirit has had to do with the destruction of the former. Yet there is fitness in this state of affairs. Nihombashi did not, like the Shinagawa licensed quarter, explicitly reject change; but perhaps it was the more genuinely conservative of the two.

On the eve of the earthquake there were probably more considerable expanses of Edo in Nihombashi than anywhere else in the city. Even today, when one has to hunt long for a low frame building of the old sort, Nihombashi looks far less like New York than do Ginza and Shinjuku. As a summer twilight gives way to darkness in eastern Nihombashi, one can still sense the sweet melancholy that Kafū so loved, and observe the communal cheerfulness that Shigure described so well.

Kyōbashi was a place of easier enthusiasms. On the north it merged with Nihombashi. To the south of the "Capital Bridge" from which it took its name, it was narrower and poorer, a district of artisans, for the most part, where it was a plebeian district at all. Considerably under half of the lands south of the bridge and the canal which it crossed belonged to the townsman.

In Meiji the Ginza district, in the southern part of Kyōbashi, changed abruptly. Some might have said that it ran to extremes as did no other part of the city. The original Ginza was the "Silver Seat" of the shogunate, one of its mints, moved from Shizuoka to the northern part of what is now Ginza early in the Tokugawa Period, and moved once more, to Nihombashi, in 1800. The name stayed behind, designating roughly the northern half of what is now Ginza. It may be used to refer to the lands lying between the Kyōbashi Bridge on the north and the Shimbashi Bridge on the south. (The ward extended yet further north.) In this sense it was the place where the West entered most tumultuously.

Kyōbashi was a very watery place, wateriest of the fifteen wards, save Fukagawa east of the river, where the transport, storage, and treatment of the city's lumber supply required a network of pools and canals. The Ginza district was entirely surrounded by water, and the abundance of canals to the east made the Kyōbashi coast the obvious place for storing unassimilable alien persons. They could be isolated from the populace, and vice versa, by water. Virtually all of the canals are now gone.

The Tōkaidō of the shoguns was the main north-south street in Meiji, and the main showplace of the new Bricktown. It still is the main Ginza street. In other respects Ginza has shifted.

Business and fun tended in a southerly direction when the railroad started bringing large numbers of people in from the south. If there was a main east-west street in this watery region it was the one the shogun took from the castle to his bayside villa, the Hama Palace of Meiji. It is now called Miyukidōri, "Street of the Royal Progress," because the emperor used it for visits to the naval college and the Hama Palace. Presently a street was put through directly eastwards from the southern arc of the inner palace moat, somewhat to the north of the Street of the Royal Progress. When Ginza commenced moving north again, with the extension of the railroad to the present central station, the crossing of the two, the old Tōkaidō and the street east from the inner moat, became the center of Ginza, and of the city. This was a gradual development, somewhat apparent in late Meiji, but not completely so, perhaps, until Taishō. Though the matter is clouded by the enormous growth of centers to the west, it might be said that the main Ginza crossing is still the center of the city. There was a span of decades, from late Meiji or from Taishō, when almost anyone, asked to identify the very center, would have said Ginza, and, more specifically, the main Ginza crossing.

Both the fire and the opening of the railroad occurred in 1872. The two of them provided the occasion for the great change, which was not as quick in coming as might have been expected. Bricktown, parts of it ready for occupancy by 1874, was too utterly new. It was the rage among sightseers, but not many wanted to stay on and run the risk of turning, as rumor had it, all blue and bloated, like a corpse from drowning. (There were other rumors, too, emphasizing, not unreasonably, the poor ventilation and the dampness.) In the early eighties, midway through the Meiji Period, the new Ginza really came to life. In 1882 horse-trolley service began on the main street, northwards through Nihombashi, with later extension to Asakusa. That same year there were arc lights, turning Ginza into an evening place. The age of Gimbura, a great Taishō institution, had begun. *Gimbura* is a contraction of *Ginza* and *burabura,* an adverb which indicates aimless wandering, or wandering which has as its only aim the chance pleasure that may lie along the way. It originally referred to the activities of the young Ginza vagrant, to be seen there at all hours. The emergence of the pursuit as something for all young people, whether good-for-nothing or not, came at about the time of the First World War.

Ginza began prospering by day as well. What was known as "the Kyōbashi mood" contrasted with the Nihombashi mood. One characterization of the contrast held Nihombashi to be for the child of Edo, Ginza for the child of Tokyo. In a later age it might have been said that Nihombashi still had something for the child of Meiji, while Ginza was for the child of Taishō, or Shōwa. Nihombashi contains relics of Meiji, and nothing at all remains, no brick upon another, of the Ginza Bricktown. The last bit of Meiji on the main Ginza street, completed as that reign was giving way to Taishō, has now been torn down. The Ginza of Meiji is commonly called a place of the *narikin*. A *narikin* is a minor piece in Oriental chess that is suddenly converted into a piece of great power. It here refers to the *nouveau riche*. As pejorative in Japanese as it is in French, the expression contrasts the entrepreneurs of Ginza with such persons as the Mitsui of Nihombashi.

The new people of Ginza were not such huge successes as the Mitsui, or the Iwasaki, with their Mitsubishi Meadow, but they were perhaps more interesting. Their stories have in them more of Meiji venturesomeness and bravery, and help to dispel the notion, propagated by Tanizaki Junichirō among others, that the children of Edo were lost in the bustle and enterprise of the new day.

All up and down Ginza were Horatio Algers, and possibly the most interesting of them was very much a son of Edo. Hattori Kintarō, founder of the Seiko Watch Company, was born to the east of the Ginza district proper, the son of a curio dealer, and apprenticed to a hardware store in the southern part of what is now Ginza. Across the street was a watch shop, in business before the Restoration, which he found more interesting than hardware. Refused apprenticeship there, he became apprenticed instead to a watch dealer in Nihombashi. He also frequented the foreign shops in Yokohama, and presently set up his own business, a very humble one, a street stall in fact. (Ginza had street stalls until after the Second World War.) The watch was among the symbols of Civilization and Enlightenment. An enormous watch is the mark of the Westernized dandy in satirical Meiji prints. Hattori had come upon a good thing, but only remarkable acumen and industry thrust him ahead of enterprises already well established. Within a few years he had accumulated enough capital to open a retailing and repair business of a more solidly sheltered sort, at the old family place east of Ginza. In 1885, when he was still in his twenties, he bought a building at what was to become the main Ginza crossing, the offices of a newspaper going out of business. The Hattori clock tower, in various incarnations, has been the accepted symbol of Ginza ever since. The same year he built the factory east of the river that was to grow into one of the largest watch manufacturers in the world.

It is not a story with its beginnings in rags, exactly, for he came from a respectable family of Low City shopkeepers. All the same, there is in it the essence of Ginza, spread out before the railway terminal that was the place of ingress and egress for all the new worlds of Meiji, and their products, such as watches, which no high-collar person of Meiji could be without. If the Rokumeikan, a few hundred yards west of Ginza, was the place where the upper class was seeking to make political profit from cosmopolitanism, the Hattori tower, there where the two trolley lines were to cross, marked the center of the world for mercantile adventuring.

Other instances of enterprise and novelty abounded. Shiseidō, the largest and most famous manufacturer of Western cosmetics, had its start in a Ginza pharmacy just after the great fire. The founder had been a naval pharmacist. He experimented with many novel things—soap, toothpaste, ice cream—before turning to the task, as his advertising had it, of taking the muddiness from the skin of the nation. His choice of a name for his innovative enterprise contained the Meiji spirit. It is a variant upon a phrase found in one of the oldest Chinese classics, signifying the innate essence of manifold phenomena. Today a person with such a line for sale would be more likely, if he wished a loan word, to choose a French or English one.

It was not only the great houses in Nihombashi that profited from an alliance with the bureaucracy. In early Meiji there were in Kyōbashi Ward two confectioneries with the name Fūgetsudō, one in what is now Ginza, the other north of the Kyōbashi Bridge. It was a model contest between the new and the old. The northern one sold traditional sweets, the southern one cookies and cakes of the Western kind. During the Sino-Japanese War the latter received a huge order for hardtack, upwards of sixty tons. The traditional Fūgetsudō admitted defeat, and the innovative Fūgetsudō, House of the Wind and the Moon, became the most famous confectioner in the city. The most successful of early bakeries, also a Ginza enterprise, had General Nogi among its patrons, and he helped bring it huge profits during his war, the Russo-Japanese War.

July 4, 1899, was a day to remember for several reasons, one of them being the end of the "unequal treaties," another the opening of the first beer hall in the land, near the Shimbashi end of Ginza. Very late in Meiji, Ginza pioneered in another institution, one that was to become a symbol of Taishō. This was the "café," forerunner of the expensive Ginza bar. Elegant and alluring female company came with the price of one's coffee, or whatever. The Plantain was the first of them, founded in 1911 not far from the Ebisu beer hall, at the south end of Ginza. The region had from early Meiji contained numerous "dubious houses" and small eating and drinking places, mixed in among more expensive geisha establishments. The Plantain was still there in 1945, when it was torn down in belated attempts to prepare firebreaks. Shortly after it opened it began to have competition. The still more famous Lion occupied a corner of the main Ginza crossing, and had among its regular customers Nagai Kafū, the most gifted chronicler of the enterprising if somewhat trying life of the café lady. One of them tried to blackmail him.

Ginza had the first gentlemen's social club, the Kōjunsha, founded in 1880. The name, a neologism compounded of elements suggesting conviviality and sincere, open discussion, was coined by Fukuzawa Yukichi, a great coiner of new words and the most important publicist for Westernization. He was the founder of Keiō University and the builder of its elocution hall, towards that same end. Japanese must learn public speaking, argued Fukuzawa, and they must also become capable of casual, gentlemanly converse. The Kōjunsha was Fukuzawa's idea, and the

The lobby of the Kōjunsha

money for it was provided by friends. It opened near Shimbashi in 1880 and is still there, just a hundred years old, in a building put up after the earthquake and already a period piece in the newness of Ginza.

The emperor himself was stumped by one enterprising Ginza merchant. On his way to Ueno in 1889 to open an industrial exposition, he saw in the northern part of Ginza a shop sign which he could not read. The name of the owner was clear enough, but the article purveyed was not, and the emperor was a man well educated in the classics. A courtier was sent to make inquiry. He came back with the information that the commodity in question was the briefcase. The shopkeeper had put together the characters for "leather" and "parcel," and assigned them a pronunciation recently borrowed from China and indicating a container. Awed by the royal inquiry, the shopkeeper inserted a phonetic guide. The shop sign became famous, and the word and the character entered the language and have stayed there. The sign was burned in 1923.

Some of the most famous modern educational institutions had their beginnings in the southern part of Kyōbashi Ward. The first naval college occupied a site near the foreign settlement. The commercial college that became Hitotsubashi University was founded in 1875 by Mori Arinori, most famous of Meiji education ministers, assassinated for his Westernizing ways on the day in 1889 when the Meiji constitution went into effect. Fukuzawa drafted the statement of purpose, a somewhat prophetic one: the coming test of strength would be mercantile, and victory could not be expected without a knowledge of the rules. His disciples learned the rules very well. Opened as Mori's private school in very modest quarters, the second floor of a purveyor of fish condiments, the college moved in 1876 to Kobikichō, east of Ginza proper. It was taken over by the city, and in 1885 by the Ministry of Education, which moved it to Kanda.

The middle school and girls' school that were the forerunners of Rikkyō or St. Paul's University had their origins in the Tsukiji foreign settlement, and by the end of Meiji had not moved far away. The origins of another famous missionary school, the Aoyama Gakuin, also lay in the foreign settlement of early Meiji, but by the end of Meiji it had moved into the southwestern suburbs.

Ginza did not, in this regard, stay for long at the forefront of Civilization and Enlightenment. The foreign settlement was gone as a legal entity by the end of Meiji, though foreigners continued to live and preach and teach there until the earthquake; but the missionary schools were moving elsewhere and all would soon be gone, leaving only the naval college as a place of higher education.

*   *   *

In another field of modern cultural endeavor Ginza quickly began to acquire a preeminence which it still in some measure maintains. Though not on the whole very popular, the Ginza brick buildings early caught the fancy of journalists. The newspaper is a modern institution, with a slight suggestion of ancestry in the "tile-print" broadsheets of Edo. The first daily newspaper in Japan was founded in 1870, moving from Yokohama to Ginza in 1879. Originally called the *Yokohama Mainichi* (the last half of the name meaning "daily"), it became the *Tokyo Mainichi* in 1906, after several changes of name between. It is not to be confused with the big *Mainichi* of today, which had a different name in Meiji, and was, with the *Asahi,* an intruder from Osaka.

The earliest Ginza newspaper—it occupied the site of the Hattori clock tower—seems to have been founded in the Tsukiji foreign settlement by an Englishman, J. R. Black. He was somewhat deceitfully treated by the government, which wished to purge Japanese-language journalism of foreigners. Offered a government job, he accepted it, and as soon as he was safely severed from his newspaper, the job was taken away. Late in Meiji an English performer in the variety halls had a certain vogue. He was the son of J. R. Black. The vogue did not last, and the son died in obscurity shortly after the earthquake.

In mid-Meiji, the Ginza contained as many as thirty newspaper offices. It was at this point that Osaka enterprise moved in, and, by its aggressive methods, reduced competition. At the end of Meiji, there were fewer papers in the city and in Ginza than there had been two or three decades before. Two of the big three had their origins in Osaka, and all three were, at the end of Meiji, in Ginza. The *Yomiuri,* the only native of Tokyo among the three, stayed longest in Ginza, and now it too is gone. Large numbers of regional newspapers still have Ginza offices, but middle and late Meiji was the great day for Ginza journalism.

Nihombashi may have had the most romantic of Meiji murders, but Ginza had an equally interesting one, of a curiously old-fashioned sort. What is believed to have been the last instance of the classical vendetta reached its denouement just north of the old Shimbashi station in 1880. The assassin, who avenged the death of his parents, was of military origins, his family having owed fealty to a branch of the great Kuroda family of Fukuoka. His parents were killed during the Restoration disturbances— victims, it seems, of clan politics. No attempt was made to punish their murderer; he was in fact treated well by his lord and then by the Meiji government, under which he made a successful career as a judge. After duty in the provinces he was assigned to the Tokyo Higher Court. The son of the murdered couple came up from Kyushu and spent his days stalking. On the chosen day, having failed to come upon his prey outside the court chambers, the vengeful son proceeded to the Kutoda house in what is now Ginza, and made polite inquiry as to the judge's whereabouts. The unhappy man chanced upon the scene and was stabbed to death. The son received a sentence of life imprisonment but was released in 1892, whereupon he went home to Kyushu to live out his days. Though vendettas had been frowned on by the old regime and were considered quite inappropriate to Civilization and Enlightenment, a certain admiration for this sturdy fidelity to old ways may account for the leniency shown in this instance. The Kuroda family moved away from Kyōbashi two years later and took up residence in the High City, not far from Keiō University. They would doubtless have left soon enough even if the incident had not sullied the old residence. It was the pattern. The area is today thrivingly commercial.

The prominence of the Ginza district in the theater was partly a result of things that happened in Meiji, when both the Shintomiza and the Kubukiza went up a few paces east of Ginza proper. It had an earlier theatrical tradition, from the very early years of the shogunate down to the Tempō edicts of the 1840s. It was the setting for a most delicious bit of theatrical impropriety: A lady in the service of the mother of the seventh shogun fell madly in love with an actor. Pretending to do her Confucian duty in visits to the Tokugawa tombs, she arranged assignations. When it all came out, the actor and the theater manager were exiled to a remote island, and the theater closed. The lady was sent off into the mountains of central Japan. One may still view the melodrama on the Kabuki stage.

Many are the delights in reading of Meiji Ginza. The ardor with which it pursued the West is infectious, and the mercantile adventuring of which it was the center has brought the land the affluence and the prestige that military adventuring failed to do. Both kinds of adventuring inform us persuasively that in modern Japan the realm of action has been more interesting than that of contemplation. Of the two the mercantile kind has certainly been the more effective and probably it has been the more interesting as well. Doubt and equivocation have characterized the realm of thought, whose obsessive themes are alienation and the quest for identity, not so very different from the sort of thing that exercises the modern intellectual the world over. It also dwells at great length on helplessness, the inability of tiny, isolated Japan to survive on its own resources and devices. Meanwhile the manufacturer and the salesman, by no means helpless, have been doing something genuinely extraordinary. The beginning of the way that has brought us to semiconductors and robots is in Meiji Ginza. Gimbura beneath the neon lights of a spring or summer evening is still such a pleasure that one looks nostalgically back to the day when Ginza was the undisputed center of the city and of the land. Yet Ginza and Gimbura have taken on a patina. There are noisier and more generously amplified entertainment and shopping centers to the south and west, and it is to them that the young are inclined to swarm. Gimbura has the look of a slightly earlier time. When it was all the rage, the person who now feels nostalgia for the Ginza of old might well have been drawn more strongly to conservative Nihombashi, where it was still possible to wander in the Edo twilight.

Had one gone about asking townsmen at the beginning of Meiji to define the northern limits of the Low City, there would probably have been a difference of opinion. Some would have said that it ended at the Kanda River or slightly beyond, and so included only Nihombashi, the flat part of Kanda, and perhaps a bit more. Others might have been more generous, and extended it to include the merchant quarters around the Asakusa Kannon Temple and below the Tokugawa tombs at Ueno. These last were essentially islands, however, cut off from the main Low City by aristocratic and bureaucratic lands.

At the end of Meiji everyone would have included Asakusa and Shitaya wards, the latter incorporating Ueno. These wards had filled up and the upper classes had almost vanished, along with many of the temples and cemeteries. Except for a few remaining paddy lands, the Low City reached to the city limits, and in some places spilled beyond.

"The temple of Kuanon at Asakusa is to Tōkiō what St. Paul's is to London, or Nôtre Dame to Paris," said W. E. Griffis. It was a place that fascinated most foreigners, even Isabella Bird, who did not for the most part waver in her determination to find unbeaten tracks. Griffis was right, though Asakusa was more than a religious center—or rather it was a Japanese sort of religious center, one which welcomed pleasure to the sacred precincts.

Griffis's description was perhaps more telling than he realized. "At the north end are ranged the archery galleries, also presided over by pretty black-eyed Dianas, in paint, powder, and shining coiffure. They bring you tea, smile, talk nonsense, and giggle; smoke their long pipes with

tiny bowls full of mild, fine-cut tobacco; puff out the long white whiffs
from their flat-bridged noses; wipe the brass mouth-piece, and offer it to
you; and then ask you leading and very personal questions without blush-
ing… Full grown, able-bodied men are the chief patrons of these places
of pleasure, and many can find amusement for hours at such play."

The description suggests "places of pleasure" in a more specific sense,
and indeed that is what they were. The back rooms were for prostitution—right there in the yard (the back yard, but still the yard) of the
great temple. More than one early foreign visitor remarked, with a certain not unpleasant confusion, upon a very large painting of a courtesan
which hung in the main hall, but no one seems to have noted the true
nature of the archery stalls.

Griffis's description extends over more than a chapter of his memoirs.
It is lively and it is sad. Today some tiny outbuildings and a stone bridge
survive from Edo, and nothing else, save a few perdurable trees. The melancholy derives not only from physical change; if most of the buildings
are gone, so too is most of the life. The main buildings, which had survived the earthquake, were lost in 1945. Asakusa continued even so to be
a pleasure center. Then, gradually, people stopped coming. Troops of rustic pilgrims still visit the temple, but the urban crowds, and especially the
young, go elsewhere. Asakusa was too confident. With its Kannon and its
Yoshiwara, it had, so it thought, no need of railroads, and it was wrong.

Asakusa and Shitaya, from what is now Ueno Park to the Sumida,
were a part of the zone of temples and cemeteries extending in a great
sweep around the Tokugawa city. One could have walked from where
the northernmost platforms of Ueno Station now stand nearly to the
river, passing scarcely anything but temples. Plebeian houses, waiting to
be flooded every two or three years, lined the river bank itself. (The riverside park of our own day was laid out after the earthquake.) Edo was
a zoned city, and among the zones was one for the dead. Not wanting
them too near at hand, the shogunate established a ring of necropoles at
the city limits. Many temples remained at the end of Meiji and a scattering remains today, making Asakusa and Shitaya the most rewarding part
of the city for the fancier of tombstones and epitaphs. A late-Meiji guide
to the city lists 132 temples in Asakusa Ward and 86 in Shitaya. Temple
lands shrank greatly, however, as the region became a part of the main
Low City, and the pressure on lands near the center of the city led to the
closing and removal of cemeteries.

Along towards mid-Meiji the metropolitan government embarked
upon the creation of an early version of the public mall or shopping center.

On land that had been occupied chiefly by chapels in attendance upon the Kannon, the city built two rows of brick shops, forming a lane from the horse trolley to the south or main front of the grand hall. The city retained ownership and rented the shops. The original buildings were casualties of the earthquake, but the prospect today is similar to that of 1885, when construction was finished. It is not displeasing. Though no longer Meiji it rather looks it, and is perhaps somewhat reminiscent as well of the Ginza Bricktown. From late Meiji into Taishō there had grown up what sons of Edo called the new Asakusa, generally to the south and west of the Kannon. Then came the earthquake, to destroy almost everything save the Kannon itself, and afterwards, those same sons inform us, the new quite took over.

"The word Asakusa," said Akutagawa, who grew up in Honjo, across the river, "first calls to mind the vermilion hall of the temple—or the complex centered upon the hall, with the flanking pagoda and gate. We may be thankful that they came through the recent earthquake and fire. Now, as always at this season, droves of pigeons will be describing a great circle around the bright gold of the gingko, with that great screen of vermilion spread out behind it. Then there comes to mind the lake and the little pleasure stalls, all of them reduced to cinders after the earthquake. The third Asakusa is a modest part of the old Low City. Hanakawado, Sanya, Komagata, Kuramae—and several other districts would do as well. Tiled roofs after a rain, unlighted votive lanterns, pots of morning glories, now withered. This too, all of it, was left a charred waste."

The pleasure stalls, said Kubota Mantarō, "are the heart of the new Asakusa, Asakusa as it now will be":

> This Asakusa took the recent disaster in its stride...
> But the other, the old Asakusa.
> Let the reader come with me—it will not take long—to the top of Matsuchi Hill... We will look northwards through the trees, towards the Sanya Canal. The color of the stagnant water, now as long ago, is like blackened teeth; but how are we to describe the emptiness that stretches on beyond the canal and the cemetery just to the north, and on through mists to the fuel tanks of Senjū, under a gray sky? The little bell tower of the Keiyōji Temple, a curious survivor, and the glowing branches of the gingkos, and the Sanya Elementary School, hastily rebuilt, and nothing else, all the way north, to catch the eye.
> Let us go down the hill and cross Imado Bridge... No suggestion remains of the old air, the old fragrance, not the earthen godown remembered from long ago, not the darkly spiked wooden fence, not

the willow at the corner of the restaurant. In front of the new shacks
... a wanton profusion of hollyhocks and cosmos and black-eyed su-
sans, in a dreariness quite unchanged since the earthquake.

It is the common view, and in the years just after the earthquake,
when these melancholy impressions were set down, almost anyone would
have thought that the old Asakusa was gone forever, and that "the new
Asakusa," represented by the flashiness of the park and its entertainments, had emerged dominant. In recent years there has been a reversal.
The life of the park has been drained away by the new entertainment
centers elsewhere, and to the north and east of the temple are still to be
found little pockets answering well to Akutagawa's description of the old
Asakusa. Not having flourished, certain back streets had no very striking
eminence to descend from.

The novelist Kawabata Yasunari used to say that, though he found
abundant sadness in the culture of the Orient, he had never come upon
the bleakness that he sensed in the West. Doubtless he spoke the truth.
Tanizaki remarked upon the diaspora to the suburbs and beyond of the
children of the Low City. He too spoke the truth. Not many residents
of Asakusa were born there, and still fewer can claim grandparents who
were born there. One may be sad that life has departed the place, but
one does not reject Asakusa. There is still something down-to-earth and
carpe-diem about it that is not to be found in the humming centers of
the High City, or in the stylish, affluent suburbs.

Shitaya and Kanda wards, to the west of Asakusa, were partly flat and
partly hilly—partly of the Low City and partly of the High. The Shitaya Ward of Meiji contained both the old Shitaya, "the valley below,"
and Ueno, "the upland stretches." Lowland Shitaya, generally south and
east of "the mountain," Ueno Park, was almost completely destroyed in
the fires of 1923. The hilly regions of the park and beyond were spared.
At the end of Edo the merchant and artisan classes possessed very little
of even the flat portion of Shitaya—a cluster south of the great Kaneiji
Temple, now the park, a corridor leading south along the main street
to Kanda and Nihombashi, and little more. Almost everything else belonged to the aristocracy and the bureaucracy. Like the busiest part of
Asakusa, the busiest part of Shitaya—the "broad alley" south of the
mountain and its temple—was a plebeian island largely cut off from the
main Low City.

By the end of Meiji the upper classes had for the most part moved west, and their gardens had been taken over by small shops and dwellings, a solid expanse of them from the Hongō and Kanda hills to the river. A brief account in the 1907 guide put out by the city suggests the sort of thing that happened.

> *Shitaya Park.* Situated in the eastern part of the ward. To the east it borders on Samisen Pond and Asakusa Ward, and to the north on Nishimachi, Shitaya Ward. It was designated a park in April, 1890, and has an area of 16,432 *tsubo.* Once an estate of Lord Satake, it returned to nature with the dismemberment of the buildings, and came to be known popularly as Satake Meadow. It presently became a center for theaters, variety halls, sideshows, and the like, and, as they were gradually moved elsewhere, was assimilated into the city. It may no longer be said to have the attributes of a park.

There is no trace of a park in the district today. The expression rendered as "assimilated" says more literally that the Satake estate "is entirely *machiya,*" meaning something like the establishments of tradesmen and artisans. Most of the aristocratic lands of Shitaya became *machiya* without passing through the transitional stages.

Northern Shitaya, near the city limits, was a region of temples and cemeteries, a part of the band streching all along the northern fringes of Edo. A part of Yanaka, north of Ueno, where the last shogun is buried and where also the last poem of Takahashi O-den may be read upon her tombstone, became the largest public cemetery of Meiji. The city has sprawled vastly to the south and west, and today almost anyone from southerly and westerly regions, glancing at a map, forms an immediate and unshakable opinion that anything so far to the north and the east must be of the Low City. In fact it was the new High City of Meiji. As temple lands dwindled it became an intellectual sort of place, much favored by professors, writers, and artists. There is cause all the same, aside from its place on the map, for thinking that it gradually slid into the Low City. Professional keeners for dead Edo would have us believe that what was not lost in 1923 went in 1945, and that most things were lost on both occasions. In fact the Yanaka district came through the two disasters well. Its most conspicuous monument, the pagoda of the Tennōji Temple, was lost more recently. An arsonist set fire to it one summer evening in 1957. The heart of the old Low City contained few temples and Yanaka still contains many. With its latticed fronts, its tiled roofs, and its tiny expanses of greenery, it is the most extensive part of the present city in which something like the mood of the old Low City is still to be sensed.

The Negishi district, east of Yanaka, gave its name to a major school of Meiji poetry. It had long been recommended for the *wabizumai,* the life of solitude and contemplation, especially for the aged and affluent, and had had its artistic and literary day as well. A famous group of roisterers known as "the Shitaya gang" had its best parties in Negishi and included some of the most famous painters and writers of the early nineteenth century. Like Yanaka in the hills and over beyond the railway tracks, Negishi still has lanes and alleys that answer well to descriptions of the old Low City, but it has rather lost class. No artistic or intellectual person, unless perhaps a teacher of traditional music, would think of living there. It is not a good address. From Yanaka and Negishi one looked across paddy lands to the Yoshiwara. In late Edo and Meiji the owners of the great Yoshiwara houses had villas there, to which the more privileged of courtesans could withdraw when weary or ill. Nagai Kafū loved Negishi, and especially the houses in which the courtesans had languished.

Always, looking through the fence and the shrubbery at the house next door, he would stand entranced, brought to his senses only by the stinging of the mosquitoes, at how much the scene before him was like an illustration for an old love story: the gate of woven twigs, the pine branches trailing down over the ponei, the house itself. Long unoccupied, it had once been a sort of villa or resthouse for one of the Yoshiwara establishments…. He remembered how, when he was still a child on his mother's knee, he had heard and felt very sad to hear that one snowy night a courtesan, long in ill health, had died in the house next door, which had accommodated Yoshiwara women since before the Restoration. The old pine, trailing its branches from beside the lake almost to the veranda, made it impossible for him to believe, however many years passed, that the songs about sad Yoshiwara beauties, Urasato and Michitose and the rest, were idle fancies, yarns dreamed up by songwriters. Manners and ways of feeling might become Westernized, but as long as the sound of the temple bell in the short summer night remained, and the Milky Way in the clear autumn sky, and the trees and grasses peculiar to the land—as long as these remained, he thought, then somewhere, deep in emotions and ethical systems, there must even today be something of that ancient sadness.

Shitaya Ward, now amalgamated with Asakusa Ward to the east, was shaped like an arrowhead, or, as the Japanese preference for natural imagery would make it, a sagittate leaf. It pointed southwards towards the heart of the Low City, of which it fell slightly short. The character of the ward changed as one moved north to south, becoming little different from the flatlands of Kanda and Asakusa, between which the point of the arrow thrust itself. The erstwhile estates of the aristocracy had been "assimilated," as the 1907 guide informs us.

Kanda was almost entirely secular. There were Shinto plots, and the only Confucian temple in the city. There were no Buddhist temples at all. The shogunate did not want the smell of them and their funerals so near at hand. The Akihabara district that is now the biggest purveyor of electronic devices in the city took its name from a shrine, the Akiba—"Autumn Leaf." The extensive shrine grounds, cleared as a firebreak after one of the many great Kanda fires, were Akibagahara, "field of the Akiba." Then the government railways moved in and made them a freight depot, and the name elided into what it is today. This is the sort of thing that infuriates sons of Edo, and certainly the old name does have about it the feel of the land, and the new one, as Kafū did not tire of saying, has about it the tone of the railway operator. Names are among the things in Tokyo that are not left alone.

The purest of Edo Low City types, popular lore had it, was produced not in the heartland, Nihombashi, but on the fringes. Quarrelsome in rather a more noisy than violent way, cheerful, open, spendthrift, he was born in Shiba on the south and reared in Kanda. It was of course in the Kanda flatlands that he was reared, with the Kanda Shrine (see page 141) to watch over him. (Like Shitaya, Kanda was part hilly and part flat.) Kanda had once been a raucous sort of place, famous for its dashing gangsters and the "hot-water women" of its bathhouses, but in Meiji it was more sober and industrious than the flatlands of Shitaya and Asakusa, nearer the river.

The liveliest spot in Kanda was probably its fruit-and-vegetable market, the largest in the city, official provisioner to Lord Tokugawa himself. Though not directly threatened by the forces of Civilization and Enlightenment, as the fish market was, the produce market of Kanda yet lived through Meiji with a certain insecurity. In the end a tidying-up was deemed adequate, and the produce market escaped being uprooted like the fish market. The big markets were where the less affluent merchant of the Low City was seen at his most garrulous and energetic. The produce market, less striking to the senses than the fish market but no less robust, is a good symbol of flatland Kanda and its Edo types.

The western or hilly part of Kanda was the epitome of the high-collar. There it was that Hasegawa Shigure, child of Nihombashi, had her first taste of the new enlightenment (see page 194). Hilly Kanda had by the end of Meiji acquired the Russian cathedral, one of the city's grandest foreign edifices, and it had universities, bookstores, and intellectuals. The Kanda used-book district that is among the wonders of the world was beginning to form in late Meiji, on the main east-west Kanda street, then so narrow that rickshaws could barely pass. Losses in 1923 ran into tens of thousands of volumes.

Kanda had the greatest concentration of private higher education in the city, and indeed in the nation. Three important private universities, Meiji, Chūō, and Nihon, had their campuses in the western part of Kanda Ward—three of five such universities that were situated in Tokyo and might at the end of Meiji have been called important. All three were founded in early and middle Meiji as law schools and had by the end of Meiji diversified themselves to some extent. Law was among the chief intellectual concerns of Meiji. If Western law could be made Japanese and the foreign powers could be shown that extraterritoriality no longer served a purpose, then it might be done away with. The liberal arts did not, at the end of Meiji, have an important place in private education. Meiji University had a school of literature, one among four. Nihon had several foreign-language departments, while Chūō had only two branches, law and economics. The liberal arts and the physical sciences were for the most part left to public universities. In Kanda professional and commercial subjects prevailed. This seems appropriate, up here in the hills above the hustlers of the produce market, and perhaps it better represents the new day than does public education. It defines the fields in which the Japanese have genuinely excelled.

The regions east of the river were the saddest victims of Civilization and Enlightenment. This is not to say that they changed most during Meiji—the Marunouchi district east of the palace probably changed more—but that they suffered a drearier change. Someone has to be a victim of an ever grosser national product, and the authorities chose Honjo and Fukagawa wards, along with the southern shores of the bay, after a time of uncertainty in which small factories were put up over most of the city.

It would be easy to say that the poor are always the victims, but the fact is that the wards east of the river, and especially Honjo, the northern one, do not look especially poor on maps of late Edo. Had there been a policy of putting the burden on the lower classes, then Nihombashi

Lumberyards in Kanda, late Meiji

and Kyōbashi would have been the obvious targets. The eastern wards were chosen not because they were already sullied and impoverished but because they were so watery, and therefore lent themselves so well to cheap transport. They were also relatively open. Many people and houses would have had to be displaced were Nihombashi to turn industrial.

Though more regularly plotted, the Honjo of late Edo resembles the western parts of the High City, plebeian enclaves among aristocratic lands. Wateriest of all, Fukagawa was rather different, especially in its southern reaches. It contained the lumberyards of the city. The lumberyards were of course mercantile, though some of the merchants were wealthy, if not as wealthy as the great ones of Nihombashi. By the end of Meiji the wards east of the river were industrial and far-from-wealthy makers of things that others consumed. Nagai Kafū wrote evocatively of the change. The hero of *The River Sumida,* returning to Asakusa from a disappointing interview with his uncle, wanders past rank Honjo gardens and moldering Honjo houses, and recognizes among them the settings for the fiction of late Edo, to which he is strongly drawn. In certain essays the laments are for the changes which, in the years of Kafū's exile overseas, have come upon "Fukagawa of the waters."

Heavily populated as the city spilled over into the eastern suburbs, Honjo and the northern parts of Fukagawa were but sparsely populated at the beginning of Meiji. Akutagawa Ryūnosuke, who was born in 1892 and spent his boyhood in Honjo, described the loneliness in an essay written after the earthquake and shortly before his suicide.

> In the last years of the nineteenth century and the first years of the twentieth, Honjo was not the region of factories that it is today. It was full of stragglers, worn out by two centuries of Edo. There was nothing resembling the great rows of mercantile establishments one sees in Nihombashi and Kyōbashi. In search of an even moderately busy district, one went to the far south of the ward, the approaches to Ryōgoku Bridge....
>
> Corpses made the strongest impression on me in stories I heard of old Honjo, corpses of those who had fallen by the wayside, or hanged themselves, or otherwise disposed of themselves. A corpse would be discovered and put in a cask, and the cask wrapped in straw matting, and set out upon the moors with a white lantern to watch over it. The thought of the white lantern out there among the grasses has in it a certain weird, ominous beauty. In the middle of the night, it was said, the cask would roll over, quite of its own accord. The Honjo of Meiji may have been short on grassy moors, but it still had about it something of the "regions beyond the red line." And how is it now? A mass of utility poles and shacks, all jammed in together....
>
> My father still thinks he saw an apparition, that night in Fuka-gawa. It looked like a young warrior, but he insists that it was in fact a fox spirit. Presently it ran off, frightened by the glint of his sword. I do not care whether it was fox or warrior. Each time I hear the story I think what a lonely place the old Fukagawa was.

The "moderately busy" part of Honjo was the vicinity of the Ekōin Temple, at the eastern approaches to Ryōgoku Bridge, one of five put across the Sumida during the Tokugawa Period. The Ekōin was found-ed to console the victims of the great "fluttering-sleeve" fire of 1657, so called from a belief that it was spread by a burning kimono. It was among the great temples of Edo, though Basil Hall Chamberlain and W. B. Morse thought it less than elevating. They said of it, in the 1903 edi-tion of their guide to Japan, that it "might well be taken as a text by those who denounce heathen temples. Dirty, gaudy...the place lacks even the semblance of sanctity."

The Ekōin attracted places of refreshment and entertainment, solace to the living as well as the departed, less varied and on the whole shab-bier than those of Asakusa. The "broad alley" of Ryōgoku fared badly in Meiji and after. At the end of Edo it was one of the three famous "broad alleys" of the Low City. Ryōgoku continued until the Second World War to be the Sumo center of the land. There it was that the big tournaments were held from late Edo down to the Second World War, but they moved away. The gymnasium was requisitioned by the American Occupation and then sold to a university, and the Sumō center of the city and the nation has for three decades now been on the right bank of the river.

Not much remains at Ryōgoku. It became a commuter point when a railway station was finished in 1903, but a minor one, serving some of the poorest parts of the city and only the Chiba Peninsula beyond. So it may be said that Honjo, once unpeopled, is now crowded and subdued. No part of the city is without its pockets of pleasure and entertainment, but Honjo has none that would take the pleasure-seeker out of his way.

On a single evening every year, something of the old joy and din came back. It was the night of the "river opening," already described, admired by U. S. and Julia Grant, E. S. Morse, and Clara Whitney, among others. The crowds were so dense at the 1897 opening that the south rail of the bridge gave way, and people drowned.

Still in late Meiji the district from northern Honjo into the northern and eastern suburbs was much recommended for excursions. It enjoyed such excursions in perhaps the greatest variety in all the city, though they were becoming victims of material progress. The 1907 guide put out by the metropolitan government thus describes the state of affairs: "Under the old regime the district was occupied by townsmen and the lower ranks of the aristocracy. It was also the site of the official bamboo and lumberyards. Today it is mostly industrial. To the north, however, is Mukōjima, a most scenic district, and in the suburbs to the east are such attractions as the Sleeping Dragon Plum and the Hagi Temple, for especially pleasant excursions." The temple survives, but the *hagi (Lespedeza bicolor)* of autumn does not. Neither do the plum blossoms of spring. Kafū's description, in *The River Sumida,* is of joyous springtide, out beyond the blight; but the blight was advancing.

"They who make the count of the famous places of Tokyo," says the guide a few pages later, "cannot but put a pair of scenic spots, Ueno and Mukōjima, at the head of their lists."

Cherries had from the seventeenth century lined the left bank of the Sumida, from a point generally opposite Asakusa northwards into the suburbs. Though gnawed at by industrial fumes from late Meiji, they still attracted throngs during their brief period of flowering that were second only to those of Ueno. The Sumida was still clean enough for bathing—or at any rate no one had yet made the discovery that it was not.

Grassy banks led down to the river on the Honjo side, and small houses lined the Asakusa bank, waiting resignedly for the next flood. The
river was open, no bridges in sight north from Asakusa, with at least
four ferry landings well within sight on either bank. As the city took
to wheels, bridges came into demand, but the ferry must have been the
pleasanter way to cross, especially in cherry-blossom time. The last of the
Sumida ferries, much farther downstream, did not disappear until after
the Second World War.

Tokyo is today, and it must have been in late Meiji, a city where one
learns to gaze only at the immediate prospect, blotting out what lies
beyond. Crossing Azuma Bridge at Asakusa, one would have had to do
this, unless a background of chimneys and smoke and utility wires could
be regarded as pleasing. Yet the foreground must have been very pleasing indeed.

The view across the Sumida from Honjo to Asakusa was quiet urban
harmony, and that in the other direction was pastoral calm, broken by
those noisy vernal rites when the cherries were in bloom. In the one direction was the "old Asakusa" of Kubota Mantarō, low wooden buildings at the water's edge with the sweeping roofs and the pagoda of the
Asakusa Kannon beyond, and Matsuchi Hill, the only considerable rise
in the Low City, slightly upstream. In the other direction was the Sumida
embankment, surmounted by cherry trees that blocked off all but the top
portions of the industrially productive regions beyond, still suggesting
that over there somewhere a few old gentlemen of taste and leisure might
be pursuing one or several of the ways of the brush.

Beyond the city limits on the left bank, in what was to become
Mukōjima Ward, was a pleasant little cove much heard of in amorous fiction of late Edo and Meiji. It was watched over by the Shrine of the River
God, tutelary to the Sumida, and it was a good place, remote and serene,
to take a geisha. No trace of it remains. The Sumida has been rationalized
and brought within plain, sensible limits, with a view to flood control.

A victim of pollution, Honjo was also subject to natural disasters. It
suffered most grievously among all the wards, perhaps, not in terms of
property losses but in terms of wounds that did not heal, from the Great
Flood of 1910. Most of the wealthy who had maintained villas beside the
river withdrew, hastening the end of the northeastern suburbs as a place
of tasteful retirement. The flood-control devices of Taishō and since have
been very successful, but they have also been somewhat unsightly. It may
be that not many in our day would wish to view the sights and smell the

Honjo in the Great Flood of 1910

Another view of Honjo during the Great Flood

smells of the Sumida (and only stuntsters venture to swim in it). Even if the wish were present, it would be frustrated by cement walls.

On maps of Edo, northern Fukagawa, the southern of the two wards east of the river, looks very much like Honjo, but the watery south is different, solidly plebeian, as no part of Honjo is. Across the river from Nihombashi, Fukagawa was nearer the heart of the Low City. Though not among the flourishing geisha quarters of Meiji, Fukagawa did in the course of Meiji get something that was just as good business, the Susaki licensed quarter (see page 181). Fukagawa was among the better heirs to the great tradition of Edo profligacy.

The Susaki quarter did not, like the Yoshiwara, have a round of seasonal observances, but it was at times a place for the whole family to visit. Shown on certain maps from late Edo as tidal marshes, the strand before the Susaki Benten Shrine was rich in shellfish, and clam raking was among the rites of summer. This very ancient shrine had stood on an island long before Fukagawa was reclaimed. All through the Edo centuries it was presided over by the only feminine member of the Seven Deities of Good Luck. So the quarter had an appropriate patroness, well established. In certain respects Susaki was more pleasing to the professional son of Edo than the Yoshiwara. Not so frequently a victim of fire, there in its watery isolation, it was not as quick to become a place of fanciful turrets and polychrome fronts. Indeed it looks rather prim in photographs, easily mistaken, at a slight remove, for the Tsukiji foreign settlement.

The Fukagawa of late Meiji had more bridges than any other ward in the city, a hundred forty of them, including those shared with Honjo and Nihombashi. Only two were of iron, and a hundred twenty-eight were of wood, suggesting that the waterways of Fukagawa still had an antique look about them.

The beginnings of industrialization, as it concerned Tokyo, were at the mouth of the Sumida and along the Shiba coast. The Ishikawajima Shipyards, on the Fukagawa side of the Sumida, may be traced back to public dismay over the Perry landing. A shipbuilding enterprise was established there by the Mito branch of the Tokugawa clan shortly after that event. It followed a common Meiji course from public enterprise to private, making the transition in 1876.

Over large expanses of the ward, however, Kafū's "Fukagawa or the waters" yet survived, canals smelling of new wood and lined by white godowns. Kafū was not entirely consistent, or perhaps Fukagawa itself was inconsistent, a place of contrasts. On the one hand he deplored the changed Fukagawa which he found on his return from America and

France, and on the other he still found refuge there from the cluttered new city (see pages 61-62). His best friend, some years later, fled family and career, and took up residence with a lady not his wife in a Fukagawa tenement row. There he composed haiku. In Fukagawa, said Kafū approvingly, people still honored what the new day called superstitions, and did not read newspapers.

The grounds of the Tomioka Hachiman were in theory a park, one of the original five. Much the smallest, it had a career similar to that of Asakusa. It dwindled and presently lost all resemblance to what is commonly held to be a public park. The Iwasaki estate in Fukagawa, now Kiyosumi Park, is far more parklike today than this earlier park. The history of the two is thus similar to the history of Ueno and Asakusa. It was best, in these early years, to keep the public at some distance from a park. Deeded to the city after the earthquake, Kiyosumi Park was the site of the Taishō emperor's funeral pavilion. The beauties of the Fukagawa bayshore are described thus in the official guide of 1907:

> One stands by the shrine and looks out to sea, and a contrast of blue and white, waves and sails, rises and falls, far into the distance. To the south and east the mountains of the Chiba Peninsula float upon the water, raven and jade. To the west are the white snows of Fuji. In one grand sweep are all the beauties of mountain and sea, in all the seasons. At low tide in the spring, there is the pleasure of "hunting in the tidelands," as it is called. Young and old, man and woman, they all come out to test their skills at the taking of clams and seaweed.

One senses overstatement, for the guide had its evangelical purposes. Yet it is true that open land and the flowers and grasses and insects and clams of the seasons were to be found at no great distance beyond the river. When, in the Taishō Period, the Arakawa Drainage Channel was dug, much of its course was through farmland.

Among the places for excursions, only the Kameido Tenjin Shrine and its wisteria survive. Waves of blue, mountains of raven and jade, are rarely to be seen, and the Sumida has been walled in. Yet the more remarkable fact may be that something still survives.

There is the mood of the district, more sweetly melancholy, perhaps, for awareness of all the changes, and there are specific, material things as well, such as memorial stones and steles. Some of the temple grounds are forests of stone. Kafū's maternal grandfather and Narushima Ryūhoku are among those whose accomplishments will not be completely forgotten, for they are recorded upon the stones of Honjo and Mukōjima. The

A mikoshi (god-seat) at the Fukagawa Hachiman Shrine festival

great Bashō had one of his "banana huts" in Fukagawa. It too is memorialized, though finding it takes some perseverance.

The other industrial zone was along the bayshore in the southernmost ward, Shiba, which was also the ward of the railroad, the only ward so favored in early Meiji. The Tokyo-Yokohama railroad entered the city at the southern tip of Shiba, hugged the shore and passed over fills, veered somewhat inland, and came to its terminus just short of the border with Kyōbashi. Closely following the old Tōkaidō, it blocked the plebeian view of the bay (or, it might be said, since Meiji so delighted in locomotives, provided new and exciting perspectives). It may or may not be significant that the line turned inland to leave such aristocratic expanses as the Hama Palace with their bayshore frontage.

Shiba at the south and Kanda at the north of the Low City were honored in popular lore as makers of the true child of Edo. The fringes were not as wealthy as the Nihombashi center, and so their sons, less inhibited, had the racy qualities of Edo in greater measure. Most of Shiba is hilly and not much of it was plebeian at the end of Edo. Edo land maps show *machiya*, "houses of townsmen," like knots along a string. There was a cluster at the north, around Shimbashi, where the first railway terminus was built, a string southwards to another knot, between the bay and the southern cemetery of the Tokugawa family, and another string southwards to the old Shinagawa post-station, just beyond the Meiji city limits.

It was through Shiba that the foreigner and his goods entered Tokyo. Had it not been for the Ginza fire, its northern extremes might have become preeminent among places for the purveying of imported goods. The region did in fact prosper. The southern cluster, by the Tokugawa tombs, did not do as well. It came to harbor one of the quarters commonly called slums, though it may be doubted that Tokyo knows what a real slum is—in that regard, it has never quite caught up with the rest of the world. Since Kanda, the partner of Shiba in producing the true son of Edo, contained no "slums," its flatlands were probably more prosperous in Meiji than those of Shiba.

Shiba was the earliest legation quarter. When Sir Rutherford Alcock, the first British minister, went to call upon the shogun, his way lay almost entirely through what was presently to become Shiba Ward. It seems to have taken him around the western or hilly side of the Tokugawa cemetery, where also there was a plebeian fringe. He makes it sound like a lesser Asakusa.

After a mile of the Tocado, our road turns off into a side street, narrower and more crowded. A Daimio's residence extends the greater part of its length on one side, with a large and imposing-looking gateway in the center, from which stretches a long line of barred windows.... A small, narrow, and very muddy moat, little more than a gutter, keeps all intruders from too close prying. But these outbuildings are only the quarters of the numerous retainers.... In many cases these extend for a quarter of a mile on each side of the main entrance, and form in effect the best defence for their lord's apartments....

We soon emerge into an open space in front of the Tycoon's Cemetery, and through it a small river runs, fringed with fresh green banks, and a row of trees.... Here, in open space above, forming a sort of boulevard, Matsuri, or public fairs, are often held, and, in their absence, storytellers collect a little audience. A few noisy beggars generally take up their position by the wayside.... Here a party of jugglers may often be seen too, collecting a crowd from the passers-by. Blondin and the Wizard of the North might both find formidable rivals here—for the Japanese performers not only swallow portentously long swords, and poise themselves on bottles—but out of their mouths come the most unimaginable things...flying horses, swarms of flies, ribbons by the mile, and paper shavings without end.

On crossing the bridge, we traverse one of the most densely populated of the commercial quarters, through which, indeed, we can only ride slowly, and in single file, amidst pedestrians and porters with their loads. Bullock-cars, Norimons, and Kangos are all here, jostling each other in contending currents. Over a gentle hill, then sharp round to the right, through a barrier gate, we approach the official quarter, in the center of which, within three moats of regal dimensions, the Tycoon himself resides. But we are not yet near to it. We pursue our way down some rather steep steps—a Daimio's residence on one side, and the wall and trees of the Tycoon's Cemetery, which we are skirting, on the other. As we emerge from this defile, we pass through a long line of booths, where a sort of daily bazaar is held for the sale of gaudily-colored prints, maps (many of them copies of European charts), story books, swords, tobacco pouches, and pipes, for the humbler classes; and in the midst of which a fortune-teller may habitually be seen.... Something very like the gambling table of our own fairs may also be seen in the same spot; but, judging by the stock-in-trade and the juvenile customers, the gambling, I suspect, is only for sweetmeats. Their serious gambling is reserved for teahouses, and more private haunts, where the law may be better defied. On festive occasions, a row of dingy booths divided by curtains into small compartments is often seen, provided for the lowest class. The Social Evil is here a legalized institution, and nowhere takes a more revolting form.

In later years a place along the other side of the tombs, the east side, was known to Clara Whitney and her friends as "the thieves' market." It also contained one of the lesser geisha districts of the time. So the old pattern may be seen once more, places of pleasure and commerce accumulating around places of worship, in this case the great Zōjōji Temple, the southern equivalent of the Kan-eiji at Ueno.

The circle of temples and cemeteries that started at the Sumida and fringed the old city came through Shiba and ended at the bay. The Zōjōji was the grandest of Shiba temples, though today the most famous is probably that which contains the ashes of the Forty-seven Loyal Retainers (see page 64). The grounds of the Zōjōji were one of the five original parks. There it was, on a moonlit night, that a moping Kafū, back from France and hating everything Japanese, had his first mystical experience of traditional beauty.

Virtually nothing remains of the old Zōjōji. As for the park, it is enough to say that the remains of the shoguns and their ladies, including the sad princess who became the bride of the fourteenth shogun, have been squeezed into a narrow walled enclosure, so that commerce may thrive. Hibiya Park, newer and some slight distance to the north, is today more open.

The hilly sections of Shiba Park were so heavily wooded, we are told, that there was darkness at noon. Today they are dominated by Tokyo Tower, of Eiffel-like proportions, while the graves of the shoguns lie naked under the midday sun. In 1873 arsonists destroyed the main hall of the Zōjōji, around which the graves were once disposed. The culprits, self-righteous young men of the military class, resented the temple's failure to separate itself from Shinto, which must be pure, uncontaminated by foreign creeds. Rebuilt, the hall was destroyed again on April Fool's Day, 1909, this time by accident. A beggar built a fire under it to warm himself in that chilly season.

To accommodate the electric trolleys of late Meiji, a street was put through almost directly south from the castle to the old Tōkaidō highway, which it joins some distance north of Shinagawa. It bisected the Zōjōji grounds. The portions east of the new street were those earliest given over to development, which has today quite engulfed them, leaving scarcely a trace of park. Yet farther east was what might be called the southernmost extremity of the old Low City, and along the bay-shore was an early center of heavy industry.

Tokyo Shibaura has been a leading manufacturer of machinery ever since its founding in 1875 by a man from Kyushu. Shibaura means "Shiba coast." Its main factories on land reclaimed by the shogunate, the company was an early manufacturer of telegraphic equipment. In spite of all these industrial endeavors, Shibaura remained the most popular of watering places. The young Tanizaki went there gathering clams.

Shibaura had clams in spring and cooling breezes in the summer, and a view up the Sumida to Ryōgoku Bridge for the "opening of the river." Meiji graphic art tends, except in certain erotica, to emphasize the clams. It was only at the end of the period that the youth of the land turned with enthusiasm to sea bathing. Advertisements from middle to late Meiji recommend it as something which, since foreigners find it pleasant and healthful, Japanese might try too. The places where pretty clam-diggers posed for photographers, skirts tucked up to reveal sturdy legs, now lie beneath a freeway, and already at the end of Meiji reclaimed lands were creeping eastwards.

Just north of the Tokyo Shibaura plant was, at the end ot Meiji, the Number One Gashouse of the Tokyo Gas Company; and just north of that, to remind us that it was not only the lower classes who had factories for neighbors, the Shiba Detached Palace, a salubrious retreat for royalty.

"Twenty years ago," wrote the novelist and playwright Osanai Kaoru, some years after the earthquake, Shibaura was a place with flair. There the geisha came, the genuine sort, for delicious assignations.

"I went the other day for a look at it, the first in I do not know how many years. I was shocked, at the wide expanses of reclaimed land, at the big new docks along the shallow bay, where there once had been beaches, at the warehouses, at the utter disappearance of the old restaurants and inns.

"Only the black pines of the Flama Palace, across the canal, remained from other years."

In its shady western hills, Shiba Park had perhaps the most famous Japanese restaurant of Meiji. Called the Koyokan, House of the Autumn Colors, it does not survive. It was built in 1881 as a sort of club for the elite, who in the Rokumeikan period saw the need for a good Japanese restaurant not associated, as most of them then were, with the demimonde. The improving spirit of the day is here again to be noted. No one under the old regime, except perhaps for a few of the more unbendingly puritanical bureaucrats, would have seen a need for the separation. Some of the most prominent names in the land were on the list of stockholders. Radically innovative in one sense, the Kōyōkan sought to be traditional in another. Kyoto food was served, and the waitresses were asked to have Kyoto accents, whether they came naturally or not. Much frequented by bureaucrats, politicians, and intellectuals, the Kōyōkan figures more prominently in Meiji literature than does the Rokumeikan.

Shiba was the most hapless of the three large early parks. We have seen how Saitō Ryokuu contrasted Ueno and Asakusa, the latter noisy and down-to-earth, the former sternly edifying. Shiba was neither the one nor the other, and since the most recent destruction of its temple, in 1945, it has seemed almost unpeopled, as that word may be understood in Tokyo. Already in Meiji it was being left behind. From a short distance south of the Tokugawa tombs a branch of the Tōkaidō led northwards into the High City—it is the route Sir Rutherford Alcock seems to have taken—while the main road led to Nihombashi. The tombs lay between the two, and on either side was a flourishing district of the sort described by Sir Rutherford. The railroad passed them by. As they declined, it was the far north of Shiba, by Shimbashi Station, that thrived.

Shimbashi, always called Shibaguchi, "the Shiba Mouth," by such cognoscenti as Kafū, did not get modernized after the great Ginza fire. It is where the old merchant and artisan city narrowed from the spread of Nihombashi and Kyōbashi to a constricted corridor leading southwards towards the city limits and Shinagawa. Before the Meiji ward boundaries were drawn, separating Ginza and Shimbashi, it could be distinguished from its northern neighbor by little save its greater remoteness from the center of things—a remoteness and a lack of affluence which made it the proper breeding ground for children of Edo. If Shimbashi had become a part of the new Ginza Bricktown it might also have become, like Ginza, the sluice through which the delightful new things of the West came flooding. It was immediately in front of the station, while Ginza was a bit removed. After the trauma of the rebuilding, Ginza did eventually retrieve its standing as a place of revelry, of tiny drinking and lechering establishments, but through most of Meiji that function was assumed by Shimbashi. It was as if, having had their look at Ginza, which of course everyone wished to see, people turned back and relaxed in Shimbashi, where they felt at home. One is reminded of the typical estate of a Meiji plutocrat, consisting of a grand Western building (by Conder, perhaps) for garden parties and foreign dignitaries, and a Japanese wing somewhere in the background for everyday use. Ginza had its broad streets and colonnades, and Shimbashi was a warren, where one felt snug and secure. A part of Shimbashi was known as Hikagechō, "Shadyville," which seems just right.

The Shimbashi geisha district, with Yanagibashi the greatest of them through most of Meiji, has been the most peripatetic. It was named from its proximity to Shimbashi, the New Bridge on the Tōkaidō, and moved northwards and then eastwards. Today, though still called Shimbashi, it is largely in the Tsukiji district, where the foreign settlement was and the fish market is. In the decades since Meiji it has done better than Yanagibashi, but it may be that the geisha profession is a dying one. Elegance and ritual survive, if perhaps the old standards in song and dance have fallen.

The original Shimbashi Station, northern terminus of the railway from Yokohama and later from Kobe, is said by experts on Meiji architecture to be something of a mystery, though it was endlessly photographed and made into woodcut prints. The original plans, by an American, have been lost, and no detailed description survives. So it was observed by millions of eyes (some three million passengers got on and off in 1907 alone), and drawn and photographed countless numbers of times—and yet we cannot know exactly what was seen by all those eyes. Among stations in the West, it seems to have resembled the Gare de l'Est in Paris most closely.

Some places have a way of coming back from hard blows, others do not. Yanagibashi is being destroyed by the ugly wall that cuts it off from its river. Shimbashi lost its station, and did not seem to notice. After 1914, when Tokyo Central Station was completed, Shimbashi was no longer

The Shimbashi Station, 1881

the terminus and the old station was no longer used for passengers. A new and less important station was built some slight distance to the west, right on top of Shadyville. Shimbashi might have languished. Because the Low City was made to feel rejected by the new central station, however, people from Kyōbashi and Nihombashi preferred to board their trains at the new Shimbashi Station. So in the warrens of Shiba Mouth there was revelry as never before. Ginza moved northwards and Shimbashi went on doing the old thing, more intensely.

At the end of Meiji, Nihombashi was no longer a center holding the Low City together. The genuine child of Edo may have been born in Shiba and reared in Kanda, but from both places, while Edo was still Edo, he looked towards Nihombashi as a height or a hub. Wonders of power and progress were achieved in Meiji, but these things do not happen without cost. The Low City was no longer what it had been through the last century or so of Edo, the cultural capital of the land, and Nihombashi, still the geographic center of the Low City, looked about it at a scattering rather than a system.

There was no reason for modern ward lines to follow the ridge line that separated the hilly half of the city from the flat half; and they did not. Each of the wards along the western fringe of the flatlands reached into the hills, and the eastern portion of Hongō, largely in the hills, lay beyond the ridge and in the flats. The boundary is somewhat imaginary in any case. The two halves were and continue to be different from each other, but the ridge line is no more than a convenience for dividing them.

The line entered the Meiji city north of Ueno and left it near the present Shinagawa Station, where the hills came almost down to the bayshore. Had one walked through Edo generally following the ridge line, there would have been only one stretch of the route where the division between High City and Low City seemed quite clear, and even so one would have had to stray eastward from the precise topographical line. There was a cultural chasm along the outer ramparts of the castle.

In Meiji it became the line separating Kōjimachi Ward and especially the Marunouchi business district, within the circle, from the several wards, notably Kyōbashi and Nihombashi, that lay outside it. Before the fall of the shogunate, the highest of the bureaucracy and the military aristocracy dwelt within the circle, to the west of the moat. To the east lay the heart of the Low City, Nihombashi and Kyōbashi.

The outer moat survived through Meiji and down to the recent past, but it was early decided that His Majesty's abode did not require such defensive works as Lord Tokugawa's had claimed. So the outer gates were quickly dismantled, and the district between the outer and inner moats put to several uses.

Great changes have come over Nihombashi and Ginza, to the east of the chasm, and Marunouchi, to the west; but on a holiday in particular the old difference is still to be observed. The outer edge of the circle teems with shoppers and pleasure seekers, the inside is dead. The former continues to be the land of the merchant and his customer, the latter is the land of the office worker, who withdraws to the suburbs on holidays, or perhaps steps across the line into Ginza for something self-indulgent.

Mention has been made of the late-Meiji photographs taken by Ogawa Isshin from the roof of the City Hall. They are striking for the unfinished look of the Marunouchi district, but among specific objects the most remarkable is perhaps the great wall that is being put up to the east, as if to keep off barbarian hordes, or to keep a restless populace at home. It is the elevated railroad to the new central station, and it did have the effect of emphasizing divisions, even though no guard was present to enforce them. As of old, the lines of commerce and passage went north and south, from the Nihombashi bridge to the Kyōbashi bridge and the Shimbashi bridge, and the station was rather for the accommodation of the executive and the office worker. The division still survives.

The mansions and government buildings near the palace, on what was to become Mitsubishi Meadow, did not all disappear at once. Some did disappear but some were for a time put to the uses of the new bureaucracy; but by the end of Meiji all were gone. The lands immediately east of the palace became public park (though not a part of the municipal park system), and Mitsubishi presently took over and began to develop its Londontown when the bureaucracy withdrew from lands farther east. In search of relics by which to remember the old castle complex, one would at the end of Meiji have come upon stones and trees, a scattering of gates and bridges, and no more. Parts of Kanda or Nihombashi repeatedly destroyed by fire would have been more redolent of Edo than Marunouchi.

To the west of what in late Meiji became Hibiya Park, still in the Kōjimachi flatlands, was the main bureaucratic complex. It was chiefly brick by a variety of foreign architects in a variety of styles, on the whole more up-to-date, from the foreign point of view, than the Classical Revival styles that were to prevail among Japanese architects. A single building, the Ministry of Justice, remains from the bureaucratic center of late Meiji. Though several German architects are usually given credit for the design, the original one seems to have been revised in the direction of simplicity. The Germans seem to have been fond of traditional frills, and it was these that were disposed of.

The first Diet building rose south of Hibiya Park, not far from the Rokumeikan. It promptly burned down, a victim of electric leakage, and was rebuilt in 1891, in a half-timbered Renaissance style, far less imposing than, for instance, the highly Italianate General Staff Headquarters, which occupied a much more imposing site somewhat to the west, perhaps the finest in all the city. In front of it was the palace moat, and beyond that the grassy embankment and the venerable pine trees beyond which a new residence had been built for the emperor. Although the symbolism cannot have been intentional, it seems to put Meiji democracy in its place.

Kōjimachi was also the diplomatic ward. At the end of Meiji it contained most of the legations and embassies, although the American embassy stood on the land it still occupies, in the northeast corner of Akasaka Ward, and two legations still remained in the old Tsukiji foreign quarter, near which there was a lesser bureaucratic center. The German embassy and the British embassy stood grandly on the inner moat. The former was the grander, and the most frequently photographed of all the embassies, part of an impressive row with the War Ministry and General Staff Headquarters. The embassies have followed the movement of the city to the south and west, and only the British, among the old ones, remains in what was Kōjimachi Ward. When in late Meiji land was chosen for the American legation and embassy, it was eccentrically far south, but the flow of the city has left it nearer the pulsing bureaucratic heart than any of the others.

Though the foreign settlement still contained hotel accommodations at the end of Meiji, the big hotel in the Western style was the Imperial. A Tokyo Hotel had been put up some years earlier in the same part of Kōjimachi, but foreign relations were proceeding briskly and treaty negotiations arriving at a hopeful stage. Something more elaborate was thought to be needed. With government encouragement and a grant of land (and some of the most successful entrepreneurs of the day among the investors), the Imperial opened for business in 1890. Almost immediately the Diet burned down, and the Imperial became temporary accommodations for the House of Representatives.

It was a three-storey wooden building with verandas and arches not at all out of keeping with the Rokumeikan, its neighbor. Sources vary on the number of guest rooms, but there were not above a hundred. So perhaps two or three hundred guests would have filled all the exotic hostelries in the city. One senses what a pleasantly remote and isolated place Tokyo continued to be, despite its emergence into the great world, and its prospect of brilliant successes in the art of war.

Prince Itō, the prime minister of the "dancing cabinet," he who was host to the masquerade ball at the climax of the Rokumeikan period,

The first Imperial Hotel, with one of the old castle moats in foreground

A lounge inside the Imperial Hotel

regularly took meals at the Imperial. The hotel replaced the Rokumeikan as the gathering place of the international set. Over the years it has moved back and forth across its ample public domains, a new one being put up on one half and itself becoming "the old Imperial" when yet another new one is put up on the other half. The first Imperial was destroyed by fire while the second one, by Frank Lloyd Wright, was under construction.

The southern and eastern parts of Kōjimachi had yet more monumental piles in the Western manner. The Imperial Theater was finished at the very end of Meiji, across from the palace plaza. Beside the outer moat of the palace as it crossed the ridge line and entered the High City was the Akasaka Detached Palace, finished in 1908. It was built on the site, expanded by gifts and purchases, of the main Edo mansion of the Wakayama Tokugawa family. There it was that the Meiji emperor, left homeless by the palace fire of 1873, spent roughly the first half of his reign. The mansion became the crown prince's residence upon completion of a new main palace. The new Akasaka palace was put up for the crown prince, who, whether he wished it or not, had a far grander residence than his father. Now serving as the guesthouse for visiting queens, popes, and the like, the Akasaka Palace consists of three floors of brick and granite in the Versailles manner.

The Imperial Theater and the Akasaka Palace were designed by Japanese architects. It is an indication of the distance come. After the first hybrid curiosities, built by Japanese "master carpenters," came the foreign period dominated by such people as Josiah Conder. Beginning with the Bank of Japan, Japanese architects commenced doing the big foreign thing for themselves. Although Wright was summoned to build the second Imperial, foreign architects would never again be so important. No one would say—as it was said in early Meiji—that Japanese foreign architecture was foreign to any known style. It could not, on the other hand, be said that there was anything very original about the Gallic exercises of late Meiji (although the Imperial Theater did, until the earthquake, bear atop its dome a large statue of a Kabuki actor). Amateur exuberance gradually gave way to a professional discipline that was perhaps too tightly controlled.

The flat parts of Kōjimachi Ward, within the outer moat and to the east and south of castle and palace, may have had no geographic features to distinguish them from the flatlands beyond the outer moat, but no son of Edo would have thought them a part of the Low City—his city. Today they are the most national part of the city, where financial and productive endeavors are regulated, and from which the land is governed. As one crosses the ridge line, following the inner moat or the avenue where the outer moat once was, one is clearly in the High City. The British embassy has perhaps the best address in the whole city, but it is more isolated than the American embassy, because the system of rapid transport has until recently been reticent about intruding upon affluent residential neighborhoods.

* * *

The High City was sparsely populated in Edo and largely emptied by the Restoration. The high ranks of the military aristocracy went away, presently to come back with titles and new mansions. The lower ranks provided some of the most successful Meiji bureaucrats, politicians, and entrepreneurs, and ample stories of tragedy and desperation as well, including those of O-den, O-kinu, and O-ume, the eminent murderesses.

Then they all went away, and the High City was turned over to tea and mulberries. The Meiji government, after initial hesitation, began a policy of confiscating unused lands and encouraging their return to agriculture. There were for a time more than a hundred acres of tea and mulberries in what was to become Akasaka Ward. The avenue that leads southwest from the Akasaka geisha quarter seems to have passed through mulberries and little else. Shibuya, beyond the Meiji city limits and one of the thriving entertainment and shopping centers of Taishō and since, was known for the excellence of its tea. The "tea-and-mulberry policy" was a brief expediency which left no lasting mark upon the High City. The tea bushes and the mulberry trees soon withered, and development came, to make the High City the half (or somewhat more than half) of Tokyo that has grown hugely in this century.

From mid-Meiji, the repopulation of the High City progressed furiously, accounting for well over half the total population growth through the Meiji years. When the population reached a million, approximately the highest Edo figure, Yotsuya Ward in the High City still had the smallest population of the fifteen, and Akasaka, immediately to the south, was the least densely populated. Their opposites were of course in the Low City, Kanda with the largest population and Nihombashi with the highest population density. The population of the city reached two million by the end of Meiji, but growth in the central wards, the Low City plus Kōjimachi, was slow, and in some places population was actually declining.

A line north and south from the center of the palace grounds would have divided the Meiji city into two almost equal parts, and on its way to the city limits at either extremity it would have passed almost entirely through hilly regions. Today the portion of the twenty-three wards that lies west of the line is larger than the eastern portion, and much more populous. A line north and south from the westernmost point of the Meiji city would divide the present city—the twenty-three wards—into approximately equally populated parts. It is a change indeed, when one remembers that the Low City had more than half the population of late Edo. The city has moved westward and goes on doing so, and the old Low City figures much less than it once did.

Though growing rapidly, the High City did not really begin splitting its seams until after the earthquake. When the novelist Tokutomi Roka, among the most popular in his day of all Meiji writers, fell under the spell of Tolstoi and wished to live the Tolstoian life, he only had to go five or six miles west of Shinjuku and the Meiji city limits to be among the peasants. This was shortly after the Russo-Japanese War—and Shinjuku was the most rapidly growing of the new transportation centers. In 1920 a part of it became the first considerable annexation to the fifteen Meiji wards.

For all these frantic changes, the High City changed less in some respects than the Low City. Class distinctions, once very clear if measured by money, tended to disappear from the Low City. They remained valid in the High City. So also, to a remarkable extent, did the pattern of land usage, the distribution of land between the affluent and the more straitened. In both parts of the city the street pattern, despite revolution and disaster, has continued to resemble that of Edo. It is sometimes said that the Japanese succeeded in putting together a rational city, by which seems to be meant one of gridwork, only when building themselves a capital in the Chinese style. In fact Edo was rather like Kyoto, the longest-lived of the Chinese-style capitals. The commercial center was laid out with reasonable consistency and thoroughness in a series of grids. The grids tended not to join one another very well, but that is another matter. Over considerable expanses the right angle and the straight line prevailed.

A map of the High City, on the other hand, puts one in mind of a vast, ancient country village, with the streets following animal tracks and the boundaries of fields. So too it is with Kyoto, a grid where the old city was laid out, but something quite different in outlying districts.

It is as if, having paid homage to the Chinese model, the Japanese settled back into something familiar and comfortable.

Finding an address in the High City is a matter of navigating in more or less the right direction, and asking aid and comfort upon approaching the bourne. It must have been worse in Edo, when there were no house numbers, and the person of the Low City rarely ventured into that cold, alien land, the High City. There is a charming Kafū story about a young girl from a Shimbashi geisha establishment who is sent on a bill-collecting expedition into the High City, and the dreadful time she has finding the delinquent customer of whom she is in pursuit, and her resolve, upon returning safely to Shimbashi, never again to accept so hazardous an assignment.

The High City is not merely a jumble of hills. It is a pattern of ridges and valleys. The main roads out from the city followed ridge lines and valleys, so that the premodern city had, and the modern city has preserved, a resemblance to the cobweb plan admired by planners. Lesser routes climbed up and down the slopes to join the greater ones. The residences of the upper classes were on the heights, and there were farmlands and plebeian clusters in the valleys and along the main roads. A map from late Meiji therefore shows, typically, a tract of undivided land, perhaps private, perhaps a parade ground or a religious or educational establishment, with a somewhat orderly arrangement of small blocks beside it, or on more than one side of it. The main streets are arteries radiating from the heart, with innumerable capillaries between them. From a combination of orderliness and confusion the modern pattern of the uplands grew, remarkably like Edo both in the configuration of the streets and the pattern of land use, except for the fact that farmlands were soon eliminated.

There were other respects as well in which the streets and roads did not change greatly. A very few of the main avenues had been widened to accommodate trolleys, but for the most part they were pitted, narrow, and badly drained. Kafū's little bill collector made her way westwards towards the city limits through a sea of mud. The novelist Tokuda Shusei recalled that in mid-Meiji the main street past the university in Hongo was as rough and narrow as a rustic lane—and this street was the beginning of a principal Tokugawa highway, running out past the Itabashi Mouth and on through the mountains to the Kansai. The hilly part of Kōjimachi Ward, to the west of the palace, where the British legation and embassy has stood for upwards of a century, is the Kōjimachi of Edo. Some think that it was the site of a yeast works, and therefore that the name means something like Yeastville. Others hold it to be a pun on *daimyō kōji,* "daimyo alley," and yet others combine the two and make it "daimyo ferment." The second and third are nicely descriptive, for the ward was given over to the residences of the lesser military orders, the *hatamoto,* the humblest who could still claim access to the shogun's presence. It was bisected by a narrow mercantile strip along the Kōshū highway, leading westwards to the Shinjuku Mouth and the province of Kai. The *hatamoto* departed. Many of their houses remained, to be taken over by the bourgeois of the new day, the bureaucrat, the merchant, the journalist. The Nagai family lived there for a time in Kafū's childhood.

Yet if the displacement of the old inhabitants was virtually complete, the district was the least changed physically of any in the immediate environs of the palace. At the end of Meiji *hatamoto* houses still survived in large numbers. The Arishima family, from which sprang Takeo the novelist and Ikuma the painter, as well as another novelist who used the pseudonym Satomi Ton, possessed one of them.

Still living in it after the earthquake, Ikuma wrote:

> I do not know whether it is a hundred years old or two hundred years old. I know from old maps that it once belonged to a lesser *hatamoto* called governor of something or other, but I do not know who might have built it or lived in it over the years. I have no notion of the joys and sorrows that came and went. Nor have I had any urge to learn.

They who come after me will probably not know about me, or have an urge to learn. It does not seem likely that there will be one among future dealers in culture who love this house for the reason that I love it, one reason only, that it is old. In the not distant future it will probably suffer the common fate and be torn down. The proverb has it that the head of a sardine can be deified if one is of a mind to do it. So we may account for my inability to think of giving up this shabby old house and its grounds. Not many are left of the *hatamoto* houses that lined the Banchō district. The fires that followed the earthquake reduced half of it to ashes.

Banchō, "the numbered blocks," Block One through Block Six, was another designation for the Kōjimachi district proper, the part of Kōjimachi Ward immediately west of the palace. Through a rearranging of numbers the British embassy was presently to acquire its fine address, Number One Block One. Arishima's reminiscences inform us that Banchō came through Meiji fairly well, and was grievously damaged in 1923. Though under new ownership in Meiji and early Taishō, it wore an aged aspect that was different from surviving parts of the Edo Low City, a graver, more sedate look. Because of massive gates and high garden walls, there was little here of the street life that prevailed in the Low City. Tiny garden plots lined the streets of the Low City, but the walled garden was virtually gone there by the end of Meiji.

Banchō had not contained the great estates of the daimyo, but the moderately ample places of the lesser aristocracy. The former became detached palaces and parade grounds and the like, while the latter were nicely proportioned to the needs of the upper middle class of the new day. In search of the look of the Edo High Town, therefore—an austere, walled-in, perhaps somewhat forbidding look—one might best, at the end of Meiji, have gone for a walk through Banchō.

The northern and southern parts of the High City have, in the Tokyo century, gone different ways. The beginnings of that difference were already apparent in Meiji. The two southern wards, Akasaka and Azabu, became the home of the highly affluent, and of the international and diplomatic set. There were such people in the north too. The Iwasaki family of the Mitsubishi enterprises had the most lavish of their several estates in Hongō. For those who wished to be near the rich and fashionable, however, and participate in their doings, the northern wards of the High City, Hongō and Koishikawa, were on the wrong side of the palace, and ever more so as the decades went by. The Low City, of course, was even farther removed from Society. The wards to the west, Yotsuya and Ushigome, tended to be rather more like the north than the south.

Insofar as they remained within the city limits at all, the good addresses came to be concentrated in the two southern wards. It says something, perhaps, that these two wards seem the least interesting of all the Meiji fifteen. They contained interesting people, no doubt, but, save for a few enclaves like the Akasaka geisha quarter, they were not interesting neighborhoods. Indeed the word "neighborhood" scarcely seems to apply. They encouraged the exclusiveness of the Tokugawa military classes.

Less wealthy, the northern wards—and to an extent the western wards too—had an artistic and intellectual tone. Sometimes the lack of wealth was extreme. Yotsuya Ward, west of Kōjimachi, contained one of the "slums" of which historians of the city seem so proud. There it was that Hanai O-ume, the murderess, died in 1916. It was almost next door to the Akasaka Palace, where the Meiji emperor spent a good part of his reign. The High City has always accommodated, side by side, the extremely well placed and the extremely poorly placed. The Yotsuya slum seems not to have been industrial, but a gathering of uprooted farmers.

It would probably be a simplification to say that the divergence north and south began with the disposition made of the grand estates. Yet that does seem to point the directions taken. Of the estates scattered around the castle, four stand out on Edo maps as rivals of the castle itself. They chanced to fall into four Meiji wards, all in the High City. The mansion and park of the Wakayama Tokugawa family, in Akasaka, became the Akasaka Detached Palace; the Nagoya Tokugawa estate in Ushigome became the military academy; the Mito Tokugawa estate in Koishikawa became an arsenal and later an amusement park, with a fragment of the Mito garden tucked somewhat sootily into a corner. And finally there was the one among the four that was not Tokugawa, the Maeda estate in Hongō, which became the Imperial University, and so Hongō, with the hilly parts of Kanda, became the student quarter of the city, and one of its intellectual and literary centers as well.

The origins of the university are complicated. It did not settle completely on the Maeda estate until mid-Meiji. Its earliest beginnings may be traced to certain institutions established by the shogunate for the study of the Western barbarian, and for more genteel Chinese studies as well. A South School and an East School each lay in a southerly direction from the Maeda estate. The Occidental and traditional branches feuded chronically and bitterly, but by the time of the move to Hongō in the eighties the former was ascendant.

Until the earthquake the Maeda family still occupied a generous—
though by old standards restricted—expanse at the southwest corner of
their old estate. Before it became the university campus the Maeda estate
had provided housing for Western persons who taught here and there
and were otherwise of service to the government. E. S. Morse lived on
the Maeda estate or Kaga Yashiki, as he called it, from the name of the
province that was the Maeda fief.

His description suggests what was happening to many of the old aristocratic tracts: "Kaga Yashiki is now a wilderness of trees, bushes, and
tangled masses of shrubbery; hundreds of crows are cawing about; here
and there are abandoned wells, some of them not covered, and treacher-
ous pits they are. The crows are as tame as our pigeons and act as scaven-
gers. They...wake you in the morning by cawing outside the window."

Immediately to the north of the university stood that most haughty
institution, the First Higher School. It was founded late in 1874 as the
Tokyo School of English and did not move to its Hongō grounds until
1889. The Hongō site is now occupied by the agricultural college of the
university, which in Meiji was in the southwestern suburbs. The First
Higher School was perhaps even haughtier than the university, which
was certainly haughty enough. All gifted and ambitious lads wanted to
attend both, and the higher school had the fewer students. Most of its
graduates who lived long enough became eminent in one way or another.
More than half the graduates of both institutions went routinely into the
bureaucracy or the academic life.

A short distance from the university on the other side was the most
elite of schools for women, the Women's Higher Normal School. When,
as soon happened, other institutions that called themselves universities
came into existence, they congregated in the regions to the north of the
palace. There were some famous boarding houses in Hongō, which, with
Kanda, had more of them than any other part of the city. The most famous produced approximately one doctor of philosophy per year during
the quarter of a century after its establishment.

At least one such house survives from late Meiji, a three-story wooden
building of a kind that fire regulations would not permit today. It was
considered so exciting an addition to the university quarter that there
were lantern processions for three nights to honor its opening. We have
seen that the Nezu licensed quarter, down the hill in the flat part of
Hongō, was moved lest it cause students to lay waste to their treasures. Upland Hongō seems on the whole to have been a sober district, its students
aware of their elite status and their responsibilities. The higher school

was relatively the rowdier, but the university seems to have set the tone. There was and has been very little in its vicinity to suggest a Latin Quarter. It is commonly thought today that the quiet was brought by the Second World War—this despite the fact that much of the district escaped the fires. It seems, however, to have been rather quiet all along.

The most famous novel about the student life of late Meiji is Natsume Sōseki's *Sanshirō,* whose title is the name of its hero. The campus pond, a survival from the Maeda days, is known as Sanshirō's Pond. Sanshirō lives in Hongō, and does not have a very exciting time of it. He sees a performance of *Hamlet,* which strikes him as full of odd remarks, but the pleasurable event described at greatest length is a viewing of the chrysanthemum dolls at Dangozaka, just north of the university. The novelist Tokuda Shūsei remarked upon how students had to go to Kanda for almost everything, from school supplies to Kabuki. Hongō was very much a part of the High City, he said, informing us, probably, that the students of the private universities may have set the tone in Kanda, but Hongō was dominated by more austere sorts, professors and intellectuals and the young men of the future.

Along its eastern border with Shitaya, Hongō extended a short distance into the flatlands. There was situated the soon-to-depart Nezu licensed quarter. At the top of the ridge a short distance south lay an older and unlicensed pleasure quarter, that of Yushima. In Meiji it was patronized chiefly by Nihombashi merchants, but the clientele also included the more affluent sort of student. There does not seem to have been any thought of doing to it what was done to Nezu.

The Yushima quarter had come into being because the huge Ueno temple complex, ministering to the Tokugawa tombs, was so near at hand. It was not proper for priests to frequent the usual sort of teahouse, and so they took their pleasure at establishments called *kagemajaya,* in which Yushima specialized. Written in a fashion that invites translation as "shady teahouses," the *kagemajaya* offered male geisha and prostitutes. Such places did not go out of business immediately upon the Restoration and the destruction of the temple. Towards the end of the nineteenth century Yushima shook off its past and became a more conventional geisha quarter.

Many professors dwelt in the vicinity of the university, and many literary persons as well, including Natsume Sōseki and Mori Ogai, the two of them the most revered of all Meiji novelists. Nagai Kafū has a memorable description of a visit to Ogai's "Tower of the Tidal Vista," not as fanciful a name as it may seem. Ogai lived north of the university, and the Hongo and Ueno rises were still much acclaimed for the views they offered over the Low City, low then in skyline as in elevation, towards the Sumida and the bay.

There was a *gakusha-machi,* a "professorial neighborhood," which has since disappeared. The Abe family, lords of Fukuyama in what is now Hiroshima Prefecture, had an estate very near the main gate of the university. Late in the Meiji Period they undertook to sell parcels at very low rates to professors, and to lend half the money needed for building houses upon them. Because the Abe had surrendered title, and the current holders could dispose of it as they wished, this admirable endeavor was defeated. In the years after the earthquake addresses to the west of the old city became fashionable among intellectuals. The professors moved there, and the Abe lands went to others. It is another episode in the westward movement of the city. Intellectuals may have had antibourgeois tendencies in some respects of intellectual import, but a good address for the businessman has been a good address for the professor *too*.

In Koishikawa, the ward to the west, the Iwasaki family attempted a similar endeavor in the years after the earthquake. Their main estate straddled the boundary between Hongō and Shitaya, and so graced both High City and Low. The Western house had been placed by Conder upon the ridge, and the main gate down at the Shitaya end. The house survives. The Iwasaki estate is probably the best place in the whole country for acquiring a sense of how the Meiji plutocracy lived. A few of the Japanese rooms that once stretched all along the west verge of the garden survive. The Western mansion was of course for show, and the lawn, more like an English park than a traditional Japanese garden, must have provided a grand setting for parties; the Japanese rooms were where the family chose to live.

The story of the survival is interesting. The holocaust of 1923 destroyed another Iwasaki mansion by Conder in Fukagawa, but spared the Hongō one, as did the holocaust of 1945. The tract and the buildings on it passed to the government as a result of American efforts to disperse the assets of rich families. Most of it was presently entrusted to the Supreme Court, which decided to clear the site for a legal institute and housing for judges. Destruction was proceeding briskly and had overtaken most of the Japanese wing when the Cultural Properties Commission intervened and declared the remainder, and the Western mansion, an Important Cultural Property under the protection of the state. The Supreme Court acceded; had it wished to have the designation revoked, it would have had to go to court like anyone else.

The Iwasaki mansion in Hongō, designed by Conder. A survivor from Meiji

Life has at times been difficult for the very rich of modern Japan. The head of the Yasuda enterprises, now Fuji, was assassinated in 1921. There are subterranean passages on the Iwasaki property. Many sinister things are said to have occurred in them, while the house was used by Americans for counterintelligence operations. Earlier occupants had in fact dug the passages, because they could never be sure when they might have to flee. From such details one may sense what life was like for the Rokumeikan set.

It would seem that even before the earthquake professorial and intellectual sorts were beginning to move westwards. A 1918 work, one of large numbers describing the "prosperity" of the city, offers brief characterizations of each of the fifteen wards. Those for the Low City are rather obvious. It may be that, compared to the High City, the Low City was static and simple to classify, not the place of the future. Kyōbashi is "high-collar," Nihombashi "Japanese." The several directions in which the High City seems to be moving are apparent, as is the divergence between the north and the south. Akasaka is the place of the aristocracy, Azabu that of "the voices of insects," suggesting wide gardens and tracts still awaiting development, there at the southern edge of the city. Hongō is the place of the student (as is Kanda, but of the sort of student who must work for his board), and Koishikawa, in the northwest corner of the Meiji city, is the place of the *gakusha,* the professor or scholar.

Koishikawa produced Nagai Kafū, the most sensitive and diligent chronicler of the city, but on the whole it was the less distinguished of the two wards on the northern tier of the High City. It had very little, in the days before a baseball stadium and an amusement park came to occupy the site of the old Mito estate, that people would wish to go out of their way for. The circle of temples along the outskirts of Edo extended westwards and southwards through Koishikawa and Ushigome. Koishikawa contained two very solemn temples, both close to the Tokugawa family, and having none of the popular appeal of the Asakusa Kannon. There were also gardens of some note, including the university botanical garden, founded in the seventeenth century as the shogun's own medicinal gardens. The oldest educational building in the city, once the university medical school, is in the botanical garden.

Koishikawa contained pockets of industry, one of them dear to chroniclers of the proletariat. The valley behind the Denzūin, one of the two grand temples in the district, was a printing center. Being somewhat better educated than most members of the proletariat, printers early acquired class consciousness, and so provided Japanese counterparts of Joe Hill. On the whole, however, Koishikawa was a region of solid if not high bourgeoisie. For some reason this northwesterly direction was not the one in which people who could go anywhere chose to go; nor was it a quarter of the city that was being pushed under in the rush to the suburbs. The outer boundary of Koishikawa was still not far from the real limits of the city.

Ushigome and Yotsuya, the wards to the west of Kōjimachi and the palace, had that same air of the modestly bourgeois. They did, from time to time, show more distinguished things to the world. Kagurazaka, in Ushigome, was for a time the only High City district of flowers and willows that rivaled Akasaka. Kafū thought it had High City sleaziness in uncommon measure, but he was difficult to please. The best time for Kagurazaka was immediately after the earthquake. Ushigome was the only ward among the fifteen that suffered no fire damage. So it drew people who, in a happier day, would have preferred the older and more conservative quarters of the Low City. Presently Kagurazaka was left behind in the great rush to the western suburbs.

Still in mid-Meiji the least populous of the fifteen wards, Yotsuya was on the most frequented of the migratory routes westwards. Just before the earthquake it was enlarged to include a part of the Shinjuku district, the most rapidly growing of the western suburbs, presently to excel Ginza as a place for shopping and pursuing pleasure.

The Arishima family bought a *hatamoto* house in Kōjimachi, and Ikuma was still living in it after the earthquake. Nagai Kafū's father bought two *hatamoto* places in Koishikawa, and tore them down to have a house and garden more suited to the new day. Only traces of the old gardens, dread places inhabited by foxes, remained in Kafū's boyhood. It would seem to have been typical. The rows of *hatamoto* houses in Kōjimachi supported one another and gave the place its tone, and so they remained. In the wards farther north and west the larger estates were broken up or put to public use, and the *hatamoto* lands in among them attracted people who were not of an antiquarian bent. So the outer wards must, at the end of Meiji, have looked much less like Edo than did Banchō.

The southern wards were lacking in places one might wish to show a country cousin. Azabu was the ward of the singing insects, but of course he had quite enough insect voices at home. Akasaka had its detached palace, through whose iron gates it was possible, at the end of Meiji, to gaze upon the Gallic pile where dwelt the crown prince.

There were extensive barracks in the southern wards, and from them the Roppongi section of Azabu got its start as a pleasure center, the only major one in the present city that is not also a transportation center. The military origins of Roppongi are not commonly remembered in our day. It is a place where pleasure-seeking pacifists assemble.

The other place for military revelry in late Meiji was Shibuya, beyond the city limits to the southwest, one of the directions in which the city was pressing most urgently. Famous for its tea in early Meiji, Shibuya was by late Meiji becoming richly suburban, the chief rival of Shinjuku in its power to draw people and money from the center of the old city.

On Meiji maps, Akasaka "of the aristocracy" looks as if it might have had noisier insect voices than Azabu. It was not the principal abode of the highest aristocracy, the court stratum. Of fourteen houses recognized as princely in late Meiji, seven were in Kōjimachi, between the inner and outer moats of the old castle, and five were scattered through the southern wards of the city, only one of them in Akasaka. One remained in the old capital, Kyoto, and one was still in the Low City, beside the Sumida above Asakusa. None were in the northern wards of the High City, which were distinctly less titled and moneyed.

Yet Akasaka had great tracts of public and royal land, and the princeliest personage among them all, the next emperor. Had one been good at scaling walls and evading guards, one could have walked the whole of the way across the ward, from the city limits to the outer moat, without setting foot on private, nonroyal land. Across certain wide expanses singing insects may have been hard pressed to survive. The new Akasaka parade grounds, to be the site of the Meiji emperor's funeral and then to become public gardens in his memory, were as dusty as the old Hibiya grounds. A scorched-earth policy thought to be good for instilling a soldierly mood prevailed in both places.

Though it did not have the smallest population, Azabu must in late Meiji have seemed the most rustic of the fifteen wards. Indeed we have the testimony of rickshaw runners that they preferred to stay away from it, and had no great difficulty doing so, for it had little need of their services. Its streets and lanes wandered their own way with little regard for the ways of their fellows, and the runner was likely to suffer the professional humiliation of getting lost.

The main thrust of the city, as it spilled over its limits in late Meiji, was directly to the west, past Yotsuya to Shinjuku. The next most powerful was to the southwest, past Akasaka towards Shibuya. So the pattern at the end of Meiji was as it had been at the beginning, energetic commerce along the radial strands of the cobweb, and residential districts of varying density and greatly varying affluence scattered among them.

The great shift of Meiji and since has been more than a matter of population. The High City was accumulating the money, the power, and the imagination. Culture tends to go where money goes, and so the Low City was ceasing to be original in this important regard. It may seem strange to say that power was leaving the Low City, since under the old regime absolute power had been concentrated in the shogun's castle. Yet, as we have seen, the aristocracy was scattered all over the Low City (especially in places with water frontage and pleasant prospects), and the wealthy of the merchant class, such as the Mitsui family, had much more power than Tokugawa theory permitted.

Today there is an illuminating confusion in defining the boundaries of the Low City. The affluent of the southern and western wards tend to think that all of the poorer northern and eastern wards are Low City. In fact, however, they straddle the ridge line that originally divided the two, and the Hongō and Yanaka districts were significant artistic and intellectual centers in Meiji, most definitely a part of the High City. The confusion is illuminating because it informs us that the great division today, especially in the minds of the high bourgeoisie, is between the richer and poorer halves of the city. It was not so in Edo and early Meiji. Then, if any generalization held, it was that the High City was the more patrician of the two, and the Low City the more plebeian.

Today, poring over rosters of literary societies, one may come upon an occasional address in the northern wards, but scarcely any in the flatlands east of the Ueno rise—in the classical Low City. Writers and artists were moving out all through the Meiji Period, as were the old military aristocracy and the mercantile elite. Few stayed behind after the great flood, and by the time of the earthquake the withdrawal was almost complete. Nagai Kafū loved the Low City, but it would not do for everyday. He lived in Tsukiji, near the foreign settlement and even nearer the Shimbashi geisha district, for a time in mid-Taishō, but several years before the earthquake he built himself a house in wealthy, hilly Azabu. His diary for the Tsukiji time is a grouchy document. The Low City was noisy and dusty.

The Low City was the home of the literature and drama of late Edo, insofar as those pursuits had to do with the new and not the traditional and academic. The drama changed gradually, because of the improvers and because of inevitable influences from abroad, and its base in the Low City was dissipated. The literature of Edo continued to be popular until about midway through Meiji, when the modern began to take over.

Of the difference between the traditional and the modern in literature, many things can be said. The popular literature of Edo had not been very intellectual. The literature known as modern, with its beginnings in the Rokumeikan decade, the 1880s, is obsessively, gnawingly intellectual. If a single theme runs through it, that theme is the quest for identity, an insistence upon what it is that establishes the individual as individual. The importance of Christianity in Meiji thought and writing, an importance which it has not had since; the rebellion against the family and the casting of the authoritarian father into nether regions; the strong autobiographic strain in modern fiction: all of these have in common the identification of modernism with individualism.

They were concerns of the High City. The Low City went on for a time reading and producing the woodcut books beloved of the Edo townsman. The leaders of modernity had utter contempt for these, and as the afterglow of Edo faded, the Low City offered no serious competition with modernity. Nor was it remarkably steadfast in its devotion to the old forms. Not many people of Taishō could, and almost no one today can, make out their antiquated, ornate language and quirkish calligraphy.

A strong sense of locale was present in the literature of Edo. One can with no great exaggeration say that Edo had its literature and Tokyo does not. Modern literature is altogether more national and cosmopolitan than Edo literature, which is not to be understood and appreciated without reference to very specific places—from Shiba on the south to Kanda, Shitaya, and the Asakusa-Yoshiwara complex on the north, and eastwards beyond the Sumida. Though people like Kafū and Kubota Mantarō made the changing city their chief subject, they were exceptions. Modern literature calls to mind not specific places like Shiba and Kanda but that great abstraction "suburbia."

To say that the Low City was the cultural center of Japan in late Edo and Meiji is to say that it created the most interesting culture. This is different from being a cultural capital, the products of which are purveyed all through the land. The boundaries of the Low City as we see them on a late-Edo map defined a cultural region. The boundaries of the High City today do not. It is bigger than it looks. The story of modern literature is, like the story of prime ministers, philosophers, and the like, a national one, something that has happened in Tokyo but is not of it.

All these several stories are interesting, certainly. Giving them a few lines and then moving on, I may seem to be dismissing the grander story, that of the transformation of a small and isolated country at a far corner of the earth into a modern technological giant, and of the intellectual and emotional processes that accompanied the transformation and made it possible. Yet it may after all be less a story of change than one of survival. The modern novelist and thinker have been dedicated evangelists for individualism, and yet the great strength of modern Japan may be in the willingness of most Japanese, even in the absence of authoritarian precepts, to suppress their individuality.

The growth of the High City in size and influence has made Tokyo more of an abstraction and less of a community. Beginning in Meiji and continuing all through the century since Meiji began, the change is a profound one. The baseball-and-television culture of the Low City of our day is an altogether lesser entity than was the culture of the Low City a century ago; and the culture of the High City is much more considerable. The High City still has poor people enough, but it has all of the exceedingly rich people. The other elements, literary and artistic and philosophical and the rest, have followed money, even when they have thought of themselves as constituting a resistance.

The High City gets higher and higher. The Low City is still the warmer and more approachable of the two, but the days of its cultural eminence are gone. They are for elegists and threnodists.

Chapter 6

THE TAISHŌ LOOK

July 20, 1912, was the day scheduled for the *kawabiraki*, the opening of the Sumida (see pages 143-144), most delightfully crowded of Low City observances. It was called off, for on that day came the announcement that the Meiji emperor was grievously ill. He had been ill for a week, and had fallen into a coma from uremic poisoning.

The rest of the summer was hushed. The street festivals for "taking in coolness," which made the oppressive heat of August a happy thing, were subdued, as was the mood of the pleasure quarters. Geisha who found it necessary to go about their business did so in ordinary dress, lest they attract attention. Even the stock market reacted, pessimistically, for there was an instinctive feeling that the end of an age had come, and no one could be certain about the one that was to follow.

Notices of the state of the royal health were sent out from the palace by pony express and put up before police boxes. There were silent crowds in the palace plaza. Public-minded persons (not, it seems, the city) provided water. There were crowds as well at shrines near the palace—Kanda to the north, Sannō to the south, the Hibiya Shrine near the Imperial Hotel. From temples poured great clouds of smoke, day and night, the burning of sesame seeds being an ancient form of exorcism, and ancient beliefs about malign spirits yet widespread.

Vehicular traffic made every attempt to move silently when it had to move past the palace. Rags muffled the sound of wheels along the trolley track that followed the palace moat from Hibiya towards Yotsuya and approached fairly close to the royal apartments on its southwest arc. From the plaza, the cannon that since 1871 had fired the *don* at noon each day was moved to a remoter spot.

Outside the palace as the Meiji emperor lay dying

The emperor died late on the night of July 29. The announcement came early on July 30, and so the forty-fifth year of Meiji became the first year of Taishō. Rain began falling a few minutes past midnight and fell as the announcement was made, but crowds, standing or kneeling, remained in the plaza all through the night.

Demonstrations of grief and affection continued through the weeks before the funeral. Theaters called off all performances upon the announcement of the death, and some remained closed until the funeral. The variety theaters seem to have been the quickest to go back into business. Many shops closed, especially in commercial districts near the palace. Sales throughout the city fell by perhaps a fifth, perhaps as much as a third, during the early days of mourning. The grief had a streak of anger in it; the house of the emperor's chief physician was stoned.

There was a movement to have the interment in Tokyo, but Fushimi, on the southern outskirts of Kyoto, had already been selected. The funeral took place on September 13. Newspaper descriptions emphasize the stillness of places usually noisy, save only the railway stations, and especially Ueno, accommodating travelers from the poor and conservative northeast. The Nihombashi fish market, usually closed only at the New Year, was silent on the day of the funeral. Shops remained closed all over the city. Asakusa was described as quieter than in the aftermath of the great flood two years before. The ladies of pleasure beneath the Twelve Storys in Asakusa observed the day solemnly.

The weather was good. The funeral was a combination of the old and the new, richly symbolic of the era that had ended. Night had always been the time for the most sacred of Shinto ceremonials, and the funeral was at night. The guards regiment fired a salute at eight in the evening. Naval vessels off Shinagawa answered, and temple bells all through the city started tolling. The cortege left the southeast gate of the palace to a bugle call and funeral marches played by the guards band. The way to Babasaki, on the other side of the plaza, was lighted by gas torches in iron baskets, while attendants in the immediate cortege carried pine torches. The funeral pavilion, at the Akasaka parade grounds, was also lighted by gas, in that latter day of gaslight. Five oxen in single file drew the hearse. Some attendants wore ancient court dress, others modern uniforms.

The cortege made its way southwards from Babasaki past Hibiya Park, westwards along the outer moat, and then south to the parade grounds, which it reached at about eleven. At Babasaki the crush was so great that there were injuries. All windows and utility poles along the way were draped in black and white, all lights were put out, and all shop signs were either draped or removed. The body was taken to Kyoto by train on the fourteenth, and that night interred at Fushimi. With the energetic Shibusawa Eiichi in charge, planning for a memorial shrine began immediately. Land belonging to the royal household in the western suburbs, beyond Akasaka Ward, was chosen for the site of the shrine proper, and the parade grounds, site of the funeral, for the "outer gardens." The iris gardens that are the most famous part of the shrine grounds are said to have been designed by the Meiji emperor himself for the pleasure of his empress, to whom the shrine was also presently dedicated. It was begun in 1915 and dedicated in 1920, although construction was not finally completed until late the following year. The outer gardens were not finished until 1926, the year in which another reign began, the Shōwa, which yet continues. On the day of the dedication a bridge collapsed, leading to a construction scandal already remarked upon (see page 49). It coincided with a scandal over gas rates. The double scandal led to the resignation of the mayor.

The most remarkable happening attendant upon the funeral was the suicide of General Nogi and his wife. It seems to have occurred as the temple bells began tolling at the start of the obsequies. The Nogi house, a modest one which yet stands, is very close to the parade grounds. In

Funeral procession for the Meiji emperor

that day when the southern wards were so little developed, it may have been visible from the funeral pavilion.

No shrine would be dedicated to the Taishō emperor, successor to the Meiji emperor, nor can his passing have seemed so clearly the passing of an age. Meiji is remote as a person, but as a symbol he remains important. Of Taishō this cannot be said. His last years were spent in shadows deep even for an emperor. A regency was proclaimed in 1921, with the crown prince, the present emperor, then a youth of twenty, as regent. Gingerly, we are told in biographical notes that the emperor had fallen ill. That the illness was mental is one of those facts which no one speaks of but everyone knows.

The Taishō reign was a short one, only a third as long as Meiji. The emperor had ceased to exist as a public figure, and his death, coming so soon after the earthquake, must have seemed an event of no great moment for the populace of the city, where manifestations of grief for his father had been conspicuous. One wonders whether, if he had died before his father and the present emperor had succeeded as a boy of ten or eleven, the period from 1912 to 1926 would be thought by historians to constitute a unit at all.

In any case, it might be described as unexciting, compared with the preceding and following reigns. The former brought huge successes, the latter brought a catastrophe of its own making and now brings successes of a quite different order. Taishō had its war, a comfortable one for the Japanese, in which the principal action was far away in Europe and certain fruits of victory lay near at hand. The expressions with which "Taishō" is most commonly associated are "the great Taishō earthquake" and "Taishō democracy," the latter a pale flower that bloomed briefly after the First World War and left nothing behind save its name. Taisho history contains little to be either very proud of or deeply ashamed of.

We are accustomed to thinking of modern Japanese history in terms of reigns, however, and so there are Taishō literature, the Taishō theater, and the like. The fact remains that the things of Taishō do have their own look.

Wandering through the more crowded parts of the Low City, one comes upon pockets that survived the conflagration of 1945, and there it is, the Taishō look. Very rarely is the Meiji look to be come upon, and almost never the genuine Edo object. One recognizes Taishō in the pressed-metal fronts of little shops, in irrelevant turrets, in oriel windows and shutters that fold rather than slide. Nagai Kafū rejoiced in the obliviousness of the regions east of the river to the call of Civilization and Enlightenment, but Taishō may be seen as the time when they started paying attention at least to its decorative elements.

In 1914 the city sponsored a great fair called the Taishō Hakurankai, the Taishō Exposition. The purpose was to honor the new reign and, in the Meiji spirit, to promote industry. It got off to a bad start. The contractors did not seem very intent upon promoting industry. Construction was incomplete on opening day, and the emperor had to make his way to the site through a sea of mud. Letters to editors objected to the inclusion of a mummy among exhibits felicitating the new era, but the exposition was on the whole a success. More than seven million people purchased tickets. Whatever it may have done for industry, it did succeed in giving the Taishō reign a certain independence from its predecessor, an identity of its own.

There were other expositions, one of which celebrated the semicentennial of the establishment of Tokyo as capital; another honored the conclusion of the war to end wars, and itself ended just a year and a half before the earthquake. But no exposition was more important than the Taishō Exposition. It introduced and established the Taishō look, right there at the beginning of the reign.

Tokyo led the way into the new era, as it had into the old. By the end of Meiji, monumental architecture in the Western style had become soberly, somewhat academically Western. The earliest exercises in Western architecture, such as the Hoterukan, had been something different—different, indeed, from anything Western. Much the same may be said of the influence which the Taishō Exposition had upon shop and domestic architecture, nowhere more conspicuously than in the pleasure quarters. Extremes of fancifulness make them look like Disneylands before their time. E. Philip Terry, that writer of colorful if not wholly reliable guidebooks, thought the Yoshiwara "Pompeiian." Looking at pictures of what was lost in 1923, others might think that it was Venetian, rather, in the exuberance and liberality of its decoration. It had something of San Marco in it.

There was a Taishō look in people too, more noticeable in women than in men. The day of the flapper did not arrive until after the earthquake. Men had for the most part taken to Western dress before the earthquake, but Japanese dress prevailed among women. The Taishō woman in Japanese dress looks more Western, somehow, than does the Meiji woman in Western dress. The bustles and bonnets of the Meiji woodcut are all very gay, and, at the remove of a century (however they may have looked to a Parisian couturier of the time, and indeed did look to Pierre Loti), seem authentic enough, but the face is of an earlier day. A languorous beauty of Taishō, by contrast, speaks of a world-weariness that has been studied well and mastered, and it is not of domestic provenance.

Two years older than Tanizaki, the painter and illustrator Takehisa Yumeji was in his late twenties when Taishō began. Among all artists and craftsmen he is the most symbolic of Taishō. His creative years were mostly in Taishō, and his illustrations, while they may not be great art, speak more eloquently of Taishō than do those of any other artist. Wan, consumptive, with sloping shoulders and lips, the Yumeji girl would have felt at home in the Germany of a century before.

Edo artists in the woodcut admired slender beauty, certainly, but it is an abstract, fleshless sort of beauty, very far from this wasted flesh. The Yumeji girl may look ill, but she smiles sometimes, albeit wanly. The Edo beauty did not smile, and the Meiji beauty did but rarely. All manner of smiles flash across Taishō paintings and posters, and give a sense that Western things have been absorbed and become part of the organism as they had not earlier been. The enterprising cosmetologists of the Shiseidō may at length have succeeded in clearing the national skin of its murkiness.

A Yumeji girl—with cat

The painter Kishida Ryūsei, who was born in Ginza in 1891, thought he found a Taishō look in men too, and especially actors. "There is a certain briskness about these handsome figures. There is something that suggests Valentino." He wrote of the quality after the earthquake, but it must have been there before. The Valentino look may be associated with the Taishō look—though "briskness" is the last word one would apply to the Yumeji girl. It is a pity that we have no Yumeji boys.

The population of the fifteen wards grew during Taishō, and the population of the prefecture grew yet more rapidly. By the time of the earthquake the former had risen to well over two million, and the population of the prefecture to almost four million.

The High City was reaching beyond the city limits in all directions, especially the south and west. At the beginning of Meiji the city did not fill the fifteen wards, and at the end of Taishō the fifteen wards no longer defined the city. The city proper was larger in area than Yokohama, Kobe, or Kyoto, but covered less than half the area of Osaka, and only a little more than half that of Nagoya. Not until almost a decade after the earthquake were the city limits expanded to encompass most of the population, and such burgeoning suburbs as Shibuya and Ikebukuro. The municipal government seems to have been reluctant to press for expansion. The city was vulnerable to incursions upon its autonomy, and any approach to the size of the prefecture meant risking a return to the old "special" status, with a governor and no mayor.

Yet it seems to have been thought inevitable that the city would expand. Aside from Tokyo itself, there was still at the end of Taishō only one incorporated city in the prefecture. Much more populous districts than that one city, Hachiōji, lay just beyond the fifteen wards. It seems to have been assumed that these would presently become wards themselves. In 1932, they did.

The governor continued to be a faceless bureaucrat from the Home Ministry, while the mayor was sometimes a man of considerable eminence. There were mayors of ministerial stature, such as Gotō Shimpei, he of the "big kerchief," who would have had the earthquake and its aftermath to preside over had he not resigned in the spring of 1923.

None of the eight mayors of Tokyo during the Taishō Period was born in the city. Gotō may have been the most famous of them, but probably the most popular was his predecessor, Tajiri Inajirō, so eminent an authority on administration that he lectured at the Imperial University. He had to resign because of the bridge that collapsed while the Meiji Shrine was being dedicated. An eccentric in a way that made people like him, he wore hand-me-down clothes and walked to his office from Koishikawa, his lunch tied up in a kerchief like that of any other worker. A tendency towards incontinence in moments of tension was taken as a mark of earnestness.

The nation enjoyed a war boom, and the city shared in it. Industrial production in 1919 was almost four times what it had been in 1910. As for finance and management, there was a rush to Marunouchi, the old Mitsubishi Meadow. In 1922 more than a third of companies with a capitalization of over five million yen had their headquarters in Kōjimachi Ward, chiefly Marunouchi. The number was about equal to the combined total for Nihombashi, the heart of the old merchant city, and Kyōbashi. The city was falling into its present shape by mid-Taishō.

Across from the central railway station, the Marunouchi Building, largest in the land, was finished on the eve of the earthquake. The Marine Insurance Building, finished in 1917, was the first to be called *biru*, short for "building." (Most office buildings are now so designated.) The two buildings represented another Taishō look, the box-like one. The small shopkeeper may have fancied oriels and turrets, but big builders were eschewing unprofitable decorations. Another lesson had been learned.

* * *

The First World War produced inflation, and at the end of it came riots over the high price of rice. They led to the formation of the first government based on political parties, an event generally held to mark the beginning of "Taishō democracy." The rioting reached Tokyo in mid-August of 1918, having begun on the coast of the Japan Sea ten days earlier.

Police dispersed a rally in Hibiya Park on the night of August 13, and marauding bands ranged through Kyōbashi and Nihombashi. There was more rioting on the evening of the fourteenth. One swath of violence began in Hibiya and extended from Shimbashi northwards through Ginza and Kyōbashi into Nihombashi. The other was more interesting. It began in Asakusa and advanced upon Ueno, where the crowd was estimated at twenty thousand, and upon the Yoshiwara, where sixty-nine houses were damaged. Arson and looting occurred.

On the fifteenth, riots struck the same parts of the Low City and for the first time moved west into the High City. On the sixteenth there was violence in Ginza once more, but in Ueno mounted troops scattered a band of eager rioters. No reporting on the riots had been allowed since the fourteenth. On the seventeenth it resumed, the papers having protested and the peak of the troubles having passed.

The riots led to the resignation of a prime minister who as a lad not yet twenty had served with the Restoration forces, they that overthrew the shogunate, and to the investiture of a new kind of prime minister, symbolic of Taishō democracy. Another important man of a new sort first came into prominence because of them. Shōriki Matsutarō was in command of the police who dispersed the initial Hibiya riot, and got into the newspapers because he suffered a gash on the forehead. He was so forceful and energetic a man that he was bound, sooner or later, to make his appearance in chronicles of the twentieth century. The riots were the occasion for his debut. Shōriki later became president of the *Yomiuri,* which, when he took charge, was fifth or sixth among the dozen or so newspapers in the city. He made it the largest of them all in terms of Tokyo circulation (and it is a native of the city, and not, like the *Asahi* and *Nichinicki* or *Mainichi,* Osakan). He may be called the father of professional baseball and commercial television; and so there are few Japanese lives upon which he has had no effect.

The provincial riots clearly originated in discontent over inflation. There is room for disagreement about the real meaning of the Tokyo riots. Probably the national government would not have been called upon to resign had the violence not reached the capital but been restricted to remote fishing villages. Yet there is always a suggestion in Tokyo rioting that participants gather for fun and excitement. In these events, a thousand were arrested. About a quarter received prison sentences, the highest fifteen years. Few of the accused seem to have been poverty-stricken.

Nagai Kafū thought that he detected certain leisurely, recreational tendencies in it all.

> I turned into a side street and noted that the rows of geisha houses were silent, their shutters closed and their lights out. Back on the main street, I was passing time in a beer hall when a young man who seemed to be a student told me of attacks on Ginza shops and on geisha establishments in the Shimbashi district.
>
> So I first learned of riots over the price of rice. From the next day there were no newspaper reports in the matter. I heard later that the rioting always occurred in the cool of evening. There was a good moon every evening during those days. Hearing that the rioters gathered menacingly before the houses of the wealthy when the evening had turned cool and the moon had come up, I could not put down a feeling that there was something easy and comfortable about it all. It went on for five or six days and then things returned to normal. On the night of the return to normal, it rained.

The city was becoming somewhat more fireproof, and the flowers of Edo were being stamped out. The biggest fire of Taishō, excluding the gigantic one of 1923, was another in the fine series of Kanda fires. It came in the first year of the reign, and destroyed more than twenty-five hundred buildings from Kanda eastwards into Nihombashi and Kyōbashi. Among Taishō fires of some note was the one that destroyed the first Imperial Hotel on the eve of the opening of the second. Improved firefighting methods may have had something to do with diminished losses, bur fireproofing no doubt played a larger part. In 1916 thatched roofs were banned for new buildings. The fire brigades of Edo, spirited and cheerful, remained on the job right up until the earthquake. The central fire department was reduced to ashes in 1923, along with most of its equipment. Such a disaster was needed to bring unified and centralized firefighting. The new system was not, of course, able to prevent the disaster of 1945, nor can it hope to be completely effective against similar disasters in the future.

The great flood of late Meiji was the last to devastate the center of the city. In 1917 the Kabukiza, east of Ginza, was knee-deep in water, but that was because a typhoon blew the bay inland. The Arakawa Drainage Channel was begun after the great flood and finished on the eve of the earthquake. Even before its completion it worked well, controlling torrential rains in the summer of 1918. The Tone River system still floods the farthest eastern wards from time to time, but the Arakawa Drainage Channel has contained the more mischievous Sumida.

The channel was the most ambitious engineering project the city had seen since the shogunate filled the marshy mouths of the Sumida to make the Low City. The money came from the national government, and the Home Ministry directly supervised operations, digging a wide new watercourse for upwards of fifty miles, from deep in Saitama Prefecture to the bay. In its upper reaches it generally followed the old Arakawa River. From approximately the point where the Arakawa changes names and becomes the Sumida, it swept eastwards, entering the bay at a point about halfway between the eastern boundary of Fukagawa Ward and the eastern limits of the present city. Sluices control the flow of water into the Sumida.

Nowhere did the new channel pass through any of the fifteen wards of the Meiji and Taishō city. The land was acquired at what was then thought to be a very great expense. Since the regions it crossed were then mostly suburbs and farm and fishing villages, the cost would have been several times as much a few years later. The endeavor showed great vision, and the results were splendid. The floors of a few houses may sometimes even now be under water from a cloudburst, but no major flood has been caused by the Sumida since 1910.

Perhaps inevitably (though one wonders why it must be so), fires and floods have been controlled at a cost of beauty. A somewhat fireproof concrete box does not have the tones of aging wood, nor has a flat roof pasted over with tar paper the appeal of a massive, deep-eaved roof of thatch. One now looks across the river not at grassy embankments and expanses of reed and rush, but at walls of splotchy concrete.

Writing in 1920, E. Philip Terry warned the tourists whom he hoped to have as readers that they need not expect night life in Tokyo.

After dark Tokyo is a big dusky village to all but the initiated, and to some an intolerably dull one. Unless one figures in the diplomatic swing, and officiates at the almost ceaseless round of entertainments enjoyed by that favored class, there is little for the average man to do outside the comfortable hotel…. On the other hand, the Japanese, who do not go in much for a fast life, and who are easily pleased, find the decorous allurements of Tokyo so potent that they are drawn to them, as by magnets, from all parts of the Empire. To hobnob perpetually with a tiny pot of insipid, sugarless tea and a tobacco-pipe with a bowl no bigger than a bullet, the while listening to the beating of a tom-tom and the doleful ditties of pantomimic *geisha,* fills them with rapture; and once installed in the capital they regard with positive pity all who are so unfortunate as to dwell outside it.

It is a lively account, and the tourist must have found truth in it. Had Terry known as much about Japan as did Chamberlain and Mason, those authors of a much superior guidebook, he would have known that there was more night life in Taishō than the city had known before. Edo had been black and silent after dark, its nocturnal pleasures reserved entirely for men, and not for many of them. The crowds that poured forth on Ginza with the coming of its bricks and bright lights were quite new. It was an innocent sort of night life, perhaps, but still it offered something for all the family, and especially for the younger adult members, who had rather been left out of the pleasures of the pleasure quarters. The great day of Gimbura, "killing time in Ginza," began in Taishō and lasted until the Second World War, though by then such western centers as Shinjuku were drawing away the youthful crowds.

Ginza and Gimbura were the heart of Taishō Tokyo. Nihombashi, the heart of mercantile Edo, was being challenged by Marunouchi as the place for big planners and managers, but it went on being the place for the big retail sell. Mitsukoshi and Shirokiya, the two department-store pioneers in the mercantile revolution of late Meiji, continued trying to outdo each other. Mitsukoshi, as has been noted, was the better of the two at advertising.

Losing crowds to Ginza, Nihombashi might have seemed to be losing its mercantile preeminence as well—for the purpose of advertising is to draw crowds. Yet one should remember that conservative, systematic Nihombashi had not been a place to draw huge crowds, and the Gimbura crowds, such a new phenomenon, were not of a sort to buy expensive merchandise. It would be decades before Nihombashi had rivals as the big shopping center of the city. Gimbura was merely a pleasant way for people about twenty years old to pass time, among people indistinguishable from themselves, the sort they liked best. It may have been the first time that the city had a place for them—and for the most part only them—to go. The expression Gimbura has fallen into disuse and the largest crowds have moved westwards; but the crowds go on being about twenty years of age.

The willows of Ginza, 1921

The famous willows, symbol of Ginza in the years when Gimbura was coming into vogue, disappeared on the eve of the earthquake. They had been badly damaged by the typhoon which in 1917 brought the waters of the bay within a block or two of the center of the district. In 1921, when the main Ginza street was rearranged to give less room to pedestrians and more to vehicles, authorities replaced them with gingkos, which were more compact, and better served the convenience of motorists.

By then, of course, the day of the motorist had arrived, and his convenience had become the most important thing, as it has remained. The first automobile is said to have come from abroad (in those years all internal-combustion engines did) in late Meiji, and to have been the property of a man with a curious name, Isaac Satō. There were taxicabs from the beginning of Taishō. By the time of the earthquake there were several hundred motorcycles in the city. G. B. Sansom, the British historian, liked to say that he had the very first one in the land. He brought it in shortly before the First World War and used it to explore the countryside.

The opening of the new Ginza main street was not a complete success. The part of the street for vehicular traffic other than trolleys had been uncertainly surfaced, and as a result was often muddy or dusty. Now it was covered with wooden blocks, the interstices filled with asphalt, a technique assuring durability and thought appropriate to the anticipated weight of traffic. On the day of the opening, heavy rains caused a large number of blocks to float, and the splashing was extreme. There was similar trouble the following year, and trouble with melting asphalt in the torrid August sun. Finally, in 1923, the street caught fire and burned up. So in a way the story of Tokyo's first half-century is bracketed by Ginza fires.

For the masses, however things may have been with the managers, Taishō was the era of Ginza and Asakusa. Only on the eve of the earthquake was the name "Ginza" officially applied to the full length of the district as it is today. It had in the strictest sense designated only the northern blocks, where the old mint, the "Silver Seat," had been. Most people would have thought Ginza the center of the city, but it was not really "downtown." It did not possess really big things, except perhaps in journalism and the theater. It was a mood, rather, not easy to define or characterize. For all the accomplished world-weariness of the Yumeji girl, Taishō had a younger culture than Meiji. It was then that the *mobo* and *moga,* the "modern boy" and "modern girl," emerged and started having fun on next to nothing. Ginza was the main place where they had it.

Asakusa is where the masses went to do what the masses of Edo had been wont to do, find performances to view and thereby ruin themselves. It was the show center, and it had the best range of little roistering places and unlicensed lechering places as well. It was traditional in the sense that the most popular temple in the city, the Asakusa Kannon, had long been friendly to such places. At the end of Edo, Asakusa had a near-monopoly on the theater and served as the final station on the way to the most distinguished of the pleasure quarters, but its great day, between the two world wars, continued the old tradition and was very modern as well.

Asakusa had a flair for the new mass culture. It kept up with the times and may have been a little ahead of them, leading the masses its way. In the years after the Russo-Japanese War, it contained the most thriving cluster of movie palaces. Asakusa was preeminent in this respect through Taishō and on into Shōwa. Kafū would go there to look at the "motion picture" posters, and so keep up with the times. Asakusa still had Kabuki. The Miyatoza, behind the temple, was looked upon by connoisseurs as the last ground of Edo Kabuki. Kabuki was not, however, the popular form it once had been in its own Low City, and cinema, though growing and favored with such talents as Tanizaki's (he wrote scripts), was still something of a curiosity.

Shopping "mall" in Asakusa

Between the two, popular Kabuki and monstrously popular movies, came the best day of the music halls, and Asakusa was where they throve. The Asakusa of Meiji may have been the noisiest pleasure center in Tokyo, but it had rivals in other cities. The Asakusa of the music halls, middle and late Taishō and into the present reign, was without rivals, the place where Tokyo outdid itself and the rest of the nation at the fine old art of viewing things.

"Asakusa opera" is the expression that covers musical endeavors in Asakusa during middle and late Taishō. It is a generous term, encompassing everything from pieces that would without challenge call themselves operas in the West, through various strains of light opera, domestic and foreign, all the way to the chorus-line revue.

Opera in the narrow sense was a form which it was thought necessary to have if Japan was to be civilized and enlightened. Very shortly after the opening of the Imperial Theater in 1911, the entrepreneurs and dignitaries who were its backers set about this new task, the importation of opera. They found a willing Italian, G. V. Rossi, in England, where he was a choreographer and director of light opera. He undertook to manage what was to be a permanent repertory troupe at the Imperial. He was somewhat disappointed to learn, upon his arrival in 1912, that the Imperial was not, as the name had suggested, the state theater of Japan, but, having been given a very large sum of earnest money, he stayed.

His first production was *The Magic Flute* with a Japanese cast. This seems unrealistic, and indeed it was. Even today, with training and competence in Western music so vastly improved, *The Magic Flute* is among the operas the Japanese are not quite up to. The Imperial production must have had a makeshift look about it. The same soprano, with a stand-in at the point where the two encounter each other, did Pamina and the Queen of the Night. Rossi decided that lighter things would better suit the available talent. Though he continued to produce Italian opera in the narrow sense, he gambled also on operetta.

The gamble did not succeed. The permanent repertory theater lasted only three years. Rossi was dismissed in 1916. The venture had not been a financial success. He had another try, at Akasaka in the High City, where he bought a movie house. It became the Royal (in English), famous in the history of Western music in Japan, but no more successful than the Imperial. The Royal closed in 1918, and Rossi left Japan for America, a disappointed man.

He was an important teacher. Many of the people who were to become famous in Asakusa were among his Imperial and Royal singers. Insofar as Asakusa opera was genuine opera, it could not have existed without him. His troupe had started deserting him while the Royal still persevered, and upon its closing they all went off to Asakusa. One might have advised the hapless Rossi to go there himself when the Imperial fired him. Akasaka has its geisha and hosts of rich people, but it was not a place to attract crowds. It was on the southwestern edge of the city, to be reached by a trolley line along which few trolleys ran. Asakusa was where things were happening.

There was another strain, a more important one, in Asakusa opera. A skit called *The Women's Army Is Off for the Front* was such a huge success early in 1917 that the date of its opening is called the birthday of Asakusa opera. It was a frivolous war piece, about the First World War. There being a shortage of men on the Western Front, a women's army is dispatched. Mostly the piece is song and dance, including a hornpipe and a Highland fling (so we are told, though descriptions make it seem more Cossack). Because of it "Tipperary" became very popular, sung along all the coves and strands of the nation. The pack day after day was such that people had to be rescued by stagehands at closing time and hustled out through back doors.

This popular strain was the dominant one, though lists of performances at Asakusa show an occasional opera of the genuine sort, such as
Rigoletto or *Lucia*. "La donna è mobile" from *Rigoletto* was among the big
hits of the years before the earthquake. A memorable event occurred in
relation to *Rigoletto*. No competent tenor being available, the duke was
once sung by a soprano. Operetta and revue prevailed, however. Among
Westerners, Suppè (of the "Light Cavalry" overture) seems to have been
the most popular. Facing each other across an Asakusa lane were a theater
that specialized in the Western and one that went in for the native. Domestic productions, tending towards the erotic, outnumbered Western.

That there should have been genuine opera at all and that it should
have been popular is remarkable. Yet it must have gone on looking makeshift, and having a somewhat traditional sound to it. The two most famous Asakusa tenors had scarcely any formal musical training. They
were both still to be heard in the years after the Second World War, and
one of them survives in this year 1982, in his eighties, still belting away
on television. His early career was with the Mitsukoshi boys' band. He
said proudly, not long ago, that when the band performed at Hibiya he
could be heard in the farthest corners of the park. How considerable an
achievement this was is hard to judge. The farthest corner is some four
hundred yards from the bandstand where the boys performed. There are
many trees to be gone through along the way, and so it may indeed have
been a feat, but the important point is that the singer seemed to prize
volume above all else. Even today there is more volume than art in his
singing. The crowds of Asakusa loved it.

Asakusa opera was astonishingly popular, especially among the young.
That eroticism is what most attracted them is scarcely to be doubted. But
a decade or two before, young men of Meiji had gone in great numbers to
see (and hear) pretty girls perform traditional music (see page 167 for the
popularity of *musumegidayū*). Their motives, too, are scarcely to be doubted. The Taishō look was different from the Meiji. In addition to the strong
foreign influence, "Tipperary" in its own right and in many a native adap-
tation, the Asakusa opera was far more open. The sudden exposure of firm
young flesh was the most obvious element in the new openness. Pretty legs
went kicking in every direction. The performer of *musumegidayū* might as
well not have had legs, for all the use she made of them. And the soprano
duke and flailing legs were alike part of Asakusa opera.

There were intellectual and bourgeois types among its followers, as
there could not fail to be, since it numbered an Italian and the Imperial among its forebears. The fanatical devotees known as *peragoro* were

young and often penniless. There are two theories as to the origin of the word *peragoro*. Everyone agrees that the first two syllables are the last two of "opera." As for the last two, some say that they derive from "gigolo," others that they are from *gorotsuki*, an old word for "thug" or "vagrant." The latter signification, whether or not it was there from the start, came to predominate. The *peragoro* were the disorderly elements that hung around the park. They went to the theaters night after night, provided unpaid claques for favorite singers, and formed gangs, whose rivalries were not limited to vehement support for singers. There were violent incidents. A *non-peragoro* could not with impunity protest the excessive vehemence in the theaters. *Peragoro* gangs would gather in the park, each having plighted its allegiance to a popular singer, one gang under the statue of Danjūrō, another under the wisteria bower by the lake. Two marches upon the theaters would occur each night, one for the more affluent at opening time, one for the more straitened when the signals sounded that half-fare time had come.

They were there for the excitement, of course, as crowds of young people are at all times in all places, but devotion to the Asakusa opera was their primary motive. That is the mark of its popularity. Their lady friends, often from the dubious little houses below the Twelve Storys, were sometimes called *peragorina*, though this expression had by no means the currency of *peragoro*.

When, in the diminished Asakusa of our latter day, old persons reminisce upon the good times, it is not the Asakusa described by Morse and Griffis that they are thinking of. It is the Asakusa of the opera. Nothing in the new entertainment districts, Shinjuku and the like, has quite taken its place. The Low City may be essentially conservative, but it changes, and good things are lost. Some of the best were lost when the crowds departed Asakusa. There is a Kafū story at the wistful ending of which the hero wearies of Asakusa and moves west. That is what the crowds did.

The division of literary history into reigns seems somewhat forced. What began happening at about the time of the Russo-Japanese War went on happening in the new reign, and if there is a Taishō look in literature it does not really become prominent until late in the reign, when it might as well be incorporated into the next one.

The theater, and especially the Kabuki, the art so central to the culture of the city, better accommodates the division into reigns. Generations of actors do correspond rather well to reigns. The most famous of Meiji actors all died in the last decade of the reign. It took a few years, during which there were many laments for the death of the form, before the generation of Taishō actors had established itself. The Kabukiza, east of Ginza, has been the grand stage for Kabuki ever since it was opened, in 1889. It was the biggest and the best situated, immediately east of Ginza, and in 1912, the year of the change of reigns, it came to have energetic Osaka management, with which to bludgeon its rivals. Morita Kanya (the twelfth of that name, who was active during Meiji—the line has continued) died a few years after the opening of the Kabukiza, which quite overshadowed his Shintomiza.

For all the grandeur, and some may say arrogance, of the Kabukiza, it had rivals during the Taishō Period—more interesting, possibly, than it was. Among these were the "little theaters" scattered all over the city. The one most fondly remembered is the Miyatoza, that guardian of tradition in Asakusa. Of the three "big" theaters of late Edo, one was gone by the end of Meiji; the other two—the Shintomiza, formerly the Moritaza, and, in southern Shitaya, a few minutes' walk from the Yanagibashi geisha quarter, the Ichimuraza—both prospered. The sixth Kikugorō and the first Kichiemon, two fine actors who survived the Second World War and brought the great tradition down to our time, held forth there.

Then there was the Meijiza in Nihombashi, today the oldest Kabuki theater in the city. It may not have provided the best of Kabuki, but its chief actor, the second Sadanji, was a worthy successor to Kanya in the matter of innovating and improving. He was the first important Kabuki actor to study abroad, and the first to act in the new Western theater.

He joined Osanai Kaoru (see page 69), one of the leading entrepreneurs of the new theater, to form, in 1909, a troupe called the Jiyū Gekijō, the Free Theater. In the years that followed, the Free Theater presented in translation plays by such Westerners as Ibsen and Maeterlinck.

This was very different from the sort of thing that the fifth Kikugorō had essayed in, for instance, his balloon ascent. A kind of realism and cosmopolitanism had been introduced in Meiji that was less a matter of style than of accessories. Little Western bibelots were introduced, and actors appeared in Western dress. All of this seems in retrospect amusing and not serious.

What Sadanji undertook was very serious. He was a Taishō man. As with the Yumeji girl, we may say that the pursuit of Western things had become more than exoticism. It had sunk deeper. Sadanji set the example. It has become common for Kabuki actors in these latter days to appear in Western or Westernized vehicles. In many a subtle way the influence of the West has insinuated itself into Kabuki. The Valentino look came to stay. Today it could be called the television look. All of this began with Sadanji.

Sadanji's Free Theater was not the only troupe that undertook performances in the Western style, in translation and by Japanese writers. From the first uncertain sproutings in the political drama of Meiji, the "new theater" increased and multiplied. There was a bewildering proliferation of troupes between the two wars, and from them emerged a most energetic movement in the experimental theater.

The most celebrated performer of early Taishō was an actress. That this should have been the case has, again, the Taishō look about it. The most celebrated female celebrities of Meiji had been murderesses.

In this regard the women of Taishō were not up to their Meiji forebears. No Taishō murderer or murderess had the appeal of Takahashi Oden, though there were interesting murders, sometimes of a technically advanced kind. In 1913 a thief used power from a high-tension line to dispose of a policeman. (Taishō was not a happy time for policemen. In the wartime and postwar inflation, police wages rose only a third as much as average wages.)

The Taishō celebrity was of a different sort, positive in her attainments, and sufficiently prominent, as no Meiji woman had been, to be called a symbol of her day. Matsui Sumako was vibrantly symbolic, and she came to the kind of sad end best loved in Japan and best suited for immortality. A country girl born in 1886, she arrived in Tokyo at the turn of the century, worked as a seamstress, was married and divorced, and entered the Bungei Kyōkai or Literary Society, a dramatic group founded in 1905 by, among others, Tsubouchi Shōyō. Shōyō was a man of many parts, a pioneer in the new novel and drama. (It was probably a production of *Hamlet* by the Literary Society that so puzzled Natsume Sōseki's Sanshirō.) Sumako had her first great success in 1911, as Ibsen's Nora. The Literary Society was disbanded in 1913, largely because Shōyō disapproved of a flamboyant affair Sumako was having with Shimamura Hōgetsu, his favorite disciple and an eminent theorist in the new movement. Hōgetsu and Sumako organized their own troupe, the Geijutsuza (Art Theater) that same year. Her greatest success was in Tolstoy's *Resurrection*. "Katyusha's Song" from that production, her song, so to speak, is held by historians of the subject to mark the beginning of modern Japanese popular music. It was popular all through the Japanese empire, and, we are told, in North China as well.

Hōgetsu died a sudden and solitary death in the influenza epidemic of 1918. On January 15, 1919, after a performance in Hibiya, Sumako returned to the Ushigome theater which the two of them had struggled to build and where, in one of the back rooms, he had died, and there hanged herself.

She was a willful woman, who seems to have caused endless trouble in both troupes, and she was also passionate and courageous, representative of the new, liberated womanhood. Taishō had other representatives of the type. The soprano Miura Tamaki, for instance, was a member of Rossi's company at the Imperial Theater and the first Japanese to perform Madame Butterfly abroad; she came into prominence for a shocking practice, riding a bicycle to music lessons at Ueno. But Sumako was first among the new women. She could not have existed in Meiji. The old ways were still too strong in Meiji for women to be among the examples that defined it.

In the Taishō Period the popular entertainments went resolutely international. It may be that similar resolve would have come to nothing in Meiji, because only with the advent of movies were international celebrities placed in front of everyone. There could have been no Meiji equivalent of the Chaplin caramels that were vastly popular before the earthquake, and made huge amounts of money for the Meiji Confectionary Company. A song from just before the earthquake has the *shareotoko,* the dapper youth, accoutered in a blue shirt, a green tie, bell bottoms, a bowler hat, and *roido* spectacles. *Roido* seems to be a transliteration of "Lloyd," from the horn-rimmed spectacles worn by Harold Lloyd. A less pleasing theory derives it from the last syllable of "celluloid." Most probably it is both, for the Japanese have always loved a pun. Lloyd and Chaplin were as well known to the populace of Taishō Tokyo as to the populace of any place on earth. Perhaps the nearest Meiji equivalent was Spencer the balloon man. Perhaps, again, it was General Grant.

With Chaplin and Lloyd in everyone's movie theater, visits of prominent foreigners may not have been quite the festivals they were in Meiji; or it may be that the city and the land, ever *more* modern, were more resistant to such excitement; or that the excitement was there, but in a less obvious form. In any case, eminent visitors in Taishō tended more towards the intellectual and the artistic than had General and Mrs. Grant.

Pavlova, Schumann-Heinck, and Prokofiev were at the head of the stream of performers who met with acclaim and good fees in Tokyo. Then there were Margaret Sanger and Einstein, whose visits were not affairs of state but caused great stirs all the same. After the visit of the former, which occurred in 1920, a local counterpart known as the "Margaret Sanger of Japan" appeared, handing out devices. Einstein's modest, somewhat comical warmth greatly affected the Japanese. He liked them too. He said that they were pleasanter people than Americans. He came to Japan the year before the earthquake and spent two months on a lecture tour. No one seems to have been called "the Einstein of Japan." Perhaps that was the greatest mark of respect the Japanese could have accorded him.

Frank Lloyd Wright was probably the most famous foreigner to come on business in the narrow sense of the term. His Imperial Hotel, the second one, under construction from 1915 to 1923, was formally opened in 1922 and finished just in time for the earthquake, which it survived so famously.

Wright had a wide variety of troubles in the building, and left Japan after the formal opening without staying to view the completed structure. There seems to have been resentment at the presence of a foreign architect, and in this one sees a contrast between Taishō and the golden Meiji days of Conder. There was labor trouble, one more new Taishō institution, and trouble with the underworld, which had strong roots in the building trades. The old Imperial was demolished by fire on the eve of the opening of the new. Wright's original backers found in the fire their pretext for withdrawing. Their real reason was financial: the enterprise was running several times over the original budget.

The result of all the trouble was worth it. The old imperial (as it would be called in the last years before its destruction in 1968, for by then yet a third—and now likewise departed—Imperial Hotel had been put up) was a fine building. It gave repose in the noisy heart of the city. Its famous performance in the earthquake did not, however, demonstrate that Wright's principle of floating piles on mud was superior to that of driving them through to bedrock. The old Imperial settled badly, while more traditional buildings in the Low City, such as the Bank of Japan, did not. Some of the corridors came to have a wavy, rubbery look about them. Perhaps it had to go, but its departure, occasioned less by the unevenness of the floors and corridors than by the implacable urge to put valuable land to more intensive use, was the greatest loss that postwar Tokyo has had to endure. The facade may be viewed in Meiji Village near Nagoya (despite the fact that it is not Meiji but Taishō). For those who know what once lay beyond that façade, it is less comforting than saddening.

The Sanger and Einstein visits were events of national moment, even though they may not have touched off quite the surge of fervor that met the Grants. The visits of Charles Beard, the American historian, were more specifically Tokyo affairs. There was one before the earthquake and one after. Beard was received by the most eminent statesmen and financiers in the land, but Tokyo was the reason for the visits. Immediately upon assuming office, Gotō Shimpei, that famous mayor whose sweeping plans for the city were known as "the big kerchief," assigned his son-in-law, resident in New York, the task of luring Beard, who would surely contribute greatly to the contents of the kerchief. Beard studied the city for six months just before the earthquake and wrote a report on the city administration that is still widely read. Many of his recommendations could have been adopted in the aftermath of the earthquake, and few were.

He made practical suggestions and some that were not so practical. He urged the installation of electric meters, because the system of charging by the number of bulbs was wasteful. He also argued for simplified administration and local autonomy. He wanted a single government for greater Tokyo—for the prefecture—a system that was not adopted until 1943. Here he may be taxed with inconsistency, since the reason for the dual structure, a prefectural office and a city office, was that it permitted a measure of local autonomy.

He admired the metropolitan bureaucracy but lamented the absence of a popular base and of control over its own finances. Though Beard is often credited with inventing the notion of Tokyo as a cluster of villages, it seems to have been almost commonplace. We have seen that John Russell Young, in attendance upon General Grant, regarded the city in that light almost a half-century before. The center of Tokyo enjoyed a certain preeminence, Beard said, *because it was* the place from which the nation was governed, but the surrounding towns were more considerable than in any other metropolitan complex of his acquaintance. He concluded that this state of affairs should be remedied by pumping capital into the central district. Today the vogue among planners is all for decentralization.

The report continues to be admired, probably because it is Beard's; but it is a chilly document, not as alive to the humanity and the variety of the city as it might be.

The neologisms of Taishō often have a High City, bourgeois sound to them, and so inform us that the Low City, which had slipped into a secondary position by the end of Meiji, was slipping ever further. Some of the new words are surprising. That English words should have supplanted native ones for the most intimate and complex of personal relationships seems strange indeed. It was in Taishō that "mama" and "papa" came into currency among the bourgeois and intellectual types of the High City.

Now they are next to universal. The explanation may be that they are easier to use than the native words, which introduce delicate honorific problems, and because of their complexity had always been unstable. What the High City chose to do in such matters, in any event, the Low City tended to follow. Cultural hegemony had passed from the Low City.

On the eve of the earthquake the sexes may have been more clearly differentiated from each other than on the eve of the Restoration. Most of the men among the Ginza crowds wore Western dress and most of the women Japanese. Even working women tended to favor Japanese dress, although nurses were pioneers in dressing Western. Photographs of telephone exchanges look very quaint, with the operators in kimono, their hair swept up in the traditional styles. (Why a telephone operator in kimono should seem quainter than one in Western dress is not easy to explain. The universal Japanese notion that Japanese dress is impractical, difficult to maintain and given to falling to pieces, may be part of the explanation.) The middy blouse, to become universal for girl students, first appeared in Taishō. So did sewing schools. Girls had learned the simple old ways of sewing from their mothers. Bathing dress became big business in Taishō.

If the sexes were clearly differentiated by dress, their hair styles tended to merge. Women took more easily to Western coiffure than to Western

The switchboard, Tokyo Central Telephone Exchange

dress. Long hair became the mark of the "modern boy" and short hair that of his female companion. Hairdressers in the traditional styles belonged to a dying trade. They had a place to go if they wished, however, because wigmakers prospered; there continued to be occasions of a ceremonial kind when the old styles were appropriate. Few women, in that day of short hair, had an adequate supply.

The "all-back" style for men, with the hair combed straight back from the forehead and not parted, became popular among the young because an American stunt pilot, Taishō successor to Spencer, affected it. For women there was something very new, the "ear-hiding" style. Ears and napes of necks had been left exposed by the old styles, and were thought erotic. Now, irony of the new day of liberation, they disappeared. The shampoo style of the Meiji geisha had sometimes obscured these points, but the "eaves" coiffure, in the Western style, had not (see page 104). Eye shadow and the hairnet also became stylish.

Fashion, in the chic sense of the term, was created in Taishō by the agency that always creates it, advertising. There had been fads and vogues in Edo, often induced by Kabuki actors, but styles of dress changed slowly until advertising took over. Advertising arranged that dress be increasingly loud and polychrome in the years before the earthquake.

Western sweets were in ever greater vogue, especially the Chaplin caramel. Chocolate was a luxury. The Taishō emperor bought some jelly beans at the Taishō Exposition. There was a soda fountain in Ginza just before the earthquake, though in this respect Tokyo seems to have been behind Yokohama. A measure of modernization has been the advance of dairy products upon this nonpastoral society. Meiji had ice cream and Taishō had "milk parlors." Butter and cheese were slower to take hold. The intelligentsia of Taishō, they who made Taishō democracy, gathered in milk parlors to engage in rarefied conversation and read the official gazette over milk toast and waffles.

From late Meiji into Taishō there was a great increase in university students, and in ideology. The Marx boy and Marx girl made their appearance in early Taishō, somewhat in advance of the words for (if not the fact of) "modern boy" and "modern girl." Students have *always* delighted in larding their speech with foreign expressions. Some of the Taishō neologisms have stayed with us, such as *rumpen*, from "lumpen-proletariat," signifying a vagrant, and *saboru*, "sabotage" converted into a Japanese verb. The latter seems to have been invented during the Kawasaki Shipyards strike of 1919. It has come in more recent years to signify cutting class, or staying away from work for no good reason.

The Meiji Period had been all in favor of education, but Taishō was the time of *kyōyo,* a word which falls within the general meaning of education, but carries connotations of enrichment, self-fulfillment, and gracious living. It lends itself to such expressions (these are taken from dictionaries) as "enrich one's education" and "enhance the level of one's culture." The modern intelligentsia had arrived.

There were all manner of new schools besides universities: driving schools, beauty schools, English-language schools, typing schools. The day of the office girl (now known as the O.L., for "office lady") dawned in Meiji, with the telephone operator, the nurse, and the shop girl, and now its sun rose radiantly. There was a popular song which began "I'm a typist, I'm a typist," and whose refrain was "Typist, typist," this word in English. Girls first appeared as bus conductors in the years before the earthquake. Theirs was an almost exclusively feminine calling until, with

The Peace Exhibition held in Veno Park in mid-Taishō.
Dignitaries included the Prince of Wales (right)

the emergence of the "one-man" (in English) bus, in the last decade or so, it went into a precipitous decline.

Proletarian education and "liberal" education may be dated to the first "labor school," founded by Christians very early in the Taishō Period. From late Meiji the city had several *himmingakkō*, rendered by certain dictionaries as "pauper schools" and "ragged schools." They were first administered by the city, then transferred to the wards. Their chief purpose was to provide classes for the children of indigents and transient laborers. The distribution of such schools at the end of Taishō gives interesting evidence of where the ragged dwelt: five were in the two wards east of the river, and the remaining six, on the other side of the river, were evenly divided between the High City and the Low. There was one in Azabu, among the richest of the fifteen wards; the High City has always accommodated extremes of affluence and penury.

The tourist bus was of course a new Taishō institution. The standard route included old things and creations of Taishō as well—Tokyo Station, the Meiji Shrine, the house and graves of the Nogis. It may be that the last will make their way back to the list one day soon, for the suspicion of military immortals that prevailed after 1945 is fading. On the whole, the monuments of Taishō have been supplanted. The standard list today is made up largely of earlier and later wonders. Here too, Taishō has the look of a valley between two eminences.

As at the end of Meiji, one might have remarked at the end of Taishō upon the remarkable tenacity of tradition. Taishō lists of annual observances are strongly traditional, though with a sprinkling of triumphal and patriotic observances from Meiji and after, and a sprinkling as well of Western events and practices, such as April Fool's Day. The seasonal pattern of the flowers, grasses, birds, and insects is familiar.

Certain places for having these natural pleasures have disappeared by late Taishō, new ones have appeared. Among the lost places and things are the chrysanthemum dolls in Hongō, visited by Sōseki's Sanshirō, and the night cherries of the Yoshiwara, but there are still places for chrysanthemum dolls and an ample selection of places for cherries, Ueno and the Sumida embankment still first among them. Although with improved transportation and the spread of the city into open lands, spots for the appreciation of grasses and flowers are sometimes more distant on Taishō lists than on Meiji ones, most of them are still present. The Yanaka cemetery glows with fireflies on a warm, damp evening and the Sumida embankment is a chorus of singing autumn insects. It is striking, indeed, that so many natural pleasures of late Taishō lie near the heart of the city. The Sumida embankment appears with some frequency, though the favored spots of Edo have clearly fallen victim to blight. Insect voices, wasted moors, and the like are farther upstream.

Among fairs and festivals on Taishō lists are many old ones, closely joined to the grasses and flowers, such as those in May at which one bought bugs, bells, and goldfish in preparation for the summer. Then-are new ones too, such as the opening of the university baseball season in September. Baseball was ever more popular.

In those same years Sumō wrestling enjoyed a renaissance. Early Taishō was for Sumō, as for Kabuki, a quiet period, when many a voice lamented its demise. The great wrestlers of Meiji had withdrawn from active service. A half-dozen years into the new reign began the flowering. The Sumō stadium burned down in 1917, just as the bud was opening. Until a new stadium was finished in 1920, semiannual tournaments were held at the Yasukuni Shrine. There was another Sumō strike in 1923 (for an earlier one, see page 169). In 1926 professional wrestlers organized a Sumō Association, an incorporated foundation. This major event in Taishō democracy is held to mark the final emergence of the Sumō world from feudalism, but in the long history of the sport, it sounds rather like one of those new names that do little to change reality.

In late Meiji and Taishō the city seemed to be growing so rapidly that its weight might bring it down. Waste disposal was among the urgent and interesting problems. There were public collection points for garbage.

Some was burned and some devoted to filling the bay or fertilizing paddies east of the bay. The burning was al fresco, and the unremitting smell of burning garbage is a detail commonly remarked upon in memoirs from east of the river.

Sewage was the real problem. The night-soil cart continued to be the chief agent of disposal. Because there was a distance beyond which cartage became impractical, the problem reached crisis proportions. From about the end of the First World War, houses near the center of the city could no longer sell their sewage, but had to pay someone to take it away. As the crisis mounted, tanks would be deliberately broken in order that the stuff might quietly slip away, or sewage was carried out and dumped during the night. Edo was no doubt a smelly city; but Tokyo as it passed its semicentennial must have been even worse.

In 1921 the city finally began to assume limited responsibility for sanitation. Still, by the end of the Taishō Period, three years after the earthquake, the city was disposing of no more than a fifth of the total mass. Tokyo was by then much larger than Edo had been, but in certain respects it had not much changed from the Edo pattern. The Low City was necessarily more advanced than the High City in this public service, because most of the High City lay nearer to farmlands than did the heart of the Low City. The crisis was less acute there.

In the lore of sewage disposal are numerous curious details. Farmers, in the days when they bought, were willing to pay more for sewage the higher the social level of the house. The upper-class product was richer in nutriment, apparently. So, apparently, was male excrement. In aristocratic mansions where the latrines were segregated by sex, male sewage was more highly valued than female. It seems that the female physique was more efficient.

Edo had a system of aqueducts bringing water from the west. It was expanded in Meiji and Taishō. Even so, estimates of the number of persons still dependent on wells within the city run as high as a third of the total. Wells were often noisome and brackish, and so water vendors still went the rounds of the Low City.

We hear more about the problem of traffic and transportation than that of garbage and sewage. Late in Meiji, Nagai Kafū used an overcrowded and badly organized trolley system for one of his most beautiful soliloquies (see pages 61-62). Matters were even worse in the years just before the earthquake. Kafū's diary is quite splashed with mud. Tanizaki, having settled in the Kansai, looked sourly back on the Tokyo of "those years":

> I doubt that in those years, the years of prosperity during and immediately after the World War, there was anyone even among the most ardent supporters of Tokyo who thought it a grand metropolis. The newspapers were unanimous in denouncing the chaotic transportation and the inadequate roads of "our Tokyo." I believe it was the *Advertiser* which in an editorial inveighed against the gracelessness of the city. Our politicians are always talking about big things, social policy and labor problems and the like, it said, but these are not what politics should be about. Politicians should be thinking rather of mud, and of laying streets through which an automobile can pass in safety on a rainy day. I remember the editorial because I was so completely in agreement. Foreigners and Japanese alike denounced our capital city as "not a city but a village, or a collection of villages".... Twice on my way from Asakusa Bridge to Kaminari Gate I was jolted so violently from the cushion that my nose hit the roof of the cab.... And so, people will say, it might have been better to take a streetcar.

That too could be a desperate struggle.... With brisk activity in the financial world, all manner of enterprises sprang up, and there was a rush from the provinces upon the big cities. Tokyo did not have time to accommodate the frantic increase in numbers and the swelling of the suburbs.... For the general populace there was no means of transport but the streetcar. Car after car would come by full and leave people waiting at stops. At rush hour the press was murderous. Hungry and tired, the office worker and the laborer, in a hurry to get home, would push their way aboard a car already hopelessly full, each one for himself, paying no attention to the attempts of the conductor to keep order... The ferocity in their eyes could be frightening....

The crowds, a black mountain outside a streetcar, would push and shove and shout, and we could but silently lament the turmoil and how it brought out the worst in people....

They put up with it because they were Japanese, I heard it said, but if a European or American city were subjected to such things for even a day there would be rioting.... Old Japan had been left behind and new Japan had not yet come.

It is to be noted that the idea of the city as a cluster of villages is not credited to Beard but rather is treated as commonplace, and that, like Beard, Tanizaki remarks upon the quality in deprecatory terms.

We are often told that "those years," the years when Taishō democracy was coming to be, were a time of sybaritism, irresponsibility, and disenchantment. The characterization itself has about it a disenchanted look, as if the burden of modernization had become too much. Meanwhile, those who were to bring about the reaction of the thirties were waiting in indignation.

Taishō was the day when such apparently definitive symbols as the Yumeji girl looked as if they themselves, and not merely their bonnets, had been made abroad. The ease with which Taishō democracy surrendered, however, tells us that tradition was strong and near the surface; and a cynicism not far from disenchantment had been affected by the son of Edo. Japan was catching up with the world in respects which had seemed desperately urgent to the people of early Meiji. So the eagerness of the chase had somewhat diminished. There is a Taishō look, but more recent decades seem to inform us that the modern boy and modern girl were not at all inclined to drop out of the race. The Taishō look was another Western element that had been studied well and mastered.

Rain in the Low City. A woodcut by Komura Settai, 1915

The song everyone was singing in 1923 was both new and old. It was called "The Boatman's Song." The music was by Nakayama Shimpei, who wrote Matsui Sumako's song in *Resurrection* and is held to have founded modern popular music.

> I am dead grass on the river bank.
> You are dead grass on the bank as well.

So went the refrain. It was thought to be very decadent, but the stylized self-commiseration would have been familiar and congenial to the child of Edo. Among the righteous and the indignant were those who held that it invited destruction, and got what it asked for on September 1, 1923.

BOOK TWO

TOKYO RISING

The City Since the Great Earthquake

AUTHOR'S PREFACE

This book is a sequel to *Low City, High City,* which told of Tokyo between the Meiji Restoration of 1867 and 1868 and the great earthquake of 1923. Most people who vaguely remember the title of the earlier book seem to think that it is *High City, Low City,* probably because "high" comes before "low" in so many conventional locutions. The reversing of the two was intentional. The book is elegiac, its emphasis on the part of the city which was the cultural center of Edo, predecessor of Tokyo, and was ceasing to be any sort of center at all. *Low City, High City* makes no claim to be political or intellectual history, and little more to be literary or economic history. It might possibly be called social or cultural history. So might this one, although, with the growing ascendancy of the High City—the wealthy hilly districts—politics and intellectual matters are bound to figure more prominently. The ascendancy is now virtually complete. The Low City, the less affluent flatlands, offered something to talk about as late as the years between the two world wars. The center of popular culture was there, in Asakusa. Since the Second World War it has offered very little indeed. The words before the comma in the earlier title have been almost completely eclipsed by the words after.

There was another reason for the emphasis on the Low City: a fondness for the place. It follows with a certain inevitability that when there is little to say about the place one is fondest of, things must be said of places of which one is less fond. Many interesting things have happened in the High City, certainly, and Tokyo, which for cultural purposes is now the High City, goes on being the city among them all in which one has the least excuse to be bored. Yet the effort has been continuous to keep grouchiness from creeping in at the ways in which the city has chosen to spend its money. If I have not been entirely successful, and if a certain grouchiness does creep in at, for instance, the internationally famous architects, I can only hope that it is balanced by affection for people like Enoken.

Low City, High City could have ended with the end of the Taishō reign, three years and a few months after the earthquake. The earthquake was the end of so much more than was the end of the reign, however, that it prevailed. If it had not, then this book might have been, more neatly, about Tokyo in the recently ended Shōwa reign. That is what it is mostly about in any event. Nothing is said about the end of the Shōwa reign because it had not occurred when the manuscript was finished. All that seemed practical was to go back and put the reign in the past tense.

The problem of what to call Tokyo has been a nagging one, since the city of Tokyo ceased to exist as a political and administrative entity in 1943. In that year the municipal government and the prefectural government were amalgamated. The prefecture may be divided broadly into the "ward part" and the "county part," the twenty-three wards as they have been since 1947, and the rest of the prefecture, off to the west of the wards. In the chapters having to do with the postwar period, I have tried to use "prefecture" whenever a government agency is referred to and whenever precise distinctions seem called for. Sometimes "city" has been a convenience. When the word is used it may be taken as referring to the ward part of the prefecture.

The annotation is like that for *Low City, High City:* minimal. The sources of direct quotations are given, and the notes contain little else. A disproportionate number refer to the writings of well-known authors, disproportionate in the sense that the passages cited are less conspicuous in the text than in the notes. It will be observed that notes become less frequent toward the end of the book. Fewer memorable things seem to be said about the city as time goes by. The well-known authors have died, chief among them Nagai Kafū, to whose memory *Low City, High City* was circumspectly dedicated, and as writers about Tokyo they have not had successors. The point is made in the book that Tokyo is not the subject for distinguished writing that it once was. The Japanese name order, with the family name first, is used throughout. Modern life, for all its complexities, does produce a simplification from time to time. One has been the tendency of writers not to have "elegant sobriquets." This means that when a single element of a name is used it can be, as in the West, the family name. "Nagai Kafū" is the major exception. "Kafū" is a sobriquet. In accord with Japanese practice, it is used when the whole name is not. The Tokyo Archives have been very helpful in the assembling of illustrations. So has the *Asahi Shimbun,* in particular Mrs. Notoya Ryōko, of the staff of the weekly magazine *Asahi Hyakka Nihon no Rekishi (The Asahi Encyclopedia: Japanese History).* Where no credit is given, illustrations are from postcards in my collection or photographs by Mr. Fukuda Hiroshi.

TOKYO IN 1927

東京市全圖

1. Kōjimachi
2. Kyōbashi
3. Nihombashi
4. Kanda
5. Shiba
6. Azabu
7. Akasaka
8. Yotsuya
9. Ushigome
10. Koishikawa
11. Hongō
12. Shitaya
13. Asakusa
14. Hongō
15. Fukagawa
16. Shinagawa
17. Ebara
18. Ōmori
19. Kamata
20. Meguro
21. Setagaya
22. Shibuya
23. Yodobashi
24. Nakano
25. Suginami
26. Toshima
27. Itabashi
28. Ōji
29. Takinokawa
30. Arakawa
31. Adachi
32. Mukojima
33. Jōtō
34. Katsushika
35. Edogawa

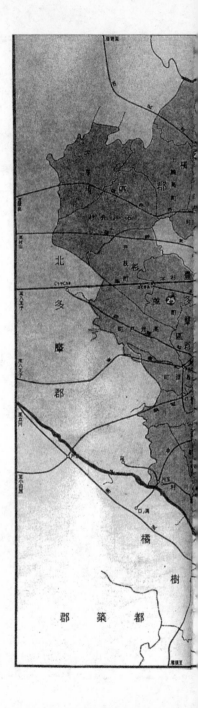

THE TOKYO WARDS,
1932–1947

Tokyo Prefecture as it has been since 1947. Certain offshore islands, not shown here, are also part of the prefecture. The four surrounding prefectures, reading clockwise from the west, are Yamanashi, Saitama, Chiba, and Kanagawa. Nos. 3 through 25 are the twenty-three wards, as follows.

3. Chiyoda	15. Shibuya
4. Chūō	16. Suginami
5. Minato	17. Nakano
6. Shinjuku	18. Toshima
7. Bunkyō	19. Nerima
8. Taitō	20. Itabashi
9. Sumida	21. Kita
10. Kōtō	22. Arakawa
11. Shinagawa	23. Adachi
12. Ōta	24. Katsushika
13. Meguro	25. Edogawa
14. Setagaya	

The remaining portions are what was after 1932 the "county part" of the prefecture. The unnumbered portion at the extreme west is all that remains of West Tama County. Everything else is now incorporated cities, except for No. 41, which is two incorporated towns. No. 44 is Hachiōji, the oldest incorporated city in the county part. The Taisho and Shōwa emperors are buried in the western part of Hachiōji. Mitaka, of the celebrated train wreck, is No. 26. Higashimurayama, wherein reposes the reservoir that has replaced the one at the Shinjuku Westmouth, is the southern of the two Nos. 35. Tachikawa of the big (the newspapers said notorious) American air base is the eastern of the two Nos. 39.

Chapter 7

THE DAYS AFTER

I n a few years the governor of Tokyo, the council, and the bureaucracy will move their offices out beyond the western limits of the old city.

Despite opposition from the eastern wards, the decision was made in 1985. Unless there are delays in building the somewhat grandiose new offices, the move will take place in 1991. The governor will then be nearer the population center of his constituency than he is now. However one may regret the departure from the old city, the reasons for the move are good ones.

The city has moved westward in the century and twenty years since it became Tokyo. So the governor recognizes the facts, and will go where the people who elect him have gone. American city halls tend to stay put. The New York city hall has not moved north or east with the spread of population, and the Philadelphia city hall has remained where William Penn put it. Perhaps the Japanese are more realistic and flexible in these matters.

Yet one does have regrets, for the move and for the shift that has made it seem realistic. Edo, the seat of the Tokugawa shoguns, became Tokyo in 1868, after the overthrow of the shogunate. The Low City, mostly reclaimed flatlands, was where the lesser orders lived, the merchants and artisans or workmen. It was the crowded part of the city, and the lively part. The hilly High City, to the west of the castle, was sparsely populated. A line north and south from the old magistracies (there were two of them) would have had the larger part of the population east of it, and the centers of commerce and culture as well. The aristocracy in the great castle complex and the High City had money and taste, but it was not imaginative or inventive. It was in the Low City that the things which interest us a century and a half and two centuries later were made and done.

By "aristocracy" is here meant the military class, the court and its court-iers having stayed in Kyoto. The military class was on the whole conser-vative. Its tastes and the tastes deemed appropriate to it were antiquarian and academic. What was new and interesting in Edo, the cultural center of the land under the last six or seven Tokugawa shoguns, was mercantile. The daimyo patronized Nō drama and the tea ceremony. The wealthy merchant patronized Kabuki and the entertainments, often of very high quality, provided by the geisha, whether in the licensed pleasure quarters or the less strictly regulated "private" quarters. Nō and the tea ceremony were elegant and elevated pursuits, but during the Tokugawa Period they became highly ritualized and formalized. If they changed, it was almost imperceptibly. Kabuki changed and grew, and so did the music and dance of the pleasure quarters. It has become common in our day to think of Kabuki, like Nō, as a crystallization of unearthly beauty, but it can be earthy, erotic, and ribald. More important, new and good things were constantly being added to it, and to the art of the geisha, as they were not to Nō and the tea ceremony. The former were living and grow-ing, the particular treasures of the Low City.

In Meiji the governance of Tokyo Prefecture moved slightly west-ward, to Marunouchi. Meiji is the era designation for the first reign after the upheaval of 1867-68. The Meiji emperor died in 1912, and the era name changed to Taishō. The prefectural government, along with the city government when there has been one, as there has not been since 1943, has been in Marunouchi ever since. And now it will move much further west, to a part of Shinjuku that was not brought within the city limits until 1932.

Even if the governor and government were not moving, we would have to admit the fact, melancholy for some of us, that the Low City has fallen far behind. It was the cultural center of Edo, and the new prefec-tural offices will lie beyond the old High City, beyond even the first of the old post stations on the highway to the mountain province of Kai. Although already declining, the Low City was still important enough in Meiji that a cultural history of Meiji Tokyo could not leave it out.

The simplest and the best explanation for the decline of the Low City is economic. Money departed. Kabuki stayed behind and so did the best geisha, but rich merchants, such as the Mitsui, moved to the High City when the class structure of Tokugawa disappeared. The chief sources of patronage came to be the entrepreneurial and bureaucratic classes of the High City. In 1923 mansions of the wealthy and aristocratic stood along the Sumida, central to the arts and pleasures of the old Low City. Most of them then disappeared. The new Sumida Park and a brewery came to occupy the tract on the east bank of the Sumida where the greatest of them, the river villa of the Mito Tokugawa family, had stood.

Except for the regions immediately east of the outer moat, now filled in, not many would notice if the Low City were to disappear completely from a postwar history. Only the omission of Ginza, just east of the old castle complex, would be certain to bring complaints. Ginza is geographically in the Low City, since it lies east of the hills that begin in the palace (once the castle) grounds, but it belongs to the whole city. If the city, sprawling and decentralized, has a center today, it is probably Ginza and districts nearby.

Amusing things were still going on in the Low City during the interwar period, but they fall in the realm of popular culture, amusing enough for an evening, but ephemeral, not likely to be of much interest to anyone except very specialized antiquarians two centuries from now. So, even without insisting upon them, the story of Tokyo since 1923 must implicitly be about the decline of the Low City and the rise of the High City.

The Low City did almost completely disappear for a time late in the Taishō reign, which ended on Christmas Day 1926. Fires raged through it for two days following high noon of September 1, 1923, and left almost nothing behind save modern buildings along the western fringes. The fires followed upon the great Kantō earthquake, which struck at a minute and a few seconds before noon on September 1. The great shift to the High City was already in process and would have occurred even without the disaster, but the disaster sped it along. The novelist Tanizaki Junichirō was born in Nihombashi, the heart of mercantile Edo, between the old castle complex and the Sumida. He remarked in 1934 that he could no longer think of Nihombashi, or indeed Tokyo, as home. The place where he had spent the most impressionable years of his boyhood now lay under asphalt, in the middle of a thoroughfare cut through after the earthquake. It is an extreme instance, but symbolic of what happened to the whole Low City. The sites were there, but denuded, stripped of history and culture.

Old things would probably, most of them, have vanished in any event. Except for grand public structures like temples, buildings were not meant to last long and did not last long. But they would not have gone so quickly. Crowded and flimsily built, the Low City could not be protected against the fires that broke out immediately after the earthquake. The

High City fared better. It too was largely built of wood, but broken to-pography and irregular building patterns reduced the damage.

The financial, entrepreneurial, and merchandising center of the city—Nihombashi, Ginza, and Marunouchi—also fared better. The offices of governor and mayor, in Marunouchi, came through so solidly that no one within was immediately aware of what had happened. Lights swayed, but it was the news that automobiles were unable to get through to the east that brought the first sense of disaster. Presently, people on their way to the safety of the palace plaza were dying of burns and having babies under the mayor's windows.

Marunouchi was less severely damaged than Nihombashi, and so the managers and entrepreneurs started moving westward, even as the city did. Marunouchi derives its name from the fact that the district lay with-in the outer revetments and moat of the castle. Developed in Meiji by the Mitsubishi enterprises, which bought it from the government, Mar-unouchi now emerged clearly dominant over Nihombashi, where the merchant class of Edo had been most affluent and powerful. The stock exchange and the Bank of Japan stayed in Nihombashi, but Marunouchi more and more became the right address for the big managers.

The Yamanote loop line of the National Railways, joining the center of the city with transfer points to the western suburbs, was finally fin-ished in 1925. The last link joined Tokyo Central Station with Ueno, the point of departure for the north. Marunouchi thus became the *genkan,* the "front door," for the whole nation. The front door of the station faced Marunouchi and, from 1926, a broad avenue leading to the palace plaza. Nihombashi, on the east side of the station, did not even have a back door. The number of big companies with offices in Marunouchi doubled between 1922 and 1924. Almost three decades, since the com-pletion of the first Mitsubishi brick building in 1894, had been required to reach the 1922 figure.

Nihombashi was also losing out to Ginza as a retail district. It had Mitsukoshi and Shirokiya, the energetic Meiji pioneers in the new, West-ern kind of retailing, but department stores in quick succession estab-lished main or branch stores in Ginza. Mitsukoshi was among them. As the lesser parts of the Low City, save only Ginza, were left further and further behind by the High City, so was proud—some might have said, arrogant—Nihombashi.

There was talk of more shattering change, spiritual and man-made this time—the physical disaster could scarcely have been more complete. Kyo-to was still officially the capital of the land in 1867, when the shogunate collapsed. There was talk of having the capital somewhere other than Edo, seat of the shoguns and the actual seat of power. It was stilled when the emperor took up residence in Edo, and not revived until 1923.

With the city so grievously damaged, might it not be better off without the national bureaucracy, and the bureaucracy without the snarls and tangles of the great city? It should be easy to find a new capital less prone to disasters. Tokyo lies in earthquake country. Another flattening earthquake was bound to come. It has not come in the more than sixty years since the last one, but the assumption that it will come someday is universal.

Among nonseismic arguments for moving the capital was that Kyoto, or elsewhere in the Kansai, would be nearer the center of the Japanese empire, by which was meant Taiwan and Korea as well as the home islands. There even seems to have been talk in the armed forces—already feeling the spur of ambition—of moving the capital to the continent. Dispersal was suggested (and again today, when concentration in Tokyo has come to seem extreme and unhealthy, it is a popular subject). Kyoto had been all this while going on thinking of itself as the Western Capital. A measure of reality might be given to the claim. The government could be in both Kantō and Kansai.

On September 12, 1923, a royal proclamation said that Tokyo would remain the capital. This is the official translation: "Tokyo, the capital of the empire, has been looked upon by the people as the center of political and economic activities and the fountainhead of the cultural advancement of the nation. With the unforeseen visit of the catastrophe, the city has entirely lost its former prosperous contours but retains, nevertheless, its position as the national capital. The remedial work, therefore, ought not to consist merely in the reparation of the quondam metropolis, but, in ample provisions for the future development of the city, completely to transform the avenues and streets." The regent, the next emperor, took a drive through the burnt-over wastes of the Low City. (He was to do it again, as emperor, in 1945)

The city burned for some forty hours, and before the last embers were out reconstruction had already begun. It was used to and indeed rather proud of fires, known as "flowers of Edo," and proud as well of the speed with which it recovered. The proper merchant insisted upon speed in these matters. If a shop had not resumed business within three days, common mercantile wisdom held, it had no future. Prepared for what must come sooner or later, merchants kept reserves of lumber east of the Sumida River. The lumberyards were very watery, and reserves of lumber had a chance of surviving the worst conflagration, as also did inventories in somewhat fireproof warehouses. Department stores quickly put up emergency markets. Ginza and Asakusa almost immediately had street stalls again, as they had them before. Already on September 3 there was a sign in the wastes of the central fish market, in Nihombashi, summoning such fish dealers as survived to discuss plans for reopening.

> Completely burned out. But see:
> The son of Edo has not lost his spirit.
> So soon, these rows and rows of barracks,
> And we can view the moon from our beds.

So went "The Reconstruction Song," popular in the months after the earthquake.

Late in September a newspaper account based on a police report said that thirty thousand "barracks" had already gone up. Here and in "The Reconstruction Song" the English word is used, in the singular, to signify a building erected hastily on the site of a disaster. The new barracks were most numerous in Asakusa, Shitaya, and Honjo wards, the northern tier of the old Low City. The smell of new wood was everywhere, faces were black from clearing the ashes, though the wares offered for sale were skimpy.

More than ashes had to be cleared away. The tallest building in the city, the Asakusa "Twelve Storys," broke in two, at the eighth story, during

Barracks begin to go up in Hongō Ward after the earthquake

the earthquake. The novelist Kawabata Yasunari was off for a look at Asakusa a scant two hours afterward. He was less impressed with the destruction than with the refugees, especially the courtesans and geisha who poured in from the north, "like a disordered field of flowers." The great Yoshiwara quarter, to the north of Asakusa, was completely destroyed and several hundred of its women were incinerated, but the fires stopped just short of Asakusa proper, where Kawabata wandered in his field of flowers.

He did describe the final disappearance, the following year, of the Twelve Storys. It seems to have been a rather festive occasion. More properly the Cloud Scraper, the Twelve Storys was a pleasure and retailing center, a somewhat ungainly brick tower completed in 1890. Army demolition squads completed the destruction.

A character in Kawabata's *Scarlet Gang of Asakusa (Asakusa Kurenaidan)* published at irregular intervals between 1929 and 1935, is speaking:

> "All around us and as far as we could see were burned wastes. A few shacks had gone up here and there, but nothing blocked the view of the park from the school roof. The elevated portion of the roof was crowded with spectators. We must have waited an hour or so. There was an explosion and a cascade of bricks. The wall at one side had not fallen. It was like a thin sword. Another explosion and the sword fell. The crowds on the school roof cheered, and then how we all did laugh! As the sword collapsed a black mass of people raced up the mountain of rubble."

Individual enterprise was so swift and forceful that some of it got in the way of larger plans. Charles Beard, the American historian, was also swift and forceful, generous with his advice. A telegram from him crossed with one from Gotō Shimpei, the home minister, now in charge of reconstruction. Mayor of Tokyo until shortly before the earthquake, Goto had once before asked Beard's advice. He was known as "the mayor with the big kerchief," which might be rendered as "the mayor with all the plans." At his invitation, Beard studied the city administration for six months in 1922 and 1923 and submitted a report early in 1923. Now Gotō summoned him back. He came, and the telegram, a stern one, preceded him. Sentimentality about the old must not be allowed to interfere in any way with plans for the new: no new buildings were to be allowed until a new street plan had been drawn up. But of course barracks were already appearing at a rate of close to ten thousand per week, if that police report was accurate.

The earthquake came at a time of political disarray. The admiral who had become prime minister in the summer of 1922 died late in August 1923. It was the age of what historians call "Taishō democracy," a somewhat liberal age between the authoritarianism of Meiji and that of the thirties and early forties. Political parties were for the first time experiencing the delights of power, and they were much given to squabbling. A successor cabinet was not easily arranged. On September 2, while the city still burned, a cabinet headed by another admiral took office. It lasted only until early 1924, but under it, and especially Gotō, the national government assumed the lead in the rebuilding. It would probably have done so even without the services of Gotō, since the city did not have the money.

Gotō's original plan covered the whole city, including the relatively undamaged High City, and almost every lesser category imaginable streets, parks, rivers, canals, transportation. A grand arterial highway some two hundred yards wide was to run north and south through the city proper from beyond the city limits at either end, passing just to the east of Ginza and the main part of Nihombashi. For a politician, Gotō was curiously unrealistic. The budget was scaled down from several billion yen to about a half billion for Tokyo, and an additional amount for the still more grievously injured Yokohama. The main emphasis in the more modest plans was upon getting roofs over people's heads and widening streets. The width of Gotō's grand avenue was reduced to a little over half, and its length greatly reduced as well. Known as Shōwa Avenue from the era designation for the reign just recently ended, it runs past Ginza and Nihombashi and on to Ueno in Shitaya Ward.

Less than the half billion yen was finally approved. The new Reconstruction Agency was not of a single mind. Some thought that matters of little immediate concern were included and that the requisitioning of land for the widened streets would be a great bother. One of the two major political parties agreed. Why, it asked loudly, should so small a part of the country make demands upon the whole country? Widened streets and some new parks remained of Gotō's dreams. The street pattern was similar to that of Edo.

The rebuilding of the city may seem like a case study in lost opportunities. It would not do, however, to suggest that nothing at all was accomplished. The city *was* rebuilt, after a nondescript fashion, and it was to an extent redesigned. Nor would it do to leave the impression that the city did nothing at all for itself. The national government took responsibility for main thoroughfares, new and widened, and the city for lesser streets. In the end almost a quarter of a million residences were moved. The proportion of streets to total area was much higher after the earthquake than before. Three big new parks were financed by the national government, all in the Low City, near or along the Sumida. The city built more than fifty small parks, many of them by waterways now gone, most of them near schools. Motomachi Park, in what was then Hongō Ward, near Ochanomizu Station, is perhaps the only one of the small parks to survive in its original form. Opened in 1930, it is a charming Art Deco composition, with something in it of Frank Lloyd Wright's Imperial Hotel as well. The erection of a memorial hall on the site east of the river where the largest loss of life occurred was the mayor's idea. It took seven years to complete, but already by the first anniversary of the quake it was receiving pilgrims to its mass graves.

One of Kawabata's short-short stories, which he called "palm-of-the-hand stories," is set on the first anniversary of the earthquake. A woman whose whole family died in the earthquake has become the companion of a clever and skillful Asakusa beggar. They go off to the memorial site. The man removes one of his shoes, and tells the woman that her questions about this eccentric behavior will soon answer themselves. He uses the bare foot to pick up coins that have been tossed at but missed the offertory

An anniversary service at the Earthquake Memorial Hall east of the Sumida, site of the largest loss of life in the fires following the earthquake

box, and puts them in the shoe. A royal emissary arrives. So do the home minister and the mayor. All of them read messages at the altar. There are wreaths from ambassadors. "At two minutes before noon all vehicles in the city stopped for one minute. The whole city prayed in silence."

The novelist Nagai Kafū tells in his diary how it was on that first anniversary, a day of aprehension for the superstitious. "The citizenry was in terror. Banks locked their doors, greengrocers and fishmongers took a holiday. The weather was good, with a fresh autumn wind."

The climax to Kafū's *The Woman in the Rented Room,* written in 1927, also occurs on September 1, 1924. "It was already dark, but the back alleys were ridiculously silent. The Yotsuya geisha quarter was, on the surface at least, taking a holiday. That was not all: even on the main trolley street there was none of the usual bustle of night stalls and shops. The trumpet from the grounds of the Military Academy, beyond Tsunokami Hill, seemed very near." The woman of the title, through whom we observe the silence of this dread anniversary, is a kept woman, and the fact that she does not expect her patron to come calling this night of all nights causes him, after a sequence of almost ludicrous mishaps, to discard her.

The origins of the panic of 1927 may be traced directly to the earthquake. The causal relationship between the two was not inevitable, but the behavior of the government gave it the look of inevitability. The Yamamoto cabinet, which took office on September 2, declared a limited debt moratorium. Under certain conditions and in certain areas payment could be deferred. In effect, the Bank of Japan was required to guarantee losses by commercial banks, and its own losses were guaranteed by the government up to a specified limit. The time limit for these arrangements was extended repeatedly. Because the value of uncollected and uncollectable instruments far exceeded the official guarantee, the Bank of Japan was affected, and through it the commercial banks.

In March 1927 the finance minister did a peculiar thing. He said in the Diet that the Watanabe Bank, an important commercial bank, would be forced to close its doors in a few hours. This was untrue. The Watanabe Bank was in trouble, but not such critical and immediate trouble. He seems to have said it to divert attention from a bank still more heavily burdened with bad instruments. There was a run, and the Watanabe Bank was forced to suspend payments. So, after a time, was the second bank, the Bank of Taiwan, in the interests of which the minister had spoken his untruth, and half the capital of which came from public funds. Efforts to bail it out were declared unconstitutional by the Privy Council. Other banks failed, including one of the five largest in the land. It was the worst financial panic in the history of modern Japan, and its remote origins were in the earthquake. The cabinet resigned, to be succeeded by that of Tanaka Giichi, an army man and an early advocate of assertive policies on the continent. So the political and economic effects of the earthquake reached far. The politicians who said that the damage to the capital was of little concern to them and the nation were wrong.

Through a moratorium, actions by the Bank of Japan, and a bit of trickery, the crisis presently came under control. The banks that reopened did so with ostentatious piles of cash by their teller windows. Much of the money was printed only on one side, for there had not been time to print both sides.

It is possible—though to state it as fact we must put complete credence in the professed motives of the culprit—that the most sensational crime of the post-earthquake years was also caused by the earthquake. On December 27, 1923, the regent, after 1926 the emperor, was on his way to the opening of a Diet session. As he passed Toranomon, "Tiger Gate," a young man pushed his way out of the crowd and fired point-blank at the regent, who escaped injury. This attempted assassination is known as the Tiger Gate Incident, from the site of a castle gate on the outer moat. (Both gate and moat are long gone.)

The young man was from a good provincial family, the son of a Diet member. He later said that he had to do what he did, and that he did it out of anger at the treatment of laborers and Koreans after the earthquake.

However matters were with laborers, Koreans were very badly treated indeed: they were massacred, as many as two thousand of them.

The would-be assassin was pummeled by the crowds and arrested. Not quite a year later, in November 1924, he was hanged at Ichigaya Prison, and that evening given a pauper's burial east of the Sumida, in the northeastern suburbs. The river embankment was very pretty, it is said, with police lanterns.

Only after the sentence was handed down did the defendant break his silence. This he did with two shouted words encouraging revolution. So the theory that he might have avoided execution had he been less vehemently revolutionary is not supportable. The court was not prepared to be merciful to someone who had done such a thing.

Nagai Kafū, a quirkish man, had his own thoughts in the matter, and set them down in his diary.

November 16. Sunday. Sunny. Big play given in all the newspapers to the execution of Namba Daisuke. Daisuke is the student who was arrested after trying to shoot the regent at Toranomon last year. Some denounce the act as the vilest treason, but I do not think it anything so very astonishing or reprehensible. The assassination of monarchs is no rarity in the West. Everything about modern Japanese life is superficial imitation of the West. Daisuke's behavior is but another instance of imitation. What is there to choose between him and a Westernized woman out dancing?

It is interesting to note, by way of comparison, what happened to earlier and later would-be assassins. In 1891 a policeman in the town of Otsu, just east of Kyoto, slashed the czarevitch of Russia with a sword. The Otsu trial was swifter than the Tiger Gate one, but the assailant was sentenced to life imprisonment rather than death. Though the prosecution asked the death penalty, the judge allowed only a charge of simple assault, holding that this attack on royalty was no different from an attack on anyone else. The fact that extraterritoriality was still in effect may have influenced the decision. The judge wished to demonstrate the independence of the courts from political pressures, and therefore the superfluity of extraterritorial consular courts. The fact remains that the Tiger Gate court did not follow the Otsu precedent.

On January 8, 1932, the emperor (the 1923 regent) was the victim of another attack. A Korean threw a hand grenade at his cavalcade as he was returning from a military parade. No one was injured, though one of the automobiles, not the emperor's, was damaged. The incident bears the name of another of the old palace gates, the Sakurada or Cherry Orchard Gate. The Tiger Gate precedent, and not the Otsu one, was followed: the assailant was put to death. The conclusion seems hard to escape that not all royalty is equally royal. The cabinet resigned after the 1923 incident, and attempted to resign after the 1932 one. It was persuaded to stay on in the latter instance because of the outbreak of hostilities in Manchuria.

The Tiger Gate Incident had an effect on the culture of the nation that could not have been foreseen. The chief of the Tokyo police was dismissed, as was the assistant chief in charge of the patrolling forces. The latter was Shōriki Matsutarō, who set forth on a new career that brought him fame and power, in the media and in entertainment. He became president of the *Yomiuri Shimbun* in February 1924. It was a time when aggressive Osaka journalism seemed to be having everything its way. Two Osaka newspapers, the *Asahi* and the *Mainichi,* each passed a million in nationwide circulation the year after the earthquake. The largest Tokyo newspaper had a third of a million. The two Osaka papers ganged up on it, undermining it so successfully that the *Yomiuri* took it over. The Osakans next turned their energies on another distinguished Tokyo newspaper, and the *Nichinichi,* the Tokyo edition of the *Mainichi* (both names mean "daily"), took that one over.

Shoriki went quickly to work. He sought to give the *Yomiuri* a common touch, without the intellectual tendencies of the Osaka newspapers. His *Yomiuri* had the first women's page and the first advice-to-the-troubled column. He also did wonders with sports, giving the *Yomiuri* a professional baseball team which the whole nation loves. He made it into the largest paper in the city. Since the war it has become the largest in the land.

So all manner of remarkable sequences of events (Shōriki was also to become a pioneer in commercial television) are traceable to the earthquake, if we may assume that the Tiger Gate Incident is traceable to it. But to return to the immediate aftermath. The governor of Yamaguchi Prefecture, whence the assailant came, docked his own pay for two months. The governor of Kyoto Prefecture, where the man had lingered on his way to Tokyo, was reprimanded. The man's father resigned from the Diet and withdrew into the stoic seclusion of the dishonored samurai. The village in which he had been born forwent all New Year festivities by way of atonement. The principal of his elementary school—he had graduated a decade earlier—resigned.

The trail of punishment and contrition following the Otsu Incident is altogether less exaggerated. The home minister resigned, and the governor and police chief of Shiga Prefecture, of which Otsu is the capital, were dismissed: and that was that. All of these people may in some measure be held responsible, whereas it is hard to think the governor of Kyoto and the rural school principal responsible for what happened at Tiger Gate.

* * *

The Taishō period, the reign of the Taishō emperor, stands almost exactly midway through the first Tokyo century, 1868 to 1968. The whole of the Meiji reign and the portion of the Shōwa reign that falls within the century are of almost equal length. Taishō stands at midpoint in another sense. The city has not ceased changing since the end of Taishō, and the early years of Shōwa were to bring a disaster that almost destroyed it once again. Taishō may have been the era when change was fastest. There is no device for precise measurement of such phenomena as cultural change. Yet one has a "sense" that it must be so. The last year of Taishō must have seemed more different from the first than 1912 did from 1897, or 1925 from 1940. The things of late Taishō and early Shōwa, the institutions and the modes of behavior, have a familiar look about them that those of the Russo-Japanese War do not. Even "Taishō democracy," which surrendered so meekly to the reaction of the thirties, seems familiar. It has come again. We have similar extravagances today. Only a prophet can say whether or not indignant, righteous men with guns will try one of these days to work a similar reaction.

The Taishō emperor

The Taishō emperor was mentally incapacitated—from how far back in his not very long life (he was born in 1879) we do not know. His birth was difficult and he was given up for dead. So it may be that he was retarded from infancy. He had already withdrawn from public life before the future Shōwa emperor became regent, late in 1920 and some months after his twentieth birthday. There was little stir over the Taishō emperor's death, certainly very little compared with that which accompanied his father's last illness. The announcement that he had pneumonia came early in December 1926. He was taken to the royal villa at Hayama, on Sagami Bay, south of Tokyo. (The villa disappeared, a victim of arson, in 1971.)

In his diary, Nagai Kafū indicated disapproval of the announcement.

December 14. Cloudy and cold. Toward evening it began to clear. I went in the evening to Ginza, which was noisy with hawkers of newspaper extras. I suppose they informed us that His Majesty's death approaches. The detail with which newspapers, morning and evening, have reported the royal illness is extreme. They do not hesitate to tell us the state of his appetite and of his defecatory processes. This sort of reporting began with the death of the Meiji emperor. With the encouragement of the authorities, the newspapers told us that the emperor suffered from uremic poisoning, and that his august countenance had turned a muddy purple…. If my opinion were asked I would give it. I would say … that a national legend is thus destroyed. While he lives our sovereign is revered as a god, and to tell us that he has died a victim of uremic poisoning shatters the poetry…. Why must these facts about appetite and defecation be made public as the royal death approaches?

The emperor died very early on Christmas morning, and so the first year of Shōwa was only a week long. Among the curiosities one comes upon in flea markets are diaries and memorandum books for the year that failed to be, the sixteenth year of Taishō. It was too late to print books for the second year of Shōwa, and so people made do with ones printed before the royal death and the change of era names.

It has been the practice since 1868 to have era names coincide with reigns. In earlier centuries they were changed more frequently. The designation "Shōwa," meaning literally "Clarity and Harmony," and conveying a hope for peace at home and amity with all nations, comes, like most of them, from the Chinese classics. It is the longest-lived era name in Japanese history, and it is an inadvertency. The royal household got scooped and was embarrassed. Among the common Japanese ways of coping with an inadvertency is to pretend that it did not occur. A newspaper published the name originally chosen, Kōbun, before it was officially released. The alternative name Shōwa was therefore substituted on a moment's notice and was with us for more than six decades. Kōbun, suggesting an age of brilliant letters, might have been more descriptive of the reign than Shōwa.

The Taishō emperor was buried in February 1927 with suitable reverence and pageantry, and great crowds in which people were trampled to death, but without the public outpourings that accompanied his father's

Interment of the Taishō emperor at Hachiōji, February 1927

obsequies. There had been disagreement about where the Meiji emper-
or should be buried. There seems to have been none in the case of the
Taishō emperor. His grave is in the western suburbs of Tokyo. Lavish
undertakings for a memorial to the Meiji emperor produced the Meiji
Shrine and Gardens. No one took the trouble in the case of the Taishō
emperor. General Nogi Maresuke, the greatest of modern military heroes, committed suicide on the first day of the Meiji emperor's funeral.
The poet and scholar who composed the official threnody died the day
before the Taishō emperor's funeral began, but not by his own hand.

All in all, a hush surrounds the Taishō emperor. It is not easy to as-
sess the political importance of the Meiji emperor, but his name rallied
the nation for the great efforts of the late nineteenth century. The Taishō
emperor is by comparison a slight, sad figure.

He was, however, the first Tokyo emperor. His father was reared in
Kyoto and buried in the outskirts of that city. The Taishō emperor lived
his whole life in Tokyo, to the extent that anyone in this mobile age lives
his whole life anywhere. His grave lies in Tokyo Prefecture. No one remembers much about him except that he was kept out of sight, but in
this one regard he was unique, an original.

Chapter 8

HAPPY
RECONSTRUCTION DAYS

The official view was that the reconstruction of Tokyo from the great earthquake was complete by 1930. A "reconstruction festival" took place in March of that year. The emperor, who had been regent at the time of the earthquake, was among those who addressed a reconstruction rally in the palace plaza. The mayor addressed a gathering in Hibiya Hall, a few hundred yards to the south. The citizenry was not much a part of these rallies, but the celebrations went on for several days and included events to please everyone—parades and "flower trolleys" and the like. These last were elaborately decorated trolley cars that went all over the city.

The Shōwa emperor, then regent, on an inspection tour after the earthquake; he is standing next to the chair

The emperor took an inspection tour, and expressed taciturn satisfaction with all that he saw by way of reconstruction and hopes for a future of unity and progress. He used the word "capital" to particular effect, as if to emphasize that there was to be no more talk of a capital elsewhere. The organizers of the tour shielded him from the masses with a thoroughness at which the Japanese are very good. Some fifteen thousand people with whom it was conceivable he might come into contact were vaccinated for smallpox. An estimated quarter of a million people were in some way involved in the planning and execution. The tour took him through the flat Low City, the regions most cruelly devastated by earthquake and fire. He stopped, among other places, at Sumida Park and the earthquake memorial (see page 299).

The park is a product of the earthquake, one of the two big new parks beside the Sumida River. It runs for not quite a mile along the right, or Asakusa, bank, less than half that distance along the left bank. The shorter, or left-bank, portion has been the more successful as a park, because it contains venerable religious institutions and the famous line of cherry trees. A new start had to be made on this last. The fires of 1923 destroyed the old one almost completely. Much of the right-bank portion is on reclaimed land. The Arakawa Drainage Channel of mid-Taishō had removed the threat of floods and made reclamation possible. When, in recent years, an ugly concrete wall was put up to contain the river, the incentive was less a fear of waters rushing down the river than of waters rushing up from the bay during stormy high tides. Title to the land for Hamachō Park, the other of the two, on the right bank downstream, presented few difficulties, since there were only three landowners. Getting rid of all the little places that had rights of tenancy was more complicated. Much of the Hamachō geisha district happened to sit upon the tract, and geisha and their patrons can be strong-willed and influential people. The quarter was rebuilt a short distance to the west.

If the official view is accepted, the city did not have long to enjoy its new self. The reconstruction had taken seven years. Only a decade and a little more elapsed before the Second World War started pulling things apart once more. Happy days were few. It may be, indeed, that the years of the reconstruction were happier than the years that followed, for the latter were also the years of the depression, the assassinations, and the beginnings of war.

The Japanese word that is here rendered as "reconstruction" is also rendered by the dictionaries as "restoration." Perfect restoration of a city is probably impossible. There may be attempts to redo a city exactly as it was before whatever made restoration necessary. There have been such attempts in Europe since 1945. The results may be faithful to all the evidence of what was lost, but they are somehow sterile. The life that produced the original is not there.

Nothing of the sort was attempted in Tokyo. Probably it would have been impossible except in limited neighborhoods. We may be grateful that the city was allowed to live and grow, and not forced back into molds it had outgrown. Yet, though few people now alive are old enough to remember what was there before September 1, 1923, one has trouble believing that the old city was not more pleasing to the eye than what came after. If perfect restoration is probably impossible, a reconstruction is generally less pleasing than what went before it. In Tokyo the reasons are not mysterious. They have to do with the fact that Tokyo and Japan had opened themselves in the decade of the 1860s to a deluge of devices and methods from a very alien culture. These had much to recommend them. They were ways of fending off political encroachment. They also tended to be cheaper and more convenient than old devices and methods. So with each reconstruction jerry-built hybrids became more common.

The citizenry seems on the whole to have been rather pleased with the rebuilding, as it was again to be in 1945 and after. Everything had become so cheerful, all that white concrete replacing all that dark plaster and those even darker tiles. Sukiya Bridge, west of Ginza, with the new *Asahi Shimbun* building reflected in its dark waters like a big ship, and the Nichigeki, the Japan Theater, like a bullring, was the place where all the *mobo* and *moga,* the modern boys and girls (for these expressions see page 324), wanted to have their pictures taken.

Fully aware that there are no rulers for measuring, and at the disadvantage of not having been there, we may ask just how much it did all change. The opinions of the best-informed and most sensitive are not unanimous. Most of what survived from Edo had been in the Low City, because that is where most of Edo was. Therefore most of it disappeared. So much is beyond denying. It is in the matter of the rebuilding and the changes it brought to the physical, material city and to its folkways—changes in spirit, we might say—that opinion varies.

In the early years of Shōwa, Nagai Kafū was spending many of his evenings in Ginza, at "cafés," which today would more likely be called bars or cabarets. In 1931 he put some of his experiences and observations into a novel, *During the Rains (Tsuyo no Atosaki).* An aging character who is in many ways a surrogate for Kafū himself—although Kafū was younger,

Kyōbashi, as rebuilt after the earthquake

and never served a prison term for bribery, as the character has—muses upon the Ginza of recent years. Every day something changes; the sum of changes since the earthquake is like a dream. The Ginza of today is not the Ginza of yesterday. The old gentleman's interests are rather narrow. He is chiefly concerned with the cafés which sprang up in large numbers after the earthquake, most of them on burnt-over tracts, and which, being outposts of the demimonde, were highly sensitive to new fashions and tastes. He speaks for Kafū, however, and Kafū found the changes devastating. The old pleasure centers were gone, and good taste threatened to go with them.

Tanizaki Junichirō, a native of the city who had been away most of the time since the earthquake, felt differently. Change had not lived up to his predictions. On September 1, 1923, he was in the Hakone Mountains, some fifty miles southwest of Tokyo. He had a famous vision of utter destruction and a splendid flapper-age rebuilding. What he saw and wrote of in 1934 was disappointing, or would have been had he still been in his 1923 frame of mind. He had changed, and was glad that changes in the city had not been as extreme as he had hoped and predicted. The Tanizaki of 1934 would have been disappointed, this is to say, if the Tanizaki of 1923 had not himself changed.

So ten years and one have now gone by. The decade which seemed so slow as it passed came to an end on September 1 of last year. I am forty-nine. And how are things today with me, and how are things with Tokyo? People say that the immediate future is dark, and that nothing is as it should be; yet looking back over the meditations in which I was sunk on that mountain road in Hakone, I feel somewhat strange. I do not know whether to be sad or happy at the irony of what has happened. My thoughts then about the extent of the disaster, the damage to the city, and the speed and form of the recovery were half right and half wrong.... Because the damage was less than I imagined, the recovery in ten years, though remarkable, has not been the transformation I looked for. I was one of those who uttered cries of delight at the grand visions of the home minister, Gotō Shimpei. Three billion yen would go into buying up the whole of the burned wastes and making them over into something regular and orderly. They were not realized. The old tangle of Tokyo streets is still very much with us. It is true that large numbers of new bridges, large and small, now describe their graceful arcs over the Sumida and other rivers and canals. The region from Marunouchi through Ginza and Kyōbashi to Nihombashi has taken on a new face. Looking from the train window as the train moves through the southern parts of the city and on past Shimbashi to the central station, I cannot but be astonished that these were lonely wastes where I would play half a day as a child. People back from abroad say that Tokyo is now a match for the cities of Europe and America.... The daydream in which I lost myself on September 1, 1923—I neglected to think even of my unhappy wife and daughter, back in the city—did not approach the imposing beauty I now see before me. But what effect has all this surface change had on the customs, the manners, the words, the acts of the city and its people? The truth is that my imagination got ahead of me. Westernization has not been as I foresaw. To be sure, there have recently appeared such persons as the stick girls of Ginza, and the prosperity of bars and cafés quite overshadows that of the geisha quarters, and movies and reviews are drawing customers away from Kabuki; but none of these places, and even less the casinos and cabarets, bears comparison with even the Carleton Café in Shanghai.... How many women and girls wear Western dress that really passes as Western dress? In summer the number increases somewhat, but in winter you see not one in ten among shoppers and pedestrians. Even among office girls, one in two would be a generous estimate.

(Since Tanizaki was born in 1886, his age is obviously by the Oriental count. "Stick girls" were female gigolos. Like walking sticks, they attached themselves to men, in this case young men strolling in Ginza.)

So Tanizaki's feelings are mixed. He is sad that he must admit his in-adequacies as a prophet and sad too that with regard to Nihombashi, at least (see page 293), his predictions were not exaggerated. Yet he does not see changes in customs and manners as Kafū does.

Writing also in the early thirties, Kawabata Yasunari is more interested in physical change, and is a subtler chronicler of it, than Kafū or Taniza-ki. (Kafū was twenty years older than Kawabata, Tanizaki thirteen.) In Hama Park he comes upon a kind of revivalism directed not at Edo and the Japanese tradition but at early Westernization. He finds Western ten-dencies, in other words, that have become thoroughly Japanized.

Everything is new, of course, Hama Park being one of the two new ones along the banks of the Sumida. Nothing is unchanged except the sea gulls and the smell of the water. Yet nostalgia hangs over the place. The new Venetian pavilion is meant to recall a famous Meiji building lost in the earthquake, the offices put up by Josiah Conder for the Hok-kaido Development Bureau. Conder, an Englishman, was the most fa-mous of foreign architects active in Meiji Japan. The music and revelry from the riverboats of Edo are too remote for nostalgia.

Kawabata does not tell us what he thinks of Sumida Park, the other new riverside one, but quotes a friend who is an unreserved booster. With its clean flowing waters and its open view off to Mount Tsukuba, Sumida Park, says the acquaintance, is the equal of the great parks beside the Potomac, the Thames, the Danube, the Isar (which flows through Munich). Give the cherry trees time to grow and it will be among the finest parks in the world. In his silent response Kawabata is perhaps the better prophet. Tsukuba is now invisible and concrete walls block off the view of a very dirty river. Only in cherry-blossom time do people pay much attention to the park, and even then it is not noticed as is the much older Ueno Park.

Kawabata has a walk down the whole length of the new Shōwa Av-enue, from Ueno to Shimbashi. Some liken it to the Champs-Elysèes and Unter den Linden. Kawabata does not. "I saw the pains of Tokyo. I could, if I must, see a brave new departure, but mostly I saw the rawness of the wounds, the weariness, the grim, empty appearance of health."

Famous old sweets, offered for centuries along the east bank of the Sumida, are now purveyed from concrete shops that look like banks. (Though Kawabata does not mention it, the mall in front of the Asakusa Kannon Temple was also done over in concrete, in another kind of re-vivalist style, the concrete molded to look like Edo. The main building of the National Museum of Ueno, finished in 1937, is among the most

Shōwa Avenue (Shōwadōri), looking northwards from the freight yards at Akihabara

conspicuous examples of the style.) The earthquake memorial on the east bank of the Sumida, where those tens of thousands perished in the fires of 1923, is a most unsuccessful jumble of styles, also in concrete. Is it no longer possible, Kawabata asks of a companion, to put up a building in a pure Japanese style? "But all these American things are Tokyo itself," replies the companion, a positive thinker. And a bit later: "They may look peculiar now, but we'll be used to them in ten years or so. They may even turn out to be beautiful."

Kawabata does think the city justly proud of its new bridges, some four hundred of them. Indeed they seem to be what it is proudest of. In a photographic exhibition about the new Tokyo, he notes, more than half the photographs are of bridges.

In 1923 Tokyo was still what Edo had been, a city of waters. The earthquake demonstrated that it did not have enough bridges. There were only five across the Sumida. They all had wooden floors, and all caught fire. That is why more people died from drowning, probably, than directly from the earthquake. On the eve of Pearl Harbor, with the completion of Kachitoki Bridge, there were eleven. Kachitoki means "shout of triumph," but the name is not, perhaps, quite as jingoistic as it may seem. Those who chose it in 1940 may well have had in mind the shout of triumph that was to announce a pleasant end to the unpleasantness on the continent, but the direct reference is to a triumph that actually came off, that over the Russians in 1905. The name was given to a ferry established that year between Tsukiji and filled lands beyond one of the mouths of the Sumida. The name of the ferry became the name of the bridge, a drawbridge that was last drawn almost twenty years ago. By the late fifties automobile traffic to and from Ginza was so heavy that there was congestion for two hours after a drawing of the bridge.

Nor were there enough bridges across the Kanda River and the downtown canals. These waterways did not claim the victims that the Sumida did, but they were obstacles to crowds pressing toward the palace plaza. Of the streets leading westward from Ginza toward the plaza and Hibiya Park, only three had bridges crossing the outer moat. The moat was now bridged on all the east-west streets, as also was the canal that bounded Ginza on the east.

Moat and canal now are gone. There was some filling in of canals from late Meiji, as the city turned from boats to wheels for pleasure and for commerce. Between the earthquake and the war several canals in Nihombashi and Kyōbashi were lost, but one important canal was actually dug, joining two older canals for commercial purposes. Other canals were widened and deepened. Both in 1923 and in 1945 canals were used to dispose of rubble, that reconstruction might proceed. It has been mostly since 1945 that Tokyo of the waters has been obliterated. In the old Low City the Sumida remains, and such rivers or canals as the Kanda and the Nihombashi, but the flatlands are now dotted with bus stops carrying the names of bridges of which no trace remains. Venice would not be Venice if its canals were filled in. Tokyo, with so many of its canals turned into freeways, is not Edo.

It was after the earthquake that retail merchandising, a handy if rough measure of change, went the whole distance toward becoming what the Japanese had observed in New York and London. Indeed it went further, providing not only merchandise but entertainment and culture. Mitsukoshi, one of the bold pioneers in making the dry-goods stores over into department stores selling almost everything, has had a theater since its post-earthquake rebuilding. Most department stores have had amusement parks on their roofs and some still have them, and all the big ones have gardens and terraces, galleries and exhibition halls.

The great revolution occurred at about the turn of the century, when Mitsukoshi and the other Nihombashi pioneer, Shirokiya, started diversifying themselves. What happened after the earthquake is modest by comparison, but a step that now seems obvious had the effect of inviting everyone in. Everyone came.

The change had to do with footwear, always a matter of concern in a land whose houses merge indoors and outdoors except at the entranceway, beyond which outdoor footwear may not pass. Down to the earthquake the department stores respected the taboo. Footwear was checked and slippers were provided for use within the stores. There were famous snarls. They worked to the advantage of smaller shops, where the number of feet was small enough for individual attention. After the earthquake came the simple solution: Let the customer keep his shoes on.

Simple and obvious it may seem today, but it must have taken getting used to. Never before through all the centuries had shod feet ventured beyond the entranceway, or perhaps an earth-floored kitchen.

Smaller shops had to follow along, in modified fashion, if they were to survive. In earlier ages customers had removed their footwear and climbed to the straw-matted platform that was the main part of the store. There they sat and made their decisions. Customer and shopkeeper were both supposed to know what the customer wanted. It was fetched from warehouses. Now the practice came to prevail of having a large part of the stock spread out for review. Floor plans changed accordingly. There was a larger proportion of earthen floor and a smaller proportion of matted platform, and customers tended to do what they do in the West, remain standing and in their shoes or whatever they happened to bring in from the street with them.

Private railways were beginning to put some of their profits from the lucrative commuter business, which in Meiji had been largely a freight and sewage business, into department stores. In this they were anticipated by Osaka. The Hankyu Railway opened the first terminal department store at its Umeda terminus in 1929. Seeing what a good idea this was—having also the main Osaka station of the National Railways, Umeda was the most important transportation center in the Kansai region—the private railways of Tokyo soon began putting up terminal department stores of their own. Thus they promoted the growth of the western transfer points—Shibuya, Shinjuku, and Ikebukuro—and their control over these most profitable of places.

The department stores discontinued old services The bourgeois ma-tron from the High City now had to come to the store. Fewer and fewer stores would come to her, as all of them had in the old days. New services were added as the railways began to open their stores and competition be-came more intense: free delivery, even free bus service to and from stores. If it asked that the matron set forth and mingle with the lesser orders, the department stove made the pvocess as painless for her as possible.

External architecture changed along with floor plans. Tiled roofs be-gan to disappear behind false fronts. The old shop signs, often abstract and symbolic and always aesthetically pleasing, gave way to signs that an-nounced their business loudly and unequivocally. Advertising was now in full flood. Huge businessman and little businessman alike had taken to it, and the old subdued harmonies of brown and gray surrendered to a cacophony of messages and colors. This seems to have been truer west than east of the Sumida. In the conservative eastern wards rows of black-tiled roofs were still visible from the street. The west bank was said after the earthquake and rebuilding to resemble a river town put up by the Japanese in Manchuria.

The first vending machines were installed at Tokyo and Ueno stations ear-ly in 1926. Like advertising, whose origins in Tokugawa and Meiji were so simple that they were almost invisible, vending machines have become an insistent presence in the years since. They now offer an astonishing variety of wares, from contraceptives to a breath of fresh air.

Like the practices and habits of shoppers, those of diners-out changed. The restaurant in which one eats shoeless and on the floor is not uncom-mon even today. Yet new ways did become common at the center, Ginza, and spread outward. Good manners had required removing wraps upon entering a restaurant, or indeed any interior. Now people were to be seen eating with their coats and shoes on, and some even kept their hats on. Before the earthquake women had disliked eating away from home—it was not good form. The department-store dining room led the way in breaking down this reticence, and the new prominence of the working woman meant that women no longer thought it beneath them to be seen by the whole world eating with other women. Before the earthquake a restaurant operator with two floors at his disposal tended to use the up-per one for business and the lower one for living. Now the tendency was to use the street floor for business. An increasing number of shopkeep-ers (a similar trend in Osaka is documented in Tanizaki's *The Makioka*

Sisters) used all the floors for business and lived elsewhere, most often in the High City. So it was that money departed the Low City.

The habits and practices of the Buddhist clergy were also changing. The priests of some sects had long married. Now there was an insurgency in a stronghold of Tendai, one of the sects that had remained celibate.

The Kaneiji Temple once occupied most of the land in Shitaya Ward that is now Ueno Park. There it ministered to the souls of six Tokugawa shoguns, whose graves lay within the premises. It was almost completely destroyed in the "Ueno War" of 1868, when the Meiji government subdued the last Tokugawa holdouts in the city. Sorely reduced in scale, the temple was rebuilt and came through the earthquake without serious damage. In the Edo centuries there were fifteen abbots, even as there were fifteen shoguns. All of the abbots were royal princes, and all were celibate, at least to appearances, though dubious teahouses in the districts nearby seem to have catered to the needs of the Kaneiji clergy. In Meiji the abbots started taking common-law wives. In 1932 one of them made bold to enter into a formal, legal marriage. The appointment of his successor was the occasion for a struggle between the Kaneiji and Tendai: headquarters on Mount Hiei, near Kyoto. Hiei demanded that the Kaneiji candidate choose between marriage and career, and did not prevail. He had both. The Hiei abbots have gone on being celibate.

The female work force was expanding rapidly. In that day when Taisho democracy was dying but not quite dead, a few people were beginning to have ideas about the equality of the sexes. Already in Meiji, women had taken over nursing and the telephone exchanges. In the years before and after the change of reigns "red-collar girls" appeared. These were bus conductors, and their trade was almost entirely feminine until its extinction after the Second World War. Up and down Shōwa Avenue, the wide new street cut through from Shimbashi to Ueno after the earthquake, were gas-pump maidens. The day of the pleasure motorist-had come, and pretty maidens urged him to consume. The day of the shop girl had also come. Sales in the old dry-goods stores had been entirely in the hands of shop boys.

The question of the shop girl and whether or not she was ideally liberated added much to the interest of the most famous Tokyo fire between the gigantic ones of 1923 and 1945. The "flowers of Edo," the conflagrations for which the city had been famous, were not in danger of extinction, but they were becoming less expensive and less dramatic. Firefighting methods improved, the widening of streets provided firebreaks, and, most important, fire-resistant materials were replacing the old boards and shingles. Except for the disasters of 1923 and 1945, there have since the end of Meiji been no fires of the good old type, taking away buildings by the thousands and tens of thousands within a few hours. The number of fires did not fall remarkably, but losses, with the two great exceptions, were kept to a few thousand buildings per year.

The famous fire of early Shōwa occurred in a department store. It affected only the one building and the loss of life did not bear comparison with that from the two disasters. It was, however, the first multiple story fire the city had known, and the worst department-store fire anywhere since one in Budapest late in the nineteenth century.

The Shirokiya, an eight-story building constructed after the earthquake, was the chief rival of the Mitsukoshi through the years of diversifying and expanding. On the morning of December 16, 1932, a fire broke out in the toy department on the fourth floor. The end of the year had traditionally been a time of giving gifts, and Christmas gifts had of recent years been added to those based on older customs. The Taishō emperor brought Christmas Day into prominence by dying on it. Christmas Eve was now becoming what New Year's Eve is in the West. The Shirokiya was bright with decorations. A technician was repairing Christmas lights and a tree caught fire. The fire spread to the celluloid toys, and the

whole fourth floor was soon engulfed. Fortunately this happened at a few minutes after nine, before the store had filled with customers. A watcher from a fire tower nearby saw the fire before it was reported. Firemen were changing shifts, and both shifts rushed to the scene. Presently every pump in the city was on hand. Not much could be done to contain the fire. The floors of the Shirokiya were highly inflammable and all the top ones were quickly in flames. The fire was extinguished a few minutes before noon.

The Shirokiya fire

Utility poles and wires along the main streets, and the narrowness of side streets, made it difficult to use ladders, though some rescues were effected. Ropes and improvised lines from kimono fabrics in the store inventories brought people down and slings up to bring more people down. Army planes came by with ropes, although, according to the fire department, they were too late to do much good. It may be that no one except a single victim of asphyxiation need have died. The other thirteen; deaths were by jumping and falling. The bears and monkeys on the roof came through uninjured, to demonstrate that the roof was safe enough—throughout. The jumping was of course from panic. The falling had more subtle causes, having to do with customs and manners—in this instance, the slowness of women in converting to imported dress.

All shop girls in those days wore Japanese dress and underdress, wraparound skirts in various numbers depending on the season. Traditional dress for women included nothing by way of shaped, tight fitting undergarments to contain the private parts snugly. The older ones among the Shirokiya women also being bolder, made it safely down the ropes. Some of the younger ones used a hand for the rope and a hand to keep their skirts from flying into disarray. So they fell. In 1933 the Shirokiya started paying its girls subsidies for wearing foreign dress, and required that they wear underpants.

From about the time of the earthquake, advertising men had been pushing Western underdress for women, which they made a symbol of sexual equality. But a disaster like the Shirokiya fire was needed to effect decisive change. It demonstrated that women were still lamentably backward, and the newspapers loved it. Underpants became one of their favorite causes and enjoyed quick success, though the reform would actually seem to have begun earlier. Kawabata noted that all the little girls sliding down the slides in Hama Park were wearing underpants.

Some years earlier another department store, the new Matsuya in Ginza, which was to be the Central PX for the American Occupation, had provided the setting for another new event. The Shirokiya had the first modern high-rise fire, and the Matsuya the first high-rise suicide. It occurred on May 9, 1926. In a land in which, ever since statistics have been kept, there has been a high incidence of suicide among the young, suicides have shown a tendency toward the faddish and voguish. Meiji had suicides by jumping over waterfalls, and the closing months of Taishō a flurry of jumping from high buildings.

In May 1932 a Keiō University student and his girlfriend, not allowed to marry, killed themselves on a mountain in Oiso, southwest of Tokyo. The incident became a movie, *Love Consummated in Heaven*, and the inspiration for a popular song.

> With you the bride of another,
> How will I live? How can I live?
> I too will go. There where Mother is,
> There beside her,
> I will take your hand.
>
> God alone knows
> That our love has been pure.
> We die, and in paradise,
> I will be your bride.

At least twenty other couples killed themselves on the same spot during the same year.

Early in 1933 a girl student from Tokyo jumped into a volcanic crater on Oshima, largest of the Izu Islands. Situated in and beyond Sagami Bay, south of Tokyo, the islands are a part of Tokyo Prefecture. The girl took along a friend to attest to the act and inform the world of it. A vogue for jumping into the same crater began. By the end of the year almost a thousand people, four-fifths of them young men, had jumped into it. Six people jumped in on a single day in May, and on a day in July four boys jumped in one after another.

On April 30 two Tokyo reporters wearing gas masks and fire suits descended into the crater by rope ladders strengthened with metal. One reached a depth of more than a hundred feet before falling rocks compelled him to climb back up again. They found no bodies. After more elaborate preparations the *Yomiuri* sent a reporter and a photographer into the crater a month later. Using a gondola lowered by a crane, they descended more than a thousand feet to the crater floor. There they found the body of a teenage boy.

The year of all these suicides seems to have been a nervous and jumpy one in general. It was the year in which Japan, having rejected the Lytton Report, left the League of Nations. The report demanded that Japan withdraw from Manchuria. Feelings of isolation and apprehension seem to have swept the land. Yo-yos were bobbing everywhere. Peak sales ran to five million a month. During the summer, the withdrawal from the League having come in the spring, everyone was out in the streets and in the parks, hopping about to the accompaniment of the great hit song of the day, "Tokyo Ondo" ("Tokyo Dance"). The music of this is by Na-kayama Shimpei, generally held to be the founder of modern Japanese popular music, and the lyrics are by Saijō Yaso, a poet of such distinction that he is given three pages in a one-volume encyclopedia of modern Japanese literature.

The lyrics do not say very much. Half of them and a bit more are meaningless chants to keep rhythm by: *sate ya-a to na sore yoi yoi yoi*, and that sort of thing. Interspersed among them are fleeting references to places and things and combinations of the two, such as the moon upon the Sumida, the willows of the Ginza, and Tsukuba and Fuji, the mountains that are supposed to adorn the Tokyo skyline but seldom do.

Advised that the dancing in Hibiya Park was disturbing His Majesty's rest, the Marunouchi police ordered it to desist at nine o'clock. At Asakusa the police did the opposite, protected the dancers. They had had reports that the movie theaters, most of whose potential customers were out in the streets dancing, had hired men from underworld gangs to break the dances up. In parts of town the dancing crowds stopped traffic, and the police were powerless either to disperse or to protect.

The number of Tokyo suicides doubled during the first decade of Showa. The number of attempted suicides doubled in three years toward the end of the decade. Despondency, illness, and family difficulties were the predominant motives. The effects of economic depression are to be detected in the last category. The number of suicides began to fall with the approach of war and continued to fall during the war.

The most famous suicide of early Shōwa occurred in the northern suburbs of Tokyo. On July 24, 1927, the writer Akutagawa Ryūnosuke killed himself with an overdose of "Veronal, etc.," as accounts of the event uniformly have it. He did not, as General Nogi did, choose the day of the emperor's funeral, but his passing has widely been taken as symbolic of the passing of the Taishō reign.

A remarkable Kawabata essay, "Akutagawa Ryūnosuke and the Yoshi-wara" ("Akutagawa Ryūnosuke to Yoshiwara"), published in 1929, associates the Akutagawa suicide with the horrors of the earthquake, and so makes it yet more symbolic.

> Hirotsu Kazuo describes in a recent story how he and Akutagawa Ryūnosuke, having seen Uno Kōji to a hospital, went off for a look at the Tamanoi district and its unlicensed prostitutes.... I had an account directly from Mr. Hirotsu, and the impression it left was more powerful than that of the story. The conclusion had a certain ghoulishness

about it, with the women of Tamanoi turning pale as Akutagawa passed, and whispering to one another: "A ghost, a ghost!"

Akutagawa had by then completed preparations for his suicide, and so I wanted to attach all sorts of meanings to the anecdote, and of course I remembered how, some five or six years ago, I went with him to look at the Yoshiwara....

I had been taking long walks through the city every day from September 1. There cannot be many who saw as well as I did what the earthquake had done. I believe I was sitting on the veranda of the Akutagawa house describing a little of it. Akutagawa himself suggested, I think, that he and Mr. Kon and I go look at the bodies in the Yoshiwara pond. Akutagawa was wearing a striped kimono and a helmet. The helmet was incongruous, like a gigantic toadstool perched on the thin face and figure. Walking along in those great strides of his, swinging his body as if about to take flight, he looked like a villain setting forth on some evil mission. He was a war-horse striding past the devastated wastes, up streets that were a tangle of charred electric lines, among survivors tired and dirty as war refugees. I was a little annoyed with him and the briskness that put him in such contrast with everyone and everything else. As I ran after him, I thought what fun it would be if a policeman or a person from the vigilance committees were to stop him and question him.

The pond beside the Yoshiwara quarter was one of those horrible pictures of hell which speak only to someone who has seen the real thing. The reader should imagine tens and hundreds of men and women as if boiled in a cauldron of mud. Muddy red cloth was strewn all up and down the banks, for most of the corpses were those of courtesans. Smoke was rising from incense along the banks. Akutagawa stood with a handkerchief over his face. He said something, but I have forgotten what. Probably it was something light and sarcastic, well worth forgetting.

He came upon a policeman in the Yoshiwara. For a kilometer or so on our way back they walked side by side, and he drew forth all manner of information about the earthquake. The policeman was an accommodating sort who answered all his questions....

For me who had so little to do with Akutagawa while he lived, the picture that comes first to mind, now that he is dead, is of that helmeted figure striding vigorously along with no regard for his surroundings. There was in it a lightness and briskness that contained no hint of death.

But when, two or three years later, he had made his resolve to die, the picture must have come back into his mind, I am sure, of those horrible corpses piled on one another in the Yoshiwara pond. He seems to have deliberated all sorts of ways to die in search of one that would leave a handsome corpse. In contrast to the handsome death, its antithesis, were those corpses in the pond.

That was the day in his life when he saw the largest number of them.

And I who was with him in observing the most repellent of deaths can perhaps visualize his handsome death better than those who have been spared the repellent kind.

All of the other persons mentioned were well-known writers. Tamanoi is a district east of the Sumida River, then in the suburbs. Until 1945 it contained an unlicensed pleasure quarter. It is the setting of Nagai Kafū's *A Strange Tale from East of the River* (see pages 335-336).

The Taishō era needed a literary symbol, and Akutagawa was a good one, embodying (or so it is widely held) the sometimes neurotic refinement and intellectualism that were products of the great Meiji endeavor to encompass and catch up with the West. The common view has therefore been that his suicide, more than the death of the emperor, brought an end to an era. It is not easy to establish that Akutagawa's mental illness was peculiar to the era. Yet he will do as a symbol, as the poor emperor will not. The emperor's illness ran in the direction of retardation, which will hardly do for either Meiji or Taishō. The Akutagawa suicide provides reasonable grounds for considering the unlikely Taishō reign an independent and in some measure self-contained cultural period.

The new and popular words of the post-earthquake years were mostly foreign. This seems proper for that relatively cosmopolitan day of Taishō democracy; people did not have to be apologetic about importing their neologisms. Things were rather different in the late thirties. The Japanese language has always been hospitable to new words. Tokyo, where the lords of the media and of advertising have their seats, has coined most of them and helped others to spread. Numbers of Osaka words have made their way into the standard language, but they have had to be adopted by Tokyo before prevailing in the provinces.

Here are some popular words and expressions from late Taishō and early Shōwa: "It," "shan," "mobo" and "moga," "Charleston," "mannequin girl," "modern life," "stick girl," "casino." The significance of some should be clear enough; some require explanation. (Among the pleasure of modern Japanese is that its use of one's own language so often requires explanation.) "It" refers to the Clara Bow quality. "Shan" is from the German *schön*. It is a masculine term referring to feminine beauty. The "mannequin girl" is a particular kind of beauty, the fashion model. Though models had been used in advertising even before the earthquake, the modeling business really got started in 1929. From the spring of that year all the big department stores began using them. Curiously, an early photograph of the Mannequin Club—like most other people, models quickly formed a club which had as its chief aim the exclusion of everyone else—shows almost all of the ladies in Japanese dress. "Stick girl" will be found above, in Tanizaki's remarks about his native city. "Mobo" and "moga" are acronyms, and among the words that might be thought symbolic of the age itself. They are from "modern boy" and "modern girl"; *(garu):* the advanced young people of the day, the ones most sensitive to fad and fashion, they who went strolling in Ginza and had their pictures taken at Sukiya Bridge.

Many a neologism has had its brief day and gone, but all of the above remain in the language and are to be found in any dictionary. "Casino," from French rather than Italian or English, might be rendered "music hall." A neologism that did not gain immediate currency but has since become very much a part of the language was first used in a women's magazine in the spring of 1929. Before the earthquake "mama" was already supplanting native words for "mother." "Mama-san," adding the common appellative, now came to indicate the lady in charge of a café or bar, also often called a "madame."

Taishō was a time of great change. Such places of entertainment as the cafés make Ginza, for instance, come to seem near and familiar. And, given that wars, especially lost ones, and economic miracles are always potent engines of change, there has been no paucity in this respect in the years since. A 1929 survey of Tokyo *sakariba* shows us a city that is in important and interesting respects different from the city of today. The biggest of Japanese English dictionaries gives "a bustling place" as one of its definitions of *sakariba*. These are places where crowds gather, and where revelry and shopping occur with the greatest intensity.

The *sakariba* covered are Ginza, Shinjuku, Ueno, Asakusa, Shibuya, Ningyōchō, and Kagurazaka. No one today would include the last two, and Asakusa would be a borderline case; and no one would leave out Ikebukuro or Roppongi. Omissions and inclusions tell of the westward march of the city. Now among the gigantic transfer points in the old western suburbs, Ikebukuro was slower to get started than Shibuya and Shinjuku, those other western giants. To the huge profit of the Seibu Railway, one of the private commuter systems, it has grown hugely this last half century. The southern wards contained no bustling places in 1929. Shibuya lay beyond the city limits. Roppongi is in the old Azabu Ward, but it is a latecomer which got its start as a camp follower. This was in the late nineteenth century, when war (a victorious one in this instance) brought military barracks to the district. It has really emerged since the Second World War, as the most highly amplified of the *sakariba* and among the ones dearest to the very young.

Ningyōchō was lively in Meiji and has been in decline since the earthquake. So has most of the old Nihombashi Ward, the recognized center of mercantile Edo. Ningyōchō is as good a place as any to go in search of the mood and flavor of the old Low City, but it is not the smallest competition with a place like Shinjuku in the matter of drawing crowds. Kagurazaka, in Ushigome Ward, to the northwest of the palace and not far from the western limits of the old city, was for a time after the earthquake among the leading *sakariba*. It was one of the uptown geisha districts for which the knowledgeable Nagai Kafū had great contempt.

Their geisha were, he thought, without accomplishments other than those of the bedroom. Kagurazaka had its period of prosperity with the destruction in the earthquake of the Low City pleasure quarters. It lay near a station on the western suburban line of the National Railways, but was not a transfer point, and so was outstripped by Shinjuku, which was.

The 1929 survey was made in the afternoon at all the places except Ningyocho, where it was done in the early evening. In none of them do women outnumber men. Shinjuku in midafternoon has the highest proportion of women, 43 percent, and of these only a third are recognizable as housewives. In Ginza at four o'clock, young men account for almost half, young women only a little over a tenth; and so those who went strolling seem to have done it mostly by themselves or with male companions. *Mobo* were most commonly without *moga*. Asakusa, as noted above, would today be a borderline instance. It drew big crowds a half century ago but does no more. In 1929 the golden age of the music halls was just getting underway; yet the survey contains ominous signs. The proportion of young men is much smaller than in Ginza, and that of middle-aged men higher. Already so early, it may be, the blight was setting in. The middle-aged crowd may spend more generously, but it is the young crowd that sets the tone and ensures that there will still be crowds for a while. When the young start to abandon a place, it is in for bad times.

The sex ratio would be different today. Ours is a much more womanized age. At four in the afternoon women would probably outnumber men in any of the places that still draw great crowds, except just possibly Ueno. Asakusa, Ningyōchō, and Kagurazaka do not.

The survey also spelled out categories, which would seem to show that a great uniformity has settled over Japanese crowds this past half century. Here is a full list of them: provincials, soldiers (Ueno had the most), shop boys, laborers, young boys, male students, youths (other than students, presumably), middle-aged men, old men, old women, housewives, young women, female children, female students, serving maids, geisha, and working women. They obviously are not carefully enough defined to be mutually exclusive, but we may assume that the surveyors could confidently, albeit vaguely, distinguish the categories one from another. Many of them would be indistinguishable today—students from other young men and women, for instance, and housewives from serving maids, or shop boys and laborers from other young men the same age. Many a provincial these days could easily cross the line and pass as a Tokyo person. There has been a leveling process which some might call democratic and others might call conformist.

Another survey of 1929, of department stores, also reveals a few interesting things. There were as many men as women. Today there might just possibly be on a Sunday afternoon, if an uncommonly large number of wives were able to drag their husbands forth on shopping expeditions. There certainly would be at no other time. The categories, again, call for notice: gentlemen, merchants, provincials, housewives, working women, serving maids. Again they are obviously rough, and they cannot be all-inclusive. Why are there no children and no students, who were in those days, as they are not now, easily detectable by their uniforms?

Yet the categories are more distinctive than they would be today. Almost two-thirds of the men are in Western dress, but only a sixth of the women—and only 2 or 3 percent of "adult women," which category is not defined. The tendency of women to stay longer in traditional dress than men seems to be universal, and was clear in Japan from the beginning of Meiji. Cosmetics seem to have been a way of distinguishing the urban lady from the provincial. Heavy applications were the mark of the provincial.

Since 1898 Tokyo had had a mayor who presided over the "ward part" of the prefecture, the fifteen wards of the Meiji city, whose limits remained almost unchanged until 1932. Appointed governors had jurisdiction over the whole prefecture, including the "county part," the towns and rural regions that lay outside the city limits. Population was already spilling beyond the city limits in 1923, and did so ever more rapidly in the years that followed. The city wished to go west, and indulged the wish more and more.

Already in 1923 the prefecture was growing faster than the city. The process speeded up after the earthquake. Because the suburbs suffered relatively light damage, many of the 1923 refugees did not return, and population increase tended toward places where land was cheaper. With 1918 considered as 100, the population of the wards stood at only 90 in 1932. It fell by about a sixth immediately after the earthquake (though this was by no means as drastic a fall as that during and after the Upheavals of 1867 and 1868 and the disaster of 1945). It quickly began to recover, but at no time before 1932 had it returned to the 1918 level. The population of the prefecture, again with 1918 as the base, stood at 156 in 1932, and the population of the city as its limits were redrawn in 1932—the population, that is, of the fifteen old wards and twenty new ones—stood at 322. Even what remained of the counties, to the west of the newly enlarged city, had risen to 129 as against 100 for 1918.

In 1920 the city still contained more than half the population of the prefecture. In 1930 the proportion had fallen to between a third and two-fifths. Four towns on the edges of the fifteen wards had more than a hundred thousand people in 1930. Fifteen had fifty thousand to a hundred thousand. The expansion of 1932 lagged far behind the facts. The city was much larger than the area the mayor had jurisdiction over.

As the old city filled up and spilled over, so did its cemeteries. The big new ones of Meiji, along the western limits of the city, were filling by the end of Taisho. Plans were completed on the eve of the earthquake for a new one, out in the "county part" of the prefecture, not far from the Tama River. It too was filling before the new reign was a decade old. This time the city looked eastward. A tract was purchased at a place named Yasumi in Chiba Prefecture. Yasumi seems a most pleasant and appropriate name for a cemetery. The commonest word for "rest" is homophonous.

The western and southern suburbs were growing more rapidly than the northern and eastern ones. So once more we have evidence of the decline of the Low City. The northern and eastern suburbs were an extension of the Low City, the southern and western ones of the High City. The southern suburbs, on the way to Yokohama and in the industrial belt that lay between the two cities, were growing fastest of all. The town of Ebara, immediately beyond the southern city limits, had more than fifteen times the population in 1932 that it had had in 1918. Only one town to the north and east had an increase of more than sevenfold during the same period.

The suburbs, particularly the western and southern ones, were the realm of the *bunka jūtaku,* the "cultural dwelling," a euphemism for the kind of dwelling the "salaryman" or office worker was expected to be happy in. ("Salaryman" is a coinage from English which seems to have come into use during the First World War.) A cultural dwelling typically had three or four little rooms, one of them in a somewhat Western style, two floors, a floored kitchen, and a bath. In more traditional houses for the middle and lower orders the kitchen had a floor of packed earth. The private bath marks a major departure from tradition. In recent years it has become more economical for a family to bathe at home than to go to a public bath, and so of course the public bath has declined grievously. The public baths of Edo and Meiji were social and even cultural centers. Many cultural dwellings had pink and blue roofs, and so we have the beginnings of the plastic look, to replace the earthen look of the older styles.

At irregular but convenient intervals among all the new cultural abodes were shopping districts, many of them called the Something Ginza. Thatch-roofed farmhouses still dotted the suburbs, and some of them still had lands to farm. In late Taishō there was farming in eleven of the fifteen wards. Today there are truck gardens and a few paddies in the twenty new wards, but none in the fifteen old ones.

Universities began deserting the old city after the earthquake. Burned out in Kanda, the University of Commerce (Shoka Daigaku); moved by stages to the place where, with the name Hitotsubashi from the old site, it now is, far out in the western suburbs. Burned out in Asakusa, the University of Technology (Kōgyō Daigaku) moved out to the paddies in what is now Meguro Ward. Keiō, one of the better regarded private universities, built itself a second campus in Kanagawa Prefecture, beyond the Tama River. In this it was abetted by one of the private railways, many of which were also energetic real-estate developers.

Title to the new land passed, without reimbursement, from the Tōyoko (Tokyo-Yokohama) Railway to the university. Today the Tōyoko is a part of the Tōkyū, or Tokyo Express, system. Keiō retained the original campus in the old High City where it had since early Meiji been an evangelical center for Westernization.

The growth of the suburbs was not only residential and educational. Industry was also moving outward. In 1932, when rebuilding from the earthquake was held to be complete, more of the large factories in the prefecture—factories with more than a hundred workers—were outside than inside the city. By the thirties the district from southern Tokyo into

Kanagawa Prefecture was emerging as one of the great industrial belts of the country, and the largest in the Kantō region. Really heavy industry situated itself across the Tama River in Kanagawa, but there were many subcontractors in what from 1932 were the southern wards of Tokyo. By that year the prefecture had passed Osaka in industrial output.

Tokyo bound far the largest number of books, printed far the largest number of pieces of paper, and made far the most pencils in the country. It excelled in what might be called the literate industries. Early in the thirties, chemicals were the largest Tokyo industry. By the end of the decade, with the war approaching, machine tools had emerged as the largest. Of the five wards with the largest industrial output, only one, Honjo east of the river, was in the old city. The largest of all was Kamata, a part of the Tokyo-Kanagawa industrial belt. The district east of the river continued to be one of light industry, while the south was heavy. Most of the printing was done in the old city, because that is where the newspapers were.

The burgeoning of the suburbs has not, as in many American cities, meant the withering away of the center. Ginza, at least, and to an extent Ueno have held their own against the growth of the suburbs and the places—Shibuya, Shinjuku, Ikebukuro—where office workers on their way to and from suburban cultural dwellings change trains. Because centers yet farther east, prosperous in Edo and Meiji, have declined with the general decline of the Low City, Ginza may no longer be at the center of a cobweb; but the westward movement of the city has not emptied it. Westernmost among the lively centers of Meiji, it is now, with Ueno, the easternmost. It is still a place upon which rapid-transit lines converge, bringing crowds. We hear of a "doughnut effect" in Tokyo. It unquestionably is there, but the doughnut is an eccentrically shaped one, not exactly penannular, but far puffier to the left, as we face the top of the map, than the right. The center is not merely a hole.

If we think of the center as a larger complex than Ginza proper, including Nihombashi to the north and Marunouchi to the west, there has been a shift. This has been remarked upon above. Nihombashi is relatively less important than it was as a retail center, having lost ground to Ginza, and as an entrepreneurial center, having been the victim of a shift to Marunouchi. Yet few people would have been inclined during the interwar years to think of Shibuya or Shinjuku or Ikebukuro as the center of the city. Some might incline toward Shinjuku today, but Ginza would probably come at worst second.

These were the great years of *Gimbura,* another of the acronyms of which the Japanese are so fond and for which they have such a gift. The first syllable is from Ginza, and the other two are from *burabura,* a mimetic word which indicates an aimless wandering or an idling away of time. "Fooling around in Ginza" might do for a translation. The *Gimbura* crowds were young. They may not have had much to spend in the newly risen Ginza department stores, but they were an animating presence. More than any other part of the city, Ginza was the place to be. Yet it was first among peers. Tokyo has always been a city with several centers. That is why it is often called not a city but a collection of villages. "A collection of cities" might better catch the truth.

The Shōwa reign was a year and five days old when, late in 1927, the first Tokyo subway line began service. It was the first in the land, and in Asia. The route was a short one, less than a mile and a half long, between Ueno and Asakusa. Four companies had franchises to dig; only one started digging. The same company extended the line to Shimbashi in 1934. The entrepreneur who owned all the land around Shibuya and brought the private commuter line into it saw his opportunity. Shimbashi must not remain the terminus. So he started digging from Shibuya, and his line was opened to Shimbashi in 1939. There were two Shimbashi stations, without free transfer between them. The two companies were brought together, and the stations united, in 1941, under a public corporation whose capital came from the National Railways and the prefecture. Remnants of the other Shimbashi subway station can be detected a short distance toward Shibuya from the one now in use.

The two halves of the Ginza line, as it is now called, show a certain difference in spirit. The northern half, from Shimbashi to Asakusa, was dug by a company specializing in transportation and interested in pleasing its customers. Some of the stations are rather charming, in Art Deco and traditional styles. The station next south and west from the Asakusa terminus was decorated with the family crests of famous actors. That was deemed in keeping, and one must heartily agree that it was, with the nature of the district served. The stations south and west of Shimbashi are uniformly drab and boxlike, the product of an entrepreneur whose chief interest was in getting hordes of people as rapidly as possible into the Tōyoko department store, on the third floor of which the line ends. So we might say that the Ginza line symbolizes transition. The northern half belongs to the past, the southern half to the emerging future.

The earliest section, Ueno to Asakusa, was a huge popular success. It had turnstiles adapted from New York ones. People would go in and

Entrance to the new subway in Asakusa

out, in and out. They could not do it on Sundays and holidays, however, when a wait of as much as an hour was required to get aboard for a five-minute ride. Stories of subway picnics seem a little unlikely, given the shortness of the route.

The subway company put up high buildings at each of its two original terminuses, Asakusa and Ueno. (For the Asakusa terminus, see page 353.) The Ueno terminus had a department store, on its front a clock, illuminated at night, said to be the largest in the world. It was some twenty meters in diameter. Both buildings have been torn down in the years since the war. Subway people do not seem to have had the heads for retailing possessed by the people of the surface railways.

The Ginza line, not quite nine miles long, was the only line in existence during the war years. Construction did not begin on a second line until 1951, when another reconstruction of the city was underway. Thus well over 90 percent of the splendid system we have today is postwar. Though not badly planned, insofar as it was planned at all and not given over to mercantile ambitions, the Ginza line was not ideally planned to alleviate congestion on the National Railways. Shinjuku was growing more rapidly than Shibuya and would have been a better terminus.

The National Railways continued to provide faster transportation from all commuter transfer points except Shibuya than did the subway.

Yet it probably helped to keep Ginza at the center of things, and for this we must be grateful. Rapid transit had terminated just south of Ginza when the railway line to Yokohama opened in early Meiji and skirted it when, early in Taishō, the National Railways began service through to Marunouchi. Now it ran north and south under the main Ginza street. Another change in the transportation system favored the suburbs. Buses grew numerous and important, and, most naturally, the trolley system entered upon the decline that has in recent years brought it near extinction. With the trolley system and the railways heavily damaged by the earthquake, large numbers of little companies sprang up to take people to and from the suburbs—almost two hundred of them, mostly short-lived, in two months. Motorized public transportation was in much confusion. In the mid-thirties there were still several dozen private bus lines, in competition with one another and with the municipal buses.

The private railways, enterprise at its boldest and most aggressive, were getting into the bus business. They still are in it, most profitably. They were also in the department-store business and the real-estate business. In both of these they were anticipated by the Hankyū Railway in Osaka, which was the first company to open a terminal department store. In one Tokyo instance, the real-estate business came first, the railway afterward. A land company that owned huge tracts in the southwestern suburbs and on into Kanagawa Prefecture built a railway, the Tōyoko, to push development and, incidentally, to make Shibuya the thriving center it is today. The Tōyoko also developed a garden city, a "city in the fields," which is today one of the most affluent parts of Tokyo. It gave Keiō that new campus, out in Kanagawa Prefecture beyond the Tama River.

With the completion of the Yamanote line in 1925, Tokyo Central Station may have become the front door to the nation, but it did not itself have a back door. The throngs poured forth on Marunouchi, where Mitsubishi had built its brick "Londontown," a showplace of Meiji. As early as the thirties it was beginning to tear Londontown down, and today almost nothing remains; and Mitsubishi was beginning also to lose its monopoly. The proportion of non-Mitsubishi offices in the district rose from a tenth to two-fifths between the wars. We need not pity Mitsubishi, however. Marunouchi had by then become the undisputed managerial and entrepreneurial center of the land.

In 1929 Tokyo Central got its rear or east entrance, facing Kyōbashi and Nihombashi. The new entrance was a limited one. For long-distance tickets people still had to go around to the front, or south to Shimbashi. It was only after the Second World War that the rear entrance began to offer full services. Nihombashi has never recovered from its earthquake losses, but the new entrance has brought a turnabout. The east side of the station, known as Yaesuguchi or "the Yaesu Mouth," has become a much livelier place for shopping and revelling than the older Marunouchi Mouth.

The name Yaesuguchi is an interesting one, and a somewhat mobile one. A Dutchman named Jan Joosten Loodensteijn had his residence and business on an inlet of the bay near what is now Hibiya Park. By the familiar acronymic process and by assimilation with an old word for "fish weir," Jan Joosten's strand became Yaesu. The inlet disappeared in the seventeenth century and so of course did the strand, but the name survived and moved northward and eastward to where it now reposes. Together with the more famous Englishman Will Adams, Loodensteijn served the first Edo shogun.

Unlike most of the High City and the suburbs, Shinjuku suffered heavy damage in the fires of 1925. A part of the district had been incorporated into the city in 1920, but the vicinity of the railway station still lay beyond the city limits. The station, the car barn, and the Musashino, the largest and most popular movie palace in the High City and beyond, were all destroyed. This was probably good for Shinjuku, famous earlier for its horse manure, clouds of which would blow up on windy days like the yellow dust storms of Peking. With wartime prosperity and the beginnings of suburban growth, it was ready to take off. Buses began to run from Shinjuku into the suburbs, and the trolley line westward from the palace was extended to Shinjuku Station. A new station was completed in 1925. It too produced a turnabout. The main entrance had faced south, on the highway westward to the mountains and the province of Kai. The new one faced northward, in the direction of the postwar and post-earthquake boom.

Mitsukoshi opened several emergency markets throughout the city just after the earthquake. In 1924 its Shinjuku market became its Shinjuku branch, the first Shinjuku department store. After a move or two it settled where it is now, a few steps east of the east entrance to the station. The forerunner of the Isetan store was in Shinjuku, on the present Isetan site, in 1926. Two big private railways had come into Shinjuku by 1930. One of them set up a retail business, called the Keiō Paradise, the second word in English, in the upstairs of its Shinjuku terminus.

Old shops were rebuilding and transforming themselves, with an eye to the sophisticated and literate sorts who had to set foot in Shinjuku every working day. The Kinokuniya, an old lumber and charcoal dealer, moved westward from Yotsuya and made itself over into a bookstore, the biggest now in Shinjuku and one of the biggest in the city. A greengrocer near the station became the Takano Fruits Parlor, one of the places everyone knows. The last two words of the name are in English. An insistence upon putting "fruit" when used as an adjective into the plural is a little idiosyncrasy of Japanese English. "Fruits punch" has long been a standard item on the menus of such places everywhere.

A jumble of the old and the new, Shinjuku was already a traffic nightmare in the twenties. Automobiles and construction projects blocked the main streets, stalls and crowds blocked the back streets, lines of sewage wagons backed up each evening. Growth continued even with the panic and depression. Shinjuku took business from such places as Kagurazaka in the old High City. By about 1930 Shinjuku was second only to Ginza as a retail center.

It was one of the "mouths," the last of the old post stations on the way into and the first on the way out of Edo. Pleasure quarters grew up at all of the "Five Mouths." The old Shinjuku quarter straggled along the Kai highway. Shortly before the earthquake it was brought together into a more compact and easily definable and controllable neighborhood, just at the city limits after the 1920 annexation of a part of Shinjuku. Like Kagurazaka, it benefited from the destruction in 1923 of the Low City pleasure quarters. It was the noisy, bustling center of Shinjuku until things began to get lively near the main entrance to the new station.

The Shinjuku of the interwar years, like Asakusa, is often referred to as second-rate, and again the standard of comparison is Ginza. According to such members of the Ginza congregation as the novelist Ooka Shōhei, Shinjuku ran altogether too easily and giddily in pursuit of the modern and "high collar," two expressions meaning very much the same thing. The modern boy and modern girl went to extremes thought unseemly and in bad taste by high Ginza. Certainly it was the place where the Marx boys gathered, as to a lesser degree were the stations along the Chūō line of the National Railways. From precisely these regions was to emerge the new intelligentsia that dominated the media in the years just after the San Francisco Treaty of 1952. The phonograph was far more conspicuous in Shinjuku roistering places than the samisen, and these places were known for their large, ribald women, with limbs such as foreign women were thought to have. Street stalls made the narrow streets yet narrower. By the early years of Shōwa, Shinjuku was probably the most crowded place in the city, at least during the prime evening hours.

It had more street musicians than Ginza. It had flower women and children, their wares both real and artificial, and fortune-tellers and beggars, a constant stream through the evening hours.

Shinjuku had all of these in the twenties, and, except that the street stalls are gone, must have been rather as it is today. In the thirties it became a sort of western capital some distance behind the eastern one at Ginza-Nihombashi-Marunouchi. It had a famous slum too, even as Asakusa had one, just north of the temple. The Shinjuku slum was just south of the department stores, a place of cheap inns, bedbugs, and a transient population of day laborers, peddlers, street musicians, hawkers.

The Shinjuku quarter was one of six licensed ones. Two, including the venerable and once-glorious Yoshiwara, now fallen sadly, were within the limits of the old city. Three lay beyond, at three of the old "mouths," or stations. The Shinjuku quarter straddled the city limits. After 1932 they all lay within. Then there were the unlicensed quarters, the "dens of unlicensed whores" *(shishōkutsu)*, the most famous of them beyond the city limits. At about the time Japan went to war with China (the Japanese have preferred to call the war an incident), Nagai Kafū wrote one of his best works about the Tamanoi quarter, by then within the city limits but before 1932 in the northeastern suburbs. A lady there reminded him of Meiji and his youth, and gave the lie to his contention that Meiji quite

The liveliest part of post-earthquake Shinjuku, near the old licensed quarter

disappeared in 1910 or so. Because of Kafū, Tamanoi was the most famous of the unlicensed quarters, but it was second in size to Kameido,
a bit to the south. The Kameido district, on the north or back side of
the Kameido Tenjin Shrine and its splendid wistaria, gave sustenance to
some seven hundred ladies. Tamanoi had fewer than six hundred. Prostitution was quite open in both places. There was little to distinguish them
from the licensed quarters, except perhaps that in the latter procedures
for obtaining employment were more complicated, hygienic facilities
were better, and the ladies did not have to work as hard. The Kameido
quarter had been there from late Meiji. Like Tamanoi, it had its best
years after the earthquake.

Shinjuku may at certain hours of the evening have had a greater press
of bodies than Ginza, and certainly that is one of the things the city loves
best, but it was still second-rate Ginza. The high life of the years after
the earthquake centered upon the cafés. In these Ginza was preeminent,
the place that other places looked up to. The early interwar period was
the full summer of the cafés, and this word almost demands the quali-
fication "Ginza."

Shibuya had about it much more the look of the one-company town
than Shinjuku. It was quite dominated by the Tōkyū Railway system. As
a place for reveling it has always been some distance behind Shinjuku,
though polls have shown that the teenage crowd prefers it. In one respect
it was at the very forefront of progress. Along with Asakusa, it offered a
multilevel transportation, entertainment, and retail complex. Representations of the future as seen from the thirties, with rocket-like objects
shooting off in all directions and shooting back again, look as if Shibuya
might have been the inspiration.

The Shibuya complex has been described as very Tokyo-like. If by
this is meant that it is very crowded and cluttered and difficult to find
one's way about in, then the characterization is apt. Shibuya has the only
subway station all along the Ginza line that is not underground. Indeed
the tracks are high above the ground, the highest of all the tracks in the
complex. The Tōyoko department store is mazelike and inescapable. Perhaps that is what the founding magnate had in mind. The arrangement
of the station is in another respect not wholly irrational. The use of the
hill beyond as a turnabout station and car barn makes it possible to run
subway trains in very quick succession. The assumption that everyone
will benefit once he or she gets the hang of it all (a little time and study
may be required) also seems very Tokyo-like.

What is now the busiest part of Shibuya, still countrified after reconstruction

At the beginning of Meiji "the flower and the willow" quite dominated the high demimonde. The former was the courtesan and the latter the geisha. It is not easy to say just what a geisha is. The expression is a vague and complex one covering a broad range of prostitutes and performing artists. Geisha of the more accomplished sort, and the literal significance of the word is something like "accomplished sort," were the ones the affluent merchants of Edo and Meiji looked to for elegant and expensive entertainment. Their accomplishments were in traditional music and dance, at their best in the pleasure quarters, whether licensed or "private," and in the theater.

There came Western incursions. Opinions will differ as to whether the nightclub entertainer and the bar girl of our day are as accomplished as was the geisha of old, but the geisha has gradually yielded to them. The story of the high life of this past century might be told as the retreat of the one and the advance of the others. If Nagai Kafū had been a century younger and, as Tanizaki was, a true son of the merchant class, he would probably have spent his bachelor nights among the flowers and willows, to the extent that he could afford them. Being a man of conservative tastes, he did not forsake these people, but far more of his nights during the post-earthquake years were spent among the tinselly flowers of the Ginza cafés.

Ginza, not Shinjuku, would have been recognized by almost everyone—and certainly by Kafū, who did not often go to Shinjuku—as the place for them. The number of drinking spots in Kyobashi Ward, which included Ginza, was twice in 1930 what it had been in 1920. This is to say that in one decade the accumulation of such places equaled what it had become through all the decades before. The big buildings of Ginza came through the earthquake and fire fairly well, but not the little ones along the back streets; so building and rebuilding were feverish in the half dozen years after. Each day the Ginza of the cafés must have indeed been as the old gentleman of *During the Rains* saw it, not the Ginza of yesterday.

These years also had bars, dance halls, and cabarets, all of these words from either French or English. Distinctions among them, though cultural historians tend to treat them as obvious, are not always clear. In a general way a café was a place, sometimes small and intimate, sometimes big and noisy, but always, when it was doing well, crowded, whose clientele drank, took light refreshments, and enjoyed the company of pretty girls. We have the testimony of Kafū, among others, that many of the girls were scarcely distinguishable from the courtesans, those other flowers of Edo. Their company could be made, if the conditions were right, to last

In a Ginza café

Crowds on the main Ginza street

through the night. Café ladies in Kafū's fiction have a way of complicating things for themselves by accepting too many after-hours engagements.

An Osaka influence is discerned in the gaudier of the Ginza cafés. (It was just before the earthquake that Ginza became what it is today, the district on either side of the old Edo-Kyoto highway that lay between two bridges, the Kyōbashi on the north and the Shimbashi on the south. Before then only the northern part had, strictly speaking, been Ginza.)

The Osaka-style bars of northern Ginza were very gaudy and very big, illuminated in many colors with neon lights and flashing bulbs and dancing spotlights. The smaller and more modest Tokyo sort prevailed to the south. Predictably, Tanizaki Junichirō, having departed Tokyo in 1923 and turned vociferously against it, preferred the Osaka version.

> All up and down the back alleys of Ginza are tiny, intimate cafés.... To be sure, Osaka cafés with their noisy bands are somewhat vulgar; but no one could possibly call these cramped little places in the smallest degree elegant. It is not as if there were only a scattering of them. They are numberless, each with its own steady little clientele. The Osaka kind may be vulgar, but they do at least require a certain investment. These Tokyo ones do not. Five or six tables crowded together in a tiny room, nondescript furnishings thrown together from nothing, dim indirect lighting to conceal the tatters, a French name

to attract ambitious young literary types: such places have sprung up like bamboo shoots after a rain.

It is peculiar for an aesthete like Tanizaki to distinguish between good and bad in terms of money spent, and the passage perhaps does damage to the impression he assiduously cultivated of the quiet classical repose to be found in the Kansai. One may suspect, moreover, that had the Osaka version and the Tokyo version been reversed, he would have preferred the former then too. There was little that he liked, or professed to like, about Tokyo in those years. Yet it does seem to be the case that Osaka capital was quicker than Tokyo to plunge into the entertainment industry—and that little cafés sprang up like (as we would say) weeds.

The principal character of Kafū s *During the Rains*, written in 1931, is a promiscuous café lady. She works in a place called the Don Juan, so crowded in among other cafés that one must be attentive to avoid going in the wrong door. It is in the northern, "Osaka" part of Ginza, and fairly large, the main downstairs room covering an area of some seven or eight hundred square feet. Stepping through the front door—over which, in Roman letters, is the name of the place supported by two naked feminine statues, or paintings, it is not clear which—one has chiefly an impression of clutter. Screens and booths and tables are everywhere, lights and artificial flowers hang from the ceiling, genuine greenery is like thickets on the Kabuki stage. One does well not to enter by the alley and through the kitchen. Bluebottle flies buzz among garbage cans, and an odor of stale cooking oil pours from a hut of corrugated metal that might have been put up just after the earthquake.

Kafū loved dressing rooms. Here is the Don Juan one:

> You kept your shoes on to climb the steep stairway from the earthen floor of the kitchen. At the head of it was a room maybe a dozen feet square all along the walls of which were mirror stands, fourteen or fifteen of them. It was a few minutes before three, the hour of the change of shifts, the morning one to the evening one. The place was so crowded that you could not find a place to sit down. The girls jostled one another as they pushed their faces forward into the mirrors.

The Don Juan seems to have kept long hours. At midday it must have been more like a European than a Tokyo café, and the ladies on the early shift must have had more of the night for sleep than did Kimie, our heroine.

A striking thing about descriptions of Ginza cafés is how familiar they look. Gentlemen with a taste for the high life gather now in Ginza and Shinjuku bars, and gathered then in Ginza cafés. The two seem very much alike. One may find it a little hard to imagine what a "milk bar" of Meiji may have been like, but not a Ginza café of early Shōwa. (Milk bars were places where intellectual and literary people went to read difficult publications and discuss constitutionalism and such things.)

The novelist Takeda Rintarō describes a café in his novel *The Eight Ginza Blocks (Ginza Hatchō)*, written in 1934. The title is an up-to-date one, referring to the newly expanded Ginza, eight blocks of it from Kyōbashi to Shimbashi. The café is making its way through a dull Sunday evening.

> From time to time the door would open. Everyone would look up in anticipation of a customer; but always there would be, and in considerable numbers, children selling flowers, and imitators of famous actors and singers, and mendicant priests with boxes inviting contributions to the Church of Light and Darkness, and violinists, and sketchers of likenesses, and lutists, and solemnfaced young men in student uniform selling pills and potions, and, with babies tied to their backs, women selling horoscopes. They would all of them glance inside and, seeing that there were no customers, be on their way.

The priests, wandering adherents of Zen, would be uncommon today in Ginza and Shinjuku bars, and guitars and accordions would be more likely than violins and lutes. The Ginza café of 1930 or so, however, does not seem so very different from the Ginza bar of today.

Eroguro, sometimes *eroguro nansensu*, is the expression held to capture more than any other the mood of early Shōwa. It is the Japanese equivalent of "Flapper Age." *Nansensu* is the English "nonsense." *Eroguro* is another product of the Japanese talent for acronyms and abbreviations. It is compounded of the first two syllables of "erotic" and the first of "grotesque," the latter made into two syllables by the Japanese dislike of consonant clusters. The radical reactionaries of the thirties were against *eroguro nansensu*, even as they were against money-grubbing. Already before the earthquake there were cries for a return to the solid and austere old ways. After the earthquake, voices were raised telling the city that it was Sodom, punished by the heavens for being so. Tsubouchi Shōyō, a distinguished man of letters and a leader of the avant-garde theater, heard a Diet member remark in London that divine punishment had come for all the looseness and frivolity, all the moral laxness. Shōyō asked why divinity had chosen to punish those tens of thousands of people east of the river who did not have enough money to be frivolous and loose. The reply is not recorded.

As it concerns the cafés, the erotic half of the word is easier to apprehend than the grotesque. Suggestions as to what the latter half signified in their regard are mixed and contradictory. Also in *The Eight Ginza Blocks*, Takeda Rintarō describes a Ginza bar as dark and spooky in an outmodedly grotesque style. This suggests something crepuscularly Gothic; yet the *eroguro* that came from Osaka would seem to have had noise and light as its most conspicuous qualities. We may conclude that "grotesquerie" refers very generally to what made a new cabaret distinctive.

When we turn to the sideshows at Asakusa and their tendency toward what anyone would recognize as grotesque, it does not seem so very new. In the Asakusa park of Meiji there were, among others, a spider man and a woman who smoked through her navel. These we may describe as reasonably grotesque. In *Scarlet Gang of Asakusa,* Kawabata Yasunari describes a worthy successor in the post-earthquake years to the woman who smoked without troubling her respiratory tract. The scene is one of the little huts in the park.

"That it may be of use to medical science," cries the man on the stage, "we will show you right before your eyes how he eats through the mouth in his stomach.

"The man with the hole in his stomach was born in Asahigawa on the island of Hokkaido. The liquor with which he fended off the snow and the cold was pure alcohol. It produced strictures of the esophagus. So the doctors at Hokkaido Medical College opened this hole in his stomach.

"Unfortunately there were no teeth in the mouth the doctors made. So he has this bill, like a bird's."

It was true. The man in white untied the cord of the cloth around the bill, an object like a tobacco pipe inserted into his stomach.

Putting a glass funnel into the pipe, he poured milk and bread crumbs inside.

"Even in his pitiful condition he seems unable to forget the taste of sake. Occasionally he has a cup. He tastes it with the mouth in his face and drinks it through the one in his stomach…. Are not the advances of medical science marvelous?"

In another story from Kawabata's Asakusa period a young man back in Asakusa after an absence for his own safety gives a quick impression of how it has changed: "It's gotten to be just like Osaka." Which, if we turn again to Ginza, brings us back to lights and noise.

The grotesquerie is more elusive than the eroticism. It may be that they were put together because they sounded good together, and the first is the dominant half of the *eroguro* pair. This does not seem so very new either, although the borders of the erotic were pushed constantly back as the years passed. It took more to arouse a person. Primly dressed young women who played and sang traditional music were erotic in Meiji, as we may judge from the crowds of young men who poured in to look at them and perhaps listen to them as well. Now a certain expanse of flesh was asked for.

In a society dominated by men, it is most natural that women should dominate the world of sensuous pleasure. The girls in the big, flashy Osaka cafés are said to have had "It," the Clara Bow thing. They were becoming more aggressive and less inhibited. In the early days, when Kafū was frequenting Ginza cafés with English names like Lion and Tiger, the ladies stayed in the background, pleasant to look at and not expected to make much noise. Men went for masculine companionship, much as they must have gone to the coffeehouses of Dr. Johnson's London.

Now the ladies emerged to take charge of the conversation. The age of the waitress gave way to that of the hostess. We are still in the latter age.

There was a "Hostess's Song," the lyrics once more by Saijō Yaso. Here are the first two of four stanzas. The other two are similarly damp and aggrieved.

> I am a bar flower
> That blooms by night.
> Rouged lips,
> Gauze sleeves,
> Mad dancing
> By neon light,
> A flower watered by tears.
>
> I am a bar flower,
> A sad flower,
> By evening a girl.
> By day a mother.
> Tear-dampened sleeves
> Concealing the past.
> They are heavy as the night wears on.
> And not with dew.

Japanese popular music is so flooded with tears that we need not take them very seriously. Though such a world is bound to have its sorrows and uncertainties, Takeda Rintarō tells us, again in *The Eight Ginza Blocks*, that the world of the Ginza cafés was tight and snug.

The same people worked all the numberless places of the Ginza back streets. They moved from place to place, rarely staying long in any one of them; they all knew all the others. They knew everything about one another: foibles and general disposition, of course, and very private matters as well. It was the same with the customers. If each stronghold had its own little troop, it was a rare customer who limited himself to one place. They moved about, and so customer and hostess and manager were all of them acquaintances. The drinking places of the back streets were one world. For the clientele it was like a club, for management it was like a chain store.

Many if not all hostesses were, like Kimie of *During the Rains*, accommodating. Prices rose as the ladies came forward to dominate the scene, and so did tips. The ordinary "salaryman" could afford to go to one of the fashionable places perhaps once a month, on payday. Takeda Rintarō tells us that students were not welcome at the café of *The Eight Ginza Blocks*. They did not have enough money. Though they were not refused admission, it was hoped that they would sense the chill in the air and depart.

So another institution, the *kissaten*, literally the tea shop, emerged to fill the gap. An impecunious student could spend a whole afternoon for the price of a cup of coffee, and look at pretty girls who did not say much of anything after they had brought the cup. This meant essentially, on the simpler levels of the entertainment and pleasure business, a reversion from the age of the hostess to that of the waitress. It is a remarkable business, leaving no need unfulfilled, providing every commodity and service, and it is what the puritan radicals of the thirties objected to; and the product of their activism has been a society in which they would find much more to object to.

Tanizaki may have been right that the tiny Tokyo-style places all had French names, to attract customers with literary ambitions and pretensions. The bar that is the main setting for *The Eight Blocks of Ginza* is called L'Automne. Some of the famous tea shops also had French names: Colombin, Mon Ami. More had English or American: Columbia, Olympic, Eskimo, and Europe, the last pronounced in a way that established it as English and not French or German. Kafū was fond of a place called Fuji Ice, half of the name a Japanese proper noun and half an English common one.

For a time after 1923 Osaka may have been the first city of Japan. Artists and intellectuals fled to the Kansai district, of which Osaka was the center, in great numbers. They started coming back once Tokyo was comfortable again. Tanizaki was the great exception. He stayed not far from Osaka for most of his remaining years, although he never lived in the city. We have already seen an Osaka influence on the Ginza cafés and on the media. Osaka was largely responsible for the growth of monster newspapers. Only the *Yomiuri* among Tokyo natives stood out successfully against Osaka incursions.

And Osaka may be blamed in part for the decline of the Rakugo comic monologue. Both Osaka and Tokyo had monologues, marvels of versatile mimicry. Even before the earthquake a form called Manzai was replacing Rakugo in Osaka. Dominant in the closing years of the Taishō reign, it advanced upon Tokyo. Not all Osaka influences can be described as baneful, but this one surely was. Manzai performers come in pairs and crack jokes, sometimes funny. The difference between Manzai comedians and good Rakugo performers is that between the stand-up comic and the actor. The latter has skills and devices and puts himself into multiple roles. The former chatters, and if he is successful people sometimes laugh at the chatter. It is perhaps the difference between art and life, the one creating a world of its own, recognizable and persuasive but apart, the other being merely itself. Manzai has not raised the quality of popular culture.

Probably through Manzai, Osaka speech began lending words to Tokyo speech, the national standard. Tourists may not be aware that when they call the traditional livery jacket a "happy" they are using an Osaka word, *happi*. Many Tokyo people are similarly unaware that *shōyū*, almost universal now to indicate the soybean condiment, is an Osaka loan word.

Already in decline before the earthquake, Edo cooking surrendered the realm of high and expensive cuisine to Osaka. The most famous riverside restaurant of Edo was a victim of the earthquake, or, more precisely, the reconstruction. It stood on land marked for the new Sumida Park. Rebuilding elsewhere would have been possible, but the owner took a good price for the land and withdrew. His clientele came in from the river, and, with wheels replacing boats, the river was not what it once had been. Today Edo cooking survives in a few proud old restaurants surrounded by Osaka ones. Here the Osaka influence is not to be called baneful. Osaka cooking is more subtle and imaginative than that of Edo. So is Nagasaki cooking, which also has spread.

But the share of the blame which Osaka must take for the decline of such popular arts as Rakugo is small compared with that which may be assigned to the rise of mass entertainment, whose day had come. Audiences had been small in Edo. Even the biggest Kabuki theaters and the Sumo wrestling tournaments had drawn only a few hundred. Now they swelled to millions.

Among the celebrities who came visiting, to great acclaim, were some whom the new age had created. They were products of the twentieth century and its mass culture, and Japan was part of the twentieth century even as it had been trying hard to be a part of the nineteenth. Entertainers had come from abroad in Meiji, but they had had limited audiences in their native places and had similar audiences in Japan. Without question the foreign visitors who raised the greatest stir in Meiji were General and Mrs. Ulysses S. Grant. Next, perhaps, was an Englishman named Spencer, who did aerial stunts. Possibly the nearest equivalents in early Shōwa to the general and his lady were representatives of high technology and high culture. The *Graf Zeppelin* flew over the city in 1929 and was

Charlie Chaplin tries a Japanese snack during his visit

moored over water some miles to the east. George Bernard Shaw came in 1933. It would be hard to say that either quite captured the eager attention of the nation as the Grants did. They did not pay it as great an honor, and the nation would probably not have been as alive to the honor if, say, Calvin Coolidge had come. All people had to do was look up as the *Graf Zeppelin* flew over; they did not jam the streets for a look at its crew. They did for Mary Pickford and Douglas Fairbanks, who came the same year. Charlie Chaplin was in town on the day in 1932 when the prime minister was assassinated, the third prime minister to be so dealt with in this century, and the second in less than two years. The prime minister's son was supposed to take Chaplin across the river to the Sumō tournament on that beautiful late-spring Sunday. Chaplin went anyway.

The mass audience is not a uniquely Japanese phenomenon, of course. It was not something the Japanese did for themselves. Though one could not reasonably say that it was forced upon them, the way had not been prepared in Tokyo as it had in London and New York. Baseball did not give way to Sumō in New York as Sumō gave way to baseball in Tokyo.

The decline of Sumō is a relative matter. Baseball did not replace it immediately and has never replaced it completely. The only spectator sport in Edo, it has had its ups and downs in the century and more since Edo became Tokyo. The years before and after the earthquake were fairly good ones. There were popular wrestlers. The Kokugikan, "Hall of the National Accomplishment," the Sumō stadium near the earthquake memorial east of the Sumida, was badly damaged in the earthquake. Money for repairs flowed swiftly in. The national accomplishment, which is to say Sumō, has gone through periodic spasms of reform and modernization.

The major one in the years after the earthquake led to the formation of a legally incorporated Sumō association. The Tokyo and Osaka bands of wrestlers came together, on the understanding that tournaments would be held alternately in the two cities. This was thought admirably in the spirit of Taishō democracy, but was not sufficient to prevent new crises. Another split came in 1932, a few kantō defectors going off to Osaka with the Osaka stalwarts to form a new band. The tournaments that resulted were not popular. Neither band had enough celebrated wrestlers to fill the top ranks. A reunion was arranged in 1933, though holdouts sulked in Osaka until 1937.

The crowds that gathered for Sumō, even in the kokugikan, were small compared with those that were to gather for baseball, which may not call itself the national accomplishment, but is. Among the very young.

Sumō was probably still more popular than baseball in the years just after the earthquake. It had a radio following and presently would have a television audience as well. Newspapers did a good business in Sumō extras. It may be that radio audiences for Sumō were as large as for baseball when popular wrestlers were doing well, but here conjecture must prevail. There were no commercials and no ratings, and NHK, the public radio corporation, had a monopoly. But if Sumō was sporadically popular, baseball has been consistently and increasingly so. Sumō is no competition at all when it conies to television huckstering.

Japanese baseball began in Tokyo, and Tokyo has been the baseball capital ever since. The early period was ambiguously amateur. The big teams belonged to the universities. A tourist guide published by the National Railways in 1933 could still say that "the biggest attractions are the matches organized by the leading universities in the spring and autumn." The big baseball universities, Waseda and Keiō, did not stint in their support of promising players. A game in 1905 raised animosity between them to such a pitch that it was thought better for them not to see each other again. They resumed play in 1925, the last full year of Taishō. The best baseball stadium was in the outer gardens of the Meiji Shrine, often called Meiji Park. The shrine and gardens are a memorial to the Meiji emperor. The gardens, complete with stadium, were finished in October 1926, when the reign of Meiji's successor had only two months to go. A three-university league, all of its members in Tokyo, was formed early in Taishō, and by the end of the period, with the accession of the perpetual cellar team, Tokyo University, it became what it is today, a six-university league.

The semiprofessional status of the celebrated university players aside, there were already in late Taishō the beginnings of professional baseball. An organization called the Shibaura Society, named for filled land by the bay where it had its grounds, assembled nonstudent players for whom the game was more than sport. Its first games were with Waseda, which won. Waseda received the larger part of the credit for the sizable crowds. Ahead of its time, the Shibaura Society moved to Osaka. Professional baseball did not really get underway until the mid-thirties. It was not the Shibaura team but a Tokyo one, Shōriki's Yomiuri Giants, named by Lefty O'Doul, that was to become the national team. Wherever they go nowadays the Giants draw crowds, as no Osaka team does except in Osaka, and Osaka teams do better even in Osaka when playing the Giants.

Shibaura is at the southern edge of the Low City, but the Meiji Gardens are on the far southwestern fringes of the old High City. An attempt after the Second World War to give the Low City a baseball park of its own was not well received. Only teams from the non-Giant league played in it, and the crowds did not come. The Giants have their home park on the edge of the High City. So baseball and television, which fill the spare hours of the Low City, do not come from there.

March 22 is "founding day" for radio. On that day in 1925 experimental broadcasts went forth from Atago Hill in Tokyo, the high place just north of the Tokugawa tombs in Shiba Park that had been popular for its view of Edo and of Meiji Tokyo. There were also broadcasts in Osaka and Nagoya. The first program was elevated and eclectic: Beethoven, classical Japanese music, a play by Tsubouchi Shōyō which sought to bring Kabuki and Shakespeare together.

The three regional radio companies were amalgamated the following year into Nihon Hōsō Kyōkai, the Japan Broadcasting Corporation, a public corporation that has always identified itself to its audiences by the English pronunciation of its initials, NHK. Through the war years NHK had a monopoly on broadcasting. Commercial broadcasting came only in 1951, a few months before the first television. Tokyo Rose's popular wartime broadcasts were over NHK.

Movies were first among the forms of popular mass entertainment. So they continued to be until television began having its day. When old people, the lucky few who are able to, reminisce upon good times in Asakusa, they are likely to be talking of the music halls, and the "opera" they offered before the earthquake and the "reviews" after. They do not speak of Asakusa as the great center for movies. That is probably because live, legitimate forms were very much *of* Asakusa, and movies were everywhere.

Yet Asakusa was the center. In 1930 it had fourteen movie theaters. The next-largest concentrations were on or beyond the city limits, at Shinjuku and Shibuya, with four each. A quarter of a century later, when television was beginning to bring bad days for the movie business and turn Asakusa theaters into game parlors, Asakusa had fallen a little behind the Ginza-marunouchi complex in number of theaters (it was still ahead in the number that showed Japanese films) and was ahead of Shinjuku by a bit.

Kawabata did a survey of Asakusa in 1930 which showed theaters with live performances to outnumber movie theaters. There was a variety of styles of the former, but no single kind had as many places in which to show itself as did the movies. Asakusa still had a half-dozen Yose, or Rakugo variety halls, not as grievous a decline as one might have expected from the dozen or so of late Meiji. It had a single Kabuki theater, a small one, whereas it had had almost a monopoly on Kabuki when the shogunate fell. Then there were review places, to be discussed, places offering traditional music of more than one kind, and places whose chief attraction was swordplay, masculine and feminine, the latter the more popular because somewhat erotic.

But mostly there were the movies. Asakusa drew its crowds from all over the city. The High City and suburban places, Shibuya and Shinjuku and the like, got few people from the Low City. Asakusa had a "theater department store." Three houses under the same management stood side by side along the main Asakusa theater street. Passageways joined the three, and for the price of a single ticket the devotee could make a day of it, wander back and forth among them, and enjoy the offerings of all. Not much remains of the street from its best days, but, thanks to their continuing to be under the same management, all three houses survive, all with yellowish brick fronts, one surmounted by battlements, one with a plain-bellied front broken only by windows, the third with decorative windows in an Art Deco style. The connecting passageways also survive, but they have been left to spiders and rats for almost half a

The Asakusa Sixth District in the great age of the movies and music halls; the three theaters shown were joined together, and they still srivive—see above

century. The survival of the middle theater, the plain-fronted Tokiwaza, is a modest triumph for the conservation movement. Until 1965 it was devoted to stage productions. Then it became a movie theater, and in 1984 it closed entirely and demolition was in prospect. Local pressures and donations from wealthy persons with attachments to Asakusa persuaded the Shōchikyu entertainment company, owner of the three, to keep it open for recitals and short-run performances.

One Asakusa motion-picture theater was famous for a noisy ceiling fan. It was very popular. The attention the fan called to itself made people feel cool. The *benshi* must have been rather sorely tried, however. These remarkable and very Japanese performers were like Rakugo monologuists. Without the use of amplifiers, they declaimed all the parts on the streen above them, male and female, and told the story as well, so that the audience might be informed. They even spoke in measured phrases, alternating syllable counts of seven and five, like balladeers of old. There were *benshi* contests, one performer per reel. The advent of the talkie brought bad times. The man known as the last of the *benshi* died in the summer of 1987. He was only in his mid-sixties, and so he was a child when talkies came. It may be that others like him still preserve the art somewhere.

The first talking pictures from abroad required *benshi*. Between 1929, when the first one came, and 1931, when subtitles were first affixed (to *Morocco*) and when also the first Japanese talkie appeared, the *benshi* went on doing what he had been doing all along, a little more loudly perhaps. A Japanese audience viewing a foreign film had a *benshi* talking away in front of it while Greta Garbo and Gary Cooper were talking away on the screen. Garbo, noisy fan, no amplifier: it must have called for a durable voice, and kept people awake.

A strike by *benshi* against technical progress was in vain. Such strikes always seem to be, and one may wonder why. If it is true, and we are assured by those who remember the good *benshi* days that it was, that people often went to movies as much to hear the *benshi* as to watch the movie, why did there not continue to be a demand for silent movies? The very notion of technical progress seems to disarm resistance except on the part of those whose livelihood is immediately affected. It seems inevitable and it seems good, and those who prefer silent movies, like those who prefer silent radios and television sets, are ashamed to admit the preference.

Silent movies had background music too, and theme songs. The most popular song of very early Shōwa was from a movie, *Tokyo March (Tokyo Kōshinkyoku)*, which is also the name of the song. It is by the Nakayama-Saijō combination of "Tokyo Dance" (see pages 320-321). There are four stanzas, about Ginza, Marunouchi, Asakusa, and Shinjuku. Here is the Ginza one:

> The Ginza willows bring thoughts of the past.
> Who will know the aging, fickle woman?
> Dancing to jazz, liqueur into the small hours.
> And in the dawn a flood of tears for the dancer.

There is at least one foreign word per stanza. In this one "jazz," "liqueur," and "dancer" are all in English (the transcription into the Japanese syllabary suggests strongly that the second is not French). The fourth stanza, the Shinjuku one, advocates running away from it all via the Odakyū, the Odawara Express, a private railway line opened between Shinjuku and Odawara, at the foot of the Hakone Mountains in Kanagawa Prefecture, in 1927. The railway objected to the recording company that if the name was to be used at all it must be used in full, Odawara Kyūkō Denki Kidō Kabushiki Kaisha. This did not fit the music very well, and the abbreviation Odakyū prevailed. The song was a huge piece of free advertising for the railway. Today no one calls it anything but the Odakyū. The invitation to flee via it has a stylish, up-to-date ring, for it runs through wealthy suburbs to what in another culture might have been called a hill station.

Some of the Asakusa theaters offered more than *benshi* and music to go with their movies. One burned incense in its pits during funeral scenes, which were frequent, bereavements being frequent. Movies were rated according to the number of handkerchiefs they made sodden with tears. One little theater jiggled and chugged as the view from an observation car passed on the screen.

During his Asakusa period, Kawabata was living just behind Ueno Park, within easy walking distance of Asakusa. He said in 1934 that he went there almost every day for three years. Sometimes he wandered about all through the night. Asakusa was a nightless place, the only part of the city with all-night restaurants. The best chronicler of Asakusa during those years, Kawabata found the crowds interesting even at the most unpromising of hours, the morning ones. Men who had passed the night in the Yoshiwara quarter north of Asakusa were on their way home, and geisha on their way to matins at the great Kannon Temple.

Yet, he said, Asakusa produced nothing of the really highest order. There had been a decline, certainly, since the last years of Edo, when Asakusa had had the best of the theater and, in the Yoshiwara, some of the best chamber performances as well. It may be that Kawabata's most famous Asakusa piece, *Scarlet Gang of Asakusa,* is a little like Asakusa itself. Mannered, diffuse, obscure, inconclusive even as Kawabata novels go, it is second-rate Kawabata; but it is interesting. Asakusa may have been second-rate by Ginza standards, but it too was interesting.

In *Scarlet Gang,* Kawabata quotes a famous songwriter approvingly:

> "Asakusa is the pulse of Tokyo.
> Asakusa markets humanity."

These are the words of Soeta Azembō.

"Asakusa of the myriads flings everything forth in the raw. All manner of desire dances there naked. All classes and all races mix into one great flow, limitless, bottomless, not distinguishing day from night. Asakusa is alive. The masses edge forward. Asakusa of the masses, melting down old forms to be cast into new ones."

In early Shōwa, Asakusa was still what it had been in Meiji, the most bustling among the *sakariba,* the "bustling places," of the city. It was the great purveyor of inexpensive entertainment. For centuries the grounds of the temple had been a place where people went to amuse themselves, often in coarse and vulgar ways. The doctrine of the temple was easygoing. From Meiji into Taishō there were new entertainments, notably the movies and the Twelve Storys, the brick tower that fell apart in the earthquake.

The Twelve Storys acquired a successor in early Shōwa. Here too, as in so many things and ways having to do with Asakusa, there was a falling off. The Twelve Storys, when it was put up, was the highest building in the city. The tower that arose over the new subway station was by no means the highest. It was only six storys, or some hundred thirty or forty feet high. Yet from the observation platform on the top floor one could see, on a clear winter day, Mount Tsukuba in the east and Mount Fuji in the west, and in the near distances a great deal of smoke, from factories, from trains, and from the brewery built on the site of the old Tokugawa estate. One riverside villa yet remained on the far bank. The new tower, Kawabata said, was in the Osaka style. All the floors except the top observation one were occupied by eating places.

The movies attracted the biggest audiences, but it was the legitimate theater that interested Kawabata, and is likely to interest us a half century and more later, when the crowds have gone the way of Kabuki and the geisha. Before the earthquake there was the Asakusa opera, and after the earthquake the Asakusa review. We learn in local histories of an opera period and a review period, as if these forms were clearly distinguished from each other. A catastrophe came between, to give the impression of a cultural break, with a conclusion on the one side and a beginning on the other. (So it was to be with the catastrophe of the forties. Before it were the reviews and after it the strip shows.) The reviews had a longer period to die in than did the opera. The reactionaries of the thirties did not approve of such things and the war years brought an end to almost all theatrical performances. Yet the several genres are not discrete. They blend into one another.

The beginnings of the reviews are in the opera, the ancestry of which was Italian. An Italian impresario named G. V. Rossi is the recognized progenitor. Though the word "review" itself seems to have come from English, the reviews were ostensibly of French ancestry. ("Opera" is probably from Italian.)

Rossi never worked in Asakusa. First at the Imperial Theater in Marunouchi and then at a place which he bought near the southwestern city limits, he endeavored to produce Italian opera, including Mozart, using Japanese performers. Some of his disciples transferred the enterprise to Asakusa. The Asakusa performances based on Italian scores must have sounded more like operetta or musical comedy, people with pleasant voices singing in a manner all natural and unrestrained. The best of them had little musical education. The performance whose opening night is considered the birthday of Asakusa opera was definitely light and scattered. The language and the writer were Japanese. It could have been called a review.

Hamamoto Hiroshi, a novelist who died in 1959 and who drew most of his material from Asakusa, said toward the end of his life that the Asakusa opera was ruined by its own most fanatical supporters. Predominantly male—women preferred the movies, where they could all weep into their handkerchiefs—they demanded eroticism. They demanded a "decadent" (Hamamoto's word) something of the singers. Then there were dancers. Singing and dancing continued after the earthquake, but were beginning to look tired. They could not carry it all off by themselves.

A new element was added: bright, fast comedy, thought to be Gallic. So the review came into being. "Eroticism and nonsense and speed," said Kawabata, "and humor in the vein of the topical cartoon, and the jazz song and legs." All the items in the medley except the last are in English. So maybe it is the most important—it and the foreignness, the fact of depending so on a foreign language.

An Asakusa review

Whether or not the review was greatly inferior to the opera, and whether or not the break between the two is a clear one, the day of the review was the last time Asakusa could be ranked high among the *sakariba*.

It may also have been the last time the Low City, center of Edo mercantile culture, could be called the center and the producer of anything cultural at all. (Ginza, as we have seen, is a special instance, in but not of the Low City.) Asakusa has not done much in recent decades to return the affection of people like Hamamoto.

July 10, 1929, is the birthday of the Asakusa review, and it was born in a little place called the Casino Folies. The founders, two brothers, had been to Paris, and they loved the follies, and combined the Casino de Paris and the Folies-Bergère to give their theater its name. The Casino Folies occupied the second floor of an aquarium on a back street, next door to an entomological museum. "It came to be," says Kawabata in *Scarlet Gang of Asakusa,* "that the girls of the Casino Folies passed the fishes in their tanks and turned in by a model of the sea king's palace to go to their dressing rooms." They also had to pass "dusty cases of flies, beetles, butterflies, and bees." The aquarium and the Bug House were "relics of the old Asakusa Park, left behind in the Fourth District."

What was known as Asakusa Park, not much of it very parklike, was divided into seven districts. The Casino Folies was some distance from the main theater district, which was in the Sixth District, much the most famous and crowded of the seven. The founding brothers, besides their love for Paris and its follies, had a modest amount of money. They rented a place somewhat apart from the main Sixth District street because they could afford it. Kawabata's *Scarlet Gang*, the first part of it serialized in the *Asahi Shimbun* from December 1929, attracted attention to the Casino Folies and made it popular. Those whom Kawabata called Ginza people started coming.

The reviews were to be more popular than the opera had ever been, but the original Casino Folies did not last long. At a disadvantage when theaters nearer the heart of the Sixth District started presenting reviews, and deserted by its most famous performers, it changed management in 1932. Ownership of the property remained with the aquarium, which survived because groups of schoolchildren were taken there to look at goldfish and turtles. Often they had to be rounded up by their teachers after sneaking upstairs and getting themselves in at reduced prices to look at the reviews. Curiously, children watching the reviews did not seem to upset the police as did children going to movies, some of which were forbidden to them.

The Casino Folies produced actors and actresses who were to become very famous. The actress Mochizuki Yūko was in her later years so successful in movie portrayals of troubled mothers that she became known as Japan's mother; she got her start in the chorus line at the Casino. She was the daughter of the caterer who delivered lunch to the troupe; an actor looked at her legs and said she might join. The actor was Enomoto Kenichi, probably the most popular of all Japanese comedians. Enoken, an acronym from the two elements of his name, is how everyone knows Enomoto. He has been called the Joe E. Brown of Japan, but he was more versatile than Brown. Besides having an impish and feckless kind of charm that made people smile before he had uttered a word, Enoken was a rather good singer and a very lithe dancer. Had Danny Kaye been around at the time, he might have been a more appropriate American analogue than Brown. The son of a shopkeeper in Azabu, one of the affluent wards along the southern tier of the old High City, Enoken defied the Azabu notion of what a schoolboy should do and went off to watch Asakusa opera. Though he made his debut at the age of fifteen in one of the Sixth District opera houses, he had to wait for the reviews before he attracted attention, and the reviews had to wait for him. The July birthday assigned to the reviews might better be the November date when Enoken came onstage at the Casino.

He left the Casino Folies in 1930 for the bigger theaters in the Sixth District, where he headed troupes with such Gallic names as Poupees Dansantes and Pierre Brilliant. From them he moved on to the big movie and management companies and the central theaters, the ones near Ginza. The reviews thus became big time, with huge troupes and budgets. The Casino had ten girls or so in its chorus line. In the big theaters there were sometimes as many as a hundred people onstage at one time. Asakusa may not have produced the very best of anything, but performers who went on to be the best at what they did got their start in Asakusa. Though the "crisis" of 1937 and after was not deemed a time when people should be funny in public, and though Enoken was in very bad health in his last years, he did not give up until his death early in 1970, at the age of sixty-five. Not even the amputation of a gangrenous foot stopped him, and indeed he showed great ingenuity in converting his disability into comedy. It was sadder in his case than it would have been for others, because in his prime his versatility included dancing and acrobatics.

An impression that Enoken alone made a success of the Casino Folies and the Asakusa reviews would be wrong. Kawabata certainly helped. Enoken himself was to say in his late years that what really brought in the crowds was a rumor that the girls in the chorus line dropped their drawers on Friday evenings. It was, he said, a false rumor. Reminiscing back over a half century, Mochizuki Yuko said that a girl did in fact one day let the cotton wraparound drop from her breasts. It was an accident, and it may have been the source of the rumor. Falling drawers would not have signified very much in any event, said Miss Mochizuki, because the girls wore their own (and this before the Shirokiya fire) under the uniform stage costume. To give more strongly a sense of Paris, they sometimes wore golden wigs.

Miss Mochizuki described the test, a simple one, which candidates for the line had to pass. They raised their skirts, so that Enoken might have a look at their legs. Legs were what was wanted. They were very young girls, and by all accounts very innocent compared with the ladies of Kafū's café pieces. The average age was sixteen or seventeen. Kawabata tells of a girl who, at eighteen, had never worn cosmetics. Many commuted to the review houses from home. In one of Kawabata's shorter Asakusa pieces several girls pass the night in the narrator's apartment, and it is all very virginal, not in the least suggestive of Kafū's orgies.

The erotic element had to do almost entirely with the lower limbs. The shoulders and a patch of the back might have been exposed, but the breasts were obscured by wraparounds of cotton. It was hardly extreme nudity. Yet the police were touchy.

They forbade ad-libbing, for one thing, because they disliked surprises. As a device to forestall it they required that scripts be presented ten days in advance. Ad-libbing had been among the principal techniques of the comedians and it went on despite the ban. They did not have time to learn their lines very well. Besides, it was often the impromptu gag that brought the best laughs.

The police also worried about the garb and demeanor of the girls and handed down regulations. Drawers must cover at least the top ten centimeters of the thigh. Flesh-colored drawers were not permitted. A portion of the back might be exposed, but the whole front of the torso must be covered from a safe distance above the breasts. There might be no suggestive lighting about the hips and pelvis, no kicking in the direction of the audience, and no wriggling of the hips. If the girls wore tights for photographs, they must also wear skirts. And so on, through nine articles. The Casino girls were one day herded off to the Asakusa police station to have their drawers measured. Enoken went with them, and had to stay behind when the measuring was over, to write out an apology for indiscretions.

Two routines in particular put the police on their mettle. One, if it had gone a bit further, would have been consummated in a kiss, right there on the stage before everyone. (It was not until after the war that the movies made bold to show an unexpurgated kiss.) The other was about Tōjin (a translator has rendered this as "Chink"—it indicates a foreigner, or a Japanese whose foreign inclinations pass bounds) O-kichi, the reputed mistress of Townsend Harris, first American minister to Japan. O-kichi has been elevated to martyrdom, on the grounds that in surrendering to Harris she disgraced herself, and did it for her country. She was a good subject for Asakusa, combining nationalism and eroticism, but from the police point of view the writers seem to have provided too little of the former and too much of the latter. Comedians and chorus girls and staff worked hard. To compete with the movie theaters, the review halls changed their programs every ten days. There were three performances a day. In a short story called "Rainbow" ("Niji." 1934). Kawabata reported that the dancers were required to stay for photographs after the last performance on opening day and that rehearsals for the next program began after the last curtain on the fourth day. So there were only two nights during every run, or six nights a month, when they could go home and fall into bed. Perhaps a half dozen dance routines and an equal number of skits had to be put together. The dressing rooms were full of sleeping dancers, and fainting from exhaustion was not uncommon. A character in "Rainbow" finds conditions so bad that he does not bother to learn his lines. Nothing polished or substantial is likely to come of the effort, and ad-libbing works best.

Here, in a passage from "Rainbow," a choreographer is meditating upon the reviews and the life of the dancers:

> But there was no time for training in any real sense of the term. An amateur would suddenly be thrust on the stage and not so much trained as told to follow the others. Those who had a certain grace would presently acquire a certain facility. The choreographer would have to put five and six dances together in three and four evenings of rehearsal. The process would be repeated three times a month; and in the weariness of it all any sort of trickery was permitted if it worked. To point out faults was taboo. Nakane, only twenty-seven years old, more often felt sorry for himself than angry at the dancers. So in the beginning he warmly argued the merits and shortcomings of the chorus line with the male actors who were in positions of authority; but he found that no one was really listening.

There is a mild inconsistency here with what has been said earlier in the same story. The count of days for rehearsal is not quite the same. That there are not many is clear, as is the slapdash nature of the productions.

So is the class structure, the distinction as to status and function between comedians and dancers. Clearest of all is that the dancers have a hard life. What have they to look forward to, Kawabata asks, but to go on kicking?

In *Scarlet Gang of Asakusa*. Kawabata records a fragment of a program at the Casino Folies, six numbers out of eleven. They include a "jazz dance," a dance to "La Paloma," an "acrobatic tango," a "nonsense" sketch called "That Girl," and a comic song.

> The changes of costume are so rapid that breasts are openly displayed in the process.
> And now we have Number 6, "Jazz Dance. Ginza."

> > On a street the width of a sash:
> > Sailor trousers, false eyebrows.
> > An Eton crop. What fun,
> > Swinging the snakewood!

Silk hat at an angle, black velvet vest, red string necktie, collar opened whitely, a thin stick under an arm—it is of course an actress impersonating a man. Her legs are bare. Arm in arm with a pair whose skirts come to their hips and who are stockingless, she sings "Ginza Today." They dance their stroll down Ginza.

Nudity seems to have been more pronounced backstage than onstage. Most of the important nouns in the song—"trousers," "Eton crop," "snakewood"—are in English. Snakewood seems to be a South American wood with snakeskin markings, much used for walking sticks.

Also in *Scarlet Gang* is a complete program from early summer of 1930. The theater is not the Casino.

1. Grand Chorus: A Selection of Famous Songs
2. Fairy Story: The Spirit of the Artist's Brush
3. Musical Comic
4. Magnificent Magic, Made Public for the Very First Time
5. Ocean Dance
6. Dramatic Vignettes
   A. One Wants a Companion on a Journey
   B. Sleeping Car
7. Cowboy Dance
8. Dramatic Vignettes
   C. Falsehood
   D. Lady Angler
9. Cannon: A Sad Tale from the Wars of the Roses
10. Modern Dance: Five Festivals
    A. The New Year
    B. The Doll Festival
    C. The Iris Festival
    D. The Festival of the Stars
    E. Chrysanthemum Festival
11. Daring Aerial Acrobatics
12. Humorous Magic: Egyptian Paradise

This program too is larded with English words. "Cowboy Dance" and "Ocean Dance" are in English. So is the curious expression "Musical Comic." Even "Modern Dance," which, given the subject matter, was probably done in traditional dress, may well have had touches of the foreign. Elsewhere Kawabata speaks of a famous Asakusa dancer who did not imitate the Japanese dance as one got it at Hibiya Hall, the best concert and recital hall in town, but rather that of the port cities, aimed at foreigners.

Kawabata continues:

> The New Tsukiji Troupe had been here late in May, with the general theme "What Made Us Come to Asakusa?" It did "What Made the Girls Do It?" and "A Secret Tale of Tsukuba" and the like.
>
> On banners billowing in the winds before the Kannon Theater in July, "It," written in three ways.
>
> The Nihonkan thought of the effective name Eroero Dance Team, and even the Shōchikuza had to reply, in big black letters, with Dance Ero. "Ero" on all the billboards. The faltering Japanese of foreign performers is better than many things. Those who wish these days to collect the mottoes on the billboards of the specious reviews will find the alleys behind the lake and its theaters the place to do it: "Diary of a Sex Lunatic"—but come along and see for yourselves, all of you, in the evening. One hears that the extortionists are out along these alleys even in broad daylight; and here are the stage doors for the "ero queens." They come out to take the evening cool. My readers will understand that when I call the Danilevskis beautiful, the distortions and illusions of the night lights are at fault. Their legs are darker than those of Japanese.
>
> The program of this Tenshō troupe is, after all, not as specious as some of them. The magicians are marvelously skillful. The expressions the young dancers turn on the audience are studiously beautiful. Alas, Tenshō herself, old enough to be a grandmother, ventures to

Another Asakusa review, at the Shōchiku

play a girl student. She appears in every act and throws herself about perhaps a bit too strenuously. Henry Matsuoka's aerial acrobatics are splendid…. But what surprised Lefty Hiko most were the wares flung out to the audience from the stage. Sawa Morino, playing the artist in "The Spirit of the Artist's Brush," wound up like a baseball pitcher and flung thirty or forty bags of sweets.

Kawabata had only this one try at a chatty style and an intimate narrative stance permitting frequent intrusions, and he was not comfortable with it. Yet *Scarlet Gang* is full of good reporting. It gives most vividly a sense of what the Asakusa reviews were like, and Asakusa itself. The passage requires comment. The three ways in which "It" is written are the two Japanese phonetic syllabaries and Roman letters. Mount Tsukuba would seem to fit in with the general theme, "What Made Us Come to Asakusa?," because Asakusa was proud of having it on the eastern horizon. Lefty Hiko is a member of the Scarlet Gang, an assemblage of young delinquents.

There were foreign performers in Asakusa, most of them, as the passage suggests, Russian refugees. In that summer of 1930 (it seems to have been June) a pair of Finns, mother and daughter, the latter only ten years old, were a big hit. They, or one of them, did an imitation of Chaplin, and they sang in Japanese and did a Japanese dance. Four Russian sisters did Gypsy, Cossack, Spanish, and "jazz" dances, and sang Japanese songs with a sweet Russian accent. (Kawabata reminisces upon his student days, just after the Russian revolution, when little Russian girls no more than twelve or thirteen were walking the streets and selling themselves at no high price.) The Casino had a popular hula dancer, but she was Japanese. An American diver performed in a sideshow somewhere, and there was a French chanteuse, a dramatic soprano, we are told in English. "Her naked, pearl-white beauty quite radiates eroticism." Asakusa is kind to foreigners, says Kawabata, and especially to foreign children.

The "ero" that is up on all the marquees is of course that of *eroguro,* from "erotic" or "eroticism." The Shōchikuza is one of the grand theaters, the property of the Osaka company that dominated the Tokyo theater and had a large chunk of the movie business as well. Kawabata is saying that this institution, which should be above cheap tricks, must go erotic if that is what everyone else is doing. The sweets flung out so vigorously were aimed mostly at children. That there were children in the audience is interesting indeed, and may seem to go against generalizations about eroticism and grotesquerie. Probably such eroticism as there was, mostly bare legs, passed lightly over the heads of children. Though the

Japanese police do sometimes treat foreign manifestations as if they were invisible (the original of *Lady Chatterley's Lover* was sold openly even as criminal litigation was in progress against the publisher and translator of the Japanese version), neither Kawabata nor anyone else tells us that the chanteuse was uncommonly naked.

Asakusa connoisseurs (again our authority is Kawabata) have said that things were actually dirtier back in the days of the Russo-Japanese War. The diving girls in the sideshows of those days were far bolder than the dancing girls of early Shōwa were permitted to be. The garb of the latter was not much different from the bathing dress of the time. And there had been wantonness in the park, right there beside the great temple, at least since the eighteenth century, when Edo came into its own as a cultural center. Wayside teahouses and archery and shooting stalls and the "famed sake places" all had had their pretty girls whose business was not only the announced one.

Yet the police of early Shōwa were being challenged. They had taken a position with regard to nudity, and the impresarios were pushing ahead in that direction as rapidly as they could. The police were also becoming more self-conscious. A spasm of puritanism was coming over the city and the nation, which had been victims of such spasms from time to time through the Tokugawa centuries.

Kawabata remarks upon the conservatism of Asakusa. In the following passage, the speaker, who is addressing a young lady of Asakusa, is Kawabata's alter ego.

> "I don't care what you say, Asakusa people are old-fashioned. They look after others and others look after them, they care for people and have a sense of duty, all of them, the dealers and hawkers at the top to the tramps and beggars at the bottom. They're like the gamblers of Edo. I'm told that the toughs in Shibuya and Shinjuku are a newer sort than the ones we have here. They don't have a tradition, and Asakusa does. It may all seem like flash and glitter, but there's nowhere else things are so on the move. It's like the Bug House too. Or an island way off somewhere, or an African village with a chief and a set of rules and bonds the modern world doesn't have."

Two important matters are involved: acceptance of a moral and ethical code, and sensual abandon. It is quite possible to have both. Not even the puritan radicals of the thirties forwent the teahouses and extralegal polygamy. For all its willingness to provide and sell almost anything for and to almost everyone, Asakusa does seem to have had moral groundings. The Bug House to which the man refers is the place with the dusty display cases next door to the aquarium and its Casino Folies.

The sentence about the hawkers and the others contains several words that are almost untranslatable. The people who look after and are looked after are *oyabun* and *kobun,* the surrogate parents and children in the social arrangements of such persons as gamblers, firefighters, construction workers, and extortionists. The qualities of sympathy and duty are the *giri* and *ninjō* so prominent on the Kabuki stage. They come down to something not far from the Golden Rule.

As there were for the reviews, there were rules for the shooting stalls, which had long been covers for prostitution. The temple grounds still contained some forty of them in the early thirties. They could stay open for twelve hours from sunrise. Drinking was not permitted, nor was "wanton" touting and hawking. Only employees were allowed behind the counter. The rules may or may not have been enforced, but the fact that they were there, and that many customers were addicted to the stalls, suggests that they were used for something besides shooting.

Kawabata adverts to Asakusa speciousness and reports upon it. He is also good at scamps and beggars, the bottom of the heap. One sideshow promises nude beach photographs to those who will put down money for tickets; inside are photographs of athletic teams training on beaches. The curious passerby must buy the suggestive magazines at the stalls if he is to see what is in the secret supplements; they contain cooking and knitting lessons. A sideshow (another chronicler, not Kawabata, tells us of this one) offers an underwater strip show; inside, beyond a tank of water, is a painting of a nude woman. The code of Asakusa did not preclude misrepresentation, but it does seem to have forbidden complaining. Those who got cheated did not go to the police or otherwise protest.

When, at least partly because of *Scarlet Gang,* the "Ginza people" started coming to the Casino Folies, beggars and vagrants started going away. Earlier they had drifted in from the park to watch the girls. One caught the smell of them as the audience thinned out.

As for the scamps, there was a young delinquent known as the Mantis. He knew his law. Arrested numerous times, he could not be prosecuted until he was fifteen. Finally he got sent off to Iwo, the remotest place under the jurisdiction of the prefecture. One member of the Scarlet Gang, also a minor, works as a "cherry" for an Indian who peddles jewelry beside the temple. A cherry is a shill, someone who buys wares by prearrangement in hopes of starting a trend. An elderly man befriends him and teaches him a new trade, cat-catching. Skill and patience are required—a little, perhaps, as in fly-fishing. A sparrow on a string lures cats to within grabbing distance. Having seized one, the boy beats it to death and takes it off to the riverbank or a secluded part of the temple grounds, there to skin it. Makers of samisens pay a good price for cat skins, which function as sounding membranes on samisens.

At the end of "The Asakusa Mynah Bird" *(Asakusa Kyūkancho)*, the bird of the title, which lives in a department store, is stolen. This exchange takes place:

> "Someone stole it? The first time since the place opened that a bird's been stolen."
> "You don't say."
> "Only in Asakusa."

The last remark catches Asakusa nicely. It seems to have been proud of its scamps. A history of the ward published in 1933 finds evidence of old-style verve and gallantry in the fact that Asakusa produced so many "knights of the town," as one dictionary defines the members of the underworld gangs.

In *Scarlet Gang* there is a labor demonstration. Asakusa did have its little touches of fashionable left-wing radicalism. From the sheet-metal roof of a theater marquee, a performer agitates the passing crowds. Unless the system is reformed, he shouts, they will all starve to death. The harangue over, several of his fellows join him, there on the roof, for a display of swordsmanship. He is not of the reviews, whose lower orders would have had every right to demonstrate against the class system of which they are victims. He is rather from one of the swordplay troupes that were another Asakusa attraction.

Kengeki means literally "swordplay," if "play" is understood in the sense of "dramatic performance." There were several such troupes in Asakusa. Like O-kichi, swordsmen appealed to old virtues, and thus satisfied the police, the radicals of the right, and the Asakusa masses. Female swordplayers were more like O-kichi than the men. They brought in eroticism, as the men could not easily do. Like plucky little Orientals overwhelming huge ugly Occidentals in Bruce Lee movies, they were always overcoming adversaries more muscular than they, and they appealed to the sympathy for the underdog which was a part of the image the son of Edo and Tokyo had of himself. Best of all, they managed, wielding their swords, to show their legs every bit as generously as the review girls were permitted to do.

Singers of Naniwabushi, Osaka narrative balladry, also answered to right-wing tastes. They were very popular in Asakusa, if not everywhere. In the late thirties a Naniwabushi man was unsuccessful in Hibiya Hall, the place for advanced performances and awarenesses, but filled the Kokusai, the largest theater in Asakusa. The heroes of their ballads were strong on old virtues—loyalty, sacrifice, duty.

All of these attractions, and more, were available in Asakusa. The movies drew the biggest crowds, as they did everywhere, but it is well to note that Asakusa, in these its last good days, offered a variety of things.

After Enoken's departure the Casino Folies went arty. The choreographer had studied under Pavlova. There were dramatizations of socially conscious novels. There were ideological pieces aimed at the May Day crowd, the early years of Shōwa still being a time when the proletariat took to the streets of a May Day.

Sometimes the suggestion is strong that the reviews were not entirely serious even about artiness. On a stage other than the Casino, Kawabata saw two Heian courtiers, one of them Genji of the long romance that bears his name, the other the great lover Narihira. To all appearances they are in Heian dress, but under their arms they each have a walking stick hidden. They sway (not wriggle) their hips and sing. No, they are not courtiers at all. Observe these, their blue collars. And these weapons are not for elegant swinging, they are for smashing. The chorus line makes sedate Heian motions, and suddenly one of its number breaks into a Charleston, so earnestly that she falls exhausted. There ensue discussions of society and politics, a fox-trot, and a final "jazz chorus" and dance.

Artiness, however, may have had something to do with the untimely demise of the Casino Folies. Asakusa was not the place for that sort of thing. Shinjuku was. Shinjuku also had a review house, the Moulin Rouge, which opened on New Year's Eve 1931. The choice of opening day was an indication that it meant to be very advanced. New Year's Eve in Japan has traditionally been somewhat akin to Christmas Eve in the West, a vaguely religious night for family gatherings. Having done what they could by way of cleaning house and clearing debts, people stayed at home and perhaps went out to a shrine. Now they were invited to go to Shinjuku and watch the girls.

The Moulin Rouge was initially an offshoot of the Casino Folies. The first manager was a Casino man, and the first shows were scarcely distinguishable from the Asakusa sort. Shinjuku, however, was a place with middle-class crowds. It was also a student and intellectual center. Waseda University lay not far away. There were railway stations nearer the Waseda campus, but crowds draw crowds, and Shinjuku had the big ones. So the Shinjuku reviews gradually became sharper and more bracing than those of Asakusa. Eroticism waned as the challenge to the mind waxed. It was the sort of thing that brought radicalism of the left and of the right together. Both disliked venal politicians and money-mad businessmen. The police do not seem to have worried about it as they worried about the girls and their drawers at the Casino Folies.

Chapter 9

DARKER DAYS

Until 1926 the mayor was appointed upon royal command from a list of candidates preferred by the city council. The practice was to appoint the candidate at the top of the list—the one who had the strongest backing from the council. After 1926 the mayor was actually elected by the council. During the four and a half decades until, in 1943, there ceased to be mayors, the city had seventeen of them, or eighteen, if the one who had two separate tenures is, like President Cleveland, counted twice. So the average term was a little over two years, and for the early years of the Shōwa reign, down to the reorganization of 1943, it was even less.

Since 1947, when for the first time a governor was elected by general franchise, there have been only four governors. The average postwar tenure has been more than a decade. Only one mayor in early Showa served a full four years. Only one governor since the war has not been elected to serve three full terms, or twelve years. The present governor is in his third term. The one exception was the "Olympic governor," who thought it best to leave after the Tokyo Olympics of 1964.

The chief causes of the prewar instability seem to have been the power of the council and the cumbersome system, typical for municipalities before the war, whereby a body of select councilmen presided over by the mayor had perhaps even more power than the council. Prey to factionalism, susceptible to malfeasance, and very intrusive in the matter of appointments, this select body could cause trouble whenever it was in a bad mood. The strong and imaginative Gotō tried to curb it, but his successor, who had been his vice-mayor, did not follow his example. The successor was the mayor who may be counted twice. He presided over the two great events of the decades between the wars, the earthquake and the expansion of the city limits in 1932, which suddenly made Tokyo the second most populous city in the world.

Scandal was endemic in the affairs of the metropolitan government. There were scandals in rich variety during the post-earthquake years: over the purchase of city buses from private hands, over the fish and produce markets, over the election of a council president, over the purchase of land for cemeteries, over gas rates. Two interesting ones may be related, if not very directly, to the earthquake itself and the reconstruction.

The Keisei (Tokyo-Narita, the name means) Railway, a private line serving the eastern wards and suburbs, had long wanted to come across the Sumida River into the main part of the city. It wanted to come into Asakusa, there to join the first subway line, initially from Asakusa to Ueno and presently to Shimbashi and Shibuya. It kept petitioning and getting rejected. In 1928 the mayor recommended rejecting a sixth petition, on the grounds that another private railway, the Tōbu (which from 1929 had the rich tourist business to the ornate Tokugawa tombs at Nikkō, some eighty miles north of Tokyo), had already been given permission to come to the subway terminus, and that the Keisei, entering through Sumida Park, would be an eyesore. The latter seems a peculiar argument, since the elevated Tōbu line, put through in 1931 to a multi-level transportation and shopping complex somewhat resembling that at Shibuya, is very visible from the park. It could not have been made, in any event, if the new park had not been among the results of the earthquake. The council overruled the mayor, and then it became known that the Keisei had spent very large sums of money on the council.

The mayor recommended to the home minister that the council be dissolved. The council got even by passing a vote of no confidence, during a session that ended in fistfights. The minister did not approve the recommendation.

The mayor then resigned, taking his three vice-mayors with him. Some eminent men were implicated, including Hatoyama Ichirō, who later became prime minister, and the ubiquitous Shōriki Matsutarō of the *Yomiuri Shimbun*.

Thus prevented from entering Asakusa, the Keisei entered Ueno in 1933. In recent years it has finally been allowed into Asakusa, where it joins a subway line (not the one it originally wanted to join) and whence it sends trains through the heart of the city. Asakusa is not the prize now that it was in the days of the scandal. Nor is the station well situated for such Asakusa business as there is. The Keisei is a poor cousin among the commuter lines.

Then there was the fish-market scandal of 1928. From the early days of the Tokugawa shogunate the market had stood beside Nihombashi Bridge, in the mercantile center of Edo. It was not a pretty place and it did not smell good, and from mid-Meiji there had been efforts to move it from what was becoming a center of modern finance and merchandising. The problem of compensation for traditional rights proved intractable. The market stayed where it was until the earthquake destroyed it utterly.

On the evening of September 3, 1923, a sign was already up at the site of the old union headquarters inviting survivors to assemble and deliberate what was now to be done. The chairman of the union had lost his whole family in the earthquake; he himself escaped by boat. The decision was against attempting to rebuild in Nihombashi. Not everyone agreed. A temporary market opened on September 17, in Shibaura, by the bay. Five hundred dealers were back in business by the end of September. The market was already turning a profit. Holdouts attempted to resume business in Nihombashi, but they were turned away, whereupon some of them went to Shibaura and some withdrew to the provinces.

More fighting ensued when former naval lands in Tsukiji, east of Ginza at the mouths of the Sumida, were proposed as a permanent site. Tsukiji was approved in mid-November, at a tumultuous meeting of dealers, a type held to be particularly quarrelsome even among sons of Edo. Opening ceremonies took place on December 1, and the new market (properly, the Central Produce Market, because more than fish is sold there) opened for business the following day. The buildings were not finished until 1935.

Tsukiji fish market

Wartime controls were invoked to solve the old problem of compensation for lost rights. It was an imposed solution, allowing less than a tenth of what had originally been asked, and it did not come until after Pearl Harbor. So more than a half century elapsed between the first attempts to uproot the market from Nihombashi and the final settlement.

The market has now been in the new location for more than sixty years and in its present buildings more than fifty, which may be counted, by Tokyo standards, as forever. There is talk of moving it again. The problem this time is not that it is smelly and unsightly, but that the city consumes too much fish. The market is cramped for space and contributes to congestion. It is also somewhat dilapidated.

Compensation for the old rights was at the beginning of the scandal. Upward of a year after the earthquake the mayor recommended a schedule of payments. The council demurred. It was the view of the council that the market had managed to obstruct the proposed move for more than thirty years. What duty had the city, then, to pay the dealers anything at all? After the change of reigns the matter was brought up again. This time, by a narrow margin, the council approved compensation. One of the sponsors of the new measure was also a director of the market. He had bought a council seat solely for purposes of promoting the interests of himself and his fellow dealers. Bribery seems to have been an open secret. Fifteen people, including ten of the forty-two councilmen, were arrested for offering and receiving bribes. The home minister voided the settlement and dissolved the council late in 1928, after several councilmen had been arrested. In 1929 came the resignation of the mayor, a "purification" movement, and new elections. The prefectural government, which was an arm of the Home Ministry, was all the while relatively free of scandals.

The city and the prefecture shared quarters, a red-brick building in Marunouchi, that red-brick quarter built largely by Mitsubishi and known as Londontown. To the left were the municipal offices and the mayor, to the right the prefectural and the governor. In front of the municipal entrance was a statue of Ota Dōkan, and in front of the prefectural entrance a statue of Tokugawa Ieyasu. Dōkan was the man who first made Edo into something more than a remote fishing village. A fifteenth-century warlord, he saw its strategic importance and put up a fastness where the palace now stands. Ieyasu founded the Edo shogunate and made Dōkan's fastness into the political center of the land. A statue of

Metropolitan and prefectural offices, Marunouchi

Dōkan, though not the original one, now stands in the courtyard behind the governor's office.

This sharing of quarters was appropriate, for the two governments were close. The Home Ministry controlled the governorship, which it usually filled with one of its own. A majority of the mayors from the change of reigns down to 1943 also came from the Home Ministry. Several had been governors before they became mayors, which suggests that the mayoralty was the more desirable position. It was, so to speak, the more visible. Gotō was not the only mayor of ministerial rank. The seventeenth (or eighteenth) and last mayor was an army general.

In 1878, when the fifteen wards came to be, the population of Tokyo Prefecture was under a million. It reached a million by the mid-1880s, and two million by 1900. A jump in 1893 was due to the cession of the Tama counties by Kanagawa Prefecture. Figures before 1920, when for the first time there was a careful census, are somewhat conjectural in any event. Definitions and methods shift, as to, for instance, whether transient population is to be included, and how much weight is to be given to family registers.

One has a rough notion all the same of what was happening. The rapid growth of the early Tokyo years was in large measure a return to the population of the late Edo years. Thereafter the rate of growth slowed down, and in times of economic depression and disaster the population even fell. Since the rate was measured from an almost consistently expanding base, however, the absolute increase was massive. The census of 1920 showed three and two-thirds million, that of 1925 almost four and a half million, that of 1930 almost five and a half million. In 1932 the population was estimated at not much less than six million. During two-thirds of a century, 1868 to 1932, the city limits changed scarcely at all. They were becoming unrealistic.

The organization of these great masses of people was haphazard. Of all the large cities in the country, Tokyo was the one whose area was most at variance with its actual population. Negligible in 1878, the population of the "county part" accounted for about a third of the total by 1920. It continued to leap forward in the two succeeding censuses while that of the fifteen wards was falling. In 1920 there were about twice as many people in the "ward part" as in the five counties that bordered on it. By 1932 the proportions had been almost reversed. Not quite two-thirds of the people in the wards and the five counties were in the latter.

All along the limits of the city, which in no direction reached as far as the prefectural boundaries, stretched a patchwork of more or less heavily populated districts incorporated as towns and villages. The only incorporated city in the prefecture besides Tokyo itself was a silk-spinning center rather far out in the western counties. Some of the towns and villages had recognizable centers; some did not. Some, like Shinjuku (which straddled the city limits), were already emerging as major satellite cities. Others were arbitrarily defined accumulations of people. Behind the confusion was the assumption that someone would come up with a good idea someday. Someone had to, for it was a necessity.

In the meantime there was reluctance and intransigence on all sides. The entities chiefly concerned—the city, the counties, the prefecture, and the national government—all wished to gain from the new arrangements, whatever they might be, and stood in danger of losing. There were numerous possibilities, from doing nothing at all, on the grounds that the apparent confusion was not discommoding anyone seriously, to the bold step of unifying the mayor's constituency and the governor's and doing away with the office of mayor. The latter would have meant a loss of autonomy for the city and a reversion to a stage even earlier than the "special cities" one that had kept Tokyo, along with Osaka and Kyoto, without a mayor for a decade in mid-Meiji when all other municipalities in the country, however diminutive, had their mayors. In the counties sentiment ran strongly toward this most extreme reorganization. There would have been economic advantages, bringing rich places and poor places together under one budget, and making the mountain people of the far western counties into children of Edo. The final solution, which fell between the two extremes, did not come until 1943. By then the Crisis, the expression that was used to make the populace aware of the sacrifices expected of it, was worse than those who had brought it about had meant it to be.

Opposition within the old city subsided, in the face of an energetic propaganda campaign by the municipal government. The opposition was partly political. The expansion seemed a stage on the way to making Tokyo different from the other two special cities of Meiji. Kyoto and Osaka, and their prefectures. Originally the distinction had been made to keep these biggest and most threatening cities in the land under tighter control. Was Tokyo to be brought back under control, while the other two went on enjoying their autonomy? And then again (the political argument was by no means clear-cut): it might be good to be rid of City Hall, so extremely subject to scandal and malfeasance, and so cumbersome. The city bureaucracy grew more than a hundredfold between 1898, when the first mayor took office, and 1932. After 1932 the expenses of City Hall seemed even less necessary. The expanded city had more than 90 percent of the prefectural population and paid close to 100 percent of the taxes.

The economic argument was clearer, and perhaps stronger. The old city was more advanced than the county part, and was not especially interested in helping the latter catch up. Just upward of half the houses in the newly expanded city, and four-fifths of the houses in the old city, had running water. The poorer eastern wards were in this regard well served, Fukagawa being an exception. A watery place troubled by land subsidence, it worried more about getting rid of water than about bringing it in. The well-to-do western suburbs, after 1932 the western wards, fell much below the average for the old fifteen, and would be an expense. Almost four-fifths of the old city by area had sewers in use or under construction on the eve of the Second World War, and this was the case with less than two-thirds, again by area, of the new wards. Before the expansion of 1932, nine-tenths of the streets in the city, which is to say the old fifteen wards, were paved or surfaced. Less than a third were after 1932.

The solution of 1932 may be thought rather timid. It left the two governments in place, there behind their twin doors and statues, but the five counties bordering on the old fifteen wards themselves became wards. Absorption of the five counties was approved by the city council and the mayor's advisory council in May 1932 and received the approval of the Home Ministry shortly afterward. On October 1, 1932, eighty-two towns and villages were incorporated into the city. The city limits thus coincided with the prefectural boundaries in every direction except the west. The city shared borders with Saitama, Chiba, and Kanagawa prefectures. So it now covered essentially the area of the prefecture of early Meiji, and what remained of the county part was what had been ceded by Kanagawa Prefecture in 1893. Twenty new wards were added, raising the count from fifteen to thirty-five. This is not to say that the twenty were thoroughly urban. Extensive farmlands remained, and limited ones still do.

If timid in its treatment of political arrangements, the settlement of 1932 was startling in its effect on the population and area of the city. The population suddenly doubled, to more than five million, and the area increased sevenfold. It became the fifth-largest city in the world by area (none of the other four was in Japan, though before 1932 Tokyo was not, by area, the largest Japanese city) and the second-largest, following only New York, in population. Many a boy in the American West, no expert in the demography of the Kantō Plain, said that that was exactly the sort of thing the sneaky Japanese would do to catch up with honest, plodding New York. Two villages from North Tama County were annexed into Setagaya, one of the new wards along the western fringes of the city, in 1936.

It was most natural, given the fact that eighty-two towns and villages were reduced to twenty political entities, that there should be disagreement and some bitterness about the naming of the new wards. Those who made the decisions in 1932 did a better job than those who made similar decisions in 1947, when the number of wards was reduced from thirty-five to twenty-two. Some of the twenty-two names have a distinctly artificial ring to them, as if an advertising agency might have made them up. Only one of the thirty-five, Jōtō, has the genuinely fabricated look, and even it is vaguely descriptive. It means something like "the eastern part of the capital." Some names came from prominent geographic features. Four of the five lost counties had their names preserved in ward names, only Toyotama being left out. The commonest device was to give the name of the most prominent town to the whole ward. This caused the most dissatisfaction. In what was to become Shibuya Ward, only the town of Shibuya favored the name. In the other towns sentiment was strong for Jingū Ward, after the Meiji Jingū, the Meiji Shrine, situated in the ward. Of the old Five Mouths, the stations on the main highways out of Edo, Itabashi became the name of the largest ward by area, the one farthest to the north and west, on the old inland road to Kyoto. Shinagawa also named a ward. Shinjuku, the oldest part of which had been within the city limits since 1920, became a ward name in 1947. So only Senjū was left out. Accounting for two of the Five Mouths, it might have received special consideration, but the name of the old county, and no one could object to that, prevailed.

Three of the new wards had populations of more than two hundred thousand, and two of them larger populations than Honjo, most populous among the old fifteen. Two of the three centered upon two of the three rapidly growing western centers, Shibuya and Ikebukuro. Shinjuku, lying on either side of the old city limits, was divided between an old ward and a new. The most heavily populated ward among the thirty-five was Arakawa, a very different case from the other two, it lay just north of Asakusa Ward, and became urbanized as the poorest of the poor were forced into it, many of them refugees from disasters, especially the great earthquake of 1923. The new wards had on the average a lower per capita income than the old ones, but the western ones were extensions of the middle-class High City wards, Arakawa an extension of the poorer Low City. The two wards east of the Sumida, Fukagawa and Honjo, had the lowest average income among the old fifteen, and the two neighboring counties, including the new Arakawa Ward (as well as Jōtō, the one with the fabricated name), were yet lower.

Asakusa Ward had the largest number of pawnshops in the city, and Honjo the largest number of night schools, for very young people who worked in the daytime. Akasaka, on the opposite side of the old city, had only a seventh as many pawnshops as Asakusa, and no night schools at all.

An important novelist (not Tanizaki, who had already fled) said of the proud new city that it got worse every day, and only made him want to flee. Yet it was tidied up, and the new city limits made sense. The crazy pattern of villages along the old limits went away, most of the population was brought within the mayor's jurisdiction, and the new city had integrity. It stood together, a unit. Almost half the people who used public transportation within the prefecture moved between the new wards and the old. The remainder was divided almost exclusively and almost evenly between people being transported within the old wards and the new wards. Movement to and from and within the remaining three counties was negligible.

The time came when the new city limits did no better at containing the population than had the old ones. There are no longer towns and villages, only incorporated cities, along the limits of the ward part. Two of the three Tama counties have quite disappeared. They have been divided into cities. Some mountain towns and a single village yet remain in the remotest of the three. So why not go the whole distance, one might ask, and do away with the county part completely? Why not have a few new wards, and finish the business left unfinished in 1932 and 1943?

It probably will not happen, at least for a long time, because there are not the compelling reasons there were in 1932 for the city to expand. There are no exploding centers along the ward limits like the Shibuya, Ikebukuro, and Shinjuku of late Taishō and early Shōwa. Books keep getting written which have the commercial and managerial center of the city, and not merely the population center, continuing to move westward, finally engulfing the tomb of that sad, weak man, the Taishō emperor. A bedroom sprawl all the way to the mountains seems more likely. The pattern of cities is not as crazy as the pattern of towns and villages was. And, finally, it would make more sense for the city—the ward part—to expand into neighboring prefectures, already on the borders of the wards, than to expand westward through what remains of Tokyo Prefecture. The reality is one megalopolis from Chiba on the east shore of the bay to Yokosuka near the mouth of the bay on the west shore. The governor of Tokyo is as likely to get jurisdiction over any part of the neighboring prefectures as the mayor of New York is to get jurisdiction over Newark and Jersey City. Meanwhile Saitama Prefecture, which borders Tokyo on the north, can worry about its own crazy pattern.

On October 1, 1932, the city suddenly had seven times the area it had had the day before, but it was not as big as some people seemed to think it was. The *Nichinichi Shimbun,* now the *Mainichi,* set a competition for a city song. The winning lyrics, by a young man in the city government, glorified the expanse of the new city, all 550,000 square kilometers of it. This would be an area somewhat greater than the squaring of seven hundred kilometers. From a spot seven hundred kilometers northwest of, let us say, Tokyo Central Station, the mountains of Siberia might, on a clear day, be in view. Set to music by a music professor, the song was widely sung.

The prime minister, the third to meet that fate during the years between the wars, was assassinated in May 1932, the month in which the great expansion gained approval by everyone whose approval was needed. The Japanese recognized Manchuria as an independent nation in mid-September, a fortnight before the expansion became a reality. Such were the times. Taishō democracy had expired, reaction and aggression were in the air. Tokyo and Japan were, like most places, in economic depression, which is commonly listed among the causes of the hotheaded activism that swept democracy (such as it was), the political parties, and peace away.

The military persons who were the chief agents of the reaction might in the jargon of a later day have been thought "concerned." They saw injustices and contradictions, and thought they saw easy solutions in a return to the virtues, chiefly loyalty and sincerity, of an earlier and purer day. Some people, such as capitalists and party politicians, seemed to thrive on depression, and far larger numbers of people were too obviously in distress. If the earthquake suggested to some that the heavens and their eight million deities were unhappy, the depression made it intolerably clear to others.

The panic of 1927, the remote causes of which might be traced to the earthquake, came under control, and need not have brought a general depression. Dependent on foreign markets and especially the American market, however, Japan could not escape entanglement in the world depression. By 1930, the year the Casino Folies opened, it had come. The late twenties and early thirties were a time of labor strife. Except for a brief time after the Second World War there has been nothing like it since. The early years of Shōwa were the full summer of left-wing activity, polemical and literary. Almost everything could and can be blamed on the depression. Whether or not the reaction of the thirties would have come had the depression not come, we will never know. Perhaps it was merely time for another seizure of puritan righteousness. Perhaps it was another of those mysterious cycles that seem to operate everywhere and in everything.

The critic Oya Sōichi (today he might be called an opinion-maker) remarked that the two Chinese characters with which printers could not, keep their fonts adequately supplied were those for "step" or "grade" and for "woman." Left-wing argumentation and evangelism would have been helpless without the former, because without it such expressions as "class struggle" and "class consciousness" cannot be written. The popularity of the latter had to do with *eroguro* nonsense. Kawabata said that two subjects monopolized the media in those days, depression and eroticism.

As early as 1929 firm measures were taken against the radical left. As for eroticism, both prosperity and depression, as suited the moods and conditions of the day, could be blamed for it. The prosperity of the First

World War brought laxness, and depression made people turn to *eroguro* nonsense for distraction and comfort. During the years of the Crisis such pleasures disappeared, to emerge in far opener and bolder form after the Second World War, or, as the Japanese call it, the Pacific War. A flood of girls poured in upon the city from the poor northeastern provinces in the mid-thirties. Rural poverty and the depression were the general causes, and crop failures the immediate ones. The fact that crop failures cannot be explained in social and economic terms made no difference. The poor girls added to the indignation, even as they made work easier for the purveyors of *ero* and *guro*. These were darker days than the days of very early Showa.

In *Scarlet Gang of Asakusa,* Kawabata reports on the beggars. More of them than usual were living in Asakusa Park in the summer of 1930. Perhaps the number was as high as eight hundred; but Kawabata was reluctant to make an estimate himself, and did not trust the estimate made by the ward office. Someone stole the hilt from the sword on the statue, up behind the temple, of the celebrated Kabuki actor Danjūrō. Asakusa had drinking places that specialized in beggars. Bare-legged waitresses would come and sit upon the tables. Kawabata observed the forbearing code of the beggars. The park benches were full on a warm night, and each of the regulars had his place, which was respected. Asakusa had in those years a beggar chief, or chief beggar, known as Goldtooth, because much of his money was in his mouth. An intelligent man rumored to be a college graduate, he lorded it over the other Asakusa beggars and took a share of their earnings. He was finally incapacitated by stab wounds.

On a level just above beggars and vagrants, ragpickers decreased in numbers in the last years of the Taishō reign, and rapidly increased during the early years of Shōwa. Their number almost quadrupled between 1925 and 1932. About half were in the new ward which many wanted to call Senjū, after the old mouth, but which was called Adachi after the county of which it was a part. Urbanization and disaster forced the very poor outside of the city limits, into what was to become Arakawa Ward, and then beyond the Arakawa, as the Sumida is known in its upper reaches, into the fens of Adachi. In late Meiji truck gardens were islands among fens and lotus ponds.

Drainage brought industrialization, and ragpickers from the old Low City put together a community on lands still too watery for industrial or ordinary residential use. It was rather as Asakusa had been a few centuries earlier, before reclamation of the wetlands along the Sumida: pilgrims made their way to a great temple, in this case the Yakushi temple at

Ragpickers hovels at Nippon in Arakawa Ward

Nishiarai, through bogs and queaches among which the few permanent dwellers eked out a subsistence livelihood. The best days for the ragpicking vocation lasted down to about 1960. Thereafter a modest amount of capital was required for what before had required none. Collectors of scrap and wastepaper now make their rounds in small trucks. In the years after the Second World War there was a smaller but more famous community of ragpickers on the right bank of the Sumida just above Asakusa. It seems to have given the language the commonest word for "ragpicker." The last syllable of *bataya* applies to any kind of mercantile enterprise, and the first two seem to be from *kawabata*, "riverbank."

The Shōwa reign was a decade old on Christmas Day 1936. Had it ended then the reign designation, suggesting peace and accord, would have been somewhat ironic. The decade had moved rapidly in the direction of obfuscation and strife. A time of some pluralism and tolerance gave way to jingoism and repression. Quite aside from the effect on left-wing radicalism, the harmless if by some standards wanton pleasures of the populace were being affected. So was the appearance of the city. The most extreme internal bloodletting of the thirties took place on February 26, 1936, precisely ten months before the end of the first Shōwa decade. The military rising of that day had among its secondary results the chopping down of the palmettos that were among the symbols of Hibiya Park, the central park of the city, immediately south of the palace plaza. The insurgents had their last fortress at the Sannō Hotel, a short distance to the west. The park became artillery emplacements and the palmettos got in the way of the guns.

The Olympic Games were a somewhat later casualty. Soon after the Los Angeles games of 1932, at which the Japanese and especially their swimming team did well, sentiment began to grow for having the 1940 games in Tokyo. By the time purposeful campaigning began Hitler was chancellor of Germany. So, had circumstances not intervened, the world would have had two sets of fervently nationalistic games in a row. The Japanese returned the franchise even before developments in Europe made the games impossible. Developments in Asia had already made them impossible, or so the official view was, for Japan. The war with China, which the Japanese go on calling the China Incident, began the year after the Berlin Olympics.

A delegation set off for Berlin in the summer of 1935. It went by the Trans-Siberian Railway and had trouble with the Russians. Among the lavish presents to Hitler was a gold sword. It was confiscated at the border, but eventually reached Berlin by diplomatic channels. The Tokyo city representative at the Berlin Olympics did not come home. He stayed on in the United States, by way of which he was returning, and took a position at Northwestern University.

Tokyo was awarded the 1940 Olympics on the day before the 1936 (or Nazi) Olympics began. The Japanese did well in them too (for the first time a Japanese woman won a gold medal), but behaved so badly that the Japanese embassy in Berlin got off a special report to the minister of education. Fighting and slashing occurred on the ship back to Yokohama. The samurai spirit was in command.

It was in firmer and firmer control at home too. The turnover of prime ministers was brisk in those days. Three of the six men who held the office during the four years after the Berlin Olympics were from the army or navy. Midway through the four years the Japanese announced that they must give up the Olympics. The reason was that not enough steel for a stadium could be spared from the China Incident. The original plans called for enough steel to build a destroyer. They were cut almost in half, but the government decided that even that quantity would be difficult to come by. The main installations were to be on the Komazawa golf links, far out in Setagaya, farthest to the southwest of the new wards. There was to be a gymnasium in Kanda. The golf links are now Komazawa Park, where a part of the 1964 Olympics took place.

Had the games been held, they would have been doubly nationalistic. The year 1940 was the Zero Year from which the famous fighting plane took its designation. It was the year 2600 by the traditional, mythical reckoning of the age of the Japanese empire—which was, in the patriotic view, now twenty-six centuries old. It was a year to be observed.

Besides the Olympics, there was to be a world's fair, which was also called off. It too would have been markedly nationalistic, and it was changed to something explicitly so, the Zero Year celebrations. The sense in high places was that something was needed to shake the populace out of its gloom and make it buoyant and positive once more. By 1940 it was becoming apparent that the Chinese problem did not admit of a simple solution. Most of the Chinese cities had fallen, and yet resistance went on, pertinaciously. Sacrifice or humiliation, or perhaps both, seemed to lie ahead.

Plans for the fair got as far as Shinto propitiatory rites to the gods whose land, by the bay in Yokohama and at the mouths of the Sumida in Tokyo, was to be disturbed. Tickets went on sale and sold well. Kachitokibashi, Bridge of the Triumphant Shout, the farthest downstream of the Sumida bridges and the newest of the prewar ones, was built for the occasion. Missions were sent abroad to stir up interest. And then, also in the summer of 1938, the government announced its opinion that the fair, along with the Olympics, should be postponed. So the city got the less expensive Zero Year observances instead. There was talk of moving City Hall to Tsukishima, the reclaimed island that was to be the fair site. Reports of profiteering caused the idea to be dismissed. The mayor, who had earlier been governor, was among the cleaner ones. It seems a pity now that City Hall did not move then. It might not now be moving out of Edo.

The twenty-six-hundredth birthday of the nation fell, by traditional if unreliable reckoning, on February 11, 1940. There were parades and a river carnival on that day but, because February is one of the coldest months of the year, the culminating celebrations occurred in clement November. In the summer the city (not the nation) had an eminent guest, Pu-yi, the puppet emperor of Manchuria. The city itself invited him, doing so, said the mayor, in cooperation with the cities of China and Manchuria, the two treated of course as separate political entities. The mayor went on to say that he had no doubt of the resolve of the city to attain to the lofty ideals upon which the nation was founded and climb to the pinnacle of world culture. Such was the rhetoric of the day.

The nation held rallies in the palace plaza on November 10 and 11. Their Majesties attended. The second rally was a big picnic at which everyone, including Their Majesties, ate army field rations. The nation was much moved, newspapers tell us. On November 12 the city had a big banquet in a restaurant across from the plaza, and on November 13

A flower trolley

a rally in the Meiji Gardens that was twice as big as the one on the tenth. It wistfully imitated the lost Olympics. A sacred flame was brought by relay from the Kashiwara Shrine, south of Nara. Built in Meiji, the Kashiwara occupies the legendary site of the palace where the first emperor assumed the throne. The flame arrived on November 11 and was kept in the mayor's office until time to run it to the gardens.

Festive observances had been banned because of the Crisis, but the ban was lifted for five days. Floats and portable shrines *(mikoshi,* or "god seats") and lantern processions were so numerous that it was as if local festivals, usually scattered over the landscape and the seasons, were taking place all together. "Flower trolleys," the vehicles decorated for great public occasions, ran all through the city. And then on the fifteenth there were posters: "The fun is over. Let's get back to work."

Secondary observances furthered the cause of bringing the eight directions (as the slogan of the day had it) under one roof, the Japanese one: international conferences for writers, educators, and young people, a conference on "building the new East Asia," a tournament in the martial arts and a more conventional athletic meet.

The closing pages of Tanizaki's *The Makioka Sisters* include scenes set in Tokyo in the autumn of 1940, as the Makioka family makes another attempt, this one successful, to marry off its third daughter. Tanizaki conveys very nicely the fervor which the Japanese are so good at mustering up on such occasions; he manages to suggest as well, from his Kansai vantage point, that it is a peculiarly Tokyo-like kind of silliness. Among the principals in the marriage negotiations is a bustling lady journalist who is busy as can be. She is speaking.

> "And the day after that a meeting to organize the Rule Assistance Association. And the festival of the Yasukuni Shrine is going on, and on the twenty-first there is a parade. Oh, Tokyo is just full of excitement. All the hotels are overflowing. That reminds me—the Imperial has twice as many people as it can handle. We got you a room, but not much of a room."

The Rule Assistance Association was an invention of Prince Konoe's to advance "spiritual mobilization," which is to say totalitarianism. The Yasukuni, northwest of the palace, was and continues to be the shrine where war dead are venerated. The Imperial is of course the Frank Lloyd Wright building that was completed just before the 1923 earthquake and came safely through it.

Among the proposals by way of getting ready for the Zero Year celebrations was that the palace plaza be made a broader and more continuous expanse by putting the streets that crossed it underground. The proposal was rejected as undignified and risky, with the sacred royal presence so near at hand, though, relying on private contributions and voluntary labor, the city did tidy the plaza up somewhat. Proposals for tunneling under the palace grounds have been dismissed in the years since for similar reasons. Far larger than the grounds of Buckingham Palace or the White House, they go on inconveniencing rapid public transit. Everything moving between Tokyo Central Station and the busiest station in the city, Shinjuku, must make a detour around them.

The authorities were having their repressive way in matters that may seem trivial and even ludicrous but to them must have seemed important. They could clearly have their way in the naming of cigarettes, tobacco being a public monopoly. So cigarettes formerly known by the English names Golden Bat and Cherry took Japanese names. Yet it is not easy to judge how much was done by force and how much by suggestion. The pressure on popular entertainers to do the popular thing must be very strong, and so it may be that some of them acquiesced in what was expected of them before they were told. A singer who had called himself Dick Mine became Mine Kōichi. Back in freer days a comedian had taken a name, Fujiwara Kamatari, that now was deemed irreverent. There had been a historical Fujiwara Kamatari a dozen centuries before, the founder of the great Fujiwara clan and so a forebear of the royal family. The comedian took a different name.

The pattern was by no means consistent, however. A minister of education sought to extirpate the words "mama" and "papa" from the language, and he was not successful. The pair was so firmly rooted that many a child would not have known what to put in its place. A comic ensemble known as the Akireta Boys, who provided song and patter to the accompaniment of a guitar, became the Milk Brothers. The second word in the earlier designation had been the English one. Now both words were English. *Akireta* means something like "absurd" or "egregious," and was thought not to accord well with the solemnity of the times. Two of the boys called themselves Shiba Rie and Bōya Saburō, which is to say, Maurice Chevalier and Charles Boyer. "Chevalier" died before the change from Akireta Boys to Milk Brothers. "Boyer" did not change his name.

Though more gradually, the war was doing to the reviews what the earthquake had done to the opera. A little Kafū vignette written in 1942 is set in the dressing room of the Opera House in Asakusa, among the places he loved best. A cannon booms onstage and the smell of gunpowder comes drifting up to the dressing room; the actors are in military uniform. Guns and gunpowder had come to the review houses some years earlier, as inspirational pieces came to prevail over eroticism.

Kafū was strongly opposed to the war, and once it had entered its Pacific phase he did almost the only thing a dissident could do: he lapsed into silence. Yet his writings for the Asakusa review houses tell us that he engaged in a kind of self-censorship, and suggest too what was happening to the houses. In 1938 he did the libretto for a two-act operetta called *Katsushika Romance (Katsushika Jōwa)*. It had a ten-day run at the Opera House. Katsushika is the name of an old county and a new ward, the farthest northeast of the thirty-five wards. After the war he wrote three skits for the Asakusa burlesque houses. One senses in these skits the somewhat lubricious thing he would have liked to write, in the operetta the sort of thing he felt constrained to write if he was to write for his girls at the Opera House at all. It is a very moral piece, preaching the good old virtues of loyalty and sacrifice. It is tearful, thin, abstract, and didactic.

There are three principal characters, each of whom has solos, and a chorus. In the first act the tenor is courting a bus conductor. Almost all bus conductors, from the earliest days of the calling, were young women. She is swept off to the city by a gang of movie people who will make her a star. They have spotted her on her bus and noted a close resemblance to a person who is already a star. This is her solo as she gets swept off:

> Location
> Through the long spring days
> Location
> Such a happy path
> Such an amusing way to live
> Sing, dance
> Dance, sing
> The scarlet lights of the city beckon
> They beckon, those lights
> Hurry home
> Fly away, automobile
> Sing, make haste
> Make haste, sing

The word "location," indicating a movie location, is in English. The syllable count irregularly follows the alternation of sevens and fives that is standard in Japanese balladry.

In the second act the tenor is married to a girl who in the first act kept a little refreshment stall on the far bank of the Arakawa Drainage Channel. The young wife is about to go off and buy medicine for their colicky baby. The tenor goes in her place, for he is a good husband and it is beginning to rain. The erstwhile bus conductor enters, forlorn and bedraggled.

> It is all a dream now
> The city excitement I yearned for
> I cast off love
> And soon was cast off by the world
> Mired in filth and shame
> A scrap of paper blown by the wind
> Down among the fallen leaves
> Trampled at the wayside
> No one to pity me....
> Bars, cafés, here, there
> And I, homeless
> A fallen leaf, soaked by autumn rains
> Going where the wind blows
> Clutching at my breast

Having allowed just enough time for the solo to finish, the young wife's uncle enters. Her father is in jail. Money is needed for the defense. It saddens him deeply to ask it, but will she not indenture herself to the pleasure quarters? The bus conductor steps forward and offers to make the sacrifice herself. She is in any event "mired in filth and shame." The

young husband and wife must live out their lives, long ones, be it hoped,
in happiness.

>Let it be so
>A body sunk in the slough
>Does not matter
>Filthy
>Let it sink
>What matters it where
>To make up for the betrayal
>To help him who was betrayed
>I gladly make the sacrifice

It is the world of Meiji Kabuki, whose mission was to praise virtue
and chastise vice. Even more, perhaps, it is the world of Shimpa, "the
New School," a hybrid melodramatic form, its origins in mid-Meiji,
that retained female impersonators but experimented with more realistic
styles of acting. The women of Shimpa are always sacrificing themselves
to men who are happy to let them do it, and scarcely seem worth the
trouble. They tend to be nobler the deeper mired in filth they are. Little
of the early eroticism remains in Kafū's operetta save the scantily clad
figure of the ruined woman.

After the war, with enfeebled police and an American Occupation indifferent to such matters, Kafū let himself go. The most amusing of his
skits for the burlesque or strip theaters is called *What Happened the Night
the Lights Went Out (Teiden no Yoru no Dekigoto)*. It is without music, one
act and three scenes. The central figure is a woman kept by an elderly
man whose business is unclear but conveniently has him out of town
for protracted periods. In the first scene she is out of the house and her
housemaid is dallying with the laundry boy.

"'Don't. It tickles.' As she writhes and seems about to fall face up from
the window frame, Yamaoka takes her in his arms. Her legs inside, her
torso outside, she reveals her thighs as she pulls herself upright. At that
moment there is a sound in the hall." It is the woman, who gets measured
in delicious detail by her seamstress.

Her patron appears and tells her that he must be in Osaka for some
days. She cajoles and caresses, and when he goes out she says, "This isn't
the easiest business in the world to be in." The second scene is a dream.
A young lieutenant and a baby figure in it. "When," he asks, "will war
disappear from human affairs?" Antiwar platitudes were de rigueur in the
postwar years. It may be said for Kafū that he had more right to utter
them than did most writers and intellectuals.

In the third scene the lights have gone out. It is something they often did in those years. A police admonition is circulated. People must be on guard, this dark night, against robbers. A young robber appears. She invites him to stay the night. He is in the process of stripping her when an elderly robber appears. (There is kissing, taboo before 1945, in the first and third scenes.) She sends an inquisitive policeman on his way, allowing the elderly robber to escape. The lights have meanwhile come on again. "Aiko smiles and turns off the light. Putting tissue in the bosom of her kimono, she kneels on the bedding. The curtain falls. Only a humming of insects breaks the silence."

What Happened the Night the Lights Went Out was presented at an Asakusa theater in March and April 1949. Another skit, called *Love Suicide at Hatonomachi (Shinjū Hatonomachi),* was presented at the same theater in 1949, and again in 1950, this time at the Rokkuza (House of the Sixth District), most famous of the Asakusa strip places. Kafū himself appeared in both versions. With a different title, which might be rendered *Springtide Passion in Hatonomachi (Shunjō Hatonomachi),* the piece was made into a movie. Hatonomachi was a "private" or unlicensed pleasure quarter east of the Sumida, successor to the Tamanoi district that had attracted Kafū a decade earlier (see pages 335-336).

In the Tamanoi "den of unlicensed whores" about 1932

All the varieties of girls and their customers pass in review, sincere ones and frivolous ones, responsible ones and irresponsible ones, girls who rather enjoy their work and girls who are in it because they have no other way to help straitened parents and siblings. A sincere man who has been betrayed by a woman and a sincere woman who has been betrayed by a man go off and commit suicide together. The high moral posture of the Katsushika piece is certainly not wanting in the postwar pieces, and we have a new strain of didacticism, the pacifist sermon. There is, however, a pronounced strain of the *ero* and the *guro,* even though it may seem bland and inoffensive by the standards of our own day. It is missing from the Katsushika piece. Patriotic ideologues made Asakusa do without these little pleasures as its best day was coming to an end.

Like Asakusa itself and its reviews, chronicles of Asakusa come to have a thin, attenuated look. Kawabata wrote little about Asakusa after his interest moved on to the snowy parts of the land (specifically, Niigata Prefecture—the first installment of *Snow Country* appeared in 1935). Kafū's diary is full of interesting bits about Asakusa and the pleasure quarters to the north and east, and he wrote poignantly of the warmth and dirt and uselessness of life in the review halls.

The most famous chronicle of Asakusa on the eve of the "Pacific War" is *Under What Stars (Ikanaru Hoshi no Shita ni)* by Takami Jun. Although almost three decades younger, and although a bar sinister intervenes, Takami seems to have been Kafū's first cousin. His mother was unmarried, and his father, a governor of Fukui Prefecture, was a younger brother of Kafū's father. *Under What Stars* is commonly treated as a "novel of customs and manners," specifically those of Asakusa. It was published in 1939 and 1940, and is set a year or two earlier. Asakusa does not by any means emerge as the sensual, tactile presence that it is in Kawabata's *Scarlet Gang of Asakusa.* The consensus is that Takami's work is the better novel of the two, and so the trouble may be that Asakusa was not, at the end of the thirties, the presence it had been at the beginning.

Much of the reporting does not go beyond what we already know. We hear, for instance, about the unjust and rigid class structure of the review houses, with the dancers forever at the bottom. We learn, as we learned from Kawabata, that they worked hard. "The Asakusa theaters are such hard work that the girls immediately begin to put on weight when they leave. Misako was doing it too, in that particular way, like a sudden bursting when the hoops that have held the staves together are removed."

There is a conspicuous new institution in Asakusa, but it lies outside of the Sixth District. Shōchiku opened its Kokusai Gekijō or International Theater (which has recently been torn down that a hotel might be put up) in 1937. Takami reports that its devotees, mostly women, marched eyes-front from the subway to their theater and back again, and did not set foot in the Sixth District. Devotees of the opera and the reviews had been mostly male. For obscure reasons, all-girl troupes attract overwhelmingly feminine audiences, and the Kokusai had one of these.

Under What Stars is occasionally amusing. It obliquely informs us that the patriots were not wholly successful at stamping out corrupt Western influences. One of the review performers has the most unlikely name Bottlernouth. This is so that his full name can be pronounced Bingu Kurosubei, which is to say, Bing Crosby. What is best about the book, however, is less a matter of character and action and (what *Scarlet Gang* is so very good at) reporting than of mood. The good days are over. The action is coming to an end.

"The famous old places of Asakusa had been abandoned. The aquarium, said to be the birthplace of the Asakusa reviews, was in a state of advanced neglect, the subject of weird stories. Late at night, it was said, you could hear the sound of tap dancing on the roof. It has since been torn down, and so those who loved the Casino Folies have lost all trace of their dream." The time is late 1938.

Asakusa owed much of its vitality in the late Edo years and on into the first Tokyo century to the fact that it was on the edge of town. To keep mischievous things from the center, the shogunate moved the Yoshiwara there, and, much later, the Kabuki as well. Still on the edge of all the urban excitement, but now on the wrong edge, Asakusa could not keep them. It had a terminal department store, the Matsuya, where the subway ended and whence a private railway departed for Nikko and other points in that direction, but for the most part it was a district of small family shops. Old ones held on with admirable tenacity; new ones did not come.

In a 1939 essay called "Nesoberu Asakusa," which might be rendered "Asakusa All Sprawled Out," or "Asakusa Supine," Takami compares Ginza and Asakusa.

> Asakusa does not have face and obverse. Ginza has a provocative surface and little of substance, a certain emptiness, behind it. Asakusa sets forth a peculiar kind of warmth right there in front of you, and does not hide an inconsistency, a makeshift quality. It is like a jazz record blaring forth in an alien tongue. When it does not blare it goes to the other extreme and becomes all shyness and awkwardness, as of a girl

The Asakusa subway tower

with an old-fashioned coiffure and an advanced bathing suit. There are none of the voguish places which, in the Ginza fashion, have cover charges. That is not quite true. We have recently witnessed the opening of "grand tea salons," such as the Purple Gold and the Grand Harbor. They do have minimal cover charges, but, like the places that depend on the subway, they lie outside the Sixth District. In sum: there may be a surface resemblance to Ginza, but it is like a ringworm. It has not penetrated to the heart of Asakusa conservatism....

Here too there is an inconsistency. The young heirs to the Asakusa shops are modern boys, not apparently conservative at all. Their hair is in I forget what advanced style and their trousers are tight. Dance halls no longer interest them. In their spare time they speed about in borrowed Datsuns. And their talk is all of Ginza....

[The girls in Asakusa drinking places] spend their holidays in Gin-za. I could give any number of examples. Asakusa yearns for Ginza....
And does Ginza do the reverse? Do Ginza people come to Asakusa on their holidays? They do not. They have a low opinion of Asakusa.

At this point Takami refer to Kawabata's view that nothing in Asakusa is of the highest quality. Takami continues:

Asakusa has an unshakable standing as a place of crowds and noise *[sakariba]*, but it is indeed of a lower quality than Ginza. The pull of Ginza for the child of Asakusa may well be the pull of the best for the next best.

Ginza, the best, always seems ready for battle. Asakusa lies supine. Pleasure seekers in Ginza are always on their mettle. Pleasure should mean relaxing, letting things go.

Further evidence that foreign poisons had not been completely ex-punged, the adjectival element in the name Grand Harbor is in English.

It is an ambiguous passage, and it may seem inconsistent with certain statements in *Under What Stars*, in which we learn, for instance, that girls from Ginza places choose Asakusa for their private conversations because they are not likely to encounter Ginza customers there. It does not much matter which is literally true. Takami is praising the openness and the conservatism of Asakusa, but he is also telling us that there is something a bit less than truly professional about Asakusa. For that, one goes to Ginza. If a Ginza girl does sometimes have a little tête-à-tête in Asakusa, that is because the Ginza clientele is the one that matters, and it is sometimes to be avoided. Takami did not think to make the com-parison that would be the most obvious today, between Ginza and the western *sakariba*, Ikebukuro and Shinjuku and Shibuya.

Kafū never seemed to give up on Asakusa. One cold night during the last full year of the war he recorded the closing of the Opera House, his Asakusa favorite. It is a touching entry. "As I passed the lane of shops ... on my way to the subway, I found myself weeping again.... I have been witness to it all, Tokyo going to ruins."

The closing of the theaters brought an end not only to the reviews but to Asakusa as a leader of popular culture. After the war came the bur-lesque and strip houses, which tended to lack imagination, and in which Asakusa often seemed to be imitating and following Shinjuku. Yet Kafū went on liking Asakusa better than any other part of the city. When, in his last years, he went into the city at all from the suburban dwelling that was his last, it was most commonly to Asakusa.

Nor did Takami immediately give up. Through the war years he went on finding reserves in Asakusa. It goes on drawing factory workers from east of the river, he observes in a 1944 essay called "Enticement and Solace" ("Ian to Miryoku"), as Kinshichō, a *sakariba* built especially for the district, does not. Kinshichō is an entertainment cluster, mostly of movie houses, in Honjo Ward, since 1947 a part of Sumida Ward, near the eastern limits of the city as they were before 1932. It was developed in the thirties by entrepreneurs who thought that what was happening along the western fringes of the city might be made to happen along the eastern fringes as well. Though it was not a complete failure, it fell very far short of becoming a Shinjuku. Not inclined to go as far as Shinjuku, the proletariat of the eastern wards still preferred Asakusa to the more convenient Kinshichō. Takami has an interesting explanation. Kinshichō "has all the facilities, but the attraction of Asakusa is simply not there. Unlike Asakusa, it has no tradition. It has theaters and they have nothing behind them. We may draw a moral from this."

It is an interesting theory, but one which the facts do not support. Shinjuku and Shibuya flourished. Newest and smallest of the Five Mouths of Edo, Shinjuku was a place with a thin tradition, and Shibuya was a place where scarcely the most delicate film of it was to be detected.

The bourgeoisie and the intelligentsia were more important than the proletariat, and they were going west. Takami did lose interest in Asakusa after the war. So did many others who had been among the celebrities during the good years. In his postscript to a collection of essays he edited about Asakusa, he says that his initial inclination was to decline the task. The Asakusa of recent years has meant so little to him. It is a statement repeated with variations in responses to a questionnaire about Asakusa carried in the same collection.

"I never go there," says Enoken. "The Asakusa I knew is thirteen and fourteen years in the past," says Mochizuki Yūko, Japan's mother. Tokugawa Musei, most famous of the *benshi* movie narrators, responds with a poem in seventeen syllables:

> The end of the year.
> The day has come
> When I neglect the place.

When Kawabata said that Asakusa offered nothing of the first quality, he cannot have been thinking of literature. The Asakusa coterie, if we may call it that—Kawabata himself, Kafū, and Takami—was superior to anything Ginza or Shinjuku has succeeded in putting together.

Asakusa attracted the attention of gifted writers as no other part of the city has been able to do, and when it went into its final decline the city lost something irreplaceable.

In a coffeehouse near where the Kokusai Gekijō, the International Theater, once stood there is a somewhat naive mural by the writer Kata Kōji. It is charming and it is sad. All the Asakusa celebrities of the interwar period are there, with Enoken in the middle. Many of them are dead and none hold forth any longer in Asakusa. The girls of the all-girl troupe at the Kokusai once patronized the coffeehouse. The guests at the hotel that has taken its place do not.

The Ginza district, generously defined so that it spills over toward Marunouchi and Hibiya Park on the west and Tsukiji on the east, had almost as many movie theaters on the eve of the war as Asakusa had. Ginza proper, in terms of movies and the performing arts, was a sort of valley between two ridges, Marunouchi-Hibiya on the west and Tsukiji on the east. Ginza proper was a place of drinking, eating, and shopping.

A large movie company dominated each of the two ridges, Tōhō the western one, Shōchiku the eastern. An Osaka firm that moved in on Tokyo late in the Meiji period, Shōchiku came to dominate Tokyo Kabuki. Its canny impresarios quickly recognized the importance of movies, and moved into them as well. Tōhō too was from Osaka. Its origins were in the all-girl Takarazuka review, Takarazuka itself being a suburb

A memento of Asakusa between the wars—Kata Kōji's mural in the Peter coffeehouse. Chaplin is seated at right; the rumpled, full-length figure in the foreground is Enoken; and Nagai Kafū stands at left, holding an umbrella

of Osaka. From the mid-thirties Tōhō began making movies. In 1932, as a company called Tokyo Takarazuka, it launched an assault on Tokyo, as Shochiku had done some decades earlier. It was never able to loosen the Shōchiku grip on Kabuki, though it tried mightily, but it did very well in the staging and distributing of reviews and movies. By the end of the decade it controlled most of the movie palaces and review and concert halls to the west of Ginza, including the Imperial and the grandest of them all, the Nihon Gekijō, or Japan Theater, on the outer castle moat. In 1943 Tōhō became the legal name of the company. It condenses Tokyo Takarazuka, making use of the first and third of the four Chinese characters with which this last is written.

The Nichigeki, as everyone calls it, had big and little movie theaters, a chorus line, and strip shows. It was not quite as big as the Shōchiku property, the Kokusai, or International. They were the two largest in the land, the one seating three thousand people, the other a few hundred more. The Kokusai was in Asakusa, however, and so fell victim to the Asakusa malaise. As has just been noted, a hotel now stands on the site. The old Nichigeki too is gone, but the Tōhō movie complex to the west of Ginza, of which a new Nichigeki is a part, now quite overshadows the Shōchiku equivalent to the east. Ginza has tended in a westerly direction, even as the city has.

Asakusa and Ginza were not in the close competition that a theater count might suggest. Greater Ginza had the Kabukiza, the "cypress stage" (the Big Apple, so to speak), which overshadowed all other Kabuki theaters. It had two other big theaters for live productions of a traditional sort. For concerts and recitals to please cosmopolitan tastes it had the Imperial and Hibiya Hall. It had the Nichigeki and the Takarazuka (known to Americans of the Occupation as the Ernie Pyle). Most important, it was the leader, the center of things, the place where one went in search of Culture. The girls at the Nichigeki could be fairly *ero* and those at the Takarazuka rather *guro,* but quality was there, as it was not at Asakusa, for those who wanted it and could pay for it.

Ginza had almost a monopoly on foreign performers, who began streaming in at about the time of the First World War, and continued to do so until the Crisis began looming too threateningly. The Shimbashi geisha was on the rise and the Yoshiwara geisha on the decline, surviving, indeed, only vestigially. The geisha of the Asakusa district proper, just behind the temple, had never had great prestige. The few children of Edo who were still around to observe Ginza so much at the center of things must have thought it all very odd. The Ginza of late Edo had not

Cafés and coffeehouses in Ginza

amounted to much in the realm of refined pleasure and vulgar entertainment, and Asakusa had been everything.

The Meiji elite had sought to improve Kabuki, by which was meant to remove it from its crass mercantile origins and make it into something elevated and edifying. The West came into Kabuki. The first and second Sadanji, gifted actors, father and son, experimented seriously with Western forms and a new realism, which did not go to the extreme of using actresses. And Western spectators came to Kabuki, and found it good, and so the Meiji effort, based largely on feelings of cultural inferiority, came to seem meaningless. Meiji wanted a theatrical form which it need not be ashamed of before the world, and was surprised to find that it already had one.

Kansai Kabuki was all the while declining. Tanizaki's Makioka sisters, all of them thoroughly and almost aggressively Osakan in their tastes, prefer Tokyo Kabuki. Several of the most famous and gifted actors of our day have Kansai origins, but they have had to make names for themselves in Tokyo.

During the interwar years geisha had their go at improvement. In 1905 the metropolitan police banned public performances by geisha. In their search for a way around the ban, the Shimbashi geisha hit upon the idea of seeking permission to sing and dance in their own theater. Determination prevailed, permission was granted, and the theater was built. Work on the Shimbashi Embujō (the second element in the name means something not far from "dance hall," though the spirit is very different) began in 1923. It ran into the earthquake and was not completed until 1925. The opening program, in April of that year, was a gala recital of classical dances by Shimbashi geisha, the Azuma Odori, Dance of the East, in contradistinction to the Miyako Odori, Dance of the Capital, or Kyoto. The geisha at first used their theater three months a year and rented it out for the other months. Having made their point, they allowed improvement to withdraw into the background. In 1934 they leased the Embujō to Shōchiku. Thereafter it became a sort of adjunct to the Kabukiza, a few paces up the canal. Dances of the East, and geisha, were less prominent. The grand recital is now an annual affair, a springtide observance.

Whatever Kawabata may have meant by the high-quality thing that was not to be found in Asakusa, the suggestion is very strong from *Scarlet Gang of Asakusa* that the sideshows in the tents and huts scattered around Asakusa Park were near the bottom. From them grew a little genre that had a very brief career and may be considered an original Japanese contribution to the performing arts. It was done in by television, a form, or device, for which Japan can claim no credit. From as early as Meiji, storytellers had used silhouette figures by way of illustration, a little as the shadow performers of southern Asia do. Early in the Shōwa Period they emerged from their shelters and took to the streets, taking with them not cumbersome figures but readily transportable cards. So the *kamishibai,* the "paper show," came to be. *Kamishibai* persons, mostly men, went the rounds of the city with their cards and boxes of sweets on bicycles. In vacant lots and the like they would summon together very young audiences, whom they would hold with illustrated stories and sell the sweets to. Their best days were in the thirties. They fell in nicely with the nationalism of the time, and those who were very young when they were flourishing tell us that their representations of Anglo-American beasts were very vivid indeed. These disappeared after 1945, though the appeal to manly little fellows who went around beating one another with bamboo swords continued. *Kamishibai* seemed an indispensable part of the city and its street life, but it quickly surrendered before television, its career having lasted a generation or so.

Another graphic form, much nearer the bottom, many would say, than *kamishibai,* also had its beginnings in the years between the wars, and continues to flourish. What are called comics are probably today the only presence gigantic enough to rival television. The cartoon, often comic, has a venerable and estimable tradition, centuries old. The panel narrative, the form that so inundates our day, had its beginnings just after the earthquake. The very earliest ones were self-contained episodes in four frames. The *Asahi* and the *Hōchi* both had cartoon strips, tending toward slapstick, from late 1923. The first extended narrative was also something the *Asahi* thought up. It began in 1926, and so "comics" became earnest. Today, in their pursuit of sex and violence, they are more than earnest. They are grim. Whether or not their origins can be blamed on the confusion that followed the earthquake, that is where they are.

Though, as we have seen, there had earlier been faltering essays in the direction of professional baseball, Babe Ruth, Lou Gehrig, and some others came to Japan in 1934, and that same year Shōriki and the *Yomiuri* put together their Giants. So professional baseball began in great earnest. A very young Japanese pitcher became a national hero by holding the Babe to one hit out of three times at bat. He finally lost this now legendary game, 1-0, but it was a moral victory if ever there could be such a thing. In 1936 a professional league got underway. It had three Tokyo teams and two each from Nagoya and Osaka. One of the Nagoya teams, the Goldfish, beat the Giants in the initial game, but the Nagoya Dragons, successors to the Goldfish, have had nothing like the success and popularity of the Giants. "Goldfish" is not a good translation. They really were the Gold Leviathans of the Castle Donjon, with reference to Nagoya Castle and the maritime monsters that decorate the ridge ends of its donjon. The names in general were more imaginative than they are today, when lions and tigers and giants, all in English, predominate. One Tokyo team was named the Senators, also in English, albeit Japan may have seen some senators but has never had one. Only the Giants (Tokyo and the *Yomiuri* still) and the Tigers (Osaka) survive of the original names.

Baseball was required to pretend, as the Crisis deepened, that it had never been anything but a Japanese game. All the American terms, "strike" and "ball" and "pitcher" and the like, part of every young person's vocabulary, were translated into Japanese. There is a very funny scene in a movie about the war in which a game has trouble proceeding because no one can remember the words with which to make it do so. The Crisis cast its shadow in other ways. A grenade-throwing contest was offered as a special attraction at a Giants game in 1942. This occurred at the Kōrakuen Stadium, which, in 1937, became the premier baseball park of the city. It stands on what had been the main Edo estate of the Mito Tokugawa family. In 1943 baseball players changed to unnumbered khaki uniforms and were required to salute one another. Professional baseball held out longer than many other diversions and in the end disbanded voluntarily. In November 1944, the Patriotic Baseball Association, as the league had become, announced a recess in its activities.

The Japanese in these years were acquiring a certain amount of international sports fame not for their baseball playing but for their swimming. If the 1940 Olympics had come to be, they might well have been a demonstration of national (not to say racial) superiority such as Hitler hoped to offer at Berlin in 1936. Though a source of great pride, however, swimming produced only intermittent bursts of enthusiasm. It was becoming sadly that way with Sumō as well. The national accomplishment has not in recent decades held the continuing interest of the nation as baseball has. Here too there were bursts of enthusiasm, a very intense one coming during the years before the Pacific War. It was brought on by the achievements of Futabayama, the most famous modern wrestler, and probably the most famous in the whole long history of the sport. He had the attention of NHK, the national broadcasting system, as no talented wrestler had had it before him.

January 15, 1939 (the year of the nonaggression pact with the Soviet Union), was a day on which the whole nation gasped. Until that evening Futabayama had had a streak of sixty-nine victories, extending over a half dozen tournaments and three years. It was and continues to be the longest in the history of Sumō. January 15 was the fourth day of the Tokyo spring tournament, so called although it takes place in the coldest part of winter. Futabayama failed to win his seventieth victory. He lost to a younger wrestler of lesser rank who some years later reached the top rank but whose place in history was really achieved during those few seconds.

Futabayama retired in 1945. For a time after the war his image suffered because of his adherence to a parvenu religion (there were scores of them in those days) that did not seem very dignified. He returned to head the Sumō Association in 1957 and clear up the confusion that had caused his predecessor to attempt suicide. This unhappy episode is one in the long history of making Sumō, or so it is said, modern and not feudal. Futabayama died, still in his fifties, in 1968. Because of the demands which great corpulence makes on the vital organs, wrestlers tend not to live long lives. Sumō did not, like baseball, declare itself out of business. It persisted through the war. Two tournaments were held in 1945, one before and one after the coming of the Americans.

In these darkling days there were other matters to keep the city interested, incidents sometimes sentimental and sometimes chilling. The city and the nation have never been afraid to risk being sentimental—or perhaps the point is that they define the expression differently, being tolerant as other places might not be of effusive emotional outpourings.

High among the warming items is the story of the faithful dog Hachikō. The name means something like "Number Eight," or possibly, since it has an intimate, affectionate ring and is masculine, "Good Old Octavius." Hachikō was an Akita dog that died on March 8, 1935. For a decade or so before that he had appeared regularly each evening at Shibuya Station, faithful to his practice of seeing his master home from work. Each night he lay waiting as train after train came in. No one could explain that the master was dead. A statue of Hachikō was erected in front of the station about a year before his death. The statue fell victim to the wartime shortage of metals, but a replacement has gone up since the war, and is one of the objects in the city almost everyone knows. Shibuya is now a most bustling *sakariba* (it was not yet within the city limits when Hachikō's master died). When people meet at the station, at Hachikō's feet is the place where they most commonly arrange to do it. There can be no mistakes.

At least one noted European was swept up in the outpourings. Shortly before Hachikō died the German architect Bruno Taut spoke admiringly in his diary of the dog he kept seeing in front of the station. (Because of

The statue of faithful Hachikō, as it is today in Shibuya

Taut's writings it was standard for a half century, especially in Japan, to deplore the architectural endeavors of the shoguns and to glorify those of the Kyoto court. A reaction has recently set in, and it is possible once more, without demonstrating one's own bad taste, to aver that that of the Tokugawas and their minions was not uniformly bad.) Hachikō had a very grand funeral, and now, stuffed, is in the collection of the National Science Museum at Ueno.

As with so many warming stories, there is another side to this one, having to do with Hachikō's motives, of which we will never know the whole truth. Such observers of his behavior as the novelist Ooka Shōhei have held that he did not go to the station in the evening at all, but hung around it the whole day through, waiting to be fed. The station attendants were kinder to him than the people at home—and it may be that they recognized a good story when they saw one. If so, they were very successful. They gave Shibuya its most famous landmark.

Tokyo criminals have always had a certain flair, and sometimes it has seemed that a wish to be apprehended is among their peculiarities. The Tokyo police probably deserve their reputation for effectiveness, and yet one sometimes wonders. How would they perform if they had the un-ruly, uncooperative citizenry of Chicago or Marseilles to put up with? There was, for instance, the preaching thief who broke into more than a hundred houses from 1927 into 1929. He never harmed anyone, and did not mind being seen. After having chosen what he wanted to take with him, he would stay for a while and talk with his victims, pointing out to them the advantages of watchdogs and well-bolted doors. He left behind fingerprints in the house of a rice merchant in Itabashi, in the northern suburbs, and yet he went on stealing and preaching for some months before he was apprehended, early in 1929. He proved to be a craftsman in the building trades.

The most celebrated criminals of Meiji were murderesses, and the most celebrated criminal of early Shōwa was a murderess. The early de-cades of the twentieth century did not produce a Tokyo murderess whose accomplishments became legendary, as did those of Takahashi O-den in early Meiji. To say, as is often said, that the newspapers turned with eager delight to the case of O-sada for relief from the gloom of the February 26 Incident, the military rising of that day in 1936, would probably be to ex-aggerate. They probably would have loved O-sada in any case. The gloom seems to have dispelled itself rather quickly, especially in the poorer parts of the city, in which O-sada did her thing. Retail sales fell off drastically in rich Nihombashi, and especially at its richest store, the Mitsukoshi, but

O-sada the murderess under arrest

were relatively unaffected at the Matsuya in Asakusa. Expensive seats at the Kabukiza went unsold, but not cheap ones. It is true that there were also empty seats at the Asakusa review houses—but we have seen that they had High City intellectual types among their fanciers.

It was in May 1936, in any event, that Abe Sada, familiarly known as O-sada, did it. For a week she had been staying at a *machiai,* an inn catering to amorous trysters, with her employer, a restaurant owner in the western part of the city. The *machiai* was in Arakawa, that most populous of the new wards, near the northern limits. The man was in his early forties, she in her early thirties. On May 18 he was found strangled. His sexual organs had been cut away and were not on the premises. On May 20 O-sada was apprehended near Shinagawa Station. She had the organs on her person, and his underwear as well.

She was sentenced to a prison term and released from the Tochigi Women's Prison in 1941. For some years she ran a drinking place on the outskirts of Asakusa. Then she disappeared. Recently she has been traced to a Buddhist nunnery in the Kansai. Predictably, she had imitators, none of them remotely as famous as she.

Much black humor was inspired by the O-sada affair. The verb "to cut" also functions as "to punch," as of a bus ticket. Great was the merriment, therefore, when the "red collar" girls on the buses would go about with their standard petition: "Allow me, please, to cut those that have not already been cut." The murder also inspired a superior work of art which demonstrates that the Japanese can still turn out fine pornography, as they did under the shoguns. The moving picture *In the Realm of the Senses* contains hard-core scenes, and has great visual beauty and a suffocating intensity; and it is a reasonably authentic retelling of the O-sada story. The actor who played O-sada's friend is still very prominent. The actress who played O-sada has quite disappeared from sight.

Voguish words of the time inform us with concreteness and immediacy of what we would have known anyway, that Taishō democracy was over and more somber times had come. Neologisms stream in and out of Japanese at a rate perhaps unrivaled among major languages, and tell us what is fashionable and socially acceptable. The minister of education did not succeed in evicting "mama" and "papa" from the language, but newspapers and radio and the advertising agencies, overwhelmingly in and controlled from Tokyo, could be brought into line and made to use only worthwhile words, appropriate to the Crisis.

As late as the mid-thirties we still have foreign words and expressions in ample numbers, some of them imported in finished form, some of them fabricated from imported elements. "Air girl," for stewardess, has disappeared from the language. "Yo-yo" might still be recognized by fair numbers of people, but the word itself is no longer to be found in standard dictionaries. "Hiking" is still very much with us.

Sufu was among the last foreign words in vogue before the decade of exclusiveness and xenophobia began, and widely used neologisms came for the most part to have native or Chinese origins. It would be as difficult to eliminate a Chinese influence from Japanese as a Latin one from English. One might as well try to eliminate the language itself. *Sufu* remains in the language, but probably most Japanese would be as slow as most foreigners to recognize its foreignness. It is an acronym from the Japanese pronunciation of "staple fiber," the phonetic patterns of the language requiring a muted "u" after each of the initial consonants. Good cotton and wool almost disappeared during the war. *Sufu* took their place. Some varieties tended to go to pieces in water, and so sea bathing suffered. Being foreign and decadent, it would have suffered anyway.

Many neologisms from the xenophobic decade, such as "spiritual mobilization," are merely cant. They do not say what they mean, in this instance "totalitarianism." Others have sinister, threatening overtones. One hopes that the age which produced them will not come again. They speak of loyalty and patriotism gone mad, and they speak of mindlessness. "The eight directions under one roof" could mean nothing more baneful than that all persons are siblings, but the mood of the times left only one possible interpretation, that it was a kind of manifest destiny for the whole world to become Japanese.

It must be admitted that some of the patriotic coinages of the decade are rather clever. "The ABCD encirclement" is good, and contains delicate irony, perhaps unobserved by the coiners. The encirclers are the Americans, the British, the Chinese, and the Dutch. It may be that the French, down in Indochina, got left out because they did not fit the alphabetic sequence. That and the nonaggression pact may be the explanation in the case of the Russians. Be these omissions as they may, the expression could not have caught on without the aid of the Roman alphabet. So a device from hated Europe was put to the uses of Great Japan and its xenophobia.

Kokutai meichō is the sort of thing that lay in wait for Taishō democracy. It is rendered by the biggest Japanese-English dictionary as "clarification of the fundamental concept of national polity." The expression "national polity" *(kokutai)* may be put in the realm of cant. It sometimes seems that among the claims of the Japanese to superior uniqueness is that they alone have a polity. The longer expression speaks of an anti-intellectual response to a reasoned and intellectual position.

In 1935 the constitutional scholar Minobe Tatsukichi, whose son was governor of Tokyo from 1967 to 1979, following "the Olympic governor," published what has come to be known as the theory of the emperor as an organ of the state. This produced a violent reaction on the part of those who thought that the emperor, if not identical with the state, presided over it as a father presides over a family. The "clarification" movement found its highest expression in *The Essence of National Polity (Kokutai no Hongi)* of 1937. Put together by the Ministry of Education, this treatise condemned individualism, and informed Japanese that they belonged unquestioningly to the emperor as head of the mystical family state; fulfillment lay in service and submission and self-denial. Minobe was prosecuted for lèse-majesté, but no sentence was handed down. He resigned from the House of Peers, to which he had been appointed after his retirement from Tokyo Imperial University. All his works were banned. In 1936 he was attacked by right-wing radicals but escaped with minor wounds. After 1945 he unsuccessfully opposed rewriting the Meiji constitution. He died in 1948, a legend and something of a national hero.

It is but one four-character expression and one series of incidents having to do with one man and his ideas, but in it we have the mood of the
times and the travails of the city, intellectual center of the land. Minobe
was an independent thinker and a survivor of Taishō democracy. The left
wing had already been broken as a concerted movement before his great
agony began. *Tenkō* is among the voguish words of the early thirties. It
means something like apostasy, recanting, or disavowal, and is applied to
persons, and especially writers and intellectuals, who renounced Marxist
beliefs and turned to serving the national polity with more or less enthusiasm. There are many ways, chief among them, perhaps, geographic isolation, to account for the fact that Japan had no organized resistance and no
selfless underground martyrs. In any event, it had none. *Tenkō* prevailed.

In 1946, after such grim wartime expressions as "Anglo American
beasts" and "a hundred million fighting to the end" (four Chinese characters state this succinctly), we again have bright and often flippant cosmopolitanism, with such expressions as "après-guerre," suggesting sometimes hedonism and sometimes new beginnings, and "hubbahubba."

As there were voguish, trendy words, so too of course there were
vogues and trends. All cities have them, but at least since a cult of rabbit fanciers sprang up in early Meiji, Tokyo has had them more furiously
and frequently than most places. In 1932 women suddenly all had permanent waves, Japan having learned to produce the equipment necessary
for creating them. The year 1933, as we have seen, was that of the yo-yo.
Slightly later there was a craze for stamps, not the postage kind but the
rubber kind, provided by famous places to give evidence that the earnest,
thorough traveler has been to them. The American writer Helen Mears
describes, in *The Year of the Wild Boar*, how the acquiring of stamps
seemed to take on its own obsessive importance, greater than the sights
behind them. Her boar year, last in the Chinese cycle of twelve, was 1935.
As cycles went in the first half of the twentieth century, it was a tranquil
one, despite assassinations and the beginnings of the Crisis. The preceding one contained the earthquake, the succeeding one the Pacific War.

Nagai Kafū lamented the loss of harmony when Western techniques and
motifs began intruding upon the streets of Edo. Yet it may be said that
the Western buildings of Meiji had their own kind of harmony. When,
in monumental public building, the wildly fanciful architecture of early
Meiji gave way to brick and stone, the major buildings and complexes
that resulted, such as Mitsubishi Londontown in Marunouchi and the

Bank of Japan in Nihombashi, may not have looked much like Edo, but
they did look like one another, and like Western prototypes, a statement
that cannot be made about the very earliest excursions into the Western.
Now concrete and all its plasticity were coming to the fore, and so, in the
years after the earthquake, the eclectic jumble—the miscellany—of today
began to emerge. It began to take shape, one might say, but it really has
no shape. The twentieth century is the century of fragmentation, and it
had come to Tokyo, which was pulled in more directions and ended up
with a larger fragment count than most cities.

There were the old and new European styles, modern utilitarian box
and Queen Anne side by side in Marunouchi, and there were old Japanese styles done in modern materials. The main building of the National
Museum in Ueno and the Kabukiza are probably the chief surviving examples of this last, but there are many others, such as the priestly lodgings behind the Asakusa Kannon. Though gutted in 1945 and renovated
with a simpler roofline, the Kabukiza is not much different from the
building that went up after the earthquake. The museum is relatively
plain and utilitarian, with a roof like that of many a lecture hall in many
a temple, though none are so big, and an entrance bay that also looks like
a temple. It was finished in 1937, on the site of a Meiji building by the
English architect Josiah Conder which was badly damaged in 1923. (The
National Museum did not become that until 1947, when jurisdiction

The Kabukiza, as reconstructed after the earthquake

passed from the royal household to the Ministry of Education.) An earlier and a later building flank this main one: a Renaissance building in stone put up late in Meiji and a very modern glass-and-concrete structure put up since the war. They are an interesting progression: reading from left to right as one faces the entrance to the main building, a replica of something Western, a somewhat traditional building in Western materials, and a building which eschews Japanese forms but in its basic principles is not far from traditional Japanese architecture. Many will say that the central building is dishonest, pretending to be something that it is not. None of the three is shockingly unpleasant, but they are diverse. They are what the twentieth century has made the city.

It must be added that many buildings from the interwar period, such as Hibiya Hall and the Daiichi Hotel in Shimbashi, built for the Olympics that never happened, are distinctly unpleasant. They look as if no one, least of all the architects, had expected them to last so long.

Then there are curious exercises in styles neither Western nor Japanese. Chief among them, probably, is the Honganji Temple in Tsukiji, not far from the fish market, the villa where General and Mrs. Grant stayed, and the site of the Meiji foreign settlement. The principal east country temple of the pietist Shin sect, the Honganji was in Edo from the early seventeenth century and has been in Tsukiji since the great fire of 1657. It was twice burned in Meiji. At the time of the earthquake the

The post-earthquake Honganji Temple, Tsukiji

complex—much grander than now exists—had a main hall in an imposing courtly style. This too was lost. The rebuilding, in stone, from
1931 to 1935, is a representation of an Indian temple. So it seeks to
take us back to the origins of Buddhism, to which the name Honganji
also adverts. One of a kind, it looks stranger, there in one of the more
unchanged parts of the city, than would a glass block from New York.
A lady in Tanizaki's *The Makioka Sisters* calls it "that odd building." It is
highly unlikely that she would have so characterized a foreign exercise
of the Western sort.

The wards of the old Low City, inundated at increasingly brief intervals through Meiji, have been relatively free from flooding since the
completion of the Arakawa Drainage Channel shortly before the earthquake. (It was on the banks of this that the young lady in Kafū's *Katsushika Romance* had her refreshment stand. See page 385.) Parts of the city
traditionally immune from such troubles, on the other hand, came to
be readily and regularly immersed when rain waters were too much for
drains. Hibiya, right at the heart of the city and in front of the royal palace, is an example. The explanation is that waters which once went into
canals had now, the canals having been filled in, nowhere to go. (Similarly, the disappearance of paddy lands in the suburbs is blamed for the
greater frequency of floods in the Meiji Low City. They acted as storage
reservoirs during heavy rains.) Land subsidence, chiefly from the consumption of underground water, has been worst in the wards east of the
river, parts of which lie below sea level; but such central and technically
advanced places as Hibiya have also been affected. Some of the older
buildings have their foundations exposed, so that they stand an awkward
distance above the ground.

The city limits had been expanded in 1932 to include the five contiguous
counties, but the debate over what to do about the duplex government,
municipal and prefectural, went on for more than a decade afterward.
The interests of the ward part, the county part, and the prefecture did
not coincide, especially as regards money. There was increasing agreement, as the Crisis dragged on and deepened, that Tokyo as the capital
called for close scrutiny, and perhaps direct control by the national government. In July 1943, by which time it was becoming clear to intelligent
and informed people that the Pacific War was not going to end happily,
reform of the Tokyo government was put through by proclamation.

The proclamation was issued on the first day of June and went into
effect on the first day of July. The discussions that led up to it were kept

secret, for it was believed that they might reveal information useful to the British and American beasts. The Doolittle raids of just upward of a year before would seem to have produced the necessary sense of urgency. Reorganization fell short of the more sweeping proposals, which would have made prefecture and city one and done away with the old county part. The latter remained. What the proclamation did chiefly was abolish the city government and the office of mayor. Tokyo-fu, the Tokyo Metropolitan Prefecture, became Tokyo-to, the Tokyo Capital District.

The powers of the wards were a matter of concern, since nothing now stood between them and the prefectural government. Fears that reform would lead to a loss of autonomy proved to be well founded. The wards had fewer powers than cities and towns elsewhere in the country.

In a sense the proclamation and reorganization only made explicit what had already become fact. It brought the city more clearly and openly under the contol of the Home Ministry, which already had control over the police, including the notorious thought police, and over the appointment of prefectural governors. Even before 1943 the Home Ministry had a very large say in the functioning of the city government. Of the nine men who were mayor during the less than seventeen years between the change of reigns and the abolition of the office, five were former officials of the ministry. By way of emphasizing that Tokyo was different from the other prefectures, the governor was called not a *chiji,* like other governors, but a *chōhan,* which means something like "chief executive." The first chief executive had been home minister under Hiranuma Kiichirō, who spent his last years in Sugamo Prison as a first-class war criminal, and mayor and military governor of Singapore, which the occupying Japanese renamed the Shōwa of the South. He had been in charge of preparations for the reorganization of 1943.

The defeat of the Olympics by a metal shortage and the expunging of foreign words from baseball were by no means the only signs of the austere times that lay ahead. The age of the ersatz arrived soon after the beginning of the China Incident. Bamboo and ceramics replaced metals for cooking and tableware. The hegemony of *sufu,* staple fiber, has already been remarked upon. In 1938 appeared the smelly, fuming, sometimes asphyxiating charcoal taxicabs that continued to symbolize deprivation in the years after the war.

The General Mobilization Law and charcoal-burning cabs came into being at about the same time. Essentially the direction of the nation's efforts was turned toward technology and production, toward bringing the Crisis to a happy conclusion. There is a similarity to the tactics used in the great postwar trade campaign. A nation's inclinations and institutions do not change easily. A major difference is that big business objected, late in 1938, to certain provisions having to do with dividends and loans, and forced a compromise. This was the only serious snarl in application of the law. When the great trade campaign was being launched after the war, the army was not strong enough to return the favor. Neither was the other natural enemy, the labor movement.

The economic mobilization of recent years has not taken the joy from life as the military kind did. Two installments of Tanizaki's *The Makioka Sisters* appeared in the magazine *Chūō Kōron* early in 1943. Then it was banned, the contents, about life in a bourgeois suburb of Osaka during the early years of the Crisis, being deemed frivolous. Tanizaki went on writing, but the novel was not published in full until after the war.

The years of the Pacific War and the years immediately preceding were grim, certainly, but the authorities did not go as far as they might have gone. Tanizaki and Kafū were never compelled to break their silence, as they might have been in a thoroughly totalitarian state. Some movie directors managed to pursue their own interests; some almost managed to make fun of censorship. Not all movie houses were required to close, though all of the big ones, and most of the Ginza ones, had closed by the spring of 1944. Some were allowed to reopen again before the end of the war. Late in 1944 the Nichigeki (the Japan Theater), near Ginza, the Imperial Theater in Marunouchi, and the Kokusai (International) in Asakusa were commandeered for the manufacture of the incendiary balloons that were intended to drift across the Pacific on westerly winds and set America afire.

Kabuki did not entirely disappear. In its very worst days there were traveling companies. The largest theaters in Tokyo, Osaka, and Kyoto were all closed in March 1944, but the Shimbashi Embujō was allowed to reopen after a short recess. The great Kikugorō was playing there on the day in 1945 when the Embujō, along with the Kabukiza, was gutted by American firebombs. Performances after the reopening were limited to five hours a day, with the same program twice repeated. This was a sad falling off from the days when the devotee could sit for nine and ten hours in a theater and not have to put up with any repetition at all. The Tokyo Theater (Tōkyō Gekijō), third in the Shōchiku trio east of Ginza, survived the bombings, and Kabuki was playing there down to mid-August 1945. It was soon to find itself belabored by the other side. Wartime censors disliked the raffish heroes of the early nineteenth century, whom, with the best Kabuki of that day and perhaps of all days, they found decadent. The American Occupation was suspicious of the grand historic tradition, which it thought militaristic.

Already a year and a half before Pearl Harbor, the Crisis was having its effect on the geisha districts. The expensive restaurants at which they entertained (the establishments commonly called "geisha houses" in English) were required to close at eleven, and geisha to cease entertaining at ten. The districts were not required to close down completely until the spring of 1944. People in a position to close them down both needed and enjoyed them. Some geisha belonged particularly to the military police, some to the ordinary police. Then there were army and navy geisha and the geisha who enjoyed the special patronage of the civil bureaucracy. They formed a considerable part of the intelligence network. This was in an old tradition. The Shimbashi and Akasaka districts had become prosperous in large measure because the military and civil services condescended to use them.

New taxes after the beginning of the Pacific War made geisha more expensive. Then finally, on March 5, 1944, all the geisha restaurants closed. They stayed open almost until dawn the night before. Many geisha donned the baggy trousers that were the feminine uniform in the last months of the Crisis and went off to work in munitions and supply factories. The apprentice geisha *(hangyoku)* of Shimbashi formed a brass band which, toward the improvement of morale, had concerts in the palace plaza. In 1942 Kafū had seen the ladies of Tamanoi mustered at a shrine to give thanks for the fall of Singapore.

The all-girl troupe at the Takarazuka Theater, immediately west of Ginza, had its final performance on March 4, 1944. The crowds were so great and dense that the police faced them with swords unsheathed.

Western popular music, so strongly under the influence of the American beasts, virtually disappeared. It did disappear as public performance, and people had to keep their gramophones low if they wanted to listen to records. Classical music was another matter. There was an inherent contradiction in the great campaign to purify Japanese culture: two of the most musical of peoples, the Germans and the Italians, were Japanese allies, and the Japanese went on hoping that the Russians would stay out of the tiff with the A, the B, the C, and the D. Russian and German music were performed almost to the end. Hibiya Hall survived the May 1945 raids that destroyed almost everything in the vicinity, including the prefectural library. The Japan Philharmonic had its last concert there in June. It presented Beethoven's Ninth, a remarkable achievement in a city many of whose musicians had gone to war and whose communications and transportation had broken down. The exhortation in the last movement that the masses hug and kiss may have been taken as another way of inviting the eight directions to assemble under one roof.

The more expensive and elegant restaurants, such as those with geisha, had all closed their doors before the heavy bombings came, but lesser establishments in large numbers—some three thousand of them, the best estimate is—remained in business all through the war. Then there were drinking places known as "people's saloons" *(kokumin no sakaba)*, which provided rather chilly comfort. Takami Jun, in his diary, described a visit to one, in Ginza. Each customer was allowed a bottle of beer, a glass of draft beer, or a flagon of sake. Discipline was not good. Customers were divided into parties of ten for admission, but when the time came for Takami's party to be admitted it contained eleven people. Someone had sneaked in. It was possible to get special favors if you knew the manager. This information Takami had from a Yose performer who did know a manager.

The Crisis had some benevolent aspects. It brought, as we have seen, a fall in the suicide rate. Whether or not the closing of gambling establishments is benevolent, it too occurred. Takami reported that until the beginning of the China Incident the regions north of the Asakusa Kannon were dotted with little gambling places, each with a lookout patrolling the street. Their patrons were such people as the wives of the neighborhood greengrocers. Then the Incident began, and they all closed down. The war was a good time for those who wished to get married. If the Japanese were a superior race and if the eight directions were to do the wise thing, why then they must be numerous. They must increase and multiply. So a metropolitan wedding hall was opened, for the inexpensive and efficient production of weddings. During its best times, midway through the Pacific War, it produced some two or three hundred a month.

The Ueno Zoo had its happy events and its great sorrow. A baby giraffe born in May 1942 was named Minami, "South," by way of encouraging the Japanese push into Southeast Asia and the islands. Then the time came, in August and September 1943, to kill dangerous animals. The corpses were dissected at an army veterinary hospital and the notable ones were stuffed. The remains were buried under a memorial stone in the zoo. In a search for funds to maintain what was left, a third as many birds and beasts as in 1940, the zoo took to breeding and selling chicks, ducklings, and piglets. At the end of the war there were vegetable patches on the grounds. The largest animals left were three camels, two giraffes (including Minami), and a water buffalo. A hundred forty firebombs, more or less, fell on the zoo on April 13, 1945. The saddest stories one hears are of the elephants. The animals were to be disposed of by poisoning. The elephants refused to eat the poisoned food. The keepers could not bring themselves to shoot their charges, which went on begging until they starved to death. The most vigorous and truculent died first. There was talk of sending the smaller of the remaining two off to Sendai, but this was rejected by the chief keeper as impractical. In their cages, out of sight behind black-and-white drapes, the two struggled to get to their feet as ceremonies for the repose of their spirits proceeded. They seemed to think that if they did tricks they would be fed.

The first American air raid, the raid commanded by Lieutenant Colonel James A. Doolittle, came just after noon on a fine spring day, April 18, 1942. Thirteen carrier-based B-25 bombers flew in low enough for strafings, earlier and from a greater distance than had been planned. A Japanese patrol boat spotted the carrier that morning and sent off a wireless message before it was sunk. The message arrived in Tokyo and was treated carelessly. The view was that there might or might not be a raid and in any event it would not come for a while. Ten minutes elapsed after the planes were sighted before an alarm was sounded. A similar insouciance, having to do perhaps with the myth that the Japanese spirit would prevail over all, is to be observed in later and far more serious raids. Three of the thirteen aircraft dropped their bombs on Kanagawa Prefecture to the south of Tokyo, and three of the sixteen that took off from the carrier went to bomb Nagoya, Osaka, and Kobe. Nagoya got more than its intended share, because the Osaka flight bombed it by mistake.

In Tokyo the damage was chiefly along the northern and southern fringes of the city, although there was also damage in Ushigome Ward, just to the west of the palace. The palace itself was not damaged. The casualty total was 364, including thirty-nine dead. About two hundred fifty buildings were damaged.

Two-thirds of the deaths were in the southern part of the city, but the single one in Katsushika Ward, at the far northeast, aroused the greatest indignation. It was the one the newspapers settled upon. A thirteen-year-old schoolboy was killed by strafing. Probably he would not have died had he not lived in a district notorious for its want of medical facilities, but evidence of what the American beasts were capable of was there for everyone to see.

So was evidence of fibbing by Japanese military authorities. The first announcement from the Tokyo army command was that nine planes had been downed. It was, as we have noted, a fine, clear spring day, and no one in the city had observed the downing of a single plane. Perhaps, the joke had it, the defenders of the city meant that they had succeeded in shooting empty air. The Japanese are great punsters, and the words for "nine planes" and "thin air" are homophonous. In fact the Japanese downed none of the planes. All sixteen flew safely across Japan and on to or just short of the Asian mainland. There the crews had varied experiences. Eight men were captured by the Japanese and three among them were put to death. The largest number fell into the hands of Chinese guerrillas and made their way home through India. General Tōjō, the prime minister, chanced to be in the air that afternoon, flying off on a military inspection. He had a close brush with the raiders.

Hibiya Park, which had lost its palmettos and become an artillery emplacement in February 1936, now lost the tops of all its trees in the direction of the palace and became an antiaircraft emplacement. Certain of the Doolittle pilots had been so brazen as to fly over His Majesty, although they had done him no harm. This must not happen again. Things got worse and worse for the park, as for other parks. The lawns and parterres presently became vegetable patches. Iron artifacts were stripped away. Some bronze remained, to meet the hostility of the Americans, who found certain of its applications warlike.

The first serious raids, on the southern island of Kyushu, were mounted from China. The Saipan landings occurred in mid-June 1944. When next, on November 1, American planes were sighted over Tokyo, they came from the Marianas. They were for reconnaissance and dropped no bombs. Bombs came on November 24. The early raids, through February, by both island-based and carrier-based planes, were heavy ones aimed at military targets, mostly in the northern part of the city and in the counties. There were waves of planes all through February 16 and 17. The chief targets were air bases in the suburbs. The Japanese loss of planes was heavy, and the ability to defend the city was grievously reduced.

The Hama Detached Palace, by the bay just south of the Tsukiji fish market, may be called a military target because, like Hibiya Park, it had been devastated to make antiaircraft emplacements. Originally the bayside villa of the shoguns, it was until 1916 the place for large royal receptions, and until the late nineteenth century it provided lodgings for eminent foreign guests. General and Mrs. U. S. Grant stayed there in 1879, though the building in which they stayed was demolished in 1899. All of the central buildings went in the raids of late November 1944.

The incendiary raids began in March. The most dreadful of them, on the night of March 9-10, did very much what the fires after the earthquake had done: destroyed the Low City. Waves of bombers came in for two and a half hours from just past midnight. The planners of the raids had hit upon what may have been the urban concentration most hospitable to fires in the whole world, and they had hit upon the proper season. As is so often the case in early spring, strong winds were coming down that night from the north and west. The progress of the war had probably made the decision for the planners. The capture of Iwo in February and March and the decimation of the Kantō air defenses in the heavy raids that preceded the incendiary attacks made mass, low-level runs as nearly safe as they could be.

Nagai Kafū's house in Azabu was among the hundreds of thousands burned that night (the damage was not limited to the Low City). Having finally found refuge in the house of a relative, he lay down to sleep, his diary entry concludes, with columns of sparks in his eyes and the shriek of the wind in his ears. No incendiary bombs landed near his house. Sparks were blown in from a considerable distance away. We have vivid descriptions of what it was like to be in a rain of incendiary bombs. It was like "a fox's wedding," a profusion of fox fires or will-o'-the-wisps. Many of the bombs burst in midair and sent out hissing blue tendrils.

Some two-fifths of the city went up in flames. The four wards between the Sumida River and the Arakawa Drainage Channel almost disappeared. Between seventy and eighty thousand people are believed to have died that night. This is some three-quarters of the death count from all raids on the city.

It was a night of horror, and the Americans and their bombers were the agents. Yet a few words may be slipped in by way of mitigation for what they did. The wards east of the river were, along with the wards nearest Yokohama, the most heavily industrialized parts of the city. The pattern of industrialization beyond the Sumida was so fragmented that it would have been impossible to separate implicitly military targets from purely civilian ones. Foresight was, moreover, lamentably bad, and measures to prevent the disaster scarcely existed. Through the first months of 1945 people were actually discouraged from leaving the city. Their patriotic duty was to stay at their posts. The contrast between the March raid and the August one on Hachiōji, out in the county part of the prefecture, is telling. Warned by handbills and quite prepared to believe them, the people of Hachiōji fled. There were only two hundred twenty-five deaths, and the number and weight of the bombs were higher than in the March raid.

Looking eastward across the Sumida after the major air raids of 1945

Defenses were totally ineffective, even though there had been defense drills from as early as 1943 and though the bombers came in low and along predictable courses. The first alarms were not sounded for the March raid until several minutes after the first bombs fell. A false alarm would have had a bad effect on morale—and who would have taken the blame if the emperor and his lady, to no purpose, had been required to dress themselves in the middle of the night and move to a shelter?

Along with most of Asakusa, most of the great Kannon Temple was destroyed that night. It had survived the earthquake. In 1923 the temple precincts had been for Kawabata a field of flowers, bright with refugees from regions to the north. Several bombs fell on the main hall at about one-thirty in the morning. It was consumed in about two hours. The pagoda went too, though some outbuildings and one gate survived. A common view was that it had been a great mistake on the part of the authorities to requisition the statue of the great Meiji actor Danjūrō that stood on the grounds and send it to war. The statue had been given credit for turning back the flames in 1923. The innermost sanctuary, a small, portable shrine or feretory, was removed and brought back to a temporary hall late in 1945, and, a decade later, to a partially rebuilt main hall. Almost no one knows whether or not it contains, as averred by the clergy, a small golden image of almost indescribable antiquity, because almost no one has been allowed to look inside. The lost buildings, from early in the Tokugawa Period, were among the oldest in the city.

Because the corpses had to be disposed of speedily and neither fuel nor manpower was available in large enough measure for cremation, most were given temporary burial. The parks along and east of the river became cemeteries. Of some ninety thousand reburials in the years after the war, eighty-five thousand were in a mass grave at the Earthquake Memorial Hall (see page 299). Identification was next to impossible. Only the remaining five thousand had claimants. Wandering through cemeteries, one is always coming upon tombstones that bear the date March 10, 1945. Few of the graves beneath contain bones.

The next big raids came in April, from the thirteenth to the fifteenth. They did great damage in the northern and western parts of the city and along the industrial belt from Tokyo into Kanagawa Prefecture. Among the casualties were the main buildings of the Meiji Shrine, southwest of the old city limits. Raids in late May took away about half of what remained of the old city, chiefly in and around Ginza and southward and westward into the High City. The main building of the palace was destroyed on May 25, and the royal family moved to a secondary building. There had earlier been talk of moving the royal residence across the Tama River into Kanagawa Prefecture. Now there was talk of moving it to the mountain fastnesses of central Japan. The move would doubtless have taken place if the army had had its way and the nation had fought to the end. It would have meant moving the capital, for the capital is where the head of state resides.

Several newspaper offices were gutted, as were the Kabukiza and the Shimbashi Embujō. Two large universities, Keiō and what was to become the University of Education, suffered heavy damages. The great Zōjōji, the southern of the two Tokugawa mortuary temples, was almost completely destroyed. The May raids also did great damage to the public transportation system. The trolley lines were virtually incapacitated. These were the last important raids on the ward part of the city. The raid on Hachiōji, the main population center of the county part, has already been mentioned.

The total number of American flights over Tokyo in 1944 and 1945 was upward of four thousand. The number of bombers in the March raid was smaller than in the major raids of mid-April and late May. There were about three hundred, as against more than five hundred on May 24 and almost as many on the two following days. If the term "casualties" is taken to include homeless as well as dead and wounded, then the effects of the April and May raids, though far behind those of March, were to some degree comparable. More than half as many people were affected in both cases.

The air raids produced rumors and magic. The rumors tended to be wishful. One of the grander ones held that Japan had developed a fleet of bombers powered by pine resin and capable of flying off to bomb America and flying back again. The Shiseidō, the most prominent maker of cosmetics and the like, active since Meiji in the endeavor (as its advertising said) to give Japanese women pellucid skins like Western women, had a big order in 1944 for expensive perfumes. Everyone learned about the transaction, which produced ominous rumors. The Russians were coming. The perfumes were to please the wives of their elite. Actually they seem to have been traded for Chinese metals.

Just as today there are magic potions, such as bean soup or a brew made from pine cones, for warding off the AIDS virus, so there were charms for keeping bombs at a distance. One was a very simple breakfast of rice and pickles—but it would not work unless others were let in on the secret. Goldfish also did good service in fending off bombs. The owners of houses that survived sometimes had a bad time. People would move in on them uninvited. Since everyone had a share in the disaster, what could be more natural than that housing should be common and undivided as well? Pilferers and looters had the same justification.

A program of offering temporary shelter to victims of the raids was abandoned as hopeless after the March attack. Thereafter the emphasis was on relocation. For the weak and obscure much of it was forced. Fearing that they might never be allowed to return, people were reluctant to leave. Those who wanted to go and were not part of mass relocations could find it difficult. The novelist Satomi Ton, in an autobiographical story called "Putting the Old Woman Out to Die" ("Obasute"), described the undignified process of obtaining tickets. "Bribery at the market rate seemed to him a nearer thing to honesty and a more manly thing than mingily going from acquaintance to acquaintance of acquaintance, finally getting an introduction to a railway functionary, and escaping with only a modest gift."

Between February and August more than four million people left Tokyo, both voluntarily and under various degrees of duress. A great many of the three million or so who stayed were without adequate shelter. The police estimated that on September 1, 1945, one in ten among the Tokyo citizenry was living in an air-raid shelter or some other sort of temporary abode.

The main municipal library had since late Meiji been in Hibiya Park. Plans for relocation in a remoter part of the prefecture took shape after the Doolittle raid. At first it was by truck, then (one is reminded of the Chinese under Japanese attack) by handcart and knapsack. It was not completed in time for the May raids. The library building and some two hundred thousand volumes fell victim to the bombs. The Hibiya library opened temporary offices in the Kyōbashi library, the only one among the branch libraries that escaped damage, and did not return to Hibiya until 1947.

Maps of the areas affected by the fires show much wider destruction than in 1923. The pattern was similar: far worse damage to the east than to the west. One of the fifteen wards of 1923 escaped fire. None of the thirty-five of 1945 did, though the scattering is sparse around the fringes, save to the south, where the northern extension of the Tokyo-Yokohama industrial belt had grown up. If a line is drawn north and south a bit to the east of Ueno and Tokyo stations, then almost everything east of it as far as the Arakawa Drainage Channel—farther east than the eastern limits of the Meiji city, this is to say—is gone. To the west large pockets were spared in the vicinity of Ueno Station. As in 1923, the flat part of Shitaya Ward disappeared and the hilly part remained. This last was suburban when Tokyo was Edo and a part of the Meiji High City distinguished for its intellectual and artistic sorts, and today it is probably the part of the city in which we can best sense what mercantile Edo and Meiji were like. It would not have survived if the wind had been blowing in the opposite direction that night in March.

The High City was, as in 1923, a patchwork of places burned and places spared. Of the twenty new wards, Jōtō, along the lower reaches of the Arakawa Channel, was almost totally destroyed, and all of the other wards along the fringes of the old fifteen, including the one that contained a part of Shinjuku, were badly damaged. An almost solid expanse of burned-over wastes stretched westward from Shinjuku as far as Nakano and the eastern borders of Setagaya Ward, the farthest of the thirty-five to the southwest. A solid and unbroken if somewhat winding band of wastelands stretched all across the city from the westernmost wards to the Arakawa Channel. There was no band by any means that extensive after the earthquake. Starting from the eastern part of Setagaya Ward and Suginami Ward and proceeding past Shinjuku and Kanda, or, alternatively, along the south side of the palace and on through Nihombashi, one could in the summer of 1945 have walked all the way to the Arakawa Channel upon nothing but cinders.

Four of the thirty-five wards suffered more than ten thousand fatalities. All were in the Low City, and among them they accounted for more than 80 percent of the total. It is a situation that once more calls to mind 1923. Punishment was then said to have come down upon decadence, and it might now be said to have come down upon military aggression. It descended most cruelly, however, on people who had little to do with decadence in the first instance and the making of aggressive schemes in the second.

Parts of the Low City were virtually depopulated. If one takes the population of February 1944 as 100, the populations of Honjo and Fukagawa, the two wards east of the river among the old fifteen, were down to 4 and 6, respectively. Fewer than ten thousand people were left in Honjo. Of the fifteen old wards, the southernmost, Shiba, had a higher proportion of bitter-enders than any other. Its population in June 1945 was still more than a third what it had been in February 1944. Of the twenty new wards, Jōtō, immediately east of Fukagawa, was down to 5 from the 1944 base. No other among the twenty suffered a loss of as much as four-fifths of its population. The old city was the worst hit, and, as in 1923, the flat parts of it worst of all. Some districts along the fringes of the city had larger populations in the spring of 1945 than in early 1944.

The war cabinet, that of General Tōjō, resigned in the summer of 1944. In May 1945 the Germans surrendered. Early in August came the atomic bombs. On one of the two days between them the Russians entered the war, invading Manchuria and Korea. On August 15, for the first time in the history of the land, the emperor made a radio broadcast. He announced acceptance of the Potsdam Declaration. Since less than half the Tokyo citizenry is old enough to remember the bombings, less than half is old enough to remember the broadcast. Many who do remember it did not understand it. Reception was generally poor, and the language was stilted. The general import was soon clear enough, however. He was obviously not exhorting them to get out their bamboo spears and await the enemy along the beaches and in the hills. So only one explanation seemed possible for so extraordinary a performance.

Some soldiers gathered on Atago Hill north of Shiba Park, thinking to hold out as supporters of the shogun had held out on that other "mountain," Ueno, three-quarters of a century before. There were suicides. The American occupiers would not have been surprised if they had encountered guerrilla war. The Japanese rather hoped that the Americans would occupy the government buildings at Kasumigaseki, and leave the commercial and financial heart of the city alone. Perhaps they already sensed that the next war would be economic. Advance scouting parties thought that Marunouchi would be easier to defend. General Douglas MacArthur agreed to the choice of the Daiichi Insurance Building for his headquarters. It is a thick-walled citadel with windows recessed behind solid square pillars and the open spaces of the moat and the royal plaza in front of it. The ineffectual defenses of the city had had their command post there.

Takami Jun's wife said that if the emperor had told them to fight to the last man and woman they would probably all of them have done it. Takami was inclined to agree. In the event, there was no resistance. The general would have been as safe if he had gone to Kasumigaseki or pitched a tent in the wastes east of the river.

The "chief executive" of the prefecture, a general, resigned late in August. A very quick succession of executives followed him, six of them between August 1945 and May 1947. The last of them, Yasui Seiichirō, who had had a brief term earlier, resigned to run for election and became the first popularly elected governor of the prefecture.

Americans were in Tokyo from late August. An advance party, heavily armed, set up tents, well surrounded by barbed wire, on the Yoyogi parade grounds, where a few days earlier some boys of the radical right had committed suicide. The purposes of the party were to test the land and to scout out buildings suitable for requisitioning. General MacArthur landed at Atsugi, southwest of the city, on August 30. He spent his first nights in Yokohama, where the guerrillas would be easier to fend off than in the middle of the gigantic capital. The surrender documents having been signed aboard ship in Tokyo Bay on September 2, the occupation of Tokyo began in earnest on September 8. The city could turn its thoughts to another in its venerable series of reconstructions.

Chapter 10

THE DAY OF THE COD
AND THE SWEET POTATO

In the early years after the war, praise for Nagoya and blame for Tokyo were much in fashion. Nagoya took advantage of the bombings to refashion itself. Tokyo was a growth which, flattened, lay flat for a time and then pulled itself together much as it had been. The redesigning of Nagoya brought wide avenues, sufficient, one might have thought, for all the vehicles likely to pass through the central business district. The corresponding district of Tokyo has a street pattern scarcely different from that of Taishō.

It is more challengeable now than it was forty years ago that Nagoya benefited greatly from the changes. Not many today think that the widening of streets can keep up with the flood of automobiles. Nagoya has its traffic jams too. Nor do wide streets seem to be among the things the Japanese are good at. They range from featureless to ugly. In Nagoya the wide streets took away the past. The bombings, it might be argued, *had* already taken it away; but one has no sense, along the broad avenues of central Nagoya, of all the people who lived there over the centuries. Not much is old in Tokyo, but the street pattern is, and makes Tokyo seem warmer and cozier than Nagoya, a much smaller city. There can be no final conclusion to arguments over the Tokyo way and the Nagoya way. Yet a person may feel that if there is going to be congestion anyway it is better had on comfortable old streets.

Tokyo might not have been able to do as Nagoya did even if it had had the wish and the will. For one thing, there were all those buildings in the way. A walk east and west through the cinders of 1945 could have taken one close to Tokyo Central Station. The prefectural offices were heavily damaged. Mitsubishi Londontown, however, the heart of financial and managerial Marunouchi, escaped. Only a very iconoclastic prefectural government could have persuaded itself to destroy good, solid buildings in a city that had lost so much.

Then there were the Americans. They left the Japanese the Marunouchi Building, the largest office building in the city and the land, but they took almost everything else in Marunouchi. Unsuccessful at persuading them that the bureaucratic quarter of the city would admirably serve their needs, the Japanese had no way of dislodging them from Marunouchi. Harassment might have worked, but there was none of that. If the Japanese had any policy in those days it was to smile and accommodate and hope that the invaders would soon go away. By 1947, when popular election of the governor brought a measure of stability to the prefectural government, retention of the old street pattern was the established condition all over the city. We cannot know whether the opportunity to do something with Marunouchi would have kindled a zeal to do something all over the city. Nagoya did not do much with its outskirts either.

As after the earthquake, the first thing that had to be done was to clear away the cinders. Again they were dumped in huge volume into the canals. There were not enough vehicles and there was not enough gasoline to take them out and, as was done with garbage in later years, dump them in the bay for landfill. Canals, along with such wide streets as Showa Avenue, put through east of Ginza after the earthquake, provided convenient receptacles. The streets, though piled high with rubble for a time, presently became usable again. The filled-in canals did not come back as usable canals; and one wonders where all the cinders will be put when the next disaster comes. Some of the canals were already so silted in that they were little more than broken puddles of stagnant water, and some of the important ones, such as the Kandagawa, the "Kanda River," were in the years of rapid economic growth to become so filthy that, as popular wisdom had it, not even typhoid germs could live in them. They bubbled and seethed with noisome gases. The old canal system thus became a broken ruin. It had been left behind in any event, and when economic growth kills something one is foolish to lament over it. Still the canals were a necessary part of Edo, for which one may pardonably feel nostalgia.

The filling in of canals and the disposition of the land that resulted were among the first stirrings as the city began coming to life again. The conspicuous presence of the Americans in Marunouchi may have been in part responsible for the new prosperity of what had been the back side of Tokyo Central Station. Perhaps more important was the filling in of the portion of the outer palace moat that ran along that east or back side, also known as the Yaesu Mouth. In the early years of the station, railroad yards and the canal cut it off in a most unfriendly way from the old Low City. Now the canal was filled in, and an eating, drinking, shopping, and watering complex arose where it had been. A Yaesu station building went up in 1947, across the tracks to the east of the old station. It burned down a few months after its completion, but it would soon have gone anyway, as the Yaesu Mouth reached up into the sky and down into the earth.

In 1953 a *meitengai,* which might hesitantly be translated "shopping center," began business at the Yaesu Mouth. The reason for the hesitation is that a *meitengai* does not provide accommodation for the automobile. It is more like a bazaar. The city had long had such places, and the one at the Yaesu Mouth led the way to ever vaster ones. It began going underground, and in the next fifteen years or so had become the largest underground complex in the Orient. The first multistory building after the war started rising, eight floors aboveground and two below, near the north end of the landfill even before the Korean War brought a great building boom. By 1954 the number of persons passing through the Yaesu Mouth exceeded that for the Marunouchi Mouth, the old front entrance, and a dozen years later the Yaesu figure reached a half million a day. So the Low City could have thought, if it wished, that an old wrong had been righted.

A similar instance is Sanjūsangenbori, the "thirty-three-ken [two hundred-foot] dig," which ran north and south just east of Ginza. The back streets to the east of the main Ginza street do not seem to have been very lively before the war. The canal, which cut Ginza off from the Shochiku entertainment center, farther east, became a cinder dump. When it was completely filled in, by about 1950, the land was divided among people who could be expected to make it a bustling pleasure center. It had pinball parlors, drinking places, cabarets, and a burlesque hall which was in business for less than a year, even though it offered such celebrities as "the queen bee of Anatahan." (The queen bee had spent several postwar years with several men on Anatahan, a small island in the Marianas.) And it had the Tokyo Onsen, the "Tokyo Spa," a pleasure palace not of a completely new kind, perhaps, but of a bold sort that seemed to bring an end to the years of deprivation. It was until 1986, when it was torn down to make way for a much higher building, a four-story watering place. There are no natural hot springs within a great distance of downtown Tokyo, but since Meiji there had been fabricated ones at, for instance, Shinagawa, at the southern limits of the old city.

The Tokyo Onsen contained big communal baths, said to incorporate the latest techniques from Turkey and Scandinavia, and private rooms as well, and for a tariff of a hundred yen, not much in those days of inflation, one could have a bath attended by a pretty masseuse. It all seemed rather shocking at the time, not because of the sexual abandon, so much a part of the life of the city that only a missionary or a policeman could object, but because of the prodigality. It seemed a luxury which the city and the nation could not afford. The builders of the Onsen were presently vindicated. They led the way into a future in which the pleasures their enterprise offered came to seem modest and even demure, and it may be that their boldness was just what the city needed in those difficult times.

The filling in of the "dig" had one consequence that cannot have been foreseen: it brought the entertainment complex east of Ginza closer to Ginza, by which it was presently absorbed. The old Kobikichō became East Ginza and then plain Ginza. The change of names had no great practical effect. The smaller districts into which the Tokyo wards are divided have no more administrative or political significance than the streets of an American city. Nor has the entertainment complex been in the television age what it was in the movie age. Yet a grand old place name was lost. Elderly people still go to Kobikichō, not Ginza, for their Kabuki. It will take time for the old name to fall completely into oblivion.

Like the cinder-filled canals, the black markets helped to get things started again. Probably they were necessary. Rationing did not provide adequate sustenance. In 1947 the death of a judge in the Tokyo District Court received much attention from the newspapers. He died of malnutrition, because he refused to eat anything purchased on the black market.

A reconstruction of the Ikebukuro black market

Every little station along the commuter lines had its little market for illicitly acquired foreign products. When the need for them passed, with the passing of rations and the presence of adequate supplies, they became the clusters of eating and drinking places where, at the end of their day, office workers fortify themselves against the rigors of home and family. There have been such places ever since there have been office workers and commuting, but the black markets contributed to the huge increase in their numbers, a far more rapid increase during the postwar years than that for enterprises in general.

The Occupation left the Japanese to do what they could by way of controlling the black markets, though they would have been impossible without the generous cooperation of many a commissary sergeant. It did wish them to keep out of its sight, and show reticence in operating where most of its operations were. So in the center of the city black marketing did not contribute to the first stirrings of revival and reconstruction as it did along the big transfer points of the Yamanote loop line.

The most thriving among the black markets was what came to be known, and still is known, though its functions have changed, as Ameya Yokochō, just south of Ueno. The Americans had their own name for it, the Ueno PX. Yokochō is "alley," and Ameya is a pun on "American shops" and "sweets shops." Sugary items, in cruelly short supply in those years, were important to Ameyoko, which offered sweet concoctions from beans and potatoes. There were repeated raids on the district. On a day in May 1946 six hundred armed police staged a very big raid. They could not cope with Ameyoko's resilience, however, and it is doubtful that they really tried very hard. A raid might briefly diminish the flow of American goods, but only briefly. Unless they were suspected of having committed more serious crimes, stallkeepers and shopkeepers were treated leniently, as if by way of recognizing that at least they were doing something, and *someone* had to do something. When Japanese started going abroad again, they of course had to come home bearing gifts. One would hear that those who were too busy or too timid to do their shopping abroad would go to Ameyoko for it.

During the second postwar decade Ameyoko began to shift from American goods to marine products, which no one would dream of importing from America. The change may be taken as a sign that the worst deprivation and confusion were coming to an end. In 1983 an Ameyoko Center, all shining metal and glass, was finished. The small retailers who moved in dealt mostly in manufactured goods. Purveyors of foodstuffs remained along the street and far outsold the food department of the

The Ameya Yokochō black market as it looks today

gigantic Matsuzakaya department store a few steps away. In very recent years Ameyoko has been the center of a new kind of black market. Japanese (or whoever) can buy easily transported goods in, for instance, New York, bring them back to Tokyo without paying duty, and sell them at a lower price than they sell at in Japan through legal channels. All of these changes, and many others, are symbolic of larger change. Step by step, Ameyoko has kept up with a changing city, and, after a fashion, represented it.

If a black-market stallkeeper risked being raided and losing a few commodities and spending a few nights in jail, things could also be risky for a more pitiable kind of black-market person: he, and very often she, who circumvented rationing by buying rice in the country and bringing it to city markets. There were occasional roundups, generally at railway stations in the northern and eastern part of the city where *katsugiya,* "bearers," as they were called, were likely to leave or change trains. (The

big Japanese-English dictionary renders *katsugiya* as "runner," with a warning that this is an Americanism.) The policeman on the beat seems to have been reluctant to take action against *katsugiya* when he did not have to. The story was told of a policeman who tapped a woman on the shoulder and said, "Your baby is wetting its pants." In those days when the almost universal way of transporting babies was by strapping them to adult backs, a woman would seek to disguise her black-

Police search a woman smuggling rice into Tokyo

market rice by strapping it and cosseting and posseting it and making soothing noises to it, quite as if it were a baby. This poor woman's sack had sprung a leak and rice was trickling out.

At the beginning of 1946 Tokyo contained an estimated sixty thousand black-market stalls. Sad reminiscences of those hard days persuade us that most of the stallkeepers were desperate men and women who would gladly have done something else if there had been anything else to do. Many, however, were under the control of gangs. Very soon after the surrender, extortion and protection gangs occupied land at each of the main entrances, the "mouths," east, west, and south, to Shinjuku Station.

The motto of the gang at the most important of them, Eastmouth, was "Let light spread forth from Shinjuku." Court action was required to return the land, now not far from the most valuable in the world, to the rightful owners, some of them, such as the Takano Fruits Parlor, among the most venerable and esteemed of Shinjuku retailers. Gang warfare was endemic at Southmouth, and we may be grateful to very great complications at Westmouth that we still have the relic of the postwar years known as Piss Alley (see page 483). A farrago of rights and claimed rights made it possible for keepers of little drinking places to buy their own land. It was a decade and a half after the war that the old black market at the Ikebukuro Westmouth was finally leveled, by court order.

There was in those days the problem of the "third nationals." It was conspicuous in the underworld and in gang squabbling. Third nationals were for practical purposes Chinese and Koreans resident in Japan. The expression put them in their place, distinguishing them both from Japanese and from the Occupation, which favored them, treating Chinese as allies and Koreans as quasi allies (enemies of the enemy). It is hard to deny that they took advantage of their position.

If the police could not intercede in behalf of Japanese gangs that thought of themselves (or at any rate advertised themselves) as Robin Hoods and defenders of the Japanese spirit, there is much evidence that they managed to aid them surreptitiously. In the "Shimbashi Incident" of 1946, American military police and Japanese police intervened to prevent an armed battle between Chinese and Japanese gangs for control of the market. The nonbattle was in effect a victory for the Japanese. It showed the Chinese, who were progressively weaker, that they could not have everything their way even in that day of confusion and demoralization.

Across the bay in Chiba, later in 1946, the police seem to have actually encouraged a showdown between Japanese and third-national gangs. It would be the occasion, the Chiba police and the American military police agreed, for rounding up gangsters of whatever nationality. The Japanese police told the Japanese gangs what was to happen and invited their cooperation. The Americans do not seem to have accorded the same favor to the third nationals. The encounter took place, a few minutes of gunfire in which several men were wounded but no one was killed, and in the end only third nationals were rounded up.

The problem of relations between the police and the underworld has always been a delicate and elusive one. At the very least the police seem to prefer organized crime to the more scattered and diffuse kind. Some elements in the police force would have to work harder if the gangs were to go, and the gangster for his part prefers police whom he knows and who know him to outsiders who might come meddling if an incident were to be prolonged.

The most powerful force in getting things moving again came fairly late. The Korean War broke out in June 1950, almost exactly at midpoint through what we may call the decade of the rebuilding. For Korea it was a terrible happening, for Japan a momentous one, with little sense of the terrible. The calm with which Tokyo and Japan assumed that someone would do something was rather wonderful. It was perhaps natural in an occupied country that had no foreign policy save to get rid of the Occupation and export things whenever and wherever possible; and an eminent editor once remarked that two subjects certain to send readers away in droves were Korea and education. Still it was rather wonderful. The prospect of losing Korea to the people (in those days the Chinese and the Russians seemed monolithic) from whom it had been won less than a half century before was received with huge indifference.

Momentous the event certainly was for all that. Japanese profits from the Korean War were massive, and they went into rebuilding city and land, and bringing them back somewhat near, in material terms, the position that had been theirs before the folly of the forties. Procurement contracts in the remaining months of 1950 ran to $180 million, and before the Korean War was over they ran to $2.3 billion. Production returned to and passed prewar levels. Direct American aid, which had been necessary in the immediate postwar years, now ceased to be. Brave beginnings had already been made toward putting things together again, but it was in the early fifties that matters went forward with speed and purpose. No one can blame the Japanese for having a delightful fish in troubled waters, and someone else would have done it if they had not. Yet it is ironic that the prosperity of a country which has renounced war (see Article IX of the postwar constitution) is founded on a war.

The days just after the surrender were very hard ones. When a middle-aged or aging Japanese remarks upon the terrible time, one must listen carefully to know which time is meant. One may instinctively suppose it to be the last months of the war, the time of the bombings, but for many the really terrible time was the first winter after the war, a time of cold, disease, and hunger. Typhus was the worst plague. There were almost ten thousand cases of it in Tokyo Prefecture during the winter of 1945 and 1946, and almost a thousand deaths. Smallpox and cholera may not have reached such epidemic proportions, but in a more settled day they would scarcely have been present at all. Typhus bespeaks lice and unclean bodies, very distressful to the well-washed Japanese. In those days not even a good hot bath was easy to come by. The city has always had fleas and chinches in ample numbers, but lice are a different matter.

A tenth of the populace that clung to the city through that winter lived in such emergency places as air-raid shelters and warehouses. The underground passages at Ueno Station, at that time the most considerable in the city, though they do not bear comparison with the honey combs that have been dug since, had the largest and most famous accumulation of beggars and vagrants in the city. From time to time they were rounded up, and ineffective attempts made at dispersal. On a night in mid-December 1945, some twenty-five hundred persons were taken in. There were deaths from exposure. Temperatures in Tokyo do not go much below freezing, but dampness can bring great discomfort even to the well-fed person. Through the last months of 1945 vagrants were dying in Ueno at a rate of two to three every day, and sometimes the number was as high as six. The second postwar winter brought improvement in the sense that exposure was not for the most part the immediate cause of death. Eleven people died in the Ueno Station complex during the first week of 1947, most of them from pneumonia.

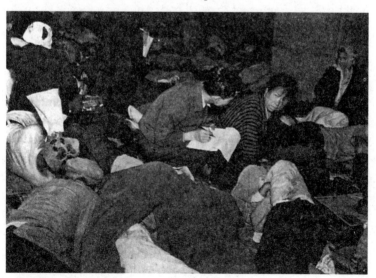

A postwar census-taker at work among the homeless in the Ueno subway station

Dance hall scene, 1946

Students sat and shivered in their overcoats in unheated classrooms, professors stood and shivered. An office in one of the best buildings left to the Japanese, such as the Marunouchi Building or the Bank of Japan, might be heated only by a charcoal brazier or a scattering of them, to which typists would turn from time to time to thaw their stiffened fingers. The bravery of dancers in unheated theaters, such as the Rokkuza, the Sixth District Theater, in Asakusa, was something to arouse admiration. Everything was rationed. One had to have coupons to eat in a restaurant. The cod and the sweet potato were the staples. Many a Japanese of a certain age cannot look at either without shuddering.

Yet there was a communal spirit over the city and the land which, in the recall, makes the shabby Japanese of the day seem more estimable than the dapper (or chic) Japanese of today. It was beautiful the way in which people shook themselves from daze and shock and looked about them, and, military expansion having proved impractical, set about having a try at another kind.

As after the earthquake, huts began going up almost immediately on the burned-over wastes. Street stalls were back in the bustling places where they had always been—Shinjuku, Ginza, Ueno, and the like. They offered food and drink before less flimsy shops were doing so. The Occupation did not like the stalls. It ordered in 1949 that they be done away with, and on New Year's Eve 1951 the last of them finally went.

Efforts at coaxing stallkeepers into other businesses were not entirely successful. Many of the stalls were finally subsumed into covered markets, in such places as the filled-in canal east of Ginza and the revetment beneath the statue of the Meiji rebel Saigō Takamori, the most famous of Ueno landmarks.

The streets of Ginza and Shinjuku thus became more passable for people and automobiles in a hurry, but what they gained in that regard they lost as gathering places. The stalls probably would have gone anyway, as the city and the country became more affluent. Occasionally an aging stallkeeper is interviewed in a newspaper, and almost always he says that he would not for the world go back to the old business, with its prickly heat and chilblains. An unsuccessful experiment with stallkeeping a quarter of a century before had demonstrated that it was not a business for dabblers and dilettantes. In the summer of 1930, as a device for relieving unemployment in those bleak depression years, the prefectural police opened some ten miles of streets in the city and the suburbs to amateur stallkeepers. More than sixteen thousand stalls quickly lined them, but within a year more than fourteen thousand had gone out of business.

Charcoal-burning taxicabs also went away, not to reappear, on that New Year's Eve of 1951. Scarcely any remained—perhaps fewer than ten still puffed about the city, as against three thousand or so during the war. Many liked the street stalls, no one liked the charcoal cabs. They were forever fuming and sputtering to a halt, choking their passengers along with themselves. Like the sweet potato and the cod, they were the embodiment of bad days.

In a sense the black market never really disappeared. We have seen that smuggled goods, often of Japanese make, can be purchased at, for instance, Ameyoko. It stopped dealing in necessities, however, as they became plentiful and were no longer rationed. The process of derationing began early. Retail derationing was slower than wholesale, which ended in 1950. Not many who visited the city for the Olympics in 1964 can have guessed that the system of coupons for meals in restaurants still prevailed. It was not discontinued until 1968, by which time it had long been meaningless. The black-market price of rice fell below the rationed price in 1959. So retail rationing withered away.

There may already have been huts among the cinders when the first Americans arrived, but the city has not done strikingly well in the matter of housing. One person in twenty was still living in a temporary shelter at the end of 1946, as against one in ten the year before, but the population had grown. The first public housing went up, on old army land, in

1948, and had three hundred applicants for every small house available. A survey of housing by the Construction Ministry showed that Tokyo had rebuilt about a third of its housing by early 1949. This was a better performance than that of Osaka, but not as good as those of a number of other cities, including Hiroshima and Nagasaki, the cities of the nuclear bombs. Despite its poor record in new buildings, Osaka had more living space per capita than Tokyo, which had fewer than three *tatami* mats per person. (A *tatami* is about two square yards.) The figure has gone up gradually and continues to go up, but in 1986 Tokyo still had fewer than eight mats per person, the lowest for any prefecture in the country except Okinawa—and Tokyo is the richest of the prefectures, and Okinawa the poorest but one or two. The average citizen of Tokyo thus has a space of about twelve feet square to call his own. Seven people may be expected to share a house or apartment with a thousand square feet of floor space. This is the average, including the affluent wards along with the poor. The eastern and northeastern wards are well below the average. Of land prices and the distance from the center of the city to which an office worker must go to find a bit of land he can afford, more must be said later. They seem to be spinning out of control. All that "planning" can really hope to do is make things more convenient and expeditious for people who must commute long distances.

Nor has the city done very well with parks. Some considerable tracts, notably along the Sumida River, were left open after the earthquake and presently developed into parks. Little of the sort happened in 1945. The problem of what exactly did happen is complicated by the fact that several sets of parks are involved: national parks, royal parks, prefectural parks, and city and ward parks. The area of park lands has increased, but the prefecture was initially slow about adding to them, other than with small playgrounds. More considerable accessions to the system or the several systems resulted from donations. An example is the Hama Detached Palace, where in 1879 General Grant and his lady were accommodated. Once the bayside villa of the shoguns, from whose hands it passed to the royal household, it was donated to the city late in 1945. Somewhat halfheartedly, the Occupation requisitioned it a year and a half later. When it was needed for American training purposes the public was excluded, but it was open during periods when the Occupation had no specific need of it.

So the city itself did not do much when so much could have been done with the charred wastes. Some prewar parks actually disappeared. Conspicuous among them is Asakusa Park, one of the original five established early in Meiji. For this the Occupation may be held in part accountable. It returned the park lands to the Kannon Temple. The temple, hard pressed for reconstruction funds, made them utterly commercial. The famous ponds in Asakusa Park existed for perhaps three generations. Only the tract behind the main hall of the temple remains unbuilt upon. Hard-surfaced, it provides parking space for tourist buses.

Per capita the area of parks is equal to that for Kyoto, larger than that for Yokohama, and smaller than those for Osaka, Nagoya, and Kobe, whose per capita park area increases in that order. It is only one-twentieth that of Washington, D.C. The absolute area is well under that in Philadelphia and only a bit over that in Detroit—both of them much smaller cities. It may be, though much depends on definitions, that Tokyo is worse off in the matter of parks than Edo was. The proportion of parks to the total areas of the city today is smaller than was that of the shrine and temple grounds that functioned as parks in Edo.

To the credit of Tokyo must be admitted the fact that large areas of the center of the city are freely open to the public. Tabulations always give Seoul a much larger per capita park area than Tokyo, but fail to note that one must pay an admission fee to every considerable park in or near the center of the city.

In these regards the city has not done well. In building to make itself more firmly what it already was, the economic center of the land—and to make it a strong challenger as well to the traditional economic centers of the world—it has done far better. The Korean War, crucial to the economic revival of Tokyo and Japan, speeded up the concentration of managers and executives in Tokyo. Gradually, it came to mean as well the waxing of Marunouchi and the waning of Nihombashi as a managerial center. Before the war and in the early years after, new construction of offices was smaller in area than new construction of residences. In the early 1960s the former area passed the latter.

The Crisis of the thirties put a stop to monumental office building, and the Korean War set it going in earnest once more. In 1951 work began on a second Marunouchi Building, across the station plaza from Tokyo Central and across the street from the first Marunouchi Building, which was finished just before the earthquake and suffered damage in it. The foundations of the second building had already been laid before the war. The prewar excavations filled with water and remained a stagnant pond through the Occupation years, with an occasional corpse floating upon it. There was a great treasure hunt when drainage and filling began, for rumors spread that a trove had been dumped there at the time of the surrender. Nothing was found.

Viewed from the station, the two buildings look like twins, both of them with uninspired tiled fronts. The second one has a somewhat different floor plan, however, with more space for Mitsubishi to rent, and so it now became what the first one had been, the largest building in city and land. It did not long remain so. A third Marunouchi Building, more properly called the Otemachi Building from the district in which it reposes, was finished in 1958. Many a yet larger building has been put up since.

Very little was being done, meanwhile, to accommodate commuters to these new buildings. For the first decade after the war transportation to the center of the city remained as it had been before the war. The third Marunouchi Building held forty thousand workers, and the crush on the National Railways was becoming frightful. The most painful (to some amusing) pictures of station attendants pushing people in tighter so that the train doors will close date from these years. A segment of a second subway line, the first to pass directly under Marunouchi, opened from Ikebukuro to Ochanomizu in 1954. It cannot have done much good for anyone except a scattering of students and scholars on their way to browse in the Kanda bookshops. It opened as far as Tokyo Central in 1956 and Ginza in 1957, but did not go through to Shinjuku, whence and whither the largest floods of commuters came flooding, until 1959, a year after completion of the third Marunouchi (or Otemachi) Building. Free transfer between the two subway lines, that from Asakusa to Shibuya and that from Ikebukuro to Shinjuku, did not come until later yet. It would probably be unfair to say that metropolitan policy consciously favored business over convenience, but that is certainly the ordering that prevailed.

In one respect things became easier for the office worker—or at least the messenger boy who ran from office to office. In the original Mitsubishi Londontown, the complex spread out before the station, the pattern had been vertical, with a company renting several floors of a segment of a building. Now it became horizontal. A company that did not have a building of its own would rent a whole floor or two from Mitsubishi or someone else.

In 1951, the second year of the Korean War and the year in which the boom in office building began, the city received the first considerable increment to its hotel space since the Daiichi of 1938, built for the Olympics that never took place. The Nikkatsu Building, with shops at ground level and below, offices on the next several levels, and hotel rooms at the top, rose at the Hibiya crossing. The hotel space is now gone, and would

The Nikkatsu building

scarcely be noticed in any event among all the huge hotels the city possesses. The builder was a movie company later done in by television. Great was the wonder in those days at the daring. Would enough foreign tourists and businessmen come to fill the rooms? They never had before. Not many seers guessed that the foreign clientele would be of so relatively little importance in keeping all the hotels filled.

Until the completion of the Daiichi, hotels, in contrast to inns, had catered almost exclusively to alien tourists and businessmen. Despite its Olympian origins, the Daiichi wished to attract Japanese businessmen and even an occasional family group, and in a measure succeeded. The tiny rooms and especially the tiny bathtubs seemed meant for them, a way of luring them gradually into something new. This new adventure in lodging lasted but briefly. The war came and hotels were destroyed, and the remaining ones, led by the Imperial and the Daiichi, were taken over by the Occupation, either for its own personnel or for "foreign traders," as they were called. When the Occupation ended, the adventure was resumed with enthusiasm, and by the time of the 1964 Olympics five times more hotel rooms were available. The clientele, especially for lavish receptions, was increasingly Japanese.

The distinction between a hotel and an inn has never been very clear. (It is a little like that between a geisha and a prostitute.) The earliest hotel in the city, the Tsukiji Hoterukan, which was of wood and went up in flames in 1872, seemed to think itself both, since the first three syllables of the generic part of the name are "hotel" and the last is a part of the commonest Japanese word for "inn." There has recently gone up in the Ueno district a place that calls itself the Hoteru Yado, to show that this ecumenical tradition perseveres. *Yado,* another reading of the *juku* of Shinjuku, "New Station," signifies a traveler's lodging.

One cannot say that hotels are in the Western style and inns in the Japanese, since many places that anyone would call an inn have beds and chairs, and numbers of large hotels have rooms in which one sleeps on the floor. Nor can it be said that hotels are expensive and inns are cheap, since either can be both. Perhaps the most definitive statement that can be made is that a hotel tends to be big, high, and fire-resistant, and an inn tends to be small, no more than two or three storys high, flimsily built, and often rather combustible.

By the end of the first postwar decade there were almost four thousand inns in the city and a dozen or so hotels. There were scores of rooms at an inn for every one at a hotel. Of the inns, more than three-quarters were of the "dubious" *(aimai)* kind, their mark the "upside-down jellyfish." It is the mark of the hot spring, the jets of steam from the water resembling a jellyfish supine, its tentacles in the air. Their business was sex, and ladies of the night were an important part of their clientele.

There is dispute as to when and where a Japanese establishment first took for itself the American designation "motel." Some say that it was in Atami in 1963, others that it was as early as 1957 at a rather remote place on the "back side" of Japan, the coast of the Sea of Japan. In any event it does not seem to have been in Tokyo, and it does seem to have been in the pre-Olympic years. Soon Tokyo had numerous specimens, and soon the secret was out in the open. The expressions "upside-down jellyfish" and "motel" had been suggestive but not explicit; "love hotel," in English, was very explicit.

Yet there remained something furtive about love hotels. A night at the Yoshiwara, in another age, had an open, rather companionable quality about it. A night in a love hotel does not. The Edo wife had no right to complain if her husband went off occasionally to the Yoshiwara. The wife of our day and days recently past thinks herself much put upon if she or a gossipy friend sees her husband emerging from a love hotel. A good part of the furtiveness has to do with arrangements for making as sure as possible that he is not detected. Family life has changed.

Officially, the recovery of Tokyo from the great earthquake was accomplished in less than a decade. There were no observances after the surrender corresponding to those in 1930 that felicitated recovery from the earthquake. In another way the reconstruction was different from that of 1923 and after. It did not stop. Building did not of course come to a complete stop in the Tokyo of the Crisis years, but depression and Crisis kept the city from changing greatly after the 1930 celebrations. It was as if they announced the end of a period of great constructive endeavor and the coming of a less active period in which to await the next storm.

Nothing of the sort has happened since the war. The building has gone on and on. There have been recessions, but there has been no major depression. Japan has been free of international involvements as probably no other major nation in modern times—free to manufacture, to export, and to build. One may expect to see from time to time in the newspapers and magazines the announcement that the postwar period is *finally* over. They are like announcements that Edo has finally died. Even as we may expect them, we may be sure that the most recent one will not be the last. "The postwar period," an expression for practical purposes interchangeable with "the period of reconstruction," will probably go on as a cultural and economic era until the next disaster brings it to a close.

Yet we may say that by the middle or late fifties Tokyo was essentially back where it had been in 1940 or so, and everything that has come since has been new growth. It took about a decade to recover from 1923, and it took about a decade to recover from 1945. In the middle fifties one started hearing Japanese say that their standard of living had returned to the prewar level.

Affluence is never evenly distributed, and the growing affluence of the city was not. Some wards had ampler housing than others. Besides taking over most of the Marunouchi business district, the Occupation requisitioned houses, more than six hundred of them in Tokyo Prefecture. With all the houses in the city and the prefecture to choose from, it naturally chose the most luxurious, and so the pattern of requisitioning follows the pattern of the domicile of wealth. A quarter of the requisitioned houses were in what is now Minato Ward and before 1947 was the three southern wards of the old city, Shiba, Akasaka, and Azabu. The American embassy is at the northern edge of it. The addition of two other wards—Ota, southernmost of the new 1932 wards, and Shibuya, centering on the bustling place of that name in the southwestern part of the city—brings the total to more than half. No houses at all were requisitioned in six wards along the northeastern and eastern fringes of the city. Scarcely any would have been left along the inner fringe even if the Occupation had wanted to have places there, but the three wards along the outer fringe were not badly damaged. Nothing in them caught the Occupation eye.

In 1956 Edogawa, one of the two easternmost wards, had the lowest per capita income. It was in those days still heavily agricultural. Of the thoroughly urbanized wards, the two immediately east of the Sumida River had the lowest income. In 1957 the weight of vegetables brought into the Kanda wholesale produce market was twice that of those brought to the Kōtō market east of the river (the two were among seven wholesale markets in the city), but the sales value was three and a half times as much. Kanda was where the expensive Ginza retailers and restaurants went for their supplies. Kōtō had no such clientele. (In 1956 Kanda sold, by value, 14 percent of the vegetables and 26 percent of the fruits for the whole nation. The value of the fruits was higher than that for any single city other than Tokyo itself, and that of vegetables higher than for any other city except Osaka.)

The population of the prefecture, which had risen above seven million in 1939 and stayed there until 1944, fell to about three and a half million in late 1945. It climbed by about a fifth during each of the following two years. Thereafter the rate of growth fell off sharply. The population once more passed seven million in 1952, and in 1962 it passed ten million. Of the seven and a third million inhabitants of the prefecture in 1940, six and three-quarters million lived in the thirty-five wards. Of about eight million inhabitants in 1955, fewer than seven million lived in the wards. This is to say that the population of the old "county part," beyond the limits of the 1932 city, had doubled, while the population of the wards had risen only by some two hundred thousand people.

The population of the wards rose to almost nine million in the late sixties, and never passed that figure. The ward part of the prefecture was saturated, while the population of the county part continued to grow. Since 1967 the population of the wards has been stable, though in slight decline over the long run. The population of the central wards and some wards in the eastern and northeastern parts of the city has, in the long view, been in decline since before the disaster of 1945. In all the wards there was an increase in population after 1945, but in the wards in question the population has never returned to the highest prewar figure.

Chiyoda Ward and Chūō Ward, the former including the Marunouchi business district and most of the government bureaus, and the latter Ginza and Nihombashi, both declined in population between the census of 1955 and that of 1960. Minato Ward had more people in 1960 than in

1955, but declined thereafter. The same was true of Taitō Ward, including Ueno and Asakusa, and Bunkyō Ward, including the haughtiest of the national universities and the Kōrakuen baseball stadium. (Estimates for noncensus years suggest that the last two wards may have been growing at a very slight rate for a year or two after the 1960 census.) Setagaya Ward, at the southwestern limits of the ward part, lost less than a tenth of its population from 1944 into 1945, and already in 1946 had more people than in 1944. It has not flagged on its way to becoming the most populous ward in the prefecture. If we combine the populations of the thirty-five antebellum wards into the twenty-three of today, then Setagaya was in 1935 fourteenth among the twenty-three, and Taito and Sumida, which face each other across the Sumida River and neither of which has returned since the war to its highest prewar population, were the most populous.

Eight of the twenty-three wards, among them all the wards that lay entirely within the old city (the city as it was to 1932), lost population between the censuses of 1960 and 1965. Two that straddled the old city limits, one of them Shinjuku, gained slightly, but estimates for noncensus years suggest that they too were already in decline by 1965. All of the new wards outside the 1932 city limits were with a single exception gaining population. The exception was Arakawa Ward, that district to the north of Asakusa where the very poor went when disaster and rising costs drove them out of Asakusa.

So it is that Tokyo moves away from Edo. The new wards grew as the old ones declined, the county part continued to grow as the ward part (seen as a bloc) declined, and when the prefecture in general started to lose population, the neighboring prefectures went on growing enormously. Inevitably there was diffusion, as the tight heart of Edo emptied and the circle around it widened, and the mass of people who might be expected to be paying attention to the same thing at the same time grew enormously. The marvel is that the city has gone on having a center at all. The daytime population of the central wards is several times the nighttime population. That is true, however, of many a large city whose center is incapable of attracting people for any purpose other than making money. People still swarm to the center of Tokyo to dissipate their money and their energies, and to consume.

The average term of governors since, in 1947, the first one was popularly elected has been ten years and a little more. This figure is certain to rise, since the incumbent has most of his third four-year term yet to serve.

Such longevity in office, as has been noted (see page 368), is in sharp contrast to the breathless comings and goings of the prewar years.

Japanese local government since the war has followed the American presidential pattern, with popular election both of chief executives and of legislative bodies. The national government has followed the British parliamentary pattern. The Japanese example does not provide strong arguments in favor of either system, since both have produced stability. The mayor before the war had endless trouble with what were in effect two city councils. The prefectural council since the war has been on the whole manageable, though since 1965 no single party has had a majority of the seats. Only one governor has completely lost control. That was the Olympic governor, most of whose attention went into staging a model sporting event. A larger part of his attention should perhaps have been on a scandal that broke shortly after the event was triumphantly staged. Since the war, scandals have been neither as frequent nor as interesting, for the most part, as before the war.

One powerful force in the workings of the city and the prefecture is not entirely under the control of the prefectural government: the police. The chief of the Tokyo prefectural police is appointed by a national police agency with the approval of the prime minister and upon the advice of a prefectural police commission, which is ineffectual. None of these agencies is under the control of governor and council. Tokyo becomes a police city when it is thought necessary to guard against the embarrassment of having someone shoot at a president or a queen or a pope. It has more than twice as many policemen as Osaka, though it is less than twice as large in population. The problem of police excesses is by no means limited to Tokyo—it was in Kanagawa Prefecture that a case of illegal eavesdropping was uncovered in 1986—but it is most conspicuous in the prefecture in which national embarrassments are most likely to occur. People complain that most of the police budget is provided by the prefecture, which does not control the size of the force. Much of it would come from Tokyo even if it were routed through the national government. The richest prefecture naturally contributes the most to national revenues. In 1946 the Tokyo police, under the influence of the Americans, had policewomen for the first time. It still has them, though many another American idea, such as decentralization, has long since been forgotten.

Even before 1947, when for the first time a governor was popularly elected, the view had come to prevail that the ward boundaries were ill drawn. They had since 1932 varied greatly in size, with the old fifteen wards on the average much smaller than the twenty new ones of that year.

Now, with bombings, evacuation, and the return from evacuation, population differences were also extreme. Sources do not agree as to whether the initiative in the matter of reducing the number and the inequalities came from the Americans or from the prefecture. The best evidence is that the prefectural government brought the Americans into a matter of little concern to them as a way of making sure that it would have its way.

In 1946, in any event, the Occupation indicated that some of the wards should be amalgamated. The chief executive set up an advisory commission in the summer of 1946. Having obtained the approval of the prime minister, he submitted a report later in the year that called for reducing the number of wards from thirty-five to twenty-two. Eleven wards would retain their present names and boundaries. They were all among the twenty new wards of 1932. The old fifteen of 1932 would all be amalgamated either with other old wards or with new ones. In a single instance, Shinjuku, two old ones were combined with a new one. All would most probably lose their old names.

The probability brought resistance, for there was great pride in the old names. Only four among the councils of the old fifteen wards indicated immediate approval. Six of the nine new ones facing amalgamation approved, for with these the pride was less considerable. Palaver ensued. It was a foregone conclusion that all thirty-five would, when talked out, agree, and all presently did; and this was despite the fact that popular opinion was in several obvious cases ignored. Thus a small residential ward in the northern part of the city wanted to join the residential ward bordering it on the south, but was joined instead to a very dissimilar industrial ward to the east. The history edited and published by the new ward, Kita, tells us that the decision was carried out quickly and without publicity.

In March 1947, very shortly before the first gubernatorial elections, the chief executive, with the consent of the prefectural council, proclaimed the reduction from thirty-five to twenty-two wards. All of the old wards did in fact lose their names, and here too public opinion was little respected. Early in 1947 the *Tokyo Shimbun* conducted a poll among residents of the twenty-four wards to be amalgamated. They were asked what names they would prefer for their eleven new wards. Only four of the names finally adopted were even mentioned. Some of the new names seem appropriate. The time did seem right for Shinjuku, that principal rival to the old business district, to become the name of a ward. Others seem merely fatuous. The worst is Bunkyō. It means something like "literary capital" or "cultural capital," probably with reference not to the Kōrakuen baseball stadium but to Tokyo University. The name has that bureaucratic ring to it.

There was no attempt to equalize the area of the wards. Even after amalgamation the central wards remained much smaller than most of those remoter from Marunouchi and the palace. The smallest of all, an amalgamation of the old Shitaya and Asakusa, was only an eighth the size of Itabashi, the farthest of the wards to the north and west. Though Itabashi had had the same boundaries since it became a ward, with the same name, in 1932, it was now thought unwieldy. It was big, certainly, some ten miles across at its widest point, and rapidly growing in population. Later in 1947 it was split in two, and so the count of wards became the twenty-three it has remained.

The new ward lines had more to do with population than with area. Looking to the future, they anticipated a ratio of one to three between the smallest population and the largest. It is not surprising that the eye to the future did not serve well. Few could have foreseen that affluence and prosperity would return and that the outer wards would grow so hugely. If Itabashi had stayed whole it would today have some twenty-two or twenty-three times the population of Chiyoda, where the palace and the Marunouchi business district are. Setagaya, the farthest to the south and west, today has the largest population, upward of eight hundred thousand, seventeen times that of Chiyoda.

In the functions permitted the wards we may see a small instance of a successful popular rising. Outbreaks of resentment at this and that policy of the government have not been unknown, but few have produced even minor change. As a part of the reforms in local government that brought popularly elected governors, "ward heads" (this is the official translation, appearing on alien registration certificates and the like) were also popularly elected. In September 1952 the national government, one of several led by the strong-minded Yoshida Shigeru, replaced this method with something less direct, the announced reason for the change being that the wards were too small to go their own undirected way. Most of the cities in the prefecture, it may be noted, were smaller than most of the wards, but they continued to elect mayors. The ward heads were now elected by the ward councils with the agreement of the governor.

Two decades later the councils of five wards adopted as their policy the designating of ward heads by plebiscite. The candidate with the highest popular vote would be commended to the governor. Three wards actually held plebiscites. This happened, we are told, in response to a popular view that a certain decentralization might be at least a partial solution to the increasingly complicated problems of the city—and indeed it was getting smoggier and more debt-ridden all the time. In 1974 the Local

Autonomy Law was amended to return to the earlier system of popular elections. Under the new law the prerogatives of the wards became as they had been under the Occupation, similar to those of incorporated cities.

There have been other little shows of independence at this lowest of administrative levels. Nakano Ward, to the west of Shinjuku, has gone against the wishes of the Ministry of Education and elected its school board by popular vote. Probably not much of significance will emerge from this smaller rising. Tokyo had a radical government, supported by both of the major left-wing parties, from 1967 to 1979. Faced with a choice between ward heads elected by popular vote and ward heads whose appointment required the consent of the governor, the Local Autonomy Agency was of the view that it did not much matter one way or the other, and that elections might actually be an improvement in Tokyo, where all the fuss was. We will never know what would have happened to the popular rising in other circumstances.

It is a bleak city that loses its sense of fun and pleasure. Tokyo did not. Pleasure quickly came back, and humor went the rounds. The jokes about General MacArthur and his Occupation may not seem exactly sidesplitting by American standards, but then Japanese humor is not American humor. The general emerged with more dignity, on the whole, from Japanese jokes than from American ones.

"Why is General MacArthur like a navel?"

"Because he is above the *chin*."

The italicized word is a first-person pronoun used only by the emperor—he used it in the broadcast of August 15, 1945. Here it signifies His Majesty himself. It is also a ribald though not grossly indecent word for penis. So the general and the navel were above the *chin* in its two senses.

Nationalist sophistry has in recent years maintained that Japan did not surrender unconditionally, since the emperor remained in place. But popular wisdom had no doubt as to where the place was, and the first meeting between general and emperor clearly established it: the emperor called on the general, and not the reverse. The general did not go to the door to receive his guest or to see him off. In the famous photograph of the occasion the general is large and relaxed, the emperor small and tense. The emperor called on the general five times thereafter, and the general never paid a return call. Among the expressions used on every possible occasion during the autumn of the surrender was: "It's MacArthur's order." He was an imperial presence, and probably he saw less of Japan than

General MacArthur and the emperor, 1946

any other American who came during the Occupation years. He shuttled back and forth between his offices by the moat and his residence in the American embassy, perhaps fifteen or twenty minutes' walk away.

One major Kabuki theater, the Tōkyō Gekijō or Tokyo Theater, a part of the Shōchiku complex to the east of Ginza, came through the bombings and burnings. The Shimbashi Embujō and the Kabukiza, the other two major parts of the complex, were both gutted. Kabuki was playing at the Tokyo through the first half of August 1945 and was still there on August 15. The theater was closed for the rest of the month, but opened again on the first of September, even before it was known how the Americans would behave. They behaved in a way that may, from a certain remove in time, seem peculiar.

Ichikawa Ennosuke, a very popular actor who had led the troupe at the Tōgeki in early August, was back there leading it again in September. In October the Shimpa, a melodramatic form less stylized than Kabuki, was at the Tōgeki, and the sixth Onoe Kikugorō, one of the most celebrated actors of the century, was at the Imperial Theater in Marunouchi. Relations with the Americans seemed to be progressing nicely. Then, in November, there was trouble. It was almost as if the grand satraps of Kabuki were asking for it, or at any rate probing the limits of American permissiveness. The first Nakamura Kichiemon, another highly esteemed actor, chose as his November vehicle at the Tōgeki a play which, unless one is used to its sort of thing, may seem demented, pushing the old military virtues, and especially loyalty, to the point of insanity and still holding them to be virtues. So it seemed to the Occupation censors, who ordered the play closed. There were censors of the arts and literature in those days, not the most democratic of people, but people who must be tolerated, perhaps, in a crisis. There was a certain air of crisis about the Occupation. It had a great deal to get done in a short time—and a half dozen years is, in the long view, a short time.

Censorship was not new to Kabuki. Wartime censors had been stern with what they thought to be frivolous and immoral elements, and especially with the idealized rogues of late Edo. There was no attempt to resist before 1945, and there was none after 1945. The effort in both cases was to accommodate. Since the show went on in both cases, it may be deemed successful.

Shōchiku promptly organized a committee to select plays that no one could object to, and to negotiate with the censors. The latter accepted a list of 174 plays of a soundly democratic nature, and said that new plays might be a solution to the problem. Kabuki has never had a fixed repertory, a canon. New plays are always being written. To this Shōchiku acceded with an appearance of heartiness. Early in 1946 it announced a sad fact it had come upon. Kabuki was in danger of fossilization. New plays were the thing.

Had the early views of the censors and the announced ones of Shōchiku prevailed, dance might have become more central to Kabuki than it had traditionally been. Kabuki has always been a highly ritualized and choreographed form. The repertory contains pieces that are entirely dance. These would have come to prevail. The "feudal" old classics quickly started coming back, however. Plays not on the approved list were being performed from as early as 1947, and the censors did not object. The play that was the cause of all the trouble in 1945 was being performed before the end of the Occupation in 1952.

The Tōgeki, where Kabuki survived the most difficult times, perhaps, in its history, does not itself survive. The building does not, this is to say, though the institution does, under a dozen or so storys of offices and restaurants. As a place for Kabuki it did not last through the postwar decade. It became a movie house with the reopening of the Shimbashi Embujō and the Kabukiza. Redone on the inside, looking very much as they had before the war on the outside, the two reopened respectively in 1948 and 1951. As had been the case on its original opening, the Shimbashi geisha who had built the Embujō had the use of it in March 1948, the month of the reopening. Once again they gave their recital of Dance of the East. To save money, Shōchiku did not attempt to rebuild the ornate prewar roof of the Kabukiza, which had collapsed in 1945. The building is nevertheless one of the grander relics of the interwar fondness for old styles in new materials. The facade, still elaborate, is in a Tokugawa style.

The Tōgeki was the only major Kabuki theater to come through the bombings, but the Mitsukoshi department store in Nihombashi helped fill the gap until the Embujō and the Kabukiza could be redone. Ever since the mercantile revolution that produced department stores, around the turn of the century, they have been cultural and amusement centers. They became these things to draw people away from the old specialized stores and make them feel at home in a confusing and threatening emporium. It is to their credit that, having drawn the crowds, they have gone on being cultural and amusement centers. Ever since its rebuilding after the 1923 earthquake, Mitsukoshi had had an auditorium which it rented out for meetings and performances. The name was changed from Mitsukoshi Hall to Mitsukoshi Theater in 1947, at which time it became a full-fledged, full-time theater. In addition to providing another place for Kabuki, a somewhat more sumptuous and elegant one than the Tōgeki, the Mitsukoshi Theater was very important in passing Kabuki on from an aging generation to an emerging one.

The postwar decade was, like the first decade of the century, a time when everyone seemed to be dying. People announced the death of Kabuki itself. The great Kikugorō, the leading Kabuki actor of his time, died in 1949, within two months of two other major actors. His last performance was at the Mitsukoshi. (In the last year of his life, Kikugorō became the first actor of any sort to receive the Culture Medal, the highest honor the nation can bestow on its literary and artistic talents. Kabuki had climbed a great distance since, a scant century before, it had been beneath the notice of the Tokugawa military aristocracy.) The first Kichiemon, who would have been on most lists as Kikugorō's leading rival, died at the end of the first postwar decade, in 1954. But death announcements for the Kabuki form as a whole were, as they had been in late Meiji, premature. The actors who are the old masters today were establishing themselves, and the Mitsukoshi Theater, more than the Tōgeki, was the place where they were doing it. The Mitsukoshi was last used as a Kabuki theater in 1951, the year the Kabukiza reopened. Since 1953 it has returned to its earlier duties, as a place for recitals and meetings.

The Meijiza in Nihombashi, the oldest Kabuki theater in the city, re-opened a few months before the Kabukiza, in November 1950. Before the new decade was over it had been gutted and restored yet another time, the fifth since its original construction early in Meiji. Early on an April morning in 1957 a fire started in the illumination room. There were no casualties.

The Tōgeki narrowly escaped requisitioning by the Occupation. The story of how it escaped is a pleasant one, though there is considerable possibility that it is apocryphal: early in 1946 Ennosuke, he who was playing at the same theater in August 1945, appeared in a modern sort of play with Mizutani Yaeko, probably the most esteemed actress of the day. They kissed, unabashedly, right there in front of the public. Never had it happened before. The critical reception was mixed, but the public approved. So did the Occupation, which thought this display of independence and emotional honesty promising and did not requisition the theater.

The Takarazuka, that big Tōhō property across Ginza from the Kabukiza and the other big Shōchiku properties, did not escape being taken over. As the Ernie Pyle, known to every American who visited the city during the Occupation years, it was a movie and stage theater in the hands of the Americans for almost a decade. It had a huge staff and served as a sort of public-works project for unemployed Japanese theater people. When Tōhō got it back, in 1955, it launched a brave effort to break the Shōchiku monopoly on Kabuki. Some famous and accomplished actors joined the Tōhō Kabuki, and Shōchiku seems to have been genuinely unsettled. It responded by having popular singers do recitals (or something of the sort) at the Kabukiza, and by finding new Kabuki talent. The brightest among the new Kabuki actors was Bandō Tamasaburō, a female impersonator who made his debut in 1967 in the play the American censors had taken objection to in 1945, and who today, in his thirties, is the most popular Kabuki actor. In the end the Tōhō undertaking was not a success. Shōchiku still has its monopoly. The Takarazuka has returned to what it was originally meant for, light and popular musicals, prominent among them those of the all girl Takarazuka troupe. Yet a decade later the troupe was to have its most smashing hit, *Rose of Versailles,* in which, as in *The Marriage of Figaro,* a woman impersonates a man (in attendance upon Marie Antoinette) impersonating a woman.

Not long after its release by the Americans and its return to the Takarazuka troupe and others, the Takarazuka Theater was the scene of another famous fire, one which, unlike that in the Meijiza, resulted in deaths. The first day of February 1958 was opening day for a musical comedy (not all-girl) about the Ainu, the aborigines who survive vestigially on the northern island of Hokkaido. The play was in progress, the house was packed. On a higher floor an audience was having a movie afternoon, and on a level yet higher a program of the Yose variety theater was underway. Along toward the end of the performance in the main theater the Ainu village which was the setting was attacked by the Japanese. The effects were partly achieved by a fire machine, a sort of flame thrower. It seems that not all the sparks and flames it threw were extinguished. Still later in the performance a curtain began to smolder. The fire quickly spread. The audience applauded these yet more dramatic effects, and did not realize that they were unintentional until a barrier was lowered between the stage and the pits. There was panic and there were injuries from trampling, but no fatalities among the spectators. Those in the theaters above, not witness to the excitement, were evacuated quietly by emergency exits. The three deaths occurred backstage—two child actors and a woman dancer.

Yose too had its troubles with censorship. Although certain feudal tendencies, such as an emphasis on loyalty and submission that runs all through Japanese society, are to be detected in Yose, the censors found nothing in the comic Rakugo monologue so undemocratic as to call for action. They did object, however, to the serious, didactic Kōdan, also done by monologuists. They thought, and they were right, that it glorified the military virtues. They were particularly suspicious of revenge and righteous violence. The form accommodated itself by devices similar to those resorted to by Kabuki. As with Kabuki, the attention of the censors presently flagged.

The most popular Yose theater in the city was for a time near the Sumida River in the Ningyōchō district of Nihombashi. It closed, for want of a clientele, in 1970. Ningyōchō, in which something of old Nihombashi yet survives, is not the bustling place it once was. It escaped the bombings, though the Meijiza, to the east, did not. In the years just after the war it seemed to beckon across the wastes to western Nihombashi, where big business and finance resided, as if asking it to come home again.

In late Edo and through much of Meiji, until the movies came along, Yose was the entertainment for the masses who did not have much money. Presently radio and baseball also came along, and then television, and a far bigger city now contains only one percent as many Yose halls as during the best years of Edo. Yet one need not despair for Yose. It has come to terms with the newer media, and they have extended assistance. The Suzumoto in Ueno, the oldest hall in the city, and now the largest, seating upward of two hundred people, was having a very hard time during the depression years, 1930 and thereabouts, and fees from NHK, the public broadcasting system and the only one there was in those days, helped it come through. Radio and television fees still give a comfortable living to the better-known performers. Yose seems moreover to appeal to the young. Scarcely a university is without its Rakugo study society. Most of the active professionals, a scattering of women among them, were born in the last reign. A single one was born in Meiji, and fewer than twenty in Taishō.

So it seems that Rakugo, and, more tenuously, Kōdan, will survive. There is today a single house in the city and indeed in the nation that specializes in Kōdan. Also in Ueno, it opened in 1950, before the censorious Americans had gone away. The name, Hommokutei, is interesting. It once belonged to the Suzumoto, which was founded in the year of Commodore Perry's landing. The Hommoku district of Yokohama was made famous by that event. So we may infer that Edo had a good idea of what was going on and was much interested.

The name Ernie Pyle does not seem to have suited Japanese taste. Takarazuka came back. Piccadilly did better. The British Commonwealth Occupation Force gave the name to a theater west of Ginza. and it was kept. We are not to understand, however, that American movies and the American movie business were held in low esteem. Marilyn Monroe and Joe DiMaggio came visiting in 1954, to huge acclaim, more of it for Marilyn than for Joe. The pack of reporters and photographers at the airport was so huge that she was hustled off the plane through an emergency exit. They had a parade into the city and up Ginza.

It was a most advantageous thing in those days for an actor or actress to have a trip to Los Angeles on his or her record. The expression *ameshon,* a most graphic one, had some currency. It is another acronym, made of "American" and *shomben,* "urination," and it refers to a sojourn in America just long enough for a good trip to a urinal. When the actress Tanaka Kinuyo returned from her *ameshon* in 1949, she too had an open parade up Ginza and on to the *Mainichi Shimbun,* from a balcony of which she blew kisses to the crowds, not at all a common or accepted thing for a Japanese lady to do. Her first word to the reporters upon disembarking from her plane is said to have been *haro* ("hello"). She was for a time an object of ridicule, but her career, a brilliant one, did not suffer. She gradually moved from ingenue to gerontic roles.

The two decades after the war may have been the golden age of Japanese moviemaking. The great directors, Ozu Yasujirō and the rest, were doing their best work. It was not, however, the best for box offices. That

came between the wars. There was a boom in the building of movie houses during the first postwar decade, at the end of which there were four
times as many such places in Tokyo as at the beginning. And then, with
television, came the decline in audiences, and bankruptcies and closings.
Ginza has dominated the age of the movie in decline. The big fashionable "road show" theaters are almost all near Ginza, if not precisely in it.
Road shows (the expression is in English), chiefly of foreign movies, are
offered in a single theater per city at a high price for an indefinite run.
They have held their own as the cheaper domestic film has declined.

As the legitimate theater had its first undisguised kiss in 1946, so did
the movies, in an otherwise forgotten film. The very first postwar commercial film has not been forgotten. It was made in what is now termed
Greater Tokyo, and its name is Zephyr *(Soyokaze)*. From it came the first
postwar hit song, a swinging smash of a hit and a charming piece of nonsense after all the fustian and doctrine of the war years. Everyone was
singing "The Apple Song" in that autumn of 1945. The lyrics are by Sato
Hachiro, a well-known humorist and writer of light verse.

> To this red apple
> My lips draw near
> The blue sky watches in silence
> This apple
> Is silent too
> And yet I know how it feels
> How agreeable is this apple
> How agreeable

The utter want of a message, and indeed of meaning, may account for
the huge appeal. The tune is agreeable as well, and, remarkable for a popular Japanese song, there is not a tear in sight, not a sob to be heard.

The age of television, both public and commercial, began in 1953. Those
of us who thought television a luxury beyond the means of the Japanese
could hardly have been more mistaken. Already in 1958, as rapid economic growth was getting underway, NHK had a million sets from
which to extract fees. Early in 1962, the first full year in which the joys
of color television were to be had, the figure passed ten million. It is hard
to imagine today that commercial television could have gone with other
than complete slickness, but the first commercial, in the sense of adver-
tisement, was run silently backwards.

Such idols of the radio age as Dick Mine may have been required to change their names as being out of keeping with the contemporary Japanese spirit. He had many a successor in the television age, however, that spirit once more being receptive to exotic things. Tony Tani, Peggy Hayama, Frank Nagai—the list is a long one. Tony, on the staff of the Ernie Pyle for a time, was very popular as a master of ceremonies on radio and television. He invented new words, or catchy variations on old ones, such as *o-komban wa,* adding an honorific prefix to the standard expression for "good evening," so that it becomes something like "estimable good evening." They seemed to have entered the language for good, but one does not hear them today. The matter of which neologisms stay and which go, in this language so extremely fond of them, defies explanation.

Puritans disapproved of those first public kisses, on stage and on screen, both for what they were and for what they foreshadowed, and they were right that more was coming, on stage and on screen. Toward the end of the first postwar decade there was a vogue for sex films that professed to be educational. They contained a great deal of suggestive posing but not much that was very revealing. More and more has been revealed in the decades since, but not, on the screen, the ultimate, not even in movies with titles like *Flesh Gate* (see pages 459-460) and *Women of the Night.* The hard-core masterpiece about Abe O-sada has not been shown publicly in Japan except in an expurgated version.

The live stage has been bolder. It is more firmly under the control of the local police than the movies, and, for reasons which are not easy to grasp, they have been spottily permissive, not to say arbitrary, in deciding what may be staged and what may not. The strip show, in any event, was something new in popular entertainment. The shows that titillated and even shocked in the early postwar years would not be worth the trouble of producing today, so mild are they compared to what everyone over eighteen (in theory—practice seems more generous) can see. More and more has been stripped away.

January 15, 1947, is recognized by historians of the subject as the day on which the strip show was born. What was known popularly as "The Picture-Frame Show" and properly as "The Birth of Venus" had its premiere on that day on an upper floor of a Shinjuku theater. In the middle of the stage was a large composition resembling a picture frame. In it a girl posed as Venus being born. She was not completely nude; she wore panties and a brassiere, and the rest of her was enclosed in gossamer. She posed for some thirty seconds. It was all, witnesses say, very artless.

This public display of flesh was far more extensive than anything the Casino Folies had ever dared offer. The house was so silent that one could hear a pin drop. People came time after time for those few seconds, and the lines at the box office were as long as ration lines. The show ran until August 1948.

The performers who had such a quelling effect on the Shinjuku audience were at Asakusa slightly later in the season. In June, Asakusa had a completely nude performance, a young lady modeling a model, so to speak. The scene was a painter's studio. It was very popular. Asakusa now proceeded to go wholeheartedly for the strip show, which expression referred at the outset not to the process of stripping but to the stripped condition. (The English word "strip" has always been used, though there are native expressions that would serve as well.) In the early years, when it was bringing comfort and diversion to large numbers of men, even as radio and television were bringing these things to large numbers of women, Asakusa had wider expanses of naked flesh than Shinjuku. Many were heard to lament the falling off which this represented from the days of the opera and Enoken.

The years immediately after the Shinjuku opening are known to cultural historians as the golden age of the strip show. Despite the strip theaters in Shinjuku and some time later in Ginza, Asakusa was the place for them. With bold competition from places beyond the prefectural boundaries and so beyond the jurisdiction of the prefectural police, Asakusa too became bolder. Posing moved into stripping, onstage and not in undressing rooms. Panties and brassieres went away, and even butterflies. In the early days of stripping (not mere posing), more than half the girls in Asakusa rid themselves of Japanese dress. In Ginza Western dress prevailed. Shinjuku occupied a point in between. Asakusa soon adopted the Ginza way. Western dress comes off more quickly than Japanese.

The strip show had its rivals. Light dramatic skits such as Kafū's were still there and popular enough. For a time, midway through the postwar decade, Onna Kengeki, "women's swordplay," threatened to eclipse even the strip show. The form had its origins in the interwar period (see page 365). For a time a half-dozen troupes were performing simultaneously in as many Asakusa theaters. Somewhat erotic from the start, Onna Kengeki held its own in the competition by taking bold steps in the direction of the strip show. The latter prevailed. The early fifties were the best years for the Asakusa strippers. A "bathtub show," replete with bubbles, made its appearance in 1951, and is credited with the triumph of the strip show. Tightrope strips and acrobatic strips also had their time of popularity.

Oe Michiko, the great star of female swordplay, 1959

The rebuilding of the Asakusa entertainment district was swift. One might have thought at the end of the post-surrender decade that it was in a position to hold its own against the upstarts out west. Only a dozen Asakusa theaters, a bit more than a third of the prewar number, survived the war intact. Some, including Kafū's Opera House, which was never rebuilt, were torn down during the war to make firebreaks, others closed for other reasons; eight were either partially or completely gutted during the incendiary raids. By the mid-fifties the count of theaters, stage and screen, was almost back to the prewar level, and for a time a few years later it was even higher.

For one not armed with sociological statistics (see page 326), the Asaku-sa of the postwar years may well have been the part of the city with the strongest, warmest sense of life. Ginza and Shinjuku were already coming to seem impersonal by comparison. All the hum and bustle made the in-between light, coming after great darkness, seem like a dawn and not a dusk.

But the revival was illusory. A 1966 history of Taitō Ward, which includes the old Asakusa Ward, quotes a newspaper article with the headline: "Deserted Place, Thy Name Is Asakusa." This is only a little extreme. The same history refers disparagingly to "Asakusa County, Chiba Prefecture." By this is meant that sophisticated, urbane crowds have gone elsewhere, and such crowds as Asakusa still draws are predominantly rural ones from the prefecture to the east, held in low esteem. Chiba Prefecture lies within Greater Tokyo as legally defined, but that fact has not much helped the prefectural image.

Old Asakusa hands have blamed the filling in of the lakes for bringing on the decline. Kubota Mantarō, a poet, playwright, and novelist who was a native of Asakusa and wrote with great nostalgia about the old Asakusa, vowed that he would never return to see the place without its lakes. He cheated on the vow, for he was seen there by many a person; but the sorrow and anger ring true. Both lakes were filled in, or all three of them, if one thinks of the larger as divided in two by a causeway. When, in the declining months of the Occupation, Asakusa Park was returned to the big temple, the latter promptly started looking for buyers. The southernmost portion of the lakes went to a movie company, which excavated part and filled part, and put a movie theater on the excavated part and an amusement park on the filled. The northern part went to a syndicate which included the ubiquitous Mitsui and which put up a pleasure emporium, practically everything except bawdy houses under one roof. The amusement park and the emporium now are gone. The movie theater remains. The old hands cannot be completely correct, for such changes are never simple. Yet Asakusa was greatly altered by what the temple and its successors to title did with the old park; and it may well be that when even the topography of a place has changed people who knew it before the change will look for other places, where the wrench of memory is less painful.

Other explanations are possible for the fact that so promising a start came to so little. Kata Kōji thinks that Asakusa was doomed because no swarms of students have campuses nearby. Enoken thought that Asakusa made the mistake of trying to be all classy like Ginza. This is interesting, and it does have a certain applicability to Enoken's Asakusa reviews. But if Asakusa imitated any of the other bustling places it was Shinjuku, and Shinjuku has not been much noted for its classiness. As for the Kata view, one may point out that Roppongi is not favored with campuses either. Students come from afar.

The essential facts can be stated simply. The Japanese seem to enjoy moving as if to the sound of a drum, and one of those sixth senses (there are many) of which they are proud seems to tell them in which direction everyone is moving. The great thrust of the city was westward, into the hills and away from the flatlands, and the best advice in the world from all the people who had explanations for the decline of Asakusa could not have done much to stop it.

Such first-run movie houses as the Tokyo Theater and the Japan Theater (the Tōgeki and the Nichigeki), to the east and west of Ginza, also had their strippers, with names like Mary Matsubara, Gypsy Rose, and Frieda Matsumoto. Early performances were elegant by comparison with what was going on in Shinjuku and Asakusa. The first performance at the Nichigeki Music Hall, in March 1952, had a pair of French artistes live from the Folies-Bergère, as well as Koshiji Fubuki, one of the great figures, and not at all a bawdy figure, in recent popular entertainment. The Music Hall loosened up a bit as time went by and it became apparent that much would be permitted which had not earlier been. Yet Ginza maintained a certain tone that the other places did not.

Even as the Meiji government had essayed to provide ladies of pleasure for early foreign visitors and residents, so the Japanese government thought to do it for the Occupation forces. Soon after the surrender there was a poster in Ginza inviting young ladies to join a "recreation and amusement association" for the entertainment of the Americans. It had a few gatherings in the basement of a Ginza department store, but soon became a cabaret for Japanese. The government early indicated a willingness to set aside a generous number of pleasure quarters for the exclusive use of the Occupation. Unfriendly to the idea, the Occupation responded by declaring houses of prostitution off-limits. So they remained. Even today the person who knows where to look can find off-limits signs on the crumbling tile and plaster fronts of what once were such houses, in districts left behind by economic growth.

Of the old licensed quarters, the two within the old city, Yoshiwara and Susaki, prospered. The Shinjuku quarter was doing well enough too. The Shinagawa quarter actually received public subsidies, because, pleasantly and conveniently situated beside the bay and the Tokyo Yokohama highway, it was popular with Americans. Under certain conditions they were permitted the company of geisha, held not to be prostitutes. The haughtier Shimbashi geisha quarter refused a proffered subvention.

The most famous of the "private" or unlicensed quarters, Tamanoi, did not come back after the bombings, but another such quarter east of the Sumida River was probably the most famous one of the immediate postwar

years. Called Hatonomachi, "Pigeon Town," it was the setting for a minor Kafū work, one of his burlesque skits (see page 388). Without having
known Tamanoi, one may imagine that Hatonomachi was very much like
it, though with the addition of an off-limits sign at every door.

A quite new kind of quarter also sprang up, becoming one of the
things people went to see. Kafū went to see it on February 25, 1947.

> Clear, and warm again. I enjoy cooking beside the well and eating
> under the eaves. In the afternoon I walked through the Koiwa district.
> Some five or six hundred yards to the west on the Chiba highway is
> a den of unlicensed prostitutes. The Kameido quarter picked up and
> moved itself en masse to an imposing complex which during the war
> was a Seikō factory and dormitory. At the cement gate is the name
> of the place, Tokyo Palace, and at the entrance is a clinic for diseases
> of the quarters. To one side is a dance hall which opens at five every
> evening and always has, I am told, thirty girls in attendance. There
> are five two-story dormitories, each with fourteen or fifteen rooms,
> and passageways joining them, and sellers of vegetables and repairers
> of footwear. One is initially startled at the size of the place. By the
> gate and all through the grounds are signs: "Off Limits," "VD." Until
> October of last year American soldiers streamed in and out, but now
> the clientele is entirely Japanese. For a half hour, a hundred yen, I was
> told, and for an hour two hundred; eight hundred to spend the night
> from nine o'clock and six hundred from eleven o'clock. I bought an
> apple apiece for two or three women who were taking sweets at the
> confectioner's and had them show me about. Then I walked back to
> the station by a different route.

The off-limits warning is reproduced in Roman letters. "Palace" is the
Japanese phonetic representation of the English word. Both Kameido and
Koiwa are east of the Sumida, the latter near the boundary with Chiba
Prefecture. Kafū was then living in Ichikawa, on the Chiba side of the
boundary. Kameido had a "den" of unlicensed prostitutes before the war,
larger than Tamanoi. Bombed out, it seems to have done as Kafū here has
it doing. Another such den grew up in the Koiwa district after the war.
Seiko is of course the clockmaking enterprise famous the world over. Tokyo Palace, one of the sights along the Chiba highway in those early years,
was a temporary expedient. The girls started moving to more central loca-
tions as soon as they could, and nothing was left in 1958 to outlaw.

These who had shelter were among the luckier ones. It was the day of
the streetwalker. She was among its symbols, and her gradual disappearance, not that she has ever disappeared completely, was among the signs

that a better day—not a day of improved morals but a day of material improvement—had come. Streetwalkers were everywhere in the early years, most conspicuous in places where the after-office crowds were densest and soldiers most numerous. Their paths as they plied their trade in Shinjuku were a factor (see pages 484-485) in changing the map of the place. In the golden age, so to speak, there were as many as five hundred girls in the vicinity of Yūrakuchō Station, just south of Tokyo Central, and immediately west of the main Ginza crossing. (Yurakuchō is often abbreviated Rakuchō, literally "Pleasureville.") On a November evening in 1953 a drunken American soldier threw a pimp over the bridge that still ran across the outer castle moat between Yūrakuchō and Ginza. The fellow drowned, and the incident got much attention from the media. Anti-Americanism was strong in the days after the San Francisco Treaty. ("Yankee go home" was among the expressions that enjoyed great vogue. The English was used.)

Streetwalkers gave the language at least one neologism which has survived. They were and still are known as "*panpan* girls." The origins of the first word are unknown. The second is the English. They had their literary spokesman. The novelist Tamura Taijiro was the leading exponent of the "carnal literature" *(nikutai bungaku)* of the day. His most famous work, a novella published in 1947, has the same title, *Flesh Gate (Nikutai no Mon)*, as the very popular movie made from it. A group of streetwalkers work the district from Yurakucho eastward through Ginza to the Sumida River, and live a communal life in the ruined dockyards. They have their code: they do not give themselves to men except for money; business is business, and any suggestion that sex is other than business is a threat to them all. The main action has to do with the punishment meted out to girls who violate the code by indulging gratis and with pleasure. The first stage, exposure, made the work obvious material for the strip theaters, which did not overlook it. The girls have such vivid names as Borneo Maya. Maya has never been to Borneo, but her brother was killed there, and she is always talking about it. Poor Maya is awaiting punishment as the story ends.

It is sometimes the case that a minor work of literature captures the sense of a time and place better than any major one. *Flesh Gate* must be called a minor work, but one would have trouble thinking of a work that better catches the desperation of those grim years, and the determination to survive. The code may not be of a very elevated sort, but the girls are expected to live by it, one for all and all for one.

Poster for the film Flesh Gate

So much for the flower of the old pair, flower and willow, courtesan and geisha respectively. The sad decline that was to overtake the willow profession of the geisha was not apparent in the immediate postwar years, although there were shifts and changes. Because of a rumor that Americans would be widely requisitioning to the south of Yanagibashi, the Willow Bridge from which the old and elegant geisha quarter derives its name, the houses farthest to the south moved north, and the whole quarter came to lie north of the bridge. The Shimbashi district was meanwhile moving eastward, though there was no similar threat, and leaving the Ginza district entirely to the dancer and the bar girl. In hindsight it is as if they were leaving the future to these latter types. Aficionados talked, as they had for a century or so, of the decline of the geisha. The new geisha had neither the accomplishments nor the brains of the old one. Doubtless the complaints had, for a century or so, been valid. The problem of the decline of the geisha, not numerically apparent until later decades though adumbrated by these complaints, is essentially a moral one. The old sense of pride and responsibility was declining. The flower and the willow were less and less distinguishable.

Already in October 1945 the police permitted the reopening of bars and cafés. The profusion of such places presents taxonomic difficulties. One is hard put to grasp the distinction between a dance hall and a cabaret. They may have been much the same thing, with the former predominant before the war and the latter after. So it is too with the café and the bar. Ginza led the way. It had the only high-rise building, six storys of it, that was cabaret from top to bottom. The opening in 1947 was segregated. There was a floor for foreigners, by which was meant Occidentals. Soon after the San Francisco Treaty it became exclusively Japanese, not admitting "foreigners" at all. Even today, this sort of racism (so it must be called) is not uncommon. Many a deal that contributed to the economic miracle, we are told, was arranged amid the din. The big Ginza cabaret came upon bad times toward the middle of the fifties, as the Akasaka district, near the bureaucratic center of the city and still the abode of elegant geisha, began to have cabarets that were tonier and more convenient. The building was sold to a large magazine in 1955.

One does not often hear the word "café" anymore. "Bar," on the other hand, is everywhere, and unquestionably English, while "café" could be French. Connoisseurs may draw distinctions between them. To the person who has not known the prewar cafés except from literary sources, they may seem very much the same. Young women of varying degrees of elegance, depending on the price, provide company in bars even as Kafū's café girls did before the war. The most elegant and expensive ones have continued to be in Ginza.

Then there were the coffeehouses, the *kissaten,* literally tea shops, though this is misleading. In them persons of more limited means could take more moderate and innocent pleasures. They proliferated in the years after the war, and the years after the San Francisco Treaty may be seen as their best ones. There were coffeehouses where a person could watch newsreels for the price of a cup of coffee until he had had his fill of them or concluded a deal of some description, and places where one could do the same to the accompaniment of popular or classical music. There were "chanson" coffeehouses, where some very famous performers got started. The coffee was not cheap, but one could stay all afternoon and evening and not feel rushed. Coffeehouses got bigger and bigger until, in the mid-fifties, they perhaps got too big. In 1955 a six-story coffeehouse opened in a busy part of Ginza, very near the six-story cabaret. It had life-size animated female dolls to greet customers at the entrance, and several live bands, and the dominant color was purple. It could accommodate six hundred fifty customers. It was not a success. People seem to have gone once and decided that it would not do for every day.

Also toward the middle of the fifties, coffeehouses started becoming less innocent. The matter of the "late-night coffeehouses" attracted the attention of the media, and in 1956 the prefecture handed down regulations for their governance. Licensing of such places had been lax. Some stayed open all night, offered curtained-off and otherwise sequestered nooks, and were much frequented by prostitutes and petty criminals. They provided inexpensive substitutes for inns. The 1956 regulations forbade such places to take customers under eighteen and overnight customers. There were raids. Intermittent fits of police sternness did not succeed in eradicating them. It may be that this was impossible in so energetically sensual a city; and it may be that the police did not try very hard.

Then there was the "*arbeit* salon," abbreviated *arusaro*. The first word is of course German, and it has since the war indicated part-time nonprofessional work, chiefly by students piecing out their income. The *arbeit* salon was a sort of cross between the coffeehouse and the cabaret. Office girls, girl students, and even housewives with spare time would be companionable waitresses during the daylight hours and dancers in the evening. It was less expensive than the cabaret, and for a time customers found the amateurishness of the hostesses pleasing. The vogue for such places had largely passed by the end of the fifties.

In 1947 an imperial edict (for the Meiji constitution was still in force) did away with publicly recognized prostitution. This in theory meant the end of prostitution. What it meant in practice was that the old public quarters, the Yoshiwara and such, turned private, like Kafū's beloved Tamanoi. The operators of the old houses became "special purveyors of beverages," and the women who wished to could work as waitresses. They were free agents, got a share of the earnings, and could depart whenever they wished. The Yoshiwara women formed a union and set up their own clinics, replacing the ones that had sought to control venereal disease among licensed prostitutes. They were supposed to be over eighteen, but many were not.

The evidence is that the change from public to private prostitution made things worse for them. It had been harder to obtain work in the Yoshiwara than elsewhere, because the Yoshiwara required stronger assurance that women would not run off leaving debts behind them. The private operators had pimps and gangsters to assure that this did not happen.

The events of 1947 have a cyclical look. Much the same sort of things had happened in early Meiji when, out of deference to what were thought to be Western notions of propriety, the ladies of the quarters were liberated. It was to happen again in 1958, when, this time by act of the Diet under the new constitution, prostitution was finally outlawed. The new law was opposed by the union, which organized an anti-anti-prostitution movement.

A clerk for the Supreme Court wrote in 1955 of the 1947 edict (Edict 9) outlawing prostitution, and the reasons for its ineffectiveness: "Many

Japanese laws fail to work as their drafters intended them to, and this is because of a failure to investigate, thoroughly and in detail, the manner in which society is likely to react. A reaction sets in, and the law becomes incapable of imposing the controls which are its reason for being. It is like an old sword that has no function except as a family heirloom. The assigned function of the law does not accord with reality. So it was with Edict 9."

In a word, society was not ready. Four decades have passed and it is still not ready. Yet the sword that has become the family heirloom does swing occasionally. It is true of many laws in Japan that they are ignored until it suits someone's convenience to enforce them. Heads then may fall.

Baseball may have replaced Sumō as the national accomplishment, but vogues for other diversions have blazed so violently that they have seemed capable of sending even baseball into eclipse. There blazed the yo-yo, and the Hula-Hoop, which even appeared on the Kabuki stage. Shiga Naoya, one of the dignified elders of Japanese letters, aroused some interest when, in Japanese dress, he had a try at it. When it began, a half-dozen years after the surrender, one might have thought that *pachinko* would blaze and fade. It has not faded. Even today, looking for pursuits that keep people mindlessly happy, one might well come up with a trio: baseball, television, and *pachinko*.

The word is an onomatopoeic one that had several uses before it settled upon the pinball machine. It was a slingshot, a catapult, and a pistol. The vogue for *pachinko* as pinball began in Nagoya, not Tokyo, but Tokyo had more than five thousand pinball parlors by 1952, after which the number fell off somewhat, though the number of machines and customers remained constant. Some were and are very grand, veritable casinos of parlors, blazing with lights and sending forth their metallic clangor to be drowned somewhat in amplified music. The balls fall vertically and not, as in Western prototypes, along an incline, and so speed and noise are increased. With premiums offered for skillful play, *pachinko* became a gambling game. Skillful players were willing to sell their premiums at prices that undercut the retail market. The underworld therefore entered the scene. Petty racketeers would loiter about to buy up premiums.

In 1956 the prefecture, along with other local bodies here and there across the country, took action against automatically fed machines, which greatly increased the speed of play, allowing as many as two hundred balls to flow through a machine in a minute. Automatic feeding led to bigger premiums and a bigger role for the underworld. "Third nationals" have always been prominent in the *pachinko* business, as owners and as buyers of premiums. More than a decade later the automatic feeders were

Playing pachinko

back again, though with the proviso that no more than a hundred balls were to be admitted to a machine per minute. In the mid-fifties upward of one divorce in ten was on grounds of prodigality. *Pachinko* often figured in the matter.

Why has *pachinko,* among all the fads that have come, most of them to go again, shown this perdurability? That it is a flight from reality, a refuge from nagging worries, seems almost too obvious. But there are many such refuges, and why the Japanese have taken to *pachinko* as no one else has, save imitators elsewhere in East Asia, is mysterious. Probably there is no simple answer, but it does seem to be the case that the Japanese would prefer to be knocked into happy oblivion by sheer noise than by most things. *Pachinko* is in any event an instance of Japanese originality.

Baseball came back quickly after the war, both the professional kind and the semi-amateur kind that draws large crowds. The Patriotic Baseball Association returned to its old name in October, and returned as well to the corrupt old terminology, largely English. The Kōrakuen Stadium once more took the English for the second element in its name, the professional teams went back to their old names, Giants and Tigers and the like, also in English, and the best pitcher by far, a Russian, reverted to his real name from the Japanese name he had been required to take during the Crisis. The first professional games took place in November, in Tokyo and Osaka. They were anticipated slightly by a resumption of the Keiō-Waseda rivalry. A game between "old boys" of the two schools was held at the Meiji Stadium on November 18. The stadium had been requisitioned by the Americans and was lent for the occasion. The Occupation was all in favor of baseball, which was peaceful and democratic and which it thought would cement relations, not that it had done much toward this end during the preceding decade.

The novelist Funabashi Seiichi was at the Keiō-Waseda game and set down what it meant to him.

> The gates having been closed off by the Americans, we had to go in over concrete rubble along the passage between infield and outfield. This was unpleasant, but I suppose inevitable....
>
> In the violence of the war, so recently over, we thought that we would never again see a baseball game. And here we were already, under autumn skies, listening to the crack of the baseball bat. It was like a dream. Today, even now, behind the net, I was witness to a squeeze play, a fielder's choice, a pitcher giving an intentional walk, a two-three count with two out and the bases full.
>
> I wanted to feel my eyes and make sure that they were open. But it was no dream. American officers, viewing a serious university baseball game for the first time, seemed to take a different view of us Japanese.

Funabashi uses the old and revived terminology, laced with English.

The Occupation was sensitive to the argument that baseball would be good for the national morale, and Funabashi's remarks suggest that the view was not groundless. The Kōrakuen Stadium, the main grounds for professional baseball in Tokyo, was in a very dreary state at the end of the war. The Scoreboard was a twisted ruin from the April bombings, the stands were artillery and machine-gun emplacements, the field was vegetable patches. Unpromising though it was, the stadium had to remain in Japanese hands if professional baseball was to survive. This was the view of the magnates of the sport, who gathered in emergency session early in November. Their resolve was initially frustrated when the Occupation requisitioned the stadium a few days later. They did not give up, however. They argued eloquently that baseball was necessary to restore the shattered morale of the nation. The requisition order was revoked in February 1946. The first postwar season began in April, at the Korakuen and at the Nishinomiya Stadium in the suburbs of Osaka. The morale of Tokyo was not helped by the fact that the Giants did *not* win the championship that year. An Osaka team did.

The Korakuen Stadium was surrounded by potholes in the early years after the war. Then in 1955 it came to be surrounded by an amusement park, the brightest and best in the city, quite overwhelming the Hanayashiki, the "Flower Garden" in Asakusa. It had roller coasters, of course, and it had skating rinks and gymnasiums too. There it was that Mishima Yukio took up boxing and bodybuilding to reshape the rather fragile endowments with which he had had to be satisfied in his earlier years.

Professional baseball had enough players and sponsors that by the end of 1949 it had enough teams to split into two leagues, the Central and the Pacific. So 1950 was the first two-league season, and in that autumn occurred the first Japan Series, on the American model. Again Tokyo was disappointed. A Tokyo team won the series, but it was not the idolized Giants. Lefty O'Doul, who had given the team its name, came visiting with his San Francisco Seals in 1949. The first night games were held in 1950, and so the language received a new word, "nighter," in modified English.

Shōriki Matsutarō, the father of Japanese professional baseball, became the first chairman of the baseball commission, overseeing both leagues. The circumstances leading up to the split into rival leagues suggest that, besides the national morale, baseball was interested in money. The Giants and the Osaka Tigers had initially been on opposite sides in the matter of admitting new teams to the old league. But then the possibility arose to haunt the Tigers of having to give up games with the Giants, the most lucrative games, if the two remained at odds. So the Tiger organization switched its vote, the teams were admitted, the split occurred, and Giants and Tigers remained lucratively matched.

The promptness with which the Occupation returned the Korakuen may have been responsible for the survival of Shinobazu Pond, a part of Ueno Park, and one of the prettiest spots in the city, especially in midsummer, when the lotuses are in bloom. A very shallow pond, it was drained after the war and put to the growing of cereals. There was a nasty scandal having to do with the disposition of the cereals thus grown. (A large part of the pond disappeared again in 1968, when excavation for a new subway line accidentally punched a hole in the floor.)

Water came back in 1949, but there was talk of putting the site to uses other than pleasure boating and the growing of ornamental water plants. A suggestion which had strong backing was that it be made into a many-level parking garage—for even in those thin days it was apparent that the number of automobiles and the proportions of the traffic problem would not stop growing. Another suggestion, and one that was very

Cultivating the drained Shinobazu Pond, Ueno, 1946

popular with businessmen who thought that Ueno, like Asakusa, might be languishing, was to make the site into a baseball stadium. The faction in favor of filling in the pond and making it useful had a majority on the Taito Ward council, and the death of the pond seemed a matter of time.

Opponents lobbied here and lobbied there, and sought to stir up public attention and concern through such devices as fireworks displays. Finally they summoned up their last measure of courage and went to see Shoriki. He listened in a friendly manner and made a call to the president of the league. It seemed, he said, that the locals did not want a baseball stadium. He thought it might be well for the league to take action appropriate to this state of affairs. So the petitioners went to the president. He nodded smiling assent to their every word and suggestion, and thus ended a battle that had lasted three years. We often hear the word "consensus" with regard to Japanese decisions. The incident might offer evidence as to its deeper meaning. One of Shoriki's visitors said that for the first time he really understood the expression "a single call from the crane." The principal Japanese-English dictionary renders the proverbial call of the crane as "a word *ex cathedra*." Shōriki might not have been as ready with his cathedral pronouncement if the Giants and those other teams had not already had the Kōrakuen at their disposal.

The Occupation was not as kind to Sumō as to baseball. The Sumō arena east of the Sumida River, the domed Hall of the National Accomplishment, was requisitioned the day after Christmas 1945. Like several big theaters, it had been used during the closing months of the war to make incendiary balloons. Except for a single tournament permitted by the Occupation in 1946 in the old arena, Sumō spent the next forty years west of the river. Its main grounds through the Edo centuries and most of the first Tokyo century had been in the east.

After several temporary sites during the immediate postwar years, including the Kōrakuen, Sumō settled on the west bank of the Sumida, just below Asakusa, and remained there for more than a third of a century. At the entrances to the temporary arenas was the warning: "Off-limits to all Occupation and non-Occupation personnel." Those who spoke the Occupation dialect understood the meaning: that no foreigners, whether with the Occupation or not, were permitted within. As a practical matter this meant persons of European or African extraction, who could be apprehended, chided, and evicted. The reasons probably had to do with overcrowding, the Occupation taking the sensible position that Japanese crowds were quite large and dangerous enough already.

When the old arena was finally returned, on April 1, 1952, the Sumō Association found the cost of rehabilitating it, and especially of removing the huge masses of concrete that had been poured into the pit, prohibitive. In 1958 it was sold to a university, which in 1981 sold it to the prefecture, which in 1983 tore it down. The site is now a parking lot. (The Meiji Stadium and the Imperial Hotel were derequisitioned on that same April Fools' Day of 1952. Important things happen on April Fools' Day in Japan because it is the first day of the fiscal year.) In 1985 Sumō returned east of the river, but not to the old grounds, which were never reoccupied. The new arena lies a short distance to the north of the site of the old one, on the other side of the railway line to Chiba.

Probably all authoritarian regimes have their arbitrary side, and the American Occupation, despite its high democratic rhetoric, was authoritarian. It was not evenhanded in its treatment of the two sports. Perhaps the Sumō Association, being somewhat insular, was not as persuasive as the baseball magnates, and of course it did not have the bond of friendship and mutual admiration which each crack of the bat calls up. Because it was very old and very traditional, it may have been, like judo, associated with the martial arts. Certainly judo did help many a soldier, Japanese and American, offensively and defensively. It is hard to believe that Sumō ever did anyone much good in a martial way.

A dozen years after the war Sumō went through another in its series of crises and challenges on the road to what is known as modernization. It has already been mentioned for its place in the career of the great wrestler Futabayama (see page 399). There were hearings in the National Diet on the obstinate refusal of the sport to become modern. Pressures mounted periodically through the first "modern" century of the sport. The president of the Sumō Association was a man who had held the highest rank and taken the professional name of Tsunenohana, which means something like "Everlasting Flower." (Sumō wrestlers often take flowery names.) The pressures became too much for him. One day in May 1957, in what was then the Hall of the National Accomplishment, on the west bank of the Sumida, he attempted a premodern kind of suicide, by disemboweling.

He recovered, but Futabayama replaced him, and in the autumn was able to push reforms through. The problem was the nagging one of how tickets should be sold. The solution was a compromise, as they all have been. Should they be sold directly through a box office managed by the association, or should they go through the traditional teahouses? Well, some would go the one way, some the other. It was a problem that also nagged Kabuki, but Kabuki reformers were more energetic and resolute. The teahouses have vanished from Kabuki sales arrangements. The formal status of the teahouses was also changed, but the change made little difference in their operations.

There were other gestures toward modernization or (another magical word) internationalization. Chairs were put into some of the stalls in which spectators had hitherto had to hunker down on straw matting. The pillars were removed from the roof over the wrestling ring. Like Nō actors, Sumō wrestlers had long performed under two roofs, that which closed the larger arena or theater off from the heavens and that which gave the stage or ring the aspect of a smaller, more intimate building. In 1952 the pillars disappeared from the smaller, lower roof of the Hall of the National Accomplishment. It has since been suspended from the higher ceiling. Safety and visibility were given as the reasons. Wrestlers were always injuring themselves against the pillars.

Futabayama retired a few months after the end of the war, and everyone said that his like would not come again. It may be true, and it certainly is true that Sumō as popular entertainment has been put in deep shadows by baseball. Yet Sumō more than survived. It returned from the ashes to have one of the most remarkable periods in its modern history. From about the end of the first postwar decade two fine wrestlers, Wakanohana and Tochinishiki, began their rise to the top, which both of them reached toward the end of the fifties. (Wakanohana is another of those floral names. It means something like "Flower of Youth.") They may not have been the very finest of postwar wrestlers, but each was a worthy rival of the other, and it takes two to make a match. There was excitement in the Tochiwaka period, as the Japanese fondness for acronyms has it, as there has not been since.

The two provided moments of great excitement, and Wakanohana won the important matches. They fought to a draw in 1958, at the end of the tournament as a result of which one or the other was certain to be promoted to Yokozuna, the top Sumō rank. Wakanohana won the rematch. In 1960 both went into the fifteenth and last day of the March tournament undefeated. It was the first time in the history of the sport that two Yokozuna had gone into the final day in that condition. Again Wakanohana won. It is true that the rank has been debased in recent years, so that there may be stars to attract crowds and the television audience. Yet it was a fine moment. The pair provided fine moments as we have not had them since.

We often hear that the invasion of the old national accomplishment by "foreigners" did not begin until the late sixties, when a Hawaiian came into prominence. In fact there had earlier been Koreans. One of them, whose Sumo name was Rikidōzan, started something, the huge popularity of professional wrestling, that would probably have started one day even without him. As in all places, professional wrestling in Japan is less sport than show. Rikidōzan, a moderately successful and popular Sumō wrestler, though he did not reach the very top, left Sumō in some pique at the feudal ways of the Sumō world, and in October 1951 was the big attraction in the first professional wrestling matches. He became a great hero. He had come upon something the age and the nation yearned for, doing brutal things to monstrous persons of European stock. It was the Bruce Lee act. Rikidōzan was proclaimed "world champion" in 1954. He had close ties with the underworld. Feeling that he needed bodyguards, he used gangsters. In December 1963 he was stabbed during an alterca-

The great Sumō wrestler Futabayama being arrested.
The religious group of which he was an adherent was
suspected of black market activities

tion in an Akasaka cabaret. The assailant was a member of the gang that controlled the place. Rikidōzan died a week later.

Besides the black market mostly provisioned by Americans, there was another market, blackish, at least, that is not often remarked upon. The Japanese armed forces had huge commissary supplies at the end of the war. Indeed they were almost the only organizations that might have been deemed affluent. The more lethal portions were for the most part turned over to the Americans and destroyed, and those that were less so found their way into the civilian market by various routes. They got many a Japanese company started on its way to recovery, and they also got Akihabara started. The Akihabara electronics market is today among the marvels of Tokyo. At Akihabara, it is said, and we who do not know must take the statement on faith, the electronically sophisticated person can find anything that has been invented.

"Akihabara" is literally "the meadow of the Akiba Shrine." Nagai Kafū insisted to the end that anyone who did not pronounce it "Akibagahara" was a barbarian. Alas, the barbarians have quite taken over, for everyone today says Akihabara. A freight yard since Meiji, it became an important passenger station when, after the earthquake, the Yamanote loop line was finally completed. In Meiji the district was known for domestic handiwork, combs and split-toed socks and the like. Between the wars it was known for its bicycle wholesalers. Such of these as remained after the bombings withdrew some distance from the station.

The radio was very important during the last months of the war and the hard times after. Often it was the only bit of advanced technology a family took with it to the air-raid shelter. Radios were the way to know when danger was coming and when it seemed to have passed. The nation might not have surrendered so meekly if it had not been told to turn on all its radios at high noon on August 15, 1945. The radio became a kind of status symbol in the months after the war. To say that one had an all-wave radio was to say that one had a particular pipeline.

So everyone wanted radios, not as easy to come by as the television sets everyone was to want in a few years' time. Akihabara was ideally situated to take advantage of the blackish market in military supplies. The first to come in were from the Chiba Peninsula, to the east of Tokyo Bay. Akihabara stands at the junction of the Yamanote loop and the line that runs eastward to Chiba and westward to Shinjuku and beyond. The last of the electronics stalls still scattered over the Kanda district moved north when, at the end of 1951, street stalls disappeared.

Electronics emerged dominant at Akihabara for another reason. Penniless young men back from the war were trying to get ahead with their schooling, and Akihabara was near the Kanda-Hongō university district. Many stood on the sidewalk and sold peanuts. A much better way to do it, for those who could, was to build radios. So they combed the Akihabara shops for parts the shopkeepers themselves often did not know the functions of, and built.

Thus began the Akihabara market, assuredly a wonder. Many of the makeshift devices and institutions of the postwar confusion have gone away, and some have stayed and prospered. Chiyoda Ward still has the largest volume among the twenty-three of retail sales in electronics equipment. It is peculiar that that place of big-time managers should lead in retail sales of anything at all, but we must remember that Chiyoda is a mating of two very unlike wards, Kōjimachi, where the managers are, and Kanda, a place of students, universities, and small enterprises.

On April 28, 1952, the great actor Kichiemon led the audience at the Kabukiza in three cheers. It was the day on which the Occupation ended and the San Francisco treaties—the peace treaty and the Japanese-American Security Treaty—went into effect. The undoing of the Occupation, the reassembling of the old combines and the like, is a long and complex story, and of course not limited to Tokyo. Neither is the story of what happened to "summertime." This last is an instance, however, of an American miscalculation that could be and was swiftly repaired. The expression is in English, and it signifies daylight-saving time, which was imposed by the Americans in April 1948 and abolished just four years later, in the month in which the treaties went into effect. It was something American that could be readily disavowed, though more rational arguments were offered. Better to have an innocent and healthy extra hour in the morning, went one of them, than an extra hour in the evening to waste on drinking and mah-jongg. Just a year later the American practice of giving women's names to typhoons was discontinued. Since then they have had only numbers. Kitty, which struck in the autumn of 1947, did more damage to Tokyo than any other typhoon in all the years since the war.

Though he cannot have intended them so, Kichiemon's three cheers might have been taken to announce the beginning of the radical years. Those who read only the newspapers during the Occupation years cannot have been prepared for what happened immediately afterward. The newspapers had suggested little except delight with the Americans and their Occupation and ways, and a resolve to move upward into the light, equal partners (in an expression much favored by a later ambassador) with the United States. Those who went occasionally to the university campuses and saw what was on the student posters may have been vaguely aware that another current was waiting to burst forth.

It did, explosively, on the third day of Japanese independence. May Day had been among the annual festivals of Taishō democracy. Laborers and progressive thinkers got out and marched. With an estimated half-million people in attendance, the observance was resumed in 1946. The seventeenth May Day rally, after the loss of a decade's worth to the Crisis, was held in the palace plaza. In succeeding years that was the place for it. Then, in 1951, the last year in which the Occupation had a say in the matter, the use of the plaza was banned. This happened again in 1952.

Riots in the palace plaza, May Day 1952

Progressives and laborers assembled in the Meiji Gardens. After a big rally there they set forth on marches over five approved routes. The march that was supposed to end at Hibiya Park was seized with an urge to go on to the plaza, just across the street. Erstwhile headquarters of the Occupation lay across another street from the plaza, and a few paces up from the intersection between the two. So General MacArthur, if he had been there, would have had among the best views in town of what happened. The marchers crossed the street and poured into the plaza, and there were met by the police, who used truncheons, tear gas, and even pistols. As they retreated back across the street the demonstrators overturned and set fire to a few American automobiles. A large proportion of the automobiles in the city in those days were American, and they still were allowed to park along main streets.

Initial announcements had one young man killed, by pistol fire. Actually two were killed. More than a hundred, more of them policemen than demonstrators, were seriously injured. More than a hundred demonstrators were arrested on the spot, and eventually more than a thousand.

Of the two hundred or so brought to trial, more than half were declared innocent by the Tokyo District Court—in 1970. Not quite eighteen years had passed. Justice grinds more slowly in Japan than in most places that have it. In 1972 the Tokyo Higher Court declared most of the convicted ones innocent. Fewer than twenty sentences were served.

Such clear-eyed witnesses as the novelist Umezaki Haruo, not of strongly radical inclinations, put the blame on the police. The first acts of violence, he said, were on their side. It may be true. The police, not the well-oiled machine they are today for containing such manifestations, may well have been overzealous. Whatever the rights and wrongs, May Day 1952 stands symbolically at the beginning of a remarkable period. Those who controlled the media seemed intent upon making the nation accept a most simpleminded orthodoxy. Every unpleasant question had a simple answer: blame it on capitalism and imperialism, and join the peaceful socialist force. Many an explanation has been given for the phenomenon, but the sudden clap of pacifist, socialist thunder after the quiet of the Occupation was certainly very startling.

The rioters of 1952 still had another dozen years to go with their court travails when it all began to quiet down. In 1960 the attempt to prevent revision of the Security Treaty failed, and showed that the media were not after all omnipotent and that the movement may have been more sound than substance. There followed fragmentation and (as in the thirties) apostasy, and the golden radical years did not return. Today they are (as the saying has it) a dream within a dream. They were remarkable while they lasted, and Tokyo was where the noise was made. Having a demonstration in Osaka or Nagoya would have been like marching on the wrong Washington.

There had been numerous instances under the Occupation of violence with political origins. In 1946 there was an occurrence the likes of which had not often, perhaps never, been heard of in earlier Japanese history, a demonstration not against evil, corrupt ministers surrounding the emperor but against the emperor himself. In the spring of 1946 a "give us rice" rally in the western part of the city was turned into a march upon the palace by the communist firebrand Nosaka Sanzō, recently back from China. Only a direct confrontation with the emperor would serve, he said. The rally marched upon the palace and breached one of the palace gates before it was dispersed. A demand was presented: that the contents of the royal pantry immediately be communized. "I have plenty to eat. You people can starve," said one placard. The first-person pronoun was the sacred *chin* (see the ribaldry on page 445), reserved for the emperor alone. A result was arraignment for lèsemajesté, the last before that crime ceased to exist. The Occupation was less sure thereafter that communist agitation was a welcome part of the new democracy.

A prominent instance of possible political violence remains a mystery. Was the violence wrought by the victim upon himself, or was it at the hands of others? We do not know. In the spring of 1949 the National Railways began a drastic personnel retrenchment. On July 4 the railway offices announced plans to dismiss forty thousand workers. The president, Shimoyama Sadanori, was last definitely seen alive on the morning of July 5, near the main Mitsukoshi department store in Nihombashi. The next morning his dismembered body was found on a track of his own National Railways in the northeastern part of the city. The finding of the official autopsy was that he was dead before being run over, but there was expert opinion to the contrary, holding that he had placed himself upon the tracks and been killed by a train. There were also those who averred that someone very like him had been seen near the fatal spot on the night of July 5. No arrests were made. If Shimoyama was indeed murdered, then his murderers were most likely radical unionists. They were much inflamed in those days, both because of the layoffs and because of a hint from General MacArthur on that same July 4 that the Communist Party might be outlawed.

Through the month of July there were literally thousands of instances of sabotage and obstruction throughout the National Railways system. The most famous incident occurred not in Tokyo but at Matsukawa in Fukushima Prefecture, on the main line of the National Railways to the far north. Three train crewmen died on August 17 in a derailment. The union members taxed with the act were not finally acquitted until 1963. Some weeks earlier there had been a bloodier though less celebrated incident at Mitaka, in the western suburbs of Tokyo. On July 15 seven railway cars ran loose down a sloping track from the Mitaka railway yards. They crashed into a house, killing six people. The suspicion was strong that the runaway was not accidental. Two union men were arrested and one was sentenced to death. The sentence was never carried out. He died in prison.

If the Matsukawa defendants were guilty (they were acquitted for want of evidence) and if Shimoyama was murdered, then the most likely explanation for all three incidents is union unrest. The thought that Japan once had militant unionism is like a faint echo from a legendary past; but indeed there was such a time. A strike against the *Yomiuri Shimbun* in 1945 brought a brief period of democratization, by which is meant control of editorial policy by the labor unions. General MacArthur interdicted plans for a general strike in 1947. Concerning the most celebrated instances of violence, the railway cases, there have been theories that someone else did everything, some strongly anti-union entity

The train wreck at Mitaka, 1949

wishing to make it *seem* that the unions were responsible. The Occupation is prominent among the suspects. In the Shimoyama instance, it is said that a peculiar grease used by Americans in ministering to their weaponry was found on the dead man's shirt.

The Mitsukoshi department store figured peripherally in the Shimoyama incident, possibly a product of labor strife, and it had some strife of its own which was rather amusing and showed how quickly the militancy was subsiding. This occurred during the year-end rush of 1951. A popular saying resulted: "You can find anything at Mitsukoshi, even a strike." Management, with the help of nonunion and part-time clerks, was prepared to open the store on the morning of December 18, but some two thousand pickets from the Mitsukoshi union and others sealed the entrances. They were joined by thirty concerned clergymen from the aggressive Nichiren sect, who marched up and down banging on ritual drums. The police informed the pickets that they would not be allowed to interfere with business, and that was that. By noon customers were pouring in.

A history of labor strife in Tokyo over the past third of a century would surely be among the shortest histories ever written. It has consisted mainly of ceremonial stoppages of which the public is informed in advance. They can be fun. Office workers who know that they cannot get back to the suburbs disport themselves later than usual and sleep in the city.

* * *

The hardships of the first winter after the war caused the death in March 1946 of the eminent Kabuki actor Kataoka Nizaemon. He was the twelfth in a line of actors bearing that name, its origins in Kyoto in the seventeenth century. He was murdered, along with four members of his family. The murderer was a young man who lived with the family. His complaint was that he was cheated on rations, given less to eat than members of the family. Having been scolded by Nizaemon s wife for stealing food, he seized an ax with the intention of punishing only her, and was surprised into attacking the rest of the family.

(In the case of the other postwar Kabuki actor of eminence to die in extraordinary circumstances, the circumstances were much more luxurious. The seventh Bandō Mitsugorō died of *fugu* poisoning in 1975. Certain parts of the *fugu*—blowfish—are poisonous. Much prized by gourmets, it is safe when prepared by professionals. Real gourmets, however, approach close to the poisonous parts and, it is said, experience a delightful tingling of the palate. Mitsugorō seems to have approached too close.)

Some of the crimes and misdemeanors of the postwar years, though they produced pains and losses, seem in retrospect chiefly amusing. On the evening of November 22, 1948, the chief of the prefectural police, off having a look at Ueno Park, a most disorderly place, was beaten up by a male prostitute. The following month the park was declared closed at night to everyone but policemen. In September 1950 a teenage chauffeur for Nihon University made off with a large sum of money, stolen from a university functionary, and also with the daughter of a university professor. The two were apprehended in bed. In the two days between their absconding and their capture they had spent some twenty-five times the beginning monthly salary of an office worker. As the police entered the room they had taken, the boy sat up in bed and said, in English, "Oh, mistake." He never explained himself, and there were several theories as to what he meant. Probably he wanted the officers to think, back in those Occupation days, that he was an American. "Oh, mistake" was among the new expressions that went the rounds that year, along with "nighter" signifying an after-dark baseball game.

Some crimes were dreadful. A man named Kodaira took advantage of the postwar hardships to rape and murder women, ten of them. He would lure them to secluded spots with promises of food and work, and there do it. The body of the last victim was found in Shiba Park on the heights behind the Tokugawa tombs, where Tokyo Tower was later to go up (see pages 517-518). He was apprehended in August 1946. Then there was what is known, with black irony, as the Kotobuki affair. *Kotobuki* means something like "good luck." In this instance it was the name of a lying-in hospital, in what was before 1947 Ushigome Ward, to the west of the palace. In January 1948 the police apprehended an automobile taking a dead infant from the hospital. Investigation revealed that the man and wife who ran the hospital had since 1945 been taking in unwanted infants for money. They had disposed of more than a hundred in several ways. Some had been allowed to die of exposure and pneumonia, some had starved to death. The largest number had been quietly suffocated.

There was a young man named Yamazaki who was eminently representative of nihilistic postwar youth. He was a member of the elite, a student at Tokyo University. He set up a usury business. It failed, and he committed suicide, in November 1949. Life is an empty play, he said, and death is nothing at all. The affair caught the fancy of Mishima Yukio, who a few months later began serialization of the novel *The Green Years (Ao no Jidai)*, based on Yamazaki's brief career.

It may be that the crime most celebrated the nation over during those postwar years was the Matsukawa derailment mentioned above. That is because it aroused intense political passions, and won the services of an eminent writer, Hirotsu Kazuo, who thought of himself as a Japanese Emile Zola and made it his mission to establish the innocence of the defendants. Probably the most celebrated Tokyo crime was the Imperial Bank robbery. (The Imperial, or Teikoku, subsequently reverted to its earlier name, the Mitsui Bank.) On the afternoon of January 26, 1948, just at closing time, a man of perhaps fifty wearing what seemed to be an official armband entered the branch of the bank at Shiinamachi, on the Seibu Ikebukuro line a short distance west of Ikebukuro. He said that he had come to administer a dysentery preventative and that all the employees must drink it. They did, all sixteen of them, and twelve died. What they had drunk was potassium cyanide. He too had a drink of the liquid, by way of demonstration, but seems to have drunk only from the layer of water on top. He made off with a considerable sum of money and a check.

A painter named Hirasawa was sentenced to death for the crime. The sentence was confirmed by the Supreme Court in 1955, and numerous petitions to reopen the case were dismissed. The sentence was never reversed, nor was it carried out. In 1985 Hirasawa was returned to Tokyo from Sendai Prison, where capital punishments are carried out for Tokyo criminals. He died in a prison hospital in 1987, at the age of ninety-five. He had been imprisoned for almost forty years, and had lived with the death sentence for almost a third of a century. All that was required to carry it out was the seal and signature of the minister of justice, and no minister ever signed and sealed. Since 557 executions did occur between 1947 and 1985, believers in his innocence have found support for their position. There had been more than thirty justice ministers during the more than thirty years between Hirasawa's final conviction and his death. Every one of those many ministers—who replaced each other at a dizzying rate so that all manner of politicians might have their time— apparently had doubts about his guilt.

The devices which led to Hirasawa's arrest, on the island of Hokkaido in August 1948, were certainly very ingenious. There had earlier been two similar incidents, one late in 1947 at a bank in the southern part of Tokyo, one a few days before the Imperial affair at a bank very near its Shiinamachi branch. Both of the latter banks were within walking distance of Hirasawa's residence. In both of the earlier cases a man of great assurance had said that, by way of disease prevention, the bank employees must drink of the liquid he offered. He was thwarted in both instances. The similarity among the three led the police to suspect the same culprit, and their attention was drawn to the name cards he (if indeed it was a single person) had left at the two earlier banks. One of them bore a fictitious name, but the other bore the unusual name of a physician living in Sendai.

Certain peculiarities in printing, having to do with the unusual name, established that the card indeed belonged to the physician. So he was set to the task of remembering the people he had exchanged cards with. Among those he remembered was Hirasawa. The two had met and exchanged cards in 1947, on the ferry from Hakodate on Hokkaido to Aomori. Hirasawa was singled out as the most suspicious, and arrested. It was all very ingenious, but it did not, in itself, prove much of anything.

Interrogation was intense. Initially it revealed nothing about the Imperial affair, but it did seem to reveal something else of interest. As the time approached for Hirasawa's mandatory release, evidence emerged that he might be guilty of fraud. At yet another bank he had, or so it was suspected, taken advantage of loose procedures and made off with a sum of money intended for another customer. So he was arraigned for fraud, and the interrogation continued. He signed a confession in the Imperial Bank matter. He later retracted it. Most of it was composed by the detectives, he said, and mental torture caused him to sign. All three of the courts that imposed or upheld the death sentence accepted the validity of the confession.

It was not quite the only evidence, though we are often told it was. A large amount of money that went into Hirasawa's bank account shortly after the crime was never adequately explained. His statement that it was in payment for a work of pornography which someone had commissioned him to do was not a part of the sworn testimony and is not convincing. Several of the experts summoned, though not all of them, said that the endorsement on the check, which was cashed on the day after the murders, was in Hirasawa's hand. Like the handwriting experts, the four Imperial Bank survivors were not in agreement. Neither were the employees of the other two banks. Some were certain that the criminal, or the would-be criminal, was Hirasawa, some were not.

Many a court would in these circumstances have held that there was reasonable doubt as to his guilt; and many a person has held that a third of a century awaiting the seal and signature of one of those justice ministers constitutes unusual and inhuman punishment.

It was a fascinating case, and not the least fascinating element is the air that hangs over it of postwar confusion and deprivation. Even the bank in which the crime occurred has a make-do look about it, not at all a

Detectives inside the Imperial Bank after the robbery

Mitsui look. To judge from photographs, it was a quite ordinary dwelling house made to do until something more banklike could be put up. One cannot imagine the cool clerks and branch managers in the glossy banks of our day accepting an unidentified drink from a stranger; but epidemics raged in those years, and the faculty called common sense had come unmoored.

Another line of investigation proceeded parallel to that of the name card. It is much favored by the radical left because it brings in the possibility of American skulduggery. The police thought it possible that the criminal was skilled in the use of chemical poisons. The biggest pool of expertise was in the Japanese army, and particularly a chemical-warfare unit once active in Manchuria. This second investigation was frustrated by the Americans, its supporters aver, because they took the unit under their protection. The Korean War broke out a few weeks before the first Hirasawa conviction was handed down, and, with a mind to launch chemical warfare against the Koreans, the Americans wished to use Japanese skills to reinforce their own inadequate ones. Rumors of chemical-warfare were rife in those days. One can say for the case that it might possibly be true, but that the evidence is flimsier than that which led to Hirasawa's conviction.

The child of Edo, who had nothing to compare his city with except the cities of the Kansai, which were not worth the time of day, may not have noticed something that early foreign visitors were quick to discern. They thought the city a cluster of villages. They were right in the sense that it was a scattered city with more than one center. What they remarked upon has been among the unchanging elements in a city of violent change. The city has gone on having not one "downtown" but several. It did not have to start decentralizing when decentralization came into vogue among planners. The process was already well advanced.

In the fifties we started hearing the word *fukutoshin*. It is literally "secondary heart of the city," and it might also be rendered "subcenter" or "satellite city." In 1960 it entered specifically into the official plans of a city that has never (and it is among the pleasures of the place) really done much effective planning. A commission presented and the prefectural council approved a plan that had specific reference to Shinjuku, Shibuya, and Ikebukuro. They were to be the first *fukutoshin,* dispersing the oppressive strength of the traditional center. The plan and the concept are notable for their westerly inclination, which is realistic, that having been the inclination of the city ever since it became Tokyo.

Shinjuku was well ahead of the other two in those days, and it is well ahead now, the only one among them that can seriously challenge the old Ginza-Nihombashi-Marunouchi center. How successful the challenge has been is a matter that must be treated later. Shinjuku grew up at the point where one of the main highways out of the city, that to the province of Kai, crossed the railroad which in 1885 commenced service from Shinagawa through the western suburbs to a point near the northern prefectural boundary. The inland road to the Kansai had in premodern times departed the city in a northwesterly direction, through Itabashi. The railroad that was to replace it began service as far as Hachiōji in 1904. It headed uncompromisingly westward from Shinjuku. Itabashi languished. Already in the early decades of this century two important private commuter lines, one of them the Odawara Express of lyric fame (see page 352), terminated in Shinjuku. Their commuter clientele fell into the habit of taking a few cups and other pleasures at Shinjuku before resuming the outward passage. Shinjuku was the place in the western suburbs that drew the biggest crowds.

In the years when the word *fukutoshin* was gaining currency, Shinjuku saw the possibility of widening its lead yet further. Indeed the possibility was becoming a certainty that it would in the near future have a big piece of land to develop. The Yodobashi Reservoir (Yodobashi was the name of one of the three wards which in 1947 were amalgamated to form Shinjuku Ward) covered a tract of more than eighty acres just to the west of the Shinjuku Nishiguchi, the "Westmouth" to Shinjuku Station. From the Taishō Period there had been talk of moving the reservoir farther west. The move actually took place in 1965, and so the story of what was done with the land can be left to later.

The Westmouth was in those years the neglected, backward one. It was not without its places for reveling. We have seen that immediately after the war underworld gangs opened markets at all three of the mouths, west, south, and east. Traces of that at Westmouth yet survive, in the cluster of one and two-story "barracks" known popularly and affectionately as Piss Alley (Shomben Yokochō). It would much prefer that the public call it Chicken Alley, for skewered chicken is, along with alcohol, the commodity it chiefly purveys, but the public does not oblige. Piss Alley it is and will be so long as it survives. It may not smell very good, but it is an object of great nostalgia for those who wish that the city had not rebuilt itself quite so thoroughly in the four decades since the war.

A more delicate vestige remains at Southmouth. A few paces east of the south entrance to the station, in against the revetment where the broad, constantly jammed successor to the old Kai highway crosses the railroad tracks, is a cluster of "barracks," shabby wooden buildings with that postwar look about them. They were once drinking places. The Construction Ministry has announced its intention to make the tract a decorative public plaza. Something of the sort is probably needed, for the pedestrian crowds at rush hours spill over onto the highway; but the owners of the buildings, or some of them, will have nothing of it. They say that the ministry does not own the land and has no right to expel them, even though it has effectively rendered most of the buildings derelict. They squatted on land that belonged to the National Railways and now belongs, in their view, to the successor company, and they themselves claim obscure rights. A court battle is in prospect. Rights are clearer in the Westmouth case. If the decorative plaza ever comes to be, it is not likely to be remotely as interesting as the vestige. In a corner of the tract is a public latrine less than ten feet square. The value of the land is estimated at not far from two million dollars at the current exchange rate. Piss Alley has no latrines. That is why it is that.

Westmouth and Southmouth were not without their reveling places, then, but Eastmouth was the really bustling part of Shinjuku. The center of the bustle had shifted in the modern century. Shinjuku, like the others of the "mouths" on the main highways out of the city, had its licensed quarter. It lay just to the north of what is now the Shinjuku Royal

Piss Alley, Shinjuku

Garden. The railway station, somewhat to the west, pulled shopping and other pleasures toward it, and in the interwar years the busiest part of Shinjuku, and the center of its café culture, was a short distance east of the station, where two roads to the west forked. With its big department stores, this is still the part of Shinjuku where women have the most fun shopping. Men came to have places farther north.

There was what was first called the Hanasono Block, from the name of the shrine against which it nestled, and then the Golden Block, the first word in English. It has never been very golden. With the clearing away of black markets from the eastern approaches to the station, a snug little pocket between shrine and trolley line became jammed with tiny drinking places, accommodating no more than a dozen customers and occupying a space no more than perhaps that many feet square. Up a very steep flight of stairs would be space for more private drinking and other activities. The district began calling itself the Golden Block from about the time of the Olympics. Even with the disappearance of the trolley line, it remained a little apart from and a little different from the much brighter and larger district that grew up to the west, and it has shown great powers of survival. The indications are that it will not survive much longer. The Seibu enterprises are buying it up, and a warren of little two-story wooden buildings is not in the Seibu class.

The story of how that brighter, larger district came to be is a most remarkable one of industry and enterprise, with a strong admixture of luck as well. Kabukichō may today be—the matter is arguable—the liveliest part of the city. It is without doubt the leading center in the city and quite probably the land for what is called "the sex industry." The industry is not quite as open, perhaps, as in Times Square, but it is more varied. There can be few proclivities to which Kabukichō does not minister. And until 1948 the name Kabukicho, much less the fact, did not exist.

Until it was reduced to cinders in 1945, the district was a nondescript one of small shops and dwellings. Noting the regularity and apparent inevitability with which the paths of the ladies of the night, as they plied their trade in the aftermath of the war, led through the district, a man named Suzuki had a dream. He had in his youth been a cook in the British and American embassies, apparently a good one. (His teacher was a man who later became head chef at the Imperial hotel.) At the end of the war he was in the food-processing business and the head of the neighborhood association of a district to the north of Shinjuku Station. His dream was that the district might be made over into a cultural center, with a variety of theaters, including a Kabuki one. It did certainly become a center, and it does have one big theater and numbers of lesser ones, but "cultural" might not be the word that best characterizes it. "Raunchy" might do better.

Suzuki and others busied themselves, and their labors seem to have been enormous, with such matters as providing utilities for and assigning lands to the owners of establishments, mostly eating and drinking ones, that would cater to the theater crowds. A new name was needed, for easy reference, because the district with which the planners were concerned extended over two of the older districts in what from 1947 was Shinjuku Ward. This gave it a divided and scattered look, when identity and integrity were required. In elaborate ceremonies in 1948, attended by such dignitaries as the first elected governor of the prefecture, it became Kabukichō.

The new name does undeniably have style, and it was expected to have a certain talismanic function as well. It was to break a jinx regarding Kabuki, to refute the old notion that Kabuki was an art form particular to and inseparable from the old Low City. Like a wildflower, it could survive only on its native grounds. As a matter of fact Shinjuku Ward had had instances supporting the generalization. A theater in the old Yotsuya Ward had what historians call second-rate Kabuki from 1917. It also had the usual history of burnings and rebuildings, and a brief period of prosperity just after the earthquake, when it was back in business before any of the Low City theaters could be. It declined as they returned and had its last Kabuki in 1937, although it survived in other capacities, to be destroyed just after the war as unsafe. A Shinjuku theater called the Shinkabukiza, the New Kabuki Theater, opened in 1929. The name having changed to Shinjuku Daiichi Gekijō, or First Shinjuku Theater, it gradually became less a place for Kabuki than for concerts, reviews, and theatrical performances of a more modern and exotic sort: for a brief period after the Second World War, when so many of the Low City theaters were gutted shells, it was again among the main places for Kabuki. It does not survive.

Possibly, depending on definitions, the jinx has been broken by the National Theater, which stands on one of the most awesome expanses of land in the High City, just across the moat from the palace. It was not, in any event, broken by Kabukichō, which never got its Kabuki theater. The first movie theater opened in 1948 and closed a decade later. It was popular with the chic left, whose great decade its one decade approximately coincided with. Kabukichō was becoming all the time more strategic, and did not really need Kabuki. The Shinjuku line of the metropolitan trolley system was rerouted in 1949 so that its Shinjuku terminus was at the southern edge of the district. The Seibu railways extended one of their lines to Shinjuku in 1952. The Shinjuku terminus was at the western edge of Kabukichō.

There was an exposition. When in doubt have an exposition: this seems to be a part of Japanese folk wisdom. In the Meiji Period there was a series of national expositions, most of them at Ueno, designed to rally the nation in the endeavor to catch up with the world. They do seem to have had an enlivening effect. Suzuki decided that Kabukichō would have one. It was held at three sites in the spring and early summer of 1950. It was a complete disaster—or would have been if good luck had not come upon the scene at this point. The fact that it was such a fiasco attracted attention, and Kabukichō was, so to speak, on the map. In 1951 Suzuki was able to arrange a land transaction between the largest landowner in the district and a movie company. It included the site of the biggest and most famous of Kabukichō theaters, the Koma Stadium. The Koma opened as a movie house in 1956, and a year later changed over to stage. The most popular entertainers in the land, such as Enoken, performed there.

Kabukichō emerged as the most bustling part of Shinjuku. The district of the interwar café bustle did not languish, but it was rather lost in the glare of Kabukichō. The pleasure quarter that was attached to the old post station did well in the years just after the war. The count of its ladies was in 1951 ten times what it had been at the end of the war. Some of the houses modernized themselves by becoming joint-stock companies and by arranging exchanges with the Yoshiwara, the most venerable of the licensed pleasure quarters. The advantage of this arrangement was that a girl could have more than one debut, and debuts were highly profitable. The two quarters had the most expensive brothels in the city.

With the second postwar outlawing of prostitution in sight, that of 1958, many a little drinking place emerged as a cover for the old business. By the time Shinjuku Ward had been in existence long enough to publish a history of its first thirty years, almost a half million people were partaking of Kabukichō each day. As many as 80 percent of them were under thirty. It is the young crowds that give a bustling place its life and its future, and so Kabukichō was doing well.

But if Kawabata thought that Asakusa had nothing really first-rate to offer, what would he have said of Kabukichō? Being of the crowd which commuted south from Ginza rather than that which commuted west from Shinjuku, he does not seem to have paid much attention. The Koma did offer performances of some quality, but, except for first-run movie houses, it was the only place all up and down Eastmouth that can

have been said to do so. Shinjuku has in this respect never been a rival of
Ginza. Nor does it offer the variety of stage performances that interwar
Asakusa did. Eastmouth is essentially a purveyor of drink and sex. It has
been increasingly that ever since it became Kabukichō. One does not
wish to sound censorious, for it is all very interesting and amusing; but
one would have liked to have, while it was still possible, a comparison of
Eastmouth and Asakusa from Kawabata.

If Suzuki and the others who worked so hard to get Kabukichō going had a sense of where it would go, they did not say so. Perhaps those
initial observations about the habits of the ladies of the night pointed in
an inevitable direction.

Shibuya, a glance at a map may inform one, is so like Shinjuku that its
failure to grow as rapidly, though it grew quite rapidly enough, may seem
puzzling. Like Shinjuku it grew around a point where a road out of the
city crossed the first railway line through the western suburbs. The highway, to a sacred mountain in the Kantō hinterlands, was not, however,
as important as the two that forked at Shinjuku. Nor did Shibuya, like
Shinjuku, stand at a crossroads of the National Railways. Private railway
systems were slower to take shape. Shibuya had its subway line into the
heart of the city a quarter of a century before Shinjuku did, but Shinjuku
had its railway connection decades before Shibuya had its subway.

Perhaps the most important difference is in the lay of the land. Both
Shinjuku and Ikebukuro are on tablelands and look as if they could
sprint off in any direction. Shibuya is hemmed in by hills which have
had a confining effect.

When, in 1883, the forerunner of Aoyama Gakuin University moved
to the campus it still occupies, there was not much below it in the Shibuya
valley. In those days the city limits more than encompassed the city, and
the new Aoyama Gakuin, founded by missionaries in the Tsukiji foreign
settlement, was in open countryside. The first Shibuya Station, a private
one later nationalized, opened in 1885. It was with the Sino-Japanese
War and the Russo-Japanese War, and especially the latter, that Shibuya
began to turn into something more than a sleepy country village. Army
training grounds lay in the countryside beyond. The road that crossed
the railway tracks at Shibuya was much used by military conveyances.
So the army is back at the beginning of all the bustle, today so little martial and spartan. As with Shinjuku, rapid growth came after the earthquake. What in 1932 became Shibuya Ward had a far larger population
than that legally required for incorporation as a city.

As the Olympics drew near, it came to seem that Shibuya would have a large, open tract of land with which to do as Shinjuku did with its reservoir. A place called Washington Heights was returned to the Japanese in time for them to make it over into the athletes' village. It lay just north of Shibuya and adjacent to the Meiji Shrine. The American Occupation had used the old Yoyogi parade grounds for family housing and called them Washington Heights. The Olympics past, the land was put to other use, but it never did for Shibuya quite what the Westmouth reservoir did for Shinjuku. The story of what it did do may be left for later.

Shibuya has continued to lag behind Shinjuku. Until the subway went through to Shimbashi in 1939 it had no direct link with the heart of the city, and until 1932 only one private railway ran from Shibuya into the suburbs. That one is today a minor part of the Tōkyū system that dominates the district. Shibuya has until recently had more the look of a one-company town, if town it may for convenience be called, than Shinjuku. It had that look even more during and immediately after the war. The two private railway systems were amalgamated in 1942. In 1948 they resumed independent operations.

So Shibuya would *seem* smaller even if it were not. In fact it is. The count of persons passing through the complex of mass-transit stations is much smaller than that for Shinjuku. One crucial indicator, however, suggests that Shinjuku may not always be dominant among the *fuku-toshin*. The very young today prefer Shibuya, and vaguely distrust Shinjuku. It is dirty and it has gangsters. Someone might come up and accost a young gentleman, or sell a young lady into prostitution.

Of the thriving centers along the western arc of the Yamanote loop, Ikebukuro seems the accidental one. Highways from Edo passed through Shinjuku and Shibuya, and any speculator would have seen them as promising places when railway stations went up beside the roads. It was not so with Ikebukuro, which was boggy, as the name, Lake Hollow, suggests. No significant road led through it, though a very important one, the inland road to Kyoto, along which many a noble procession made its way during the Tokugawa years, passed through Sugamo, just to the east, and the Itabashi way station, where travelers could rest and indulge themselves.

If the development of the railway system had been different, our speculator might have looked to Sugamo or Itabashi as the place to plunge. The first railway station in the district was put at Mejiro, to the south of Ikebukuro, on the line that passed through Shibuya and Shinjuku and continued northward past Ikebukuro. Had the loop line gone through before the north-south one, Sugamo would have been the obvious place for the germination of a *fukutoshin*, but it was not until 1903 that the loop began its turn to the east. The original plan was for the two lines to fork at Mejiro. Not as alert as it might have been to the speculative possibilities which this proposal opened, the local populace opposed it vehemently. So the forking was placed at Ikebukuro, too insignificant for a local clamor to be heard, and a station was built there, and so began the third of the *fukutoshin*.

It was slower to develop than the other two. Until a subway line went through to Tokyo Central Station in 1956, there was no direct and rapid transportation to the center of the city, and Ikebukuro had no surface link until a freeway went through in 1969. One had to wander back and forth on this and that street or take the roundabout sweep of the Yamanote if one wished to get to Ikebukuro from Ginza or Marunouchi.

Ikebukuro, like Shibuya, acquired a missionary school, but much later, when rapid urban growth was beginning. St. Paul's or Rikkyō, another product of Tsukiji, moved there at about the time of the earthquake. Also like Shibuya, it has been dominated by a single railway company. In 1915 what is now the Seibu Railway opened a line from Ikebukuro to a town in Saitama Prefecture. It has greatly expanded, and now goes into Shinjuku as well as Ikebukuro.

Inevitably, the Seibu went into the department-store business, though it was late in doing so. Ikebukuro was the natural place (not that there was anything very natural about the growth of Ikebukuro) for it to choose. A Musashino Food Company began business just before the outbreak of the Pacific War. It became the Musashino department store, and in 1949 the Seibu. Musashino was the original name of the Seibu. It means Musashi Plain, Musashi being the province in which Edo was situated. Seibu, more modestly, is Western Musashi.

The Seibu enterprises, one of which is headed by the man named by *Forbes* magazine in 1987 as the richest nonroyal person in the world, are very big all over the city, and they loom over Ikebukuro. One may complain in both Shinjuku and Ikebukuro about the impediment which the railroads and their stations present, requiring a detour for anyone who wishes to go from Westmouth to Eastmouth or the reverse; but in the case of Ikebukuro one's complaints might better be directed at the Seibu department store, which blocks off the eastern approaches to the district like the Kremlin or the Berlin Wall.

The stroller through the Ikebukuro Eastmouth has the Seibu department store to the west of him, and until 1971 there was an even more darkly glowering fortress to the east. Had Sugamo Prison been built in later years it might better have been called Ikebukuro Prison, for it was much nearer Ikebukuro Station than Sugamo Station. The reason for the name is that the institution dates back to a time when Ikebukuro was but an inconspicuous part of the rural expanse called Sugamo. Several prisons occupied the site from 1895. The last of them, the Tokyo Detention Center (Tokyo Kōchijō), was put up in 1937. It replaced the Ichigaya Prison, where such celebrated Meiji criminals as the murderess Takahashi O-den were beheaded. The last persons to be executed at Sugamo were seven Class A war criminals, including the wartime prime minister, Tōjō Hideki, who were hanged two days before Christmas in 1948.

The prison was returned to the Japanese in 1958, and seemed prepared to go about its old business. Opposition was intense, and powerful, having commerce behind it. Ikebukuro was by then emerging as one of the great shopping and entertainment centers along the Yamanote. A person could look right down on the prison grounds from the Seibu or the Mitsukoshi, which has a branch at the Ikebukuro Eastmouth. This was altogether too grim a prospect, and the prison was torn down in 1971. The site resembling all that newly opened space which Shinjuku had at its Westmouth, the debate was intense as to what should be done with

Sugamo Prison

it. Some favored recreation, some favored commerce, and the latter won. The highest building in the city, if Tokyo Tower (see page 517-518) be excluded as not quite a building, now occupies the site.

* * *

All three of the *fukutoshin* grew up as strategic points in the mass-transit system. These they have remained in the automobile age. Despite the Olympics and the building of freeways, the inadequacies of the street system have been an automatic limitation on the automobile. In 1947 forty thousand automobiles were registered in the city. By the end of the first postwar decade the number had reached a quarter of a million, and in the next two decades it was to increase another tenfold. Already by the mid-fifties the busiest intersection in the city was accommodating three times the number of vehicles considered the maximum for free and easy movement. This was Iwaitabashi, at the south end of the palace plaza and the north end of the Kasumigaseki bureaucratic complex. Thirteen other intersections at the heart of the city were accommodating traffic above the ideal maximum. Subsequently the "doughnut phenomenon" saw the worst congestion moving out to places like Shinjuku. Subsequently too there were freeways; but the problem is insoluble, and there are alternatives to the automobile, as there are not in most American cities. Trains on various levels go almost everywhere. The sensible person takes them.

The number of trolley passengers rose rapidly in the years after the war. It reached a peak of more than six hundred thousand per day in 1955—and even this was a mere trickle compared with the clientele of the suburban railway lines, public and private. There was modest expansion in total trackage as well, and from 1960 it too began to decline. With the approach of the Olympics, as Tokyo was getting itself ready to appear before the world, there were rumblings about doing away with the trolley system; it was almost completely accomplished during the post-Olympic years.

Meanwhile there had been an experiment with the trolleybus, making use of trolley wires but doing away with rails. Its career lasted from 1952 to 1968. The routes were predominantly in the northern and eastern parts of the city (the non-Olympic parts). The arc of its waxing and waning lagged somewhat behind that of the postwar trolley. The total mileage of the routes began to fall off from 1961, and the last route was discontinued in 1968. The trolleybus was the product of a gasoline shortage, and occupied an uncomfortable middle position, less of a drag upon the freedom of the automobile than the trolley, but more than the unattached bus.

Public transportation on the streets was thus left to the bus and the taxicab. The fifties were a time when cabdrivers were uncommonly lawless even for a lawless breed. The refusal by cruising cabs to take passengers, quite without explanation and quite without legal sanction, became so common that the police staged roundups. One series of them, toward the end of the decade, netted two dozen miscreants, surely a tiny fraction of the total. All manner of contradictory explanations were given for the phenomenon, but it was chiefly a matter of too few cabs and inadequate incentives. At one time it was so bad that Ginza bars were hiring buses to take their employees home after work.

The fifties were the time of the Kamikaze cabdriver, who acquired the designation from the suicide pilots in the last stages of the Second World War. The phenomenon had to do with fare and meters. When the meters were changed so that the fare mounted even during motionless intervals, drivers became more tolerant of them, and calmer. Until 1959 all drivers worked for companies. In that year for the first time owner-drivers were permitted, specifically for purposes of alleviating the abuses; and indeed it was from about then that things started getting better. Owner-drivers were older men with good records, and of course it was their own property they sent hurtling through the streets and their business that would suffer if they happened to be in the tiny minority caught in a roundup.

Among the voguish words of 1955 was *noiroze*, from the German word for neurosis. Affluence was returning, and indispositions of affluence. The Japanese may have disliked giving names to typhoons, but each of the periods of especial prosperity that have come along has had its name. The earliest was Procurement Prosperity, following upon the outbreak of the Korean War. At the time of the first postwar decade there was the Jimmu Prosperity. Jimmu was the legendary first emperor of Japan, and the name implies that nothing like it had been seen in all the days since his reign.

Then there were the *zoku*, the "tribes" or "breeds" that were in the news. The progression of *zoku* also tells of increasing affluence. Shortly after the war there was the Shayō Zoku, the Setting Sun Tribe, the name deriving from a novel about a ruined aristocratic family. The novelist, Dazai Osamu, was himself a ruinous type, but his malaise went back to his youth, long before the disaster that ruined so many once-eminent families. A couple of years later we have Shayō Zoku again, but written differently, to tell us that business is getting back on its feet. The tribe in question is the expense-account one. At the end of the decade, along with Jimmu and neurosis, we have the Taiyō Zoku, the Sun Tribe, whose designation is from the title of a short story about pampered and rebellious youth. The author, Ishihara Shintaro, may once himself have been a member of the tribe, but he is no more. He is a conservative member of the National Diet.

The dispelling of darkness, from the busy entertainment districts at least, was becoming as nearly complete as human hands can make it. Tanizaki Junichiro may have deplored it in his famous eulogy to shadows, but only limitations on fuel cut down the voltage. In 1953 Ginza acquired the largest neon light in the world, a globe eleven meters in diameter which, set atop a building near the main Ginza crossing, advertised Morinaga sweets. Though it was turned off immediately after the "oil shock" of 1973, it came back again, and was for three decades among the marvels and symbols of Ginza. Finally in 1983 it was judged obsolescent and torn down.

Toward the end of the first postwar decade the drug problem emerged. It was and continues to be mild compared to the American one, but transgressions were frequent, and profits huge. There were fourteen thousand arrests in Tokyo in 1954 for selling illegal pep pills, and profits were fifty and a hundred times costs.

In 1951 tuberculosis slipped into second place as a cause of death. By the end of the first postwar decade it had fallen to tenth, and the fatality rate was only a quarter of the highest prewar rate. Midway through the fifties we started hearing complaints about how difficult it was to find domestic help, and how expensive, incompetent, and intransigent such help was when found. Tokyo had its first supermarket, not at all inexpensive, in 1953. We started hearing too of luxurious physical examinations known as *ningen dokku,* which might be rendered as "human dry dock," and luxurious surgery. Young ladies would go to plastic surgeons with photographs of those they wished to be made over into. Wide, round eyes were especially popular.

The day of the cod and the sweet potato was rapidly withdrawing into the past.

Chapter 11

OLYMPIAN DAYS

Baseball may have helped to restore the shattered national morale, and the Korean War did much toward restoring the national economy. Yet strong feelings of inferiority persisted, and a sense of isolation. Japan continued to be something of an international pariah. Any sign of recognition was eagerly received. In 1957 an international literary gathering in Tokyo was front-page news. It would probably have taken a terrorist bomb to put such a gathering on the front pages of European and American newspapers.

The Japanese seemed to take the view that any international notice is good notice. Arthur Koestler came to Tokyo in 1958 and denounced the literary organization (it was the Japanese branch of the International PEN) that had arranged the gathering of 1957. He thought, and he was right, that its attitude toward freedom of letters was tepid, not to say contradictory. This was the great day of easy left-wing solutions, when apology was made for most actions of the Soviet Union, including the obstacles interposed to Boris Pasternak's receiving the Nobel Prize that same year. Koestler's views were also front-page news.

The first postwar Olympic games came and went, and Occupied Japan had no part in them. That Japan would have had a superb swimmer to show off if only it had been there was a matter of great chagrin. He was a genius (and he had only nine fingers), the best swimmer Japan has produced since the thirties. He had blossomed and, as swimmers will, rapidly faded by the time the next Olympics came. He had to make do with a few international victories in America. No one but the Japanese paid much heed to them, but he probably did as much for the national morale as baseball.

In 1951, the last full year of the Occupation and the first of the Korean War, and the year General MacArthur went home, Japan was readmitted to the Olympics. A Japanese team went in 1952, and did less than brilliantly. But the important thing was being there—as the Olympic charter suggests. The next task was to repair the loss incurred when the games of 1940 failed to take place. London, the other city that lost Olympics because of the war, got the first postwar games.

Already in 1952 the governor announced that Tokyo would bid for the 1960 Olympics. The bid was duly made, and was unsuccessful. There were seven candidates. Tokyo placed last in the vote. When the 1956 Olympics were over the prefecture set up a special office to entice the 1964 games. In January 1958 a commission went to work on particular and specific preparations. In May the bid for the Olympics was formally entered. The persuaders sent off to Munich, where the international Olympic Committee met in 1959, included the governor, his predecessor, and a prince of the blood who (unlike most of the imperial family) was a man of great personal charm. This time there were four candidates: Tokyo, Detroit, Vienna, and Brussels. They placed in that order on the first ballot. Tokyo had a solid majority. Literary gatherings could not again expect to make the front pages.

The city and the prefecture took the games very seriously. A new governor, Azuma Ryūtarō, was elected in the spring of 1959 as if for the specific purpose of presiding over them. He was also chairman of the Japanese Olympic Committee. The only one not to run for a third term and the only one who utterly lost control of the prefectural council, he was perhaps (though some would give the nod to his successor) the least successful of the four governors the prefecture has had. His was the administration that had the best scandal of the postwar years, one which turned into a political fiasco. Yet the whole world seems to agree that the city, the prefecture, and the nation did a superb job of staging the Olympics. They were an opportunity to show the world what Japan had been up to since 1945. The opportunity was made good use of, and Japan regained much of its self-esteem and international standing.

"Direct expenses" for the Olympics were a small fraction of those generally listed as indirect, perhaps as small a fraction, depending on definitions and categories, as a thirtieth. Direct expenses and indirect provided a good way to get money from outside the prefecture for solving a few prefectural problems. The national government took care of more of the direct expenses than the prefecture. There are no surprises on the list of these. The money went for athletic installations and accommodations for athletes and the like.

As for indirect expenses, funds came overwhelmingly from borrowing. The "bullet express" to Osaka made up about a third of the total. Its relation to the Olympics was certainly very tenuous, although the showing of Japanese organizational and technical skills was among the main reasons for having the games in the first place. Another third, almost equally divided between the two, went into streets and subways. Had the games come at a later day the division might have been different. The traffic problem was at crisis proportions, and freeways and wide nonexpress avenues were seen as a solution. The system of freeways went on growing after the Olympics, but the time passed when it was seen as a solution to much of anything. The athletic installations, and especially the main stadium and the gymnasium, are some of them very imposing, but the "Olympic thoroughfares," as they were and sometimes still are called, the freeways and the widened streets, were the most prominent change which the Olympics brought to the contours (as the regent's post-earthquake proclamation had it) of the city. It would have been remarkable if the effects had been distributed evenly over the city. The concern was to get people from the airport, then in the farthest south of the wards and near the bay, to the downtown hotels and then to the Olympic installations. These were concentrated, though not exclusively, in the southwest, the athletes' village and the gymnasium in Shibuya Ward, the main stadium in Shinjuku Ward, and a considerable complex in Setagaya Ward, out beyond Shibuya. Had someone been away for a couple of years before the Olympics and (sensibly) come back when the excitement had died down, and been asked, as the returning person always is, whether he did not find the changes in the city perfectly astonishing, he might with reason have replied, "In Shibuya, yes, perfectly."

In the old center of the city the freeway system was relatively inconspicuous because it used old public rights-of-way. Only a tenth of the land used for the whole system had to be wrested from private hands. The rest was in the public domain, as streets and canals. The original system passed discreetly by the bustling center of Shinjuku. Shibuya was the *sakariba*, the bustling place, which it cut uncompromisingly through, opening a way into and out of the very heart of the place which had not been there before. Dropped down at Shibuya Station and suddenly surrounded by the concrete and the roar, the returning person (and we are to assume that he knew the place well) might have wondered where he was.

Minato and Shibuya wards, to the south and southwest of the palace and the old downtown district, were the wards in which the Olympic freeways were the most conspicuous. Among the most affluent of the wards, they were the ones upon which Olympic blessings, perhaps mixed, poured in the greatest profusion.

A very small beginning toward a system of elevated and subterranean freeways had been made before it was even known that Tokyo would have the Olympics. After all the cinders had been dumped and such pleasure and consumer centers as Tokyo Spa and the Yaesu Mouth complex at Tokyo Central Station had been built, the filling in of canals went on. In Kawabata's *Scarlet Gang of Asakusa* there is a boy who is the son of a boatman and whose home is the boat. His father drops him at Asakusa in the morning so that he may attend school on the temple grounds. He must wait until night and sometimes all through the night for the boat to come again, and so he becomes a child of the park and its gangs. It is a way of life that has quite disappeared. The filling in of canals brought a loss of channels and moorings, and a new law that had to do with longshoring brought complete extinction to life upon the waterways, so important in Edo and Meiji.

The canal that had been the outer moat of Edo Castle was in the late fifties filled in along the border of Chiyoda Ward (which lay within the moats and the old castle revetments) and Chūō Ward (which lay without). This was the canal between Yūrakuchō and Ginza into which the American soldier threw the pimp (see page 459). The bridge from which the unfortunate man was thrown was Sukiyabashi, where all the modern boys and girls wanted to be photographed. It was especially famous in these years because it figured in a tear-provoking, Evangelinesque, and very popular radio serial called *What Is Your Name? (Kimi no na wa)*, about love frustrated by the bombings and their aftermath. (Frank Nagai's biggest hit was based on the serial.) The bridge was demolished in 1957, and at the site a wistful plaque now says, in the hand of the *What Is Your Name?* playwright, "Sukiyabashi was here."

The freeway, extending less than a mile from a point just north of Shimbashi Station along the filled-in canal, did not amount to much, and did scarcely anything toward relieving congestion on the main north-south Ginza streets. Today it is joined at either end to the larger system of freeways and is used mostly for parking. In another respect it was put to better use than most of the newer freeways have been. Two shopping arcades went into business in 1957 and two more in 1958, making use of the space beneath. In two of them the shops occupy sequestered space, cut off by walls from neighboring spaces. The other two are more like the "blocks of famous shops" *(meitengai)* or "shopping centers" in the basements of the big department stores. Stalls share a common space.

The city financed the filling and the building and sold some of the space and rented out some at less than it was worth. The leases will soon expire. The site of the old bridge is at about midpoint through the complex, which is the boundary between the two wards. Except for a rare happening such as the pimp incident, which the police to the east of the canal initially took charge of, the canal area did not much matter while it was an expanse of mud and stagnant water. Now, with money coming in, the two wards started fighting for jurisdiction. A boundary line was presently drawn that runs now down one side of the old canal and now down the other, and sometimes down the middle.

The system of Olympic freeways, which is to say, the freeways that were ready in time to serve the Olympics, extended for some twenty miles, and affected only the central district (Ginza, Marunouchi, and Nihombashi) and the wards to the immediate south and west. Freeways ran northward from the airport to the center of the city, and westward along two routes, to the heart of Shibuya and to the vicinity of the main Olympic stadium. The gymnasium and the athletes' village lay between the two.

It was not for some time that the northern and eastern parts of the city were favored with freeways. Early post-Olympic accretions were also in the central and southwestern wards. The first considerable extension to the north came only in 1969, when a freeway joined Ueno with Nihombashi. The northern and eastern parts of the city are in general the more slowly changing parts. Though slow to come, such improvements as freeways have had a more pronounced effect in uglifying the backward parts of the city than the advanced and affluent. It might almost be argued that freeways, clearing away some postwar shabbiness, have been an improvement for parts of the south and west. The argument would be quite impossible in the case of the freeway that runs along the east bank of the Sumida and onward to the north. It sits like a lid on the famous line of cherry trees. This is not to say that the freeways have not had unhappy effects elsewhere in the city. Nihombashi Bridge, the most celebrated in the land, is still there, and it still crosses a canal, but it has been sadly diminished by the freeway that passes overhead. Even the sacred view from the palace has been blemished by freeways. The mileage has grown to upward of four times what it was in 1964.

The widening of nonexpress streets was also most evident in the southwestern wards. Aoyama Avenue, as it is called from a district through which it runs, is much the most conspicuous instance. A street was widened to twice its earlier width all the way from the outer castle moat to Shibuya. The expense was huge. On charts of indirect Olympic expenditures the cost of nonexpress streets runs to some five times that for freeways. Low buildings had to be bought up one by one and moved back into the somewhat higher buildings that line the widened street. So we came to have "pencil buildings," several storys high, thin as pencils. They are said to be earthquake-proof, but they do not look it.

Less than a month before the Olympics began, a monorail was opened from the airport to Hamamatsuchō, some distance south of Ginza and Shimbashi. Neither the worst nor the best location that could have been chosen, Hamamatsuchō is not within easy walking distance of anything except the park on the site of the old Hama Palace. Not many people can get there without changing a time or two from some other mode of transportation. Despite this disadvantage and despite initial unpopularity—people may have been frightened at the Olympic crowds—it has been a commercial success. It is the best way to get to the old airport, whence domestic flights still depart, and it is fun. In 1980 it was carrying more than two million passengers a month. It was not the city's first monorail; several years earlier one had been put through joining two sections of the Ueno Zoo. But it was the most ambitious in Japan and, indeed, the whole world.

Diggings for new subway lines began at about the time the Korean War began, and much digging had been accomplished in time for the Olympics. It has gone on since and is still going on. Besides its freeway Shinjuku now had a subway line to the center of the city. The same line, the first postwar one, sweeps southeastward through the center of the city and then westward, and had earlier joined Ikebukuro with Ginza. By 1962 it had pushed on past Shinjuku to Ogikubo, near the western limits of the ward part of the prefecture.

It encountered an interesting difficulty as it made its way past Ginza. Near Hibiya Park the diggers came upon great boulders, which had to be demolished, at a great cost of time and money. It was established that they were underground foundations for the outer revetments of Edo Castle, most probably abutments for the Sukiya Gate from which Sukiyabashi took its name. They were probably put there in the seventeenth century by Date Masamune, most famous of the lords of Sendai. Not many old things remain above the Tokyo ground, but under it many an archaeological specimen is yet to be discovered.

A new and most imposing Ginza subway station was ready just in time for the Olympics. It joined the new line with the prewar Ginza line. Probably more than the underground complex at the Yaesu Mouth of Tokyo Central Station, to which few visitors from distant lands were likely to go, it showed the world what marvelous diggers the Japanese are.

It cannot be charged that the northern wards were left out in the building of subways as they were in the building of freeways. They were present at the creation of the subway system, and the earliest trackage of the second line (the first postwar one) ran to the north and northwest of the palace. The farthest northern wards were linked to the center of the city by Olympic time, and work had begun on yet another line, its eastern stretches aboveground, which would in the post-Olympic years cross the city east and west from beyond Shinjuku to well beyond the border with Chiba Prefecture. It too passes north of the palace. The increment to the system between 1954 and October 1964, the Olympic month, was almost a hundred kilometers, or upward of sixty miles.

As if by way of confusing Olympic visitors, the subways were complicated in those years by the founding of a new system. The prefecture had long wanted to take over the old system, which, though a public corporation, was not under prefectural control, and among the most striking attributes of which was that it was very profitable. Failing in this endeavor, the prefecture started its own system. Digging began in 1958, and when the first stretch of tracks was opened, in 1960, it offered service to the wards east of the Sumida River, untouched by earlier diggings. The first city-owned line was in operation through the center of the city and on to the vicinity of Shiba Park in time for the Olympics. Transfer between the two systems is possible but not easy, and it is expensive. The city-owned system has higher fares and does not show a profit. It got started too late, and for that reason might better not have started at all, though it did serve the neglected eastern wards. The old system had already dug its way through the best routes on several levels in the Ginza-Marunouchi district.

The expansion of the trolleybus system in the years before the Olympics looked ahead to dispensing with the clumsy old trolley cars. The latter were among the things Tokyo would as soon not have shown the world, but it could not do everything. The Olympics had trolleys as well as the proud new freeways and subways. The almost complete demolition of the system was left to the Olympic governor's successor, who set aggressively to work on it in 1967. Trolleybuses had their largest passenger load in 1965, and, as the trolleys went, they went too.

After streets and transportation, the largest items on compilations of indirect Olympic expenditures are for water and sewers, the latter slightly larger than the former. The Tokyo region had a severe drought in the summer of 1964, and a water shortage. For a time in August, seventeen of the twenty-three wards had water only nine hours a day. Parts of the High City were completely dependent on water trucks. The national government, prudently, had a special minister of state in charge of Olympic affairs. He turned so energetically to the drought problem that he became known as the minister of the waterworks. The present governor of Tokyo, Suzuki Shunichi, had made a career in the national bureaucracy before the Olympic governor appointed him vice-governor and assigned him particularly to Olympic preparations. He too was much concerned with the waterworks.

Tokyo did not at the time have access to the Tone River, the largest in eastern Japan, but water was coming across Saitama Prefecture from the Tone to the Higashimurayama Reservoir, in the county part of Tokyo Prefecture, in time for the Olympics. Water continues to be a problem which the prefecture has not really solved. Farming has prior rights to a considerable portion of the water that flows into the city supply when farmers do not need it. When they do they get it and the city does not.

There was a serious water shortage in 1987. The governor would like to dam the Shinano River, which flows into the Sea of Japan, and bring water across the mountains to the Tone, whence it would flow into the Tokyo system. The governor of Niigata Prefecture is understandably in the opposition, for the main mouth of the Shinano is right there in the main city of his constituency. The project is not one which the governor and the government of Tokyo can see to by themselves.

The major part of the sewage effort was directed at hiding the most obvious manifestations of what was still a very inadequate system. In 1964 only about a third of the population of the wards had the use of sewers. Obviously not much could be done to put a bright modern face on the matter, and Olympic visitors would probably not have the inclination or the means to inquire deeply. Something could be done, however, to render the *kumitoriya*, the carters of night soil, less of an assault upon the senses. Vacuum trucks replaced the old cart-and-dipper arrangements in most parts of the city likely to be on display. Statistics released by the city, however, showed that two decades after the Olympics *kumitoriya* had not disappeared from the eastern wards, where fewer than a quarter of the population had the benefit of sewers.

The year of the Olympics brought the opening of the last bridge across the Sumida, from east of Ginza to the oldest bit of filled land at the river mouth. This occurred six weeks before the games began. So the last ferry across the river was discontinued, and Tokyo became a bit more what it seemed to wish to be, no different from other cities. The ferry had been in service for three hundred years. Meiji Village near Nagoya wanted the last boat, but an elderly boatman who had worked the ferry for forty years was successful in his insistence that it remain in Tokyo. This was a most striking success in a day when no one seemed to care much whether anything of historic interest remained in Tokyo.

Also by way of preparation for the Olympics, the Construction Ministry and a public corporation charged with the nurturing and development of water resources undertook to flush out the Sumida River, which was in such a state that the expensive restaurants along its west bank smelled like sewers (and indeed it was a sewer) when the wind was right. In August a channel was completed, expressly for flushing purposes, from the new Higashimurayama Reservoir to the upper reaches of the river. Fresh reservoir water poured through for about a month just preceding the games. An announcement came toward the end of October that the results had not been disappointing. The algae content at Ryōgoku Bridge, just below the Yanagibashi geisha quarter, was down by half, and farther upstream it was down by as much as three-quarters. Oxygen had scarcely existed before, and now was up to a half gram per ton at Ryōgoku, as much as two grams upstream. This was still far from enough to keep fish alive, but it was better than nothing. The smell of the river was much improved. Delicate incenses in the restaurants could overcome it.

During the Olympic years the city began to do something for itself in the matter of parks. In earlier postwar years it had waited for windfalls such as the Hama Palace. In 1958 it bought a famous iris garden at Horikiri, some distance east of the Sumida, a relic of the nurseries that once fringed Edo. The site has changed radically over the centuries, but there it still is, never built upon except for small pleasure pavilions through the three centuries of its history.

The clearing away of beggars and vagrants from the parts of the city the world was likely to notice has a little of the scent of authoritarianism about it. Many went into institutions; harassment caused many to pick up and move to places held by their intelligence network to be more friendly. Such harassment would not have been possible in a litigious city like New York. A few years later, after the "oil shock" of 1973, they all came back (or perhaps they were different ones), and life was somewhat easier for them, with so many more diggings to sleep in and so many vending machines to obviate unpleasant encounters with shopkeepers and waitresses.

Preparation for the Olympics was a big effort, national and local, and the Japanese did most of it by themselves. Such was the distance they had come. To point out that they asked for just a little help is not to belittle the effort and the success. Since there were contingency plans for an athletes' village, something would doubtless have been put up somewhere in the couple of years at Japan's disposal even if the decision had been against letting them have the American military housing complex called Washington Heights. The complex, in Shibuya Ward, just beside the Meiji Shrine, close to the freeways, and offering space for installations besides the village, was certainly the best of possible sites. It was returned less than a year before the Olympics, with the proviso that the Japanese provide substitute housing for Americans. There is an item on the list of indirect expenses, a small item, less than 1 percent of expenditures on most lists, that is designated "construction of American military housing in the Chōfu paddies." Chōfu is a city out beyond Setagaya Ward in the county part of the prefecture.

So, the degree of readiness very high, the Olympics began, on the Double Ten, October 10, 1964. Rain threatened on the day of the opening ceremonies, but forbore. The general view is that the games were a huge success and marked a great step forward in the emergence of Tokyo as one of the grander cities of the world. Japan won sixteen gold medals, the third-largest number, after the United States and the Soviet Union. A certain amount of arranging was required to achieve this result. Japan had a remarkable women's volleyball team thanks chiefly to the efforts of a relentless coach known as "the demon," and of course it enjoyed a certain advantage in judo. Both of these sports became Olympic events for the first time.

The gold medal won by the volleyball team was only the second to be won by Japanese women, the first having been won at Berlin in 1936. There were sad happenings afterward, signifying that such events can be taken too seriously. A Japanese marathon runner who had been thought a possible winner was in second place, well behind the great Ethiopian Abebe (who this time ran with shoes on), as he came into the stadium. He was overtaken in the last two hundred yards by an Englishman—and right there before the stadium multitudes. A woman hurdler who had been

Aerial smoke rings mark the opening of the 1964 Tokyo Olympics

expected at the very worst to win a bronze medal came in fifth. Both later killed themselves.

Perhaps when everything was over some Japanese wished that the arranging had never taken place, for it brought a great national embarrassment. The volleyball team duly won its gold medal on the last day of competition. On each of the three preceding days Japanese won gold medals in the three weight divisions of judo, but on this day, in the contest that really mattered, the open-weight division, a Dutchman, Anton Geesink, took the medal. There was weeping in the streets. He said afterward that the struggle against the hostile crowd was worse than that against his Japanese opponent. That there should be weight divisions in the first place rather damaged the mystique of judo, which held that the little fellow, the Bruce Lee, uses the big fellow's weight to defeat him.

The famous director Ichikawa Kon was commissioned to do the official film document. The minister of the waterworks did not like it. He said it may have been art but it was no document.

The 1956 games were the first ones held in Oceania, one of the five Olympic circles. They had not yet been held in Asia, another of the five. That the prostrate country of 1945 should have held them made it feel that it had, perhaps, something which the rest of the circle did not have. National feelings of inferiority did not disappear in 1964, but the emergence of confidence was striking. That year is sometimes put beside 1867, 1923, and 1945 as the momentous ones in the history of the city.

This is surely an exaggeration. Yet the Olympics were an event of great moment in the life of the city, spiritual and material.

"The Tokyo Olympics were not merely a sports festival. They were a ritual marking the fact that for the first time since the defeat Japan had formally been accepted by the world. For a time on opening day, traffic in the city came to a stop. A happy excitement welled up that the nations of the world were extending their hands in congratulation. And then, after a time, all the noise and confusion of people and vehicles came back again." So wrote one observer of the scene.

The nation gave voice to its happiness in what might be called poetry, but would more safely be called verse. It has been much given to expressing itself thus, in joy and in sorrow.

> Seventy thousand see Abebe into the stadium,
> No change upon his face or in his pace.

And again:

> One and then another, ninety-four flags.
> Some, perhaps, have met on battlefields.

The "perhaps" may be taken as a mark of the Japanese tendency to soften things a bit.

On December 8, in Japan the twenty-third anniversary of the attack on Pearl Harbor, though the choice of date can hardly have been intentional, the Seibu department store in Ikebukuro had a big sale of furniture and utensils from the athletes' village. It sold out in an hour.

Tokyo acquired its first important hotel since the thirties in 1951, and then there was a pause, and then a great rush in preparation for the Olympics. A half dozen big new hotels went up near the palace and along or near the avenue that had replaced the outer castle moat. One of them, with seventeen floors, was for a time the highest building in the city. Another, the new Imperial, went up on a part of the land occupied by the old, or second, Imperial. The management did not get around to destroying this second building, designed by Frank Lloyd Wright, until several years after the Olympics. Wright's niece, the actress Anne Baxter, stayed in the then newest Imperial, which has since been replaced by a glossy tower, and delighted in it. She said that it made her uncle's work look better than ever.

A new pattern was emerging, in which the Japanese home market, reserved almost exclusively for Japanese, made foreign businessmen bilious with envy. It quickly became apparent that all these new hotels would rely very heavily on the home clientele to keep themselves profitable. The building of hotels did not stop when the Olympics were over. In 1986 there were well over twice as many hotel rooms in the city as in the Olympic year.

There was another indicator, initially somewhat disheartening. Retail business actually suffered from the Olympics. In Ginza and Shinjuku sales during October 1964 were well below the average for the run of Octobers preceding it. Japanese customers stayed away, even as they at first stayed away from the monorail. They did not want to get caught in the press of foreigners. Cameras were almost the only items that sold well, but not the more expensive ones. Shopkeepers found the tendency of customers to haggle over prices not to their taste. The important matter, the drop in sales, had its sunny side. It showed that the Japanese custom, which would come back when all those foreigners had gone away, was the one that mattered. Japanese retailing has not suffered perceptibly from foreign competition. The growth of a huge Japanese domestic market skillfully shielded from foreign incursions is among the important developments of our time.

Among the *sakariba,* the bustling places of the city, Shibuya was the one that was most visibly affected by preparations for the Olympics, and it was the one most directly caught up in the aftermath. The Shibuya district proper, the vicinity of the mass-transit complex, did not change at an especially dizzying rate compared with the other bustling places even after the freeway went through. It became part of a larger complex, however: a triangle northward from Shibuya to the Meiji Shrine and, beside it, the site of Washington Heights and the Olympic village, eastward to Aoyama Avenue, the street widened in preparation for the games, and back to

Shibuya along this last. The northeast corner of the triangle came close to the outskirts of Roppongi, another rampant pleasure district, and on to the north Roppongi merged with Akasaka of the cabarets (such as the one in which Rikidōzan was stabbed) and the geisha. So one vast entertainment, shopping, and to a degree managerial district was growing up all the way from the outer castle moat to Shibuya. For convenience, though the expression has no currency in Japan, we may call it the Southwest.

With the Olympic village at one end of the main street leading through the Harajuku district, and Aoyama Avenue, the main access by rapid transit to Ginza and the old center of the city, at the other, the Olympics brought a great increase in the number or late-night purveyors of pleasure. In the beginning it was a matter between athletes and purveyors, but the female adolescent crowd loved all the exoticism and lingered on. A decade earlier the idle young tended not to have money to spend. Now they did. The fame of Harajuku spread, and it became a place with a powerful attraction for curious and mildly rebellious youth the whole land over. Great swarms of schoolboys and schoolgirls have always converged upon the city, especially during the clement seasons, to improve themselves. In days of old they came in tightly mustered groups and looked reverently at the royal residence and the Diet building. Now they preferred to look at Harajuku, and the teachers who were their wardens were powerless to stop them.

There, in the post-Olympic years, one seemed to see the future most clearly. In those years we first started hearing of the Harajuku addition to the *zoku,* the "tribes" which followed one another through the postwar decades. Harajuku has disappeared as the official name of a district, but it survives as the name of the Yamanote station next north from Shibuya, that nearest the Olympic village (and that whence the bodies of emperors depart for their final repose). In popular usage it signifies the regions eastward from the Meiji Shrine and the Olympic village to Aoyama Avenue—the northern side of the triangle. The expression "Harajuku Zoku" might be freely rendered "flaming youth." They have been perhaps the most perdurable of all the tribes, for, changing as fads and rages change, they are with us yet. They have their sports cars and their hot rods and motorcycles, and the police have seemed unwilling or unable to stop them as they race back and forth along that northern side of the triangle, Yoyogi Park, where the Olympic village was, to Aoyama Avenue.

They also have flamboyant styles of dress and lawless ways, among them the taking over of any bit of unguarded and unoccupied property. It was in the post-Olympic years that the English words "event"

Street performers on a Sunday in Harajuku

and "happening" entered the language, to designate the exhibitionist behavior of the young, especially in Harajuku and Yoyogi. The Sunday afternoons of a quarter of a century have been rendered deafening by the noises from their amplifying devices and riotous by their dress and dancing. Happenings and events are concentrated in front of the staid Meiji Shrine, at the northwest corner of the Shibuya triangle.

Many have been distressed by them, some have thought them a hopeful sign—for a small measure of pluralism in Japan, most conformist and undifferentiated of nations, might be good for all of us. Thorstein Veblen thought the Japanese opportunity would pass when, as must inevitably happen, premodern ways of behavior no longer prevailed. It might finally be happening. Yet in some ways the Harajuku tribe does not seem so very rebellious and decadent after all. Detailed maps of Harajuku are striking for the lack of the sort of places so numerous in Shinjuku, the sex places. The events and happenings are alfresco.

The Harajuku-Aoyama district was becoming the center of high fashion in an ever more highly fashioned city. Such expressions usually have reference to feminine elegance, and this one does here. The center of masculine elegance has stayed in Ginza.

Men were wearing Western dress with reasonable competence during the interwar decades. The emperor may look a bit overdressed in the famous pictures of that first interview with the general, but he does not look badly dressed. Since emperors of Japan never wear Japanese dress on public occasions save the most elaborately ritual ones, such as coronations, it was during the interwar years that he got his practice.

And when did it happen for women? The disasters of 1923 and 1945 both brought sudden increases in the frequency of Western dress for women—although the victims of the 1932 Shirokiya fire, as we have seen (page 319), were still in Japanese dress. In the postwar years Japanese dress became so uncommon that it also became uneconomical. Low demand brought high prices. Old weavers died, old techniques fell into disuse, and those who had to have Japanese dress, such as geisha, had to pay high and ever higher prices for superior pieces.

There came a time, along toward the end of the first quarter or third of a century after the surrender, when women at length began to look as if Western dress were meant for them—not women of the diplomatic and banking sets, who came to grips with the problem much earlier, but housewives and students and office girls. With women's dress as our indicator, we may say that it took almost a century from the Meiji Restoration for Western appurtenances to rest other than awkwardly. Today Japanese ones are coming to seem that way, as when young ladies kick at the skirts of the kimonos they put on for graduation day or a wedding. Their stride goes better with Western dress.

Yet another part of Washington Heights, parts of which became Yoyogi Park and the Olympic gymnasium, became a new center for NHK, the public broadcasting corporation. The old building, near Hibiya Park, had been "Radio Japan," whence the Tokyo Rose broadcasts went forth to gladden young American hearts all over the Pacific. In 1972 NHK sold the old building to Mitsubishi. The price was over thirty-four billion and a few-odd million yen. Even in those days of a strong dollar this figure converted to almost a hundred million dollars. The new complex, very glassy, was completed with the opening of NHK Hall, for concerts and the like, in 1973.

Roppongi was the earliest of the brassy, amplified entertainment districts. It had its tribe, its *zoku,* years in advance of the Harajuku one. The origins of Roppongi are similar to those of Shibuya: military. There were training grounds beyond Shibuya, and there were barracks near the main Roppongi crossing. So Roppongi developed in response to the military demand. This occurred during the two big wars of Meiji. The barracks were taken over by the Americans, and Roppongi went on responding.

During the American years it was not an especially lively place, though it contained many a little bar that stayed open late at night to please the soldiers. When Tokyo Tower went up in 1958 (see pages 517-518), Roppongi was like the darkness at the foot of the lighthouse. The tower blazed, and Roppongi did not. The place on the edge of Roppongi where the tower went up was a dark, lonely one, well suited for murder (see page 479).

In the early sixties, the pre-Olympic years, Roppongi started to become the sort of place people knew about. The Americans moved out of the barracks in 1959. Providentially, a very big television studio opened there the same year. In those early years of its fame, Roppongi was new among the pleasure centers of the city in more than one sense. It was of course the newest in point of time, and it was the only one among them that took a little trouble to get to. Asakusa languished because it was not an important transfer point and was not served by the National Railways. Roppongi was not served by any kind of rapid transit. It did not have a subway line until 1964, the Olympic year, and it has never had an elevated line, private or public. Young people came in droves all the same. Unlike the hot-rodders and motorcycle gangs that were later to converge on Harajuku, not many of them had their own transportation. And what was it that lured them, despite the inconvenience? What if not television? When the American clientele departed Roppongi, the television one took its place, and young people went to ogle, and to imitate, and to dance and eat pizza. The mass media were talking about a Roppongi Zoku from about 1960. It did the things just enumerated. The pizza and dancing were exotic, and the people of television were at the bright cutting edge of progress. The exotic and the advanced were what the Roppongi Zoku were after, and what they signified.

The Yoshiwara, when it flourished, was known as "the nightless city," but it was less nightless by far than places like Roppongi have become in the years since the Olympics. Though the Yoshiwara may have been in business all through the night, there were no crowds in the streets during the early-morning hours, and the biggest noise was that of the wooden clappers exhorting caution against fires. It is not so with Roppongi and other parts of the Southwest. Especially before a holiday, they are lighted, crowded, brassy, and amplified all through the night, nightless as no Japanese place had been before. They are like Times Square on New Year's Eve or Greenwich Village on Halloween.

Television has also figured in the prosperity of Akasaka, just to the north. Once dominated by the geisha, it is an older and was a more elegant pleasure center than Roppongi or Shibuya. The geisha dominates no more. Her decline of recent years has been precipitous. Akasaka was one of the great geisha quarters of Meiji, very much of Meiji in the sense that it had been a dark, silent place of noble estates under the shoguns and began to bustle only in Meiji. It lay on one of the guard points along the outer moat and near the southwestern limits of the Meiji city. During the interwar years it was favored with a station on the earliest subway line, and after the war it became one of two points at which transfer between the first and second subway lines was possible (Ginza was the other).

The Akasaka geisha prospered because of her proximity to the bureaucratic center of the city. After the war Akasaka was the most conspicuous place for *machiai* politics, thought infamous by the newspapers, which invented the term. The word *machiai* is rendered by the big Japanese-English dictionary as "an assignation house." It is the institution more popularly rendered as "geisha house." *Machiai* politics had to do with the big deals in which businessmen and politicians worked hand in glove and with the arrangements whereby rival political factions formed their shifting coalitions.

Akasaka supplanted Ginza as a cabaret center. It had the gaudiest ones in the city, both because of *machiai* politics and because of all the big hotels that came with the Olympics. It too had its big television studios, and so, like Roppongi, it was a place to go for a look at the people who were making the future. There was no Akasaka Zoku, however. Only one *zoku*, the expense-account one, seemed made for Akasaka, but it was scattered everywhere.

The Shibuya-Aoyama-Harajuku triangle lies almost completely beyond the limits of the old city; Akasaka and Roppongi lie within. The separate parts have their several histories, some reasonably old and some very new, but none of them amounted to much of anything before Meiji. They are still somewhat separate, though the cordons of quiet between them are not wide.

One would be hard put to say whether the Olympics or television was more important in the rise of the Southwest. Roppongi had taken off well before the Olympics came, and so it may be that the young would have gone to that part of town in search of the future even if the Olympics had not worked their change on the Shibuya triangle. The Olympics did come, however, and they brought other ingredients of the future—freeways and boutiques and high fashion and exoticism. It has long been the case, though the Japanese remain astonishingly faithful to old modes of behavior (whether Veblen was right or not is still in doubt), that they look abroad to see what the material future will be.

While the Southwest was thus leaping forward, Shinjuku and Ikebukuro were in the Olympic years making more modest progress, and plans. The first postwar subway line joined the two, and took a circumspect route that joined both of them to the old center of the city. The old Eastmouth at Ikebukuro became a plaza for automobiles, that at Shinjuku returned to places for eating, drinking, and shopping. Ikebukuro may thus have erred. It has less chance of one day catching up with the old center of the city than has Shinjuku or Shibuya. Its Westmouth is not in serious competition, as a provisioner of drink and sex, with Kabukichō in Shinjuku.

Shinjuku started burrowing as the Yaesu Mouth of Tokyo Central Station had done, and by the Olympics had a grand subterranean promenade leading under the railroad tracks and joining Eastmouth and Westmouth. Grander plans were still largely plans. They had to do with the reservoir, and included everything a planner needed to keep himself happy—streets, plazas, parks, parking, big buildings. Two years before the Olympics water started flowing into the new Higashimurayama Reservoir, out in the county part of the prefecture. The year after the Olympics the old reservoir ceased to function. So the post-Olympic years were the time for making plans come true.

Though Shinjuku went on having a larger count of bodies in transit than Shibuya, it might have fallen behind the Southwest if it had not had the reservoir. Barring the rise of bustling centers out in the county part of the prefecture, however, its decline could only be relative. It has gone on being a gigantic blaze and din, and in one respect it remained well in the lead of the Southwest even before the Westmouth started reaching upward into the light: the sex business. For all the grotesqueries of Harajuku and Yoyogi Park and the kinky clubs of Roppongi, they were places where a boy could go walking with his high school sweetheart, in from the country, with no fear of embarrassing her or giving her the wrong idea about him. The difference is rather like that between Times Square and Greenwich Village. The Village may offer all manner of perverse pleasures, but it keeps them out of sight. For the open thing, one goes to the Square.

Certain farsighted companies, knowing what was to come, started putting up big buildings at Westmouth even during the Olympic years. An insurance building was finished in 1961; another, about twice the size, in 1964. Neither outdid buildings in the center of the city in size or height, but they looked very big and rather lonely there at Westmouth, the undeveloped side of Shinjuku. Today, viewed from the east, they are like foothills against the range that was thrust up later.

Just after the Olympics, Shinjuku had a *zoku*, a tribe. The Fūten Zoku were more aggressive dropouts from society than the Harajuku Zoku.

Fūten is the first adjective in the title of the famous Tanizaki novel *Diary of a Mad Old Man*. In this ease it means something more like "delinquent" (and indeed the Tanizaki title could have been rendered *Diary of a Senile Delinquent*). The Futen Zoku had as their habitat the plaza in front of the newly rebuilt Shinjuku Eastmouth, what was then the main entrance to the station complex. They were the equivalent of the flower children of San Francisco, and they could have chosen almost any place in which to loiter had they not craved attention. That they did want it, and so clearly, gave their doings an air of the theatrical. They got their attention as they lolled about, quaffing and sniffing mysterious things. Then they started having a social conscience, and it was the beginning of the end. Japan may be a little discommoded by dropouts, but it knows how to deal with political and ideological dissent. In 1967 the Fūten Zoku joined certain anticommunist (which is to say, more radical than the communists) student factions in a famous attack on the Eastmouth police box. It was the first of several such attacks in those years when the left-wing establishment was falling apart and the student left was growing ever more violent. When the violence died down the Fūten Zoku was no more.

Marunouchi was in these Olympic years tearing down its London-town, those blocks of red-brick buildings left from Meiji. The process was not completed until the post-Olympic years, when the first to go up was the last to come down. There was no murmur of protest when it did

The Bankers' Club, a Taishō building surviving in Marunouchi

come down, but there has since been a vigorous movement to protect from demolition two brick buildings yet remaining in the Marunouchi district, the Bankers' Club and Tokyo Central Station. Both date from Taishō. Only in the past two decades has Tokyo come to have some sense that there might be objects worth preserving in its material heritage. Not quite everything of Meiji has disappeared from Marunouchi. Each of the Londontown buildings contained, high up in its attic, a Buddhist image. The images and the lightning rods are preserved in the basement of the Marunouchi Building, saved by the Mitsubishi executive who oversaw the destruction.

Despite the beginnings at the Shinjuku Westmouth, there was no indication that the business center of the city had any intention of jumping westward across the palace grounds. Except for the two Shinjuku insurance buildings just mentioned, all the major office buildings put up in the early sixties were in the three central wards, Chiyoda, Chūō, and Minato, the largest number in Chiyoda, which is to say, greater Marunouchi, the Marunouchi district proper and the districts immediately to the north and south. It is hard to know why insurance companies should have been the boldest in moving out beyond the central fastnesses. Perhaps, feeling less vulnerable to foreign incursions, they have felt less need to be near the bureaucracy. Two years after the Olympics another big insurance company moved its headquarters to the old site of the American school, in Meguro Ward, south of Shibuya.

There continued to be, however, significant movement within the central wards, consistently away from Nihombashi, which in Edo and Meiji had been the unchallenged financial and retailing center of the city, and toward Marunouchi and Ginza. For retailing the new center was Ginza. In financial matters the transfer to Marunouchi was accomplished with finality during the Olympic years. The Bank of Japan and the stock exchange remained in Nihombashi, but twelve of the thirteen metropolitan banks moved across what had been the outer castle revetments to greater Marunouchi.

Only the Bank of Tokyo, postwar successor to the Yokohama Specie Bank, which had been such a help in financing Japanese expansionist policies, remained in Nihombashi. The metropolitan banks are the ones which, though privately owned, are deemed to be national banks, as distinguished from myriads of local banks. The departure in 1960 of the Mitsui Bank was symbolic. It had stood on its Nihombashi site, across the street from where the Bank of Japan had been since late Meiji, for more than eighty years. Its first building on the site, gloriously prominent among early Meiji exercises in "Western" architecture, was the subject of numberless ukiyo-e woodcuts. Now its main office moved to Yurakucho, just south of Marunouchi. (As the Imperial Bank, its name from 1945 to 1954, it provided the setting for the most interesting postwar mass murders; see pages 479-480.)

Retailing has not since the earthquake been as centralized as finance and management. Three very big department stores remain at Nihombashi. Two of them were the great competitors in the mercantile revolution of Meiji which produced department stores in the first place. Mitsukoshi still has its old name. Shirokiya now bears the name Tōkyū, from its new owner, the railway company that owns so much of Shibuya. (The Honolulu branch is still called Shirokiya. Perhaps Americans are thought to have stronger sentimental attachments to old names than Japanese.) Then there has been the great surge forward to the *fukutoshin,* the satellite cities along the Yamanote, as retail centers.

It may have been in the Olympic years that Ginza could for the last time confidently claim the fealty of that very important crowd: adolescents and those slightly older. Two other tribes came and went during the Olympic years, and Ginza was their base. The Miyuki Zoku took its name from the Miyukidōri, Street of the Royal Progress, in Ginza, along which the Meiji emperor passed on his way to the Hama Palace. It was

Members of the Miyuki Zoku, 1964

also known as the Oyafukōdōri, Street of the Unfilial, or possibly Street of the Prodigal Son. The first element in Ivy Zoku is borrowed from English, indicating a presumed resemblance to the Ivy League style of the United States. The two came in such quick succession and were so similar that it is not easy to distinguish between them. Perhaps it is useless to try, since both designations were invented by the mass media. Both favored casual dress, plaids and stripes and tight high-water trousers for the boys, long skirts, sweaters, and blouses for the girls, big shopping bags without distinction as to gender. The dress could be rumpled and ill-shaped, but, frequently imported, it tended not to be inexpensive—hence the element of prodigality. Ginza has not had *zoku* since. The very young crowds have tended to favor the Southwest, though in recent years there have been signs that they may be coming back to Ginza.

The building that seems most representative of the Olympic years, the gymnasium at Yoyogi, is by Tange Kenzō. So is the main prefectural building, the one in which the governor now has his office. So is the building under construction in Shinjuku, where he will presently have his offices. The one in use today was begun in 1953 and finished in 1957. It is not the largest building in the prefectural sprawl occupying an expanse just south of Tokyo Central Station and on both sides of the railway tracks, where there would have been room for rebuilding, had there been a will. It is true that the governor and his people might have been inconvenienced during the rebuilding. A statue of Ota Dōkan, who built the first Edo Castle, had stood in front of the old city hall. A new statue was unveiled a year and two days after completion of the new city hall. At first it stood on the north or front side of the main building, as the old one had stood at the door of the old city hall. Now, because of diggings in the vicinity of the station, it is out in back. No place is set aside for Dōkan in Shinjuku.

The highest structure of the second postwar decade, and still the highest in the land, is Tokyo Tower, not really a building at all in the sense

The Olympic Stadium, designed by Tange Kenzō

of an enclosed and roofed space that keeps off the elements. It is a big framework, a third of a thousand meters high, with observation towers at the hundred-twenty-five-meter and two-hundred-fifty-meter levels, and containing four thousand tons of steel. Finished in 1958, it so resembles the Eiffel Tower, though it is a bit higher, that the historian Umesao Tadao called it a monument to the Japanese lack of originality. One might indeed have wished that advances in the almost eight decades since the Eiffel Tower went up might have been put to more novel use; but perhaps it was good for the Japanese spirit, in those days when economic growth was barely getting underway and the spirit craved sustenance of any kind. The chief purpose of the tower, which serves few other purposes than sightseeing, may well have been to rise higher than the Eiffel. Hopes that it might be put to use in the electronics age came to little, but as a

The Tokyo Tower

sight for seeing it was a success from the start. People waited in line two and three hours to take the elevators. If there was symbolism in the date chosen for the opening, it has not been remarked upon. General Tōjō and his fellows were hanged in Sugamo Prison a decade, to the day, before.

The site, on the hilly side of Shiba Park, is a storied one. There it was that the elite of Meiji had their Kōyōkan, House of the Autumn Colors, where they could invite foreign gentlemen to elegant dinners without having to patronize the quarters of the flower and the willow. There too it was that the last of the Kodaira murders occurred (see page 479).

Ota Dōkan is thought to have finished his castle in 1457. Although there had earlier been a fishing and farming village on the site, 1957 could therefore be taken as the quincentenary of the founding of the city. Among the undertakings to mark the event was the erection of a big concert hall in Ueno Park. Mostly for Western music, it was finished in 1961, of proportions not much inferior to the insurance building going up at about the same time at the Shinjuku Westmouth, and was widely regarded as a great step forward on the way of the city and the nation back into the esteem of the world. Certainly it was a great improvement on Hibiya Hall, until then the main concert hall in the city. The exterior of the Ueno Park hall may not be to everyone's taste. Modern architecture has not yet come to grips with the fact that unfinished concrete soon begins to look nasty in a damp climate. The interior and the acoustics are good, however. So even before the Olympics the Japanese had technical accomplishments to show off to the world.

In another part of Ueno Park the National Museum resumed construction after a lapse of a quarter of a century. In 1962 a hall went up to house treasures from the Hōryūji near Nara, the greatest reliquary of early art in the land. It is similar in conception to the main hall, finished in 1937: traditional forms are added to modern materials. For its next and most recent building, finished in 1968, the museum discarded old forms. It is a glassy, flat-roofed building which incorporates old Japanese concepts, such as openness and an absence of supporting walls, even as it discards traditional forms.

So the National Museum is a sort of sampler for modern Japanese architecture, a record of the struggle to come to terms with the West. All that is missing is the "Western" architecture of early Meiji, the reverse of the main hall and the Hōryūji hall. In the beginning superficial Western details were added to traditional methods and materials. The oldest surviving building, from 1908, is of the day when reproduction of Western prototypes from start to finish was the thing. It is a handsome enough

Renaissance building with a central dome and lesser domes at either end—in concept a little like Tokyo Central Station, though it is in stone and not brick. Then come the buildings of 1937 and 1962, in a hybrid style. Then comes the most recent building, the hall of Oriental (as distinguished from Japanese) art. It was beginning to dawn on Japanese architects that modern architecture had come to them and they did not have to go to it. Modern architects, or some of them, were doing something not dissimilar to what the Japanese had been doing from time immemorial.

The Olympic decade was in some respects incoherent. Toward the end of it came the games themselves and the warm glow of cosmopolitanism. Midway through it came a great xenophobic rising, the protest demonstrations against revision of the Japanese-American Security Treaty.

They had the city paralyzed for several weeks during the summer of 1960, and produced one fatality—or two, if the principal assassination of the postwar period, that of the chairman of the Socialist Party, is attributed to anti-treaty unrest. It occurred at a public meeting in Hibiya Hall, but after the summer of discontent had passed and the city was back to something like normal once more. The assassin was a teenage boy of the radical right (he later killed himself in prison).

It was a most xenophobic time, and particularly an anti-American time. "Yankee go home" was among the things people were saying (in English). Even unintellectual, down-to-earth Asakusa was caught up in the mood. In April 1960 the Rokkuza (Sixth District Theater), where one of Nagai Kafū's postwar skits was performed (see page 388), offered a play called *The Tachikawa Base: Ten Solid Years of Rape*. The Tachikawa base was American, a big air base out in the county part of the prefecture.

The play is largely flashback. At the outset a young man is being arrested for murder. The police accede to his request that he be allowed to explain his reasons for killing the young lady he loved. So the flashback begins. The young lady was doing welfare work among ladies who were doing the only thing a lady could do, aside from welfare work, in Tachikawa: selling themselves to American soldiers. The girlfriend was raped by an American and acquired a loathsome disease. That is why he had to kill her.

Such was the mood of the city in those days. The play was erotic entertainment, of course, but it had its message, not too remote from the "one of us will get one of them" principle on which the extremists of the interwar years acted. Japan being a peaceful country, the ladies of Tachikawa, in one of the little sermons with which the piece is studded, are exhorted to get one of them by nonviolent means, such as infecting them with loathsome diseases. It was rather marvelous, the way the people of Tokyo had of assuring one that nothing personal was intended. The dislike for smutchy outsiders seemed very genuine. They threatened the purity of the island nation, left to itself until they came along.

The cabinet fell, but not before the treaty revisions went through; and the left never again rose to such heights of militancy. Indeed it started going to pieces. Violence continued, but it was fragmented and largely internecine. The Communist Party came to seem mild and restrained compared with the factions that broke away from it and went about flailing at one another with pipes and staves and hijacking airplanes. They did great harm to the universities in the post-Olympic years, but this does not mean that they continued to be a significant political force. Universities are defenseless against bands of fanatics unless they call the police. When they refuse to do so and the police refuse to come unless called, they are in serious trouble. The next great rising should have come in 1970, and it did not. In that year either party to the treaty could legally renounce it.

Another sort of political or social violence, if these kinds may be distinguished from ordinary criminal violence, might have developed into something serious in another country. The fact that it failed to satisfy expectations may have to do with the imprecise language that raised the expectations. Loan words, most commonly from English, can be most misleading. News that there is unrest in the Detroit slums is cause for alarm. News that the big police box in the Sanya *suramu,* north of Asakusa and the Yoshiwara, is being stoned again is routine. Such things happen and no one need feel threatened. People go off to watch, as they would go off to a display of fireworks. The stoners may be genuinely indignant at the police, but the Sanya *suramu* is not genuinely a slum.

Sanya is, along with the Kamagasaki district of Osaka, the most famous of the "slums." Purists draw a distinction between the Meiji slums, preeminent among them the Samegahashi or Sharkbridge one in Yotsuya, west of the palace, and Sanya. They assign the latter the designation *doyagai,* though "slum" is certainly much commoner. *Doyagai* is from the underworld argot that reverses the two syllables of a bisyllabic word. *Kai* or *gai* is "district" or "street," and *doya* reverses *yado,* which is "inn" or other temporary lodging. "Flophouse" might be the best rendition.

Thus a slum is, to purists, a place where poor families dwell as families. Sharkbridge was for the least fortunate of provincial families who came flooding in upon the great city. A *doyagai,* on the other hand, is a place of cheap lodgings for single and transient lodgers. In the popular

Sleeping rough in the Sanya "slum"

mind, Sanya is a slum for all that, and a stoning of the police box no different linguistically from a rising in Detroit.

In Edo and on into Meiji, Sanya accommodated people away from home. They were mostly of two sorts: travelers to and from the northern provinces, for Sanya lay where the main northern highway entered and left the city; and the staff and clientele of the Yoshiwara, for it lay on the canal that offered water access to the quarter from the Sumida. In 1976 the canal was filled in except for a hundred yards or so at the mouth. A Meiji edict regarding the operation of lodging places put Sanya in the lowest class. The opening in 1897 of what is still officially called the Sumida freight yards, though more popularly it is Shioiri, Tidewater, gave Sanya the particular character it has had ever since. It is just south of the freight yards, and it provided the most convenient lodgings for workers there.

Sanya has had a public employment agency since late Meiji, but access to work, in recent years mostly in what the Japanese call dirtwood business, which is to say roads and construction, has been overwhelmingly through less formal channels, brokers often under the control of underworld gangs. The system provides no security and no insurance, but it does provide freedom from embarrassing questions.

The *doya* of Sanya have improved. In the first years after the war they were tents, then there were large common rooms. These have mostly disappeared, though bunking arrangements with eight men in a room some twelve feet square are not unusual. Prices have risen, though not at rates greater than general inflation. Space in a shared room can still be had for under a thousand yen a night, and a man can have a tiny room with television for two thousand. Life in Sanya is not intolerable when there is work. It allows drinking, gambling, and inexpensive sex. Long rainy periods are the bad times.

A 1970 survey revealed that not many very young men lived in Sanya. Sixty percent of those polled were in their thirties and forties. More than half had been in Sanya for five years or more. So, although still a place of cheap, pay-by-the-night *doya,* Sanya was not exactly a temporary abode. The age of the residents has observably risen in the years since. The day may come when the *doya* business will disappear and Sanya will be little different from other residential districts in the northern and eastern parts of the city. The laboring population is well down from a peak of some fifteen thousand during the Olympic years. Even now, during most hours of the day, it looks little different from many another shabby neighborhood. The best hours for observing that it is in fact somewhat different are in the early morning, when crowds of men await transportation by bus and truck to the day's working place, and others lie sleeping in the gutters. In the early-evening hours it can be rather jolly, somewhat like Piss Alley at the Shinjuku Westmouth.

Sanya may not be as grim as parts of Detroit, but it has reason for discontent. The nation started moving ahead in the fifties, and Sanya did not move with it; and there was a common feeling that the police with their mammoth box, which went up in the summer of 1960, were arrogant and threatening. Indeed they are not the most friendly and helpful of police. The first big riot came that same summer, which was the summer of the treaty disturbances. There may have been a spillover. Three thousand men gathered at the mammoth box, and stoned it, and tried to set fire to it. A policeman was injured.

There have been frequent Sanya incidents since, the same police box being the main target. Perhaps because the early ones received much attention from the media, later ones came to seem random and ritualistic.

Ordinary criminal violence was not as big or as horrid as in the early postwar years. There was nothing to compare with the Imperial Bank case or the Kotobuki and Kodaira cases. Perhaps the most widely publicized

Tokyo incident was one involving a television "idol," as victim and not as culprit. On January 13, 1957, in the Kokusai (International) Theater in Asakusa, a nineteen-year-old girl flung hydrochloric acid in the face of Misora Hibari, among the most popular and perdurable of postwar entertainers. She appeared as a child at the Ernie Pyle. During her most vigorous period, the Olympic years, she was able to fill all three thousand seats at the Shinjuku Koma twice a day for a run of two months. (A month at the Koma is the cachet, the sign that a popular singer has reached the top.) Her popularity is unabated even now, though her vigor has been diminished by poor health. The girl said that she did it out of an affection so overwhelming that she wished it to be attached to a cicatrized visage. Miss Misora was laid up for three weeks and came back uncicatrized. Numbers of similar incidents have occurred in the years since.

There went on being curious little incidents to suggest that Japanese criminals rather enjoy getting caught and so render the role of the police less difficult than in most places. In September 1961 a man came into the detective offices at the Ueno police station. He wished to say hello to the detective who had sent him up for extortion two years before and to report how well he had been behaving himself since his release from prison. An old man came in to report that someone had taken his watch over by the railway station. He recognized the earlier caller as the thief.

In 1965 a man in Meguro, in the southwestern part of the city, killed his common-law wife and entombed her in cement. Several months later—he had been living with the cement block all the while—he was arrested trying to peddle his interesting story to a weekly magazine.

Crime was becoming more white-collar and intellectual. It was in the sixties that the *sōkaiya* came into prominence. Though their business is rarely thuggish enough to attract the intervention of the police and the public procurators, at its heart are extortion and intimidation. The expression shows how concise the Japanese language can be when it wishes to. The literal meaning is "general-meeting business," but the big Japanese-English dictionary must go to these lengths to make the real meaning quite clear (and thus tells us implicitly that the European languages have no need for such a word): "a person who holds a small number of shares in a number of companies and attempts to extort money from them by threatening to cause trouble at the general meeting of the stockholders."

It is a somewhat longer definition than necessary. The words "attempts to" are superfluous, for the *sōkaiya* have been very successful at getting hush and protection money from the biggest and most highly esteemed companies in the land.

In part the companies have themselves to blame. The underworld and people who occupy the twilight zone between the underworld and the great radiant world of finance and industry might not have noticed how profitable a thing it could be to own a few shares if they had not been called in for union busting and the stilling of protests against pollution and such things. The general willingness to buy off *sōkaiya* must inevitably suggest to the outsider that the great ones of finance and industry have things which they would prefer to keep out of sight. The general-meeting business, in any event, is more subtle than even a subtle bank robbery, such as the robbery of the Imperial Bank, and tells of a day when a certain margin to think things over and make a few calculations had returned.

In the post-Olympic years English-speaking *sōkaiya* began making their appearance at meetings of foreign companies. The most capable among them was a former intelligence interpreter for the American army who had studied in the United States. The labors of the *sōkaiya* have not been limited to Tokyo, but Tokyo, where most of the big companies have their headquarters, offers far the best opportunities. Like all Japanese, the *sōkaiya* are very industrious, to remind us of an important and neglected truth, that industriousness is not in itself necessarily a virtue.

In the summer of 1965 the Olympic governor, Azuma Ryūtarō, announced that he would not run for reelection. He was then midway through his second term. He had ample reason, aside from the fact that the Olympics, the occasion for his seeking office in the first place, had been accomplished. Both his predecessor, the first elected governor, and his successor, the radical governor, served three terms, or twelve years. The present governor, another conservative, is effective and popular, and, now in his third term, may well seek an unprecedented fourth one (unprecedented in Tokyo, though by no means unheard of in the provinces).

The main reason for the decision not to run was a scandal and its effect upon the conservative base. They might have prevented reelection in any event.

The metropolitan government had an aura of scandal hanging over it most of the time. The prefectural government of the postwar years has not been without scandals, though they have for the most part not been as big or as interesting as the prewar ones. A scandal surrounded the election of Azuma to his second term. Then came the biggest one of the postwar years.

The prefectural council elected a president in March 1965. It was a very dirty election, involving bribery and intimidation. The president himself was arrested, as were almost a score of others. Dissolution of the council was obviously called for, but it had to await amendments to the Local Autonomy Law. In June, pursuant to provisions of the new law, the council unanimously voted its own dissolution. New elections were called.

While the campaign was in progress, from late June into July, a huge plague of flies descended on the wards east of the Sumida River. The skies and the earth were black with them. They came from a spot of land out in the bay called Yume no Shima, "Dream Island." Dream Island is a garbage fill. Initial efforts of the Self-Defense Force (the Japanese army by another name) to exterminate the flies seem initially to have had only the effect of spreading them. Finally a scorched-earth policy worked. Dream Island was for a time a cinder on which not even flies could live. It is doubtful that the governor could have done much to foresee or forestall the scandal, though he might possibly have guessed what garbage fills are capable of. The timing, in any event, was unfortunate.

The election, which occurred late in July, was a free-for-all, great fun to watch, however one may have felt about the results. Councilmen awaiting trial ran for reelection. Several known gangsters were among the candidates. The results were a thorough renunciation of the Olympic governor and his administration—less than a year after they had acquitted themselves so nobly of their main task. The conservatives, who had a majority of the council after the 1963 elections, lost almost half their seats and were left with a third of the total. No single party has since had a majority. Coalitions have been the rule. All of the other parties gained, and the socialists became the first party, with seven more seats than the conservatives.

This fiasco for the conservatives looked ahead to the next gubernatorial elections, when the socialists and communists offered a persuasive candidate, Minobe Ryōkichi, son of the professor whose ideas found so little favor with the radical right of the interwar years (see page 404). Minobe was a television personality with a large following, particularly among women. The problem of garbage disposal, which had such an unfortunate effect on the Azuma administration, was among the consuming interests of the Minobe administration.

The matter of addresses and place names in Edo and Tokyo has always been such a complicated one that efforts to improve it often bring new complications. The theory of the address is two-dimensional rather than, as in the West, unidimensional. A huge effort would be required to change from the former system to the latter, and one of the complexities would only become more complex, the fact that place names are always changing. In possession of a slightly outdated map and an up-to-date place name, a person can find the effort to reconcile the two utterly bewildering. So it can be too with tracing a place name from a century or so ago. Several changes have probably occurred before it at length arrived at the designation which it has today (but may not have tomorrow).

By a two-dimensional system is meant one in which addresses are scattered over a tract of land. In a unidimensional system they are dots along a line. Complications become formidable when there is no perceptible ordering to the numbers here and there over the tract.

Attempts at simplification and rationalization have taken dual form, reducing the number of separately named tracts (which means of course that many houses acquire new tract designations) and bringing some order to the arrangement of numbers within each tract, so that there is at least a reasonable chance that adjacent spots will have consecutive numbers. The amalgamation of tracts to reduce the number has gone on sporadically through the century and more since Tokyo became Tokyo. It became systematic during the Olympic years, and it cannot yet be thought finished. There is still a welter of small tracts in what before 1947 was Kanda Ward, and there is one in the old Ushigome Ward, to the west of the palace. Yet, though the problem of how to match an address with an outdated map has if anything become worse, the endeavor accomplished something. One can often find a new address without the help of the police. It is often true that numbers move back and forth along traverse lines, rather as if the lines of a book were to read alternately left to right and right to left, but one does get the hang of the system, and at least it is a system. The old one was that only in a very primitive way, having to do with the order in which buildings went up, and the outsider could scarcely be expected to know that.

One may carp at the ordering of numbers, and find ways in which it can be improved; but that it is an improvement seems hard to deny. The other half of the endeavor, the amalgamation of tracts (the old *machi* or *cho*), is more controversial. It is here as it was with the 1947 reduction in the number of wards. Old names go, and a coating of history goes with them.

"Reminded that the district around the Shirahige Shrine was known in the old days as Terajima Village, I might once have thought first of the country villa of Kikugorō."

So writes Nagai Kafū at the beginning of *A Strange Tale from East of the River*. On his first visit to the Tamanoi quarter that is the site of the principal action, he passes a secluded villa, and has this thought. It is a little disingenuous, because the region surrounding Tamanoi was still known as Terajima. It would be more to the point today. Terajima is among the place names that have disappeared. It was an old and famous one, giving a family name to a celebrated line of Kabuki actors, the Kikugorō. Today Kafū would not have to pretend that he is reminded of a name now gone. Its going makes the history of the place seem remoter.

Not all places were unhappy about the change of names. The Yoshiwara and Sanya thought that new names might improve their images, and got them. In neither case has the new name been accompanied by great social improvement, but that is another matter. Suzugamori, at the far south of the Meiji city even as the Yoshiwara and Sanya were at the far north, was similarly pleased. It was known chiefly as one of the places where the Tokugawa magistrates had people's heads lopped off.

One place felt so strongly about its name that its citizenry brought an administrative action suit, in 1965, to keep it. The action was successful. A part of Bunkyō Ward continues to be called Yayoichō. Why the authorities should even have thought of tampering with so great a name is difficult to understand. It was in Yayoichō, in mid-Meiji, that artifacts were found which gave the name Yayoi to a great cultural epoch, some five centuries straddling the beginning of the Christian era.

Most attempts at resistance were unsuccessful. Sometimes the citizenry was divided. Kobikichō, east of Ginza, where the Kabukiza stands, was as important as any part of the city in the history of the Edo theater. Romantics and antiquarians wanted to keep the name. Businessmen thought that having the element "Ginza" in the name would be better for business. So it became East Ginza. (Actually this happened before the systematic rationalization of addresses. In the course of this last, the "East" was dropped, and the district became simply Ginza.)

Sometimes an old name was assigned to a larger district, so that if an old name disappeared at least it was subsumed under another old name. Often the new name was merely arid and bureaucratic. The city is dotted with Easts and Wests and Outers and Middles and Inners. Devotees of the Yose variety theaters used to greet favored performers not with their names but (so much better a way of showing that one was a real connoisseur) with the names of the districts in which they resided. It sounds nothing like as good, one of them pointed out recently, when the names must be Outer A and Middle B.

Simplification produced complication both because many old addresses had to be changed and because sometimes the old names remained in certain capacities. The subways and railways have declined to change the names of their stations merely because at street level the old name has been canceled. The two subway stations between Ueno and Asakusa bear names no longer to be found in the regions above. Shiina-machi, where the Imperial Bank murders took place, no longer exists, but it is the name of a station on the Seibu Ikebukuro line. This can be puzzling. Simplification itself becomes a complication.

August 1, 1965, was a sad day for Asakusa. The name Rokku, Sixth District, signifying the section of the old park where show business flourished, ceased to exist. On the same day the Tokiwaza closed its doors for stage performances and became a movie place. Most of the big Asakusa names from Taishō and early Shōwa had appeared upon its banners.

What was surely among the big events of the second postwar, or Olympic, decade was one in which city and prefecture played no part. Prostitution was again outlawed, this time by the National Diet. Four years after the end of the Occupation, in May 1956, an anti-prostitution law was enacted. It took effect on April 1, 1958. The previous outlawing was at the instance of the Occupation. This time the feminine electorate and women Diet members, both of them postwar institutions, were instrumental. It might never have happened without woman suffrage, and it certainly would not have happened so soon, a mere decade after the much-ignored Edict 9 (see pages 462-463). Men, such as brothel keepers, were certainly behind the opposition to the new law (the anti-antiprostitution movement), but the openest and most outspoken opposition was feminine. It was an amazonian battle—not that the conclusion was other than foregone. More than one opposition movement took shape early in 1956 as passage of the law, which had languished in the Diet for several years, seemed imminent. Two socialist members of the Diet were expelled from the party for being active in organizing a movement, in Asakusa. The Socialist Party may have wobbled and tergiversated on some issues, such as the need for revolution, but it was firm about prostitution.

There was even a grand coalition against anti-prostitution. It was called the Tokyo Federation of Unions of Women Workers. But the law was passed, of course. In the interim before its tentative application, still clinging to a hope, brothel keepers organized a National Autonomous Association for the Prevention of Venereal Disease. A Diet member was arrested for taking bribes from it. The 1958 date is the one generally accepted for the disappearance once again of prostitution, but the law theoretically went into effect a year earlier, on April 1, 1957. The following Aprils Fools' Day was the one on which the meting out of punishments was to begin.

Even as it was a foregone conclusion that the law would pass, it was a foregone conclusion that prostitution would not disappear. More than a hundred thousand women the country over were affected by the new law, and they and their associates would find ways. Yet to say that the new law made no difference would most certainly be in error. The great and venerable world of the flower and the willow, so central to the arts of Edo and early Tokyo, had over the years fallen into a malaise, and the new law made it even sicker. Of the two licensed quarters within the old city limits, the newer one, Susaki, went out of business. The Yoshiwara shifted over to a closely related business.

The Yoshiwara and Susaki had both been destroyed in 1945. Susaki rebuilt in a quiet, conservative, and, given the materials at hand, not at all tasteless fashion. The Yoshiwara began its convalescence with the shacks called "barracks," but within a half-dozen years after the war was its gaudy old self again. It had some of the most expensive pleasure palaces in the city, charging the equivalent of thirty dollars a night, a very large sum of money in those days. The architecture of the brothels was as eclectic and uninhibited as it had been before the war. The lavish courtesan processions of an earlier day were resumed, by way of advertising.

Which would have prevailed, the Yoshiwara way or the Susaki way, if the first Tokyo century had not been so rich in disasters? These are usually blamed when someone from outside remarks upon the hodgepodge which the city for the most part is—an eminent European intellectual referred to it as "this tortured use of space." What else can a place be, retorts the son of Tokyo, when it is twice wiped out, and subjected to many a lesser disaster between the two major ones? It is true that such a place has to work hard even to survive. Yet, though we can only speculate, the eclectic and uninhibited Yoshiwara way seems the genuine Tokyo way.

Wandering through Susaki today, one still comes upon a scattering of house and shop fronts that announce what the places once were. Blocks and blocks of nondescript landfills had in any event removed Susaki from the bay shore that had been among its principal charms. It may have been the newcomer among the licensed quarters in and on the edges of the city (it opened only in Meiji), but the Fukagawa district in which it is situated was prominent among the "hilly places," the unlicensed flower-and-willow districts of Edo. (There is disagreement as to why they were called hilly places, though the word "hill," *oka,* is an element in a number of expressions indicating remoteness from the place where the action is, in this case the Yoshiwara.) People like Nagai Kafū could go there and

Hatonomachi as it appears today. The small mosaic tiles are among the identifying signs of a bawdy house

linger with melancholy pleasure over vestiges of Edo. The going of Susaki brought a sense of loss.

Some of Kafū's "dens of unlicensed whores" went too, including what was probably, along with the Tokyo Palace, the most famous postwar one, Hatonomachi, Pigeon Town (see page 458), east of the Sumida River. The houses of Pigeon Town all closed their doors late in January 1958, some two months before the date from which they could all in theory be fined. Stenciled "Off-Limits" warnings to the men of the Occupation grow fainter and fainter as the years go by, but even today they are to be found in the district that still calls itself Pigeon Town, if one knows where to look for them.

The Yoshiwara was not so docile about leaving the old business behind. A few of the more distinguished houses, proud of themselves and their past, quietly closed their doors and sold their land. A great many others became what were called Turkish baths until recently. A Turk objected. Now the standard though not universal designation is "soapland." The Toruko (the Japanese metamorphosis of "Turk") was, and the soapland is, a place, often expensive, where a man can go and have a ritual bath and massage and the undivided attention of a young lady. It is a brothel by another name. The count of soaplands in the Yoshiwara is now almost two hundred, and that of soapland ladies some twenty-five hundred.

*Exuberant architecture in the Yoshiwara. Once known as Turkish baths,
the brothels are now called "soaplands"*

The Yoshiwara had since Meiji been noted for its architectural extravagances, often of a fancifully cosmopolitan kind. One may not come upon much that looks Turkish beside a Yoshiwara street, but the more ornate styles of Europe and the ancient Orient are most of them there, with an occasional touch of Egypt among them. It is all very interesting and amusing, but a result of anti-prostitution has been to make the Yoshiwara slip yet a bit further from the heights of other ages. The more dignified houses went away, and the less dignified ones stayed and became less dignified all the time.

Many a den of unlicensed prostitutes followed the way of the Yoshiwara rather than that of Susaki and Pigeon Town. The view of the police seems to have been that the law was unenforceable from the outset. It is a view in keeping with that of the Supreme Court expert (see pages 462-463) who commented on the preceding disappearance of prostitution. Those who formed the association for the prevention of venereal disease may have felt themselves vindicated. Police detected a sharp rise among prostitutes during the post-anti-prostitution years.

The years between the next-to-last and the last outlawing of prostitution were those of the *akasen,* the red line. The expression seems to have originated as police jargon, the prefectural police thus designating the districts to which the edict applied. The old distinction between licensed and unlicensed prostitution thus disappeared. The Yoshiwara and Pigeon Town were alike red-line districts. Another distinction now grew up to replace the old one, as if there were a reluctance to let anything go. Places such as the Golden Block of Shinjuku, in which prostitution was covert and somewhat secondary, came to be known as *aosen* or blue-line districts.

In 1963 there came tacit recognition from reliable quarters that prostitution yet survived, and could be a problem. The style manual of NHK, the public broadcasting corporation, decreed that those who had hitherto been called BG would henceforth be OL. Both are acronyms from English expressions, "business girl" and "office lady." Both signify working women, but NHK feared that the former might be taken to signify "prostitute."

The Yoshiwara has had no great fires on its own, none that it did not share with the rest of the city, in more than three-quarters of a century. The fire of 1910 was among the last great conflagrations of which the city has been a victim, save for the disasters of 1923 and 1945. Among postwar fires, one which occurred in the northern part of the city in April 1963 and destroyed thirty-six buildings is the most extensive given notice in the centennial history of the Tokyo Fire Department. The chronology appended to the centennial history of city and prefecture notes a fire that destroyed fifty-eight buildings east of the Sumida in 1957. It does not matter which was the larger. They were of generally the same proportions, and neither would have been much noticed during the full summer of the Flowers of Edo.

The most sensational of postwar fires included one in a department store and one in a hotel. The former, which killed seven people, occurred on August 22, 1963, in the Ikebukuro Seibu. The day was a holiday for the store, but several hundred maintenance men, decorators, and the like were on the premises. Among them, in the seventh-floor dining room, was an anti-cockroach squad. One of its members, about to have a post-luncheon smoke, threw his match into a heap of paper impregnated with insecticide. In the scramble to extinguish the flames, a can of insecticide was knocked over. Though the store really had no one to apologize to, it took the occasion for an act of contrition, a big sale, which almost turned into another disaster. The crowds at opening time were so gigantic and threatening that the store closed its doors in less than an hour. It was not wholly cleared of crowds until noon. Many a housewife demanded repayment of her train fare, and was obliged.

The toll was smaller than that of the Shirokiya fire, but still the third largest from any postwar fire in Tokyo. The hotel fire, in 1982, took thirty-three lives. In 1963 nineteen firemen died in a warehouse fire in the southern part of the city.

Yanaka Pagoda, as it was before being burned in a love suicide in 1957

The most lamentable fire of the postwar years was a case of arson. It wrought great damage upon the material heritage of a city that has never been very strong in that regard. One of three surviving wooden pagodas in the city stood in the Yanaka cemetery near Ueno. On July 6, 1957, it was damaged beyond repair by fire. A campaign to rebuild it is only now getting underway. The foundation stones remain, a few steps from the graves of the famous murderess Takahashi O-den and Nagai Kafū's grandfather. Two bodies were found among the cinders. The proprietor of a tailoring establishment in the neighborhood and a woman employee less than half his age had chosen the pagoda as the place in which to carry out their suicide pact. The pagoda had been built late in the eighteenth century and is the subject of a famous and once widely read piece of Meiji fiction, Kōda Rohan's "The Five-Story Pagoda" ("Gojūnotō"). Rohan made his hero, the master carpenter who built the pagoda, the embodiment of all the old virtues.

In 1957 there occurred a double suicide that seemed to have as much potential for setting off a vogue as the Oiso suicides of the interwar years (see page 320). It did not, but, for reasons that quite defy explanation, a suicide in 1972 did. About a hundred fifty people have jumped from the roofs of the Takashimadaira apartment complex in the northwestern part of the city since, in that year, a woman first did so. The setting and circumstances of the 1957 suicides were far more romantic, and set off no vogue at all.

On an early-winter day the bodies of a young boy and girl, dead of gunshot wounds, were found on Mount Amagi, on the Izu Peninsula in Shizuoka Prefecture. It was established that the boy, in accepted fashion, had killed the girl and then himself. They proved to be schoolmates from Tokyo. The girl's name was Aishinkakura Eisei, a most unusual one for a Japanese. The family name is the Japanization of Aishingyoro, the family name of the Manchu emperors of China. (Like Kim, the commonest of Korean names, it means "gold" or "money.") She was the niece of Pu-yi, the last emperor of China and the only head of the Japanese puppet state in Manchuria. The Japanese wife of the emperor's brother appears briefly in the movie *The Last Emperor.* She is conspicuously pregnant, and it is probably with this girl, who was very pretty and not, by all accounts, especially unhappy. The act was probably one of romantic abandon more in keeping with the Japanese half of her nature than the continental. The mystery remains that there were no imitators, while the altogether more pedestrian suicide at Takashimadaira had scores and scores.

The burning of the Yanaka pagoda was the greatest loss by fire which the city has suffered since the war. And what was the greatest loss by death? Perhaps that of Nagai Kafū, late in April 1959. He was the writer among all modern Japanese writers who most particularly made Tokyo his subject, and he was the most industrious and among the best at evoking its moods and describing its places. Toward the end of his life he expressed a wish to be buried among the courtesans in a little temple north of the Yoshiwara. Had he known that the Sunshine Building, highest in the city and the land, would come to loom gigantically over the Zoshigaya cemetery, where he is buried, he might have insisted more strongly on the temple. He did not like such places as the Sunshine, or what it stands for.

Takami Jun and Kawabata Yasunari, who wrote so well about Asakusa, died a few years after Kafū, the former in 1965, the latter, probably a suicide, in 1972. Neither was as faithful as Kafū in his attentions to Tokyo. Takeda Rintarō, who wrote so well about Ginza, died in the spring of 1946, a victim of the postwar confusion. Most biographical dictionaries say evasively that he died of a sudden liver attack. One or two hint at something nearer the truth. His death was indeed sudden, and it was from drinking methyl alcohol in a little place in Shibuya. Inexpensive beverages were not safe in those days.

Tokyo has had no one like any of them since, no writer to express its individuality as his own. The trouble may be that, vast and inchoate, it no longer has much individuality.

Along with its peculiar crimes and its voguish suicides, Tokyo has quirky deaths. On November 10, 1964, exactly a month after the opening of the Olympics, the paid announcement that the Rakugo monologuist Sanyūtei Kimba had died came out in the first person. "I am safely dead. You may put your minds at rest in that regard. It has been my wish all along that I receive no floral offerings, natural or artificial. Asking you to forgive my petulance, I mean to stand by it. We will meet again, perhaps, centuries hence, in the heavenly pavilion, or among the dew-drenched leaves on the banks of the stony river. In the meantime, have long lives, all of you. I thank you for your many kindnesses during my own lifetime. November 8. Sanyūtei Kimba."

The Buddhist writ contains many hells. In the one referred to here, children pile stones in heaps only to have the heaps knocked down by demons. The general sense is that we will meet again one century, in heaven or in hell.

The dozen years between the cooling off from the white heat of 1960 and the "oil shock" of 1973 were years of rapid economic growth. It almost seemed during those summer months of 1960, so completely was the city under the control of the anti-treaty demonstrators, that all they had to do to consummate their revolution was march upon the television stations, the Tokyo equivalent of the Winter Palace. The cooling was rapid. Youthful factions went on fighting, but it was mostly with one another and with the universities. In a land where business has never been below second on the list of important things, it was first again.

Among the loan words in vogue from the late fifties into the sixties were "glamour," "vacance," "leisure," "topless show," "*otomee fujin*," and "instant." Most of them tell of new and affluent ways, one or two ask for explanation. The next to the last is a hybrid, the first element being an abbreviation of "automated" or "automation," the second a Japanese word for housewife. The last refers to instant food, making things easier for the automated wife.

Among the tribes or *zoku* not already mentioned were the *yoromeki,* the *kaminari,* and the *ereki*. The first took its name from a very popular novel by Mishima Yukio called *The Faltering of the Virtues (Bitoku no Yoromeki)* and suggests wantonness and infidelity. The second is literally "the Thunder Tribe." Its members raced about on motorcycles. They outraced the police, who were left to pretend that they were not there and to hope that they would go away. The last is another abbreviation, of "electric." It signifies amplified music, and especially the electric guitar.

In these tribes and their names is the spirit of the day. There were also an Anchūha and an Angoha. The first syllable in both cases signifies the Japanese-American Security Treaty, and the second is respectively "during" and "after." The third is "faction." So, in contrast to the faction that was all caught up in the disturbances, there was already by the early sixties a faction that had come to the fore after they subsided. For them 1960 was already ancient history.

Pearl Harbor was prehistory. In 1959 a group of forty-five students at a Tokyo middle (or junior high) school was set without warning to the task of composing an essay about the significance of December 8, the anniversary of the attack, corresponding to December 7 in the United States, that day once expected to live in infamy. Only two knew the principal significance, and many another significance was attached: the day Christmas sales begin, the day on which a famous Sumō wrestler got married, the day Grandfather died. Probably a similar group of American students would not have done much better with Pearl Harbor, but it would most likely have spread its ignorance more impartially, offering little help as to the significance of August 6 (Hiroshima Day) either. This last day, when Japan could claim to be the injured party, is remembered.

There were also the years of (in English) "my car." The word *doraibu* was already in vogue by the beginning of the Olympic decade. It signifies a new pursuit, pleasure driving, and it is the Japanization of the English "drive," used as a noun. At first most of the drivers out on the road for the fun of it were businessmen with expense accounts, and civil servants, but within a few years driving clubs with cars for rent made half their money from students.

In the next decade private automobiles became so numerous that the parking-lot business began, the first Tokyo specimen opening in 1959. In 1963 it was made illegal to keep the family automobile in the street space in front of the family house. Little garden plots all over the city fell victim to the higher demands of the automobile. In general driving conditions were much improved from the days early in the century when Tanizaki was getting his nose bloodied against the roof of a taxicab. By the early eighties virtually all the streets in the wards had hard surfaces. Conditions were not quite so good in the county part of the prefecture, but the surfaced mileage passed 90 percent for the prefecture as a whole. Three decades before, it had been well under half.

The so-called Jimmu prosperity of the mid-fifties recalled the semi-legendary founding of the Japanese nation, Jimmu being the legendary first emperor and the expression signifying that there had been no such prosperity in all the centuries since his reign. The sixties and seventies were not without their little setbacks, such as the one occasioned by oil shock, but the dominant note was of growth, prosperity, and increasing national confidence. The names given to periods of prosperity suggested that they were getting better all the time. There was the *iwato* or "cave" prosperity, and later, in the years after the Olympics, there was the Izanagi prosperity. Each took us further beyond Jimmu and back into the legendary origins of the nation. The "cave" referred to the one into which the Sun Goddess withdrew after a quarrel with her fractious brother, causing darkness to fall upon the land. Izanagi was an ancestor of the Sun Goddess a few generations earlier. Each of these periods of prosperity outdid the others in department-store sales. If there had been anything like them in the days of the Sun Goddess and Izanagi, there had not been since.

The supermarket, almost everyone agrees, is an American invention. It is among the American ideas that have proved more exportable than American products. It has not developed in quite the same way in all the places to which it has been exported. In America supermarkets began during the depression, to provide food at low prices to the jobless and otherwise straitened. They appeared in Tokyo during the first postwar decade. One might have expected, in those years of the cod and the sweet potato, that supermarkets would have some relation to straitened circumstances; they did not. The first self-service food emporiums that could call themselves supermarkets opened in the southwestern wards where rich foreigners and rich Japanese alike were concentrated. They were expensive.

The food departments of the big department stores had been similarly all-purpose, but they had not been arranged so that the customer could serve himself. As is in the nature of department stores, comestible items had been segregated, kept separate from noncomestible. The supermarket somewhat nearer the original American kind, purveying to the less than wealthy, did not make its appearance until the Olympic years, when almost everyone was wealthier. It put both kinds of commodities, comestible and noncomestible, in the same space, and caught on because of this not very startling innovation.

In 1964 two supermarket chains, one native to the city and the other from Osaka, got started in Tokyo. Their competition, which was intense, took place at first in the western suburbs, where neither commuting husband nor automated wife wished to spend much time shopping. Sociologists associate the emergence of the supermarket with the emergence in those same western suburbs of the two-generation "kernel" family.

The time came in the pre-Olympic years when the Japanese could no longer say with much conviction that they were poor. Consumption was becoming conspicuous. In 1962, to much publicity, an Asakusa clothing wholesaler offered a necktie for fifty thousand yen. It was snapped up. Every thread of the weft was different from every other, and an expert weaver spent three days weaving it. A reasonably expensive tie of the more ordinary sort would have cost no more than a thousand yen. A government survey in 1964 showed that 50 percent of Japanese thought themselves middle-class. The number was probably higher in Tokyo. Three years later a survey showed that 90 percent of Tokyo women thought themselves middle-class.

Among the new words of 1964, the Olympic year, was *kagikko,* "key child." It gives concise statement to the new realities of life in the High City (the Low City, as in most things, lagged behind): the nuclear family, the apartment, and, her numbers increasing, the automated wife. A key child is one who, the expectation being that no one will be at home when he or she returns, carries a key. The following year a newspaper remarked upon the growing number of fat children. Though the report was highly impressionistic and offered no statistical criteria for its findings, it confirms one's own impressions. Eating habits were changing, in the direction of fatty foods. The key child, since he usually had money and no one to tell him he ought to stop eating and get some exercise, could spend all his time with the vending machines. The number of these the nation over increased a hundredfold during the decade of the seventies. In addition to junk food the key child could, if he wished, put money in the vending machines for whiskey, condoms, and pornography.

The year 1964 may also be counted as the Year 3 of the Mansion Age. "Mansion" is an example of a foreign word put to new use upon arriving in Japanese. "Barrack," another instance, had already been a familiar word in Japanese for almost a half century when "mansion" came in. Given the principal significance which the former word had taken, one might have expected the latter to mean something very like the opposite, the one a flimsy and temporary hut, the latter a grand dwelling. The meaning of *barakku* does bear some resemblance to one of the two principal meanings of "barrack," a large building in which large numbers of people live uncomfortable lives. It has no military significance. Other words fill that gap. The want of comfort is present in a *barakku,* even though the largeness may not be.

"Mansion," in English, is different. In 1962 a developer first used the word to designate his developments, which were condominiums. A mansion became any condominium, large or small, plain or extravagant. (The word is still occasionally applied to apartments for rent.)

There were apartments for rent in Tokyo before the war. A public corporation put up apartment clusters, at least three of which survive, here and there over the city. The individual buildings were small and low. As early as 1910 there was near Ueno Station a wooden building, five storys high, with more than sixty units, that called itself an apartment house (an *apaato).* The first building said to be in the American style, a four-story one in fireproof materials, went up near Tokyo University in 1925. It survived as a sort of youth hostel until 1986. One might have guessed from its name, Culture Apartments, that it was from the interwar period.

Mostly such places were for unmarried persons. It was only in the postwar years that very large apartment houses started going up and people started flooding into them. The expression *danchi,* which scarcely a Japanese above infancy can be unfamiliar with, is postwar. It is an abbreviation of "public corporation housing," or public housing in big apartment complexes. Tokyo contains some huge ones. They tend to be not very cheerful places, badly painted and maintained. (That famous suicide place, Takashimadaira, in the northwestern part of the city, is a *danchi.* See page 534.) Surveys have shown that there is even less intercourse among the tenants than in similar American suburban developments.

The Japanese run to extremes when a notion such as privacy grips them. The first *danchi* went up about a decade after the war. So there are second-generation *danchi* people who are now adults, have known no other residence, and think of the *danchi* as their hometowns, their "native places." The advent of the mansion and other multi-unit dwellings with common entrances is something new to the Tokyo and indeed the Japanese experience. The "long house" or row house, in which the several dwellers under a common roof have their own individual entrances, is very old. Scarcely anyone wanted to move into the new Ginza brick buildings in early Meiji, and here everyone was moving into buildings little different from them in principle.

Mansions and *danchi* tend to combine American want of community with Japanese flimsiness. The traditional view of a building—that it will not last long in any event and so durability need not be a consideration—has persisted in the construction of multistory buildings. There are exceptions, especially in such places as Shinjuku and Marunouchi, but the life expectancy is far lower than for similar American or European buildings. The surviving apartment complexes from the post-earthquake period are historical curiosities. New York is full of apartment houses that are decades older. The problem of rebuilding has not been faced and is bound to be painful. If the owners do not have the means and the will to rebuild, Tokyo may for the first time have slums that bear comparison with Europe and America. It may have slums and not *suramu.*

The expression Capital District has had more than one meaning since, in 1956, it achieved legal status. A Law for the Ordering of the Capital

District (Shutoen Seibihō) passed the National Diet in that year. It was modeled on the English plan for Greater London. A more specific plan drawn up two years later defined the expression to signify an area within a radius of a hundred kilometers from Tokyo Station. This includes the whole of Saitama, Chiba, and Kanagawa prefectures, bordering Tokyo on the north, east, and south; a part of the fourth prefecture with which Tokyo shares a boundary, Yamanashi, the old province of Kai, off beyond the mountains to the west; and parts of the three northern Kantō prefectures. In 1966 the district was redefined to include all of the seven Kantō prefectures and Yamanashi.

Faced with opposition from local agencies and developers, the system of green belts that is so important to the London plan may be deemed a complete failure. A pair of bedroom towns out in the county part of the prefecture and some bypass and loop highways are the chief tangible results to be detected from the big plans. Yet the concept is significant, for it tells us what Tokyo has become. So is another expression, Greater Tokyo, variously used. Most commonly it includes all of Tokyo, Chiba, Saitama, and Kanagawa prefectures and part of Ibaragi Prefecture, most importantly the new academic and research complex at Tsukuba. Greater Tokyo has thus grown to well over thirty million people, and the Capital District to not far from forty million. A third or more of the population of the land resides in a space which, were it not for all the motor vehicles, a vigorous marcher could march across in a long weekend. There are still farmlands between Tokyo and the population centers of the northern Kantō, and indeed there are farmlands within the Tokyo wards; but the area of unbroken urbanization includes the bay littoral from Yokosuka on the west shore to beyond Chiba on the east shore. The dwindling of farms means that if the day of the sweet potato comes again it will be worse than last time.

The Sumida was flushed for the Olympics, and has gradually accumulated oxygen and little fishes. In other respects it has not been treated well. The stroller along the banks cannot even see the river for considerable stretches because of high concrete retaining walls, and the boater upon the river can see little except the walls. The ultimate reason for these was a big storm a hundred fifty miles away. In September 1959 a storm called the Ise typhoon—since the center passed over Ise Bay, at the head of which Nagoya stands—left upward of five thousand dead. It was the worst storm to hit in either the Shōwa reign or the one preceding it. Ise Bay, unhappily at flood tide when the typhoon struck, rose by some five meters. The highest point in Chūō Ward (Ginza and Nihombashi) is not that high. The Sumida was already being walled in. Now the walls were made higher, against the possibility that a similar disaster might hit Tokyo. So by the end of the sixties concrete walls six to eight meters above water level stretched for some fifteen or sixteen miles along the two banks of the Sumida. During the following decade the two principal canals draining into the Sumida, the Nihombashi and the Kanda, were also walled in.

Doubtless the sort of vision that protects the lowlands of the city against a disaster which might come one of these centuries is laudable. It has not come yet, and meanwhile we may lament that the walls are so ugly.

The Sumida has been mistreated in other ways. An expressway, put through in the post-Olympic years, crosses it from Nihombashi and proceeds upstream along the left bank to well past Asakusa. Like the walls, it is not beautiful. The Sumida once flowed home to the sea past strands where the gathering of shellfish was among the popular diversions. Now it must pass bleak landfills extending as much as two miles beyond the old coastline. One of them is Dream Island, of the pestilence of flies (see page 526). Again the concept is laudable. The city must expand, it seems, and if it can do so over garbage dumps and not paddy fields, something is saved and nothing is lost.

It should not be impossible to convert reclaimed land into something pleasing. The old Low City demonstrates as much. Yet in recent years it has seemed impossible. The tract called a park on Dream Island is probably the best thing the prefecture has done over the whole reclaimed expanse. It is occupied almost entirely by athletic facilities, freight yards, and apartment complexes. The inability to make a garbage dump look like anything but a dusted-over garbage dump is among the reasons for misgivings about plans for a "city of the future" to occupy yet more of the bay.

All in all, the Sumida is an ill-used little stream. Probably the fact that it is little is the reason. The distance from wall to wall is no more than a couple of hundred yards. The Arakawa Drainage Channel, the artificial stream farther east, is more imposing. A little stream running through a great city is bound to get dirty. When it has the obstreperous ways of the Sumida it may expect to find itself walled in as well. Yet the lady who said "It ain't the Grand Canal" had a point. The Grand Canal too is a narrow little strip of water, and it remains beautiful.

One of the great observances of Edo, the opening of the Sumida, was discontinued for a decade, beginning in 1937, because of the Crisis. It was resumed in 1948 and discontinued again in 1961, because it was thought to be a fire hazard and because the odor of the Sumida had so

One of the few remaining geisha restaurants along the Sumida, squeezed between modern buildings

taken away from the pleasure. The opening came late in July and signified the advent of hot weather, when the river, before it got so dirty, added much to the beauty and pleasure of the city. It was the occasion for a huge display of fireworks, and that these could be dangerous was demonstrated in Kyoto when a display set fire to one of the buildings in the old palace compound. The cessation was presumed to be permanent, but in 1978 the fireworks were resumed, farther up the river, near Asakusa. They attract a million or so people each year, and are among the events most disliked by the police.

The million gather along the two banks near Asakusa, and not, as they once did, near Ryōgoku Bridge downstream. So the Yanagibashi geisha district lost a valuable drawing card. Its restaurants ("geisha houses") had been much the best places for viewing the fireworks, and had commanded huge prices. Reservations had to be made literally years in advance. A place in a Yanagibashi restaurant on the night of the opening was the badge of membership in the Establishment.

Yanagibashi was far more grievously wounded by the walling in of the Sumida. All the indications are, indeed, that the wound is fatal. The river remains visible above the walls from upstairs windows, but mendicant musicians no longer come rowing up to Yanagibashi gardens. The gardens were extensions of the river bottom, and they are no more. Yanagibashi may have been doomed in any event. The geisha business has done badly in recent decades, and Yanagibashi, in the old Low City, is a part of town to which captains of government and industry do not go in the ordinary course of things. Among the once-great geisha districts Yanagibashi is the one that seems nearest to expiring. Aficionados hold that in its good years it was the most Edo-Iike of the districts, the worthiest successor to the Fukagawa district, which flourished across the river in late Edo.

There was no attempt to make Sumō, like judo, the other traditional sport with a mass following, into an Olympic event. It may have been too utterly Japanese. In most lands and sports, obesity and athletic prowess do not go together. Sumō was not having a bad time. The postwar "golden age," opened by Wakanohana and Tochinishiki, went on. Taihō, the most accomplished wrestler since the departure of the above two, was arguably the most popular champion the sport has ever had. He had the television audience, not comparable to that of baseball and especially the Giants, but no small thing all the same. Although it did not make the Olympics, Sumō was becoming a little more cosmopolitan. The first non-Oriental to reach the top ranks, a Hawaiian, did so in 1967. It was also advancing technologically. In 1969 videotapes were used for the first time in settling challenged decisions. (Any one of several judges may challenge the decision by the referee.) There were technological failures. On September 20, 1960, a light exploded in the Hall of the National Accomplishment while a match was in progress. The two wrestlers, who had been locked in combat, fled. They returned and started wrestling again twenty minutes later, the damage having been repaired. One of them had been treated for burns, from fragments that lodged inside his loincloth.

In 1963 the famous writer Ishihara Shintarō, he whose second published story gave the Sun Tribe its name (see pages 494-495), complained publicly that a Sumō match had been fixed. The match took place in Fukuoka, but Tokyo, where all the wrestlers live, can be held responsible. The Sumō Association said that such things did not happen, and that was that. The common wisdom is that such things do indeed happen. Not exactly the fix, perhaps, but the friendly, warmhearted understanding between wrestlers has long been a part of the sport. A wrestler badly needs a win, or perhaps the association needs one to keep people interested, and the wrestler who is asked to lose would be unfeeling and disloyal, among the worst things a Japanese can be, if he did not oblige.

Somewhat later an accomplished wrestler made an uncommonly frank statement. "Wrestlers going into the last day of a tournament with seven wins and seven losses always win. Even when the matches are big ones you know who is going to win."

A division remains between the northern and eastern parts of the city, not rich and not quick to change, and the southern and western parts, quite the opposite. It is a rough and generalized division, but not invalid for that fact. Those who are looking for old Japan, or unchanged Japan, or something of the sort, would be well advised to do their looking amid dirt and poverty, in Sanya rather than Shibuya. Shabbiness does not change, while the world of the rich and powerful seems to change by the minute.

The idea of having a baseball stadium that the Low City, the eastern flatlands, could call its very own was a delightful one. Geologically the Kōrakuen, home grounds for the Giants, is of the Low City, for it lies in a Kōshikawa valley only a few feet above sea level. Historically it is very much a part of the High City, for it stands on land which was the main estate of the Mito Tokugawa family; and in recent decades, because of the Giants, it has been chief among the jewels of commercial television and of advertising.

When plans were announced for a new stadium, to be home grounds for a less popular professional team, within an easy walk of Sanya, the possibility that the Low City baseball crowds might stay home and keep a little life there was buoying. Tokyo Stadium, as it was called, opened its gates in Arakawa Ward, just across the boundary from the old Asakusa Ward, in 1962, and waited for the crowds to come. It waited for some years, and was sold to the prefecture in 1977. Now it is used for sandlot baseball. The stands are gone. The crowds continued to go to the Kōrakuen.

For a time early in the Olympic decade a saying about television seemed almost as popular as television, and it was not a friendly one. It did nothing to diminish the power of television, which has grown and grown. Even the haranguers on the campuses, whose style was once stiff and jerky, have taken on the glibness of television newscasters and masters of ceremonies. The saying was the creation of the critic Oya Sōichi, and it had to do with the Japanese television audience: "A hundred million reduced to idiocy." A neat half-dozen Chinese characters, it had its time of popularity in 1956.

Chapter 12

BALMY DAYS
OF LATE SHŌWA

On a day in the spring of 1965, the portion of the Shōwa reign to occur after the surrender of 1945 became longer than that which had gone before. On a day early in the summer of 1970 the Shōwa emperor had been on the throne longer than his grandfather, the Meiji emperor, who had reigned longer than any of his predecessors whose reigns can be dated with any certainty. On Christmas Day 1976 the emperor became the first in Japanese history to greet a golden jubilee. On Christmas Day 1986 came his diamond jubilee.

The first of these four dates no one seems to have noticed at all though it would have been a good day on which to declare that elusive entity, the postwar period, finally over. The second received brief notice in the newspapers. The other two were occasions for formal observances, though in neither case did the observances occur on the precise Christmas anniversary. On November 11, 1976, to celebrate the golden jubilee, there was a gathering in the Hall of the Military Way, the Olympic building north of the palace in which the Japanese had won and lost those judo medals just over twelve years before. On April 29, 1986, the emperor's eighty-fifth birthday, there was a gathering to celebrate the diamond jubilee, in the new Hall of the National Accomplishment east of the Sumida River. Both occasions were formal to the point of stiffness, as if those in charge felt that they must be held, but with limited fanfare. There is a strong and growing tendency to pretend that the first two decades of the reign never happened. Children learned astonishingly little about them in school. (For evidence of their nescience, see page 537.)

There had been a great deal of peace, and, though the war was still remembered on August 6, Hiroshima Day, and though the nation often found it convenient to go on being postwar, which is to say deprived, the bad days were beyond the memory of most Japanese, and further away each day. In the year of the golden jubilee the number of Japanese born after August 15, 1945, passed the number born before—and of course only those born no later than 1940 or so can have clear recollections of that day and its remarkable broadcast.

As the golden jubilee approached, several events took place that may be held to mark the end of one stage and the beginning of another. In 1968 the dollar started slipping. The exchange rate of three hundred sixty yen to the dollar had been set by the Occupation in 1949 and had come to seem almost sacred. Now it was a failing god. In 1973 came the "oil shock." The international consortium of oil producers had made it certain that the price of imported oil, and Japan had scarcely any domestic oil, would rise.

So the age of rapid economic growth, which had lasted from the years when the Korean War was being put to such good use, was at an end. The years immediately following were ones of hesitation and uncertainty. Bankruptcies occurred with greater frequency than at any other time since the war. It came to seem possible that rapid growth would be replaced by no growth at all, or even a diminution. The effect on the life of Tokyo was immediately noticeable. Most prominent among the lights to go out was the Morinaga globe in Ginza. Elevators were put on furlough, lights in hallways were dimmed. Broadcasting hours and movie hours were shortened. Filling stations took holidays. Another sacred institution, the expense account, seemed threatened.

The city and the nation emerged from it all with greater confidence than ever. It was in those years that one began to hear that Japan, after a century and more, had nothing to learn from the world, and the world, if it had any sense, should start learning from Japan. Though slow economic growth would be the thing, the continuing slide of the dollar was the best indication that the national foreign policy, export and export and export some more, had been a success. The lights started going on again. By the end of the decade the city gave little indication, in its surface aspects at least, that the shock had occurred.

Inflation proceeded apace. In 1975 prices in the ward part of Tokyo were four times what they had been a quarter of a century before, when the wild inflation of the immediate postwar years had been brought under control. The higher price of energy of course made domestic manufactures more expensive. The lower price of the dollar might have been expected to make foreign products, and especially American products, cheaper. Deflation in this regard was scarcely to be detected. It certainly did not occur at the rate at which the dollar declined. Economic growth would continue, at a reduced pace, and the country had proved itself capable of handling both expensive imports of raw materials and cheap imports of manufactured goods. The new confidence seemed quite justified. Opinion will differ as to whether or not it made Tokyo a pleasanter and more livable city.

Quiet was returning to the campuses by the early seventies. The violence and the apparent ability of students to do as they wished with their universities began to subside with the fall of what the media called Yasuda Castle. Yasuda Hall is the main administration building at Tokyo University. Radical students who had made it their "castle," expelling the president and all the other administrators, were themselves expelled in the summer of 1968. They occupied it again, and were again expelled, in January 1969, after a fierce battle with close to ten thousand police-

Fire hoses drench students holding out at Tokyo University during the battle of "Xasuda Castle," 1969

men, watched by the whole nation on television. Among the popular words of those years were *gebaruto* and *gebabō*. The former is the German *Gewalt* ("force, power"), and the latter combines its first two syllables with a Japanese word for "stick" or "stave." It refers to the staves with which radical students flailed at the police and rival student factions.

Mishima Yukio died on November 25, 1970. It was too complex an incident, and he was too complex and intelligent a person, for us to see it as merely an instance of misguided nationalism. He knew the youth of the land too well, and the changes that were coming over it, now that the turbulent sixties were out of the way, to expect that the army (more properly, the Ground Self-Defense Force) would rise up and follow him in bringing about a Shōwa Restoration. A repetition of the 1960 demonstrations against the Security Treaty was expected in 1970. It did not come off, and 1970 may be seen as the year in which the Socialist Party lost all credibility as a possible alternative to the conservatives who had been in charge of the country since 1948. Those who wanted change became splinter groups. Conformity came to prevail, and an appearance of democracy in which it would not be possible to turn the rascals out.

After standing on a balcony for a few minutes and urging the assembled soldiers at the Ichigaya barracks to rise and follow him, Mishima withdrew into the office of the commanding general, and there, with help, met his end (it was technically murder and not suicide). The recorded shouts of the soldiers are more suggestive of amusement and derision than sympathy—and it is hard to believe that Mishima expected them to be otherwise.

His death speaks of the times, in a very negative fashion. He did not like the emerging consensus and conformity. In all manner of ways, from dress to sexual behavior, he was a nonconformist. He did not have

Mishima Yukio's last oration, Ichigaya, 1970

much to say about democracy in the lands of its origin, but he thought that in Japan it was a sham and a pretense. He had hoped that the anticipated anti-treaty demonstrations of 1970 would bring a genuine confrontation and the emergence of something more honest, even if the honesty might be revealed in ungentle ways. It is clear that he started making preparations for his death during the summer, when the confrontation seemed possible. Motives other than disappointment must have been present in his last, drastic deeds. We may reasonably think that it was among the motives, however. The city was entering a time of ever bigger and brighter material objects and ever greater conformity, and no one turned up to protest, on the last occasion when genuine protest might have been possible.

In the spring of 1977 four young men who had been members of Mishima's private army attacked the headquarters of the Federation of Economic Organizations, just north of Marunouchi. Even as there are splinter groups on the radical left, there are such groups on the right and Mishima and his death are among the inspirational sources of the latter.

The day when such happenings will be of importance is a great if not infinite distance away, but they serve to remind us that the city and the nation chose to take one course and some by no means stupid people wished them to take another.

For bright young people who conformed there might be a room at the top of one of the high new buildings. These were very new, something the city had not seen before, the first buildings worthy of the name skyscraper. The city started reaching upward as New York had done a half century before. In this way too the years just before the golden jubilee and after the Olympics seem to mark the beginning of a stage.

The relatively permanent, fireproof, and advanced parts of the city had low, fairly even lines in the interwar period and the years just after the war. On one of her visits from suburban Osaka to Tokyo, Sachiko, the heroine of Tanizaki's *The Makioka Sisters,* finds the avenue with the palace moat and plaza on one side and the office buildings of Marunouchi on the other—it is the avenue on which General MacArthur had his headquarters—almost the only thing in Tokyo, aside from the Kabuki, worth looking at.

It was, by comparison with its condition today, a modest, quiet sort of avenue. The big Marunouchi office buildings, including the Marunouchi Building, the biggest of them all, did not exceed seven and eight storys, in a day when New York was flinging the Empire State Building into the heavens. Reasons of dignity and reasons of prudence were argued for this state of affairs. The royal residence must not be dwarfed by huge towers (for the same reason headquarters of the prefectural police, at Cherry Orchard Gate, were kept to a modest level); and skyscrapers would not do in a city of earthquakes.

Somewhat higher buildings began to rise in the years after the Korean War. The biggest and highest of the Olympic hotels was seventeen storys high. The reasons of dignity just mentioned are closely related to aesthetic reasons, and these last seemed to be forgotten. The hotel, the New Otani in Akasaka, looms over a surviving segment of the old outer moat, until the Olympics (when it also got freeways) one of the prettiest places left from the old city. When the time came for *real* skyscrapers, however, aesthetic considerations asserted themselves once more. A race seemed in prospect to see who would have the first such building. The competition was between the Marine Insurance Building in Marunouchi, on Sachiko's avenue and General MacArthur's, and a building which Mitsui proposed to erect just south of the Kasumigaseki government complex.

The former got embroiled in a controversy over the integrity of the avenue. Time passed before an accommodation was reached which cut several storys from it. The new Mitsui building meanwhile went up, to be the first of the "super high-rises," as the Japanese expression for the genre may be translated.

The Kasumigaseki Building was finished in 1968, and it is thirty-five storys high. We are told that prudence was kept in mind. The building, along with other supers, we are assured, is perfectly earthquake-resistant. It is in any event a nauseating experience, like seasickness, to be high in one of them when even a mild earthquake strikes. When the building was new the largest annex to the American embassy stood right across the street from it. People would rush to their windows and watch it rock. Looking up at the supers, one may wonder less whether they will stand through a big earthquake than whether all that glass will come showering down into the street. The Kasumigaseki Building was a new adventure for Japanese builders, but it does not look very daring, save for its height. It is a large block.

It did not long remain the highest building in the city. In the years since it was finished it has slipped to tenth place or so. In 1970 a World Trade Center (Sekai Bōeki Sentaa) was put up at Hamamatsuchō, a short distance south of Ginza and Shimbashi. It is forty storys and a hundred fifty meters high. Though it was not yet built when the Olympic monorail was put through to the airport, it now functions as the northern terminus.

The highest structure in the city continues to be Tokyo Tower, and the highest building in the narrower sense of the term—a structure of walls and rooms—is the Sunshine, finished in 1978 on the site of Sugamo Prison in Ikebukuro. It is sixty storys and a bit more than two hundred forty meters high, plus three underground levels.

The Shinjuku Westmouth, however, is the true place for supers. It has a cluster of them, while those mentioned above stand in isolation. The cluster too wears an air of isolation when viewed from anywhere except the middle of the cluster itself. From a distance it goes on looking as if the city had not made adequate preparations for it and did not quite know what to do with it.

The prefecture kept a part of the old reservoir site for its own use, and it is there, toward the western end, beside Shinjuku Central Park, that the new prefectural offices are under construction. The rest of the tract was turned over to private developers. The park is made over from the well-wooded grounds of an old shrine that still occupies a corner of it.

The old Yodobashi reservoir, later site of the Shinjuku Westmouth skyscrapers

A new station building rose at Eastmouth in the year of the Olympics. Besides being the main Shinjuku station for what were then the National Railways, it is an elaborate shopping and feasting complex with an English name, My City. Traffic and crowds were put into a kind of order at Westmouth before the high buildings started going up. The Westmouth plaza was finished in 1966. The pleasant station plaza that had stood near Piss Alley at the undeveloped Westmouth quite disappeared. A complex on several levels took its place, accommodating many, many vehicles, public and private, and people and shops. It became possible to have a covered, rain-free walk eastward from the old reservoir site past one subway station and on to another, a distance of a kilometer or so, with subterranean entrances to shops and department stores and rapid transit all along the way. Not many cities can have the digs that Tokyo has. It is like a coal mine.

No one seems to have foreseen that the Westmouth plaza could easily be clogged by people who chose to clog it. On a day early in October 1968 students for whom the Communist Party was too conservative started hurling chunks of pavement, mostly at the police but somewhat randomly, and occupied a police box. Then, by way of preparation for an "antiwar day" later in the month, all the paving blocks were taken up in the course of a single night and replaced by asphalt. Windows were boarded over. My City closed early in the evening. Some twelve thousand policemen were massed in readiness. The station was occupied by student factions all the same, and in chaos. Fires were set, stones were hurled, tear gas was used.

Thereafter for a time skirmishes were almost nightly affairs, and fun to watch. Folksinging and dancing of a militantly nonmilitant sort succeeded the violence. They too led to clogging and police action. The police eventually succeeded in putting a stop to the singing and dancing, but it was a great bother to them. The Shinjuku Incident of October 1968 and the fall of Yasuda Castle early the following year were probably the most conspicuous events in the great show of youthful spirits. We have seen that the Delinquent Tribe of the Eastmouth was a part of the action, and got dispersed as a result of it. What with mouths and plazas and tribes and factions, Shinjuku was in those days a very lively place.

The first super high-rise on the old reservoir site was the Keiō Plaza Hotel, finished in 1971, forty-seven storys, but still under two hundred meters. Also in Shinjuku, another Mitsui building, finished in 1974, went up fifty-five storys and some twenty meters over the two hundred mark. Critics of architecture do not find much to praise in these supers. The new prefectural offices will, however, be something to look at. If they look like big pieces of latter-day Gothic, they will do so with some honesty. Notre Dame of Paris is the admitted inspiration. The offices will be, we are told, a monumental specimen of "postmodern" architecture.

This very fashionable expression is elusive, but one of the things it seems to mean is that architectural forms will once more hark back to periods remoter than the present century. While all this was going on at Westmouth, Eastmouth did not cease to bustle. The immediate Eastmouth remained one of the best places for shopping, and crowds of ladies with money poured in upon it every afternoon from every direction. The district farther east, where the old post station had been, became somewhat specialized. It evolved into the homosexual capital of the nation, and surely it is well in the running for the designation homosexual capital of the world. The homosexuality is not exclusively male, but that predominates.

As a place for masculine bustle of the commoner type, Kabukichō, with its neighbor the Golden Block, was leaving the competition behind in Shinjuku, certainly, and arguably in the land as well (though the Kansai cities were often pioneers in the kinkier things). In 1984 and 1985 the police had another fit of puritanism, and it was generally agreed that Kabukicho provided the occasion. It was becoming altogether too open and brazen with one of its two staples, sex. The other staple, alcohol, was not a problem unless it led to drunken driving, and this was dealt with

Kabukichō at night

sternly. Nor has noise, a by-product, been thought a problem. Tokyo and its police have in this regard always had a high threshold.

The puritanical fit removed from the streets the most obvious signs of what was going on. Touts became more reticent about laying hands upon passersby who seemed in a mood for something; the latter had to look a little harder to find it. Gaudy billboards and lights were no longer there to direct them. Yet it had taken a quarter of a century to create Kabukichō in its present image, and it was not prepared to revert to an earlier existence, or convert to something else. Detailed maps of the place go on showing something of a titillating nature at almost every Kabukichō number.

A recent one is packed full of mysterious runes and codes, and the key to them may be translated thus: "peep show; crystal; health girl; massage in private rooms; telephone club; love room; television games; video; girl companions; private sauna; pantyless tearooms; special baths; adult toys." About half the key is in what seems to be English. It would take a genuine expert to say exactly what all the terms mean, and whether they are carefully defined and mutually exclusive categories. That the sex business is large and subtle, however, must be apparent to anyone.

The most mysterious item is the second, "crystal." It is in the Japanese phonetic syllabary, and seems to be from English. The English word was already present in the Japanese language in such expressions as "crystal glass," "crystal diode," and "crystal microphone." In this case it seems to

Love hotel in Kabukichō

A Kabukichō eating and drinking establishment, unfortunately named

derive from the title of a popular novel, *Somehow Crystal (Nan to naku Kurisutaru)*, written in 1980 by a student named Tanaka Yasuo. It is an almost plotless piece, really a novella, which would run to no more than thirty thousand words in English translation; and it contains 442 footnotes identifying details, predominantly exotic, that might otherwise puzzle the reader. We may presume that the use of the word here also signifies something exotic, though a recent inspection of Kabukichō turned up no very convincing answer to the question. The "crystal" places seemed no different from the run-of-the-mill purveyors of "adult" gadgetry.

Another recent tabulation, compiled at about the time the police were beginning to have their puritanical seizure, covered only the southern half of Kabukichō, the half in front of the Seibu station and nearest to Eastmouth proper. It contains twenty "consolidated pornography houses" (pornography emporiums, so to speak), twenty-one places offering massages in private rooms, two strip theaters, twenty-one "nude shows in private rooms," four pornographic movie theaters, seventeen "soaplands" (which would earlier have been called Turkish baths), four houses offering video in private rooms, thirteen peep shows (including places that offer these in private rooms), two pantyless tearooms, seventeen pornography shops, and eleven enterprises which (most ingeniously) fell into none of the above categories—a total of a hundred thirty-two. There were also fifteen love hotels, and some two hundred touts swarmed the area, no more than five hundred yards across east to west and two hundred north to south.

The strip shows deserve a special word. Always rather demure from the outside, with perhaps no more than a sign saying "New Art Theater" surrounded by a stream of white lights, they were little affected by the police crackdown. They were and are uninhibited. The girl who stood in the picture frame as Venus can scarcely have dreamed what ways she stood there at the head of. Complete nudity and the most wanton of dances prevail. They are under the control of the gangs, some thirty of which, large and small, independent and cartelized, are said to operate in Kabukichō. What the arrangements are between them and the police only the one or the other can tell us.

Many a thing goes on in Kabukichō that the laws of the land and the regulations of the prefecture do not permit. An obvious solution would be to bring the laws and regulations into better accord with what actually prevails; but righteous forces would rise up against that. Probably the police could not stop all these things if they had the will to. Their solution seems a sensible one: keep them out of sight as much as possible.

The events of 1985 were known to American devotees of Kabukichō as the Valentine's Day Massacre. It was on and near that day that the disappearance of the strip girls of Kabukichō seemed imminent—or at any rate their return to the frills and furbelows of an earlier era. Indeed, a certain hush and sense of caution did come over the scene for a while. The hush remained upon the streets, but behind doors things were soon as noisy and abandoned as ever.

The political center of city and prefecture will soon shift to Shinjuku. Does this mean that a great reversal has taken place, comparable to the great shift through the first half of the Tokyo century from the Low City, the cultural center of Edo, to the High City, where almost everything of an original and "creative" nature is today? Has there been a great reversal, with Shinjuku—the leading one among the *fukutoshin*, or satellite cities—now the main center, and the old center—Marunouchi, Ginza, Nihombashi, and southward and westward into Minato Ward—now the satellite? It is a view that has been commonly argued since Kabukichō became so big and sinful and the cluster of supers went up at Westmouth.

There is little evidence to support it. In only one field, or set of fields, related to sinning and toping, might it be asserted with some force that Shinjuku is ahead of the old center. It has most definitely not become the managerial and entrepreneurial center. That is still Marunouchi, somewhat broadly defined. Big insurance companies do have their headquarters at the Shinjuku Westmouth. The first considerable building to go up there, aside from the terminal department stores, was an insurance building. For the rest, headquarters have stayed mostly in the old center. The huge real-estate companies, Mitsui and Mitsubishi and Sumitomo, have stayed there, and rented out space in their Shinjuku supers to lesser companies, cultural institutions, and the like.

In 1982 almost three-quarters of companies with capitalization of a billion yen and more had their headquarters in the three central wards, and the figure was 80 percent for those with capitalization of ten billion and more. Close relations between business and government make Tokyo offices essential even for companies (such as Toyoda) whose head offices are elsewhere. The Tokyo offices of the biggest among these are also in the central wards. All of the "metropolitan" banks, the ones held to be national in their operations, have their head offices in the central wards, most of them in Chiyoda (Marunouchi).

Shinjuku is not a very cultural sort of place, unless "cultural" is defined as signifying all the things that make a culture what it is, which is to say, all the things that people do. Though people do many things in

Shinjuku, it does not excel in high culture. Recently there have been reports of schools in Kabukichō to teach Japanese to foreign persons. These might in another place suggest culture and that yet higher cultural entity, international cultural exchange. Kabukichō is a curious place for them. They seem in fact to be arrangements to get easy visas for pretty Southeast Asian girls, especially Filipinos, and put them to work in the bars and cabarets and strip halls of the district.

Kabukichō set out to become a dramatic center, and it did not. It does have its Koma Stadium and the largest cluster of movie theaters in the city. The Koma is the largest theater in the district for concerts, recitals, and stage performances. Popular entertainers are dominant. The "road show" movie houses are mostly in the Ginza district. The inner wards, with Ueno, a bit to the north, are where a symphony concert or an opera is most likely to occur, or a foreign performer to hold forth (sometimes commanding ticket prices that run to four hundred and more dollars at current exchange rates).

None of the big newspapers—the national ones, to correspond to the metropolitan banks—has moved its offices to Shinjuku. They are no longer in the Ginza district proper, but they remain in the three central wards. There has been no tendency on the part of publishing houses to move to Shinjuku. Some big ones have their offices in Shinjuku Ward, but in places where they have been for many years, along the eastern or inner fringe of the ward. (The station and its Westmouth and Eastmouth are at the southwest corner, a couple of miles away.) One big television company has its studios in Shinjuku Ward, but they are in the center of the ward, at a considerable distance from the station. The others are all in the inner wards save NHK, the public broadcasting corporation, which is in Shibuya Ward. A great deal of printing occurs in Shinjuku Ward. That too is most of the way across the ward from the station and its mouths. The heart of the advertising business—the Madison Avenue of Japan—continues to be in the central wards. So it cannot be said that in this day of information the huge and growing information industry has done much to make Shinjuku the new center of the city.

There is very little chance that Shinjuku or any of the other *fukutoshin* will ever replace Ginza in popular lore. According to a history of Chūō Ward published in 1980, there are almost five hundred Ginzas the country over—places of a more or less bustling nature that have taken the name This Ginza and That Ginza. There can be no doubt about the eponym. The history counted the name Ginza in the titles of fifty-one popular songs. Kyoto figures in thirty-two and Mount Fuji in thirteen. Shibuya and Shinjuku were not even in the running, as place names or as song titles. Where the characters for "new station," which is to say Shinjuku, appear in a place name, the pronunciation is often different from that of *the* Shinjuku, and the origins are almost always independent. Ginza is a part of Chūō Ward and so the historians had an interest in establishing its preeminence. Yet allowance for exaggeration still leaves Ginza unique in the popular esteem. If no other part of Tokyo rivals it, neither does any part of any other Japanese city.

The department stores of the private commuter lines that have their terminals at the Shinjuku Westmouth were renovated and expanded in preparation for the crowds to descend upon them from the super buildings, and the buildings themselves and the underground passages leading off toward them are full of expensive boutiques. At Eastmouth there has been no great change in the merchandising business since the years of recovery from 1945. The inner wards, meanwhile, have been adding much to the supply of slickness and opulence. The most conspicuous addition is a big merchandising and entertainment complex where the Nichigeki (Japan Theater) and the *Asahi Shimbun* used to be. Popularly called, in English, the Yūrakuchō Mullion, though it has a more formal name, Yūrakuchō Center, it does have a great many mullions. Indeed it is all vertical lines, metallic mullions and glass up and down the whole twelve storys of it. Theaters, one of them bearing the old name Nichigeki, and an assembly hall open from a central well with glistening escalators and hanging illumination. It is dizzying in its shininess and cold whiteness. On either side are two huge department stores, both belonging to private railway lines, the Hankyū of Osaka and the Seibu, which, having consolidated its initial hold on Ikebukuro, has moved on to acquire many other bases.

If shadows and easeful ligneous surfaces were essential to the old Japanese notion of an interior, then it must be said the Mullion is about as un-Japanese as a place can be (except perhaps for a few other places in Tokyo, and the Trump Tower). Doubtless it is also among the places that lead the way into the future. In this regard one can only conclude that Ginza is marching more boldly ahead than Shinjuku. The complex opened for business in 1984. In 1986 some two hundred thousand shoppers and viewers were said to enter it every day. Long before it accommodated the Nichigeki and the *Asahi* the site was that of one of the two Edo magistracies, the southern one. A history of it might without great exaggeration be taken for a history of the city this century and more.

The two Mullion stores were not the only big ones that opened in the Ginza district in 1984. It was the year of what was called the Ginza-Yūrakuchō War. Earlier that year a big supermarket chain opened a most swanky and expensive department store and gave it a swanky French name, Ginza Printemps. It is only a few steps from the Mullion, although it is in Ginza proper and the Mullion is in Yūrakuchō. There were already a half dozen other big department stores in Ginza, three of them prewar, three of them (invasions by Kansai and Nagoya capital) postwar. So Ginza, with Yūrakuchō, has more than Shinjuku to draw the daytime, feminine shopping crowds.

The Mullion must be given its due. It, more than any other force, has brought a rejuvenation of Ginza, which in the post-Olympic years had begun taking on a middle-aged look. (Middle age may be held to begin in Japan with the throwing off of blue jeans and with conversion to the religion that is the corporation.) The Ivy and Miyuki tribes were the last ones to have their main base in Ginza. The glitter of the Mullion had the effect of bringing young people back in the daytime, and there has been a rash of new beer halls, open later hours, to keep them from wandering off to Roppongi and beyond when the big Mullion stores and movie houses close.

The Mullion complex and related complexes nearby have put Ginza more firmly in control of the first-run road-show business, which it has dominated since the war. The Mullion contained five theaters, including the old Nichigeki, when it opened in 1984. Two more have since been added. Tōhō has remade the block across the street from its Takarazuka (later the Ernie Pyle) into one of the slickest things in town. Along with the vast department stores, these vast spaces for sitting and watching things have brought youth back to Ginza.

But in sex and drinking Shinjuku, especially Kabukichō, leads. A count in 1987 established that in Kabukichō alone there were not far from three thousand bars, clubs, cabarets, and other eating and drinking establishments. This is about equal to the count of permanent Kabukichō residents and larger than a similar count for the whole of Ginza, which has hovered at about two thousand. A count for the three central wards combined would outdo that for Shinjuku, but would be a misrepresentation, since it would be scattered over a much larger area. Roppongi and Akasaka in Minato Ward are a considerable distance from Ginza, and there is not much revelry in Shinjuku Ward that is not an easy walk from the station. So the preeminence of Shinjuku and especially its Eastmouth demands recognition. It may be added that Ginza continues to be the more elegant place in ample measure. Perhaps Shinjuku is the genuine successor in our day to Asakusa, a place of crowds in search of diversions varied but not of the most ethereal sort.

The conclusion must be that the center holds. When the prefectural offices move to Shinjuku they will not be moving to a new center. They will be leaving a remarkably strong and durable old center behind. A city that has always been more decentralized than the American cities of the railway age has avoided becoming the doughnut that so many American cities of the automobile age are. It may be that in already decentralized cities the centrifugal pull of the lesser centers is weaker than in a centralized city such as Los Angeles once was. The center remains stronger in almost every regard than any of the bustling places along the outer circle. It is of course possible to view this state of affairs in more than one way. Those who first gave currency to the expression *fukutoshin,* "secondary center" or "satellite city," thought that the center had accumulated too much and a distribution of its assets would be good. Charles Beard—it is true that he was not looking at the same city but at that of a half century before—thought that the outward-moving forces were too strong.

Though concentration of any kind can be excessive, it does seem to be the case that vitality at the center of a city has a vitalizing effect on the whole city. The Ginza crowds, human and vehicular, can be maddening when one is in a hurry; but to have them all abandon the area in favor of the county part of the prefecture would be far worse.

It may be, though precise measuring devices are not to be had, that Shibuya, with the adjoining Aoyama and Harajuku, outdoes Ginza in one respect, the chic and the ultra-European.

Since the Olympics two things that Shibuya has done and had done to it are of importance. It has pushed out of its tight, constrictive valley, and it has come to seem less of a one-company town. It has acquired a Park Avenue (Kōendōri). Few Tokyo streets have official names; some have popular names. Insofar as it had any name at all, the street leading up the hill northward from Shibuya Station to the Meiji Shrine and what was Washington Heights and the Olympic Village used to be called the ward-office street. Now, because it leads up the hill to Yoyogi Park, the old Washington Heights, it is Park Avenue. The name is entirely popular and unofficial. It was part of a forceful advertising campaign, for a department store, and then several of them, called Parco. The English word "park" has established its place in the Japanese language, in both the Central Park and the parking-lot sense. Something with more tone was asked for, and so the Italian word was chosen. (Probably the French one was rejected because it would have been indistinguishable from the English.)

The advertising campaign brought the two important new Shibuya developments together, for it was at the hands of the company that became genuine competition with the Tōkyū railways for hegemony over Shibuya. The Seibu enterprises, their groundings in another private railway system and in real estate, moved aggressively into Shibuya in the post-Olympic years. Both Seibu and Tōkyū opened stores in the direction of the park and at a remove from the main station complex, where Tōkyū had been supreme. It was the beginning of the climb out of the valley.

Soon after the Seibu opened its Shibuya store it opened the first of its Parco places, also in Shibuya. The Parco slogan was: "Park Avenue in

Park Avenue in Shibuya

Shibuya, where the person you pass is beautiful." The Parco places are not so much department stores as elegant and expensive bazaars. They have as concessionaires the elite in fashion and food. Affluent Tokyo was by these post-Olympic years becoming one of the ultra-chic places of the world, and Shibuya was becoming what Ginza long had been (and neither Asakusa nor Shinjuku ever was, really), the highest of the highly fashionable. "Shibuya" may here be understood to include the rest of the southwestern triangle, Harajuku and Aoyama. So few years had passed since women left behind the shapeless bags of the years of war and defeat.

The Tōkyū enterprises were not slow or timid in fighting back. They opened elegant and ingenious bazaars of their own on the slope leading up the park, and gave them such names as Hands and 109. The good, solid English of the former suggests everything the amateur builder and engineer can possibly want, and that is what the stores by that name offer. The latter is a pun. Advertising renders it in Roman letters, One Oh-Nine. It is then divided in two, One-Oh or Ten, and Nine, and the Sino-Japanese readings for these figures are *tō* and *kyū*; and it becomes Tōkyū, the abbreviated name of the railway system.

The Southwest, in the broad sense in which the expression was used in the previous chapter, designating the great shopping and entertainment complex from the outer moat to Shibuya, contains most of the places that are even slicker than the Yūrakuchō Mullion. Most striking among them, it may be, is the complex called Ark Hills, finished in 1986. The second word is English; the first might seem to be as well, but in fact is an acronym from Akasaka Roppongi Kaihatsu, "Akasaka Roppongi Development." A few steps from the American embassy, astride the boundary between Akasaka and Roppongi, or the old Akasaka and Azabu wards, it contains a concert hall, luxury apartments, office space, and a very shiny hotel. It seems to have succeeded in doing what it set out to do in one regard, attracting international finance. Highly advanced communications devices are available around the clock. The hotel is a marvel of shiny surfaces and bright lights. Like many shiny surfaces, it seems impenetrable. It seems to turn away all attempts at getting close to it.

Ark Hills has not succeeded, apparently, in becoming one of the new sights of the city, a place to which all the bunches and buses must go, a magnet like the Yūrakuchō Mullion, drawing hundreds of thousands of people every day. Experts find the reasons for this failure in a certain want of integrity. It is concrete and pretends to be something else. This may possibly be true, though one doubts that the multitudes who have failed to show up are aware of such niceties.

Whether or not it is popular today, Ark Hills has the look of what tomorrow is likely to be. Shinjuku is probably ahead of Ginza in sin and roistering, and Shibuya and the Southwest may be ahead in the shiny things of the future. They are most definitely in advance of Ginza and the land in offering advanced things for women to buy and put on. They also have a stronger hold on the adolescent crowds, despite the return of youth to Ginza and the Mullion.

The Sunshine Building, sixty floors and two hundred forty meters, was finished in 1978 on the site of Sugamo Prison, near Ikebukuro Station. It is the highest building in Japan, though not as high as Tokyo Tower, and it requires getting used to. It may not be as forbidding as the prison was, but it does have a remote look about it. The routes of access from the station, which is a fifteen-minute walk away, are obscure; and, at the northwest side of the city, the direction whence cold winter winds blow in from Siberia, the building has, even more than the cluster of supers at the Shinjuku Westmouth, a lonely, unaccepted look about it, quite the opposite of the sunniness which the name seeks to call up.

When one has overcome obstacles physical and mental and set foot inside the doors, it proves, with subordinate buildings, to be a city in itself. Sunshine City is the name of the whole complex, even as Sunshine Sixty, from the number of storys, is the full name of the biggest building. The complex contains galleries, a planetarium, an aquarium, all manner of shops, a hotel, a theater, a concert hall, a trade-promotion center (as if

The Sunshine Building, Toyko's tallest, seen from the freeway

that sort of thing were really needed these days), government offices, a branch of the Mitsukoshi department store, which has another branch nearer the station, and many another facility. In a corner of the grounds is a melancholy piece of stone, a memorial to the "war criminals" who were hanged there late in 1948.

Open space yet remains at the Ikebukuro Westmouth. It belongs to the prefecture. This is in itself no obstacle to development, since the prefecture owned the lands at the bottom of the Shinjuku reservoir as well, and allowed a perfect frenzy of development to occur there. It has thoughts of something more cultural for the Ikebukuro Westmouth.

Despite the presence of Seibu, one of its Parcos, one of Tōkyū's Hands, and Sunshine City, Ikebukuro goes on looking a little insubstantial. The bustle has subsided and the district seems to have exhausted its resources some time before one reaches Sunshine on the walk from the station. It asks for comparison not with Shibuya and Ginza but with Shinjuku. Like Shinjuku, it is somewhat wanting in class, and it is this with nothing comparable to the Shinjuku intensity, magnitude, and variety. The comparison is not to be understood as saying that Ikebukuro is dull and dreary. A want of finish brings a particular kind of vigor, not innocent, perhaps, but eager. A century or so ago Ikebukuro offered little promise indeed, and so it may be called the miracle among the bustling places. It is the boom town way out on the wild prairies.

The Seibu Parco in Ikebukuro

Greater Tokyo contains half the university students in the land, and there is only one four-year university, the Merchant Marine Academy, anywhere in the Low City. It has been said, probably truly, that many a provincial student goes through his four years of higher education in Tokyo without ever seeing the Sumida.

Some of the Low City wards have done brave and imaginative things of a cultural nature. One of the wards east of the river has established an ethnological museum devoted to the customs and physical aspects of the Edo Low City. It does its work well. Earlier there was a smaller museum, devoted to the same subject, beside Shinobazu Pond in Taitō Ward. This last ward, which has been energetic in preservation and restoration as few Japanese agencies are, has moved and restored a Meiji concert hall which was in danger of being torn down. It sends forth Occidental sounds once more in the setting in which Japanese first heard them. The ward has done the same for an apparently doomed sake shop, also of Meiji, in the Yanaka heights behind Ueno Park.

It has sought to bring drama back to its old center, Asakusa. Kabuki, on which Asakusa had almost a monopoly in late Tokugawa and early Meiji, has returned. So have more modern and realistic forms that got their start in Asakusa. They have only short runs, however.

Such accomplishments emphasize the hopelessness of the task. A decade and a half after the surrender, before television had really started having its tyrannical way over other dramatic forms, there were three dozen theaters in Asakusa. They were not very innovative, to be sure, but still there they were, in numbers worthy of the old Asakusa. By 1987 the number was down to sixteen, including two strip theaters and three movie theaters specializing in soft-core pornography (the hard-core thing is not yet to be had in any Japanese movie theaters, though it is present in the strip shows). For mildly serious theater there yet remained a pair of variety halls, one specializing in Yose and the other in concerts and light reviews. Of the eight nonpornographic movie theaters only one showed foreign films, and they were second-run. The point is worth remarking upon, not because foreign films are necessarily better than Japanese, but because new films that have attracted favorable notice abroad are the ones still capable of fetching good crowds and admission fees in greater Ginza. In 1976 the Denkikan, "Electricity Hall," the oldest movie theater in the land, was torn down. In 1985 a hotel went up on the site of the International Theater (Kokusai Gekijō), once the largest in the Orient, and the home theater for the Shōchiku all-girl troupe, now disbanded. This had sought to compete with the Takarazuka company of

The most extensive remains of prewar Asakusa—the three linked theaters between which one could move for the price of a single ticket

the other big theater owner, Tōhō. The Takarazuka, its popularity undiminished (and its audience overwhelmingly feminine), still holds forth at its main theater in greater Ginza and at its original establishment in the Osaka suburbs as well.

Ueno and Kinshichō, the other two somewhat prominent entertainment and shopping districts in the Low City, remain much as they were. This is to say that they have declined relatively. Kinshichō, the only *sakariba* or bustling place east of the river worthy of the name, is still a cluster of theaters with a thin coating of bars and restaurants. Ueno is bigger, but falling behind Shinjuku and the others all the same. It draws the biggest crowds in the city for the few springtime days when the cherries in the park are in bloom. In those days the Sumida embankment also draws crowds, but its famous cherries are sadly squeezed in between the concrete of the freeway above and the concrete of the river wall below.

Of bars and cabarets Ueno has many, but by no means as many as Shinjuku. In 1978 the count for Taitō Ward was only a third that for Shinjuku Ward. Since Taitō Ward also includes Asakusa and the Yoshiwara, the Ueno count was perhaps a quarter that for the Shinjuku Eastmouth. The Shinjuku number has grown more rapidly in the years since. And so, despite its pleasant and interesting ethnological museums, we may say that a blight has settled upon the Low City and will not leave.

There is a tendency to blame those third nationals, the Koreans, for the failure of Ueno to bustle as Shinjuku does. It is true that Koreans own many of the taller buildings in Ueno, but whether, like oak trees, they establish openings around themselves that discourage other life is doubtful. The largest concentrations of Koreans are not in places like Ueno but on the outskirts of the city, in the northeastern wards and the industrial south. They are spread fairly evenly over the city. In only four of the twenty-three wards are they other than the most numerous of alien residents. In these four they are second by only a short distance. There are a few more Americans in Chiyoda Ward (Marunouchi and the palace) and Minato Ward (Roppongi and Akasaka), and a few more Chinese in Chūō Ward (Ginza and Nihombashi) and Toshima Ward (Ikebukuro); and not many people of any description have permanent residences in Chiyoda Ward or Chūō Ward. The largest number of Chinese is not in Toshima Ward, where they slightly outnumber Koreans, but in Shinjuku Ward, where they are slightly outnumbered. The Chinese and American concentrations are certainly better placed, to harm or to benefit, than the Korean.

The street leading south from Ueno Park past the big department store was one of the *hirokōji* of Edo, the "broad alleys" widened as firebreaks, three of which became lively shopping and entertainment districts. The Asakusa district stagnates, and the Ryōgoku district has been quite left behind by the shifting currents of fashion. One of the great bustling places of Edo, even less apologetic for its vulgarity than Asakusa, it lies at the east flank to the earliest bridge across the Sumida. It now has again, as it had down to 1945, the Sumō arena, the Hall of the National Accomplishment. It was once a gateway to the provinces, minor compared to Ueno, for it served only the suburban regions east of the bay. The station is now almost deserted, because it has been bypassed. Trains go directly from the suburbs to Tokyo Central. A yet bigger ethnological museum having to do with the city and its past will go up on the expanse of concrete and weeds behind the new Hall of the National Accomplishment. That may help a little, but the prospect remains bleak. There has been talk of a fashion center east of the river, from Ryōgoku to the Kinshichō amusement district, to rival Shibuya. It is a brave idea and one wishes it well but cannot be optimistic. Affluent maidens and matrons do not live in that part of the city, nor are many of them likely to think that they can find something better at Ryōgoku than at Shibuya.

The literature of Edo was very much of Edo. In the last century or so of the shogunate it was so self-contained as to approach the autistic, and so happy with its own little part of the world as to approach the arrogant. Yet the best of Edo writing did have the power to make Edo a sensual presence. Something of the sort prevailed for parts of the city, Asakusa and to a lesser extent Ginza, down to the war. One feels Asakusa in the Asakusa writings of Kawabata, and a wider expanse of the Low City in the writings of Nagai Kafū. The intensity is much diminished in the Asakusa writings of Takami Jun, only a very few years later than Kafū's curious tale of that bawdy house east of the river. In stories in which Ginza figures— by Kafū once more, and by Takeda Rintarō—one may get a glimpse of this and that place in Ginza, a bar, a café, a street corner, but one has little sense of what Ginza was and why people went there. Asakusa is dense and palpable, Ginza is diffuse and evasive. Asakusa is an individual presence, Ginza an abstraction.

Many a novel has been set in postwar Tokyo. One has no trouble finding descriptions of the black markets and the burnt-over wastes, or the sun and moon coming through the collapsed roof of Tokyo Central Station. The black market at Ikebukuro figures prominently in one of the best novels of the immediate postwar years, *Drifting Clouds (Ukigumo)*, by Hayashi Fumiko. In others Tokyo Tower looms over things, to take on what one vaguely assumes to be symbolic functions, though what they are symbolic of may be in some doubt. Niwa Fumio's *Love Letter (Koibumi)* gave its name to an alley near Shibuya Station. Tamura Taijirō and his streetwalkers have already been remarked upon. The part of the city in which they have their lynchings is a wasteland, as if to emphasize that they are primordial creatures, not part of any civic body. In a very popular novel called *Free School (Jiyū Gakkō)*, by Shishi Bunroku, a husband and wife separate that they may have their freedom, and come back together again, having concluded that they can have it only with each other. The husband's ambages take him to such places as the ragpicking village on the embankment above Ochanomizu Station and the company of such persons as a band of smugglers.

Many other examples could be cited. Sketches of this and that place in the city are often skillfully done. If Asakusa and Shinjuku stand in contrast to each other in terms of bustle and prosperity, however, Asakusa consistently getting the worse of it, so also, their positions reversed, they stand in literary contrast. Unless some fine author and his works wait to be discovered, we may say that no novel addresses the subject of Shinjuku as *Scarlet Gang* addresses Asakusa. No novel conveys a sense of Shinjuku as a place, no novel is suffused with affection for it. Shinjuku has no regional literature. It may be said indeed that Tokyo has had none since the war.

Not even prewar writings about Asakusa convey a sense of Tokyo as writings from the closing years of the shogunate convey a sense of Edo. In 1933 the critic Kobayashi Hideo wrote an essay called "Literature That Has Lost Its Home" ("Kokyō wo Ushinatta Bungaku"—the first word is more like "hometown" or, as the Japanese say, "native place").

> Looking back over my life and how I have lived it, I see that it is very much wanting in the concrete. I do not see there someone firmly emplanted, a member of a social entity. I do not see a native of Tokyo but an abstraction, someone who was not really born anywhere. Meditations upon this abstraction can doubtless be made into a kind of literature, but it wants a substantial, tangible backing. From it is likely to arise the peculiarly abstract wish of the weary heart to be free of society and back with nature. Nature set off from society is certainly a world of substance, but literature tends not to come out of it.
>
> Mr. Tanizaki has spoken of "literature in which one finds a home [kokyō] for the spirit." My own problem is not literary. It is far from clear that I really have a home.

Kobayashi was born in the far south of the Meiji High City to a family long in Tokyo. He did not, to be sure, have a very long life to look back over. He was but a little past thirty when he wrote the essay. He was always old for his years, however, and we need not make too much of the point. The essay contains an element of the prophetic. Already in 1933, when people like Kafū and Kawabata were finding in the Low City not home, perhaps, for neither of them lived or grew up there, but still a mooring place—even then Kobayashi felt that he had no home.

Almost all Japanese writers live in Tokyo today, and none of them write of it as if it were home; and so the problem has become general. Kobayashi was very much a part of the High City, while Kawabata and Kafū distributed themselves more widely, taking in the smells of the Low City along with the odorless rarefaction of the High City intellectual world. Perhaps what has happened to the High City, now so close to being the whole city, is among the things encompassed by that voguish expression "postmodern." A city that is urban in the abstract may be what the future holds.

An element of the television and baseball age, probably a necessary and inexorable one, has been a diminution of street life. By this expression is here not meant the life, mostly very young, that floods the streets of Shibuya, but rather that which once flooded the streets of any ordinary neighborhood. People may fly up from Osaka to participate in a

Sunday afternoon in Harajuku and Yoyogi. They do not pour out upon the streets of their neighborhoods as they once did on fine, warm summer evenings. This sort of street life was more important in the Low City than in the High. The salarymen and professors of the High City have always kept to themselves as the shopkeepers and craftsmen of the Low City have not. Then too there are class differences in the High City, with the fishmonger and the magnate living in close juxtaposition. Despite claims, perhaps in some respects justified, about the communal, consensual nature of Japanese working practices, classes do not mix any better in Japan than they do in most places.

In Edo and Meiji Tokyo, the Low City amused itself in the places that lay readiest, its streets. Especially on summer evenings, they became as much assembly places as corridors for passage. The poorer classes of the city did not have much money to spend and seldom went far from home, and the street in front of home was more interesting than home itself. So the streets of the city teemed far more evenly than they do now.

These tendencies still remained strong in the years just after the war, especially on clement evenings when there was a street fair, perhaps a garden fair or a shrine fair. With television and its nightly baseball game all through the summer, home (or, for the privileged myriads, the baseball stadium) became more interesting than the street, and the street began to lose its life. Now the ordinary and undistinguished street tends to be hushed in the evening and on Sunday, which has become an almost universal holiday. The big summer garden fairs by Shinobazu Pond in Ueno and behind the Kannon Temple in Asakusa attract fewer stalls and strollers each year. They may never quite dwindle to nothing, but they are ever more attenuated.

It may be argued that the people of Meiji and earlier poured forth into the streets because their lives contained so little by way of diversion. For most of them there were only the Yose house and the bathhouse in the cold months, and the street was an addition beyond pricing in the warm months. These things have been crowded out by more interesting things. A life that offered so little was a deprived one, and now life is richer. So it may be argued. Yet variety is lost, uniformity prevails, and for some this is a development to be lamented. Certainly a stroll through the Low City of a summer evening is not the fun it once was.

The Olympic governor still had more than half of his second term to serve when he got the Olympics out of the way. No governor of Tokyo has died in office or resigned since popular elections began in 1947.

Governor Azuma decided, as none of the others have, not to stand for a third term. Because of the scandals already remarked upon, he had lost control of the prefectural council.

Conservatives do not get voted out of the prime ministership of the land, but they do get voted out of important regional offices. The shock of the post-Olympic scandals was strong and lasting enough to lose them the governorship, which they had held for twenty years. Two university professors ran against each other in 1967. Minobe Ryōkichi, candidate of the socialists and communists, was the winner. It was not by a landslide. With four and a quarter million votes cast for the two main candidates, radical and conservative, Minobe led the other professor by about a hundred thirty thousand votes, and votes for lesser candidates were enough to keep him from a majority. There were no elections for the prefectural council that year, and so the situation after the 1965 elections prevailed. The socialists and communists did not have a majority. Minobe was able to arrange a working coalition, however, as his discredited predecessor had not been. In succeeding council elections during the Minobe years, the communists did better than the socialists, until, in 1977, both slipped badly, suggesting that the prefecture was ready for a change, which it had in 1979.

Despite the closeness of his initial victory, Minobe was a popular governor. He had no trouble being reelected twice. His popularity was in large measure due to his television personality, of which his famous smile was a crucial part. This is always referred to as the Minobe *sumairu*, and why a Japanese word would not have done as well as the English is mysterious. It would seem that the language requires a constant supply of loan words in order to maintain its vigor. "Talent" candidates (again the English word is used)—television personalities who use their exposure for getting elected to public office—are not in good repute with the media. The media blame them on the conservative rascals who cannot be voted out of power, and forget that Minobe was among the earliest.

He was a successful politician. Whether or not he was a successful governor is open to argument. The city budget was in the red all through the Minobe years, and at the end of them the proportion of prefectural expenditures for debt management was twice the average for other prefectures. Many elaborate explanations are given for this state of affairs, and many external causes cited, such as the oil shock of 1973, which threw everyone's plans out of joint. It is true that Minobe and his administration are not wholly to blame. The budget had already slipped into the red during the first term of Governor Azuma. Yet Minobe made things worse all through his tenure, and it is hard not to believe that prodigality and loose administration were chiefly responsible.

Asked what was so wrong with Minobe, an eminent newspaperman replied. "Almost everything, I think, that he could have brought this rich city to the edge of bankruptcy."

Suzuki Shunichi, who had earlier been important in the national and prefectural bureaucracy, was elected governor in 1979, and continues to serve. The conservatives recovered well from 1965, their worst year. From 1969 they were only a dozen or so seats short of a council majority, and had more seats than the socialists and communists combined. Governor Suzuki immediately began a program of personnel retrenchment. During his first term, after two decades, the prefectural budget returned to the black once more. The matter of the black and the red is a technical one. Since the prefecture goes on issuing bonds, it cannot be said to be paying its way in full. Yet the current account is in balance.

One expects mayors—and Minobe may be considered a mayor, though he was technically a governor—to face such problems as crime and drugs. But, though pep pills have been a nuisance and the occasion for numerous arrests, drugs have not been the problem in Japanese cities that they have been in American. The low incidence of random street crime, however matters may be with organized crime, is something in which Tokyo takes boundless pride. These in any event are police problems, and the prefectural police are not under the control of the governor. It may be that the most considerable problem Minobe faced was garbage. Certainly the "great garbage war" got much attention in the media. For a time it was as famous as the Minobe smile.

It had been smoldering for some time. In 1971 it broke out angrily when the council of Kōtō Ward, east of the river, passed a resolution opposing the passage of garbage trucks through the ward on their way to the fills, such as Dream Island, off its bay shore. It was Dream Island whence all the flies came in 1965 (see page 526). Every ward, the council said, should take care of its own garbage, and Kōtō had no duty to be the dumping grounds for the wealthy and, it thought, irresponsible western wards.

Some two-thirds of metropolitan garbage was then being disposed of along the garbage fills of Kōtō Ward. Nine of the twenty-three wards had no garbage-disposal facilities whatsoever. The governor agreed that this was an inequity, and that disposal plants should be built elsewhere. The indignation of Kōtō Ward was aroused chiefly by Suginami Ward, one of the westernmost and wealthiest of the twenty-three. The announcement in 1967 that a garbage-disposal plant of an advanced technological kind would be built in Suginami brought violent opposition from residents. There was similar opposition in Meguro, a rich southwestern ward that shared with Suginami the distinction of being chosen for the first new plants. Five thousand garbage trucks a day continued to pass through Kōtō Ward, trailing filth and bad smells behind them, and creating traffic jams. In 1973 the Kōtō council voted to use force to turn back trucks from Suginami.

An agreement was finally reached in 1974 that in principle every ward would contain facilities sufficient unto its own garbage. The controversial Suginami plant was built, the feelings of the eastern wards were mollified, and the war was over. Dream Island became the park and athletic field, more the latter than the former, that it is today. In 1971 the twenty-three wards produced more than twelve thousand tons of garbage every day, and three wards in the High City accounted for a third of it. The total was three times what it had been a decade before. The population of the wards had in that decade risen by less than a twentieth. Among the things that the economic miracle produced was garbage. By 1977 the percentage of burned garbage had risen to almost 90 percent. So it may be said for the Minobe government that it did well by garbage.

As for sewage, the whole population of only seven of the twenty-three wards had the use of sewers in 1986. The figure for all the wards was 83 percent, for the county part of the prefecture 64 percent. The easternmost wards were the poorest served. One of them, Adachi, had sewers for only 46 percent of its population, and for the other two the figure was under 60 percent. Kōtō Ward and Suginami Ward, the chief combatants in the garbage war, had sewers for more than 90 percent of their population. The goal of the prefecture is to have sewers for everyone in the wards by the turn of the century. There is still a city out in the county part of the prefecture that has no sewers at all.

There are now ten sewage-disposal plants taking care of the wards. During the last years of the Olympic governor industrial wastes that had poured into the Sumida began going into one of the plants. The river has much improved in smell, color, and general livability.

Tokyo and New York have been sister cities since before the Olympics, and Governor Minobe, despite his unfriendliness toward American systems and institutions, did nothing to change the relationship. It has for the most part seemed that Tokyo is the younger sister, since it has done New York the honor little sister accords big sister, imitating it in numerous superficial ways. Whether, with its new eminence, it will relax a bit and sit back and wait for others (who knows, even possibly New York) to imitate it remains to be seen.

Certainly in the early sororal years imitation was quite open. Articles of clothing bearing the legend "I" and a heart and "New York" had counterparts in Tokyo with only the proper name changed. It almost seemed that "I-heart-Tokyo" might become the motto of the city. But then during his first election campaign, in 1979, Governor Suzuki came up with a new motto, if not for the city and prefecture, certainly for his administration. "My Town Tokyo" it is, and, as with the other, two of the three elements are borrowed from English. He promised a city free from fires, earthquake damage, and pollution. Much progress had already been made on the first and third freedoms before the governor took office, though perfection is unattainable. As for the second, a great earthquake will one day come to tell us how substantial the progress has been. Governor Suzuki also promised generous welfare programs for the aged, who are an increasingly serious problem in a land without adequate pension programs. By the mid-eighties a million residents of the city were sixty-five and more years of age.

Tokyo is less heavily burdened in this regard, however, than the nation as a whole. Charts which divide the population by age show that it has a higher proportion than the nation at large for all ages between fifteen and fifty-five; for ages above and below the proportion is higher for the nation. For the early twenties, Tokyo has proportionately half again as many people as the nation. After twenty-five the figure drops, though not with complete regularity. So it goes on being, by national standards, a youthful city. People tend to return to the provinces when the time comes to face the end. Many youngish men leave their wives and children in the provinces.

Whether or not the governor's goals, as enumerated thus far, are capable of full realization, at least they are capable of definition. An altogether more enigmatic and elusive part of My Town has to do with its functions as a gathering place for and leader of the world. "Internationalization" has been one of the voguish words of recent years. If it means establishing the city as a financial center to rival London and New York, a place where a person can know instantly and always all that there is to know about the markets of the world, a twenty-four-hour place, then that too is capable of definition, and realization is certainly not beyond the capabilities of the ingenious Japanese. If, on the other hand, it means a magnanimous acceptance of people and their ways from all over, such as characterizes New York, then the matter is more doubtful.

For all the huge physical changes that have come over it and all the talk of the "new people" of Harajuku and such places, Tokyo remains a very insular city. Its inhabitants are far from ready to accept the pluralism of a New York. It has not changed so very much since the centuries when the shoguns kept almost all foreigners out. No one would dream of excluding them today; yet in many ways they are effectively excluded. They are in no significant way a part of its life, and it sometimes seems that the workings of the international economy, making it possible for the Japanese to buy the world and next to impossible for the world to buy the tiniest part of Japan, may work toward seclusion every bit as successfully as the policies of the shoguns did. The permission of the Bank of Japan is required for any purchase of real estate by a nonresident foreigner. It is automatic when the purchase is small and there are no special considerations, such as the possibility of criminal activities; but the unrealistically high value of the yen on the foreign-exchange market discourages if it does not prohibit even small purchases.

Its sufficiency unto itself, precluding the "Americanization" of which it has always been accused, has given the city the individuality that has made it interesting, and a refusal to abandon old values has been the chief strength of the land. It is the Japanese who say that they wish to internationalize, however, and the prefecture that puts internationalization among its goals, and so one is permitted to remark upon the unlikelihood that genuine internationalization will ever occur, to make Tokyo as calmly accepting of variety and eccentricity as New York is.

*   *   *

The population of the wards, which had been falling slightly since about the time Governor Minobe took office, began to rise in the early eighties.

Then in 1987 it fell again. The fall, only a little more than one person in three hundred, hardly suggests a stampede to get out of the city, whose population may be termed stable. The population of the Tokyo region has continued to grow at a much more rapid rate than that of the nation. United Nations statistics now put Tokyo-Yokohama behind Greater Mexico City in population, but well ahead of Greater New York.

Tokyo has most things thought useful and appropriate to the advanced society. The supply of old things diminishes all the while.

The closing months of 1967 and the early ones of 1968 were a bad time for those who believe that old things should be saved even when they are not making money. Destruction of the "old" Imperial Hotel began in December 1967. The following month screens and scaffolds started going up preparatory to the destruction of the Mitsubishi Number One Building in Marunouchi.

What was then called the old Imperial was not the oldest but the Frank Lloyd Wright building put up just before the great earthquake. A Society to Protect the Imperial Hotel was organized in the summer of 1967. It was not successful in its main endeavor, to keep hands off the Imperial, but that there was a movement at all is significant. Until then the populace of the city had accepted the destruction of old buildings in favor of more profitable ones as among the facts of life. Henceforth the profit-seekers must think of possible resistance if their destructive ways threaten something that may be called "cultural property." The conservation movement continues to be erratic and uncertainly organized, however. Tokyo Central Station and the Bankers' Club, both in Marunouchi and both Taishō buildings, are the objects of well-publicized preservation campaigns; and the last Queen Anne building of Meiji left in the center of the city was recently torn down. Originally the Imperial Hemp Building, it stood at the north flank of Nihombashi Bridge. A glassy thing will go up in its place. Nor were voices raised to save Mitsubishi Number One. It quite went away. Designed by the British architect Josiah Conder and finished in 1894, it too was Queen Anne, and a good if somewhat tattered example of the style. The rooms were dark and moldy and the three storys were unworthy of Mitsubishi's next-to-priceless land. Yet one misses

The facade of Frank Lloyd Wright's Imperial Hotel, now standing in nonfunctional splendor in a theme park near Nagoya

it. Fragments of the old Imperial survive, the largest in Meiji Village, near Nagoya. One need not go all the way to Nagoya to see lesser fragments, which are to he found in such Tokyo places as the new lmperial and the Foreign Correspondents' Club. The old Imperial closed its doors on November 15, 1967. Demolition began a little more than a week before the last trolley passed through Ginza. Things moved fast in the early Minobe years. In addition to fragments, reflections of the old Imperial survive here and there over the city. The tufaceous stone to which Wright took a fancy when he found it in garden walls and which gave his Imperial its pleasant brownish tinge had not before been used in buildings. It came much into vogue. The most conspicuous surviving example is the prime minister's residence, done by a Wright disciple. A most marvelous Ginza beer hall, the Lion, erected in 1933, shows the Wright influence clearly.

The city virtually did away with its trolley system during the years after the Olympics. Among the prides of Meiji, it had at its most extensive some two hundred twenty miles of trackage. There were minor additions until 1958, and stretches of track were from time to time put out of service through the postwar years down to the eve of the Olympics. In 1963 and 1966 two long stretches of about five miles each went out of service westward from Shinjuku and northward from Sugamo—outward, this is to say, from the Yamanote line.

The Shinjuku one was troublesome, and in any event had not long been a part of the metropolitan system. A single-track line running west as far as Ogikubo, marketing center for an affluent residential district, it was bought from the Seibu system in 1951. Moving trolleys were a great annoyance for the automobile, and stationary ones were far worse. There were always stationary ones up and down the track, because they had to wait at sidings for moving ones to pass.

Resolute abandonment of the system began in 1967 and was completed by 1971, with a single line remaining. Even before 1966 the prefecture had begun disposing of trolley cars. It might be thought that scrap would be the only fate for a trolley car without tracks, but numbers went to parks and playgrounds, where the nostalgic may still observe them and perhaps clamber aboard. The earliest trolley line in the city was among the first to go. Service was discontinued along twenty miles of track on December 9, 1967, and on that night the last trolleys ran along Ginza, the Number One route. There were outpourings of regret and affection. Thousands gathered to say goodbye to the very last Ginza trolley. Governor Minobe, in his first year of office, made some remarks. Much be-

The last remaining Tokyo trolley line

hind schedule, it passed southward through Ginza late in the evening. All-night operations began immediately to remove the tracks.

By 1972 most of the trackage all through the system had been removed. A single route survived both because there was strong popular sentiment for keeping something, and the Minobe government was not cold and remote in this regard, and because it was a peculiar sort of line, planned and executed in such a way that it inconvenienced the automobile less than the others did. For much of its length it runs on its own right-of-way, and where it shares the way with the automobile there are relatively few of the latter. It runs in an arc through the northern part of the city, from just below Waseda University in Shinjuku Ward to Minowa in Arakawa Ward, not far from Sanya, the most successful of the "slums" in getting its name in the headlines and on the screens, and the unsuccessful Tokyo Stadium.

Like the Seibu line west from Shinjuku, the surviving trolley was built as a private railway, to take fanciers of cherry blossoms and maple leaves to Asukayama, Asuka Hill, a famous place for those things. Now in Kita Ward but in the northern suburbs when the line was built, it was the only one of the original Meiji parks that lay beyond the city limits. The Oji line, as it was called (it is now called the Arakawa line), was put through westward most of the way to Waseda in 1911 and eastward to Minowa in 1913. It is very popular, and for some reason less expensive than the buses.

On a fine Sunday afternoon one must be prepared to wait in line for several cars to depart if one wishes a seat.

The trolleybus, that generally unsatisfactory compromise between the tracked vehicle and the freewheeling one, had a much shorter career, only sixteen years. The last trolleybus disappeared before the last-but-one of the trolley lines. The first line, from Ueno to Imai east of the river, was also the last. At 9:45 on a September evening in 1968 the last trolleybus left Imai for Ueno. It was crowded, though the event did not get the attention which had gone to the last Ginza trolley a few months before. Things of Meiji had been around long enough to be a part of everyone's memory and a part of the city scarcely anyone had known it to be without.

The subway system was all the while growing, and it continues to grow. Besides expansion of subway trackage proper, there has been huge expansion because of linkage between subway lines and suburban commuter lines. Though all four terminal stations for the earliest two lines, the only prewar one and the first postwar one, are at points whence lines depart for the suburbs, no effort was made, and indeed it would have been impossible because of incompatible gauges, to run trains through from the inner-city system to one or more of the suburban systems. The concept was slow to die that the inner system should be sealed off from the other and in the public domain.

The breakthrough came in 1962. Two suburban lines began running trains directly from their own tracks via subway tracks into the central wards. Today every one of the suburban systems has connections with the inner system. The commuter seldom has to exert himself further than a stroll across a platform between trains. It is a splendid system, some will say the best in the world. If land prices prevent the average salaryman from living near his place of work, commuting over considerable distances has been made as easy as one can conceive of it being.

It might seem that the old transfer points, Shinjuku and the rest, had lost their reason for being. The commuter need not pause in them. Old habits do not die easily, however. The old *sakariba* continue to bustle furiously during the after-work hours. Many a salaryman, we may infer, prefers to spend in Shinjuku time that might otherwise go into discussing the household budget and disciplining the children.

The subway system (more properly the two subway systems) carries huge numbers of passengers. The public corporation carries far more than the prefecturally owned system, both in absolute numbers and relative to trackage. The former has some eighty-two miles and so outdoes the latter by only about two and a half to one, and carries more than four times as many passengers. It would be easy to blame public administration for this state of affairs, but the essential fact is that the corporation was in business earlier and got the best routes. The two oldest lines, neither of which is connected to suburban commuter lines, carry the largest number of passengers, the one about nine hundred thousand and the other about seven hundred thousand per day.

The number of automobiles grows, but there are incentives, such as are lacking in American cities, not to drive. Frequent trains, underground and otherwise kept beyond reach of automobiles, departing at predictable intervals, see a person to or through the heart of the city in less time than automotive transportation, even by freeway, can be counted upon to do. The freeways choke up frequently, and so have proven to be what at the outset they might have been expected to be, no solution at all to the congestion problem.

The Minobe administration found a new use for a few of the streets that seems completely laudable. It established the institution of the *hokōsha tengoku,* the "pedestrian paradise." There had been experiments in the United States with closing streets to automobiles and giving pedestrians free use of them, and there had been a brief experiment in Yokohama as early as 1960. The first regular and systematic program of pedestrian paradises began in Tokyo and several lesser cities, the largest of them Kobe, in the summer of 1970—toward the end of the first Minobe term.

On a Sunday afternoon early in that season the main streets of Ginza, Shinjuku, Ikebukuro, Asakusa, and, out in the county part of the prefecture, Hachiōji were closed to automobile traffic. Pedestrians poured forth in huge numbers to enjoy their new hegemony. This was good, for if they had not the experi-

*The "pedestrian paradise" in Harajuku on
a Sunday afternoon*

ment would probably have been deemed a failure. In the event the pedestrian paradise became for Tokyo an apparently permanent institution, and it has spread all over the country. Retail sales actually rose on paradise days along the streets affected. There are now paradises in Tokyo places other than the earliest ones, such as Ueno and Harajuku.

Bus and taxi drivers may complain about the pedestrian paradises, which are an inconvenience to them. There are not many success stories that do not inconvenience someone, and the pedestrian paradises are a success story. They have brought new street life to the city, which means a new accession to its supply of life in general. For several hours each week some of the busiest streets turn into parks.

The Minobe administration need not be blamed, at least not in full, for another pedestrian innovation, the overhead crosswalk. This is in theory an increment to the convenience and security of the pedestrian, for it gets him or her across busy intersections without having to wait for traffic lights and without the risk of being run down. Many a pedestrian thinks it a scarcely tolerable nuisance.

The first one went up in the southern part of the city in 1962. By the beginning of the Minobe administration there were more than thirty, and by the end of it they were everywhere. A welcome sign of the Japanese capacity, minute, perhaps, but not completely absent, for civil disobedience was the marked rise in jaywalking. People would march across a forbidden intersection (crossing at street level is generally forbidden when there is an overhead crosswalk) rather than climb all those stairs. If the walks fall in considerable numbers when the next big earthquake comes, fire trucks will be unable to get through, and the fires after an earthquake have a way of being worse than the earthquake itself. We are assured that they are quake-proof. Of that we cannot yet be sure.

Another sort of pedestrian crosswalk, to the theory of which scarcely anyone could object, is the pedestrian bridge across a watery place. The most considerable one is Sakurabashi, Cherry Bridge, across the Sumida north of Asakusa, opened in 1987. It is a pretty bridge, pleasant to stroll across, and it was meant to bring a bit of life back to the Low City. For this it is unfortunately placed. Off to the right as one crosses from the Asakusa side is the famous sweep of cherry trees, one of the most famous since the centuries of the shoguns. Though the trees are confined by the freeway above and the Sumida wall below, they are certainly very handsome when in bloom. The trouble is that they are all of them on the right or downstream side. Cherry Bridge is out of things. Not many people are likely to go out of their way to cross a bridge. It must be at a point where they wish to cross anyway. Not even the soaplands of the Yoshiwara draw people north of Asakusa in great numbers these days, and the flank at the left or east bank is even more remote. Yet Cherry Bridge is pleasant, and the fact that it is there makes the district a little more conspicuous.

It may be that there has been some abatement in the parade of *zoku,* "tribes," in recent decades. One has not heard so much of them. In the post-Olympic years the parade, mostly in Shinjuku and the Southwest, was bewildering. Among those not yet mentioned was the Angura Tribe, which had its main though not exclusive base in Shinjuku. *Angura* is an abbreviation of the Japanese pronunciation of "underground," and it signifies the flamboyantly unconventional young people who frequented the little underground or avant-garde theaters, the most famous of which held forth in a bright red tent on the grounds of the Hanasono Shrine in Shinjuku. The Shinjuku Golden Block (see page 485) nestles in against the walls of the shrine. Performances in the Hanasono tent were most conspicuous for their lurid colors. Another "tribe" that went in for lurid colors was the Saike. *Saike* is from the first two syllables of "psychedelic." They dabbed psychedelic paints over their clothes and the exposed parts of themselves. In 1969 there was a conflict with the law when the shrine closed its grounds to the red tent. Without permission, the troupe moved to the new Central Park at the Shinjuku Westmouth. The riot police took speedy care of the infraction and arrested several people, including the manager, who, however, has continued to prosper. In 1982 he won the most coveted prize for new writers with a story based upon an actual incident, the murder and cannibalization of a Dutch girl by a Japanese boy in Paris.

The Harajuku pedestrian paradise, the closing of the main Harajuku street to vehicular traffic (except stunting motorcycles), has brought a very special kind of street life, associated with one of the more recent tribes to come into prominence, the Takenoko or Bamboo Shoot Tribe. *Takenoko* had an unpleasant connotation during the years of the cod and the sweet potato. It signified shedding one's belongings layer after layer in order to buy the necessities. Beginning about 1980 or a little before, it acquired a more cheerful connotation, even though it was not necessarily pleasing to everyone. The name came from the Harajuku boutique which provided the baggy, haremlike dress that was the mark of the tribe. It already had Yoyogi Park in which to do its things, but the Harajuku pedestrian paradise provided more exposure and presumably more exhilaration, a street being a somewhat unconventional place for performances.

The Bamboo Shoot Tribe is still there, but the larger and later Hara-juku Tribe dominates things. The Harajuku phenomenon has been lik-ened to the spasms of dancing that have swept the country in times of crisis (see page 320). Since there has been no discernible crisis in recent years, it is more likely rebellion against the boredom of peace, prosperity, and the life of the office worker and spouse. One senses something like a longing for insecurity. The mass media, active in such things as never before, have also played a big part in keeping Harajuku noisy.

The expression "tribe" has become so broad and imprecise in recent years that its meaning is in danger of dissolving. There is the Silver Tribe, which some Americans might call "senior citizens." The appellation de-rives not, as one might expect, from the color of elderly hair or from silver anniversaries, but from the silver-colored seats set aside on public vehicles for the elderly and disabled. There is the High Yen Tribe, people who take advantage of the high price of the yen as against the dollar, etc., to do things which they would not have dreamed of doing in other years, such as buying Parisian frocks and paintings and weekending in Honolulu.

Tokyo holds itself, and is commonly held by others, to be a model among the cities of the industrialized noncommunist world for its freedom from street crime. The claim is a valid one: but there are other kinds of crime. The elusive nature of organized crime and the police attitude toward it have already been adverted to. Another kind of crime has many apolo-gists and yet remains crime: politically and ideologically motivated vio-lence. The apologists assign sincere motives, and these are not to be gain-said in Japan.

After the treaty disturbances of 1960 factions of young people first broke with the Communist Party, then started fighting with one anoth-er. At first *uchigeba* referred to fights between the Communist Party and the noncommunist (often called Trotskyite) left. Then, the party image having become a peaceful, cuddly one, it became chiefly fighting among nonparty factions, and sometimes fighting for control of a faction. It grew more murderous. The goal was to wound and maim, and eventually to kill. The staves and pipes and even axes of the attackers were aimed directly at the heads of the attacked. There have been scores of fatalities, and the count continues to rise. Extremists in Europe may have been more suc-cessful at killing politicians and bankers, but none have been more suc-cessful than the Japanese at killing one another. The most murderous incident took fourteen young lives. It was a factional purge which oc-curred in 1972 at a mountain lodge to the northwest of the Kantō Plain, in a faction whose headquarters (like those of most of them that have not gone overseas) were in Tokyo.

By no means may all violent incidents in public places be blamed on *uchigeba*. There was always the fight against authority and the state of the world. The demonstrations of 1960 were unlawful but nonviolent, except for the occasional use of bare fists against the police. From the late sixties staves and rocks started being used, and then homemade bombs and Molotov cocktails. The argument from sincerity went on being invoked. The first bombing occurred in the Meiji Gardens in 1969. Thirty-seven people were injured. The Molotov cocktail had become a weapon in the anti-Establishment struggle as early as 1952, the year the Occupation ended. The first really damaging one was flung in Ginza in 1968. Sixteen people were injured. This was also the time when assaults upon universities were reaching their high point.

The announcement in 1966 that a new Tokyo International Airport would be built at Narita, in Chiba Prefecture, offered a new outlet for the sincerity of the young. After the fall of Yasuda Castle in 1969 academic turmoil subsided, and so, in Tokyo, did large-scale violence in general. Much of it was exported to Chiba. The airport was not finally opened until a dozen years later. Numbers of violent incidents occurred in the interval, and the airport must still be among the most closely guarded (and inconvenient) in the world. The fact that some of the farmers on the site did not want to give up their land provided a cause.

So did rumors, which may one day prove true, that the airport was really a military base in disguise. The planting and throwing of small bombs reached a climax in about 1971, when several factions used them against police boxes and the riot police. On Christmas Eve of that year a Christmas tree exploded behind a Shinjuku police box, injuring eleven people. Also in 1971, the wife of an important police official was killed by a bomb that came in the mail.

In 1974 there was a much bigger bombing, the first of a series. In August a bomb exploded in the Marunouchi offices of Mitsubishi Heavy Industries. Eight people were killed. The eight people convicted of the bombings belonged to a faction which called itself the Anti-Japanese Armed East Asian Front (Higashi Ajia Hanhichi Busō Sensen). Divided into working parties with far more vivid names—Wolf, Scorpion, Fang of the Continent—it proved to have had its origins among a group of classmates at a private university in Tokyo and was dedicated to rectifying the baneful effects of Japanese imperialism. The faction had no relations with other factions, which is to say that it was not a product of the

The bombing of Mitsubishi Heavy Industries headquarters, Marunouchi, 1974

fragmentation that followed upon the disturbances of 1960. The members passed as quite ordinary office workers and housewives. So discontent may be deeper than one fancies it to be in the conformist middle class.

Public and political crime has overshadowed private, personal crime in recent years. It may be a mark of maturity, of having caught up with the world and shed feudal vestiges. There was much public crime in early Meiji, but there were also picturesque and popular murderesses. The interwar years had assassinations, including those of three prime ministers, but they also had O-sada. Perhaps the absence of women from recent annals of crime has made the annals less interesting.

The most talked-of kidnapping was political, and international as well. On the afternoon of August 8, 1973, Kim Dae-jung, the most prominent leader of the South Korean opposition, was abducted from his hotel room just below the Yasukuni Shrine. Spirited off to Osaka by automobile, he was put aboard a ship and released at his home in Seoul five days later. He seems to have come very close to being murdered at sea. The culprits were Korean intelligence agents. The evidence is that they were not acting on orders from the top levels of the Korean government.

The prime minister of Japan, Tanaka Kakuei, who would later be convicted of bribery, told reporters that the incident struck him as *kiki kaikai*, which might be rendered "weirdo." Though the media expressed great indignation, the two governments reached a "political settlement," which meant that the not very adequate explanations by the Korean government were accepted by the Japanese. The Japanese government has never been very skillful in its dealings with truculent Korea. (It does better with fatherly America.) Later, during his American exile, Kim said that he considered the incident still unresolved. He put much of the blame for this fact on the Japanese.

On a less political and more private level, white-collar crime has continued to flourish. The *sōkaiya,* those who specialize in disrupting general meetings (see pages 524-525), are most if not all of them high-class extortionists. Laws have been passed to thwart them, and occasionally a hapless businessman receives unwelcome publicity and a dressing down for having had dealings with them, but they are a resourceful lot and have found ways to persevere. They become publishers of periodicals, for instance, and solicit "advertisements" from the companies that are their targets. They have also made use of a device of which politicians are fond, the coerced sale of very expensive tickets to "parties." Just as American insurance companies find it easier to raise their rates than to fight mischief suits, Japanese companies find it easier to pay off than to face a showdown in the stockholders' meeting. Of some thirteen hundred *sōkaiya* thought to be in business the country over, more than nine hundred do their work in Tokyo.

In 1968 there was a robbery of unprecedented magnitude. It is interesting in itself, and just as interesting for the failure of the police to solve it. The choice of a site suggests that the robbers had a sense of humor. It occurred right beside Fuchū Prison, in the western suburbs of Tokyo. On the morning of December 10, a man on a motorcycle who looked for all the world like a policeman stopped a bank truck and said that explosives were alleged to be planted aboard. The truck contained the year-end bonuses for a Tōshiba plant in Fuchū. Four other men got out of an automobile, and, using the automobile, the party made off with not quite three hundred million yen, which at the exchange rates of today would convert to not far from two and a half million dollars. The automobile and the locker which had contained the money were found in another suburb the following spring, but the robbers were never apprehended. No suspects were announced and no arrests were made, even though the robbers must have been insiders of some description, and the mystery should have lent itself to relatively easy solution. Under the statute of criminal limitations, prosecution became impossible in December 1975. Civil redress ceased to be possible on December 9, 1988.

There was one of those heartwarming incidents, though one over which a suspicion of misdoing hangs heavily. A poor man struck it rich, and, as the newspapers put it, he did so in a fashion so improbable that it was the stuff from which *meruhen* (which word, from the German *Märchen*, "fairy tales," is preferred to anything English has to offer) come. On a drizzly spring evening in 1980 a truck driver noticed a parcel wrapped in a kerchief on a guardrail just east of Ginza. He stopped, picked it up, took it to his residence in one of the poor wards east of the river, and found that it contained a hundred million yen. The money became his when no claimants turned up during the next half-year. The most likely explanation for the absence of claimants is that there was something wrong with the money. It was not counterfeit, but its sources must have been such that it was worth a hundred million yen to someone not to have them revealed. The truck driver sensed something amiss about his trove. He quit his job, resorted to disguises, brushed up on his martial arts, took to wearing a bulletproof vest, and hired himself three bodyguards for twenty-four-hour duty.

It was in the late seventies that we started hearing the expression *yukaihan,* which might be rendered "fun crime." The police seem to have been the inventors of the term. It refers to crimes that create a great stir and the pleasure which the stir gives to the agent of the crime. The most obvious such crime is arson. In 1977 it passed smoking as the chief cause of fire in the city.

The days when General and Mrs. Grant held the city in thrall are more than a century in the past, and they seem every bit that far away. Tokyo is no longer easily stirred. Among foreign dignitaries only the queen of England and the Pope have caught the public imagination with anything like the force of the Grants; and they are unique specimens, the only pope and the only monarch who still moves about with something like monarchical grandeur. Lesser royal personages come and go and few people notice. So it is too with former American presidents—which is what General Grant was in 1879. Incumbent American presidents would probably not much interest the Tokyo citizenry were it not for security measures thought by many to be at best exaggerated and at worst illegal. It would have been a great thing indeed if President Eisenhower had come in 1960. He did not, because of the anti-treaty disturbances. Today presidential visits are next to routine. These evidences of maturity and self-possession are doubtless good, but the eagerness of 1879 must have been good too.

Famous entertainers are another matter. They capture the city with no trouble at all. No one did for a dozen years after Marilyn Monroe, but that was because no one of adequate celebrity made the effort. Then in 1966 came the Beatles. Delayed by a typhoon, their airplane arrived in the dead hours of early morning. This was as well. The elaborate preparations made by the police proved unnecessary. A helicopter was to take the guests to the Ichigaya army (or self-defense) base if the crowds proved unmanageable, and from there to the Hilton Hotel in Akasaka patrol cars would serve. If it seemed clear in advance that the crowds would be unmanageable, the plane was to divert the Beatles to an American air base in the suburbs.

They gave five short concerts in the Hall of the Martial Arts, the Olympic structure north of the palace and near the Yasukuni Shrine. Two thousand policemen were on hand for the opening concert, and more than eight thousand policemen saw action during the five days of the visit. Thousands of overzealous young persons, mostly female, were taken into custody, but no further punishments were meted out. Ringo Starr said that he felt like a bug in a cage. (Prince Philip, also with reference to the elaborate security measures, asked the pearl divers at Toba, beyond Nagoya, whether they had been boiled.)

The Beatles made sixty million yen. Gross proceeds were a hundred million yen, and the impresarios made nothing at all. The security measures cost the prefecture ninety million yen. The sound trucks of the fundamentalist right were on the streets denouncing the event as a national disgrace. They seem to be among the institutions (motorcycle gangs are another) which the police are unwilling or unable to restrain. They make of the regions around the Soviet embassy a constant bedlam.

The city has been repeatedly captured in the years since, by such personages as Michael Jackson and Madonna. Whether the personage be male or female, the crowds are predominantly the latter.

In the realm of high culture and the intellect the French have prevailed. Sartre and De Beauvoir came in 1966, the Venus de Milo in 1964, a few months before the Olympics, and the Mona Lisa in 1974. France got credit for all four even though the last two are not exactly French products. The Mona Lisa was the biggest popular success. A million and a half people, or some two hundred thousand for each of the six-day weeks that she was on display, poured into the National Museum at Ueno and jostled and elbowed each other to have a glimpse of her. It was not much of a glimpse. Railings kept the crowds at a distance. Amplified voices told them in ceremonious but commanding terms that they must not dally.

Among the popular diversions, baseball has pursued its steady way. This is to say that for the Giants the ups have prevailed over the downs. They have gone on being far the most popular team in Tokyo and in most parts of the country (almost everywhere except Nagoya, Osaka, and Hiroshima) that do not have local teams to worship. They are the main-stay of the whole system. It would collapse if they were to.

The Kōrakuen in Tokyo is the baseball capital of the land. It has kept up with the times. We have seen that in 1950 it had the first night games ("nighters"). In 1959 it acquired a baseball museum and hall of fame like those in Cooperstown. In 1976 it had the first artificial turf, a peculiar thing to have, one might think, in a city so rainy that the problem is not to grow natural turf but to keep it under control. Now it has the first covered stadium. This is Tokyo Dome, the second word in English. It is the air-supported kind. Giants fans are advised to come with mufflers and throat sprays. Not even the Seibu enterprises, so capable in most things, have prevailed in baseball. They have their team, heavily promot-ed, but it has nothing like the popular following of the Giants.

Sumo, the national accomplishment, goes on being at best second to baseball in the national regard. Efforts have been made to liven it up a bit. The ring has been widened so that matches have a chance of being over in less of a hurry, and preliminary rituals have been shortened so that they can get started in more of a hurry. The rituals were traditionally allowed to go on indefinitely, until some sixth sense told the wrestlers that they had gone on long enough. Radio broadcasting brought time limits, varying with the rank of the wrestlers, and television brought further reductions. Now the top wrestlers posture and glare for no more than four minutes. This still is not fast enough for the television audience, which is drifting away from Sumō. Baseball is also thought by many to be a slow sport, but not even a faltering pitcher takes four minutes for his windup. A gigantic Samoan-American has ascended to a higher rank than any non-Oriental had in the past. He weighs more than five hundred pounds.

Publicists and historians of Sumō tell us that it is having yet another golden age. Though there have been two or three very good wrestlers in recent decades, we may be suspicious of the fact that this golden age fol-lowed so close upon the last, and of the rate at which Yokozuna, wrestlers of the top rank, have come and gone. Of the sixty wrestlers who have held the Yokozuna rank in the not quite two and a half centuries since chronicles of the sport became reasonably precise, twenty-two have been promoted to it in the last four decades and a bit more. There must be Yokozuna and golden ages if the television audience is to be held. Some

Yokozuna have been good neither at wrestling nor at holding the audience. Some have been downright unpopular. In 1987 the Sumō Association took the unprecedented step of stripping a Yokozuna of his rank and his right to compete. He had been behaving in a boorish, overbearing, and indeed violent manner. He had been much touted by the media and the agencies as a "new man." This carries connotations of the liberated and the cosmopolitan. So it may be that the new has gone about as far as it can go if the old is not to disappear completely.

The chronicles of Sumō over the years have resembled those of phoenixes; but if each golden age is going to look more thinly plated than the preceding one, and if the advent of a new one is to be announced every decade or so, the prospects are not bright. At the very worst Sumō will survive vestigially, as do so many "cultural properties"; but that will be a sad survival for those who have known a genuine golden age or two.

A third sport, golf, may have overtaken Sumō as a national accomplishment, or at any rate as a popular diversion. It is participatory. Tournaments get their time on television and crowds follow popular heroes, even as at Pebble Beach and Augusta; but essentially it is the businessman's sport, and that of the politician and the bureaucrat. It has not thrown off the moneyed origins which, as a Japanese sport, it shares with baseball. The first Tokyo golf club, founded in 1914, had among its members some of the most eminent businessmen and politicians of the time. One of them became finance minister and was assassinated. He had tried to teach the Japanese the lesson they have learned so well since the war, that economic penetration is far more tenacious and durable than military. The links, at Komazawa in Setagaya Ward, later provided one of the Olympic sites. There had earlier been golf courses in Kobe and Yokohama. Early amateur tournaments were won by foreigners, but the Japanese came into their own in 1918, at the first one held in Tokyo. They posted the best five scores.

The popularity of golf among politicians, bureaucrats, and businessmen may have something to do with the decline of yet another national accomplishment, that of the geisha, the "accomplished person." That there has been a very sad decline is undeniable. Tastes and ways of life are changing. The traditional music and dance which were the geisha's accomplishments do not interest the ruling classes as they once did, or provide the incentives they once did for a young girl to endure the severities of geisha training.

The "geisha house," which is to say the expensive restaurant where the geisha holds forth, was once the place for concluding big deals, political and entrepreneurial. Increasingly, the golf course is. It has the advantage that electronic snooping is less of a problem. When a businessman or politician is playing golf, he is probably doing more than playing golf. He is making awesome arrangements which he might have made in a restaurant in another day.

The decline of the geisha may be dated from the second postwar decade, when rapid economic growth was beginning. So it would not seem to be true, as is often averred, that the geisha was simply too expensive. It takes dozens of evenings at an expensive geisha restaurant to dissipate a sum equal to the membership fee in one of the golf clubs important people belong to; and the expense-account crowd started turning away from the geisha just at the time when it was beginning to have more than ample money.

Local histories and official publications have become rather demure and coy in recent years. They do not pay the attention they once did to geisha. A Meiji guide to Tokyo published by the city in 1907 obligingly guides its readers to the pleasure quarters and tells them how many geisha they can choose from. It is a rare ward history in recent years that has anything at all to say on the subject. The talk is rather of schools and welfare and day care and the like. It may be that the bureaus and the historians responsible for all these documents are only a little in advance of the times when they treat the geisha as if she did not exist. Such bits of information as one comes upon suggest that it will not be long.

The history of Chūō Ward (Ginza and Nihombashi) published in 1980 is one of the exceptions, rare and refreshing. It tells us that "in the recent past" there came to be fewer than half as many Shimbashi geisha as in the fifties, fewer than two hundred as against more than four hundred. (It will be remembered that "Shimbashi" here really means Tsukiji, east of Ginza.) Matters were even worse with other districts in the ward. The Yoshichō district in Nihombashi and the Shintomichō district near Ginza had almost ceased to exist. In Shimbashi, the district clinging most pertinaciously to life, almost half the *okiya* consisted of an owner-geisha and no one else. An *okiya* is the residence of a geisha, typically, in better days, several of them. *Okiya* were becoming condominium apartments, and geisha restaurants were moving into high-rise buildings. Getting into an elevator to go to a "geisha party" represents a change indeed. Before the river wall went up one could enter a Yanagi-bashi restaurant by boat. A sense of the seasons and the elements has always been an important part of the geisha ambience.

All over the city, geisha quarters are disappearing. Shimbashi had been one of the three great quarters of modern Tokyo. Yanagibashi was another. Elegant restaurants once lined the right bank of the Sumida River north of the Kanda. Now only two are to be detected. Akasaka is probably the strongest of the three, because it is so convenient for politicians and bureaucrats, not in a part of town that takes them out of their way; but even there the decline has been marked. Akasaka had only a third as many geisha restaurants in 1984 as it had had a dozen years before. The Maruyama district on a hill above Shibuya had three hundred geisha at its postwar peak, during the years of the Korean War. In 1984 there were only seventy, and most of them were over fifty years of age. They still played the samisen, but few essayed to dance. Presumably the quarter will be extinct when the seventy die or retire. The fall in the count of geisha restaurants was even more striking than the fall in the count of geisha: down to eleven from a hundred forty. So not even the geisha who persisted in the business could expect many engagements.

The same history of Chūō Ward remarks upon the fact that even as the tides of popularity and prosperity withdraw from one part of the ward they flood in upon another. The bars of central Ginza flourished even as the geisha places to the east languished. The theaters and the pleasures of drink and sex always having been in a most intimate relationship, it also remarks upon changing tastes in the latter, corresponding to those in the former: from the stylized traditional forms to more realistic Westernized ones. It might have commented upon a yet deeper change, the decline of the popular theater as it was in the Asakusa of the interwar years.

This is not to be understood as saying that there is no theater. All the varieties, conservative and advanced, that are to be found in the West are in Tokyo, and some traditional, homegrown ones besides. There are more theaters than in New York. When, not long ago, a magazine carried photographs of what it thought to be the twenty most interesting theaters in the city, its trouble was not in finding interesting ones but in choosing among the large number of them. It came upon some that few people can have known of, in such unlikely parts of the city as Fukagawa, east of the Sumida River.

But fragmentation prevails, and in lamentable measure snobbishness. If any theater with its own troupe is as popular as the Asakusa reviews were during the interwar years, it is the Takarazuka of the all-girl troupe. The Koma Stadium in Shinjuku is the Big Apple of popular entertainment, but it does not produce its own performers as the Asakusa theaters did. They are big-time before they get there, and television makes them that.

There certainly are vulgar forms, in the several senses of the adjective. The more advanced and bold of the strip shows, however, are expensive and draw tiny audiences. Yose is not expensive, but it too draws small audiences, and, as we have seen, there are not many theaters left. The largest among them seats only two hundred and a score or two of viewers, and is seldom full save on Sundays and when several tourist buses happen to show up at once. There were until recently tiny theaters—"huts," as the jargon has them—where strolling players held forth with a hybrid of the traditional and the modern. They have gone, though they are still to be found in the provinces. All of these lesser forms combined have less than the drawing power of a single Asakusa theater back when Enoken was playing there.

Television has replaced them all, and a good many other things besides. In place of the devoted local constituency that Asakusa had, there is a single national constituency—or there are as many constituencies as there are channels. Remote local audiences that before had scarcely anything now have something, which is probably good; and the big city has lost something.

Television has combined with another hugely popular form to be a threat not only to traditional forms but to the printed word. Television scenes speed by at such a great rate that no one has time to say much of anything, and there is very little room indeed for what may be called distinguished language. *Manga* dispense with words almost entirely. They are frighteningly popular. In 1987 one and two-thirds billion copies of *manga* magazines were sold. The word *manga* is generally rendered "comics," but it is not a good rendition. The big Japanese-English dictionary has among its definitions "cartoon," which is better. There is little humor in these magazines. The cartoon, humorous and bloodcurdling, has a venerable history in Japan. Of recent years the latter has come to prevail, along with the erotic. Such words as there are to slow the devotee down on his gallop through a *manga* magazine tend strongly toward the imitative or onomatopoetic. They do not convey a meaning so much as an immediate physical experience. They cut through the descriptive functions of language, and splash and splatter and otherwise seek, like Aldous Huxley's feelies, to strike immediately at the senses.

The Japanese language has always been rich in such words. The argument has been made that because of them it is uniquely suited to such anti-rational modes of belief and conduct as Zen. They bear a much larger share of the burden in manga than in ordinary language. Some of them are rather amusing. A newspaper article in 1970 listed these: *ashe,* for cutting someone's face open; *zuzu-u-u zuzu-u-u,* for slurping noodles; *chu chuba,* for a kiss; *pattaan,* for a punch in the jaw; *murereri murumuru,* for the impatience of a young lady awaiting her young gentleman. They are many of them sounds that would convey nothing at all independently of their *manga,* which is to say that they are outside of and beyond language.

These developments are of course not unique to Tokyo, and it cannot be said that Tokyo has always led the way. It certainly leads the way in television and advertising, but in sex and violence Osaka is often the pioneer. Many a subtle new direction in the cutting edge of *manga* can be traced to Osaka. Yet it is difficult to describe the city as it is and as it is coming to be without describing such spiritual changes as this, along with all the physical changes.

Even as the Low City and its culture were melted down by the great media waves emanating from the High, so the city itself and the provinces are being fused into one great mass. The mayor of Honolulu has observed that his city is by way of becoming a suburb of Tokyo. Even Osaka, for all its originality in the realm of the sensually explicit, might make the same observation; and the son of Tokyo might complain, as Tanizaki did not cease to complain, that his city too is losing something in the process. Its chief claim today might be that it is more Japanese than Japan, in the sense of having far the greatest concentrations of glass, steel, and computerized information. A loss of individuality has occurred even as the concentration of money and power in Tokyo has approached totality.

It may be almost impossible for foreigners to buy a bit of Japan unless it be in the remote provinces, and it is becoming impossible for most Japanese to buy a bit of Tokyo.

One of the most popular little stunts at drinking places has to do with the ten-thousand-yen bank note and the price of land. The note, the largest printed by the Japanese government, is worth about eighty dollars, value shifts somewhat from day to day. A person is told to fold one of the notes as tightly as possible. Take it down to Ginza and drop it, the instructions continue; it will not buy the bit of land upon which it falls.

There are pieces of information that go the rounds, such as that if the lands on which the palace stands were to be sold and converted at going exchange rates, the dollars that resulted could buy the whole state of California. The exchange rate, a product of trade balances, here has its magical effect, because dollars buy far more than yen do in relation to their values on the exchange. So the piece of information has as much to do with exchange rates as with real values. The stunt too is a little exaggerated. Experiment determines that a ten-thousand-yen note can be folded into an area of about two square centimeters. So it would take five thousand of the notes, or fifty million yen, or some four hundred thousand dollars (in which once more the magic of the exchange rate has its effect), to cover a patch a meter square. The annual survey of land prices by the National Land Agency determined that at the end of 1987 the highest price for land sampled in Ginza, near the main Ginza crossing, was thirty-four million yen. So it is an exaggeration, though it is within the bounds of the pardonable, and, as with the matter of the palace and California, emphasizes the fact that land in Tokyo is insanely valuable.

Seven of the ten most valuable pieces of commercial property are in the three central wards, Chiyoda, Chūō, and Minato. As for residential property, the first nine are in the three wards, the tenth is in Shibuya. The most valuable piece of residential property, in Chiyoda Ward just to the northwest of the palace, commanded a price of a little more than twelve million yen, or not far from a hundred thousand dollars, per square meter.

On the assumption that the salaryman cannot risk more than five times his annual pay on a bit of land and a house, the price of the land must be kept within a hundred fifty thousand yen per square meter. Only on the northern and eastern fringes of the old city—the northern part of Asakusa, the wards east of the Sumida—do land prices fall below a million yen per square meter. Nowhere to the west or south do they do so. A square meter may be had for less than a half million along the other fringes of the ward part of the prefecture, and nowhere within the wards does the price fall below a hundred thousand. For this one must go out west where the mountains begin, a distance of some fifty kilometers, or more than thirty miles, from the center of the city.

The situation is little better in the neighboring prefectures, though prices do not rise to such heights. The most expensive land in central Yokohama is worth under ten million yen per square meter. Yet one must go as far as Narita Airport and a kilometer or two onward from the station by other means to find land in Chiba Prefecture for under a hundred thousand yen. One must go to the farther reaches of Saitama Prefecture for such land, and the makers of the survey found none at all in Kanagawa Prefecture (Yokohama).

Narita is about sixty kilometers from the center of the city. This is now considered reasonable commuting distance. One can get to the airport by the fastest express trains in an hour if one happens to be at Ueno Station, but of course commuters tend not to live either in the station or in the airport, nor are express trains always at hand. The commuting life has produced a subculture. The proliferation of sensational photograph and cartoon magazines answers to the needs of people who do not sleep very well on trains and do not want to think. Then there has been the rise of the *chikan*, rendered by the big Japanese-English dictionary as "a molester of women" and "American slang: a masher." No pretty girl who rides crowded trains is free from his attentions, though they are seldom more serious than pawing and pinching.

So the middle class is giving up hope of owning houses in the Tokyo wards. Even the tiny condominium apartment is slipping beyond its dreams. In recent years we started hearing the word *okushon*. This sounds very much like the Japanization of "auction," and was probably in part suggested by it, but more than that it is a variant and pun upon *manshon* or "mansion," which for practical purposes means a multistoryed condominium building. The first syllable of "mansion," homophonous with the word for "ten thousand," is converted to *oku*, "a hundred million." So an *okushon* is a condominium apartment that sells for a hundred million yen, not far from a million dollars at present exchange rates. A recent survey by an association of builders and realestate dealers concluded that the average price for a new condominium of twenty and more square meters within Tokyo Prefecture has now passed a hundred million yen.

There remains a small glimmer of hope, the public-housing condominium. It is very small. Four of the five complexes that drew the largest number of applicants were in neighboring prefectures, and only one, third in popularity among the five, was in Tokyo, in the ward farthest to the north and west of the twenty-three. The most popular complex was on filled land near the western edge of Chiba Prefecture, in the town of Urayasu, which also contains Tokyo Disneyland. There were more than three hundred fifty applications for each available apartment.

The problem is very much one of land speculation, and very much a Tokyo problem. Until recently land prices were rising in the Tokyo region at about three times the national rate, more than three times the rate for the Osaka region, and almost eight times that for the Nagoya region. Very recent surveys suggest that prices may be leveling off and even falling slightly. Real-estate companies are going bankrupt at a rate that cannot be explained by the general state of the economy, and if bankruptcies are ever welcome they are in these circumstances. Government measures, such as tax penalties, restrictions on credit, and licensing in the case of

The huge Westmouth buildings rise beyond the trees of Shinjuku Royal Gardens.

large transactions, may be having an effect. It may be too that a ceiling must inevitably be reached. Speculation works only as long as there is a purchaser who will pay more than the seller did.

The decline, if there is one, is far from enough to make the city once again accessible to the middle class, and a sharp decline is highly unlikely. Bank assets are very intimately associated with land prices. The banks are at the center of the Establishment, which cannot be expected to inconvenience itself unless a massive popular rising forces it to. In some countries we might expect exactly this to happen. In Japan the commuter sighs and goes on commuting. So the "my" in the governor's My Town seems by way of referring to billionaires and ragpickers and scarcely anyone between.

If there is a threat to the position of Ginza as the mercantile heart of the city, it is probably land prices. Perhaps Ginza is being strangled by its own desirability. Transactions in Ginza land are rare, but such recent ones as have occurred suggest that it is even more valuable than the 1987 survey has it, approaching forty million yen per square meter. There are spots in Shimbashi and Shinjuku where land prices approach the Ginza level. Marunouchi, which is managerial and not mercantile, rises to Ginza levels. Yet Ginza is the place that has most clearly the look of being choked by land prices. Ginza shops that have expanded into chains make their money from branches elsewhere and keep their main Ginza stores for advertising. The assets of the ones that have not expanded are mostly in real estate. So it has been aptly observed that Ginza has become a place of advertising and real-estate enterprises. This is worrisome for those who hope that the Ginza center holds, though it does not take into account enterprises, such as the department stores, big enough to make money even on Ginza land.

For about a quarter of a century there has been talk, the first serious talk since 1923, of moving the capital from Tokyo. In 1963 the construction minister, he who was known during the Olympic years as the minister of the waterworks, proposed building a new capital in the hills above Hamamatsu, which is at about the halfway point between Tokyo and Osaka. The National Land Agency has undertaken studies of the matter. The prime minister has directed the removal of minor parts of the bureaucracy from Tokyo. Among other places suggested for a new capital have been Sendai, to the north of Tokyo, and Osaka. The president of the Suntory whiskey company remarked of Sendai in 1988 that it is in the land of the Kumaso. By this he meant "barbarians," but he got his tribe wrong: the Kumaso, mentioned in the earliest chronicles, dwelt at the other end of the realm, in southern Kyushu. He made a political and tactical error as well. The Tohoku district, of which Sendai is the largest city, organized a boycott which had a pronounced effect on Suntory sales. A politician—not, of course, from Osaka, and therefore immune to reprisals—called Osaka a spittoon. So talk of moving the capital has had its diverting moments.

It is very unlikely to occur, barring another disaster. The interests of too large a part of the Establishment are too much a part of Tokyo. Even effective and outspoken critics of Tokyo as the overwhelming center of everything worth being a center of are doubtful that it will occur. Among the most effective of them has been Hosokawa Morihiro, governor of the land of the Kumaso, Kumamoto Prefecture in Kyushu. He does not look forward to anything very drastic.

"There is talk of several capitals and of moving the capital. The proposal to move the functions now concentrated in the capital to the slopes of Mount Fuji or Sendai or some such place does not seem to me realistic. It will not be practical for the crucial agencies charged with finances, foreign policy, and defense. Yet I do think that when no great weakening of government functions is likely to occur plans should be made for moving to the provinces. I think of the Hokkaido Development Board and the Okinawa Development Board.... For the Japanese islands to be a balanced organism and not just an oversized head, greater vitality must be looked for in the provinces, even as Tokyo goes on developing."

Of course the big managers will stay where the "crucial agencies" are. Nearness to the center is very important to them, even though some of them too may feel the Tokyo pinch. Shinnittetsu, the biggest Japanese steel company, owned a Marunouchi building (actually in Otemachi, just to the north) jointly with Mitsui until 1967. Now it rents from Mitsubishi at four billion yen a year, or well over thirty million dollars. Without land in the center of Tokyo, and it has none, not even Shinnittetsu could construct a Tokyo building of its own if it wanted to.

No Marunouchi land has changed hands in the past ten years. If a bit were to come on the market and a potential buyer asked to make an offer, it would probably be: "Whatever you want." Mitsubishi says that some three hundred fifty companies are waiting for Marunouchi space, and that to accommodate them all some fifty acres of new space would be required.

Governor Suzuki agrees with Governor Hosokawa. "The other forty-six prefectures, even Saitama, all have offices in Tokyo.... It will not be practical in undisturbed times to move the capital from Tokyo. In the absence of natural disasters and bombings and revolutions such as the Meiji Restoration, it will not be easy."

The three stops in Urawa, prefectural seat of Saitama Prefecture, are the third, fourth, and fifth beyond the Tokyo limits on the main commuter line to the north. Even this proximity, the governor is saying, is not enough. The pull of Tokyo is so strong that even Saitama must have offices there.

The concentration of money and power in Tokyo is to a degree unthinkable in the United States. A reasonable estimate might be that a third of large American companies have their head offices in or near New York. Many of them are trying to get away, and succeeding. There is little indication, despite costs that would seem prohibitive in most places, of a similar efflux from Tokyo and the Kantō region. It has been influx the whole time. Until the Second World War the Kansai might salve its wounded pride at having ceased to be the political center of the land by saying, and not without grounds, that it continued to be the commercial center. While it is true that the Kansai is more wholeheartedly commercial than the Kantō, and may thus make the ancient argument of sincerity and dedication, the argument no longer has much force.

When a big company (examples are Matsushita and the big automobile companies) does not have its head office in Tokyo, it has a branch office so large that the distinction between the two, main office and branch, seems to come down to long-term finance and management on the one hand and day-to-day operations on the other. Some companies make this fact more obvious by having head offices both in Tokyo and in Osaka.

Nor is the concentration only economic and bureaucratic. A "literary" memorandum book which happens to be at hand lists the addresses and telephone numbers of some four hundred institutions and organizations likely to answer to the needs of literary and artistic persons. Only seven of them have the high postal numbers that reveal them to be situated at a distance from the center: an association of photographers in Osaka, a publishing house apiece in Osaka and Kyoto, a paper manufacturer in Shizuoka, and three advertising agencies, in Nagoya, Osaka, and Kobe.

Of the nine hundred or so artistic and intellectual types listed in the same memorandum book, only about a tenth reside beyond commuting distance of Tokyo. Of these a considerable number are university professors residing in Kyoto, to remind us of a rare element in Japanese cultural life in which a modicum of decentralization remains. Kyoto University continues to be the other university, the only one with something like the prestige of Tokyo University, and offering its graduates something like the same ticket of entry to the realm of the elite.

In one field it offers the better ticket. Kyoto University produces winners of Nobel Prizes in the sciences, and so that is where the brightest would-be scientists go. Governor Suzuki recently called our attention, with wry humor, to the fact that his grandson had just entered the college of physics at Tokyo University, and that it was the only college in the university short of new students. Those who passed both in Tokyo and in Kyoto chose to go to the latter. In the realm of power—law, politics, economics—it is the opposite. Most of the very bright boys and girls of the land, when they have passed the entrance examinations of both universities, choose Tokyo. Its ticket is much the more reliable. This fact is behind moves on the part of Kyoto University to have its entrance examinations held on the same day as Tokyo University, and so make it impossible for even the brightest to pass both. They must choose in advance, and spare Kyoto University humiliation.

The concentration of students and universities in Tokyo is impressive, if not quite so impressive as the concentration of big companies, publishing houses, and artistic types. A third of the colleges and universities in the country are in Tokyo, and half the students. There has been some dispersal of universities from the ward part of Tokyo, but the concentration in Greater Tokyo remains. The new Tsukuba university and research complex in southern Ibaragi Prefecture more than makes up for the old

University of Education, its core, once situated in the same ward as Tokyo University. (Among the principal attributes of Tsukuba is its dull-
ness. One might have expected an explosion, with tens of thousands of
hot-blooded young people suddenly put down in the middle of nowhere,
and Narita Airport and all its controversy so near at hand. It has not happened. The day of pulverizing universities mysteriously passed—though
the explosion may be hanging fire.)

Such general statistics fade into insignificance beside the fact that
graduates of Tokyo University, and to a lesser extent Kyoto University,
will one day rule the land. The graduate of a provincial university is lucky
if he gets a position with City Hall or the local police force.

Osaka has now been subjected to the indignity of becoming the third-
largest city in the land. It has been passed in population by a Tokyo bedroom city, Yokohama. Though it is a considerable center in its own right,
the fact that Yokohama is a bedroom city is clear. The proportion of its
daytime to its nighttime population is the lowest for any of the ten largest Japanese cities.

So Tokyo is and has almost everything, and many a son of the city
might say that it has lost the most important thing, its identity. Americanization, though often blamed, is not responsible. Not much of Tokyo
looks like an American city, and very little of it feels like one. The loss
of identity is the result of the very Japanese process of homogenization.
Everything is subsumed unto Tokyo and Tokyo is subsumed unto everything; and the nation marches victoriously on, untroubled by the insistence on separateness and difference that troubles so many nations.

Plans and dreams for the future of the city do not have to do exclusively
with high technology and company offices, but they tend strongly in
those directions. Nor, though again the tendency is strong, do they have
to do entirely with the central wards. High-rise blocks, many of them under the auspices of the various wards, will be scattered over the city if the
plans come to fruition. There will be new "new towns" out in the county
part of the prefecture, and better facilities, such as transportation, for the
ones already there.

Though the madness of land prices suggests the saturation of the
central wards, expansion yet seems possible. Open spaces are still to be
found, and landowners see the possibility of more intensive land use than
is presently the case. Mitsubishi says that if Marunouchi can be made
to go the super way, like the Shinjuku Westmouth, it can have ten to
twenty times the office space it now has. The Shiodome freight yards,

just east of Shimbashi and south of Ginza, where stood the first railway terminus in central Tokyo, will be sold and developed, so that the successor company to the National Railways may ease itself of a bit of its gigantic debt. Something highly advanced, including, like the Ark Hills complex in Minato Ward, residential units, will probably rise. The housing is certain to be for the wealthy. Then there is the expanse of land just south of Tokyo Central Station where the prefectural offices now stand. The prefecture does not, apparently, mean to let commercial developers have it. The thought is rather that it will become a grand convention and "cultural" center.

What is called, usually in English, the "new frontier" remains. It is the waterfront, river and bay, more grandiosely the latter. Claude Lévi-Strauss recently said that he saw the future of Tokyo along the Sumida. When such a person sees something, others start seeing it too. So there are projects for high-rise blocks up and down the river. One is already under construction, on the left bank of the Sumida just opposite the busiest part of Asakusa. It is on land formerly occupied by an Asahi brewery, which Nagai Kafū hated because of its part in making the river unlovely. He would not have liked the replacement either. It is more conspicuous, and not distinguished architecturally. There will be three high buildings and some low ones. The Asahi breweries will have a big beer hall, the most attractive detail of the plans, in one corner.

Arakawa Ward, one of the poorer wards, north of Asakusa and the Sanya "slum," envisions what it calls a *kawanote* complex. The expression derives from *yamanote*. The latter might be rendered "the hilly region," and "the river region" might do for the former. The projected site for the *kawanote* is on the inner side of the bend where the Sumida turns south to flow into the bay. About half of it is the Shioiri or Tidewater freight yards, which played such a part (see page 522) in turning Sanya into a "slum." The rest is athletic fields and a small residential district. The tract is almost four times as large as the reservoir bed on which the Shinjuku Westmouth went up. Plans for the new development are by the internationally famous Tange Kenzō, the man who designed both the old and the new prefectural offices. They are uninteresting, a collection of tubular and cuboid objects. One does not want to think that Tange is losing his touch, but the evidence grows that he might be. His name is omnipresent in plans for the future of the city.

The bay front is the more tempting frontier. Nothing remains in Tokyo of the bay shore of Edo. The woodcut artists of Meiji loved to show steam trains running along the shore en route to Yokohama. Now the east side of the tracks is filled land all the way to Yokohama, where the bay once more comes in sight. Nearly four thousand hectares have been reclaimed from the bay within the bounds of Tokyo. (A hectare is a hundred meters squared, or just under two and a half acres.) There are also ample filled lands in the other two bay-shore prefectures, Chiba and Kanagawa. Yokohama has big plans for putting its filled land to use. They include what will for a while be the highest building in Japan, higher than the Sunshine in Ikebukuro. On the Chiba lands just to the east of the border with Tokyo, in Urayasu, the town in which Tokyo Disneyland is situated, four big hotels have been built and a fifth will follow soon. For advertising purposes the district is called MaihamaTokyo Bay Resort City. The last three words are in English, and the very last one is commonly written in Roman letters. Maihama is a part of Urayasu.

Of Tokyo filled lands, almost half have been put to use, for factories and docks and athletic grounds and the like. Of the remaining two thousand or so hectares, the prefecture has a scheme for 440, of which it owns 320. On not quite a quarter of it a "teleport," it is said, will be built. By this is meant the ultimate in a communications center, with satellites, etc., at its disposal. There are also to be two dozen high office buildings, condominiums (to accommodate perhaps fifty or sixty thousand people, a very small drop in the Tokyo bucket), and sports and cultural facilities. The land stretches southward from east of Shimbashi to the Shinagawa offing.

Such is the picture of the future that emerges from the drawing boards, and the future that is to an extent already with us. It is a spotty picture, a bit here and a bit there, and a conjectural one. Not all the big projects for doing away with the last frontier will ever be realized. There would be too many of them even if they were not hugely expensive. The teleport has a better chance than most, even though it is estimated to cost more than thirty billion dollars. The prefecture, unless it changes its mind about the whole thing, will need the help of the big companies, which they will be happy to provide.

The picture contains little if anything that offers hope to the middle class, now being driven to the far suburbs and the neighboring prefectures. Nor is it an aesthetically pleasing picture. Such of the filled lands in the bay as have already been built upon can only be described as bleak. One mile of dust and concrete leads to another. An old district of shops and family houses in, say, the wards just north of the palace may have a somewhat random and discursive look to it, the owner of each building having a slightly different notion from all his neighbors as to what

Center of the new Tokyo—here, at the Shinjuku Westmouth, the new prefectural government buildings are under construction

a building should be, but at least it has the feel of having grown from something. The newly filled tracts have none.

It is understandable that the most moneyed city of our day should wish to go on being that, and make its plans for the things that money desires, communications and information and the like. To do much of significance about the greatest problem the city faces, its inaccessibility to the less than heavily moneyed, may well be impossible. With regard to the aesthetic problem, questions may at least be asked. Must what results from doing away with the last frontier, the newly reclaimed lands, have the dreariness of its predecessor, the reclaimed lands already built upon? Must the cuboids to be scattered over the city have the cold glossiness of Ark Hills and the dinginess of the *danchi*, the public-housing complexes? One cannot be optimistic. These are fields in which the Japanese have not shown flair. The jargon that goes with the plans is uninventive and derivative in the extreme. "Postmodern," already remarked upon, is everywhere. So is "space," which almost seems to proscribe aesthetic judgments. So often, hearing an object described as an interesting space, one has wished to stand up in the middle of a lecture and say, "Well, yes, I suppose it is an ingenious sort of air container, what with all those pits and bulges; but isn't it the *ugliest* thing!"

When the United States was the moneyed country of the world, it created the grandeur of New York. When the maritime countries of western

Europe had the money, they put together the low, subdued harmonies of Amsterdam, Paris, and London. Tokyo will have unprecedented concentrations of communication and information, but these do not immediately meet the eye. What will is unlikely to have either grandeur or harmony.

NOTES

p. 24 *"he regained consciousness."* Akutagawa Ryunosuke, in *Daitōkyō Hanjōki (A Chronicle of the Prosperity of Tokyo)*, in two volumes, 1928; *Shitamachi (The Low City)*, 13-14.

31 *A Dutch observer.* Pompe van Meerbevoort, quoted in *Tōkyō Hyakunenshi (A History of the Tokyo Century)*, in six volumes; 1. 1973, 1521-22.

34 *wife and daughter.* Tanizaki Junichirō, *Setsuyō Zuihitsu (Osaka Essays)*, 1935, 229-33. Tanizaki uses the French/English "vaudeville."

36 *"Edo townsmen."* Hasegawa Shigure, *Kyūbun Nihombashi (Ancient Tidings of Nihombashi)*, 1935, 232.

43 *by the solar.* The solar or Gregorian calendar was adopted on January 1, 1873. That date corresponded to December 3, 1872, under the lunar calendar, and so the remaining days of the lunar year were dropped. Except when otherwise specified, dates through 1872 have been converted to the Gregorian calendar.

46 *Edo as it was.* *The Poems of Tanizaki Junichirō*, 1977, 348. Composed on August 19, 1962.

48 *drank himself to death.* Hasegawa, *Kyūbun Nihombashi*, 63.

51 *"houses are built."* W. E. Griffis, *Guide Book of Yedo*, 11.

51 *into the river.* John Russell Young, *Around the World with General Grant.* Two volumes, 1879. II, 597-98. The Enriokwan, or Enryōkan, was the guest house at the Hama Palace.

52 *Fukuzawa Yukichi.* Seiyō Jijō (The Situation in the West), second part, 9. In Fukuzawa Yukichi, Collected Works, II, 1898.

57 *florid decorations.* Tanizaki Junichirō, *Yōshō Jidai (My Boyhood)*, in Collected Works, XXIX, 1959, 181-84. "Sanctuary of the Instincts"

is Honnōji. A temple by that name, where occurred perhaps the most famous assassination in Japanese history, that of Oda Nobunaga, is situated in Kyoto. Here the name is, of course, used sportively.

58 *an interrupted dream.* Kitahara Hakushū, in *Daitōkyō Hanjōki, Shitamachi*, 166-67. Kinoshita Mokutarō was a well-known poet. Eau-de-vie de Dantzick is in Roman letters in the original.

62 *transfer to Fukagawa.* Nagai Kafū, Collected Works, V, 1948, 80-81.

62 *"Mitsukoshi is today."* Hasegawa, *Kyūbun Nihombashi*, 14.

64 *water from embankments.* The novelist Kikuchi Kan described a more interesting sort of gaffe in the case of the postal service, begun even before the opening of the railroad. The two characters on the post boxes were misconstrued as "urinal." *Meiji Bummei Kidan (Curious Tales of Meiji Civilization)*, 1948, 60.

71 *a school of whitefish.* Osanai Kaoru, *Okawabata (The Bank of the Big River)*, 52-53, 55-56. Masao is of course the hero, closely resembling Osanai. Kimitarō is a geisha. Some of her colleagues go for English lessons to the Summer School in Tsukiji, attended by the young Tanizaki. Nakasu was a restaurant and theater district in Nihombashi. Today it lies mostly beneath expressways.

72 *The River Sumida.* Widely published. See, for instance, *Nihon no Bungaku (Japanese Literature)*, XVIII, 1967, 138.

73 *Mitsui the millionaire.* W. E. Griffis, *The Mikado's Empire*, 1906 (eleventh edition; first published 1876), 365-66, 370.

74 *"latrines of later years."* Ishii Kendō, *Meiji Jibutsu Kigen (Origin of Things Meiji)*, Part 2, 1944, 734.

74 *une laideur Americaine.* Pierre Loti, *Ouevres Complètes*, undated, IV, 473.

75 *"structural hodge-podge."* Philip Terry, *Guide to the Japanese Empire*, 1920, 143.

76 *a famous artist.* Kishida Ryūsei, in *Daitōkyo Hanjōki, Shitamachi*, 360.

78 *someone would say.* Tanizaki, *Yōshō Jidai*, 91. The Kairakuen, in Nihombashi, was the first Chinese restaurant in Tokyo (see page 113). Genchan, son of the proprietor, was a close friend of Tanizaki's.

78 *connoisseur of fires and firefighting methods.* E. S. Morse, *Japan Day by Day*, 1936, I, 31-32; I, 133; II, 125-26.

80 *willows in full leaf.* Kubota Mantarō, Collected Works, XII, 1948, 250-51.

81   *"capital of the Tycoon."* Sir Rutherford Alcock, *The Capital of the Tycoon*, 1863, I, 115.

84   *dim in mists.* Kubota, Collected Works, XII, 210-11.

89   *lights were to be discerned.* Takahama Kyoshi, in *Daitōkyō Hanjōki, Yamanou (The High City)*, 63-64.

93   *"cry out in astonishment."* Natsume Sōseki, *Gubijinsō (The Poppy)*, 1908, 255.

93   *"wait for pretty boys."* Tanizaki, *Yōshō Jidai*, 73, 75.

95   *"passed away forever."* Griffis, *The Mikado's Empire*, 550.

96   *"Edo was destroyed."* Tayama Katai, Collected Works, XV, 1974, 539.

102   *"old one had not been."* Hasegawa, *Kyūbun Nihombashi*, 117-18.

106   *"trees and foliage."* Basil Hall Chamberlain and W. B. Mason, *Murray's Handbook: Japan*, 1903, 115.

106   *acting to the end.* Cf. *Titus Andronicus*, II, IV: "Enter Demetrius and Chiron, with Lavinia, ravished; her hands cut off, and her tongue cut out."

116   *"erected immediately."* Clara Whitney, *Clara's Diary*, 1979, 257.

117   *"to our honored country."* Ibid., 260-61.

128   *"chatters on and on."* Quoted in *Nishikie Bakumatsu Meiji no Rekishi (A History of Late Edo and Meiji in Woodcuts)*, X, 1978, 82. I have not been able to trace the source in Ryokuu's writings.

129   *behind the grand hall.* Kubota, Collected Works, XII, 55-57.

132   *in vacant lots.* Nagai Kafū, *Hiyorigeta (Good-weather Footgear)*, widely published. See, for instance, *Nihon no Bungaku (Japanese Literature)*, XVIII, 1967, 440-41. The Japanese names of the weeds referred to are *kayatsurigusa, nekojirashi, oka no mamma, ōbako*, and *hakobe*.

140   *of her short stories.* Higuchi Ichiyō, "Takekurabe" ("Growing Up"), widely published. See, for instance, *Nihon no Bungaku (Japanese Literature)*, V, 1968, 98.

144   *oscillations of the boats.* Morse, *Japan Day by Day*, I, 129-31.

144   *hopeless condition spiritually.* Whitney, *Clara's Diary*, 93-94

146   *sharp and cold.* Nagai Kafū, "The Fox." Widely published. See, for instance, Collected Works, XII, 94. The Japanese title is "Kitsune."

154   *shiver, pleasantly.* Tanizaki, *Yōshō Jidai*, 120-21.

154   *"out of patience."* Whitney, *Clara's Diary*, 277.

155　*illuminate his face.* Morse, *Japan Day by Day*, 1, 28-29.

155　*"clean away the decay."* Quoted in *Japanese Music and Dance in the Meiji Era*, compiled and edited by Komiya Toyotaka. Centenary Culture Council Series, III, 1956, 191-92.

160　*"what he had left was Yose."* Osanai Kaoru, quoted in the magazine *Hon*, distributed for advertising purposes by Kodansha, June, 1980.

163　*busy holiday-makers.* Chamberlain and Hall, *Murray's Handbook: Japan*, 1891, 85 and 87.

165　*upset no one.* Tanizaki, *Yōshō Jidai*, 109-10.

172　*a romantic setting.* Quoted by Kubota, Collected Works, XII, 94.

176　*would not soon forget.* Higuchi Ichiyo, "Growing Up." Widely published. See for instance *Nihon no Bungaku*, V, 98.

194　*air of the degenerate.* Tayama Katai, in *Daitokyo Hanjoki, Shitamachi*, 300-3, 304-6. *Owai*, "excrement," was the cry of the night-soil draymen as they made their way through the city. "Spectacle Bridge," Meganebashi, was another name for Yorozuyobashi, also known as Manseibashi, in Kanda. The English word "degenerate" is used.

194　*today, assembled.* Hasegawa, *Kyūbun Nihombashi*, 163, 165-66.

195　*affluence in party dress. Ibid.,* 233. *Danna*, something like "master" or "head of the house," is the word rendered "men of affluence."

205　*"Nôtre Dame to Paris."* Griffis, *The Mikado's Empire*, 378.

206　*"at such play." Ibid.,* 388.

207　*"a charred waste."* Akutagawa Ryūnosuke, quoted by Kubota Mantarō in Collected Works, XII, 31-32.

208　*since the earthquake. Ibid.,* 33-34.

209　*attributes of a park. Tokyo Annai (A Guide to Tokyo)*, 1907, II, 448. The area of the park converts to about thirteen and a half acres. The Satake were lords of Kubota, the present Akita.

210　*that ancient sadness.* Nagai Kafū, from *Udekurabe (A Test of Skills)*. Widely published. See for instance *Nihon no Bungaku (Japanese Literature)*, XVIII, 1967, 221.

214　*old Fukagawa was.* Akutagawa, in *Daitōkyō Hanjoki, Shitamachi*, 3, 30, 46. Regions within "the red line" were under the Edo magistracy. In effect it marked the city limits.

214　*"semblance of sanctity."* Chamberlain and Hall, *Murray's Handbook: Japan*, 1903, 88.

215   *"at the head of their lists."* *Tokyo Annai*, 1907, II, 598, 650.

219   *clams and seaweed.* *Ibid.*, II, 745-46.

222   *a more revolting form.* Alcock, *The Capital of the Tycoon*, I, 111-13. *No-rimono* and *kago* are two words for "sedan chair." The Tocado is more properly the Tokaido.

224   *"from other years."* Osanai Kaoru, in *Daitōkyō Hanjoki, Yamanote*, 547.

235   *half of it to ashes.* Arishima Ikuma, *Ibid.*, 94, 96.

237   *"cawing outside the window."* Morse, *Japan Day by Day*, I, 15.

253   *"that suggests Valentino."* Kishida Ryūsei, in *Daitōkyō Hanjōki, Shita-machi*, 362-63.

256   *it rained.* Nagai Kafū, *Hanabi (Fireworks)*. Widely published. See for instance, *Kafū Zuihitsu (Kafū's Essays)*, III, 1982, 14.

258   *dwell outside it.* Terry, *Guide to the Japanese Empire*, 133.

276   *had not yet come.* Tanizaki, *Setsuyō Zuihitsu*, 215-21.

295   *"avenues and streets."* *The Reconstruction of Tokyo*, Tokyo, Tokyo Municipal Office, 1933. iv.

296   *"from our beds."* Quoted in *Tōkyō Hyakunenshi (Tokyo Centennial History)*, Tokyo, Tokyo Prefectural Office, in six volumes, IV, 1972, 1241.

297   *"field of flowers."* Collected Works, Tokyo, Shinchōsha, II, 1970, 54.

297   *"mountain of rubble."* *Ibid.*, 55.

300   *"prayed in silence."* Collected Short Stories, Tokyo, Kōdansha, 1964. 338.

300   *"fresh autumn wind."* Collected Works, Tokyo. Iwanami Shoten, XIX, 1964, 332.

300   *"seemed very near."* Collected Works, VIII, 1963, 94.

302   *"woman out dancing."* Collected Works, XIX, 334.

305   *"royal death approaches?"* Collected Works, XX, 1964, 86.

311   *"a generous estimate"* Collected Works, Tokyo, Chūō Kōron Sha, XXII, 1959, 157-59

312   *"appearance of health."* Collected Works, XII, 1970, 39.

313   *"to be beautiful."* *Ibid.*, 33.

320   *"be your bride."* *Shōwa Ryūkōkashi (A History of Shōwa Popular Music)*, Tokyo, Mainichi Shimbun, 1977, 59.

323   *"the repellent kind."* Collected Works, XXIX, 1982, 232-34. A more recent version of the collected works than that cited elsewhere.

340   *"after a rain." Op. cit.*, 197.

340   *"into the mirrors."* Collected Works, VIII, 236.

341   *"on their way."* Collected Works, Tokyo, Shinchosha, III, 1977, 14.

342   *"medical science marvelous?"* Collected Works, II, 28-29.

343   *"just like Osaka."* Collected Works, III, 28.

343   *"not with dew."* Shōwa Ryūkōkashi, 51-52.

344   *"a chain store." Op. cit.*, 14.

348   *"spring and autumn."* p. cxc.

355   *"for the dancer."* Shōwa Ryūkōkashi, 48-49.

353   *"into new ones."* Collected Works, II, 30-31.

354   *"song and legs." Ibid.*, 31.

355   *"the Fourth District." Ibid.*

359   *"was really listening."* Collected Works, III, 356. The passage is a single
      sentence in the original.

360   *"stroll down Ginza."* Collected Works, II, 33.

362   *"bags of sweets." Ibid.*, 128-29.

362   *"quite radiates eroticism." Ibid.*, 109.

363   *"world doesn't have." Ibid.*, 86.

365   *"only in Asakusa."* Collected Works, III, 75.

376   *"want to flee."* Chikamatsu Shūkō, quoted in *Tōkyō Hyakunenshi*, V,
      1972, 900.

384   *"of a room."* New York, Alfred A. Knopf, 1957, 483.

386   *"make haste, sing."* Collected Works, XII, 1963, 402-3.

386   *"at my breast." Ibid.*, 408.

386   *"make the sacrifice." Ibid.* ,413.

387   *"in the hall. Ibid.*, 422.

387   *"to be in." Ibid.*, 430.

387   *"from human affairs?" Ibid.*, 432.

388   *"breaks the silence." Ibid.*, 437.

389   *"together are removed."* Collected Works, Tokyo, Keisō Shōbō, 1, 1970,
      153.

340   *"of their dream." Ibid.*, 241.

392 *"letting things go."* Collected Works, XIX, 1974, 551-52.

392 *"going to ruins."* Collected Works, XXIII, 1964, 439.

393 *"moral from this."* Collected Works, XIX, 570.

393 *"neglect the place."* *Asakusa*, edited by Takami Jun, Tokyo, Eihōsha, 1955, 272.

408 *"that odd building,"* p. 96.

418 *"a modest gift."* Collected Works, Tokyo, Chikuma Shobō, IX, 1978, 17.

452 *"how agreeable."* *Shōwa Ryūkōkashi*, 141.

458 *"a different route."* Collected Works, XXIV, 1964, 180.

463 "with Edict 9." Murata Hiroo, in Takami, *Asakusa*, 240.

465 *"of us Japanese."* Quoted in *Shōwa no Sesō (Aspects of Shōwa)*, edited by Harada Katsumasa, Tokyo, Shōgakkan, 1983, 140. The Harada volume is an appendix to the Shogakkan history of the Shōwa Period.

494 *"came back again."* Akatsuka Yukio, quoted in *Edo Tōkyō Gaku Jiten (The Edo Tokyo Encyclopedia)*, edited by Ogi Shinzō et al., Tokyo, Sanseido, 1987, 239.

506 *"things a bit."* Quoted in Harada, *op. cit.*, 254.

515 *"oversaw the destruction."* It may be a mistake to say that nothing else survives of Mitsubishi Londontown. Fragments of the Ginza Bricktown of early Meiji, thought to have been utterly lost, have turned up in the course of demolitions, excavations, and rebuildings.

523 *"helpful of police."* When a friend and I tried to photograph the mammoth police box we were told that regulations forbade it. Inquiry with police headquarters revealed that there are no such regulations.

527 *"villa of Kikugorō."* Collected Works, IX, 1964, 111-12.

530 *"use of space."* Arthur Koestler, as we were having a stroll.

535 *"Sanyūtei Kimba."* Quoted in *Shōwa no Sesō (Aspects of Shōwa)*, edited by Iwasaki Jiro and Katō Hidetoshi, Tokyo, Shakai Shisōsha, 1971, 269.

542 *"had a point."* The lady, obviously American, winked and smiled and made the remark as she got off the riverboat from Asakusa. I was waiting at Shibaura to board the same boat in the opposite direction.

544 *"going to win."* Tamanoumi, in *Bungei Shunjū ni Miru Shōwa Supōtsu shi (A History of Shōwa as seen in Bungei Shunjū)*, II, 1988, 526. The article is reprinted from the magazine *Bungei Shunjū* for April 1970. Tamanoumi became a Yokozuna in 1970 and died while still an active wrestler.

570 *"have a home."* *Shōwa Bungaku Zenshū* (a uniform edition of Shōwa writing), Tokyo, Shōgakkan, IX. 1987, 44.

573 *"edge of bankruptcy."* Fukuda Shintarō, president of the Jiji News Service, in conversation.

599 *"goes on developing."* *Tōkyōjin (The Tokyoite)*, March-April 1988, 134-35.

600 *"not be easy,"* *Tōkyōjin*, special issue, July 1988, 22-23.

INDEX

Note: Page numbers in italics refer to illustrations.

ABCD encirclement, 404
Abe family, 239
Abe Sada (O-sada), 402
addresses, 228-29
Adults' Day, 144
advertising, 118, 271, 213, 558
air raids, *416*, 418
Aishinkakura Eisei, 534
Akasaka, 511-12
Akasaka Detached Palace, 40, 230, 236
Akasaka Ward, 228, 232, 249
akasen (red line), 532
Akihabara district, 211
Akihabara electronics market, 471
Akutagawa Ryūnosuke, 24, 110, 214, 321
Alcock, Sir Rutherford, 81, 221, 224
alleys, 96; broad, 163, 568
American Occupation, 420-94; end of, 473; housing and, 439-40; pleasure quarters and, 457; street stalls and, 433; theaters and, 449; wards and, 443-45; *see also* post-war period
ameshon, 451
Ameya Yokochō (Ameyoko), 426, *427*

Anchūha, 536
Angoha, 536
anti-Americanism, 459
Anti-Japanese Armed East Asian Front, 585
Aoyama Avenue, 499-500, 507, 508
Aoyama Gakuin (missionary school), 202, 488
Aoyama Gakuin University, 488
Apple Song, The," 452
"apres-guerre," 405
aqueducts, 95, 275
Arakawa Drainage Channel, 72, 219, 257, 308, 386, 408, 415, 419, 542
Arakawa River, 180, 257
Arakawa Ward, 376, 379, *380*, 441, 545, 579, 603
"arbeit salon," 462
architects, 81
architecture, 81-89, 231, 252, 519-20, 345; aesthetics and, 603; brick buildings, 74-75, 90; Edo (Tokugawa period), 81; following 1923 earthquake, 312-13; government buildings, 228-31; 1930s, 406-08; of department stores, 316; skyscrapers, 550-51; Western buildings, 81-82; Yoshiwara,

532 *and illus; see also individual buildings*
Arishima family, 234, 242
Arishima Ikuma, 242
aristocracy, 32, 186, 187, 242, 244
Ark Hills, 563-64, 603, 605
Arnold, Sir Edwin, 129
art, *see* prints; woodcuts
artists, 209, 244, 345
Art Theater (Geijutsuza), 266, 556
Asahi Shimbun (newspaper), 283, 309, 356, 559
Asakusa Kannon Temple, 138, 205, 312
Asakusa opera, 261-64, 353-54
"Asakusa Mynah Bird, The," 365
Asakusa park, 128, 163, 342, 255, 356, 379, 397, 434-35, 456
Asakusa Twelve Storys (Ryōunkaku), 84-86
Asakusa Ward, 52, 99, 152, 191, 206, 209-10, 376, 456, 545; character of, 363-65, 390-92; decline of, 456, 566; Ginza compared to, 390-92; literature and, 668-70; new, 207-08; rebuilding of, 455; reviews, 353-67, *361, 365*; as *sakariba,* 324-25, 353; during Taishō, 260-64, *261*; temples and cemeteries in, 206; theaters, 566, *567;* World War II and, 385-89, *394; see also* Kawabata Yasunari; *Scarlet Gang of Asakusa*
assassinations, 146, 308, 405, 586
Asuka Hill, 138, 579
Asukayama Park, 128, 134, 135, 136, 579
automobiles, 34, 64, 294, 302, 334, 422, 433, 466, 474, 492, 513, 537, 581
Azabu Ward, 325, 563
Azuma Bridge (Azumabashi), 71, 72, 216

Azuma Ryūtarō, 496, 525-26

Baldwin (balloonist), 117
balloons, 117
Banchō district, 235
Bandō Mitsugorō, 478
Bandō Tamasaburō, 449
bankara (style of dress), 111
Bankers' Club, *514,* 515, 577
Bank of Japan building, 87-88, 90, 188, 192, 196
Bank of the Big River, The (Okawabata) (Osanai), 69-70, 160
Bank of Tokyo, 515
banzai, shouting of, 105
barbershops, 103-04
barracks, 296; military, 242
bars, 309, 311, 338, 339, 341, 386, 460, 493, 558, 560, 567, 593
Barton, William, 84
baseball, 105, 169-71, 274, 303, 347-49, 398-99, 450, 463, 464-67, 544, 545, 590; night games, 466, 478; World War II and, 398-99, 364-65
bataya (ragpicker), 380
bathhouses, 103
baths, public vs. private, 103
Bauduin, E. A. F., 126
Baxter, Anne, 507
bay front, 603-04
bazaars *(kankōba),* 123
beaches, 114
Beard, Charles, 51, 268-69, 276, 297, 561
Beatles, 589
beauty school, 104
beef, eating of, 111-12
beer, 105
beggars, 379
benshi, 351-52
Bird, Isabella, 74, 81, 205
Bird Fair (Tori no Ichi), 140, 176

birds, 137
Black, JR., 203
black markets, 425 *and illus.*, 426, 569
blossom-viewing, *see* cherry blossoms; peach blossoms; pear blossoms; plum blossoms
"Boatman's Song, The," 277
boats, pleasure, *38*, 68
bombings, 585; *see also* air raids
Bonin (Ogasawara) Islands, 47
boundaries of Tokyo, 47-48
Boys' Day, 142
bread, 111
brick buildings, 74, 75, 90, 515, 540
Bricktown (Ginza), *61*, 74 *and illus.*, 86, 90, 122, 188, 197, 198
bridges, 68, 69, 71-72, 313-14; *see also specific bridges*
British embassy, 228-29, 231, 235
British legation, burning of (1863), 31
broad alleys *(hifokōji),* 163, 568
brothels, 55, 174-75, 177, 487, 530, *532*
Buddhism, 408
Buddhist clergy, 317
Bummei Kaika, *see* Civilization and Enlightenment
Bungei Kyōkai (Literary Society), 266
building, 540; *see also* architecture
bunka jūtaku (cultural dwelling), 328
Bunkyō Ward, 441, 528
buses, *61*, 332, 333, 369, 402-03, 493, 563
bureaucracy, Edo, 3
business girl, 533
butchers, 112

cafés, 309, 310, 311, 324, 336, 337, 338, 339-45, 386, *396*, 460-61; *see also* bars; coffee houses; tea shops

calling cards, 106
canals, 59, 68-69, 96, 190, 197, 298, 314, 408, 423, 497, 498, 542
Capital District, 48, 409, 540-41
cartoons (comics), 397-98, 594
"casino," 323-24
Casino Folies, 355-67, 378, 390
cemeteries, 39, 125, 131, 139, 171, 205, 206, 209, 222, 327, 417
chairs, 110
Chamberlain, Basil Hall, 106, 162, 214, 258
chanoyu (tea ceremony), 36, 37
censorship, 410, 447, 450
Chaplin, Charlie, *346*, 347
Chaplin caramels, 267
"Charleston," 323, 366
cherry blossoms, 125, 126, 127, 135, 138, 139, 168, 176, 579
Chiba Prefecture, 52, 456, 458, 501, 596, 597
chikan (masher), 597
children, 142; reviews and, 356, 362
Children's Day, 142
China Incident, 381
Chinese cuisine, 112
Chinese people, 429, 568
Chiyoda Ward, 440-41, 472, 498, 568, 596
cholera epidemics, 40, 94, 114, 116
Christianity, 40, 244
Christmas, 318
chrysanthemums, 109, 135, 138, 176
Chūō University, 212
Chūō Ward, 186, 440, 498, 542, 558-59, 568, 592, 593
Citizens' Day, 48
city council, 48, 368, 375, 442
City Hall, 90
Civilization and Enlightenment (Bummei Kaika), 34 38, 49, 93, 102-03, 105; meaning of, 52, 53

clams, 134, 137, 219, 223
class distinctions, 97, 190, 233
clock tower, Hattori, 199, 203
clothing: footwear, 315; men's, 509; women's, 319, 326, 510; *see also* dress
cod, 432, 433
coffee houses, 113, 461-62; *see also* cafés
colleges, 601; *see also* universities
comic monologues, 37
comics, *see* cartoons
communists, 514, 526, 572
commuting life, 597
Conder, Josiah, 81-82, 83-84, 90, 124, 231, 239, *240*, 312, 577
conformity, 549
conservatism, 36, 141, 145, 190, 196, 363, 392
constitution, Meiji, 35-36, 49, 105, 202, 404, 462
cooking, 345-46
corporate offices, 600-01
cosmetics, 326
courtesans, 171-72, 174-75, 337; *see also* geisha
crime, 401-03, 573, 584-88; gangs, 429-30, 556; and criminals, 43, 102-03, 165-68, 203-4; in Olympic years, 524-25; organized, 429-30, 584; political, 584-87; postwar period, 475-76, 478-82; *sōkaiya*, 524-25, 587; white-collar, 524-25, 587
crosswalks, overhead, 582
cultural center, Tokyo as, 99

Daiei Building, 87
Daiichi Hotel, 407, 437
Daiichi Insurance Building, 421
Daiichi Kangyō Bank, 192-93
Daimaru store, 62, *63*, 187
dairy products, 111, 271

dances, Niwaka, 176
dancing, 109, 113, 320-21, *432*, 447
danchi, 540, 605
Dangozaka, 138, 238
Danjūrō (Kabuki actor), 27, 116, 155-57, 159, 167, 416
Dazai Osamu, 493
de Beauvoir, Simone, 589
democracy, Taishō, 255, 276
department stores, 118-19, 119-20, 314-15, 516, 559; fires in, 318-19, 533; Ginza district, 559-60; *see also specific stores*
detectives, private, 105
depression, economic (1930s), 378-79
Diary of a Mad Old Man (Tanizaki). 514
diet, changes in, 111-12
Diet building, 228, 508
DiMaggio, Joe, 451
diving girls, 363
dollar, value of, 547
doraibu (pleasure driving), 537
"double life," the, 101, 118, 145
doughnut effect, 329, 492
drainage channel, 219, 257
drama, *see* theater
dress: Meiji, 103, 104, 107, 109, 111, 120, 174; Taishō, 252, 270
Dream Island, 526, 542, 573, 574
Drifting Clouds (Hayashi), 569
drug problem, 494, 573
During the Rains (Kafū), 309-10, 338, 340, 344

Earthquake Memorial Hall, 299 *and illus.*, 417
earthquake of 1855, 26, 40
earthquake of 1923, 23-27, 33-34, 295-99, *296*, 319-23
East Ginza, 425, 528

Ebara, 327
Echigoya (store), 193
economy, 300-01, 377-80, 547
Edo (the pre-Restoration city), 24-44; architecture of, 81; aristocracy of, 32; as capital and bureaucratic center, 31; demise of, 28, 184-85; foreigners in, 40; literature of, 245-46; pleasure quarters of, 30, 36, 37, 38-39, 150-51; population of, 32, 42; renamed Tokyo (1868), 44; rice riots in (1866), 41-42; stores in, 118; streets and alleys of, 96; theaters of, 37-38; transportation in, 37-38; Yose (variety or vaudeville halls) of, 37
Edo castle, 46, 498, 500, 517
Edo culture, 30, 36-39, 49-50, 98, 150-51, 245-46
Edogawa, 440
education, 99, 202; during Taishō, 272-73; *see also* colleges; schools; universities
Eight Ginza Blocks (Takeda), 341-42, 344
Einstein, Albert, 267-68
Ekōin Temple, 163, 214
elderly people, 425
Electricity Hall, 128, 566
electric lights, 93
electric power companies, 94
elevators, 120, 519, 547
Elocution Hall (Enzetsukan), 76
embassies and legations, 53, 228-29
emperors: Shōwa, *307*, 308, 420, 445-46 *and illus.*, 475, 546-47; Taishō, 301-06, *304, 305*
Enchō (Yose performer), 160-61
English period in architecture, 81
enkashi (street minstrels), 167-68, 168, 171
Ennosuke (Ichikawa Ennosuke), 446, 449

Enomoto Kenichi (Enoken), 356-57, 358, 393, 394 *and illus.*, 456, 487
epidemics, 33, 35, 40, 482
era names, 40, 305
Ernie Pyle, 395, 449, 451, 453, 560
eroguro (erotic-grotesque), 341-43, 362, 378-79
Essence of National Polity, The, 404
ethnological museum, 566
"event", 508-09
exchange rate, 547, 595-96
exports, 547
expositions, 93, 123-24, 126, 127, 251, 487

factories, 98, 114, 115, 212, 214, 328, 604
fads, *see* vogues
fairs, *see* expositions
Faltering of the Virtues, The (Mishima), 536
farmland, 99, 231-32, 328
feast days, 139, 163, 195
February 26 Incident (1936), 401
ferries, 216
festivals, 141-44, 274; Yoshiwara, 175-78
films, *see* movies
fire(s), 26, 33, 40, 51, 77-80, 293-94, 318, 414-15, 533-35; of 1872 (Ginza), 72-73; of 1881 (Kanda), 66, 77-78; of 1911 (Yoshiwara), *77*, 177-78; after 1923 earthquake, 25-27, *41*; during Taishō, 256, 260
fire baskets, 78
fire department, 78, 256
firefighting methods, 78-80, 256, 317
fireflies, 137, 273
First Higher School, 170, 237
First National Bank, 158, *189*, 192
First National Industrial Exposition (1877), 123

fishing, 99
fish market, central, 94-95
fish market scandal of 1928, 370
Five Mouths (post-stations), 178-81
Flesh Gate (Tamura) (novella and film), 453, 459, *460*
flood control, 216-18, 257
floods, 72; of 1910, 97, 216, *217*, of Taishō, 257
flowers, 134-39, 273
"flowers of Edo" (fires), 33, 78, 140, 256, 295, 317, 533
food, 111-12
footwear, 122-23, *see also* shoes
foreigners (foreign population), 114-18, 250-51, 576, 595; in Edo, 31, 40; in Ginza, 202; in Tsukiji, 53-58; violence against, 113, 117; *see also* American Occupation
foreign legations and embassies, 53, 228-29
Forty-Seven Loyal Retainers, 64, 222
"Fox, The" (Kafū), 145-46
Free Theater (Jiyu Gekijō), 265-66
Free School (Shishi), 569
freeways, Olympic, 497-99
Fūgetsudō (confectioner), 200
Fuji, Mount, 143; miniature, 128-29
Fujiwara Yoshie, 168
Fukagawa Ward, 55-56, 212-14, 218-20, 376, 420, 530-31
Fukuchi Genichirō, 176-77
fukutoshin (subcenters), 482-92, 516, 561
Fukuzawa Yukichi, 49, 52-53, 76, 201
Funabashi Seiichi, 465
funayado (boat lodge or boating inn), 68-69, 184
Futabayama, 399, 469, 470, *471*
Futen Zoku, 513-14

gakusha-machi (professorial neighborhood), 239
Gambler's Meadow, *see* Mitsubishi Meadow
gambling, 412
gangs, 429-30, 556
garbage, 526, 573-74
gaslights, 92-93, 154
gebabō, 548
gebaruto, 548
geese, wild, 137
Geijutsuza (Art Theater), 266
geisha, *104*, 172-75, 292, 325, 395-96, 411, 543-44 *and illus.*; decline of, 511-12, 591-93; definition of, 337; earthquake of 1923 and, 297; postwar period and, 458, *460*; residences of, 592-93; theaters of, 396-97; "town", 181-82
geisha districts, 181-85, 325, 411, 543-44; *see also specific districts*
General Mobilization Law, 409-10
General Staff Headquarters, 228
German embassy, 228-29
Gilbert, W. S., 44-45
Gimbura ("fooling around in Ginza"), 75, 198, 205, 258, 330
Ginza district, 28, 30, 60, 69, 123, 187, 190, 193-94, 197-205, 224-25, 227, 294, 324, 325, 330, 425, 433, 452, 494, 501, 516-17, 558-59, 593; Asakusa compared to, 390-92; as city center, 293, 324, 325, 355, 558-59; Bricktown in, 74-77 *and illus.*, 198-99; cafés in, 200, 336, 338 *and illus,* 339-41, 344 *396,* 461; canals of, 197; department stores, 560; during Taishō, 258-60; educational institutions in, 202; fire of 1872 in, 72-73; following 1923 earthquake, 295-96, 309-10; foreign

settlement in, 202; gaslights in, 92-93; growth of suburbs and, 329; in 1870, 73; land prices in, 595-96, 598-99; main street of, 197, 259-60; *nankin* (*nouveau riche*) of, 199; newspapers in, 203; rebuilding of (after 1872 fire), 73-76; theaters in, 204, 394-96; willows of, 76, 259 and illus

Ginza Printemps, 560

godowns (warehouses), 41, 71, 78, 146, 190, 194, 218

god performances (Kagura), 163-64

god-seat festivals, 142

god-seats (*mikoshi*), 139, 141, 144

Golden Block, 485, 533, 553

Golf, 591

Goten Hill, 136

Gotō Shimpei (mayor of Tokyo), 48, 49, 90, 254, 269, 297, 311

government, 48-49, 368; Beard's views on, 268-69; earthquake of 1923 and, 298; offices of, 371-72 and illus; postwar period, 441-45; prewar instability, 368-69; reorganization of (1943), 408-09; scandals and, 369-71, 496, 525-56; wards and, 442-45; westward movement of, 291-92; *see also* city council; mayors

government buildings, 228-29

governors, 368, 571-75

Graf Zeppelin, 346-47

Grant, Julia, 114-15, 151

Grant, Gen. Ulysses S., 114-17, 143, 151

grasses, 135-36, 138, 273

gravel scandal (1920), 49

Green Years, The (Mishima), 479

Great Meiji Flood (1910), 72, 216, 217

Greater Tokyo, 541

Griffis, W. E.. 44, 51, 73, 89, 95, 113, 117, 165, 205-06, 264

grotesqueries, 342-43

hair styles, 103-04, 271

Hachikō, 400-01 *and illus.*

Hamachō geisha quarter, 191, 308

Hamachō Park, 308

Hamamatsuchō, 500, 551

Hamamoto Hiroshi, 354

Hama Palace, 83, 197-98, 414, 434

Hanai O-ume, *see* O-ume

Haneda, 99

Hanasono Block, 485

Hanasono tent, 583

"happening", 508-09

Hara Takeshi, 48

Harada Kinu, *see* O-kinu

Harajuku, 508-11, *509*, 561, 583

Hasegawa Shigure, *see* Shigure

hatamoto (lesser military orders), 234

Hashimoto Gahō, 124

Hatonomachi (Pigeon Town), 457-58, 531 *and illus.*

Hatoyama Ichirō, 369

Hattori Kintarō, 199

Hayama, Peggy, 453

Hayashi Fumiko, 569

Hearn, Lafcadio, 33

Heian Period, 36

Hepburn, J. C, 106

Hibiya, 408

Hibiya Hall, 395, 407

Hibiya Park, 130-31, 222

High City (Yamanote), 27, 49-50, 52, 97, 97-98, 231-46, 291-93; earthquake of 1923 and, 25, 30; grand estates of, 236; north-south differences in, 235-36; pleasure quarters of, 30; streets of, 232-34; *see also specific districts and wards* "high-collar," defined, 104-05

Higuchi Ichiyo, 98-99, 140, 176

Hikagechō, 225

hikitejaya (teahouses), 173, 174

hilly places, 530

Hirasawa, 479-82

hirokōji (broad alleys), 163, 568

Hirotsu Kazuo, 322-23, 479

Hitler, Adolf, 381, 399

Hōgetsu, 266-67

hokōsha tengoku (pedestrian paradise), 581-82

holidays, 46; *see also* feast days; festivals; seasons and seasonal observances

homeless, the, 417-18, *431*

Home Ministry, 254, 257, 371, 372, 375, 409

Hommokutei, 451

homogenization, 602

homosexuality, 553

Honganji Temple, 407 *and illus.*

Hongō Ward, 235-36, *296*, 299

Honjo Ward, 212-14, 216-18, *217*, *296*, 376, 420

horse-drawn transportation, 60

hospitals, 116

Hosokawa Morihiro, 599

Hoterukan (hotel), 54-55, 58, 76, 81, 187, 252

"Hostess's Song", 343

hotels, 437-38, 506-07, 550; *see also* inns; motels; *and specific establishments*

house numbers, 105-06

housing, 328, 433-34, 439-40, 539-40, 596-98, 603

Hula-Hoop, 463

Ichikawa Ennosuke, 446

Ichikawa Kon, 506

Ichimuraza theater, 152, 159, 164, 265

Iemochi (shogun), 42

Ikebukuro Ward, 315, 324, 376, 377, 489-90, *491*, 512-13, 533, *565*, 569

Imperial Bank robbery (1948), 479-82, *481*

Imperial Hotel: first, 83, *229*, 230 *and illus.*, 256, 268; second, 230, 268, 384, 507, 577-78 *and illus.*

Imperial Theater, 82, 121, 158, 159, 184, 230, 231, 261, 354, 410

Imperial University, 236-39

individualism, as new outlook, 244, 245

industrial zones, 212-15, 220; *see also* factories

industry, 328-29, 558

inflation, 547-48

information industry, 558

inns, 437-38

Inoue Kaoru, 108-09

insects, 137, 273

insularity, 576

insurance companies, 515, 557

intelligentsia, 194, 271, 272, 334, 393

internationalization, 469, 575, 576

International Theater (Kokusai Gekijō), 390, 524, 566

In the Realm of the Senses (film), 403

irises, 137

Iriya district, 137

Ishihara Shintarō, 494, 544

Ishikawajima Shipyards, 218

"It," 323-24, 343

Itabashi district, 175, 180, 376, 444

Itō, Prince, 113, 158

Itō Hirobumi, 31, 108, 109

Iwaitabashi, 492

Iwasaki estate, 219, 239

Iwasaki family, 235, 239

Iwo Islands, 47

Izu Islands, 47, 99, 320

Jackson, Michael, 589
Japanese-American Security Treaty, 473, 520, 536
Japanese language, *see* language
Jiyū Gekijō (Free Theater), 265
judo, 171, 469, 504-505, 506
Jōtō Ward, 375, 376, 419, 420
jujitsu, 171

Kabuki, 37, 38, 39, 93, 97, 116-17, 151-60, 292, 346, 394-96, 566; censorship and, 447-48; crimes as material for, 165-67; dance and, 447; during Taishō, 260, 264-65; in Ginza, 204; in postwar period, 446-49; lighting for, 152, 155; Low City and, 486; modernization of, 469; movement for improvement of, 155-56; Tokyo vs. Osaka, 396; World War II and, 410-11
Kabuki actors, 57, 118, 150, 156, 271
Kabukichō district, 485-88, 553-58, *555*, 560
Kabukiza, 157-59, 265, 395, 397, 406 *and illus.*, 410, 417, 446, 448, 448
Kachitokibashi, 314, 382
Kafū (Nagai Kafū), 30, 34, 69, 75, 80, 114, 135, 161, 172, 184, 201, 211, 222, 233, 238, 242, 244, 251, 264, 275, 300-02, 323, 325, *394*, 408, 415, 454, 520, 527-28, 531, 569, 570, 603; death of, 535; on Akihabara, 472; on Asakusa, 392; on cafés, 357; on changes after 1923 earthquake, 309-10; on death of Taishō emperor, 304-05; on Fukagawa, 61-62, 213, 218-19; on Honjo, 213; on Negishi, 210; on postwar pleasure quarters, 458; on riots of 1918, 256; on Western

style architecture, 405; Tamanoi quarter and, 335-36; "The Fox," 145-46; The River Sumida, 72, 136, 159, 174, 213, 215; "A Song in Fukagawa" (*Fukagawa no Uta*), 61; World War II and, 385-89, 410; *see also specific works*
Kaga estate, 53
Kaga Yashiki, *see* Maeda estate
kagemajaya (shady teahouses), 238
kagikko (key child), 539
Kagura (god performances), 164-65
Kagurazaka district, 182, 241, 325
Kairakuen restaurant, 112
Kameido district, 136, 336
Kamikaze cabdrivers, 493
kamishihai (paper show), 397
Kanagaki Robun, *see* Robun
Kanagawa Prefecture, 47
Kanda, 28, 95, 123, 194, 221, 232, 238, 241; Akihabara district of, 211; fire of 1881 in, 77-79; produce market of, 211; universities of, 212; used-book district of, 212
Kanda River, 137, 314
Kanda Shrine and festival, 141
Kanda wholesale produce market, 440
Kan-eiji temple, 45, 125
Kaneyasu, 33
Kannon Temple, Asakusa, 28, 38, 138, 205, 312, 352, 416, 435, 571
Kantō earthquake, *see* earthquake of 1923
Kanya (impresario), 151-59 *passim*, 265
karizashiki ("rooms for rent"), 174-75
Kashiwara Shrine, 383
Kasumigaseki Building, 551
Kata Kōji, 394 *and illus.*, 456
Kataoka Nizaemon, 478
katsugiya (runners), 428

Katsushika Romance (Kafū), 385-87, 408

Kawabata Yasunari, 208, 378, 392, 397, 535, 570; on Akutagawa suicide, 321-23; Asakusa reviews and, 354-60; on earthquake of 1923, 297, 299-300, 312-13; Kabukichō and, 487-88; *see also Scarlet Gang of Asakusa; and other works*

kawanote complex, 603

Kawarazaki Gonjuro, 57

Keiki (Yoshinobu) (last shogun), 42, 125

Keiō Plaza Hotel, 553

Keiō University, 53, 76, 83, 112, 201, 204

Keisei Railway scandal (1928), 369

kengeki (swordplay), 365, 454

key child (*kagikko*), 539

Kichiemon, 265, 446, 448, 473

kidnapping, 586

Kikugorō (Kabuki actor), 57, 117, 154, 167, 265, 410, 448

Kim Dae-jung, 586

kimono, 107

Kinshichō, 393, 567, 568

Kinoshita Mokutarō, 58

Kinoshita O-tsuya, *see* O-tsuya

Kishida Ryūsei, *see* Ryūsei

kissaten (tea shops), 344, 461

Kitahara Hakushu, 58

Kita Ward, 579

Kiyochika (artist), *63*, 65-67

Kiyosumi Park, 219

Kobayashi Hideo, 570

Kobayashi Kiyochika, *see* Kiyochika

Kobikichō, 202, 425, 528

Kodaira, 479, 519, 523

Kōdan, 450, 451

Koestler, Arthur, 495

Koishikawa Ward, 137, 241

Kōjimachi Ward, 148, 149, 227, 229, 231, 234, 235, 254

Kōjunsha *and illus*, 201

Kokugikan, 169, 347

Kokusai Gekujō, 390, 394, 566

kokutai meichō (clarification of the fundamental concept of national polity), 404

Koma Stadium, 487, 558, 593

Konoe, Prince, 384

Kōrakuen Stadium, 398, 464, 465, 466

Korea, 568, 587

Koreans, 27, 429

Korean War, 424, 430, 435, 436, 482, 493, 495, 496, 500, 547, 593

Koshiji Fubuki, 457

Kotobuki affair (1947), 479

Kōtō Ward, 573-74

Kotsukappara execution grounds, 35 *and illus, 165*

Kōyōkan restaurant, 224

Kubota Mantarō, 80, 84, 129, 172, 207, 216, 245, 456

Kudan Hill, 132

Kudan shōkonsha (shrine), 133

kumitoriya (carters of night soil), 502

Kuroda family, 203, 204

Kyōbashi, 28, 30, 69, 74, 91, 98, 186, 187, 197-205, 240, *310*; see *also* Ginza district

Kyoto, 46, 48, 134, 233; and establishment of Tokyo as capital, 44, 46

Kyoto University, 601, 602

labor, 378, 476-78

landfills, 530, 542; *see also* canals

language: *manga* magazines and, 594-95; neologisms, 269-70, 271, 323, 403, 453

laver seaweed, 99, 134

law schools, 212

leftists (1930s), 378; *see also* communists; Socialist Party

legations and embassies, 53, 228
Lévi-Strauss, Claude, 603
libraries, 419
licensed quarters, 171-81, 335-36, 457-58, 530-31; *see also* geisha districts; pleasure centers; *and individual quarters*
lighting: for Kabuki theater, 152, 154-55; street, 92-94
Lion café, 201
Li Po, 172
Literary Society (Bungei Kyōkai), 266
literature, 393-94, 459, 568-70; traditional vs. modern 245; *see also specific authors and works*
Lloyd, Harold, 267
Local Autonomy Law, 526
Londontown, 90-91, 228, 332, 371, 405, 422, 436, 514-15
Loodensteijn, Jan Joosten, 333
Loti, Pierre, 74, 83, 107, 114, 252
lotuses, 137-38
Love Consummated in Heaven (film), 320
Love Letter (Niwa), 569
Low City (Shitamachi), 24, 28-30, 28, 97-98, 188-89, 232, 233, 244-45, *277*; air raids and, 414-15, 420; areas comprising, 28; baseball and, 348-49; boundaries of, 205, 243-44; cultural developments in, 566; decline of, 292-93; earthquake of 1923 and, 24, 25, 28, 293; fires in, 78; in Kubota's writings, 80; Kabuki and, 486; pleasure quarters of, 30; population of, 49; street life of, 570-71; suburban growth and, 327; *see also specific wards and districts*
lumberyards, 213 *and illus.*, 219, 295
Lytton Report, 320

MacArthur, Gen. Douglas, 421, 445, *446*, 474, 476, 496, 550
machiai, 174, 183, 402, 512
machiai politics, 512
machiaijaya (rendezvous teahouse), 181
Madonna, 589
Maeda estate, 126, 137, 236, 237
Magic Flute, The, 262
Mainichi (newspaper), 203
Makioka Sisters, The (Tanizaki), 134, 383, 396, 408, 410, 550
"mama", use of term, 269-70
Manchuria, 302, 316, 320, 378, 382, 420, 482, 535
manga magazines, 594-95
"mannequin girl", 323-24
"mansions", 539-40, 597
Manzai comic monologues, 345
Maria Luz affair (1872), 174
Marine Insurance building, 34, 254, 550
Marunouchi Building, 34, 254, 423, 432, 435, 436, 515, 550
Marunouchi district, 89-91, 227, 254, 329, *514,* 515, 577, 602; as city center, 292, 294; growth of, 435; Londontown, 332, 405, 422-23, 436, 514-15; in postwar period, 422-23; real estate and, 600
Masakado (tenth-century general), 141
masher *(chikan).* 597
Mason, W. B., 106, 162, 258
Matsui Sumako, *see* Sumako
Matsushita, 600
Matsuya department store, 319, 390, 402
May Day 1952, 473-75, *474*
mayors, 48, 94, 95, 254, 368, 372, 374, 444, 573
Mears, Helen, 405
meat, eating of, 111-12

Meguro Ward, 328, 515
Meiji Confectionery Company, 267
Meiji constitution, 36-37, 49, 105, 202, 404, 462
Meiji emperor, 24, 31, 40, 44, *50*, 67, 137, 159, 230, 236, 516, 546; funeral of, 114, 243, 248-50, 306 *and illus.*; illness and death of, 252-3 247-48 *and illus.*, 292
Meiji Gakuin (school), 170
Meiji Restoration, 40, 99, 600
Meiji Shrine, 49, 137, 254, 273, 306, 348, 376, 417, 504, 509
Meiji University, 212
Meijiza theater, 159, 191, 265, 449, 450
meitengai (shopping center), 424, 499
Metropole Hotel, 58
Mikado, The (Gilbert and Sullivan), 44-45, 155
mikoshi (god-seats), 139, *220*, 383
military barracks, 325
milk bars, 341
Minamoto Yoshiie, 116
Minato Ward, 439, 440, 557, 560, 568, 603
Mine, Dick, 384, 453
Ministry of Justice, 228
Minobe Ryōkichi, 526, 572-74
Minobe Tatsukichi, 404
misdemeanors, 102, 478
Mito Tokugawa estate, 236
Mishima Yukio, 16, 110, 466, 479, 536, 548-50 *and illus.*
Misora Hibari, 524
Mitsubishi enterprises, 88, 109, 235, 294; bombing of, 585-86 *and illus.*, Londontown, 90, 332, 405, 422-23, 436, 514-15
Mitsubishi Meadow (Gambler's Meadow), 87-91, 93, 95-96, 98, 123, 133, 158, 169, 199, 228, 254

Mitsui Bank, 86, 94, *187*, 192 *and illus.*, 192-93, 479, 515
Mitsui building, 551, 553
Mitsui Club, 83
Mitsui dry-goods store, 119
Mitsui family, 243
Mitsukoshi Department Store, 25, 86, 94, 190, 448, 476, 477, 565
Mitsukoshi Theater, 448
Miura Tamaki, 267
Miyatoza theater, 158-59, 260, 265
Miyukidōri street, 516
Mizutani Yaeko, 449
mobo (modern boy), 260, 309, 323-24, 325
Mochizuki Yūko, 356, 357, 393
modeling business, 324
modernism, 244
"modern life", 323
moga (modern girl), 260, 309, 323-24, 325
Molotov cocktails, 585
Mona Lisa, 589
monorail, 500, 507, 551
Monroe, Marilyn, 451, 589
Mori Arinori, 202
Mori of Nagato, 42
Mori Ogai, *see* Ogai
Morita Kanya, *see* Kanya
Moritaza, *see* Shintomiza theater
morning glories, 135, 137
Morse, E. S., 59, 63-64, 78-80, 81, 102, 143-44, 154-55, 190, 215, 237, 264
Morse, W. B., 214
motels, 438
Motomachi Park, 299
Moulin Rouge, 366
Mount Fuji, 142, 353, 559, 599; miniature, 128-29
movies, 267, 349-52, 410, 450, 451-52; *see also specific movies*

movie theaters, 128, 260, 350-51, 394-95, 452, 566
Mukōjima district, 84, 215, 219-20
mulberry trees, 231-32
murderesses, 154, 231, 266, 401, 586
music, 167, 172, 320-21, 366, 411-12; *see also* opera
music halls, 128, 261, 325, 349; *see also* Yose
musumegidayū (theater music), 167, 263
My City (railway station), 552-53

Nagai, Frank, 453, 498
Nagai Kafū, *see* Kafū
Nagoya, postwar reconstruction of, 422
Nagoya Tokugawa estate, 236
Nakamura Kichiemon, 446-47
Nakasu Island, 70
Nakayama Shimpei, 277, 321, 351
Namba Daisuke. 301-02
Naniwabushi, 366
Nara, 45, 383, 519
narikin (*nouveau riehe*), 199
Narita airport, 596, 602
Narushima Ryūhoku, *see* Ryūhoku
nationalism, 170, 171, 358, 397, 548
National Museum (Ueno), 127, 312-13, 406, 519, 589
National Theater, 161, 486
Natsume Sōseki, 9, 62, 93, 124, 238, 266
Negishi district, 210
Nemuro district, 48
neologisms, 323, 403, 453; of Taishō period, 269
"Nesoberu Asakusa" (Takami), 390-92
neurosis *(noiroze)*, 493
New Chronicle of Yanagibashi (Ryūkyo Shinski), (Ryūhoku), 182

New Otani, 550
New Shimabara licensed quarter, 54, 152
newspapers, 203, 302-03, 345, 558
New Year, 139, 142, 144
New York, 574-75
Nezu district, 175, 181, 237, 238
NHK (Nihon Hōsō Kyōkai), 348, 349, 399, 451, 452, 510, 533, 558
Nichigeki (Nihon Gekijō) (Japan Theater), 309, 395, 410, 457, 559, 560
Nichinichi (newspaper), 303
Nihombashi Bridge, 86, 94, 122, 186, 188, 192, 194, *196*, 370, 499, 577
Nihombashi River, 188-89, 190
Nihombashi Ward, 28-29, 32, 33, 39, 62, 71, 77, 91, 98, 186-97, *191*, 226, 227, 232, 240-41, 293-94, 325, 329, 332-33, 435, 450, 516, 592-93; as financial center, 472, 193; fish market in, 94-95, *189*, pleasure quarters in, 191, 195; pride of place of, 196; shrines and temples of, 191; during Taishō, 258
Nihon Hōsō Kyōkai (Japan Broadcasting Corporation), *see* NHK
Nihon University, 478
Nikolai Cathedral, 51, 84-85, 132, 194
Nikkatsu Building, 436, *437*
ningen dokku (physical exams), 494
Ningyōchō, 324, 325-26, 450
Niwa Fumio, 569
Niwaka dances, 176
Normanton incident (1886), 110
Nō drama, 133, 292
Nogi Maresuke, Gen., 114, 306
noiroze (neurosis), 493
Nosaka Sanzo, 475

Occupation, American (after World War II), 128

Odakyū, 352

O-den (murderess), 154, 165, 166 *and illus.*, 209, 231, 401, 491, 534

Oe Michiko, *455*

office buildings, 435-36

office lady, 272, 533

Ogai (novelist), 9, 156, 238

Ogasawara (Bonin) Islands, 47

Ogawa Isshin, 90, 227; photographs by, *86, 104*

Okawabata (The Bank of the Big River) (Osanai), 69-71

okiya (geisha residence), 592

okushon (condominium), 597

Olympics, 381-82, 399, 495-96; 1964, 437, 496-508, *505*

Olympic Stadium, *517*

O-kinu (murderess), 165, 231

omnibuses, 60, 193

Omori, shell middens of, 63

Omura Masujirō, 45

Onna Kengeki, 454, *455*

Ooka Shōhei, 334, 401

opera, 261-63, 353-54; Asakusa, 261, 263-64

operetta, 262, 263

O-sada (Abe Sada), 401-03 *402*, 586

Osaka, 44, 48, 53, 98, 134, 150, 158, 302-03, 315, 339, 340, 345-46, 366, 595

Oshima, suicides on, 320

Osanai Kaoru, 69, 160, 171, 184, 224, 265

Ota Dōkan, 371, 517, 519

Otemachi Building, 436

Otsu Incident (1891), 301-03

O-tsuya, murder of (1910), 89-90

O-ume (murderess), 154, 191, 231, 236

Oya Sōichi, 378, 545

Ozaki Yukio, 48, 94

Ozu Yasujirō, 451

pachinko (pinball), 463-64 *and illus.*

palanquins, 37, 60

panic of 1927, 300, 378

"panpan girls," 459

"papa," use of term, 270-71, 385, 403

Parkes, Sir Harry, 113

Parco department store, 561-62, 562-63, 565 *and illus.*

Park Avenue (Shibuya), 561-62 *and illus.*

parking-lot business, 537

parks, 96, 124-32, 299, 434-35, 435; *see also specific parks*

parties, during Rokumeikan era, 109-10

peach blossoms, 136

pear blossoms, 136

Pearl Harbor, 537

pedestrian paradise, 581-82 *and illus.*, 583

Peers Club, 83, 110

people's saloons, 412

"pencil buildings", 500

peragoro (Asakusa opera devotees), 263-64

performers, street, *509*

Perry, Commodore Matthew Calbraith, 40, 132, 182, 218, 451

Peter coffeehouse, *394*

Piss Alley, 429, 483-84 *and illus.*, 552

place names, 526-28

planning, city, 602-06

Plantain café, 200-01

plastic surgery, 494

pleasure centers (or quarters), 55-56, 163; of Edo, 30, 36, 37, 39, 151; in postwar period, 457-58; Shinjuku, 334-36, *335*, television and,

511-12; *see also* licensed quarters; unlicensed quarters; *and specific quarters and districts*

plum blossoms, 135-36, 139, 154, 215

police, 358, 363, 367, 396, 442, 453

police boxes, 148, 247, 585

political parties, 255, 298, 378

population, 49-50, 52, 232, 576; of Edo, 32, 42; during Taishō, 253-54; following 1923 earthquake, 327; 1932 expansion and, 373-7; in postwar period, 440-41

ports, opening of, 40

Portsmouth Treaty (1905), 147-48

post-stations (Five Mouths), 178-81

postwar period, 422-494; black markets and, 425-29 *and illus.*, *427, 428,* 433; crime and, 476-77, 478-82; emperor and, 446; gangs and, 429-30; geisha and, 458, 460; government and, 442-45; homelessness during, 431 *and illus.*; housing and, 433-34; population during, 440-41; rationing and, 432, 433; *see also* American Occupation

preaching thief, 401

prints, 65-67, 75-76, 110

private detectives, 105

produce market (Kanda), 211

professorial neighborhood (*gakusha-machi*), 239

prosperity, naming periods of, 493, 537-38

prostitution, 37, 117-18, 173-74, 206, 461-62, 462-63, 487, 529-33; outlawing of (1958), 178, 180; *see also* brothels; courtesans; geisha; geisha districts; licensed quarters; pleasure centers; pleasure quarters; soaplands

public transportation, 60, 332, 376, 417, 493; *see also specific types*

Pu-yi, 382, 535

rabbits, 112

radio, 349, 450-51, 472

ragpickers *(bataya),* 379, 380 *and illus.*, 598

railroads, 62-64, 178-80, 220, 294, 315, 324-25, 329, 331, 332-33, 352, 476, 492; prints of, 65-67

"Rainbow" (Kawabata), 358, 359

Rakugo comic monologues, 345, 346, 349, 351, 450, 451, 535

rationing, 425, 428, 433

reading from left to right, 105

real estate, 576, 595-99, 602-06

reconstruction (after 1923 earthquake), 295-96, 308, 312-13

restaurants, 316, 412, *543*

retail business, 294, 314-16, 507; *see also* department stores

reviews, 354-67, *355, 361,* 385-87, 593-94

rice riots (1866), 40-41, 42

rickshaws, 58-60

right, radical, 549-50, 589

Rigoletto, 263

Rikidōzan, 470-71, 508

riots, 473-75, *474,* 520, 536, 548, 549; of 1918, 255-56, after Portsmouth Treaty (1905), 147-48; rice (1866), 41-42

rivers, 68-72; *see also* floods

River Sumida, The (Kafū), 72, 136, 159, 174, 213, 215

Robun (journalist), 166

Rokumeikan, 67, 82-83 *and illus.*, 108-10, 229

Rokumeikan era, 107-10, 113

Roppongi, 147, 242, 325, 510-11

Rossi, G. V., 261-62, 267, 354

Royal movie house, 262
Rule Assistance Association, 384
Russia, 114
Russo-Japanese War (1904-1905),
    147-49
Ryōgoku, broad alley of, 214-15
Ryōgoku Bridge, 214-15
Ryogoku district, 568
Ryokuu (novelist), 127, 224
Ryōunkaku (Twelve Storys), 27, 84
Ryūhoku (journalist), 182-83
*Ryūkyo Shinshi (New Chronicle of
    Yanagibashi)* (Ryūhoku), 182
Ryūsei (painter), 163, 253

Sadanji (Kabuki actor), 265-66
Saigō Takamori, 127, 433
St. Luke's Hospital, 56
Saijō Yaso, 321, 343
Saionji, Prince, 158
Saitō Ryokuu, *see* Ryokuu
Salvation Army, 117-18
sakariba (bustling place), 324-25,
    353, 355, 392, 393, 400, 497,
    507, 567, 580; *see also specific
    places*
Sakurabashi (Sakura Bridge), 582
"salaryman", 328, 344
San Francisco Treaty, 334, 459, 461
Sanger, Margaret, 267-68
Sanjusangenbori, 424
Sannō festival, 141
Sansom, G. B., 259
Sanya, 521-23, *522*, 528, 603
Sanyūtei Enchō, *see* Enchō
Sanyūtei Kimba, 535-36
Sartre, Jean-Paul, 589
Satō Hachirō, 452
Satomi Ton, 234, 418
Sawamura Tanosuke, 106
scandals, government, 49, 369, 371,
    442, 525, 572

Scarlet Gang of Asakusa (Kawabata),
    297, 342, 353, 355, 359, 379,
    389, 397, 498
schools, 98-99; missionary, 202;
    Taishō, 273
school uniforms, 111
sea bathing, 114, 223, 403
seasons and seasonal observances,
    134-44, 273-74
Seibu enterprises, 485, 490, 562,
    590
Seibu Parco, *567*
self-image, national, 495, 506
Seiyōken Hotel (now restaurant),
    58, 126
Senjū (post-station), 178, 180
Setagaya Ward, 419, 441, 497, 504,
    591
sewage disposal, 95, 274, 503, 574
Seward, William H., 114
sexual equality, 317, 319
sexual mores, 343-44, 354, 357-58,
    363-64, 449, 454, 554
shadows, Tanizaki on, 92-93
"shan", 323-24
Shiba Detached Palace, 114, 223
Shibaguchi, *see* Shimbashi
Shiba Park, 223, 224, 349, 420,
    479, 501, 519
Shibaura, 223
Shiba Ward, 178, 221; temples and
    cemeteries of, 222
Shibusawa Eiichi, 80-1, 85, 153,
    254; mansion of, 86
Shibuya, 242, 315, 336, *337,* 376-
    77; as chic, 561-63; as *fukutoshin,*
    488-89; Hachikō, 400-0 *and illus.*;
    naming of, 375-76; Olympics and,
    497, 498, 504, 507-08; public
    transportation and, 332, 336; as
    sakariba, 324-25, 393; Shinjuku
    compared to, 488-89

Shibuya Station, 64, 400, 497, 561
Shiga Naoya, 463
Shigure (playwright), 16, 35, 49, 62, 101, 102, 103, 160, 185, 194, 195, 197, 211-12
Shimamura Hōgetsu, *see* Hōgetsu
Shimazu Saburō, 60
Shimbashi Club, 169
Shimbashi district, 69, 76, 220-21, 225, 592, 593; geisha quarter in, 183-84, 225
Shimbashi Embujō, 396, 410, 417, 446, 447
Shimbashi Incident (1946), 429
Shimbashi Station, 27, 63, 64, 83, 94, 114-15, 121, 203, 224, 225, 226 *and illus.*, 498
Shimizu Kisuke, 54
Shimooka Renjō, 66
Shimoyama incident, 476-78
Shinagawa district, 175, 178-80, 376, 457
Shinjuku Central Park, 551
Shinjuku Daiichi Gekijō, 486
Shinjuku district, 47, 95, 175, 178-80, 232, 315, 443; air raids and, 419; as city center, 329, 557-58; as *fukutoshin*, 483-85; growth of, 333-36; literature and, 569; moving of government offices to, 292; Olympics (1964) and, 513; pleasure quarters, 334-36, *335*, 560-61; reviews in, 366-67; as *sakariba*, 324, 324, 393; Shibuya compared to, 48-89; slums, 335; street stalls, 433; strip shows, 453, 454; *see also* Kabukichō district
Shinjuku Eastmouth, 514, 567
Shinjuku Southmouth, 429, 483-84
Shinjuku Westmouth, *288*, 515, 519, 523, 551, *552*, 557, 559, 564, 583, 602, 603, *605*
Shinkabukiza, 486

Shinnittetsu, 600
Shinobazu Pond, 11, 124, 125, 126, 137, *138*, 466, *467*, 566, 571
Shintomiza theater, 116, 151-52, 153-54 *and illus.*, 155, 157, 158, 159, 204, 265
Shinto religion, 134
Shioiri, 522, 603
Shirokiya (Tōkyū) department store, 118, 120, 121 *and illus.*, 258, 294, 315 *and illus.*, 319, 357, 510, 516
Shiseidō (cosmetics firm), 200, 252, 418
Shitamachi, *see* Low City
Shitaya gang, 210
Shishi Bunroku, 569
Shitaya Park, 209
Shitaya Ward, 25, 205, 208, 209, 210-11, 298, 317, 419
Shōchiku, 158, 394-95, 448, 449
shoes, 110-11
shooting stalls, 84
shop girls, 62, 120, 319
shops and shopping, 118-23, 314-17, 333-34, 424, 432-33, 472-73; *see also* bazaars; black market; department stores; supermarkets
Shōriki Matsutarō, 255, 302, 369, 466
Shōyo (novelist/dramatist), 266, 341-42, 349
Shōwa, meaning of term, 305
Shōwa Avenue (Showadori), 298, 312, *313*, 317, 423
Shōwa emperor, *307*, 308, 421, 445-46 *and illus.*, 475, 546
shrine festivals, 141-42
shrines, 132, 139-40, 162, 191; *see also* god-seats; god-seat festivals
sideshows, 75, 209, 342, 363, 397
Sino-Japanese War (1894-1895), 142, 146, 147, 175, 200, 488

Sixth District (Asakusa), 128-29, *350*, 356, 357, 388, 390, 391, 432, 529

skyscrapers, 550

slang, *see* neologisms

slums, 221, 236, 521, 540, 579

snow viewing, 134-35, 139

Society for Improving the Theater, 155-56

soaplands, 531, *532*, 556, 583

Socialist Party, 520, 529, 548-49

Soeta Azembō, 353

sōkaiya (general-meeting business), 524, 525, 587

Somehow Crystal (Tanaka), 555-56

Spencer (balloonist), 117, 154, 157, 267, 271, 346

spiritual mobilization, 384, 403

sports, 399; golf, 591; *see also* baseball; Sumō wrestling; swimmers

spring, 135-37, 140-41, 144-45

standard of living, 439

"stick girl," 311, 323, 324

Strange Tale from East of the River, A (Kafū), 323, 527-28

street life, 235, 397, 570, 571, 582, 583

street lights, 92-94

street minstrels *(enkashi),* 167-68, 171

street numbers, 105-06

street pattern, 50-51, 96, 233, 298, 422, 423

street performers, *509*

streets, 96; High City, 233; house numbers on, 195-96; naming of, 561-62; widening of, 499-500; traffic on left side of, 105

strip shows, 354, 395, 556, 566, 594

students, 237-38, 271, 344, 473, 548 *and illus.,* 552-53, 601-02

student uniforms, 111

suburbs, 326-29

subways, 34, 497, 501, 528-29

sufu (staple fiber), 403, 409

Sugamo Prison, 409, 491*and illus.,* 519, 551, 564

Sugawara Michizane, 136

Suginami Ward, 419, 573, 574

suicide, 319-23, 412, 534-35

Sullivan, Arthur, 44-45

Sukiyabashi (Sukiya Bridge), 498, 500

Sumako (actress), 172, 266-67

Sumida embankment, 135, 136, 139, 216, 273, 274, 567

Sumida Park, 293, 308, 312, 345, 369

Sumida River, 24, 41, 142, 159, 295, 308, 323, 369, 415, 434, 440, 441, 450, 457, 459, 468, 501, 503, 526, 531, 546, 593; flood-control devices on, 216-17, 257; flooding of, 72; "opening" of, 115, 142, 247

Sumō wrestling, 156, 168-69, 214-15, 274, 347-48, 399, 468-71, *471*, 544, 590-91

Sunshine Building, 535, 564 *and illus.*

Suntory (whiskey maker), 599

super high-rises, 551

supermarkets, 494, 538, 560

Supreme Court, 239, 480, 532

Susaki district, 457, 530-31

Susaki licensed quarter, 218

Suzugamori, 528

Suzuki Shunichi, 486-88, 573, 575, 600

Suzumoto, 450-51

sweet potato, 432, 433

swimmers, 495

swordplay troupes, 365

Tachikawa Base: Ten Solid Years of Rape, 520

Taihō, 544
Taira Masakado, *see* Masakado
Taishō democracy, 255, 276
Taishō emperor, 250-51
Taishō era, 298, 304-06 *and illus.*,
    305, 317, 323-26, 329-30
Taishō Hakurankai (Taishō Exposi-
    tion) (1914), 251
Taishō look, 251-53, 276
Taishō Period, 251-77
Taitō Ward, 441, 456, 566, 567
Tajiri Inajirō, 254
Takahama Kyoshi, 89
Takahashi O-den, 154, 165, *166*,
    209, 401, 491, 534
Takami Jun, 389, 412, 421, 535,
    569
Takano Fruits Parlor, 334, 429
Takarazuka theater, 117-19, 176,
    178, 305-6, 335
Takeda Rintarō, 341, 342, 344,
    535, 569
Takehisa Yumeji, *see* Yumeji
Tama district, 47
Tamanoi district, 321-22, 336, 388
Tameike Pond, 137
Tameike reservoir, 68
Tamura Taijirō, 459, 569
Tanaka Giichi, 301
Tanaka Kakuei, 586
Tanaka Kinuyo, 451
Tanaka Yasuo, 555-56
Tange Kenzō, 517 *and illus.*, 603
Tani, Tony, 453
Tanizaki Junichirō, 29, 46, 69-70,
    153, 199, 293, 310-12, 339-40,
    494; at English school, 56; and
    fire baskets, 78; on shadows and
    dark places, 92-93; *see also Maki-
    oka Sisters, The*
Tatsuno, 64
Taut, Bruno, 400-01

taxis, 60, 160-61, 259, 409, 433,
    493, 537, 582
Tayama Katai, 96, 193
tea bushes, 231-32
tea ceremony *(chanoyu)*, 36, 292
teahouses, 55, brothels and, 173,
    175, 178, 238; rendezvous *(machi-
    aijaya)*, 181; shady *(kagemajaya)*,
    238; theater, 152, 153-54, 157-58
tea shops *(kissaten)*, 344, 461
teeth, blackening of, 101, 102, 207
telephone service, 120, 270 *and il-
    lus., 317*
television, 397, 451, 452, 511-12,
    545, 558, 566, 594
temples, 139, 163, 191, 206, 209-
    10, 241
Tempō sumptuary edicts, 39
Tennōji Temple, 209
tenkō (recanting), 405
Terajima, 527-28
Terry, Philip, 74-75, 252, 257-58
theaters, 248, 394-97, 446-49, 566-
    67 *and illus.*, 593; of Edo, 37-38;
    Kabuki, *see* Kabuki theater; movie,
    128-29, 260; Nō, 133; Western,
    265-67; *see also* movie theaters; Nō
    drama; reviews; Yose theater; *and
    individual establishments*
"third nationals," 429, 463, 568
Tiger Gate Incident (1926), 301,
    302, 303
Tochinishiki, 470, 544
Tōhō, 394-95, 449, 560
Tōjin O-kichi, 358
Tōjō Hideki, 414, 420, 491, 519
Tokaidō highway, 178, 186, 223
Tokiwa bridge, *29*
Tokuda Shūsei, 234, 238
Tokugawa castle, 77
Tokugawa cemetery (tombs), 126,
    221
Tokugawa Musei, 393

Tokugawa regime, 28, 32, 40, 42, 43, 130; end of, 40-45, 46

Tokutomi Roka, 232

Tokyo: boundaries of, 47, 254; as capital district, 48; as a collection of villages, 51, 269, 276; establishment of, as capital, 44-46; government of, 48, 269; pronunciations of name, 44; *see also* Edo; High City; Low City

Tokyo Central Station, 62, 63, 76, 82, 87, 89, 90, 123, 225, 294, 332, 377, 384, 422, 423, 490, 498, 501, 513, 515, 517, 520, 569, 577, 603

Tokyo Hotel, 229

Tokyo International Airport, 585

Tokyo March, 351

"Tokyo Ondo" ("Tokyo Dance"), 320-21

Tokyo Onsen, 424-25

Tokyo Prefecture, 47

Tokyo School of English, *see* First Higher School

Tokyo Shibaura (manufacturing firm), 223

Tokyo Stadium, 545, 579

Tokyo Theater (Tōkyō Gekijō; Togeki), 545, 579

Tokyo Tower, 223, 479, 492, 510-11, 517-18 *and illus.*, 551, 564, 569

Tokyo University, 33, 53, 126, 348, 443, 479, 540, 548 *and illus.*, 601, 602

Tomioka Hachiman, 219

Tōkyū (Tokyo Express), 328, 336, 489

Tōkyū (Shirokiya) department store, 516, 562, 563

totalitarianism, 384, 403

tourist buses, 435, 594

Tōyoko department store, 330, 336

traffic, 492

traffic on left side of street, 105

transportation, 58-65, 97, 275-76, 483, 488-90; in Edo, 37-38; Olympics (1964) and, 496-502; *see also* public transportation; *specific modes of transportation*

Treaty of San Francisco, 334, 459, 461

tribes *(zoku),* 493-94, 508, 516, 536, 553, 560, 583

trolleys, 60-62, 223

trolley system, 60, 62, 94, 275, 332, 486-87, 492, 578

Tsubouchi Shōyo, 266, 341-42, 349

Tsukiji fish market, *370*

Tsukiji quarter, 53-58, 53

Tsukuba university and research complex, 601-02

tuberculosis, 494

Turkish baths, 34, 531, *532*, 556

Twelve Storys (Ryōunkaku), *26*, 84, 85-86 *and illus.*, 129, 249, 264, 296-97, 353

typhus, 430-31

uchigeba (politically motivated fights), 584, 585

Ueno, 45, 91, 124-25, 208, 324, 326, 330, 331, 567-68

Ueno Park, 25, 45, 113, 125, 126, 137, 206, 208, 312, 317, 352, 466, 478, 519, 566, 568

Ueno Station, 125, 206, 316, 419, 431, 597

Ueno Zoo, 412, 500

Uguisudani (Warbler Valley), 137

Umesao Tadao, 518

Umezaki Haruo, 475

Under What Stars (Takami), 389, 390, 392

underworld, 268, 429, 463, 470, 525

uniforms, student, 111
United States embassy, 148, 228, 231, 439, 446, 551, 563
United States legation, 51, 58, 229; attack on (1905), 148
universities, 212, 237, 328, 566, 601-02
unlicensed quarters, 335-36, 457-58
Ushigome Ward, 325, 413, 479, 527

vacant lots, Kafū on, 132
variety or vaudeville halls (Yose), 37
vending machines, 316, 503-04, 539
violence, 205-6, 253-4; *see also* crime
vogues: happenings and events, 508-09; *pachinko,* 463-64 *and illus.*; suicide, 319-23, 534-35; yo-yos, 320; *see also* tribes

Wakanohana, 470, 544
Wakayama Tokugawa estate, 230, 236
wards, 226-27, 240-41, 375-76, 442-45
Waseda, 139
Waseda University, 366-67, 579
Washington Heights, 489, 504, 507, 510, 561
waste disposal, 95, 274-75
watch of the twenty-sixth night, 140
Waters, Thomas, 73, 81
water supply, 47, 95, 502
water vendors, 95, 275
waterways, 37-38, 68, 69, 106, 218, 299, 314, 498; *see also* canals
weddings, 105, 412
weeds, Kafū on, 132
wells, 27, 32, 95, 237, 275
Westerners, *see* foreigners
Western influences, 101-49
westernization, 131, 201, 311, 312, 328

Westmouth (Ikebukuro,) 565
What Happened the Night the Lights Went Out (Kafū), 387, 388
What Is Your Name? (radio serial), 498
white-collar crime, 524, 587
Whitney, Clara, 110-11, 116-17, 144, 154, 215, 222
willows, 76, 259 *and illus.*
Wirgman, Charles, 66
wisteria, 136, 219, 264
Woman in the Rented Room, The (Kafū), 300
women: clothing of, 107, 319, 326, 510; cosmetics and, 326; department stores and, 316; in the performing arts, 167, 172; in police force, 442; in reviews, 356-58; in *sakariba,* 325-26; Sumō and, 168; during Taishō, 252, 266, 270-71; tooth-blackening by, 102; working, 317-18
Women's Higher Normal School, 237
woodcuts, 32, 68, 126, 194
World Trade Center, 551
World War I, 254, 255, 262
World War II: air raids. 413-20, *416;* Asakusa and, 385-93, *394,* baseball and, 398-99; government reorganization and, 408-09; reviews and, 385-87; surrender, 420-21; *see also* postwar period
Wright, Frank Lloyd, 268, 507, 577-78 *and illus.*
writers, 244-45

xenophobia, 27, 146, 403, 404

Yaesuguchi (Yaesu Mouth), 333
Yamamoto cabinet, 300
Yamanote, *see* High City
Yamanote line, 332, 578

Yamazaki, 479

Yanagibashi 69, 225, 225, 543-44; geisha quarter in, 182-83

Yanaka district, 209, 244

Yanaka Pagoda, *534*, 535

Yasuda Castle, 548, 553, 585

Yasuda Zenjirō, 49

Yasui Seiichirō, 421

Yasukuni Jinja (shrine), 133, 135, 139, 274, 384, 589

Yayoichō, 528

Year of the Wild Boar (Mears), 405

Yodobashi reservoir, 483, *552*

Yokohama, 44, 56, 60, 62-63, 63, 106, 602, 604

Yomiuri Giants, 170, 348-49

Yomiuri Shimbun (newspaper), 302-03, 369, 476

yoromeki, 536

Yose (variety or vaudeville halls), 37, 160-61, 162, 349, 450-51, 528, 566, 571, 594

Yoshichō district, 592

Yoshida Shigeru, 444

Yoshiwara, 28, 37, 39, 40, 47, 77, 171-78, *173*, *177*, 210, 487, 511, 528, 530, 532, 533; after 1923 earthquake, 297, 321-23; festivals in, 175-77; fires in, 77 *and illus.*, 177-78; rebuilding of (after 1911 fire), 178

Yotsuya Ward, 47, 52, 178, 232, 236, 486

Young, John Russell, 51-52, 269

Yoyogi, 517

yo-yos, 320

yukaihan, 588

Yumeji (artist), 252, 259

Yumeji girl, 252, 253 *and illus.*, 260, 276

Yūrakuchō Mullion, 559, 563

Yūrakuchō Station, 459

Yushima quarter, 238

Yushima Shrine, 136

Zephyr (film), 452

Zero Year celebrations (1940), 382-84

Zōjōji temple, 222

zoku (tribes), 493-94, 508, 516, 536, 553, 560, 583

TUTTLE CLASSICS

LITERATURE (* = for sale in Japan only)

ABE, Kobo 安部公房
The Woman in the Dunes 砂の女 ISBN 978-4-8053-0900-1*

AKUTAGAWA, Ryunosuke 芥川龍之介
Japanese Short Stories 芥川龍之介短編集 ISBN 978-4-8053-1450-0*
Kappa 河童 ISBN 978-4-8053-0901-8*
Rashomon and the Other Stories 羅生門 ISBN 978-4-8053-1463-0

DAZAI, Osamu 太宰治
No Longer Human 人間失格 ISBN 978-4-8053-1017-5*
The Setting Sun 斜陽 ISBN 978-4-8053-0672-7

HEARN, Lafcadio ラフカディオ・ハーン
Glimpses Of Unfamiliar Japan 知られざる日本の面影
    ISBN 978-4-8053-1025-0
In Ghostly Japan 霊の日本 ISBN 978-0-8048-3661-6;
    ISBN 978-4-8053-0749-6*
Kokoro 心 ISBN 978-0-8048-4886-2
Kwaidan 怪談 ISBN 978-0-8048-3662-3; ISBN 978-4-8053-0750-2*
Lafcadio Hearn's Japan ISBN 978-4-8053-0873-8

INOUE, Yasushi 井上靖
The Samurai Banner of Furin Kazan 風林火山 ISBN 978-0-8048-3701-9

KAWABATA, Yasunari 川端康成
The Izu Dancer and Other Stories 伊豆の踊り子 ISBN 978-4-8053-0744-1*
The Old Capital 古都 ISBN 978-4-8053-0972-8*
Snow Country 雪国 ISBN 978-4-8053-0635-2*

MISHIMA, Yukio 三島由紀夫
Five Modern Noh Plays 近代能楽集 ISBN 978-4-8053-1032-8*
Spring Snow 春の雪 ISBN 978-4-8053-0970-4*
The Temple of the Golden Pavilion 金閣寺 ISBN 978-4-8053-0637-6*

MORI, Ogai 森鴎外
The Wild Geese 雁 ISBN 978-4-8053-0884-4

NAGAI, Kafu 永井荷風
Geisha in Rivalry 腕くらべ ISBN 978-0-8048-3324-0

NATSUME, Soseki 夏目漱石
And Then それから ISBN 978-4-8053-1141-7
Botchan 坊っちゃん ISBN 978-4-8053-1263-6
I Am a Cat 吾輩は猫である ISBN 978-0-8048-3265-6;
    ISBN 978-4-8053-1097-7*
Kokoro こころ ISBN 978-4-8053-0746-5*
The Three-Cornered World 草枕 ISBN 978-4-8053-0201-9*

TANIZAKI, Junichiro 谷崎潤一郎
  In Praise of Shadows 陰影礼賛 ISBN 978-4-8053-0665-9*
  The Makioka Sisters 細雪 ISBN 978-4-8053-1189-9*

OTHERS

Donald Richie Memories of the Warrior Kumagai 熊谷直実
  ISBN 978-4-8053-0847-9*

EDOGAWA, Rampo Japanese Tales of Mystery & Imagination 乱歩短編集
  ISBN 978-4-8053-1193-6

John Allyn 47 Ronin 四十七士 ISBN 978-4-8053-1465-4

OE, Kenzaburo A Personal Matter 個人的な体験 ISBN 978-4-8053-0641-3*

OOKA, Shohei Fires on Plain 野火 ISBN 978-0-8048-1379-2

Richard Neery Japanese Mistress 2号さん ISBN 978-4-8053-0656-7*

SUMII, Sue The River With No Bridge 橋のない川 ISBN 978-4-8053-0650-5*

TAKEYAMA, Michio Harp of Burma ビルマの竪琴
  ISBN 978-4-8053-1488-3*

TSUBOI, Sakae Twenty-Four Eyes 二十四の瞳 ISBN 978-4-8053-0772-4*

YOSHIKAWA, Eiji The Heike Story 新平家物語 ISBN 978-4-8053-1044-1

ANTHOLOGY 選集

Ellery Queen's Japanese Detective Stories 日本傑作推理１２選
  ISBN 978-4-8053-0851-6*

Arthur Waley The Noh Plays of Japan ISBN 978-4-8053-1033-5

Donald Keene (compiled & edited)
  Anthology of Japanese Literature ISBN 978-4-8053-1014-4*
  Modern Japanese Literature 現代日本文学 ISBN 978-4-8053-0752-6*
  Japanese Literature 日本文学の手引 ISBN 978-4-8053-0753-3

Ivan Morris Modern Japanese Stories: An Anthology 近代日本文学
  ISBN 978-4-8053-0751-9*

Yei Theodora Ozaki Japanese Fairly Tales 日本のお伽噺
  ISBN 978-4-8053-0881-3

CLASSICS

IHARA, Saikaku 井原西鶴
  Five Women Who Loved Love 好色五人女 ISBN 978-4-8053-1012-0
  This Scheming World 世間胸算用 ISBN 978-4-8053-0643-7

KINO, Tsurayuki The Tosa Diary 土佐日記 ISBN 978-4-8053-0754-0

Mother of Michitsuna The Gossamer Years 蜻蛉日記
  ISBN 978-0-8048-1123-1

MURASAKI Shikibu 紫式部

Kencho Suematsu *(tans.)* The Tale of Genji 源氏物語（末松訳）
ISBN 978-4-8053-1464-7

Arthur Waley *(tans.)* The Tale of Genji 源氏物語(ウエイリー訳)
ISBN 978-4-8053-1081-6

Edward G. Seidensticker *(tans.)* The Tale of Genji (2 Volumes)
源氏物語(サイデンステッカー訳) ISBN 978-4-8053-0921-6*

Naoshi Koriyama & Bruce Allen *(tans.)* Japanese Tales from Times Past
今昔物語集 ISBN 978-4-8053-1341-1

William N. Porter *(tans.)* A Hundred Verses from Old Japan 百人一首
ISBN 978-4-8053-0853-0

YOSHIDA , Kenko Essays in Idleness 徒然草 ISBN 978-4-8053-0631-4*

HISTORY

A.L. Sadler Shogun: The Life of Tokugawa Ieyasu 徳川家康の生涯
ISBN 978-4-8053-1042-7

B.H. Chamberlain Kojiki 古事記 ISBN 978-4-8053-1215-5

Charles J. Dunn Everyday Life in Traditional Japan 江戸の暮らし
ISBN 978-4-8053-1005-2

Edward G. Seidensticker Tokyo From Edo to Showa
ISBN 978-4-8053-1024-3

Edwin O. Reischauer Japan: The Story of a Nation (4rd ed.)
日本：その歴史と文化(第四版) ISBN 978-4-8053-0666-6

Hans Brinckmann Showa Japan ISBN 978-0-8048-5088-9

Helen Craig McCullough The Taiheiki: A Chronicle of Medieval Japan
太平記 ISBN 978-0-8048-3538-1 ISBN 978-4-8053-1010-6*

Jonathan Clements A Brief History of Japan ISBN 978-4-8053-1389-3

R.H.P Manson and J.G. Caiger A History of Japan 日本の歴史
ISBN: 978-08048-2097-4; ISBN 978-4-8053-0792-2*

George Karr Okinawa: The History of an Island People
ISBN 978-4-8053-1479-1

Stephen Mansfield Tokyo: A Biography ISBN 978-4-8053-1329-9

JAPANESE SOCIETY & NON-FICTION

Boyé De Mente

Japan's Cultural Code Words ISBN 978-0-8048-3574-9;
ISBN 978-4-8053-1104-2
Japan: A Guide to Traditions, Customs and Etiquette ISBN 978-4-8053-1442-5
Samurai Strategies ISBN 978-0-8048-3950-1; ISBN 978-4-8053-1249-0*

Donald Richie Japanese Portraits ISBN 978-0-8048-5053-7

Edwin O. Reischauer The Meaning of Internationalization 真の国際化とは
  ISBN 978-4-8053-1034-2

NAKANE, Chie Japanese Society タテ社会の人間関係
  ISBN 978-4-8053-1026-7*

Ruth Benedict The Chrysanthemum and The Sword 菊と刀
  ISBN 978-4-8053-1491-3

R. Davis Japanese Culture ISBN 978-4-8053-1163-9

R. Davis and O.Ikeno The Japanese Mind ISBN: 978-0-8048-3295-3;
  978-4-8053-1021-2*

SAMURAI, BUSHIDO

NITOBE, Inazo Bushido 武士道 ISBN: 978-4-8053-1489-0

O. Ratti and A. Westbook Secrets of the Samurai ISBN 978-4-8053-1405-0

R. Hillsborough
  Shinsengumi 新撰組 ISBN 978-4-8053-1119-6
  Samurai Tales ISBN 978-4-8053-1353-4
  Samurai Revolution ISBN 978-4-8053-1235-3

Stephen F. Kaufman Musashi's Book of Five Rings ISBN 978-0-8048-3520-6

TABATA, Kazumi Secret Tactics ISBN 978-0-8048-3488-9

Thomas Cleary
  Code of Samurai ISBN 978-0-8048-3190-1
  Soul of Samurai ISBN 978-0-8048-3690-6

ZEN & SHINTO

SUZUKI, Daisetz Zen and Japanese Culture ISBN 978-4-8053-1199-8*

Nyogen Senzaki and Paul Reps *(trans. And compiled)* Zen Fresh, Zen Bones
  ISBN 978-0-8048-3186-4 (paperback); 978-0-8048-3706-4 (hardcover)

ONO, Sokyo Shinto ISBN 978-0-8048-3557-2; ISBN 978-4-8053-1106-6*